Family and Marriage
Cross-Cultural Perspectives

Edited by
K. Ishwaran
York University

WALL & THOMPSON
Toronto

Canadian Cataloguing in Publication Data

Main entry under title:

Family and Marriage

Bibliography: p.
Includes index.
ISBN 0-921332-10-6

1. Family - Cross-cultural studies.
2. Family - Canada.
I. Ishwaran, K., 1922-

HQ518.F35 1989   306.8'5   C89-093465-7

Cover: A wedding in New Guinea.
Unicef.

ISBN 0–921332–10–6
Printed in Canada.
1 2 3 4 5   93 92 91 90 89

TABLE OF CONTENTS

Preface

Chapter 6
WOMEN, THE FAMILY AND CHANGE

Susannah J. Wilson, Oasis Management Consultants, Long Beach, California

PART III
THE SOCIALIZATION PROCESS / 91

Chapter 7
GENDER ROLE SOCIALIZATION

Charlene Thacker, University of Winnipeg

Chapter 11
PATTERNS OF MATE SELECTION

G. N. Ramu, University of Manitoba

Chapter 12
MATE SELECTION:
A Theoretical Perspective

Jarmila L.A. Horna, University of Calgary

PART IV
THE MARITAL SYSTEM / 195

Chapter 13
MARRIAGE: A Developing Process

James M. White, University of British Columbia

Chapter 14
POWER AND AUTHORITY IN THE FAMILY

M.B. Brinkerhoff and Eugen Lupri, University of Calgary

PREFACE

Despite a multitude of modern challenges, both family as a group and marriage as the process that generates it continue in some form in all societies. Structural and functional changes, no doubt, have been great, and many alternatives to the traditional families and marriages are being devised and used. These facts, however, do not point to the disappearance of family and marriage as social institutions but, instead, confirm the diverse ways in which familial and marital institutions can be organized in response to the pressures and opportunities of wider societies. The task of a truly modern sociology of the family and marriage is to document and analyze the diversities of familial and marital forms and processes in order to identify and explain both changes and continuities in terms of various levels and kinds of generalizations about socio-cultural patterns and processes that generate them. This study is an introduction to some of the results of the efforts that are being made to accomplish this sociological task.

The diverse and alternative family and marital forms and processes—as these are forming and re-forming all over the world—can neither be grasped nor explained within the parochial perspectives in which the North American situation is conceptualized as *modern* while situations elsewhere, especially in the so-called Third World, as *traditional*! The traditional operates in the closely inter-connected modern human world and the modern world, no matter how modern it may become, does not operate in a vacuum without traditions. What, therefore, needs emphasis is not the polarity of modern/traditional, even though this emphasis has long been prominent in sociology in general and in the sociology of family and marriage in particular. What needs emphasis is the selective combinations of the modern and the traditional in particular empirical contexts—be they in the western or in the non-western world.

The central implication of the above observations is that the sociology of the family and marriage, in order to accomplish further developments in its efforts to describe, analyze, and generalize, must adopt systematically, not just superficially, the cross-cultural perspective. Such a perspective can display the empirical diversity, both in continuities and change, of the familial and marital forms and their generative processes; it can also present the theoretical, conceptual, and methodological challenges that must be identified and tackled to ensure advancements in the sociology of family and marriage. The studies in this volume use and extensively document the kind of cross-cultural approaches that we think is urgently needed.

This book covers a wide range of topics relevant to a sociological understanding of the familial and marital forms and processes within the cross-cultural perspective we advocate. Such topics relate not only to the traditional aspects—such as socialization, mate-selection, and so on—but also to contemporary problem aspects in the field of the sociology of family and marriage.

The pedagogical value of the book is ensured not only by the extensive list of suggested readings at the end of each chapter from which both instructors and students can make their own selections, but also by a list of important terms and concepts in each chapter and a repertoire of issues for discussions in the class or in term papers. These lists of readings, concepts, and topics are intended, of course, as points of departure for a wide variety of ways in which the material in the chapters of this book can be used according to the requirements of particular courses and classes.

Finally, thanks are due to the contributors whose painstaking researches and reportings make it possible to submit this volume to those interested in the fascinating sociological tasks of documentation, analyses, and generalizations in the context of family and marriage in the cross-cultural perspective.

K. Ishwaran
York University
North York, Ontario, Canada

PART I

CROSS-CULTURAL PERSPECTIVES

Reverse: Among the Nayars of Malabar trial marriage is practiced. Women have equal rights with men in terminating unsatisfactory unions. These are wives of the Malabar Coast, wearing the "tali" or marriage cord. © Wiele and Klein

Chapter 1

INTRODUCTION
Some Issues and Contexts in Family Studies

K. Ishwaran
York University

The social grouping that we call "the family" has a variety of forms and functions. Like other social groupings, both the forms and functions have been changing virtually everywhere in recent times. The family, as generally thought of in North American society, has been under great pressure from rapid changes in other spheres of social life. For example, there are more single mothers in Western societies than ever before. A great deal is heard about the breakdown of the family. But deeper understanding requires a perspective on the family that is not confined to North America. The arguments presented in later chapters of this book highlight some aspects of the family as a dynamic social reality, especially as it is found in contemporary North America. This chapter discusses some of the issues that are generally regarded as important in contemporary family sociology.

For descriptive convenience, the issues are classified into two categories: conceptual and substantive.

CONCEPTUAL ISSUES

The Universality of the Family

Is the family found in all societies and at all times? In other words, is the family a universal social institution? A sociological answer, in the light of modern knowledge, involves complex definitional and empirical matters (Reiss, 1965). These may best be identified and discussed through an examination of four atypical cases: the Israeli Kibbutzim, the Nayar of southern India, the early post-revolutionary Soviet Union, and the Chinese under socialism.

The Israeli Kibbutzim

The kibbutzim in Israel have existed now for four generations. In 1985, there were 268 kibbutzim in the country. They were established to initiate economic and social changes in order to achieve national goals of economic development and defence (Spiro, 1956; Talmon, 1962). Thus, their overriding concern has been, and continues to be, community development and welfare. The basic operating principle was that the individual should subordinate his or her interests to the overall interests of the community. As a result, the family was initially perceived as an impediment, since it created an interest distinct from the community interest. Economically, the Kibbutzim involved agricultural collectives, communal property, and communal production and consumption. Socially, this type of organization implied communal living and communal child-rearing. Members of the same family—the husband and wife—were assigned work in different workplaces. But what is significant is that the Kibbutz functioned as a kin-like group, involving intense interpersonal interactions, without the biological bond of kinship. The sense of family was systematically eroded by collectivistic education (*chinuch meshutaf*) of children from infancy in a dormitory environment. The significant agents of socialization were outside the family—peers, teachers, and specialized nurses. In short, the traditional *family* functions were performed by agencies and persons outside the "family." But all this effort to reduce the role of the family has not succeeded. As Kibbutzim developed through the years, husbands and wives began to enjoy more privacy in their semi-detached homes and were able to spend more time with their children in their dormitory and bring them home for weekends. In consequence, even though children were separated and socialized by specialists, emotional ties with their parents seem to have increased over the years. Thus, the Kibbutz experiment shows that it is possible to do away with the family structure, but not its basic functions, such as providing psychological security for the young. Indeed, as recent studies show, the family that was once totally subordinate to the community has gained status (Rabin, 1982).

The Nayars of South India

The second atypical case is the matrilineal Nayar family of Kerala in the eighteenth century (Gough, 1960, Mencher, 1965), which was a family system without a father. But can one refer appropriately to a family if there is no father in the family structure? The Nayars in this period had a matriarchal and matrilocal social organization. The community followed the practice of marrying off girls between seven and twelve, before puberty, to a male from the corresponding subcaste, but this was a ritual marriage. The ritual husband was allowed to deflower the bride, but after a four-day celebration of the marriage, he left the house to render his caste duty as a Kshatriya to the local Raja or the feudal chieftain.

In the Nayar system, the female tie was central, and descent was through the female line, as was inheritance. The traditional household comprised kin descending from a common female ancestress. Usually, this meant a woman, her children, children of her daughter and grand-daughters, her brothers, kin through her sisters, and her relations through the deceased female ancestress. Men lived, not with their wives, but with their mothers. The system, allowed the woman to take a second type of husband called *Sambandham*; in this she was generally assisted by her uncle or father. There was no limit to the number of husbands

she could take this way, and it was quite common for a Nayar woman to have six or seven husbands. If she became pregnant, it was open to her to designate any male of the suitable subcaste to serve as the putative parent. The legitimacy of the child was ensured by the designated male bearing the incidental expenses regarding delivery and offering some gifts.

The Nayar example lacks one of the crucial components of the family structure, the husband-wife relationship, in an enduring form. It is therefore arguable that the Nayars had no family, and hence the family is not a universal institution. However, the functions of reproduction, child-rearing, and socialization do get performed by certain members of the family though not by the persons taking on the roles of father and husband. The Nayar could be therefore be considered to have a family form of their own.

The Nayar case illustrates, not the absence of the family, but the absence of a specific model of the family. Nayar community or society could not dispense with the functions of the family, but the system of roles it had evolved does not conform to the nuclear family paradigm.

The Case of the Soviet Union

Both the Soviet Union and the People's Republic of China exemplify attempts to abolish the traditional family on ideological grounds. In the West, anti-family ideology goes as far back as Plato, who, in his *Republic*, recommended a system of community of wives, on the grounds that the family represented a serious threat to the unity and functioning of the *polis*. In the Soviet Union, similar considerations led to measures from 1917 to 1934 calculated to eliminate the individual household (Geiger, 1968). But from 1936 to 1944, the system made a revolutionary reversal of this policy and initiated measures to strengthen the family in order to stabilize the new society. Earlier Marxist thinkers, Engels and Lenin, had conceptualized the family essentially as a basic component of bourgeois, capitalistic society, and hence regarded it as irrelevant to a socialist society (Engels, 1884). Soviet ideology viewed the capitalist family as possessing three undesirable features, which had to be countered. These were: the role of the husband as the sole income-earner, the wife's role as the exclusive manager of the household economy, and the role of the parents in child-rearing and socialization. The measures introduced from 1917 to 1934 which attempted to destroy these features included an extreme liberalization of divorce (1917), the provision for non-registered marriages (1927), legalization of abortion (1920), abolition of inheritance rights (1918), abolition of adoption (1918), abolition of the legal distinction between legal and illegal offspring, granting full equality to women with men in the work-force, and a general elevation of the socio-cultural and economic status of women (Hazard, 1939). While these measures had succeeded in eroding the family to a significant degree by 1930, they had also created disorder and social de-stabilization. The Soviet return to the family can be explained by the fact that, unlike the Kibbutzim, the Soviet state had virtually destroyed the family, without providing any substitute infrastructural complex to handle the family functions.

From 1933 to 1944, Stalin was forced to restore the family in order to tackle such social problems as vagrancy, widespread delinquency and demographic depletion. The new pro-family measures included the strengthening of the marriage institution (1936), and stiffening of the divorce law. Though both the anti-family policy and its reversal had roots in ideological considerations, note that the restoration of the family was forced on the Soviets as a pragmatic necessity.

The Case of China

Pre-revolutionary China had a social system that was predominantly familistic. Even the political system was modelled on the family, with the Emperor conceptualized as a father. But the dominant structure was not the family as such, but the clan or the *tsu*, the largest familial unit. In fact, the family derived its strength and identity from participation in the clan system. The clan system also served as the backbone of the traditional polity in China. The *tsu*, as a crucial social institution, performed a variety of functions, including policing, education, local administration and justice. Although the small family was not absorbed into the *tsu*, it played a relatively lesser role in rural China than the *tsu*. In the urban areas, the *tsu* was unable to root and flourish. The increasing urbanization and modernization prior to the revolution had already weakened the *tsu* by 1930, even in the province of Kwangtung, its traditional stronghold.

The traditional family, the *chia*, was not a nuclear family but an extended family comprising parents (often involving a number of wives as well as concubines), their sons, sons' wives and children, and unmarried daughters. Also included in a household were servants and artisans. This was the pattern of family composition for the ruling landlord class (Levy, 1949). The *chia* was functionally supported by the larger clan (*tsu*) group, which was able to place at the service of the family resources needed for such occasions as a wedding, a funeral, a sickness, or some financial crisis. The relationships within the *chia* were highly authoritarian and male-dominated, and roles were ranked on the basis of generation, sex, and age. While the well-to-do farmers had large families and extended family arrangements, the ordinary peasantry had smaller families. The moral basis of the family, whether large or small, whether that of the landlord or the common peasant, remained the Confucian ethic of kinship bonds. At the heart of this ethic was the centrality of the father-son relationship. As Mao put it, in the traditional family, "...Men oppressed women. The old oppressed the young..." (Mao Zedung, 1954).

Even prior to the Communist revolution, Sun Yat-sen's modernization programme found the traditional family an obstacle to be drastically modified, if not abolished. The main thrust, however, was not directed against the family as such, but only the *tsu* system.

The Communist Revolution in 1949 betokened a systematic onslaught on the traditional family itself, as in Soviet Russia from

1917 to 1934. The first step in this direction was the Marriage Law, proclaimed on 1 May 1950. But by 1953 it was apparent that the provisions of this law, milder than the anti-family measures of the Soviets, had produced large-scale marital disruption and demand for divorce. The Communist attack on the traditional family was actually an attack on some of its features considered incompatible with the ideology of the regime. For instance, the principles of age hierarchy and group loyalty, which formed the foundation of the *tsu* system, were found to be a threat to the new revolutionary regime. Moreover, the new regime found it ideologically necessary to transform the economic function of the traditional family which was based on the private ownership of the means of production. With the cooperativization of the rural economy, this function was automatically taken out of the purview of the family. From the rural sector, the process was extended to the urban sector and included the whole country by 1958. By 1962, there was evidence that the leadership was interested in continuing the family. The only direct consequence of the anti-family measures was the elimination of the *tsu* system, whose functions came to be taken over by the governmental agencies.

Universality of the Family: Conclusions

Any number of cases may be examined to support what the four cases discussed above demonstrate: (i) certain functions, focused on early socialization of children, nurturance, and biological survival, often called family functions, are universal; (ii) they may be performed within a wide range of social arrangements, as widely different as the Israeli Kibbutzim and the Nayar system; (iii) the particular structural form of the nuclear family, usually considered in modern Western societies as the only family form, is not essential for the performance of the so-called family functions; (iv) if, as the Soviet and the Chinese cases show, the traditional family, whatever it may be, is destroyed, then, so long as alternative social arrangements for the performance of family functions are not

made, the result is disorder. Briefly then, while family functions, in the sense noted, are universal, no particular structure of the family is so.

Universality of the Nuclear Family

Three of the four cases outlined above—the Israeli Kibbutzim, the Nayar case, and the Chinese family during the revolution—are quite sufficient to show that the nuclear family, comprising a set of married couples and their unmarried children, is not universal. In his examination of 549 societies, Murdock found 248 societies (45.12% of the total) in which the nuclear family existed and operated independently of wider kin groups (Murdock, 1957). Murdock's samples were globally collected. Regardless of what statistical arguments one may have with Murdock, his findings are quite sufficient to establish that the nuclear family is not universal.

Those who claim the universality of the nuclear family do so not on the grounds that the nuclear family is or has been universal: they do so in terms of a trend. They argue that, with increasing urbanization and industrialization, all family forms tend to assume the nuclear structure. But urbanization and industrialization take many forms which do not lead universally to nuclearization of the family.

Moreover, the nuclear family form is not in all cases the result of urbanization and industrialization. Evidence shows that food-gatherers and hunters, due to the logistics of their food quest, are likely to live in nuclear families. The Inuit, for instance, and segments of modern industrialized societies, may tend to display the same family type, that is, the nuclear family (Damas 1976).

The theory that postulates the universality of the nuclear family as a result of increasing urbanization and industrialization also claims that agrarian families are essentially non-nuclear. On the basis of their Indian data, Chekki and Ishwaran (1977) however, have shown that the expected extended family is more of an ideal than a reality (Chekki, 1974; Ishwaran 1977). Because of poverty, housing scarcity, and the shrinking of land per capita, the reality is more likely to tend toward nuclearization of the family.

Nuclearization of the family structure can arise from a variety of ecological circumstances and is by no means inevitably connected with modern forms of urbanization and industrialization.[1]

Isolation of the Nuclear Family

A related assertion, promoted by Parsons and others, is that, because of the same forces of urbanization and isolation, the nuclear family becomes isolated from larger kin groups. The available evidence, however, challenges this assertion.

Bennett and Despres (1960) hold that any form of kinship system can be compatible with urban-industrial circumstances. Others have challenged the Parsonian thesis that interaction with larger kin groups decreases in frequency with increasing urbanization (Axelrod 1956; Litwak 1959–1960; Reiss 1962; Sussman 1959). Irving (1972) found the relationship with parents and parents-in-law in Canada emotionally powerful, and Meissner (1964) demonstrated the importance of the families of origin of married couples. Axelrod (1956) has shown that, in terms of visiting patterns, urbanites visit their kinsfolk more frequently than non-kinsfolk, and Garigue (1956) has drawn attention to the intensity of interactions with parents and siblings. Technological improvements in communication—telephones and automobiles—associated with urbanization and industrialization actually increase rather than decrease interactions with kin outside the nuclear family.

Such interactions between the nuclear family and wider kin groups may often reflect personal considerations rather than kin loyalty, though a sense of obligation may also be displayed (Piddington, 1968; Osterrich, 1968; Ishwaran, 1977). Males and females differ in these interactions: interactions between women and their parents are likely to be more frequent and intense than interactions between men and their parents. This indicates the prominence of unilateral kinship systems in some modern Western societies, as noted by Komarovsky (1967), Reiss (1962), and Young and Willmott (1957).

The interactions between the nuclear family and wider kin groups often serve a useful purpose in everyday life. Sussman (1953) shows that they may relate to financial aid, gifts, services, and counsel. Also, as he shows, in inter-ethnic marriages, parental support may be highly significant. Others corroborate and add to this list (Litwak, 1960a; Sussman and Burchinal, 1962; Adam, 1968).

All this, however, does not mean that the interactions between the nuclear family and wider kin groups are always happy and supportive. Interventions from mothers-in-law may generate marital conflicts; once "disturbed," interactions with wider kin groups may be rejected (Bell, 1962). However the issue here is that in urbanized-industrialized Western societies, the nuclear family does not usually operate in isolation from wider kin groups. No doubt such societies are often highly competitive and mobile, and thus the possibility of isolation may be always there. But the bulk of the evidence suggests that this possibility itself generates various links, however voluntary, between the nuclear family and wider kin groups (Wellman, 1977). It is quite possible, then, that the assertion or thesis about the "isolation of the nuclear family" reflects a deep-rooted cultural compulsion of some Western societies to emphasize primary loyalty to spouse and children (Reiss, 1960; Komarovsky, 1967), even though that primary loyalty actually operates in a matrix of wider kin relations.

---

[1] There is no conclusive evidence to support the claim for the universality of the nuclear family on the grounds of urbanization and industrialization. The claim is simply an instance of Western ethnocentrism that lurks in many spheres of current sociology. As Coult and Habenstein (1962) note, "... theoretical considerations alone indicate that the universalistic ideology of America could not unilaterally determine social behaviour..."

Changing Functions of the Family

The pre-industrial family in the West, together with the Church, regulated individual life from birth to death through a wide range of contexts—affectional, biological, economic, educational, protective, recreational, religious and status assigning. In today's urbanized-industrialized West, the family's functions have been drastically reduced.

Such functions are now largely performed by a variety of specialized structures and agencies. Economic functions are now performed by the factory, the store, the office, and a host of production and service organizations. Educational functions are carried out by schools, colleges, and professional institutes. Recreational functions are fulfilled by the cinema, the park, the club, commercially organized games, and so on. The Church and related agencies focus on religious functions. The State and its agencies provide the protective functions. It is often noted that social mobility has shifted the status-assignment role of the family to the individual. It would seem that, under the circumstances, the family has lost, or is losing fast, all its functions, and is destined to vanish, sooner or later.

The loss of family functions, in the sense noted above, has been going on for some decades in the West and is alarming many sociologists and laymen. These sociologists have argued that although many of the traditional family functions have been taken over by non-familial, specialized agencies, the family performs certain functions which no other social institution can undertake (Ogburn, 1933).[1] The universal functions that these and other sociologists mention are basically two: biological reproduction and child socialization. But, as we noted earlier, the other functions fulfilled by the family in earlier times are now carried out by a variety of non-familial structures.

What, then, can be said about the functions of modern families, especially in the urban-ized-industrialized West? The answer is that even though the modern family has given up some of its direct functions to a wide array of specialized agencies, it has acquired a new and enormously significant coordinating function: coordinating the effect of those specialized agencies and institutions in the everyday life of the growing child. This coordinating function has yet to be properly studied. Some sociologists have noted that the modern family in the West has changed from an institution (with its well-defined roles, rights, and obligations) to "companionship" (Burgess, Locke and Thomes, 1963). Others have pointed out that membership in a family still tends to define the life-chances of an individual (Porter 1957; Adams et al, 1971). These are significant approaches to studies of functions of the modern Western family, but their significance emerges fully only if they are explored as aspects of the new coordinating function of the family, indicated above.

This concludes our comments on some of the conceptual issues in the field of family sociology today. The following section focuses on the issues that are primarily substantive.

SUBSTANTIVE ISSUES

Children of Working Mothers

The rapid increase in the number of women engaged in gainful employment, especially those with infants and children, is a relatively recent phenomenon in all industrially advanced countries. For instance, between 1977 and 1984 in Canada, the proportion of mothers with pre-school children in the labour-force grew from 37.3% to 53.6%. Such a significant increase in the participation of mothers in the labour-force must have had important consequences for their children.

In the 1960s the relevant sociological literature claimed that maternal employment and

---

[1] Such universal functions are, according to Davis (1949), biological reproduction maintenance, placement, and socialization; according to Murdock (1949), they are reproduction, socialization, economic cooperation, and sexual gratification. According to Reiss (1965), however, the family has only one universal function: "nurturant," that is, socialization.

juvenile delinquency were positively correlated, though some studies found that the two variables were associated with the other factors, namely, class background and the experience of a broken home (Glueck and Glueck, 1957). Subsequent studies showed that the situation was very complex as the correlation between maternal employment and delinquency or withdrawal behaviour did not hold constant because of different sets of contributing factors (Hoffman, 1968). The most significant factor was the mother's work satisfaction, which is indirectly associated with social class. Higher class status offers access to better and more satisfying jobs. Also there were studies indicating the relevance of the urban-rural distinction to the working mother-child relationship (Roy, 1961). However, none of these studies offered any general conclusions, because they did not deal with other relevant variables such as the mode of child-care used by the working mother and the quality of her involvement with the child when she was at home.

In the mid-seventies, the issue took a new turn because of new circumstances. By this time, it had become the normal pattern, rather than the exception, that the child was taken care of by somebody other than the mother during the important periods of his or her waking time. This new development raised obvious questions: Who looks after these children? What are the consequences of impersonal, institutionalized caring?

At this stage of our knowledge, it is difficult to make firm generalizations about the nature of the fathering and mothering being provided in dual-career families. However, it can be claimed with certainty that the care of a majority of North American children is now entrusted to daycare centres. For instance, in Canada, in 1981, as many as 52.2% of pre-school children were entrusted to private and public daycare centres, some of which were commercial and profit-oriented. The available data do not warrant the sweeping conclusion that this situation is harmful to children, who, however, remain under the pressures of mothers caught between dual roles (Etaugh, 1980).

The Storm and Stress of Adolescence

Adolescence has become a relatively recent field of systematic research (Muus, 1968). It is often described in sociological literature as a period of uncertainty—no longer a child, but not yet an adult. This uncertainty has been investigated from several perspectives.

One perspective focuses on the adolescent sub-culture arising from the anxiety of adolescence (Sebald, 1977). This is a peer group culture, normatively and behaviourally in conflict with the parental generation. According to Davis (1940), the generational conflict is structurally inherent in the dynamics of modern society. Winch (1971) relates this conflict to the value dissonance between generations. While the generational conflict is likely to be acute at times in modern Western societies, it is by no means unique: one can find it in many societies, past and present, provided that the cultural norms in such societies define a period of adolescence—neither child nor adult.

Some of the anthropological evidence endorses the above assertion. Margaret Mead describes the initiation and induction rites in life-stages in pre-modern Samoa: such rites eliminate the uncertainty experienced by the modern Western adolescent. Elimination of this adolescent uncertainty, apparently, also eliminates generational conflict (Mead, 1928). Ruth Benedict (1954) goes further. She suggests a typology of societies which produce generational conflict and those, which on account of special institutional arrangements, avoid it. According to Josselyn (1948), modern Western society, lacking the needed institutional arrangements to avoid generational conflict, produces it.

Comparative Canadian data, though meagre, suggest that where community social structure emphasizes cultural isolation and cultural identity, there may be harmony, rather than conflict between generations (Elkin and Westley, 1957; Ishwaran and Chan, 1978). The community, if deeply involved in religious self-definition, may foster harmonious handling of generational conflicts. But so long as adolescence is culturally conceived as an undefined phase in human growth, the generational conflict is always bound to be there.

One of the grounds of conflict is sexuality. Adolescence and sexuality are often associated. But it is difficult to correlate puberty (a biological factor) with the culturally defined adolescence (Kinsey, Pomeroy and Martin, 1948).

Unlike pre-modern societies, modern ones lack clear-cut rites of passage from childhood to adulthood. Such societies have developed some indications of segments in the growth process; for example, the debut, graduation from school or college, completion of apprenticeship in a trade or profession, moving out of the natal home, doing military service, and marriage. Normally such indications are relatively informal and rarely ritualized, except, in some cases, the debut (Bossard and Boll, 1948).

All in all, adolescence in North America is dominated by two themes: sex and career. Both seem to have affected the growing-up of the adolescent in a competing and complex world.

Mate Selection: Romantic Love and Other Factors

Mate selection has been conceived in terms of two concepts: homogamy and heterogamy. The first postulates attraction between similar personalities; the second, between dissimilar personalities (Winch, 1955; 1958). Both assume romantic love as the crucial factor and connect it with sex. Romantic love—for that matter love in general—is a powerful passion, capable of causing great social disruption. Therefore, all societies structurally regulate love, (Goode, 1959), even though instances of violation of such regulations occur in all societies. In a sociological perspective, love by itself is not enough to sustain marriage (Mowrer, 1927; Elliot and Merrill, 1950). In this perspective, romantic love has been regarded as the opposite of conjugal love and stable marital life.

But there have also been more positive assessments of love as beneficial (Lasswell and Lobsenz, 1980). Romantic love has been situated within the wider value system of modern society, based on individualism, liberty, and self-development. In a society where the individual feels rootless and psychologically restless, romantic life is seen as a source of marital stability (Parsons, 1949b). The importance of romantic love in North American society is derived from three factors: first, the youth-idolising culture weakens family ties and encourages falling in love; second, love substitutes for kinship in stabilising individual marital role behaviour; and finally, the structural isolation of the family promotes strong, affective, love relationships.

In fact, the sharp dichotomy between romantic love and unromantic love has no basis in reality, since empirically one finds a continuum between the two. It is true that in the modern West, especially North America, the romantic end of the continuum dominates, whereas, in Japan or India, the opposite end may be more significant. The continuum model is better able to capture the richness and diversity of the empirical reality (Goode, 1959). It is therefore a matter of relative dominance; no societies are wholly characterised by one kind of love. All societies need to offset the disruptive effects of romantic love through structural mechanisms like stratification and assigned status within the family. Even marriages based on romantic love take into account non-romantic factors. In traditional societies, such as Indian culture, the non-romantic type is the norm.

In Canada, as in many other countries, religion plays a significant role in mate-selection. The demographic data of 1972, for instance, shows that 80% of marriages among Protestants, Catholics, and Jews are between partners of the same religious group (Heer and Hubey, 1976).

Educational factors play an important role in mate selection. A common educational level facilitates the selection process. Recent census data bears this out: 44% of husbands married wives with similar educational levels, as opposed to 26% of men who married women with higher levels. Also educational level itself relates to socio-economic level. Hence, while romantic love does play an important role in modern societies, it is certainly regulated by a host of other factors.

Chapter 1 / K. Ishwaran

Traditional Versus Modern Sex Roles

In virtually every society, the division of labour is sex-based to some extent (Murdock, 1937), but the extent of overlap between sexes in work is culturally determined (Davenport, 1977). This practice rests on specific assumptions about the roles of men and women. On a cross-cultural basis, there exists a universal practice of socializing the girls to become "nurturant" and boys to become "instrumental" (Barry et al., 1957).

Traditionally, in every society women have been assigned the tasks of infant-care and child-care, though in most societies, men have been expected participate to some degree (Stephens, 1968). These tasks have been biologically based, and on the same basis women have been excluded from roles and tasks involving physical prowess and aggressiveness. Beyond such roles, there has been considerable variation in women's roles across cultures. For instance, in agrarian societies, crop-tending and harvesting can be done by either sex.

Sex-based role socialization starts at infancy and is later reinforced by non-family agencies like school and the mass media. Within the family, boys and girls dress differently and engage in different kinds of activities. This pattern is strengthened later in peer group association. The sex-typed roles are internalised subconsciously through interaction with peer groups. Parental behaviour serves as a role-model, boys looking up to their father and girls to their mother. Girls tend to participate in household chores under mother's tutelage. The girls may also see the mothers working away from home either for extra income or merely to keep busy. This is a continuous process of socialization.

The school carries on and reinforces such socialization into sex-based roles. The mass media and even children's toys strengthen this process. Such socialization from childhood to adolescence prepares the individual to play appropriate roles in adult life in terms of occupation, education, and aspirations. Women are socialised into expecting relatively lower educational attainment and away from prestigious and remunerative occupations, such as those of university teachers, physicians and surgeons, pharmacists, psychologists, lawyers and notaries, industrial engineers, and dentists. In Canada, in 1981, only 24.6, 17.1, 41.3, 52.0, 15.1, 12.2, and 7.9% of women respectively were in these professions (1971 census and 1981 census, vol. 3.2, Table 8). Since then, the situation, which is similar to that in the USA, has not changed appreciably.

Aging: Poverty and Isolation

The problem of old people is important in all societies, but it acquires poignancy and sharpness in modern, industrial societies because of patterns of residence which spatially separate the generations (Parsons, 1942). Since the end of the nineteenth century, the decline in family size and the increase in longevity have meant that parents are left with about a quarter of their married life to live after the last child moves out of parental residence (Deutscher, 1962). In pre-modern societies, old age was expected to bring psychological and biological loss, but was compensated for by being accorded virtues of wisdom and a venerable status. In modern society, this is denied to the old, for whom the increase in longevity means increased years of isolation, boredom, powerlessness, and sheer despondency (Philbert, 1965).

Two important issues that concern the elderly shall be discussed briefly at this point: their financial hardships and dependence, and psychological deprivation. We all would like to assume that working people will be able to save enough during their working lives to give themselves economic security in old age. But in reality, the income from pension and welfare benefits is not sufficient to cover the requirements of old age. The combined effect of the declining value of savings, the rising cost of living, and the absence of any assistance from relatives makes old age an unbearable burden in most cases. Only a small minority of Canadians and Americans, who come from the upper and upper-middle levels of society, can welcome their retirement as the golden age of life. As for the rest, who constitute an overwhelming majority, old age is a period of deprivation and anguish. In Canada, for instance, the number of elderly men and women living below the poverty line in 1981 was 189,000 and 415,000 respectively. In 1982, 60% of single Canadians, aged 65 and above, were below the poverty line (Lowrey, 1980; 14).

Advanced industrial societies face a dilemma because advances in life-expectancy and health-care have created a sizeable elderly population. At the same time these societies have alienated the old by enforcing arbitrary retirement. While the demand for gender equality in these societies has made a sharp impact, resulting in a relatively better deal for women, the demand of the old for minimum living conditions has hardly been raised.

It is not merely poverty that afflicts the old in these societies, but the fact that they are also driven into social isolation. The social relationships traditionally available to the old are no longer there because of changes in the extended family and the spatial dispersal of relatives and friends. Though there are reports that in certain countries, such as England, working-class parents are looked after in their old age by women, especially daughters, many parents themselves seem to prefer the State to attend to their needs. The old seem to be more worried about isolation from their family than about material care. As one person expressed it, "If you ask me, children don't look after old people now-a-days, they just can't be bothered...There is a different atmosphere now altogether, I can tell you..." (Roser and Harris, 1965: 269, 285).

Physical and economic dependence, reinforced by the psychological despair induced by old age, have forced the old to live a life of loneliness and isolation. Statistics Canada (1983, 6) reported that the aged also suffer urban victimization as they find it unsafe to walk in their own neighbourhoods.

The aged themselves view their time of life to be worse than the earlier stages—worse, for example, than adolescence. The adolescent has a future to look forward to, whereas the old have no future, only a past, a remembered one. Their only future is the crumbling of the body, culminating in death. There may be some who enjoy their leisure and derive satisfaction from a life well lived or a "job well done" or from a positive orientation toward what is left in the future. Most old people do not seem to salvage even this kind of satisfaction. They seem to be resigned to old age as a period of "ill-defined choices, separation, loss and victimization" (Cumming and Henry, 1961).

SUMMARY

It is asserted that the family is less significant in modern societies and that it is changing both in structure and functions. In the context of these assertions this chapter considers two kinds of issues: conceptual and substantive.

A basic conceptual issue raised in family sociology is whether the concept of the family corresponds to a universal phenomenon or whether it conceals multiple phenomena subsumed under one term. This question is examined with reference to four specific cases: the Israeli Kibbutzim, the Nayars of South India, early post-revolutionary Soviet society and society in China. These cases establish that the family does perform certain universal functions such as socialization of children and their nurturance and biological survival and that these functions may be performed by a variety of forms.

Citing recent cross-cultural studies and employing a comparative focus, it is shown that the nuclear family is not a universal category and that its universal claims reflect simply an ethnocentric bias.

The assertion in sociological literature that the nuclear family is isolated from the wider kin group in modern industrial society, seems to be untenable. Recent studies have shown that the nuclear family maintains functional links with a wider kin group.

The pre-industrial family in the West regulated the life of its members in every aspect and thus performed many functions. Industrial society has divested the family of some of its traditional functions, especially economic and educational roles. But the loss of old functions has meant the addition of new ones, especially that of coordinating the roles performed by extra-family agencies.

Industrial society generates an economy in which women are increasingly involved as participants in the labour-force. They now face new problems, especially the problem of ensuring that their children are cared for while they are away at work. While the children of working mothers are increasingly entrusted to the care of agencies outside the family, there is inadequate evidence regarding the quality of care they receive. It has also been found that variables like social class and urban-rural distinctions are relevant to an understanding of the relationship between working mothers and their children.

Another important issue in family sociology is the nature and significance of the period of adolescence. This is a critical period, a period of storm and stress, characterised by an identity crisis, because the adolescent is considered neither a child nor an adult. While pre-modern societies handled this period in a structured way, modern industrial societies tend to be ambiguous about it. In North American society, adolescence has been shown to be a period in which two themes dominate the life of the adolescent, namely sex and career.

Mate selection is a crucial phase in the formation of a family, and quite rightly it has become an important issue in family sociology. Here the major issue is romantic love as a mode of mate selection. Sociologically this has been distinguished from conjugal love. After indicating various factors other than love that go into the process of mate selection, it can be suggested that pure romantic love is a myth and that there is no empirical evidence to sustain the romantic-unromantic dichotomy.

In all societies, sex-based roles tend to be institutionalised. In pre-industrial society, they were sharply demarcated. Even in modern industrial societies, although such role division may have been reduced, it still survives. Feminists have tried to mount an offensive against sex-based roles as a part of male dominance. But here again, there are variables, like class, which also affect the specific roles assigned to the sexes.

One of the acute issues before modern industrial society is old age. In traditional societies, old age was treated in such a way that the aged did not become isolated from their own families, and, in some of them, they even dominated the society. In industrial society, the care of the old has been shifted from the family to agencies outside it. While improved modern health facilities have resulted in increased numbers of the elderly due to improved longevity, it has also made the question of the aged an important live issue. The old have been found to be victims of multiple deprivations, economic, social, and psychological. The issue of old age, which involves such questions as retirement, is likely to persist as a major problem for advanced industrial societies.

TECHNICAL TERMS

EXTENDED FAMILY—A family consisting of members of more than two generations who share common residence, kitchen, property and worship together.

FAMILY—A relatively stable group related by descent, marriage, or adoption, who live together with a view to procreate and bring up children.

INSTITUTION—A stable cluster of norms, values, beliefs, roles and statuses that develop to fulfil the basic needs of society.

KINSHIP—A network of people related by blood, marriage, or adoption.

MATRILINEAL FAMILY—A type of kinship system in which descent is traced through the female line.

MODIFIED EXTENDED FAMILY—A network of nuclear families related by *family* descent, marriage, or adoption for mutual aid.

PATRILINEAL FAMILY—A type of kinship system in which descent is traced through the male line.

Chapter 1 / K. Ishwaran

QUESTIONS

1. Show how family issues have changed from time to time because of the changing conditions in society. Give examples.

2. Is the human family necessary for the survival of the individual and society? Argue for and against by drawing upon relevant historical data.

3. Can we say that with increasing industrialization families all over the world will converge on a single model like the North American family? Discuss the problem in the context of convergence theory.

4. Compare and contrast the family experiments in Bolshevik Russia and Israel and show their gains and losses.

SUGGESTED READINGS

- Mark Hutter. *The Changing Family: Comparative Perspectives*. Toronto: Collier Macmillan, 1988.

  A good textbook that systematically utilizes a cross-cultural perspective throughout the study of the family life cycle. It draws upon a variety of cross-cultural and historical examples to explore the dynamics of family change, general trends and variations.

- M.F. Nimkoff, ed. *Comparative Family Systems*. Boston: Houghton Mifflin, 1965.

  A fine collection of papers dealing with the major variations in the organization of the human family: what they are, what causes them and what differences they make.

- William N. Stephens. *The Family in Cross-Cultural Perspective*. New York: Holt, Rinehart and Winston.

  This study presents family customs and behaviour in non-American societies by drawing upon a wide variety of literature.

FAMILY STUDIES
An Historical Account

K. Ishwaran
York University

CLASSIFICATION OF FAMILY STUDIES

The family has long been the object of interest and study across a variety of cultural traditions. This interest first manifested itself in oral folklore and subsequently in the work of ancient classical philosophers. It was transformed into a systematic scientific enterprise in more recent times. Christensen (1964) identified four stages in the origin and development of family studies; to these we may add one more stage, which has been dominated by the writings of feminists and radical critics since 1970. These are: (1) the pre-sociological tradition up to 1861; (2) the tradition focusing on origins and evolutionary schemes, from 1862 to the 1920s; (3) the tradition of investigation into poverty, social disorganization and other social problems confronting the modern industrial society, from the 1920s to 1950; (4) the crystallization of a more systematically and self-consciously scientific tradition, characterised by great methodological skill and sophistication; (5) the feminist orientation towards the family. These stages should be viewed as inter-linked and evolving, rather than as isolated historical segments. Themes and concerns, even techniques and methodological tools, cut across such tidy and neat periodizations. The present scientific status of the study is a cumulative historical product, and the stages we refer to are no more than rough-and-ready signposts to a massive and complex historical process. Thus, this schema is in some ways arbitrary, but very useful as a heuristic device. It must also be taken as a continuum.

THE FIRST STAGE: PRE-SOCIOLOGICAL

In the West, family study can be dated as far back as the period of the Holy Scriptures. Outside the Western tradition, we find it discussed in the sayings of Confucius in China and in the socio-ethico-religious writings of Manu in India prior to the Christian era. Beyond these, both preceding them and co-existing with them, has been folk literature and literary classics in several languages—Shakespeare's plays in English, Kalidasa's plays in Sanskrit, and the writings of Goethe in German. The Hebrew scriptures make abundant reference to the family and its institutional and behaviourial aspects. For instance, we have references to the *bayith* (house), *mishpachah* (clan), and *mohar* (dowry). Among the themes discussed are engagement, dowry, marriage, parent-offspring relations, divorce and inheritance. The fifth commandment assigned marriage the role of being the very foundation of the social order and invested it with religious sanction. Condemnation of incest, support of endogamy and upholding of morals rooted in family life, disapproval of anti-family practices like prostitution and adultery, all these constituted an essential part of the socio-religious tradition of ancient Hebrews.

The laws of Solon testify clearly to the ancient Greek interest in marriage as a crucial social institution, in terms of both public and

Left: van Eyck, Flemish. 15th Century.

private good. Homer's epics draw attention to the structure and hierarchically-based social order. Given this perspective, Manu disapproved of hypergamy, that is, the marriage of a upper caste woman with a lower caste male. On the issue of woman's role, Manu clearly supported the view that she should be subjected to the dominance and authority of man, but he also stated that the health of family life depended on the well-being of the women and that the honour of a family was based on the honour of its women-folk. In emphasizing such a view Manu was not unique since such norms can be found in many ancient civilizations and cultures across the world.

The foregoing literature on the family, largely incidental, unsystematic, and impressionistic, was essentially non-empirical and largely moralistic.

THE SECOND STAGE: FOCUS ON ORIGIN AND EVOLUTION

The study of society, in general, and the study of the family, in particular, received considerable stimulus from the publication of Darwin's seminal work, *On the Origin of Species* (1859), and his *Descent of Man* (1871). The concept of evolution exerted enormous influence on the study of humanity and society, as attempts were made to transpose the biological-evolutionary model to the social realm, leading to *social Darwinism*. Marriage and the family came to be examined from an evolutionary perspective, involving a progressive development through recognizable and successive stages. The most notable students of society who pioneered this approach were Johann Jakob Bachofen, Henry Main, John F. McLennan, Herbert Spencer, Edward Westermarck, and Friedrich Engels, from Europe, and Lewis Henry Morgan from the USA. All of them adopted some form of evolutionism (Bardis, 1964).

Johann Jakob Bachofen (1815–87)

Johann Jakob Bachofen, a trained jurist interested in philosophy and classicism, published *Das Mutterrecht* (The Mother Right) in 1861,

using a unilinear evolutionist framework. His schema of successive stages of development of society postulated as the earliest stage a society characterised by promiscuity, sexual permissiveness and sexual communism. This was followed by the stage *gynaecocracy* in which the family was matriarchal and the chief deity was the feminine moon as opposed to the male deity, the sun. This was succeeded by patriarchate, involving an institutionalized male dominance. The family was patriarchal and succession patrilineal. Man's authority over women and minors was absolute. His method of historical reconstruction was based on a reinterpretation of cultural survivals such as temple prostitution, involving *jus primae noctis* (the law of the first night). This was assumed to be an indication of sexual promiscuity, violating the marital norms of sexual exclusiveness. Bachofen's evolutionary theory was rooted in a metaphysical-moral position, involving the assumption of a progressive human transcendence of animal and material levels. Evolution was seen as a process of increasing spiritualization or humanization. It presupposed male superiority over the animality and the evil represented by the female.

Sir Henry Maine (1822–88)

Henry J. Sumner Maine published his seminal work, *Ancient Law*, two years after Darwin's *Origin of Species* and one year before Bachofen's *Das Mutterrecht*. He rejected the universal evolutionist schema, especially the matriarchal thesis. Taking a line directly opposed to Bachofen, he argued that private property and mother right were mutually exclusive principles.

His theory depended heavily on a reinterpretation of the scriptural history of Hebrew patriarchs. Maine's own evolutionary schema postulated a progressive historical shift from traditionally ascribed group status to contract—from customary rights and duties to legally enunciated rights and duties. He explained this shift in terms of intensified urbanization, leading to a weakening of kinship and family ties. Ancient systems of law were oriented towards group life, whereas the modern systems derived from the supremacy of individual life. This process meant that individuals became strengthened at the cost of social groups, including the family. State intervention through civil law raised the status of women, consequent upon the decline of the family role. Hence, he saw a causal relation between decline in family power, increase in the power of the state and the rise of individualistic ethos. His sources for such historical interpretation were Latin and Sanskrit epics. In the end, while rejecting Bachofen's evolutionism, Main advanced his own kind of evolutionism based on patriarchal universalism.

J.F. McLennan (1827–1881)

McLennan attempted to derive his evolutionism from ethnographical data on the family. Apparently uninfluenced by Bachofen, he too arrived at an evolutionary theory which assigned a central role to matriarchal descent in the development of the family (Lowe, 1937). He accepted the nineteenth century paradigm of parallelism or universalism in respect of the family from the stages of savagery to civilization. He contributed two key terms to scientific sociological vocabulary—*endogamy* and *exogamy*. He used them both in regard to tribe and family. He held that the earliest tribes were exogamous, that is, married outside their social group, and thus became involved in endless conflict. This was because a wife from outside could be acquired only through violence. The earliest human stage was characterised by sexual promiscuity and intertribal warfare. Since girls were at the root of such violent conflict, female infanticide was practised, and this led to a depletion in female population first, and then to exogamy. Another consequence of this was polyandry within a tribe. Thus, he saw interdependence between exogamy and polyandry.

Herbert Spencer (1820–1903)

Although he was a professional student of society and biology, Spencer became the historical channel through which the sociological and biological streams in evolutionism came to mingle. He attempted to provide a biologi-

cal foundation to social evolutionism. He viewed sociology as a systematic treatment of supra-organic phenomena within an evolutionary frame. Though he took great pains to intermesh biological and sociological phenomena into a single theoretical framework and even resorted to organic analogy, he also tried to separate biological and sociological theory from biological analogy, using the latter merely as "scaffolding" because "inductions will stand out by themselves!" (Spencer 1896). However, Spencer's sociological theory could never purge itself of biological analogy and organic terminology.

Based on the Darwinian notion of inherited characteristics, Spencer held monogamy to be innate, a consequence of a natural law by which the numerical equality between sexes was established. He rejected the theory of primitive promiscuity. He argued that the function of procreation diminished in importance as society advanced, because the period of youth became prolonged. This increased the scope for individuality and self-development. This led eventually to a decline in the role of the family, turning marriage a matter of individual choice.

Edward Westermarck (1862–1939)

Westermarck was a Swedish Finn whose reputation rested on his great work, *The History of Human Marriage* (1891). He advanced the notion of a multilinear evolution, and offered his own interpretation of social institutions like monogamy and incest. He questioned the methodology of reconstructing historical structures on the basis of the evidence of survival of customs. He held that "many lines of development may have occurred in the evolutionary process." Convinced of the universality of marriage in some form, he rejected the thesis of primitive promiscuity, on the ground that "the horror of incest" is universal. He warned especially against the uncritical use of classical literary sources. Using Darwin's citation of ape sexual behaviour, he argued against the possibility of primitive promiscuity or early sexual communism. He held aversion to incest to be a natural corollary of living together closely. Such closeness, in fact, led to exogamy.

He held strongly to the monogamous thesis, and believed that the food-gatherers and hunters were monogamous. According to him, Christianity simply accepted monogamy as it was part of the historical progress of societies. He prophesied that monogamy would become more dominant in Western civilization. This conclusion was based on the observation that women were becoming politically stronger, especially in the field of social legislation.

Lewis Henry Morgan (1818–1881)

Morgan, like, Main and McLennan, came from a legal background. He was both an imaginative theorist and a meticulous ethnographer. He was able to gather vast data about the North American aboriginals. His *Systems of Consanguinity and Affinity of the Human Family* (1870) contained kinship data for more than 200 tribes. His method combined direct observation with indirect reports of traders, missionaries and political agents. His best known work, *Ancient Society* (1877), offers a sweeping theoretical frame for interpreting sociologically both the classical Graeco-Roman and the Amerindian socio-cultural systems.

His evolutionary schema, too, assigned a central role to primitive promiscuity and matriarchy. He advanced a three-stage universal schema, comprising successively *savagery, barbarism* and *civilization*. Each stage was further sub-divided, and was underpinned by a structure of correlation with specific levels of economic and intellectual achievements. For instance, savagery preceded pottery, barbarism was associated with ceramic techniques, and civilization produced the art of writing. Given his overarching and universal frame, he could interpret ancient Graeco-Roman institutions with the help of Amerindian data. He took a Darwinian position in holding that the class structure resulted from natural selection, involving the rise and diffusion of a superior civilization. For the family itself, six successive stages were identified. They were: (1) promiscuity, (2) group marriage between siblings, (3) organization of family into gentes, leading to exogamy, (4) emergence of a marital pair as a basic social unit, (5) the rise of the patriarchal family and (6) the monogamous family.

Holding succession to be a crucial element in marriage, he argued that matriliny preceded patriliny. This process was interpreted in terms of change in property relations and rules of inheritance. In empirical terms, his most scientific contribution was the study of comparative kinship. He divided kinship terminology into two categories—classificatory and descriptive. The former emphasized kin solidarity and common class category more than precise genealogy. He maintained that the primitive social order was *classificatory* while the modern was *descriptive* in its kinship system. Like other evolutionists, Morgan tended to interpret empirical and historical data to suit pre-conceived evolutionary schema. His kinship theory has been criticized by subsequent scholarship as too schematic.

Friedrich Engels (1820–1895)

The impact of Social Darwinism in general and the evolutionary schema of Morgan in particular are clearly evident in Engels' work, *The Origin of the Family, Private Property and the State*, first published in 1884. Relying on Morgan's evolutionary theory, Engels traced the family through the three stages of human history—savagery, barbarism, and civilization—and argued that each stage was associated with its own type of family. In his view, a particular family type was linked to a particular form of technology.

In the first stage, savagery, society was characterized by communal living, communal ownership of property, rule by women, group marriage, and a polygamous marital system. Life was then adapted to nature. In the next stage, characterized by domestication of animals and cultivation of land, rule by women gave way to masculine domination; women and children were now exploited by men for economic gain. For Engels, this stage clearly signals the emergence of private property, along with slavery and private wealth. The third stage was characterized by the bourgeois capitalistic family, an economic arrangement in which not love but property was the single most important factor influencing family relationships. In the final stage, communism would prevail, heralding the disappearance of the family as an economic institution controlled by men and ushering in the liberation of women from masculine dominance.

Engel's ideas about patriarchy and the exploitation of women and children by men through privatization of the family have received particular attention from feminists today. They have renewed interest in his document on the origin of the family, which points to the historical causes for the subjugation of women and promises their liberation.

Contribution of Social Darwinists

Overall, the social Darwinist literature addresses two central issues: (1) Were the original human societies promiscuous or monogamous? (2) Was the earliest family form patriarchal or matriarchal? Both these issues emerged as crucial only because the social Darwinists were in search of the alleged origins of social institutions. Subsequently, sociological study shifted its focus from origin and evolution to an empirical and systematic understanding of the structure and functioning of social institutions, including the family. Hence, from the modern perspective, social Darwinists suffered from a thematic and methodological limitation. More recently, sociology seems to have come full circle to raise the kind of theoretical and empirical issues that social Darwinism raised in its day.

The evolutionist pioneers were constrained by limited data and perhaps inadequate conceptualization. Their problems required a systematic examination of historical data, folklore data, and data secreted in myths and legends. In fact, today, scholarship is better equipped to ask and answer the type of questions with which social Darwinism was deeply concerned. The pioneers had at their disposal partial or incomplete data, uncritical and even downright misleading data. This led them to simplistic interpretations and naïve theorization. Their excessive dependence on biological models and philosophical speculation pre-

vented a more rigorous and systematic sociology. Above all, their deterministic and unilinear theoretical framework tended to block and obscure sociological reality, rather than clarify the issues raised. Evolutionism was subsequently found to be value-loaded and ideologically biased. Its Eurocentric orientation also tended to perpetuate a distorted view of non-Western societies and peoples. These limitations, coupled with their simplistic tools of enquiry, have brought evolutionism and social Darwinism some discredit. Even their one great strength, historical analysis, was vitiated because of their historical determinism. Their attempt to understand primitive man and his society on the basis of contemporary primitive groups was methodologically flawed because of its deterministic extrapolations. No less questionable was their attempt to use cultural survivals to re-construct man's primitive past. Their interpretations on this basis were frequently arbitrary and untrustworthy. Their work was a mixture of empirical data, fanciful interpretation, ideological obsession, moral prejudice and methodological naïveté.

THE THIRD STAGE: FOCUS ON POVERTY AND SOCIAL DISORGANIZATION (1920–1950)

The third historical stage of family studies was dominated by the notion of social reform based on desirable social goals. In this respect, this approach was not dissimilar to the evolutionists. They differed not on the goal of social change *per se*, but on the values in which social change was conceptualised. The early evolutionists subscribed to an optimistic framework of historical progress. But this optimism was soon belied by the social problems of urbanization in nineteenth century industrial society. Slums, overcrowded areas, inadequate sanitation and the constant threat to orderly and peaceful social life—all undermined Victorian optimism and generated a critical attitude towards industrialism and urbanism, which could not fit into an optimistically interpreted evolutionary schema of progressive incrementalism. The prevailing atmosphere of doubt and anxiety, as well as critical scrutiny, could not help but influence the emerging discipline of systematic sociology.

The most decisive blow against evolutionist optimism was the First World War. Spencerian evolutionism held that social evolution had reached a stage of international interdependence which ruled out the possibility of wars between modern industrial societies. Thus, evolutionism had to be either drastically reformulated or totally abandoned. In fact, the focus shifted from evolutionism and social change to social structure (Becker and Barnes, 1952). As a result, emerging social problems came to be conceptualized in structuralist terms as problems of social organization, disorganization and breakdown, and social malfunctioning. The major social theorists such as Durkheim found themselves involved in the theoretical problem related to social structure and its structural conflicts/contradictions.

Durkheim in France

Emile Durkheim (1858–1917) was the first social theorist to conceptualise the family in structuralist terms as a component of the social structure. In his classic study of suicide, he assumed a systematic relationship between industrial behaviour and group structure. His interpretation of suicide (1897) in anomic terms presupposed a social structure the normal functioning of which depended on social norms, that is, the principles of its structure. In his framework, a distinction was made between earlier societies based on *mechanical solidarity* as their structural principle, and modern societies, increasingly characterised by the qualitatively new structural principle of *organic solidarity*, based on division of labour. His problem was to relate the disintegrative implications of division of labour to its co-existence with social solidarity. He interpreted the problems of strife and conflict—deviations from social integration—in terms of social norms and values, rooted in *collective sentiment*. His social structure, therefore, came to rest on essentially psychologistic foundations. The anomic consequences of division of labour had to

be structurally countered by organizational solidarity, arising out of collective loyalties, feelings and attitudes. Even as he was trying to discover a way out of the dilemmas of modern industrial society, Durkheim was not unduly optimistic, as can be seen from his preoccupations with the problem of anomie.

Le Play: The Pioneering Student of the Family

Frederick Le Play (1806–1882) was a pioneer in the systematic study of the family. He, like Auguste Comte, was concerned with the problem of contemporary social organization, especially the social impact of the French Revolution. They were both interested in the problem of restructuring the social order after the revolution. Both believed that the solutions to the problem could only be found through systematic and empirical study. Le Play, a sociologist and economist, pioneered in the mid-nineteenth century a new way of presenting sociological knowledge—namely, scientific monographs on family standards of living. He not only pioneered the survey method, but he also inaugurated the interdisciplinary problem-solving tradition by enlisting the co-operation of economists, engineers, and political scientists in his studies. He evolved a methodology of identifying the simplest and most basic social units and then constructed more complex structures. He endeavored to identify the social conditions conducive to stability and the industrial progress of a nation. Since the nation was too large and complex an entity, he resolved to arrive at an understanding of this structure through a study of select families, which served as his basic units of observation and as a representation of the larger whole. He believed it was possible to generalize about the larger unit from the knowledge of the simpler one. He studied select working-class French families in detail, focusing on life-style, roles and role-relationships and using the survey method.

The Family as a Basic Unit

Le Play used the family as the basic social unit, and focused on the family budget as a means of understanding social facts. Since the family had to sustain itself on the basis of work, and since the work involved the place of work, his sociological framework tended to emphasise the place-work-family triadic relationship. Moreover, Le Play's choice of the working class family was dictated by the fact that this class was a majority in the population, and hence imparted its characteristics to the larger social whole. He is believed to have discovered a systematic interrelationship between the consumption pattern of the families and their social activities, and also between the consumption habits and the social policies of a nation. He took care to choose average families for his study. He also lived with the family as a participant-observer. Le Play forged a quantitative technique for computing the different dimensions of family life. He emphasized the importance of such data as necessary to eliminate vagueness and uncertainty. He prepared a detailed standard outline, which was to be applied uniformly to all units of observation. It was designed to elicit precise quantitative data about such items as the family size and composition, internal ranking, its pattern of work, recreational activities, consumption pattern, health and hygienic condition, and religious habits. In his methodology, direct observation was supplemented by personal interviews based on questionnaires. The interviews were meant to enable the interviewer to make "an outpouring of the heart."

Le Play viewed the family in terms of complex interrelationships between the economic situation, emotional life, and ideology within the family. He theorized that a social structure promoting well-being comprised seven components—acceptance of universal moral laws and parental authority, religion, government, material prosperity of the community, individual property, and patronage. He held that the upper and the middle classes set the mores, and the third class provided the means of livelihood.

Booth and Rowntree in England

The positive consequences of the work of Le Play came to be reflected in the work and writings of two well-known statisticians and reformers in England in the later half of the nineteenth century—Charles Booth (1840–1916) and B.S. Rowntree (1871–1954). Booth's *Life and Labour of the People of London* and Rowntree's *Poverty: A Study of Town Life*, (1908), demonstrated the relationship between poverty, misery and depravity. It also gave an account of the life-situation of the various social classes. Booth made systematic use of the census and other official sources to gather data about income, occupation, number of dependents, and number of rooms available for living. However, he found this approach too quantitative and aggregative to yield any qualitatively meaningful propositions. He began increasingly to use methods of detailed and direct observation. His aim was to work out a socio-economic classification of East Londoners living at the time, but using the family as a unit and the poverty-line as a cut-off point. For this purpose, he employed the method of the large-scale interview. Thus he combined the statistical approach with what may be called the case method. One major flaw in his data was his occasional outbursts of subjective feelings and emotions. To counter the possibility of his subjects refusing to give genuine personal information, Booth resorted to the direct, participant observation method. Booth's work remains monumental in the history of modern sociology, not so much for his statistical data as for his realistic and graphic account of the social reality, as he encountered it in East London.

Rowntree's follow-up study of urban poverty, *Poverty and Progress: A Second Social Survey of York* (1941), dealt with labour and family life in a small town, not dissimilar to the concerns of Booth. Rowntree was able to put forward a hypothetical standard of minimum family need, measured food values in caloric terms, and computed carefully the quantum of cost of energy necessary for a worker and his family. His concept of minimum subsistence included such items as house rent, cost of clothing, purchase of household equipment. He also introduced the notion of secondary poverty which indicated the level at which income would have been adequate but for certain items of expenditure, both useful and conspicuous. While Booth estimated that 30.7% of the whole of London's population lived in poverty, the Rowntree study put this figure at 27.8% for York. The significance of these studies is that they document empirically the existence of substantial poverty among families in some of the wealthiest areas of the world during periods of their economic expansion. Such findings became the basis for later reformist activity.

The Chicago School: 1920–1950

In this phase of the evolution of sociology as a scientific discipline, a notable part was played by a group of sociologists collectively known as the *Chicago School*. The most important members of this school were: Charles H. Cooley (1864–1929), W.I. Thomas (1863–1947), Robert Park (1864–1944), Florian Znaniecki (1882–1958), and Ernest Watson Burgess (1886–1966). At a time when evolutionism was becoming a spent force and the neo-positivist trend was yet to appear, the Chicago School pioneered what might be called psychological sociology. Besides the sociologists already indicated, the philosopher George Mead was also closely associated with the Chicago School.

Cooley's most significant contribution was the concept of the *primary group*, the self, and the looking-glass self. Society was conceived by him as rooted in the mind and imagination of the individuals composing it. Cooley located the source and development of individual psyche in the activity of the primary group and social interaction/communication. Self, therefore, was seen as a dynamically evolving entity within a bounded social context. In Cooley's own words, "…There is no sense of 'I' …without its correlative sense of you, he, or they…" (Cooley, 1902). On this basis, he developed his celebrated concept of reflected or "looking-glass" self, characterized by three chief features—the imagination of the self by the others, the imagination of oneself in the other's situation and understanding other's feelings, and self-feeling, as reflected in pride or hurt.

The distinctive property of the primary group is intimate, face-to-face, interpersonal interaction, resulting in direct cooperation and conflict, and comparatively free expression of personality and sentiment. For him, the most important primary groups were the family, the play group and the intimate neighbourhood. They were primary because they were essential constituents of human nature itself. They gave rise to such universal values as faith, service, kindness, acceptance of social norms, and individual freedom. Indeed, their emergence was an index of the degree of realization of the goals of progress and democracy. Cooley's social theory tended to idealize the relationship between the individual and society. He argued that progress from the simpler to more complex societies was accompanied by increasing mechanization, the formation of secondary groups, a decline in human nature, religious intolerance, and a general routinization of institutional behaviour.

W.I. Thomas and Florian Znaniecki

Thomas (1863–1947) and Znaniecki (1882–1929) were no less interested in the notion of social disorganization, but their approach differed from the approaches of Cooley and Durkheim. Thomas and Znaniecki were concerned with the growth of urban America and the supply of cheap labour. Thomas had accumulated data on the Polish immigrants in America by the time he met the Polish philosopher-sociologist, Znaniecki. They collaborated in producing their classic study, *The Polish Peasant in Europe and America* (1918). They used family life history to re-construct the process of social development in a cross-section of the population studied. They used personal documents, diaries, and personal correspondence. The authors were also interested in evolving a typology of individual life organization, structure of social organization, and specific notions of personal and social disorganization. All these illuminated the structure and functioning of the Polish immigrant family. Their study pioneered the use of modern anthropological concepts in comprehending rapid cultural change, social organization and socio-cultural adaptation in advanced industrial societies such as the USA. They effectively argued that deviant behaviour was the result of breakdown of social organization under tension.

Park and Burgess

Robert Park was a renowned teacher whose students contributed substantially to sociological literature. He was one of those great scholars who preferred inspiring others to writing himself. His disciples became intensely involved in the study of urban life, and focused especially on the problems of social disorganization in American cities. They attempted to interpret social phenomena from an ecological perspective, as in such works as E.R. Mowrer's *Family Disorganization* (1927), F.M. Tharsher's *The Gang* (1927) and H.W. Zorbaugh's *The Gold Coast and the Slum: A Sociological Study of Chicago's Near North Side* (1929). *The Gold Coast* contrasts a wealthy neighbourhood in Chicago to a slum area in the same city. While works like this gave realistic and detailed accounts of social organization and disorganization in urban life, their chief motivation was to promote reform and re-organization of local society. This is evident in Park's study, *The City* (1925). The same ecological perspective dominated *The Urban Community* (1926), edited by Ernest Burgess. Burgess was born in Tilbury, Ontario, Canada in 1866 but emigrated to the USA at the age of two and a half. He graduated from the University of Chicago and taught there from 1916 to 1966 when he died. The scholar who influenced him most was Robert Park. The Park-Burgess team was very productive. Disillusioned with contemporary social work, Burgess, as a social reformer, believed that solutions to social problems should be sought in social research. His research led him to the view that contemporary society had *declined* to a state of disorganization from a prior stability and orderliness. He located the source of disorganization in the processes of industri-

alization and demographic mobility. However, he believed that this was a prelude to an era of social re-organization.

Burgess soon shifted his attention to the family, and, in particular, to the theme of marital harmony. His knowledge of Russian and a personal visit to Russia enabled him to examine the impact of Communist ideology on family structure. He was also encouraged by S. Franklin Frazier's study of the Negro family in Chicago. In 1926 Burgess's paper, "The Family as a Unity of Interacting Personalities," set out the program of his future research activities.

In 1939 Burgess published *Predicting Success or Failure in Marriage* in collaboration with Leonard L. Cottrell, Jr., which was a landmark in the interactionist study of the family. Burgess hoped that a search for predictive variables might lead to the identification of more complex variables, capable of providing a conceptual framework for understanding marital dynamics. He also believed that predictive variables would have practical application in the work of marriage counsellors and other relevant professionals. Meanwhile, Burgess, in collaboration with H.J. Locke, was engaged in writing *The Family*, a comprehensive treatise representing twenty years of study, research, and teaching. When published in 1945, it established itself immediately as a standard textbook on the family.

The postwar period was dominated by studies of social disorganization. These studies focused on problems of slum clearance, loneliness, estranged relations with relatives and superficial contacts with neighbours in the new urban settlements. They revealed the stress and strain in urban family life that continues today.

Since 1950: Towards a Theory of the Family

A variety of theoretical models and frameworks to explain family structure and behaviour have appeared since 1950. These have generated empirically testable and interrelated propositions claiming universal validity and possessing the property of parsimonious presentation. [1] The names that stand out are William Goode, M.F. Nimkoff, Ivan Nye, Reuben Hill, Bernard Farber, and Marvin Sussman.

In this period, family studies were acquiring respectability all over the world, because of the shift in sociology from a pragmatic approach to a more academic and theoretical concern. Hill and Hansen's important paper, "The Identification of Conceptual Frameworks Utilized in Family Studies" (1960), discussed five dominant theoretical-conceptual frameworks in family studies in this period. According to them, a theory is, "a set of interrelated concepts, a set of underlying and unifying assumptions, and a set of postulates," whereas a conceptual framework "might be viewed as a set of concepts which are rather loosely held together which are not in any definite sense interrelated" (1960: 300–301). Hence, a conceptual framework cannot be strictly called a theory. Broadly speaking, the new scientific approach brought to the study of social phenomena a new set of values and commitment such as value-neutrality, objectivity, and empiricist epistemology. The overall impact of this development has been to encourage a conservative orientation and a certain squeamishness regarding certain areas in regard to family study. Yet the gains have been both methodological and substantive. New problem areas, apart from marital adjustment, such as normal pre-marital activities like dating, courtship, and mate selection, have been opened up for systematic investigation.

Since the 1940s, empirical investigations of the several aspects of family life have proliferated (Hill, 1958). In the USA, the themes relating to marriage and family have been in the forefront of sociological study, ranking fourth among some 24 identified fields of sociological investigation. A 1963 survey of sociological research found family studies in second position in terms of quantity and concern (Nye and Bayer, 1963). The USA accounted for a little more than half of all the family-related research publications from thirty countries, according to a 1958 survey (Hill, 1958). New and more sophisticated infrastructural styles have entered the field of family studies. Research investigations have become more elaborate and complex, with an increasing stress on a multi-disciplinary focus. Admittedly, the course of these developments have been beset with problems arising out of the nature of the phenomena studied. Family life is a sensitive area, a very private preserve, and people are resistant to scientific intrusions into it. This was particularly true of the earliest crop of family studies. A landmark in the institutionalization of family study within the sociological tradition of the USA was the emergence of bodies like the National Commission on Family Relations (1938), a special section for family studies in the American Sociological Association, the White House Conference on Children, and the Family Study Centres. At the international level, there were: the International Seminar on Family Research and the Committee on Family Research of the International Sociological Association. Another manifestation was the increasing efforts at cross-cultural studies on the family.

THE FOURTH STAGE: TOWARDS SOPHISTICATION

From the 1950s onwards, the study of the family became more sophisticated with the designing of an investigative hypothesis and the employment of elaborate techniques for data-collection, analysis, and interpretation. The practice of cumulative theory-building be-

---

[1] Though it has been asserted that real theory-building in regard to the structure, functions and dynamics of the family began only after 1950 (Christensen, 1966), it should be pointed out that the evolutionist school was also similarly concerned. But what is certainly true is that it was in this period that systematic and coordinated attempts were made at conceptualization and theorization on the family.

came part of the whole enterprise of the scientific study of society. More rigorous sampling techniques, greater dependence on direct observation, better constructed questionnaires, and more controlled testing procedures, came to characterise family study. [1]

An important survey of the years 1947–61 (Nye and Bayer, 1963) noted the following trends: the practice of establishing linkages with previous research work through documented references to them, the use of formally articulated hypothetical propositions, and use of tests of significance. The questionnaire and the interview became more frequently used. Direct observation ranked lowest and declined even more rapidly in the period 1952–61. According to Nye and Bayer, the important variables studied were: dating/courtship/mate selection, marital satisfaction, marital roles, parent-child relationship, and sex-related behaviour. While these were dependent variables, the independent variables were sex, social class, age, religion, education, and residence. From 1950 on, new research tools and techniques came to be increasingly applied, such as direct observation of family behaviour, tape-recording of material relating to interviews and other interactions, projective methods, socio-metric tools, record linkage and controlled experiment (Hill, 1958; Hill, Katz, and Simpson, 1957).

Current innovations and improvements in methodology are due to family research today becoming self-critical and critically self-conscious. One indication of this is the increasing attention that is being paid to the criteria for evaluation of research material. [2] In the area of theory-building, significant developments have been the appearance of critical and evaluative literature and comprehensive surveys of the field. Attempts have been made recently to integrate the different findings of various family studies in order to generate hypotheses.

THE FIFTH STAGE: THE FEMINIST PERSPECTIVE ON FAMILY STUDIES

The feminist movement in the West started on a limited scale at the beginning of this century, but its significant effects became visible only in the 1970s, and on a global scale. In almost every society today, from the least developed to the most, an elite minority of women is seriously challenging men's domination of society.

One area where the feminist challenge has been articulated with particular sharpness is the literature on family studies. In the 1960s, there was little attempt to deal with the abuses and neglect suffered by children and women in the existing social structure. If we take a look at the widely used textbooks on family sociology in the 1960s, we find that their central preoccupations were the basic functions of the family, both in its universal and society-specific aspects and the relevance of these functions for the integration, maintenance and survival of societies. Particular emphasis was laid on the function of the family as a provider of love, care and emotional sustenance to its members. However, the issues and concerns of the textbooks that have appeared in the mid-seventies and after were not those of the previous decade; they tend to focus on such disturbing themes as "violence in the family," "battered child syndrome," "wife-battering"—all highlighting the darker side of the family life. (Scanzoni and Scanzoni, 1981; Lasswell and Lasswell, 1982; Bell, 1983; Broderick, 1984; Leslie (1985). This perspective reflects the growing feminist concern for children and women, with special attention to the

---

[1] From a global perspective, it is interesting to note that the USA held a relatively lower rank than Europe and Asia, in the matter of representative samples and direct observation, but it ranked higher in the employment of stochastic analysis, hypotheses-testing and analytical frameworks.

[2] These criteria include technical competence, theoretical achievement, relation to ongoing research, qualitative understanding of the family, originality in interpretation of data, potentiality for practical application, relevance and status of problem, innovativeness in techniques and lucid exposition and explanation (Foote, 1957).

violence perpetrated on them in a male-dominated society.

The Death of the Family

Dissatisfied with the traditional division of labour, involving injustice to, and exploitation of, women both at the macro-societal level and at the micro-level of the family, radical feminists question the very relevance and need for the family.

This critique contends that the family is not a functional necessity for modern societies. The arguments are as follows: First, the only two functions now left to the family, reproduction and socialization of children, will soon cease to be family responsibilities as agencies outside the family are taking over these functions. Second, the increasing abuse of children and the mounting incidence of violence within the family refute the claim that the family is a desirable place, "a haven in the heartless world" (Lasch, 1977). Third, the symptoms of the collapse of the family as a functional institution are evident in the galloping divorce rate, disruptive and aggressive individualism, selfishness, dominating intra-family relations, and the utter neglect of the old. The family has been always a necessarily exploitative institution, a discriminatory and privatized institution working to maintain male dominance at the cost of children and women; the family is a dying and anachronic survival from a male-oriented history. Assuming the death of the family to be an established fact, the advocates of this critique are now engaged in discovering alternatives to the family to serve human needs.

Redefining Concepts and Re-structuring Theories

Since the beginning of the 1980s, feminist sociologists have been actively engaged in rewriting family sociology, its concepts, theoretical frames and overall perspective, to generate a new feminist family sociology. It is too early as yet to assess the outcome. One cannot, however, ignore their work, as it may have some

potential. They question the very concept of family, as elaborated in traditional sociology. They argue that we must make a clear distinction between "the" family, a historical institution rooted in a male-dominated civilization, and the family in a more generic sense. As a result, they advocate what they call a multidimensional approach. Their argument is that a monolithic approach leads to serious biases in data collection. If the concept of multiple family types is accepted, it would enable us to look at dimensions invariably ignored in a monolithic approach (Eichler, 1988, 10). A multidimensional approach would eliminate the risk of imposing the observer's model on the actor's model. In the monolithic approach, the varieties of models people hold tend to be overlooked. Methodologically, they recommend a de-construction of the dominant model, so that the way is cleared for a more realistic and empirically valid picture of the family.

In the next chapter, Cheal argues that the feminist theoretical framework represents an alliance between feminism and Marxism; this alliance can be seen in the interest demonstrated by their radical policy, and their sharing of a materialist epistemology and methodology with Marxists. This means that they both employ a materialist methodology in explaining social causation. The patrimonial family, for instance, is viewed by the feminists as an effective instrument for exploiting women, both socially and economically. So they contend that the existing social system leads to the "internal stratification of family life," skewed essentially in favour of men, and legitimises their dominance.

The feminist literature of the '80s reveals the following crucial assumptions: (1) The family is an ideological construct, manipulated by men for men. Therefore, it is unrealistic to recognise only one family concept. (2) The family is not a place where psychological needs are satisfied, but, on the contrary, it is a place where women and children are exploited and suppressed by men. (3) The family as a human institution is fast dying out, giving way to other, new social arrangements and structures, which cater to the needs of people more successfully.

Although the feminists make too many unrealistic claims, they deserve credit for having drawn the attention of sociology and its practitioners to certain significant but neglected aspects and features of family life. They deserve credit for increasing social awareness of social abuses, such as discrimination against women and abuse of wives and children, both within and outside the family system. This has alerted policy-makers to work out remedial measures for the victims of social injustice and has resulted in a considerable social and legal reform, aimed at setting right such abuses. Their claims that the family is only detrimental to society, that it is a dying institution, and that it deserves to die are not realistic. For we know that most societies across time and space have looked to marriage for the production of children and to the family for the rearing of children. We also know that there has always been, and continues to be, a small number of people who reject the family framework but do so within socially sanctioned limits. Vast numbers of children all over the world are born into families, and their parents have been willing to look after their welfare and happiness, despite the trials in the working of the family system. It is one thing to argue for reform or even radical change, but it is quite a different thing to condemn the family and welcome its alleged death.

The current hostility to the family as an institution should best be viewed as a symptom of a society in flux, and it is worthwhile to await the emergence of a re-fashioned family system, functioning under altered rules and norms, before passing negative judgements on the family.

SUMMARY

The purpose of this brief survey is to review the changing perceptions and conceptions in the sociology of the family in the West since the beginning of the nineteenth century. The survey points to a theoretical tradition, capable of changing its frameworks and preoccupations in response to changing social reality. It also draws attention to some of the difficulties and dilemmas, even paradigm shifts, that have characterised the history of family studies. It focuses on five stages in that history: (1) the pre-sociological tradition up to 1861; (2) the tradition, emphasizing origin and evolution of the family, from 1862 to the 1920s; (3) the social problem-cum-social reform tradition, emphasizing the issues of poverty, social disorganization, and other social malaise plaguing a modern industrial society, from the 1920s to the 1950s; (4) the emergence of a more self-consciously scientific tradition, involving methodological and theoretical sophistication, from the 1950s to the 1960s; and (5) the period of feminist critique with Marxist overtones, from the 1970s to the present. However, these stages should be seen as inter-linked and overlapping, not sharply demarcated.

The first stage is characterized by an absence of methodological, theoretical and thematic coherence. It is largely the product of ancient and classical societies, and is essentially moralistic and non-empirical in approach. It may best be described as pre-sociological, belonging to the time prior to the birth of modern sociology.

The second stage may be broadly called social Darwinism, reflecting the ethos of evolutionism inaugurated by Charles Darwin. The social Darwinists raised many interesting problems, but their conceptual tools were not precise and their data not scientific. Further, they also assumed uncritically and ethnocentrically that Europe was most advanced in the evolutionary process. While they had brilliant speculative insights, they also left problems which can never be resolved in principle.

The third stage was dominated by the practical concern for identifying and solving the problems arising in the working of a industrial society. Sociology and social theory were a byproduct of this concern for social reform and amelioration. The overall contribution of this approach can be summed up as "psychological sociology," a development that took sociology away from the evolutionist concerns, but did not as yet blossom into an empirical and scientific tradition.

The fourth stage is the one in which family study, as part of the wider discipline of sociology, became empirically oriented and organised as a positivist scientific discipline, modelled on the natural sciences. For the first time, family studies became recognised as sharply focused in terms of theory, theme and technique. A substantial body of theory, resting on empirical data and amenable to testing through scientific investigation, came to be produced. Perhaps one major limitation in this stage was the inability to formulate a general theory of a cross-cultural nature, and the tendency towards an ethnocentric elevation of the North American family model.

The fifth stage is more critical than consolidating. The feminists have produced a powerful and up-to-a-point necessary critique of the dominant male-oriented family, especially drawing attention to the exploitative nature of the family, in which women and children are the chief victims. While the ideological content of its critique is valid, this approach seems to overreach itself in failing to note the universal persistence of the family.

TECHNICAL TERMS

ENDOGAMY—A cultural pattern prescribing marriage within one's own social group.

EXOGAMY—A cultural pattern prescribing marriage outside one's social group.

DARWINISM—The theory explaining the survival of societies in terms of an evolutionary scheme based on natural selection.

MECHANICAL SOLIDARITY—Social cohesion characteristic of small-scale, preindustrial societies and based on a consensus of values, beliefs, and norms.

MONOGAMY—The marriage of one person to one other person.

ORGANIC SOLIDARITY—Social cohesiveness characteristic of large-scale industrial societies and based on the functional interdependence of its members.

SOCIAL EVOLUTION—The process of development of societies from simpler to complex social forms.

URBANISM—A way of life typical of residents of cities.

QUESTIONS

1. What is meant by the term *social evolution*? Select any one social evolutionist and examine his contributions to family sociology.

2. Describe the contributions of the Chicago school toward our understanding of the family in the urban context.

3. Can we say that the feminist orientation to family studies allows us to regard their solutions as problems and their questions as solutions?

4. Critically examine the remark that early evolutionists, like the neo-evolutionists today, were ethnocentric in their interpretation.

Chapter 2 / K. Ishwaran

SUGGESTED READINGS

- Gary S. Becker. *A Treatise on The Family*. Cambridge: Harvard University Press, 1981.

  An economist's view of the family. It presents a theoretical analysis of the family from an interdisciplinary perspective.

- Harold T. Christensen. *Handbook of Marriage and The Family*. Chicago: Rand McNally, 1964.

  A collection of papers dealing with the literature on family studies and theoretical and conceptual approaches that have emerged in the literature.

- Lee Gray. *Family Structure and Interaction—A Comparative Analysis*. Philadelphia: J.B. Lippincott, 1977.

  The study examines theory, methodology, and various aspects of the family from a comparative point of view.

The Bunz family of Saskatchewan stands four generations deep beside their first home which was built around 1904.

Chapter 3

THE MEANINGS OF FAMILY LIFE

Theoretical Approaches and Theory Models

David Cheal
University of Winnipeg

The theory of family life is one of the most challenging areas in sociology today. This is not due to any past neglect of theoretical issues by family sociologists. Sociologists of the family have always been interested in studying family life, of course, but in recent years many other social thinkers also entered the field. Some of them became involved in family studies in order to find ways of improving social policies affecting family members. Others sought to change the ways in which we think about—and live—family life. The latter is especially emphasized by feminist theorists, whose work is increasingly recognized for its power and originality (Ritzer, 1988).

Sociologists have often disagreed about what is the best approach to studying family life, and they were already doing this before the re-emergence of feminism during the 1960s. Recent debates have revived some of the differences of opinion that existed when the sociology of the family was first established (Mowrer, 1932: 6–11), but which were not visible in the period immediately after the Second World War (Hill and Hansen, 1960). In all of these discussions the meaning of family life has been interpreted and reinterpreted in many different ways. As a result, we cannot properly understand the sociology of the modern family by thinking about "the family" in only one way (Vanier Institute of the Family, 1981). Rather, we must learn to think about the different meanings of family life as they appear to different groups of theorists. That is one reason why the study of family life is so interesting to many social scientists. It is also why we need a separate chapter on theoretical approaches to family life in this book.

Thinking about the variety of ideas held by different family theorists is not always easy, but it is necessary. To begin with, if we are to decide for ourselves which ideas are most helpful, we need to know what alternatives exist. We will therefore be interested in comparing the contents of different theoretical approaches in order to weigh their advantages and disadvantages. This is the task of theory description. Second, if we think about the different theoretical approaches carefully we will eventually wonder why it is that so many approaches exist at all, and what we should do about it. The next step is to examine the relationships between the different schools of thought in order to find out more about how sociological theories are developed. That is the task of meta-theory. In this chapter we are going to do a little bit of both of these types of thinking, beginning with meta-theory.

Thinking About Family Theory

In order to understand family theory today, we must start by considering the uses that theories have in the social sciences. Social scientists work with two different kinds of theories. A variety of terms have been used to describe these two types of theories. Nye (1980) has called them "mini" theories and "general" theories. We will refer to them here as *theory models* and *theoretical approaches*. A theory model is a set of propositions that is intended to account for a limited set of facts. The limits to a model's relevance are often set out in definitions, assumptions or statements of limiting conditions. Theory models are useful because a small number of propositions can be used to explain a much larger number of observations (Cheal, 1983). Since they help us to summarize information, models have an important part to play in discussions of social policies affecting families (Eichler, 1985a; 1987).

Theoretical approaches (also known as theoretical orientations, conceptual frameworks or paradigms) are much broader than theory models. They usually contain a number of models, together with general statements about the relations between them. Theoretical approaches have five important uses. First, they provide us with concepts which we use in analyzing and communicating our observations of social life. The key concepts in theory models are usually derived from these conceptual frameworks. Second, theoretical approaches suggest the kinds of questions we should be asking, and hence they direct our attention to certain kinds of events rather than others. Third, they provide us with ways of answering questions, in the form of orienting assumptions and guides to observation. Fourth, they help us to interpret what we observe, and thus they structure the process of perception. And fifth, theoretical approaches often (some would say always) involve value-judgements about how social science knowledge should be applied in social affairs. Those value-judgements may have their origins in radical or conservative ideologies, as has often been the case in current debates about marriage, gender, and the family (Berger and Berger, 1983).

Theoretical approaches clearly have the most profound effects upon the nature of what we judge to be valid social scientific thought. Two effects have been particularly important in shaping the forms of family theory found in contemporary sociology. They concern the nature of knowledge itself (that is, epistemology) and the nature of the units of analysis (that is, ontology).

Theories are developed by social scientists in order to expand our knowledge about the world in which we live. Theoretical approaches must therefore contain some answer to the most basic question of all—what is knowledge, and how do we get it? One of the most influential answers to this question has been that social scientists should imitate natural scientists, and seek to uncover general laws of social organization. That point of view, known as *positivism*, has given rise to a distinctive method for developing family theory. It is the method of *theory construction* (Burr, 1973).

According to the theory construction program, the goal of the social sciences should be to produce an integrated set of propositions about the family that is both general and true. Investigators who hold this point of view believe that it will eventually be possible to produce one general theory. They also believe that many of the elements for that theory already exist in the hypotheses that have been tested by researchers. It follows that there are thought to be two principal tasks for sociological theorists. First, there is the task of cataloging (or "inventorying") propositions which are known to be sound. Second, there is the task of integrating those propositions within more general statements. That is to be done through techniques such as the "interdefining of concepts" and the "specification of hypotheses," in which a variety of models are linked together.

For more than two decades American social scientists have put an enormous amount of work into these projects, with some impressive results (Goode et al, 1971; Burr, Hill et al., 1979). However, the value of these results has been criticised in recent years (Osmond, 1987; Thomas and Wilcox, 1987). The main criticisms have been that the theories developed in this way have been uniformly conventional, often conservative, and in the past they overlooked women's particular concerns (Eichler, 1985b). These limitations occur because any theory is based upon some set of assumptions, or presuppositions, which are affected by our common sense views of the world, including those related to gender. This does not mean that the theory construction method is a complete waste of time. What it does mean is that its real value lies in coordinating the work of those who share the same fundamental beliefs. Others who hold different beliefs will develop different theories, using methods that uncover new meanings (Currie, 1988).

Debating the utility of methods for developing family theories is one of the two principal effects of different theoretical approaches, which were mentioned above. The other effect is that theorists often have different ideas about what it is that they are studying. Defining the object of investigation, or unit of analysis, is an important activity in the social sciences. The principal unit of analysis is often not the same in different theoretical approaches, even when a common term like "family" is employed. The term "family" has often been used to mean different things by different theorists, and in some cases "the family" has been replaced by other units of analysis in family studies. Further discussion of this point will be postponed until after we have described some of the major theoretical approaches and theory models in the sociology of family life.

Standard Sociological Theory

In the standard theory of family life the unit of analysis is the family, conceived of as an adaptive system which mediates between the individual and society. Defined in this way, the family is believed to perform essential functions for family members and for the larger society. It is thought that when a society changes, the form of family life will be reshaped to ensure that societal needs continue to be met. Standard theorists have claimed that in the modern western societies the family has adapted to meet the needs of an industrial economy. The dominant type of family in industrial societies is described as the "conjugal family" (since it is founded upon the marriage relationship) or the "nuclear family" (since it is a minimal social group). Talcott Parsons'

model of the nuclear family is one of three standard theory models that have shaped much sociological thinking about the modern family.

I. Nuclear Family Model

Parsons claimed that the conjugal or nuclear family is the only type of family that does not conflict with the requirements of an industrial economy (Parsons, 1964). Consisting of husband, wife, and children (if any), it is small enough to be highly mobile. Furthermore, the obligations of members to kin outside the nuclear family are separated from occupational commitments, and thus individuals are relatively free from kinship pressures at work (Parsons, 1949b). Parsons described the American kinship system as consisting of interlocking conjugal families (Parsons, 1943). Each conjugal family, Parsons claimed, usually lives as an independent nuclear family household (Parsons, 1943; 1971). Parsons concluded that the nuclear family household has two main functions in modern societies. They are the socialization of children, and the "personality stabilization" (or "tension management") of adults. He thought that in general the functional importance of the family was in decline, since many of its traditional functions had been transferred to other social structures. In particular, Parsons stated that the modern nuclear family was no longer engaged in much economic production (Parsons, 1955).

According to Parsons (1949), in the middle class American family economic resources are provided by the employment of the husband/father, while the wife/mother stays at home to serve the emotional needs of family members. Parsons thought that this differentiation of the sex roles was necessary, because otherwise competition for occupational status between the spouses would undermine the solidarity of the marriage relationship. He described the husband/father as the "instrumental leader" of the normal family, and the wife/mother as its "expressive leader."

Parsons' views on the family have always been controversial. Among standard theorists, the most influential criticisms were directed against Parsons' emphasis upon the structural isolation of the conjugal relationship (Lenero-Otero, 1977; Lee, 1980). In contrast to the isolated nuclear family model, Litwak proposed an alternative model which he called the modified extended family (Litwak, 1960a).

II. Extended Family Model

Litwak drew a distinction between the "classical" extended family, which is a group of related persons living in close proximity, and the "modified" extended family, whose members are physically dispersed. According to Litwak, modern communications technologies and the existence of a money economy enable people to overcome the physical barriers to interaction arising from separation. In Litwak's opinion, nuclear families keep up their extended family connections mainly because of the "emotional, social and economic aid" which they receive. The nuclear family is a small group, with limited resources. In emergencies those resources may be insufficient. Extended family kin therefore continue to be important in contemporary society, because they "provide supplemental resources to the isolated nuclear family" (Litwak and Szelenyi, 1969: 469). In particular, intergenerational aid permits families to respond to the different kinds of needs that occur at various stages of the family life cycle (Hill, 1970).

III. Developmental Family Life Cycle Model

The nuclear family model and the extended family model are static theories. They describe family life as the result of a fixed arrangement of roles. Models of the family life cycle, on the other hand, are dynamic models. They look at family life as a process that unfolds over time. In standard theory models of the family life cycle family development is described as a series of stages (Hill and Rodgers, 1964; Aldous, 1978). The passage from one stage to another occurs when there is a change in family composition. Such changes in turn affect various aspects of family well-being, including the pressure upon economic resources. It is therefore claimed that at each stage the family faces distinctive tasks whose completion is essential

for individual development (Duvall and Miller, 1985).

The developmental family life cycle model has been subject to considerable criticism over the years (Nock, 1979; Cheal, 1987b; Eichler, 1988), although efforts at conceptual refinement continue (Mattessich and Hill, 1987). The principal difficulty has been the impossibility of fitting all of the many different living arrangements that exist into a universal set of stages. Some critics have suggested that the family life cycle concept should be retained, but that its status needs to be re-evaluated (Goode, 1977). Other critics prefer approaches with assumptions different from those of standard theory, such as symbolic interactionism (Elder, 1977; 1984).

Standard Theory: A Critical Appreciation

Critics of standard sociological theory have adopted a variety of alternative approaches, but they are all agreed on one thing. Standard family theory is believed to have paid insufficient attention to the real diversity of experiences in family life. Parsonian images of the family have been especially heavily criticized as dominated by a rigid, exaggerated and oversimplified view of marital interaction in general, and women's experiences in particular (Laws, 1971; Oakley, 1974; Beechey, 1978). Although Parsons' work has not been representative of standard theory for some time, its subterranean influence is still detected in sex-role theorizing (Beechey, 1978; Edgell, 1980; Thorne, 1982). Can standard sociological theory respond to these and other attacks, or will it disappear to be replaced, perhaps, by feminist theory? (Stacey and Thorne, 1985)

Standard sociological theory has undergone many changes in past decades, and it continues to change today. In its early version, known as *structural functionalism*, the structure of roles in the family was thought to be determined by the functions it performs for society, as illustrated in Parsons' work. That point of view is no longer widely accepted, since the "fit" between family and society seems to be quite loose. In some societies, notably England, the isolated nuclear family existed long before industrialization. Furthermore, in late twentieth century industrial societies the major changes in family life, such as increase in divorce, are unrelated to requirements for occupational mobility. Partly for these reasons, standard sociological theory has changed. Today, standard family theorists are most likely to identify themselves with the principles of family systems theory (Broderick and Smith, 1979; Morgan, 1985). A system is understood to be a set of interacting elements (the parts of the system), which is capable of maintaining a boundary between itself and the outside world, and which enters into transactions (or interchanges) with its environment. The concepts employed in this approach are derived from an interdisciplinary *systems theory* that was introduced into family studies by family therapists (Kantor and Lehr, 1975; Piotrkowski, 1979), and by the sociologist Reuben Hill (1971; 1977) and his associates.

The great advantage of thinking about the family as a boundary-maintaining system is that it is possible to analyze whatever changes occur in family life as simply one more aspect of the family's continuous adaptation to a changing environment. Ahrons and Rodgers, for example, have recently argued for a developmental interpretation of divorce. In their view a more flexible model of the family life cycle is needed, in which the post-divorce family is described as the bi-nuclear family, made up of two independent but related households (Ahrons and Rodgers, 1987).

Standard family theory is likely to remain a vital part of the sociology of the family for some time to come. Before we take a look at the major alternative approaches, its achievements should be acknowledged, as they have helped it to survive despite considerable opposition (Nett, 1982). At the macro level its achievements have included examining the links between types of families and types of societies. At the micro level standard theory has done three things. It has analyzed relationships within the family household (as nuclear family roles), family relationships beyond the household (as extended family ties), and

changing family relationships over time (as consequences of the family life cycle). Finally, theorists such as Rodgers have shown that creative innovations are still possible within standard sociological theory. Standard family theorists may have been slow to respond to recent changes, such as women's employment experiences (Hare-Mustin, 1988), but there is no reason to suppose that this approach has gone into irreversible decline. The theoretically most significant questions lie elsewhere, having to with units of analysis. The most fundamental question is: is the family really a system at all? One school of thought which contends that the family is not a system is symbolic interactionism.

Symbolic Interactionism

The emphasis in *symbolic interactionism* is upon individuals and their social relations. The most influential statement of this position is Burgess's definition of the family as a unity of interacting personalities (Burgess, 1926). Burgess stressed that whatever unity exists in family life can only be the result of interactions between family members. He therefore set out to study marital adjustment as a social process (Burgess and Cottrell, 1939). This process continues to be an important interest of family researchers (Adams, 1988). It has since become apparent that the theoretical implications of Burgess's definition point in two directions—on the one side to stability (and system), and on the other side to instability (and unpredictability).

On the side of stability, symbolic interactionists have often felt that individual behavior can only be understood within the context of the family role that an individual occupies (Stryker, 1968; Turner, 1970). Interactionist accounts of behavior in families can therefore be easily fitted into standard theory models of the family role structure (Burr, Leigh et al., 1979), with which they share the assumption of family unity. In this way, symbolic interactionism took on the principal form of a specialized social psychology within family studies. On the side of instability, Elder has argued for studying the family as a set of mutually contingent careers (Elder, 1984). The focus here is upon the individual life course, and on how it affects and is affected by the life courses of other individuals, in ways that produce both conventional and unconventional patterns of behavior in families. Interactionist work on shifting patterns of family life also includes studies of the ways in which behavior is negotiated and re-negotiated among family members (Backett, 1987; Finch, 1987).

Interactionist themes have been given a strongly individualistic thrust in work influenced by *phenomenology*. McLain and Weigert, for example, have objected to the assumption, which they attribute to standard theorists, that "some construct called family actually behaves" (McLain and Weigert, 1979: 187). Instead, they claim that only individuals behave. Focusing on individuals rather than families means that not all intimate performances are described as occurring within family situations. Interactionist sociologists have been particularly interested in intimate encounters that occur in alternative relationships. They have given us a number of useful studies of sexual encounters outside of the family, which illustrate how sexual behavior may be detached from family roles (Atwater, 1979). The choices that individuals make between family roles and non-family roles also receive explicit attention in exchange theory, where emphasis is placed on mutual feedback in the development of close relationships (Scanzoni, 1987).

Exchange Theory

Exchange theory has been the preferred starting point for much theorizing about family interactions, most notably in the United States (Aldous, 1977). One of the advantages of exchange theory is that it enables the investigator to think about gratifications provided within the family, and gratifications provided by sources outside the family, as alternatives between which individuals choose (Anderson, 1971). A theory of choice is in fact at the heart of the exchange-approach to family interaction (Nye, 1979).

In exchange theory it is assumed that individuals choose between lines of action so as to minimize their costs and maximize their rewards. Exchange theorists believe that individuals will engage in interaction only if it is profitable for them to do so. It is therefore thought that family life takes the general form of the exchange of goods and services (Nye, 1980). Most exchange analyses of the family have been concerned with relations between husbands and wives. Relevant topics include the choice of marriage partner (Murstein, 1973), the quality of the marriage relationship (Lewis and Spanier, 1982), and marital separation (Levinger, 1979). One of the best-known applications of exchange theory has been Scanzoni's work on marital interaction as a bargaining process (Scanzoni, 1972: especially 62–70).

Scanzoni stresses that his concept of marriage bargaining is different from the concept of marital adjustment. The latter concept, he says, has the effect of "emphasizing stability, consensus, and equilibrium" (Scanzoni, 1979b: 296). Bargaining within marriage may be explicit or implicit. According to Scanzoni, it occurs whenever one of the partners in a series of transactions wants to change the rules of exchange. Those rules determine "who gives how much of what benefits in return for how much of what other benefits" (Scanzoni, 1979b: 307). If marriage partners cannot agree on the rules of exchange, then open conflict may occur. Scanzoni has noted that the conflict strategies which individuals employ sometimes include coercion and physical violence (Scanzoni and Szinovacz, 1980). Discussions of such issues have been particularly prominent in feminist writings about the oppression of women within the family (Dahl and Snare, 1978).

Feminism

The central contribution of *feminism* to the sociology of family life is to describe women's oppression in marriage as the outcome of patriarchal relations. The term *patriarchy* is used to describe the political and social control of women by men (Coward, 1983). Processes of control and domination are thought to come into play whenever men and women interact.

Patriarchy is therefore seen as "a relatively autonomous structure written into family relations" (Kuhn, 1978: 51). It produces an internal stratification of family life, in which men receive superior benefits to those of women (Delphy, 1979).

Although patriarchy is an autonomous system of relations, it is often described as having especially strong effects upon family role structures. That is because men's relations with women are thought to take the principal form of control over the production of people, in biological and social reproduction (Fox, 1988). Patriarchy is therefore believed to include the social construction of women's desires to nurture and care for children.

In order to expose the underlying structure of patriarchy in family life, scholars working in the feminist tradition argue that we must "deconstruct" (Barrett and McIntosh, 1982: 90) or "decompose" (Thorne, 1982: 8) existing concepts of the family. What they mean by this is that the concept of the family as a social system should be replaced by the concept of the family as an ideology. That is to say, "the family" is thought to be a set of ideas which obscures more fundamental relations, such as the sex/gender system. Feminist theorists argue that the only reason why we continue to think of "the family" as an adaptive system is because of the ideological aura of sanctity that surrounds family life in capitalist societies (Barrett and McIntosh, 1982: Wearing, 1984). Rapp has claimed that "the concept of family is a socially necessary illusion" (Rapp, 1978: 281).

Feminists have criticised much research into family life for being committed to a view of the family as an adaptive system, or "agent" as Hartmann puts it (Hartmann, 1981). Hartmann has argued that instead we should study the ways in which the production and redistribution of resources takes place. As she sees it, the family is "a location where people with different activities and interests in these processes often come into conflict with one another" (Hartmann, 1981: 368). Those conflicts are the results of men and women having different economic interests due to their differ-

ent positions in the division of labour. How the connections between economic interests, gender and family life are to be conceptualized is of great concern to other theorists, including Marxists.

Marxism

A common focus on economic struggle has encouraged close links between feminism and *Marxism* in family studies (Brenner and Laslett, 1986), particularly in Canada (Cheal, 1988). Among Marxists this focus is expressed theoretically as economic determinism. The determining influence on social life is held to be the process by which goods are produced, or in other words, the mode of production. In the capitalist mode of production the most important economic relationship is that between owners of capital (that is, capitalists) and the wage labourers who work for them. Marxist theorists argue that families are necessary for the maintenance of capitalism, because they produce the labour power employed in factories and offices (Blumenfeld and Mann, 1980). Marxist studies of family life have therefore focused on the *political economy* of reproduction that is performed in the household (Mackintosh, 1979; Luxton, 1980).

Most housework is performed by women, and *Marxist-feminist* theorists emphasize that domestic labour is unequally distributed according to gender (Smith, 1981). It is thought that in capitalist societies the nature of domestic labour, and therefore of women's work, is determined by the fact that it is performed outside the labour market and is therefore unpaid. The consequences of this state of affairs are held to include the privatization of family life (Zaretsky, 1977; Barrett and McIntosh, 1982), the economic and social dependency of wives (McIntosh, 1979), and the exploitation of women's unpaid labour (Bennholdt-Thomsen, 1981).

Although Marxism is the last theoretical approach to be discussed in this chapter, it is clearly not the final word in family theory (Marshall, 1988). The principal objections to orthodox Marxism are that it is overly deterministic, and that it stresses selected economic variables to the exclusion of other factors (Miles, 1985). The extent to which capitalists and capitalist institutions are in fact able to control the internal arrangements of families is open to debate. Certainly the issue of whether or not families possess any significant autonomy in modern societies is a most important question (Cheal, 1987a). It is a question to which family systems theories and Marxist theories propose very different answers.

Conclusion

Two decades ago it could be claimed in good faith that the sociology of the family was entering into a phase of systematic theory building (Broderick, 1971). Theory construction techniques seemed to offer the promise of a growing integration of propositions, leading to one comprehensive family theory. Much has happened since then. Efforts to develop a unitary theory of family life continue, but they can no longer be imagined as constituting the pinnacle of family theorizing. Rather, the program of family theory integration must be seen for what it is, namely one specialized activity among many.

The fragmentation of family theory during the past two decades has appeared to some observers to be a serious crisis that threatens to undermine the value of social scientific studies of family life. In the short run, it is true, the babble of competing voices does undercut the authority of social science experts. Perhaps that is as it should be. In the long run, one thing is clear. Greater understanding can only lie in the direction of embracing the most difficult questions about social scientific knowledge. Several of these important questions have been exposed in the debates about the modern family. In this chapter we have focused on one such question, namely the issue of the units of analysis in family theory.

Recent discussions in family theorizing have clarified the fact that "the family" means different things to different people. That is true not only in the social sciences, but also in everyday life. Family life has many different meanings, and those meanings are reflected in the variety of family theories. Each theory of family life deals with a limited aspect of a complex reality. That reality is not encompassed by any one theory, and it never will be. As family life changes, people create new meanings with which to interpret their activities. Those meanings are eventually reflected in new sociological concepts. In this chapter we have seen that a variety of theoretical approaches exist in the field of family studies today, and they receive different emphases in different national traditions. Five conceptualizations of family life have proven to be most useful.

First, there is the concept of the family as an adaptive system that meets the needs of all its members, as well as certain specialized needs of the society. This concept is dominant in standard sociological theory, both in the older form of structural functionalism and in the newer form of general systems theory. Second, there is the concept of the family as a situation, or arena, for interaction between autonomous individuals. This concept can be incorporated into several different theoretical approaches, depending on how the family situation is described. It is most prominent in symbolic interactionism and in certain branches of feminism. Third, the fundamental unit of analysis in family studies is sometimes not the family at all, but individuals who are involved in intimate relationships of various kinds. This point of view is most commonly found in phenomenology and in exchange theory. Fourth, the family may be described as a deep structure of ideas that defines the surface appearances of family roles. Feminist analyses of familial patriarchy are the best known examples of this viewpoint. Fifth, family life may be conceived as composed of the transactions that take place within the household. That is the point of view of Marxism, and especially of Marxist-feminism which focuses on the division of household labour between men and women.

There are, then, five meanings of family life in family studies today. The sociology of the modern family includes all of them. We should not think of this state of affairs as a theoretical crisis, for it is one of the great strengths of contemporary family studies. A multiplicity of theoretical approaches is needed to describe the multiple realities of modern family life.

TECHNICAL TERMS

EXCHANGE THEORY—A theoretical approach which studies transactions between individuals as outcomes of the rational pursuit of individual self interest.

FEMINISM—A theoretical approach which defines and studies the injustices experienced by women.

MARXISM—A theoretical approach derived from the work of Karl Marx, which studies the internal contradictions of capitalist societies.

MARXIST-FEMINISM—A branch of feminism, sometimes referred to as an independent theoretical approach. It studies the material basis of patriarchy in the capitalist mode of production.

PATRIARCHY—The political and social control of women by men.

PHENOMENOLOGY—A theoretical approach which studies the life-world of personal experience.

POLITICAL ECONOMY—Studies on the possession of economic resources and the uses of power in their distribution.

POSITIVISM—A scientific method in which the procedures of the natural sciences are believed to provide the methodological foundations for the social sciences.

STANDARD SOCIOLOGICAL THEORY—A theoretical approach which studies social systems, including the family system.

STRUCTURAL FUNCTIONALISM—A branch of standard sociological theory which studies the functions that social structures fulfill for social systems and for their individual members.

SYMBOLIC INTERACTIONISM—A theoretical approach which studies how human behavior is shaped by the meanings communicated in social interaction.

SYSTEMS THEORY—An interdisciplinary theoretical approach, also a branch of standard sociological theory, which studies how a variety of forms of life can be understood as self-reproducing systems.

THEORETICAL APPROACH—A way of thinking about the world in terms of a set of general concepts.

THEORY CONSTRUCTION—A method for developing a comprehensive and logically integrated set of propositions.

THEORY MODEL—A set of propositions intended to explain a specific field of phenomena.

QUESTIONS

1. How much autonomy from social determination do you think the family possesses? State which of the existing theoretical approaches you think provides the best solution to this question.

2. In recent years there has been a tendency to shift the unit of analysis in developmental models from the family to the individual. What is the significance of that change in emphasis?

3. Describe some of the different meanings that are attributed to family life in everyday discourse, and show the extent to which they have been used and modified in social science concepts.

4. What are some of the problems with the idea that there should be only one unitary family theory? Show how that idea is related to theories of societal totality in structural functionalism and in Marxism.

5. Describe some of the contributions made by feminism to family theory. What is the status of feminism in family studies today? Is it a way of focusing on women's issues that can be applied to all theoretical approaches, is it a way of asking questions about gender that has a special affinity with one theoretical approach, or is it a distinct theoretical approach in its own right?

SUGGESTED READINGS

- Wesley Burr et al., eds. *Contemporary Theories About the Family*, Vol 1. New York: Free Press, 1979.

  This book consists of a comprehensive set of articles on family issues, many of them by authorities in their fields. The contributors were instructed to summarize and systematize recent theoretical developments on topics with established research traditions. This is an essential introduction to mainstream American family theory in the 1970s.

- Wesley Burr et al., eds. *Contemporary Theories About the Family*, Vol 2. New York: Free Press, 1979.

  Lengthy review articles are presented on exchange theory, symbolic interactionism, the general systems approach, conflict theory, and the possibilities for a phenomenological sociology of the family. At the time this was a pathbreaking attempt to relate the model-building efforts of family researchers to the theoretical traditions in sociology. More radical perspectives on family life in feminism and Marxism subsequently took up most of the space once occupied by conflict theory.

- Barrie Thorne and Marilyn Yalom, eds. *Rethinking the Family: Some Feminist Questions*. New York: Longman, 1982.

  The editors gathered a diverse collection of papers dealing with selected issues in family life that became controversial

with the rise of feminism. This book is a useful companion to Burr et al. (above).

- D. H. J. Morgan. *The Family, Politics and Social Theory*. London: Routledge and Kegan Paul, 1985.

  The author combines a selective discussion of family issues with an eclectic commentary on social theory. This book is particularly strong on revisionist interpretations of the family drawn from family history and feminism, with an emphasis on British politics.

- Marvin Sussman and Suzanne Steinmetz, eds. *Handbook of Marriage and the Family*. New York: Plenum, 1987.

  See especially Chapter 4 on "The rise of family theory: a historical and critical analysis" by Thomas and Wilcox, and Chapter 5 on "Radical-critical theories" by Osmond. The authors of these chapters attempt to come to terms with, and to expand upon, some of the recent changes in theorizing about family life.

- David Cheal, "Theoretical Approaches to the Study of Family Life." In *Marriage and the Family in Canada Today*, ed. G. N. Ramu, Chapter 2. Toronto: Prentice-Hall, 1988.

  The author reviews developments in family theory in Canada. The chapter includes discussions of standard sociological theory, feminism, marxism, political economy, and exploratory approaches to neglected dimensions of diversity and complexity in family life.

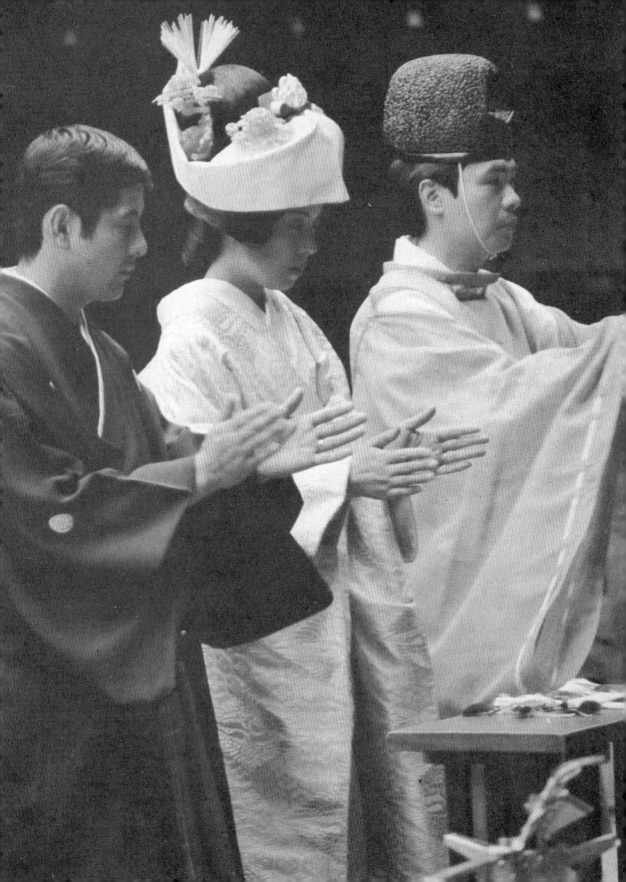

Chapter 4

FAMILY PATTERNS AND CONTEMPORARY GLOBAL TRENDS

Stanley R. Barrett
University of Guelph

Love and romance are on the march. In India, arranged marriages are giving way to individual choice based on mutual attraction (Prakasa and Rao 1979: 13). In China, the family heads no longer command the authority to sign the marriage contract for their offspring (Queen and Habenstein 1967: 96). In contemporary Africa, educated women look to marriage as a source of companionship rather than primarily as a basis for child-rearing (Little 1979a: 53). A similar trend has occurred in Poland (Lobodzinska 1979), where marital choice based on class and wealth has been sharply reduced by the socialist revolution. Even among those small-scale societies of anthropological fame, such as the Tikopia in Oceania (Firth 1965: 109) and the Aboriginals in Australia (Berndt 1965: 103), personal choice of marital partner has made its mark.

The world-wide trend towards romantic love would seem to be only one piece in an emerging marriage and family pattern that includes monogamy and the nuclear family. It might be suggested that these developments are indicative of an evolutionary trend—the final stage of a trajectory which has successively passed through early communal or group marriage, matriarchy and patriarchy. Or one could point to the structural and functional fit of the isolated nuclear family with an increasingly industrialized world. Whatever the explanation, it would seem to be clear that what we are witnessing is not merely global convergence—a melting-down and merging of cross-cultural differences; instead, it is Westernization pure and simple.

The trouble with this portrait, once one of the masterpieces in the sociologist's gallery, is that it is fundamentally distorted. Recent scholarship—often a synthesis of sociology, anthropology, history and demography—has provided us with a much clearer picture. First, although romantic love may well be sweeping the world, individual choice of marital partner, even in North America, has never been free of structural constraints. Second, the fit between the family and other social institutions—notably the economy—is far from airtight; we shall see, for example, that the assumed relationship between industrialization and the isolated nuclear family is questionable. Third, the degree of variation in family and marriage type *within* particular regions, such as preindustrial Europe and present-day North America, has been and remains extensive. Fourth, recent changes in family and marriage have been uneven around the world, with ample evidence of the persistence of old patterns such as polygyny.

The purpose of this chapter is to sketch out the main features of contemporary family and married life. To comprehend how these institutions have changed in recent decades, we must know what they were like in the past, and this is where we shall begin.

Types of Family

The main distinction that will guide our discussion is between the nuclear and the extended family. The nuclear family consists of a man and woman and their children; sometimes it is referred to as the conjugal family (other terms are the elementary or biological family), in order to emphasize the central importance of the marital relationship. The classical extended family usually consists of two or three generations with descent traced in the male (agnatic) rather than the female (uterine) line, occupying a common residential unit, cooperating in productive enterprises, with authority wielded by a senior male (the patriarch).

Two other varieties of the family can be conveniently subsumed within the extended type; the stem family and the joint family. The stem family consists of two adjacent generations constituting a productive and residential unit. The typical form is a man and his wife (who are affines) plus one of their married sons. The stem family has existed in rural Ireland (Humphrys 1965), rural Quebec (Verdon 1980), and rural Japan (Kamiko 1977). In the stem family, only one son is slated to inherit the family enterprise. In the joint family, in contrast, two or more brothers, and sometimes their cousins and their blood relatives (consanguines), joined by their living parents and wives and children, form a productive unit, pooling their resources, and often sharing a common residence. The joint family has been a prevalent type in India (Nimkoff 1965, Kolenda 1968); the *zadruga* in Yugoslavia, consisting of two married brothers and their families (see Davis 1977: 169–172), also falls into this category.

Let us now turn to the assumption, once widely accepted, that with industrialization the extended family is transformed into the isolated nuclear family, and the corollary that the extended family impedes the industrial process. This argument, forcibly presented by influential scholars such as Parsons (1943, 1955) and (perhaps less dogmatically) Goode (1963, 1982), stressed the importance of geographical and status mobility, unhindered by kinship constraints, in a technological society. A massive body of literature soon emerged to challenge this argument, including an impor-

tant study by Young and Willmott (1957), which showed that relatives in a London community retained extensive contacts and relied on each other for financial aid. There is no room here for me to review this literature. Suffice it to say that the notion of the isolated nuclear family in industrial societies was dismissed, as Sussman (1959) put it, as more fiction than fact.

This did not mean that the family in the process of industrialization had not changed at all. In an attempt to clarify matters, Litwak (1960a, 1960b) distinguished between the "classical" and the "modified" extended family. The latter, which he saw as characteristic of contemporary USA, differed from the former in that it was not a tightly-knit unit, with common residence and a family patriarch; instead, it consisted of a loosely-based network of nuclear families whose members maintained meaningful contact with each other. In a further attempt at conceptual clarification, Firth (1969) introduced the term "extended-familial kin" to describe the contemporary Western family; Firth stressed that authority had become dispersed among the several inter-connected nuclear families, rather than held by a senior male.

The other side of the argument is that the extended family was the basic type in pre-industrial society. That argument, too, has been virtually destroyed. Lazlett and Wall (1972), Singer (1968: 423) and Hareven (1977: 339) indicate that in England, indeed in Western Europe generally, the most prevalent family type from the 16th to the 19th century was the nuclear family. Greenfield (1961–62) pointed out that the nuclear family existed in Barbados without industrialization and urbanization. With a slightly different twist, Beteille (1964) argued that the joint family in India actually facilitated industrialization, and Kamiko (1977: 157) pointed out that in Japan the stem family, although it has been reduced in the wake of industrialization, continues to exist.

The Soviet Union represents an especially interesting case, because the family, according to Marxian theory, was supposed to wither away under socialism. Yet not only has the family resurfaced as a basic structure in Soviet society, but it has also taken a particular form: the three-generation family (Geiger 1965 and 1968, and Adams 1980: 52–56). What has happened is that an aging female relative, usually the grandmother, has assumed the responsibility of caring for the young children while both parents work outside the home.

Industrial societies have also been described as neolocal in residence pattern, meaning that the newly-weds set up an independent household, rather than living with or near either the husband's parents (patrilocal) or the wife's parents (matrilocal). Yet in Turkey (LeVine 1963) members of the extended family sometimes occupy separate flats in the same block of apartments. In Corsica, I have found large compounds, consisting of several independent residences, in the new sectors of coastal towns, in which all the occupants are kindred.

Further confounding the old assumption that the extended family is to pre-industrial society as the nuclear family is to industrial society is the wide variety of family types *within* a single geographical region. Sussman (1971: 520–521), for example, stresses that in North America what we usually find existing side by side is the nuclear family, the remarried family, and the dual-work family; to this he could surely have added the common-law family and the homosexual family. Then, too, family structure and norms vary across class and ethnic lines (Adams 1980, Clayton 1979). The white middle-class family in the USA is more likely than the working class (white or black) to embrace a "futuristic" orientation— deferring immediate pleasure in order to realize long-range goals such as a university education or a cottage in the country.

Europe, too, has had its share of family variations, including a form of fictive kinship— godparenthood—which has extended kin ties and responsibilities (Davis 1977: 167). Commenting on the joint family in India, Beteille

(1964: 239) stressed that it was only one of several existing types. In a remarkably successful attack on the assumption that pre-industrial societies were "simple" in social organization, Bascom (1948: 19) pointed out that in what used to be known as the country of Dahomey there were no less than 13 types of marriage. Also prevalent in West Africa— among the Yoruba, for example (Lloyd 1966: 491)—is an institution called fictive marriage, in which both spouses are women. This is not a lesbian relationship. Instead, a wealthy woman, often one who was barren, would choose a suitable man (the genitor) to impregnate her spouse (the genetrix). The children became the legal property of the wealthy woman who in effect was the sociological father or pater. Fictive marriage, it may be realized, has much in common with a relatively recent phenomenon in North America: the surrogate mother. However, while women in North America who agree for payment to bear children for others (usually childless couples) are the subject of considerable controversy, in West Africa fictive marriage has been an acceptable means for a woman of wealth to enhance her status.

In a study of the family in Martinique, Slater (1977) showed that in this one small society we can find the matrifocal family (dominated by the grandmother), the extended family, the conjugal family, as well as a family type consisting of mother and offspring but devoid of any rule of legitimacy; that is, children are born outside the context of marriage, and the male, rather than being part of the family, plays only a procreative role. The last part of this statement is significant, because several outstanding social scientists (Malinowski 1927, Radcliffe-Brown and Forde 1950, and Gough 1959) have argued that marriage exists universally (or almost so) for one fundamental purpose: to provide legitimacy to offspring.[1]

---

[1] An influential alternative perspective on the universal functions of the family and marriage can be found in Murdock (1949). Incidentally, Gough's work on the Nayar of India, who distinguish between "ritual" and "visiting" husbands, is often cited as one of the basic cases to demonstrate that marriage is not a universal institution, although that conclusion was eventually rejected by Gough herself.

Also adding to the confusion is the process known formally as the developmental cycle of the family (and marriage). Thus, at one point in time a study of the family in India may show it to be primarily of the joint type. Another study at a different time may show it to be primarily nuclear. Similarly, as Clignet (1987) has indicated, a person in West Africa may move into and out of polygynous marriage in his or her lifetime.

Two important arguments, in addition to those offered in Chapter I, relating to the links between family type to the wider society remain to be discussed. The first is the contention, put forth by Parsons and Murdock, that the nuclear family is universal. Not only is it supposedly characteristic of industrialized societies, but it is also said to be the modal type in hunting and gathering societies, and indeed the basic and identifiable unit in *all* forms of family organization, including the extended family and the large lineage systems of tribal societies. It is a fact that we do find the nuclear family among hunters and gatherers; indeed, in anthropological jargon, the formal designation of the nuclear family is the "Eskimo type." But two points must be made. First, even in Murdock's (1957) cross-cultural sample, 21 hunting and gathering societies actually took the extended family form. Second, as Bohannan (1963: 73) has suggested, if we must speculate about the universal form of the family, it makes much more sense to focus on the matrifocal (or matricentric) family, composed of a mother and her children.

A closely related argument is that the nuclear family exists in subsistence-level societies, while the extended family emerges in agricultural peasant societies, where a larger economic surplus permits both stratification and sedentary lifestyle (see Nimkoff 1965: 38). Again, evidence contrary to this argument abounds. Segalen (1980), for example, makes it clear that among the peasants of rural France, the domestic unit in the past was overwhelmingly of the nuclear family type.

A few words are in order about descent groups. It is here that we cross the line from the family to kinship in the anthropological sense.

To oversimplify to an almost unforgivable degree, we can make a distinction between the North American bilateral system, in which a person traces her or his heritage through both parents and the category of close kinsmen is small, and the large corporate descent groups or lineages in which thousands of individuals trace their descent to a common ancestor (or ancestress), real or putative. One of the determining principles of descent is the sex of the parent. In some societies the father-child or agnatic link is considered critical, in others the mother-child or uterine link. These result in patrilineages, in which descent is traced through the male line; and matrilineages, in which descent is traced through the female line. The northern Yoruba (Lloyd 1966) is an example of a patrilineal society, and the Hopi (Queen and Habenstein 1967) of a matrilineal one. In a patrilineage, one's own mother is an outsider; she belongs to the lineage into which she was born, not into which she married. Her major function is to provide her husband's lineage with offspring. In a matrilineage, it is the husband who is an outsider; his main function is to provide his wife's lineage with offspring.

While there is no reason to believe that the forces of technology, industrialization and urbanization have totally obliterated these large corporate descent groups, it is clear that they have been weakened, if for no other reason than the emergence of the state as a rival basis of organization. Land, for example, which formally belonged collectively to the descent group rather than to the individual, now can be purchased by individuals, becoming their private property. In matrilineal systems, a man's main responsibility is toward the children of his sister, not his own offspring. There is some evidence that this system, known as the avunculate, is breaking down: men are increasingly interested in the welfare of their own (biological) children. Another change is the growing pattern of neolocal residence among groups such as the Yoruba (Lloyd 1966: 491); but as elsewhere in the world, there also is evidence that the Yoruba and other ethnic groups in Africa sometimes re-establish the

Chapter 4 / Stanley R. Barrett

kin-based residential unit in urban neighbourhoods. And certainly a number of kin-based and voluntary organizations in the cities sustain kinship, ethnic, and regional identification.

Types of Marriage

There are two basic types of marriage: monogamy and polygamy. Often a third type—group marriage—is included in textbooks on the family, but it has been extremely rare. According to Linton (see Clayton 1979), group marriage was practiced among the Marquesans of Polynesia, and it has not been unknown among utopian movements such as Oneida in the USA (Muncy 1974). In a West African utopia that I studied (1974, 1977, 1982), there was a great deal of experimentation with marriage, including a period in which free love operated. Free love, not group marriage, would also seem to be the more precise term for "complex marriage" in Oneida. Whatever the terminology, it is obvious that we are talking about small, atypical communities, not entire societies.

The two forms of polygamy are polygyny and polyandry. In the first, one man is married to two or more women. In the second, one woman is married to two or more men. Polygyny has been immensely more widespread than polyandry. The latter was the modal type of marriage in Tibet (Prince 1965). According to Burch (1982), it existed to a minor degree among the Eskimo (or Inuit), although they also had polygyny, monogamy and co-marriage (spouse exchange). Polyandry, where it has occurred, has often taken a fraternal form, with several brothers married to a single female.

Polygyny, as Murdock (1957) has clearly demonstrated, has been the *preferred* form of marriage (at least by men) in the vast majority of societies. Nevertheless, monogamy has been the widest *practiced* form of marriage, even in those societies where polygyny has been preferred. The key factor here is economics. While sometimes polygyny can be an economic asset in productive activities, more often it is a *symbol* of material wealth and status; that is, only men with sufficient economic assets can afford to have more than one wife. In contrast, polyandry usually is found in circumstances of bare subsistence; it is a marital form that avoids the fragmentation of economic assets, especially land. As anthropologists sometimes put it, for much of the world's population, monogamy has been practiced when men have been too poor to be polygynous, while polyandry has emerged when men have been too poor to be monogamous.

Also relevant to any discussion of marriage are rules of exogamy and endogamy. The first specified groups of persons whom one is forbidden to marry. The second specifies categories of persons from which one ought to select a mate. One example of endogamous marriage is preferential patrilateral parallel cousin marriage in North Africa—that is, a man is expected to marry his father's brother's daughter (Khuri 1970). A second example is the levirate among the Yoruba of West Africa; in this case, if a man died, his wife was obligated by customary law to marry her deceased husband's junior brother, or even the dead man's son of another polygynous union.

It may be thought that "mainstream" North America, except for the incest taboo (itself a cross-cultural variable), is noteworthy because of the absence of either exogamous or endogamous rules. Yet a number of factors restrict the individual's free choice. Both religion and ethnicity (or race), as Wakil (1971: 322) has pointed out, remain huge barriers to cross over when choosing a mate. In Canada, for example, marriage between Jew and Gentile often generates opposition from both sides (Barrett 1987: 350), and in the Greek-Canadian community there is pressure not to marry non-Greeks (Chimbos 1980). There may be somewhat more fluidity across social class lines, but people on the whole tend to end up marrying within their own class, if only because that is where their contacts with available partners has been. In the upper class ranks, the restriction of marital partner to a "social equal" is much more conscious and active. Then, too, there is the question of propinquity: the tendency to marry someone who lives in the same vicinity. In a study based in Seattle, Washington, it was found that most couples prior to marriage had lived within three miles of each other (Catton and Smircich 1964). Just as free choice is far from absolute in North America, it is far from absent in those societies with endogamous rules. In North Africa, for example, only a small percentage—as little as 10%—of all marriages actually exhibit the patrilateral parallel cousin form, and in the levirate system a man has the option of not marrying his deceased father's wife. There is, in other words, a wide gap between the ideal and the actual forms of marriage, so that even in those African societies that featured child betrothal, individual choice of partner was not entirely absent.

Is polygyny on the wane, overwhelmed by a world-wide trend toward monogamy? Certainly the pressures against polygyny have been extensive. In the newly urbanized and industrialized settings of Third World nations, polygyny has become even less affordable: how does a man of modest means provide formal education for his children in the modern school system? Then there are pressures in the form of values. One of the aims of the United Nations Commission on the Status of Women in 1947 was to eradicate polygyny. Monogamy, in other words, has been interpreted as a tool with which to build gender equality.

It would be erroneous, however, to conclude that polygyny has become an obsolete form of marriage. Burnham (1987: 46) flatly states that polygyny in Africa is not on the decline. While well-educated African women (Karanja 1987: 258) are opposed to polygyny, Steady (1987: 211) refers to a survey conducted in 1960 that showed that 85% of women in the Ivory Coast favoured polygyny over monogamy. Steady adds that in her judgement the same results hold for the 1980s; she also indicates (1987: 212) that in some cases, such as in a fishing village in Sierra Leone where the wives processed and distributed the fish caught by their husbands, polygyny can actually benefit women economically in today's world.

It does seem that polygyny has been partly redefined in some parts of Africa. Burnham, for example (1987: 46), indicates that functional alternatives to polygyny have emerged, namely the distinction between "inside" and "outside" wives. The first consists of one's formal or legal wife, the second of one's mistresses or concubines. Sometimes Nigerian women, especially well-educated ones, separate male suitors into "Mr. Right" and "Mr. Available" (Karanja 1987). The first include men whom they would want to marry, often fellow university students. The second consist of well-established, wealthy men, such as senior civil servants and successful entrepreneurs, who can provide them with gifts, spending money, and perhaps a trip abroad. In Senegal (Parkin and Nyamwaya 1987: 12), men sometimes humorously distinguish between their *femmes de cour* (who run the rural households) and their *femmes de coeur* (their town-dwelling sweethearts). With all this in mind, Karanja (1987: 257) has suggested that we need a new classificatory scheme: that between public and private polygyny.

To sum up, monogamy probably has increased across the globe in recent decades, but polygyny is not merely a distant memory. Finally, even where life-long monogamy is the preferred form of marriage, as in North America, it is not always the sole form; one only has to reflect on the rate of divorce and re-marriage (can we speak of serial monogamy?), the degree of adultery, and the incidence of single-parent families. Obviously, it is not only in endogamous North Africa that the gap between the ideal and the actual forms of marriage is considerable.

Other Trends

Two of the most significant changes in family and marriage have been the shift in focus from the kinship unit to the married couple, and the transformation of the family from a unit of production to a unit of consumption. In pre-industrial societies, marriage was not seen as merely a union of two individuals; instead it was regarded as an alliance between two families and their broader kinship affiliations.

Chapter 4 / Stanley R. Barrett

The emphasis today on the conjugal relationship has been partly the effect of the second major change: the shift from production to consumption, or the decline of the family enterprise. In his classical study, Nimkoff (1965) observed that until the advent of the industrial age, the chief integrating factor in marriage was the division of labour between husband and wife in shared economic enterprises. Among the Inuit in the past (Vallee 1971: 409), marriage was foremost an alliance between spouses in productive activity, their mutual interdependence sharpened by the harsh environment in which they lived. In rural Quebec (Verdon 1980) and rural France (Segalen 1983), the housewife was more than a housewife: she was also an indispensable partner in the daily work on the family farm. As Segalen (1983: 190) correctly points out, the family farm *per se* has not disappeared; indeed, fully 85% and 75% of the farms in France and the USA respectively remain family enterprises. But the woman's role has changed. Partly due to the mechanization and big-business character of the contemporary farm, rural women, over the past century, have become increasingly confined to the domestic domain.

There also, at least in Western society, has been clear evidence of a lowering of the age of marriage. Ogburn and Nimkoff (1955: 58) showed that since the turn of the century, the age of marriage in the USA has fallen steadily; there has been a similar trend, report Wakil (1971) and Segalen (1986: 140), in Canada and France. Nevertheless, there are exceptions. In Canada, for example (Wakil 1971: 333), the higher the education of women, the later the age of marriage. And in Africa, the emerging trend among women (Little 1979b: 211) is to postpone marriage until they become economically secure.

It is often assumed that the fertility rate has dropped significantly in this century. It is a fact that women who work outside the home, and highly-educated women, tend to have small families. A similar result has been achieved in countries like China where a limit on population growth has been formal state policy. Yet there is a serious flaw in the underlying impli-

cation: that the family in peasant and feudal society was large. As Segalen (1986: 21) points out, in pre-industrial Europe, couples married late, and the fertility rate only barely reached replacement levels. The low fertility rate was a result of factors such as famine, the high rate of infant mortality, as well as of the death of women during childbirth. The apparently widespread practice of celibacy in peasant Europe also should not be overlooked. Certainly celibacy was prevalent in Corsica, where I have done research; nor was it unknown in what we now refer to as developing societies: Tikopians, for example (Firth 1965: 108), practiced celibacy. In addition to the obvious religious motives, there were economic ones; celibacy was a mechanism, where economic assets were minimal, that avoided the fragmentation of land and property. Generated by similar economic considerations, polyandry, albeit rare, was an alternative means to depress the fertility rate.

There is one feature of fertility that is not always appreciated: its political significance. In several Eastern and Western European countries, the rate of population increase has been minimal. In some cases, political leaders, concerned about the implications for economic expansion—and, more covertly, worried that the "empty spaces," demographically-speaking, may encourage an influx of alien immigrants—have introduced incentives for people to have larger families. The racial connotation surrounding demography sometimes is expressed more forthrightly. White supremacist organizations (and what Western nation today does not have its share?) operate on the assumption that the white race is destined for extinction unless drastic steps to maintain its purity are taken (Barrett 1987). Then there is the reaction among some in the Third World to the friendly advice of Westerners to limit the size of their families in order to increase their standard of living: such advice, it has been suggested, contains a hidden agenda—the effort of "white" nations not to be overwhelmed numerically.

New Strains

With the shift in focus from the larger kinship unit to the conjugal relationship, marriage has become an emotionally super-charged institution, with the family serving as a refuge in an increasingly impersonal and hostile world. What this would seem to mean is not that marriage and the family have lost their functions, but rather that these functions have changed, rendering marriage and the family even more important in the "expressive" as opposed to the "instrumental" realm. Yet the more prevalent interpretation, at least among lay people, is that the family, due partly to its shrinking size and functions, is falling apart. The proof? Divorce! The rate of divorce in the USA has in fact increased significantly during the past century (Adams 1980: 374). Yet in cross-cultural terms this rate cannot be considered high. In some societies, as among the Tiv (Bohannan 1963: 117) and the Inuit (Burch 1982: 115), divorce has approached the 100% level. In itself, however, a high divorce rate does not necessarily mean that marriage and the family are in bad shape, nor does divorce have the same causes or meanings in all cultures. In Arab countries, where divorce, as Goode (1963: 155) has remarked, has been the poor man's polygyny, only men could set a divorce action in motion. Among the Yoruba (Lloyd 1968: 70), only women could do so. With the Somali (Lewis 1962: 35), their high divorce rate was the result of the rapid circulation among men of fertile women, and the rejection by men of barren wives. Among the Gonja (Goody 1962), women tended to return to their home compounds (their families of orientation) after menopause. Although divorce occurs less frequently in patrilineal than matrilineal societies, among the patrilineal Yoruba the rate is high, caused in part by the fact that Yoruba women enjoy a considerable amount of economic independence from their husbands, and partly because these women are only alienated from their own descent groups to a minor degree (Lloyd 1968: 79).

What really is distinctive about divorce in North America and other advanced industrial societies is not the high rate but the anguish that surrounds it. As Burch (1982) points out, divorce among the Inuit was not a traumatic affair, either for the spouses or their offspring. Heinrich (1979) argues that divorce actually provided an integrative mechanism for Inuit society as a whole, significantly increasing the number of kinship ties. In mainstream North America, in contrast, divorce is often interpreted as failure.

Also relevant is the element of re-marriage. In those pre-industrial societies where divorce was prevalent, the same was true of re-marriage. Among the Yoruba the concept of the divorcée (or the unmarried widow or widower) was hardly comprehensible. Re-marriage, of course, also is prevalent in Western society. As Segalen (1986: 157) states, rather than looking at divorce, which often leads to re-marriage, as a rejection of marriage, "...one could say that it is a sign of the health of the institution of the family."

Another indicator of the disintegration of the family is the supposedly sharp increase in recent decades of illegitimate births. Yet Goode (1963: 2) indicates that the illegitimacy rate has actually dropped slightly over the past century. Illegitimacy per se does not necessarily mean that there are underlying social problems. In Nigeria, according to Karanja (1987), pre-marital pregnancy has become a prerequisite for marriage: men have proof of fertility, and women have leverage to point men towards the altar. The "rational" context of illegitimacy is apparently evident among the Athapaskan of the Yukon (Cruikshank 1971). Due to several factors, including government aid to single mothers, a woman with children is more economically secure if she does *not* have a husband.

This last comment leads us directly to a highly-controversial form of the family: the matrifocal type, where the male is absent or subdominant in the domestic unit. Some commentators, not all of them lay people, have portrayed the matrifocal family as a pathological type. Nowhere is this viewpoint more evident than in relation to the black family in the USA. In the now famous (or infamous) Moynihan Report (1965), it was indicated that about five million black households, or 40%, were fatherless. That alone, Moynihan argues, has been to a very considerable extent the cause of poverty among black Americans. According to Billingsley (1968), however, only one million black families were female-headed, while fully four million white families were matrifocal. In a close analysis of the Moynihan Report, Clayton (1979) persuasively argued that the image of the black family in America as pathological is mostly a myth. It would be silly to suggest that the number of single-parent families in North America is not substantial. But this is not a phenomenon restricted to black families, nor is it representative of Western families in general. As Segalen (1986: 32) has remarked about the family in France, it actually is *more* stable today than it was a century ago, when marriage frequently ended with the death of a spouse, when children from several different re-marriages lived together, and when orphans were scattered among distant kin.

Women and Equality

This has been the century of a revitalized feminist movement, legislation to remove gender inequality, the "new woman" in socialist regimes, dual-career families in the West, and an increasing focus within developing agencies on women's work in the Third World. With all this in mind, and with the International Women's Decade (1975–1985) behind us, can we happily conclude that the world today is a better place for women than at any previous point in history?

Well, if we examine the status of women in earlier times, the answer would seem to be a resounding "yes!" In the upper-class extended family of traditional China (Freedman 1968), wives were defined as troublemakers, at least until they became senior enough to dominate the wives of their sons. In the extended family system in general, solidarity of consanguines was the rule: a man was expected to take the side of this brother, mother, or other blood relative in any quarrel involving his wife. Men, of course, wielded authority in patrilineages; but in matrilineages, too, it was the men who

were in charge. Even where marriage took the form of polyandry, it was not the wife who held the reins of power; instead, as in the case of Tibet (Prince 1965: 199), it was the most capable (not necessarily the eldest) of her husbands. Then, too, there is the publicly subservient position of women in the peasant communities of the Mediterranean region, where complex norms involving honour and shame (Peristiany 1966) have held women metaphorically hostage to men, and where even in the privacy of the home one can observe to this day in the mountain villages of Corsica elderly women standing by themselves and eating apart from the rest of the family.

In contrast, women in North America, whether for self-actualization or economic necessity, have entered the public labour force in increasing numbers, aided in part by an expansion of child-care facilities. In West Africa, according to Lloyd (1969: 177), men—especially highly-educated ones—are more willing than ever before to share child-rearing responsibilities. Some writers (Cruikshank 1971: 42–43) and Matthiasson (1980: 278) have suggested that Native women in northern Canada have gained more than Native men from modernization. For these women, there are new employment opportunities, such as becoming clerks, cooks and cleaners; for the men, there more often than not are no jobs—a situation, incidentally, that has placed considerable strain on the marriage relationship among Native people.

This last somewhat jarring note aside, the tune that I have been playing of steady progress for women is pleasant indeed. Yet there are a number of less harmonious melodies. One of these deals with gender relations among hunters and gatherers. The consistent argument (Atkinson 1982), with minor disagreement (Friedl 1975, Lamphere 1977), is that it is not the advanced industrial societies of today's world that have been the most egalitarian in human history. Instead, that honour belongs to hunting and gathering societies (or what Marxists would refer to as "pre-class societies" in general).

Even if it is accepted that hunters and gatherers were relatively egalitarian, can we not assume that the transition from the (sometimes mythical) large extended family of feudal times to the (again sometimes mythical) nuclear family of the industrial age has been marked by steadily increasing gender equality? Again, the answer appears to be no. Part of the explanation is that while peasant women of the past were the pawns of men on the public stage, behind the stage, in the privacy of the household, they exercised considerable power and authority. A much more significant explanation, in my judgement, concerns the transformation of the family from a unit of production to a unit of consumption. With that transformation, women became increasingly tied to domestic duties, with their power and status declining accordingly. To some extent, those women who have adapted by seeking employment outside the home have reclaimed their lost power and status. Yet women's wages remain significantly lower than men's wages. And in the majority of families, working women continue to bear the lion's share of household duties—cooking, cleaning, and caring for the children. Even when modern appliances have been made available in the home, such as a dishwasher, the proportion of domestic work done by working women may not have decreased, because the reaction of other members of the family often has been to do less.

Granted that the progress of women in the advanced industrial societies of the West may be partly illusory, surely this cannot be the case in socialist nations, where the newly liberated woman was supposed to emerge from the debris of the disintegrated family. It is certainly true that women in socialist countries have been integrated into the work force: in Bulgaria, for example (Ilieva and Oshavkova 1977: 387), 81% of adult women are employed outside the home. But as I indicated earlier, the family in socialist nations has made a comeback. Moreover, like their North American counterparts, it is the working women in nations like the Soviet Union who are stuck with most of the household duties (Adams 1980:

55). In Cuba, where there is guaranteed employment for men, but not for women (Cebotarev, forthcoming), sexism continues to deprive women of full equality in the political and occupational spheres (Cole 1982: 495–496). As MacKinnon (1982: 523) has observed, Marx's promise of gender equality has simply not materialized.

Finally, what about the progress of women in the Third World? Although polygyny persists, at least in modified form (public versus private polygyny), monogamy probably has become more widespread, at least in the sense of being the ideal form of marriage. Yet as Nimkoff (1965: 64) observed a generation ago, monogamy per se doesn't lead to equality; monogamy, after all, has been the ideal form of marriage in the West since Christian times, but only towards the twentieth century did women obtain the franchise. It should also be pointed out that any attempt to measure women's progress in the Third World must appreciate the degree to which the position of women varied across cultures in the past. In Nigeria, for example, Yoruba women were highly independent of their husbands. A Yoruba woman did not work on her husband's farm, nor did she share her own earnings with her husband; when she died, it was her own junior siblings, or others in her descent group, not her husband, who inherited from her. Igbo women, in contrast, worked alongside their husbands in the fields, and had little economic autonomy. When an Igbo family moved to an urban area—an increasing pattern—and the wife became employed outside the family unit, with her own income, the changes were much more far-reaching than in the case of the Yoruba, who incidentally, were considerably urbanized even prior to colonial contact.

While issues such as monogamy and indigenous cultural patterns are not irrelevant, neither of them goes to the heart of the matter, which is as follows: Third World women today, as a result not only of colonialism *but also* of development programs and policies, enjoy less equality than ever before, or at least than since the hunting and gathering epoch. This has been the consistent judgement of knowledgeable scholars such as Boserup 1970, Lamphere 1977, Whitehead 1979, and Rapp 1979; Nkwi (1987) indicates that it is valid for Cameroon, as does Cebotarev (forthcoming) for Latin America in general. Cebotarev, indeed, goes one step further. She contends that one institution in particular has been responsible for the failure to achieve equality and basic human rights for Latin American women: the male-dominated family.[1]

Conclusion

The family does not exist in a vacuum. In a world transformed by politics and technology, the family too has changed. These changes, however, have not been in the same direction or at the same rate everywhere. Contemporary global variations in marriage and family patterns have been generated by several factors. One of these is no more complex than the fact that the starting point, due to historical cross-cultural differences in family and marriage type, has not been identical for all societies. A second factor has been the widespread variation in marriage and family types within specific geographical regions; the viewpoint, often implicit in earlier scholarship, that each region was homogeneous, is erroneous. A third factor is the looseness of fit between family type and the wider society; the cost of assuming the contrary has been clearly shown: the mistaken argument that the extended family necessarily steps aside for the isolated nuclear family in industrialized societies.

Accompanying the changes in marriage and the family have been new forms of strain. Not all of these, however, fit the lay person's stereotypes. The divorce rate in North America, for example, is not particularly extensive in cross-cultural terms. Nor does it appear that the battle for gender equality has passed over the hump. While family life around the world has changed significantly in this century, with modified functions and new forms of strain, both the family and marriage, for good or bad, are alive and well in the contemporary world.

TECHNICAL TERMS[2]

AFFINES—Relatives by marriage.

AGNATE—Relatives by patrilineal descent.

AVUNCULOCAL—Post-marital residence of a couple with the husband's mother's brother.

CONSANGUINES—Relatives by birth (or "blood" relatives).

DESCENT GROUP—A kin group dictated by rules of descent through the father's line, the mother's line, or a combination of the two.

DOMESTIC GROUP—A group of people sharing a central dwelling house, with family property often held in common.

ENDOGAMY—The restriction of choice of marital partner within a specific category or group of people.

EXOGAMY—Rules specifying that one's marital partner must exist outside a specific category or group of people.

EXTENDED FAMILY—Two or more nuclear families, linked through parent and child or sibling ties, often constituting a domestic group.

INCEST TABOO—The prohibition of sexual relations between culturally-defined immediate kin.

LEVIRATE—The expectation that a brother (or other close kinsman) of a dead man will marry his widow.

---

[1] As Tiffany (1978: 47) has observed, it has been primarily Marxist-oriented scholars who have argued that with industrialization the status of women has declined. Structural-functionalists, in contrast, have been inclined to assume not only that gender inequality was highly pronounced in pre-industrial societies, but also that the status of women has gradually improved as societies have become industrialized.

[2] For a fuller discussion of these technical terms, the reader is referred to Roger M. Keesing, *Cultural Anthropology* (New York: Holt, Rinehart and Winston, 1976).

MATRILINEAL—Descent traced through the female line.

MATRILOCAL—Post-marital residence with the wife's kin.

MONOGAMY—One woman married to one man.

PATRILINEAL—Descent traced through the male line.

PATRILOCAL—Post-marital residence with the husband's kin.

POLYANDRY—One woman married to two or more men.

POLYGAMY—A marital state characterized by two or more wives or two or more husbands.

POLYGYNY—One man married to two or more women.

UTERINE—See MATRILINEAL.

QUESTIONS

1. Is the family becoming much the same in structure and function around the world?

2. What is the relationship, if any, between family type and level of technology?

3. Is the family disintegrating?

4. Is the family a conservative institution?

5. Are gender relationships more egalitarian today than in the past?

SUGGESTED READINGS

- E. Boserup. *Women's Role in Economic Development*. New York: St. Martin's Press, 1970.

  A pioneering work concerning the role and status of women in the process of industrialization.

- H. Geiger. *The Family in Soviet Russia*. Cambridge: Harvard University Press, 1968.

  An outstanding contribution to the understanding of the Soviet family in the context of the Marxist assumption that the family was destined to wither away.

- W. Goode. *World Revolution and Family Patterns*. Glencoe, IL: Free Press, 1963.

  Essential background reading for students attempting to grasp the state of theories about family change on a global scale.

- D. Parkin and D. Nyamwaya, eds. *Transformations of African Marriage*. Manchester: Manchester University Press, 1987.

  A collection of articles reflecting the major changes, stresses and patterns in marriage in contemporary sub-Saharan Africa.

- M. Segalen. *Historical Anthropology of the Family*. Cambridge: Cambridge University Press, 1986.

  A fine example of the recent trend towards an interdisciplinary approach to family studies, in this case applied primarily to Western Europe.

- M. Young and P. Willmott. *Family and Kinship in East London*. London: Routledge and Kegan Paul, 1957.

  One of the early studies that stimulated social scientists to re-examine the concept of the isolated nuclear family in industrial society.

Reverse: A farm family in St. Charles County,
Missouri, 1939.

PART II

THE FAMILY AND SOCIAL CHANGE

Reverse: "Pro-choice" activists argue that every woman should have the right to decide for herself whether or not to terminate a pregnancy. Part of a 1975 National Abortion Campaign demonstration in London, England.

Chapter 5

ALTERNATE LIFESTYLES
Variations in Household Forms and Family Consciousness

Jacqueline A. Gibbons
York University

In this chapter we explore some nontraditional types of family. We define these alternative family patterns and households according to whether or not they have a legal basis; whether or not they are lifelong; whether they are sexually exclusive; what the sexual preferences are; whether children are living with one or both parents; whether and if there is a defined or legitimized economic and ideological head of household; and whether there is openness to experiment and change, in the sharing of family life.

The cultural patterns of the 1950s had emphasized denial of personal feelings and impulses and adherence to the strictly defined tenets of traditional family life and gender roles. The onset of the 1960s saw an awakening of the "personal as political." The quest for experimentation in alternative family living became a movement. It was well documented with a literature on nontraditional forms of the family. Although many of these forms had existed for a long time, their relevance for today is particularly salient as new facets of the family structure have been forged and legitimized.

We see an increasing trend towards freedom of choice in marriage, though most people do still marry. We find a greater tolerance and acceptability of cohabitation and also of alternative sexual preference, such as gay coupling. Feminism and an increased awareness of women's issues have pointed the way to greater gender equality, which intersects both work and home. With the work ethic addressed by both men and women, we look at commute couples and find greater societal tolerance and acceptance of single or lone parents as bone fide members of the nontraditional family. The classic writing of the 1960s on sexual permissiveness and "liberal" attitudes was the source of literature on alternative family units such as communes, and an important source point for shaping an egalitarian ideology for the late 1980s. This permissiveness was also a backdrop to writings, old and new, on uses and values of non-monogamous sexual relations. It is clear that alternative and variant household forms are part of what is now the study of new family lifestyles. And we should remember that these newly forged styles are grown from both choice and necessity. Let us explore some of these patterns.

Old Alternative Households: Communes and Intentional Communities

During the 1960s the commune movement, a style of domestic group living, attracted much attention. Numbers of students and other young adults turned to various kinds of group living that went against the norm of coupled marital union. The people who were attracted to this style of domestic life ranged from left to right on the political spectrum; from traditional to radical in household structure; from connectedness with other such groups to isolation; from limitations on non-members to relative openness to new members; from communal to individual ownership of property; from equality of the sexes to inequality; and from authoritarian to egalitarian types of organization. (See Metcalf: 1984)

Such groups varied in their sexual composition and in the kind of sexual relations permitted. Some were rural, others urban, and their internal social structure varied with their location.

Communal living has been a domestic arrangement among certain social and philosophical experimental groups and for religious communities for many centuries. Though the communal choice has significantly decreased in the 1980s, this style has represented a new way to "do" the extended family for the post modern society.

An example of an egalitarian, non-monogamous utopian community was Kerista Village in San Francisco (Pines and Aronson: 1981). Members talked of having "successfully" grappled with the problems of sexual jealousy as they explored what they call "polyfidelity." They talked about their emotions and their relationships freely, and they made a long-term commitment to their group family unit before they became sexually involved. They came from all parts of the United States and had a definite feminist orientation in their openness, expression of feelings, and group parenting. They regulated the amount of money a person could make per month: they pooled all incomes, and the group voted on how this income is spent.

The members of Kerista Village shared a philosophy that argued that the intellectual, emotional, theoretical and cultural realms were the stuff of their connected reality, and they drew emotional security from the theories and ideals they had developed in the course of the group's development.

Another interesting American experiment in group living that has taken place over the last two decades has been the Synanon Foundation, (Blanton: 1980). It has been estimated that 18,000 people have lived in this type of community, which is privately run and is non-profit, and whose goal is to re-educate people with character disorders and/or who have suffered from drug or alcohol addiction in the past. They see themselves as a therapeutic and educational community and stress communal child rearing as in the traditional kibbutz. The children are described as "more verbal, polite, neat, and socially poised than most middle-class children of their age" (Blanton ibid: 114); however these children studied have not yet reached puberty, and thus the full effect of communal child rearing is yet to be documented. Synanon stresses the merging of home values with school values. They educate their children in the community, and the emphasis is on the group rather than the individual.

In contrast to some American data, though in agreement with the Dutch research, Jansen (1980) found that there was much diversity among the Dutch communes. They were most similar in their raison d'être which tended to be based on friendships or kinship between the members. This research was based on a study of 52 communes in the Netherlands.

The research by Van Ussel (1970, 1975) in the Netherlands shows that these communes are attempts to overcome some of the disadvantages of the nuclear family. These disadvantages are seen to be: the high monopoly that the family had on affection and intimacy, the restricted social experience of the nuclear family and the children's dependence on their mother, which is believed to hinder the development of the child's autonomy.

Communes as Prototypes to Modern Relationship Principles

The qualities that were embraced by these "classic" alternative forms of family life stressed egalitarian relations, shared resources, and experimental sexuality. They offered the alternative of the time to legitimized marriage which appealed to the youth of the day. Although the commune movement largely disappeared by the mid-seventies, except perhaps in pockets such as Oregon, California and British Columbia, the values of equality and sharing have carried through to the 1980s in alternative family form. We will see that cohabiting and same sex couples exhibit some parallel patterns of economic, emotional and egalitarian power relations. We will also see how nurturance of children has been more broadly and liberally defined with single-parent, male or female centred, new families.

Lone-Person Households and Singles

There is in Canada a growing trend for the young and the old to live alone, and with the increase in the population over 65 years of age, this tendency is growing.

In the recent decade, the number of people living alone has increased significantly. The number of widows also rose in this period, and since women live longer than men, and men usually marry younger women, the proportion of the population made up of older single women also grew in this decade, along with the number of singles of the baby boom generation who had reached maturity.

Partly as a result of a previous liberalization of the divorce laws, the 1970s showed a tripling of the numbers of divorced persons, although this rate of divorce seems to have evened out in the 1980s. Such family alterations led to an increase in the number of single households, most of which tend, in Canada, to be urban. In fact, 1 in 10 adults in the city live alone, while in rural areas the ratio is about 1 in 20 (Statistics Canada: 1984a).

Men living alone are more likely than women to own their home, though there are high ownership rates among both widows and widowers. This suggests that each of these groups continues to live in the family home once their spouse has died.

In the Netherlands, single living is rising rapidly (Jong-Gierveld and Aalberts: 1980), as in other Western countries. The data analyzed by these researchers in the Netherlands show a mix of "creative singles" and others for whom choice in remaining single may be defined in different terms, often ones of loneliness. The data indicate that women who live alone tend to value being alone more positively than men. It is argued that new ideologies that emphasize individual fulfillment over the importance of commitment to others may be making some impact on this alternative life-style.

Cohabitation

It is estimated that there were 890,000 unmarried couples living together in the US in 1976, and between 1977 through 1979 the increase in cohabitation in the USA was 40%. An important random sample of 2,143 men and women was examined by Yllo (1978). The respondents' ages ranged from 18 to 70, although 60% were under 30. While there was a progressive decline in the number of cohabiters in the age range 30 to 60, there was a dramatic increase from 3% in the 51 to 60 age bracket to 9% for the over-60s. The researchers did not find a significant difference between blacks and whites, though it is said that this finding should be regarded with caution.

Among the cohabiters, Catholic women were overrepresented compared with Protestant women. This finding is consistent with other studies. One explanation is that Catholic women are more anxious for the new relational experience after the stricter shackles of their homes. Another explanation is that Catholics may be experimenting more before marriage because they know divorce is not an option later. A third explanation is that cohabitation may be the only possibility after a dissolved marriage because of the rules of the Catholic Church.

Clayton and Vans, who studied 2,510 young men in a nationwide US sample, found that "18% of the respondents had lived with a woman for 6 months or more outside the bonds of matrimony, but 65% of these men had done so with only one partner" (Clayton and Vass 1977: 282). They found that about twice as many black as whites had cohabited. It was also found that cohabitation was more common in large cities and in the Northeastern and Western regions of the United States. This suggests that urbanization and more liberal sociocultural values (as are found in California for example) are more conducive to this alternative lifestyle. They found a large proportion of their sample were high school drop outs or were involved in unconventional activities such as "studying an Eastern religion, or philosophy, using illicit drugs, and experiencing sexual intercourse at an early age" (p. 282–

283). Their data also suggest that men who have been formerly married may be more likely to establish a cohabital liaison after that marriage than men who have never been married. They find that cohabitation "served as a temporary or permanent alternative to marriage" (p. 273).

Arafat and Yorburg interviewed student cohabiters at a large urban northeastern university and found that these students were as likely to come from working class as middle-class homes. The female respondents espoused an ideology that showed a new similarity to male ideology regarding self-image, attitude and behaviour. These data showed that 3/4 of the women and the men "characterized themselves as aggressive, independent and outgoing" (Arafat and Yorburg: 1973: 104). Similarly, Newcomb and Bentler (1980) in their study of cohabitation before marriage found that:

> males who had cohabited perceived themselves as more androgynous, attractive and less religious than males who did not cohabit. Females who cohabited saw themselves as more interested in art, attractive, extroverted, intelligent, liberal, androgynous and having more leadership qualities; while being less religious, clothes-conscious, and law-abiding than women who did not cohabit. Couples who cohabited showed significantly greater sexual experimentation and self-perception accuracy than couples who did not cohabit (Newcomb and Bentler 1980: 65).

The Canadian data in the 1980s shows a 36.5% increase in common-law unions from 1981 to 1986. This style of coupling is being increasingly seen as a viable form of domestic partnership for this decade.

When we look at cohabitation in the Nordic countries, the highest cohabitation rates in the world are found in Sweden and Denmark (Trost 1981). About 99% of married persons have cohabited for varying periods of time before marrying. There is a tradition of marriage, however, and sooner or later, cohabitants tend to marry in these societies. The wedding, when it takes place, is clearly a "rite de confirmation," rather than a "rite de passage."

It is normally a solemn occasion and is accompanied by the usual traditional festivities.

It is clear that these countries view cohabitation and marriage as identical social situations, and to a large degree, they are treated similarly under law.

In Denmark, according to the Central Bureau of Statistics for 1977, 90% of couples living together are married, and 10% are cohabiting outside of marriage. A decrease in the marriage rate in Denmark started in 1970 and an increase in cohabitation occurred in the late 1960s. This pattern is about the same in Sweden, although there is not such a significant decrease in marriage among older persons in Denmark as in Sweden.

Another Nordic country, Iceland, has a high rate of children born to unmarried mothers, which when examined is the product of children born largely to cohabiting couples. In Sweden, too, the number of children born of unmarried mothers is very high. According to 1979 figures, 38% of the children born are born to unmarried women, much of this being explainable by the norms of cohabitation. The Swedish census data (which are not a sample but a study of the total population) of 1975 show that about 11% of all cohabiters are unmarried. This may seem low, because with census data it is very likely these are minimum estimates. When these data are divided by age, more than half the cohabitants are aged 20–24 and for men this is almost three out of four. When we look at the under-30 age group and the facts of cohabitation before marriage, we find that all of this group have been cohabiters before they married.

Clearly cohabitation without marriage in Denmark and Sweden should not be seen as a deviant phenomenon: rather, it can be viewed as a "social institution" (Trost 1981: 419). An indication of this, as previously mentioned, is that the law increasingly equates the two forms, as do local authorities and social organizations. "In today's Sweden and Denmark, couples do not choose to cohabit instead of to marry; they just cohabit" (p. 421). There is too, as we have seen, a social expectation that they will eventually marry if the relationship remains intact: "the couple lives together with or without marriage, they have children together with or without marriage, they buy furniture and household goods together. They look upon themselves as a unit, they are looked upon by their close friends and relatives as a unit, and they are looked upon by society as a unit" (p. 420). When these researchers examined the situation in Finland and Norway they found that these two other countries had the same rates of cohabitation as Sweden and Denmark had some years before (p. 421).

Thus, though cohabitation in other countries is a common phenomenon among college students and in "unusual" milieu it cannot be said to have the institutionalized normalcy that it has in Denmark and Sweden. One reason offered for this is that the private individual in Denmark and Sweden is less integrally related to Church and Christianity than in many other countries. It has been argued therefore that there is a stronger belief in the sanctity of private life in these particular countries, than in others.

In Denmark (Koch-Nielson: 1980), the question of one-parent families is related to the question of cohabitation, since a number of one-parent families are joined, sooner or later, by another, or others. It is argued that the one-parent family in Denmark is therefore indicative of a new stage in the family life cycle rather than a lasting status.

Cohabitation Compared with Marriage and Same Sex Couples

One of the most significant recent studies on this topic is the one by Blumstein and Schwartz (1983). They point out some important trends among modern married, cohabiting, gay and lesbian couples as these are compared. On the issue of monogamy in the relationship, they find that where extramarital sex (e.m.s.)/non-monogamy is given permission, on some level, between married, cohabiting and lesbian couples, then the relationship has a higher "mortality" rate than where e.m.s. is done secretly. The exception in their findings is among gay men, where after the first few years it seems that homosexual men have a greater ability to

separate sex from emotional involvement and a greater tolerance in their dyad towards e.m.s. after their initial "bonding" of the relationship.

The researchers also find that where their subjects had been recently involved in e.m.s. (at the beginning of the research), that by the end phase of the field work, these couples were more likely to break up than those couples who had not been indulging in e.m.s. in their previous immediate history.

When they look at a comparison of cohabitants, and cohabitants who married, they find that the cohabitants who have married tend to do so at the beginning stage (up to two years) of their relationship. They also find that these marrying cohabitors tend to be fairly traditional about their roles and their relationships, thus indicating the significance of the marital bond in identification with legally legitimized tradition.

Where Blumstein and Schwartz examine the role of money in their four categories of domestic relations, they find that couples need to agree about money allocation and that breakups between married, cohabiting and lesbian couples are linked to women's interdependence and dependence on the marital economic dyad. In fact their data give validity to the well-held notion that wives stay in marriages because they do not have the economic wherewithal to leave that relationship. For cohabiting partners the findings show that where each member of the couple has equal influence in spending decisions, this equality of "power" keeps the relation together. They also find that there is only one type of couple in the study where equality inside the dyad is *not* linked to the survival of that relation: This is the married couple. Does this not indicate, we argue, how powerfully an institutionally legitimized union can bind, whereas in other kinds of domestic unions, inequality has the tendency to create instability. In an age when equality is such an issue in the public sphere, it is not surprising that the dramatic rise of documented cohabiting and same-sex couples may be paving the way for new forms of relationship equality in both private and public sphere.

Lone Parenting

Lone parenting has become a more acceptable family form in recent years, and the Canadian statistics show that from 1981–1986 their numbers increased by 19.6% across the nation (Statistics Canada: 1987).

Though these families are very largely headed by women, there is a recent shift in socio-cultural perceptions in the courts and at the community level, so that fathers are being slowly but newly defined as caretakers. At the same time we note that female-centred lone-parent households have also risen significantly in every province in Canada.

The lone-parent statistics reflect not only marital, separation and divorce patterns, but also family migration patterns; thus one-parent families may have moved to the more affluent provinces because of job market advantages in these parts of the country. Whether through choice, or by necessity, single mothers command the lowest average family income and spend more of their total income on "reasonable" shelter than other forms of families. In fact, single mothers with children under 16 years of age at home were the group with the highest percentage of low-income recipients (Statistics Canada: 1984b). We argue that it has been economically, pragmatically, and emotionally viable for men traditionally to pass children across to the mother for caretaking. Yet as Ambert has shown, the quality of childcare and the economic hardships in lone-parent households are connected and detrimental to children's well being (Ambert: 1984).

In the last 20 years there has been a rise in the number of single mothers who have not been married. We suggest that this reflects the new social norms of greater acceptability to be single yet bear and raise children.

Parallel or Co-Parents

The reasons for the dissolution of families include the availability of reliable methods of birth control, geographic and occupational mobility, greater secularization of our post-industrial society, changing sexual mores, greater female participation in the labour force and changes in divorce laws. These alterations of family structure result in new ideologies of the family, and the literature on the re-constitution of families has proliferated in recent years.

One style of new family structures is co-parenting (Galper: 1978), which occurs when the parents have separated or are divorced, but continue to share their children's lives and emotional, physical and financial needs. In other words, the needs of the child are defined in terms (through the courts and/or through mutual parental agreement) that define the father and mother as being equally important in the continuing parenting process. Thus as these writers argue, where the marriage ends, the family continues, and there develops a form of working relationship that addresses and hopes to serve the needs of the child. Co-parenting is a concept that has gained recent legitimacy; it means that there is a conscious attempt to negotiate parenting that follows marital dissolution. Unlike the past, this style of family split does not aim to set the child against one of the parents. Rather, the role of lawyers and parents is defined as one of conciliation and negotiation. In such a situation the children may spend equal time at each of their parents' new homes and the parents exchange information in order to arrange the child's schedule to suit those of both parents. The notion of joint custody addresses these questions. The legal realities tend, however, still to be coloured by traditionally trained lawyers who still advocate adversarial or one-sided remedies to family problems.

Non-Monogamous Marital Relations

The research on open marriage addresses notions of marital satisfaction—its maintenance or enhancement as respondents describe their spousal and extramarital relations. Despite modern fears of AIDS and thus a greater caution in embarking on or developing non-monogamous sexual discourse, the fact remains in the 1980s that non-monogamy is an attractive proposition for a number of couples, both straight and gay. We will look at the earlier marital literature for the moment.

Chapter 5 / Jacqueline A. Gibbons

One of the most widely read books on intra- and extramarital sex was *Open Marriage* (O'Neill and O'Neill: 1972). The authors described this style of marriage as open and honest in communicating feelings and sharing fantasies. They encouraged role flexibility in that new ideas were not only encouraged through exploration but also through experimentation.

The authors recommended that open companionship be encouraged so that the marital tradition of coupledness could be accompanied, if desired, by frank discussion of a spouse's extramarital affairs. The O'Neills' concept of marriage stressed equality of power and responsibility. They also emphasized that one must trust one's spouse with the open knowledge of emotional alternatives; thus they discouraged the tradition of hiding affairs and the accompanying tradition of lies. They looked at marriage as a partnership where openness and honesty were qualities that should, above all, be respected.

A Dutch study, Buunk (1980b), examined 50 couples who had experienced at least one extramarital relationship (e.m.s.).

The findings showed that e.m.s. was more than incidental: 88% have had at least one long-term extramarital relationship and 86% had at least one short-term involvement. About half the sample had participated in an exchange of partners, but this normally occurred only once. More men than women reported that their partners were jealous.

The respondents indicated that while e.m.s. was satisfying in some ways, it caused problems too, such as the fear of threatening the marriage, feelings of guilt and jealousy, and problems in dividing one's time between the marriage and the extramarital relationship.

One-third of the respondents said that permission from or consultation with their spouse was desirable regarding the extramarital involvement, and they also agreed that if their spouse asked them to end the other relationship, they would do so. In other words, they expressed the need to subordinate the external situation to the marital dyad. Thus, "ground rules" were seen to be necessary in extramarital relations.

In addition Buunk (1980a) studied 100 respondents from an urban population in the Netherlands. 17% of the males and 14% of females reported at least one long-term extramarital sexual relationship in the last year. Sexual intercourse occurred more frequently outside the marital (cohabiters were included) relationship: 26% for men and 18% for women.

Comparing Dutch and North American data, it seems that, according to this sample, there may be a greater tolerance of e.m.s. in Holland. The Dutch findings correlate with North America in linking low religious affiliation to more liberal sexual attitudes. Another similarity between the two countries is that extramarital intimate relationships may be more common among the more highly educated. The Dutch data found more e.m.s. among younger women than older ones but no difference regarding age and e.m.s. among men; this result corresponds with some American findings.

An interesting difference between American and Dutch data is that e.m.s. is concealed more in the United States than in Holland, where the sample showed a fairly large proportion of people having extramarital relations with the approval of their spouse.

In their study of Japanese and American women, Maykovich (1976) found that, though attitudes towards e.m.s. were more liberal in the United States than in Japan, the presence of opportunities for e.m.s. was an important variable in each of the cultures. Thus experience was not always in keeping with normative attitudes among these 200 middle-aged middle-class women in suburban cities of the US and Japan.

Such data point to the importance of looking at normative attitudes and actual experiences as we study how people in different cultures work out their concept of marital satisfaction.

Gay Coupling, Parenting, and Bisexuality

Blumstein and Schwartz (1977) looked at bisexuality in the formation of a "sexual career." They did extended interviews with 156 men and women in Seattle, San Francisco,

New York, Berkeley and other American centres during 1973–75. Their respondents ranged in age from 19 to 62 and had varied occupational, education and sexual histories.

They found that there was "a deliberate attempt to create a bisexual community" in San Francisco where people could get together and share support and collective wisdom. They also found that sex-object choice and identification could change in many ways over the life cycle and that the determinants of adult sexuality were not necessarily found in childhood or adolescent experience.

They found that bisexuality emerged as a theme from their respondents in three key ways: first, experimenting; second, emergence from group sex or other such liberal and/or pleasure-seeking environments; and third, they describe the emergence of an "erotic utopia" in which the ideology was one of "humanistic libertarianism" and love and/or sex was seen as a means of communication.

The authors found some intriguing differences between men and women as they participated in same sex relations. Women found lesbian experiences easier than did homosexual men. The men described their relations as somewhat traumatic: they indicated that they were afraid that homosexual relations might have implications for their sense of sexuality, their masculinity. Both men and women also described the first experience of same gender sex differently. Women found these first experiences were the outgrowth of close friendship or of a strong emotional attachment. Men found that they were more likely to have had their first heterosexual relations and first homosexual relations with strangers (such as prostitutes, "or homosexual tricks.") The implications are that same-sex relations are personal and or emotional for women, but for men they are impersonal, if not, we might argue, alienated, in these introductory contexts.

Ambisexuality

Blumstein and Schwartz point to the Kinsey (1948) data that found that 37% of the total male population had experienced some same sexual experience, which suggested that the "erotic biography" of persons of mixed sexual experience was not abnormal. These researchers suggest the term "ambisexuality" as their respondents talk of sexual relations and relationships, and they point out that erotic and emotional socialization in society in which mixed gender experience is a reasonable presumption on the basis of these and other data, and makes for a life cycle course that can change, according to the stage and life circumstances of individuals.

Harry and Lovely (1979) in their research on gay marriage examine homosexual men (241 around Detroit). They found that in communities where there is a gay sexual orientation, the values that support a homosexual orientation are found to be more like those of married couple dyad than in places where there is no such community norm. In addition they found that the "couple" lifestyle was supported and that such liaisons were very likely to be fairly sexually exclusive, while they lasted, and that the couple would be likely to live together. They did not find that homosexual relationships lasted any longer in gay communities, but there was evidence supporting stability and relative monogamy of these relations.

When we look at lesbian women, we find that they are more likely to have sexually exclusive relations with their partners than are homosexual men. Moreover, they place more importance on emotional intimacy and on equality in their relationships than gay men do (Peplau: 1982).

Gay Parenting

The research on gay parenting indicates a slow change of attitudes in the courts as judges have gingerly given greater visiting privileges to gay parents (Hitchens: 1979). It is clear, however, that the giving of custody to the parent who chooses to live with a homosexual lover is still regarded as problematic in our society. This indicates that our society views sexual orientation as more important than the quality of parenting: an intriguing paradox for the 1980s.

Chapter 5 / Jacqueline A. Gibbons

Elderly Alternatives

There have been various lifestyle alternatives for elderly living that have been documented. One of these is share-a-home, where individuals live together in small groups for economic and health reasons rather than for reasons of ideology. The share-a-home concept (Streib and Hilker: 1980) offers built-in caring and a mutual support system for the elderly in a real home. The Share-A-Home Association started in 1969 with a group of 20 elderly persons who jointly owned a 27–room house. The idea is to offer a small group alternative to the larger institutions that are often common for the elderly when they need help. These people share outings, birthdays, and expenses and are said to have overcome the loneliness of being older (Streib: 1978).

The Economics of Cohabitation for Elderly Persons

In 1977 the US Census showed 85,000 unmarried heterosexual couples living together, where the head of household was 65 or over, while the 1970 US census data puts this figure around 18,000 (Dressel and Avant 1978: 34). This trend is said to be due to Social Security regulations and also to the desire to protect one's children's inheritance. Thus living together as an alternative lifestyle for the elderly has different reasons than the ones we have explored among younger persons.

The alternatives for elderly intimate living are further complicated by the fact that single older men (over 65) are six times more likely to marry than single older women (Dressel and Avant, 1978). This fact, coupled with the biological reality that women outlive men, means that we may see small groups of women living together as family units in the future—an interesting possibility in the light of notions promulgated by the Women's Movement of collectivity consciousness and the principles of feminism.

Commute Couples and Separated Households

There is a growing literature on commute couples, where there are two households or where the family must be separated for periods of time, as a regular course of events. Orchestra conductors, actors, dancers, musicians, and artists, often have to spend time in other cities and countries as part of their regular schedules. Special project workers on pipeline construction, or oil rig drilling are required to be away from their home base for varying periods of time, sometimes months. In some cases the commuting couple have two home bases, as is increasingly being reported in the recent literature on two-career professional couples. Gerstel and Gross (1983) examine the costs and rewards of such chosen separate family or couple lifestyles, and they find that couples learn to value certain aspects of home life that most couples take for granted. Their research shows that couples who live apart value the interpersonal intensity of the periods that they can have together. When they have to move apart after a time of being together, they say that they rediscover parts of their relationship, and they recount the periods of time together as being "special." They do not handle domestic choices in traditional ways according to traditional gender and job related home work; thus women report newly won ability to handle care maintenance or house repairs, while men report new learned tasks of sewing on buttons or preparing meals.

Commuting and Fidelity

Commute couples speak of disapproval from relatives, who tend to view marriage in more conventional terms, particularly when there are young children. Such couples also report strain in their social relations because much social life is couple-oriented and to be a "married single" is to be somewhat deviant. It was found that the large majority of couples who were separated behaved in many ways as they had before they were apart; thus if they had been monogamous when they had one home, they tended not to have affairs when they were apart, while those who had not maintained monogamy while they were together tended to continue in their similar pattern. This suggests, unlike some other data, that marital fidelity is linked to internalized value systems, as these researchers found.

They found that women in commute marriages tended to be the primary beneficiaries because, as the nurturers, they had previously had to accommodate others. They did stress, however, that separation produced considerable stress, and most indicated that their preference was to live together with their husband and family.

In their study on the families of the Great Lakes merchant marine, Gerstel and Gross mention the importance of the higher salary that their husbands earn when they are away from home, and how much they sense that their husbands love their work. These couples—whose marriages have lasted from 3 to 41 years—"regularly separate for months at a time during the long nine-month sailing seasons" (Gerstel and Gross 1983, 188).

Gross (1980) examines dual-career marriages of persons in their '30s with high educational and occupational attainment. The women in these relations gave their personal relationship a higher priority than did their husbands. The men tended to "view the rewards associated with work as emotional equivalent to the rewards of interpersonal relationships" (1980: 571).

In a study of Inuit men, their employment and relations with their families (Hobart, Walsh et al., 1980), family separations were accepted as part of the necessary working lifestyle of the home; however, respondents pointed out the emotional costs of separation. The women were more worried when husbands trapped than when they worked for the oil companies, perhaps seeing the danger element as a variable component. In general the research on commute and/or separated families shows that there is least stress when the incomes are high. The research also shows that such relationships are easier without children in the home, and they are also easier when couples can be reunited regularly, for example, at weekends.

Voluntary Childlessness

In the 1960s the contraceptive pill became available as never before, and this new technique of birth control offered an alternative to traditional ways of making families.

Having children became, we may argue, an optional mode rather than one that had been defined as being more *de rigueur* in previous times. Nevertheless, the couple that today chooses to remain childless still challenges the long held traditional belief that one of the purposes of marriage is the begetting and raising of children. As Veevers (1980a, 1983) has argued: "deliberate childlessness still clearly violates the dominant family and fertility mores of our culture" (1983: 93).

Child free couples talk about being able to continue pursuing their interests and hobbies; of being able to go out in the evening without finding a babysitter; of not having to schedule their lives around school schedules, ballet classes, childhood diseases, school clothing, lunches or the emotional problems of adolescence. The schedules of childless couples emanate from the personal needs and constraints of the adult twosome. They are free to holiday when they can make time in their own personal schedules. These schedules depend on time constraints that they impose on themselves as these relate to their work, economic, emotional and intellectual interests.

Data from the Netherlands (Den Bandt: 1980) show that social disapproval of marriages where the couple has chosen not have children has decreased in the public opinion polls from 66% in 1965, to 16% in 1975.

A study in 1974 by some psychology students at Groningen University examined the deliberate childless choice of these students and found that 60% of those who intended not to have children were under age 30; 26% were between 26 and 30. There was an 80% reporting of non-religiosity (compared with an approximate 22.5% of the total Dutch population in 1973), and most of the couples in this sample had a high education level and a higher income than average (Delleman et al. 1975). The most frequently cited reasons for remaining child free were over-population, pollution, shortages of food and natural resources, and fear of a third world war.

The Den Bandt (1980) study examined 1200 women scattered throughout the western Netherlands. Almost a third of these women reported that they or their husband had been sterilized or that they planned to be soon. These were average women rather than people of high socio-economic status, which led the researcher to speculate that there may be a broadening of a trend towards childlessness among cohabiting and married couples.

Feldman (1977) finds that the childless are less traditional in their ideology and less sexist. This research also showed that such couples valued female assertiveness without devaluing "femininity," and they showed that these spouses had high interaction in their relationships.

New Patterns among Non-Western Societies

As we continue looking at the notion of "alternative" as being nontraditional, then a glance at a number of non-Western societies reveals certain changes that fit this pattern.

The changing patterns in Chinese families indicate that juvenile delinquency is increasing, because families spoil their children and shelter them when they violate the law (Zhangling: 1983). A new problem is how to bring up and educate the single child, since one child per family is the modern edict. There has been a tendency to marry later, and the divorce laws have been relaxed; however, there continues to be a problem with mistreatment of women and of the elderly, and it is noted that the inequalities between husbands and wives are greater in rural China than in the cities.

Whyte (1979) finds that young people have more freedom in their choice of a spouse in modern Chinese society than they did in earlier times. However, though the place of the new bride is strengthened, patrilocality continues, and this is re-enforced by Chinese official policies, which use patrilocality to keep the peasants rooted in their villages, thereby ensuring the working population necessary for food production.

The new patterns in Libya indicate that marriage and courtship patterns are undergoing a transformation. In his study of university students, Al Nouri (1980) finds that co-education and the influence of the foreign media makes for new and extensive interaction between the sexes. His study indicates that some marriages do not follow traditional kin and patrilocal traditions, and these are the marriages of the new generation. This research indicates that educated urban women who embark on neo-local, non-kin marriage enjoy greater freedom from interference from their in-laws. This style also deals a blow to polygyny because "they no longer worry about the vexing likelihood of having to compete with co-wives" (1980: 231).

Linked with this is the fact that since more of these women are entering occupations previously reserved for men, they are less dependent on men and "more discriminating in choosing their partners and less prepared than ever to put up with the inconveniences of polygyny" (1980: 231).

Another side of this intriguing change in the society, is that men seeking wives tend to prefer women with only a high school education, since the older, better educated women tend to be "too domineering and independent, a quality still somewhat feared by Libyan males," as the study shows.

It is clear that urban migration in many countries is effecting changes in family structures as women, men and children cope with increasing industrialization, and changes in labour markets.

In the Barbados (Stouffle: 1977), the men who migrate to urban areas and who are unemployed or under-employed often find a cohabital union to give them some domestic comfort in the new environment. These are usually men who are already married with families in the rural areas and are thus "unable to meet the cultural prerequisites of marriage."

In Mexico the migration of men in search of jobs increases matrilocal households in certain towns (Olsen: 1977), which makes for an increasing self-sufficiency and greater political strength among women in those towns of origin. Other studies show that younger urban wives who have some formal education are starting to challenge traditional husband-wife relations where they may, in the past have endured infidelity, physical violence and other forms of abuse (Le Vine: 1986). In South America Zimmerman (1975) notes that where fathers have deserted to urban regions, leaving wives and children at home, there are new gangs of boys who have "outgrown their mothers' apron strings." He calls this the "Faginization" of disrupted families.

In Iran (Paydarfar: 1975) it had been hypothesized that with modernization, the size of households would diminish. This prediction has not been born out, because, as the research shows, families keep their servants, and thus the household size does not yet show significant change.

In many parts of Africa, the children of city women are often "shipped" to rural areas to be cared for by grandparents or other relatives or friends. In contrast, a number of studies note that urban migration by family men results in polygyny as they settle into a marital type of union close to their place of work.

An interesting finding regarding African women who migrate to urban areas (Keller: 1979) is that they may have more economic independence, but they no longer have the elders of the village to turn to, and where they turn to use the courts to settle problems, there are complaints about the impersonality of magistrates. The practice of clitoridectomy appears to be diminishing in some societies such as Egypt (Assad 1980). While rural families might have killed their daughter if she had a broken or damaged hymen before marriage, they are now sharing new knowledge and new tolerance, as health care professionals share their newer and feminist-inspired insights on these old habits. Of the women that were interviewed in this study, both illiterate and semi-literate, 95% had been circumcised and half had their own daughters circumcised.

In their research on the traditional and modern Arab family, Tormeh (1982) points out that women's status in these families are changing

as nation states alter their social structure. The custom of finding a spouse through relatives is declining; there is a decline in polygyny, which reduces patriarchal dominance and the emerging educated middle classes are showing new emphasis on romance, egalitarianism and some freedom of choice in marriage. The greatest change along these lines is cited in Lebanon, and although love relationships are showing Western influences, these are still "confined to verbal expressions of affection and admiration" (1982: 45).

In India, the sex segregation of family tasks is diminishing, so that slowly, urban families are sharing one another's roles, and understanding one another better (Lal: 1979). The role of education in the changing attitudes and values of women in India makes for greater economic independence and a new sense of self confidence for many (de Souza: 1975). Miller (1980) points out the continuing costs of marrying daughters in India. Though marriages are generally occurring at an older age, and the data indicate a decline in pre-pubertal and under-age marriage (Zaman 1982).

Industrialization and Male Dominance

As women move from employment in primary sectors to secondary and tertiary sectors, the matrilineal customs of some tribal societies in India show signs of a patrilineal system, "where the position of women as decision makers and owners of property goes under" (Sachidananda: 1978). This shows industrialization makes for male dominance of which there is also much evidence in Africa, as the economy "modernizes."

Summary

We have seen that cohabitation has become an increasingly viable and more acceptable new family form. The 70s and 80s have shown us that women and men have different marital and relationship agendas. The ideologies that have espoused individualism, personal growth and self-actualization of the last few years point towards a proliferation of households where we find single, solo-parent, and re-constituted family forms in the new family matrix. Perhaps we can argue that the newly constituted second family is a post-modern extended family form for the industrial societies of the West.

There is, however, a double-edge for family life in many other parts of the world. As rural people in non-Western societies "upgrade" monetary and occupational opportunities by moving to the cities, childcare becomes increasingly problematic for the women. They also discover a job structure where the genders are more ghettoized and where family and workplace are polarized.

We learn then, that alternative and new family forms are differentially shaped, depending on levels of industrialization, women's educational opportunities, and gender-specific cultural views on sexual preference and practices. In all of these new forms there is a testing of boundaries and experimentation with contemporary ideas. New household forms are the cutting edge of family life. They lay the foundations of aspirations, traditions and values. And it is these very same forms that lay the basis for the upcoming legal and normative codes of our society.

TECHNICAL TERMS

E.M.S.—Extramarital sex.

COHABITATION—A domestic socio-emotional partnership that is held together by philosophy and volition.

LONE PARENT—Single parent households, female or male.

COMMUNES AND INTENTIONAL COMMUNITIES—A style of group living in a domestic unit that was usually grounded in political, educational, cultural and often egalitarian philosophy, and which may or may not have held to monogamous norms. Particularly common in the 1960s.

SAME-SEX COUPLES—Gay/homosexual men or lesbian women in a domestic socio-emotional partnership.

NON-MONOGAMOUS RELATIONS—Where the sexual relation is not exclusively enclosed within the primary cohabital, marital or gay partnership.

AIDS—Acquired Immune Deficiency Syndrome.

COMMUTE COUPLES—Where the marital or domestic partnership is geographically separated for periods of time because of work-related necessity (e.g., musicians, actors, dancers, immigrant workers, corporation transfers).

QUESTIONS FOR DISCUSSION

1. How does the economy and educational opportunity relate to gender in regard to lone parents?

2. Cohabitation has become an increasingly viable domestic option for couples in the 1980s. How does the state treat this in Scandinavia as compared with North America?

3. Despite the decline of Communes and International Communities, in the 80s some have argued that the egalitarian and philosophic components of these

group family forms have been continued in modern feminist family ideals. Discuss.

4. There has been some public debate in the 1980s about the rights of gay parents to raise their own children. How do social mores, sexual preference and individual rights intersect in this debate?

5. It appears that formal education is a key component in the changing values and views of women in developing nations regarding their perception of marital rights and duties. Discuss.

Chapter 6

WOMEN, THE FAMILY AND CHANGE

Susannah J. Wilson
Oasis Management Consultants, Long Beach, California

The postwar years have been marked by a number of important changes in family life, some of which have been discussed in the previous chapter. While marriage remains an important life goal, divorce, single living, and nonmarital cohabitation have become increasingly common. Fertility has declined, and childbearing is delayed for many women. Childlessness too has become more acceptable, although most young people continue to desire and expect children. North American women now spend less than one-quarter of their lives involved in childbearing and childrearing if they in fact become mothers. An increasing number of women will be single parents, and an estimated 40 to 50% of American children will be raised for a period in a single-parent household (Bloom, 1982). By 1990 it is expected that only 25% of American households will consist of married couples and their children (Glick, 1984). Perhaps the most important change is the high rate of female labour force participation in most of the industrialized world. For most women the responsibilities of motherhood will be combined with paid employment, whatever their marital status.

Despite the growing emphasis on individual self-fulfillment and a growing acceptance of nontraditional lifestyles, most North Americans expect to marry and have children. Young girls are particularly receptive to the ideology of romantic love (Women's Bureau, Labour Canada, 1986). The traditional view of marriage and family finds less support among adolescents (see Baker, 1985) and adults. Public opinion polls and attitude surveys show a shift to more egalitarian views of gender roles. "Rising divorce rates, declining fertility and the increase in women's participation in the paid work force are trends that make women's traditional roles more costly to them and that thereby set the stage for women's adoption of an egalitarian ideology" (Mason and Lu, 1988: 42). Because they accept the fundamental validity of arguments supporting gender equality, or because they recognize the financial contributions of their wives' employment, men too have begun to express more egalitarian attitudes.

These changes in behavior and attitude combine to provide an impetus to sociological analysis and to initiatives to improve the legal status and quality of life for women. In most countries of the world the Women's Movement has been an important force for change. Since the 1960s women have renewed their efforts to establish legal equality, gain educational opportunity, control reproduction, and so on. In sociology, as in other disciplines, feminists have challenged a myriad of sexist biases, assumptions, and practices. Attention has been drawn to previously ignored issues including sexual violence and housework. Recognition of the pervasiveness of gender inequality has stimulated a reassessment of a number of assumptions and models. Much feminist research contains an implicit critique

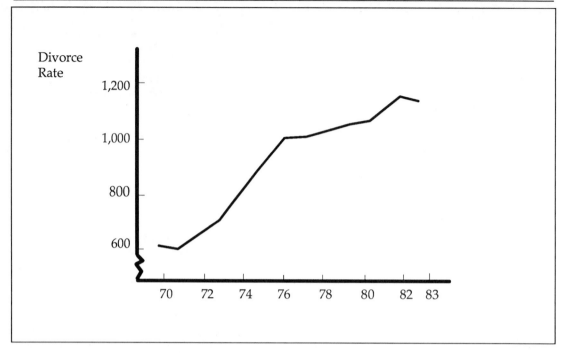

FIGURE 6–1: DIVORCE RATE, 1970–1983
SOURCE: Statistics Canada, Women in Canada, 1985, p. 3.
Ministry of Supply and Services

of existing social arrangements and includes an agenda for change. Textbooks have begun to reflect the contributions of feminist scholars, and most undergraduate programmes now include courses focusing on women.

This chapter describes changes in women's lives, and the consequences these have had for the family lives of men and children. The chapter reviews in turn major demographic changes in family structure, trends in female labour force participation, and the impact of these on family living. Although attitudes have become more liberal, the organization of domestic life and the care of children remain a woman's responsibility, whether or not she is otherwise gainfully employed. The responsibilities women assume for domestic maintenance and childcare are at the root of gender inequality in employment and in political life. For women it is a "double burden" and "double bind." Labour force segregation and low pay make economic self-sufficiency improbable, yet married women contribute an increasing amount to family income. The final section

of the chapter focuses on the increased involvement of women in public life and reviews the major accomplishments of the Women's Movement.

Demographic Trends

While marriage remains the norm, there has been an increased acceptance of singlehood, of marital dissolution, and nontraditional living arrangements, including nonmarital cohabitation and homosexual unions. Between 1970 and 1980 there was a significant drop in the number of American men and women in their early twenties who had married. "This change may mean only that more young adults are postponing marriage. On the other hand, it could mean that a growing proportion of adults are committing themselves to staying single or cohabiting" (Glick, 1984: 22). About 10% of adult North Americans never marry, but approximately four times this are currently single. Singles include predictable age and sex groups. Because women tend to marry men who are slightly older, there are more single

Chapter 6 / Susannah J. Wilson

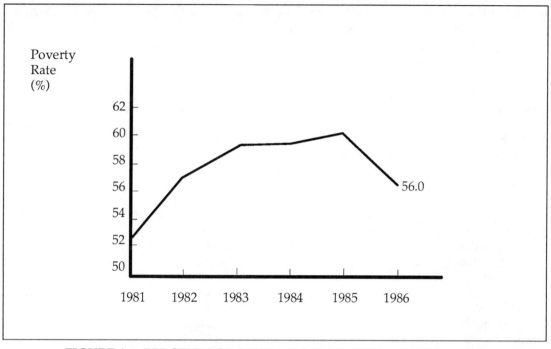

**FIGURE 6–2: PERCENTAGE OF SINGLE-PARENT FAMILIES BELOW
THE POVERTY LINE, 1981–1986**
SOURCE: National Council of Welfare, Poverty Profile 1988, p. 32,
Ministry of Supply and Services, Canada

men under twenty-five than single women. On the other hand, since women typically out-live men, there are far more older single women than men. Both widowed or divorced men are more apt to remarry than widowed or divorced women. Since half of all recent mar-riages end in divorce, it is clear that the vast majority of women now under twenty will be economically self-supporting either by choice or force of circumstances for some part of their adult lives.

For most of the nineteenth century divorce was rare, although we have no way to measure the number of marriages ended by separation or desertion. In the United States, divorce rates began to climb slowly at the end of the nine-teenth century and continued to increase dur-ing the first half of the twentieth century. Rates increased during both wars and dipped dur-ing the Depression and again in the 1950s. Since 1960 the American divorce rate has in-creased sharply but may have begun to taper off, perhaps because of the increased age at

first marriage. In Canada, divorce rates re-mained low until the 1968 legislative change, liberalizing grounds for divorce. From 1968 until 1982, divorce rates increased annually (See Figure 6–1). Since 1983 there has been a slight decline in the numbers of Canadian cou-ples seeking divorce, although it is too soon to determine the effects of 1986 legislative changes. In the United States half of all recent marriages end in divorce, giving this country one of the highest divorce rates in the world. The US rate (5.19 in 1980) is substantially higher than in the USSR (3.50), Britain, the Scandinavian countries, or Canada. Interest-ingly, Australia also has a very high divorce rate (4.75) (United Nations Demographic Year-book, 1981).

High divorce rates do not indicate a rejection of marriage. Although the remarriage rate is dropping, in Canada three-quarters of di-vorced men and two-thirds of divorced women remarry. However, for most women, divorce signals a drop in their standard of living. Without the economic and emotional support of another adult, time and money pressures create a stressful situation for women and their children.

In the last fifteen years there has been a significant increase in the number of single-parent female-headed families living with little or no economic support from the absent husband or father. Less than one-third of absent fathers pay the agreed upon amount of child support (Bohen, 1984: 258). One in ten Canadian families in 1981 was lone-parent, female-headed. The majority (56%) of these women were separated or divorced, 33% were widowed, and the remainder were never married (Statistics Canada, *Women in Canada*, 1985). Over half of single-parent female-headed families have incomes below the poverty line (See Figure 6–2). While the figures show a slight dip from 1985 to 1986, female-headed families are more than four times more likely to be poor than male-headed families. The "feminization of poverty" refers to the fact that in almost every category (age, marital status, employment status, etc.) women run a higher risk of being poor.

The postponement of childbearing, the tendency to have smaller families, and the increased number of couples who remain voluntarily childless have resulted in below replacement birth rates in most industrialized countries. On the other hand, births to unmarried women in North America have increased despite the general availability of contraception. This is a far more serious issue in the United States than in Canada. Since fertility rates generally have decreased, this trend seems to indicate an increased acceptance of unmarried parenthood, at least among some groups of women. Births to unmarried women under twenty present a particular problem. "The United States has the highest teen pregnancy and birth rates among developed nations, even though it has roughly comparable rates of teen sexuality. Pregnancy rates are twice as high as those in Canada, England, and France " (Swager and Fishbein, 1988: 8). For many of these young women pregnancy means leaving school prematurely. Forty per-

cent of female high school dropouts cite pregnancy or marriage as the reason for leaving school. Lifetime earnings of teenage parents are half the earnings of those who become parents after age twenty.

As these trends imply, it is no longer reasonable to make life choices based on the assumption that husbands or fathers provide lifelong economic and emotional security for women or children. Yet, although attitudes have become more liberal, and alternate family arrangements more socially acceptable, the idealized version of the family (breadwinning father, homemaking mother, and their children) remains a strong cultural mandate. A study of Canadian schoolchildren found that young girls expect to marry and become mothers and assume that a husband will be provider. "There do not seem to be any unmarried mothers, deserted wives, widows or divorcees among the imaginary women Canadian schoolgirls expect to become" (Women's Bureau, Labour Canada, 1986: 56). Adolescents, particularly those who have experienced living in a single-parent household, are somewhat more realistic about their future lives. Only 75% of the girls and 64% of the boys in Baker's (1985) Canadian study of adolescent aspirations expected to be married by age thirty. Most expected to marry eventually, but some thought they might live singly or cohabit first. A few anticipated the possibility of divorce, yet were generally unrealistic about its implications.

Feminists, including Baker (1985: 165), argue the importance of making young people more aware of the realities of their future. Anti-feminists, on the other hand, hold tenaciously to the image of the traditional family. Calling themselves pro-family, these groups are concerned about a breakdown in family structures and the values on which traditional family life was based. Drawing support from religious conservatives, the Right to Life Movement, and the political Right, anti-feminists stress the centrality of women to family and the family to society (Chafetz and Dworkin, 1987: 57). The family these groups hold dear is founded on an exchange relationship between hus-

TABLE 6–1: PERCENT OF WOMEN (AGED 15-64) IN THE LABOUR FORCE: WORLD REGIONS

WORLD			47
	More Developed Countries	59	
	Less Developed Countries	43	
	Less Developed Countries (excluding China)	38	
AFRICA			44
	Northern Africa	8	
	Western Africa	52	
	Eastern Africa	62	
	Middle Africa	49	
	Southern Africa	47	
ASIA			46
ASIA (excluding China)			40
	Southwest Asia	27	
	Middle S. Asia	36	
	Southeast Asia	48	
	East Asia	55	
	China	55	
	Japan	54	
NORTH AMERICA			60
	Canada	59	
	United States	60	
LATIN AMERICA			30
	Middle America	29	
	Caribbean	38	
	Tropical S. America	29	
	Temperate S. America	31	
EUROPE			52
	Northern Europe	59	
	Western Europe	50	
	Eastern Europe	65	
	Southern Europe	41	
U.S.S.R.			71
OCEANIA			53

SOURCE: Taken from *The World's Women: A Profile*. Population Reference Bureau, Washington, D. C., 1985.

Chapter 6 / Susannah J. Wilson

bands and wives. Wives offer mothering and homemaking and in return receive the protection and economic support of their husbands.

Any policies which upset this balance are seen as threatening to family life. Anti-feminists in the United States are thus opposed to the Equal Rights Amendment which would give women legal equality. Similarly anti-feminists in Canada opposed entrenching women's rights in the Constitution. For the same reason, anti-feminists oppose reproductive control, demands for measures to ensure labour force equality, or publicly supported day care. They hold the women's movement responsible for the deterioration of the family, ignoring the fact that climbing divorce rates predate the contemporary women's movement, and that increases in labour force participation have more to do with large scale economic trends than with changing attitudes. In contrast, feminists, including Bergmann (1987: 11), stress that we can only recapture what was good about the traditional family through reforms that take into account new realities of family living. Feminists argue for "the recognition of alternate family arrangements in public policy and in law, in the organization of the economy and in beliefs about legitimate choices concerning sexuality and reproduction" (Thorne, 1982: 5). The feminist agenda includes new habits of distributing domestic responsibilities, new schedules of work, and new services to meet the needs of men and women in different family situations.

Domestic responsibilities and inequalities in the labour force and in public life are two sides of the same coin. The assumption that women are primarily responsible for domestic maintenance and men for economic security means that women do not have access to economic resources on the same basis as men. Consequently they are subordinates in all aspects of life (Hartmann, 1981). For most women, economic security still depends on a relationship with a man. The availability of contraception, access to education, and job opportunities are beginning to change expectations and chip away the constraints. While strong barriers exist, we have seen some important evidence

of change. Many consider labour force participation to be the key.

Labour Force Participation Rates

In the 1950s the typical female employee in Canada was young, single and childless. During the 1960s it became customary for married women to be gainfully employed, although unusual while children were young. During the 1970s participation rates for all women of working age passed the 50% mark, and the rates continue to climb. At this point, paid employment became the norm for women and the housewife a minority position. In the 1980s the proportion of mothers of infants and young children in the labour force crossed the 50% line. In the past, middle- and upper-class women were the least likely group to be in the paid labour force. Now, it is these women, armed with professional degrees, who not only remain in the labour force, but often reject marriage or childbearing in favour of a career. Now, women who become full-time housewives, without labour force experience, are more likely to be from less privileged backgrounds.

In the 1980s many Canadians still felt the labour force participation of mothers to be less than desirable. As recently as 1982 over half of Canadians polled felt that married women should not take a job outside the home if they have young children (Women's Bureau, Labour Canada, 1984). In Baker's (1985) study of Canadian adolescents, less than one-third of the girls expected to be full-time homemakers, but half of the boys expected this of their future wives. Nevertheless, it seems likely that as more women enter the labour force and delay marriage and childbearing, attitudes to maternal employment will continue to become more liberal (Giele, 1988: 309). As a number of studies have found, husbands and children of employed women are more apt to hold egalitarian views.

Worldwide, the proportion of women in the labour force varies from a low of 3 or 4% in some African countries and parts of Southwest Asia to a high of over 85% in other African countries. (In Africa, most employed women

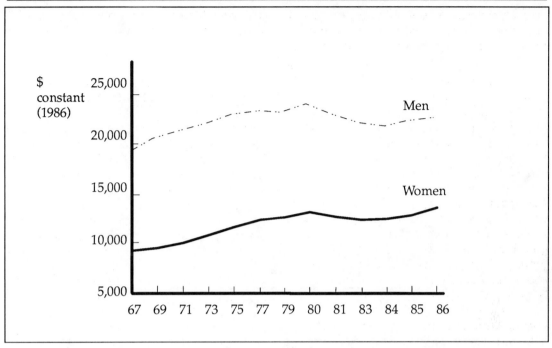

FIGURE 6–3: AVERAGE EARNINGS, WOMEN AND MEN, CONSTANT (1986) DOLLARS, 1967–1986
SOURCE: National Council of Welfare, Poverty Profile 1988, p. 101,
Ministry of Supply and Services, Canada

work in agriculture.) Generally high rates are found in Scandinavia, Eastern Europe, and the USSR. Sweden has the highest rate in this group. Among OECD countries, Canada ranks third behind Sweden and the United States. Table 6–1 shows the percentage of women in the labour force by world region.

The rapid movement of women into paid employment paralleled the changing structure of the labour force and the expansion of clerical, sales, and service sectors. Women were both qualified (having taken advantage of general increases in educational opportunities) and available for these jobs. Throughout the industrialized world, women dominate in low-status clerical, sales, service, and health occupations. In Canada in 1981 over one-third of the female labour force worked in clerical occupations, another 15% worked in service, 9.6% in sales, and 8% in medicine and health. Over three-quarters of all clerical and health workers are women.

Labour force segregation and unequal pay "have their roots in historical processes that have been unravelling for 300 years" (Cowan, 1987: 164). The association of men with productive work and women with reproductive and domestic labour has deep historical roots. It is so well entrenched as to resist the effects of industrialization and the consequent impacts of war, economic depression, and changes in the structure of the labour force. If the boundaries between the family and the economy, private and public life were ever as strict as the ideological supports, they certainly are now far more permeable.

As has been consistently reported, women earn approximately 60% of what men earn (See Figures 6–3 and 6–4). Female university graduates earn approximately as much as male high school graduates, which is far less than their male classmates at university will expect to earn. Only about one-third of pay differences can be explained by differences in edu-

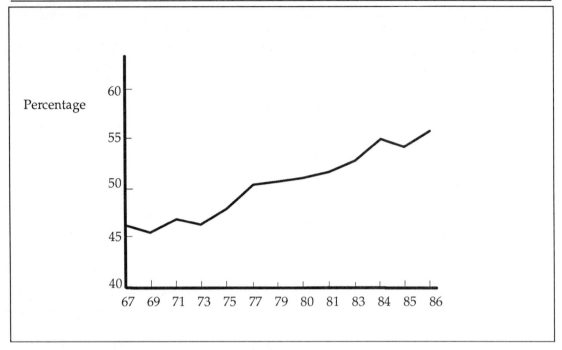

FIGURE 6–4: AVERAGE EARNINGS OF MEN AND WOMEN AS A PERCENTAGE OF AVERAGE EARNINGS OF MEN, 1967–1986 (1986) DOLLARS, 1967–1986
SOURCE: National Council of Welfare, Poverty Profile 1988, p. 101,
Ministry of Supply and Services, Canada

cation and experience, although a number of economists continue to insist that both occupation and low pay can be explained by a choice model. (See Bergmann (1987) for a critique of Human Capital Theory). One explanation of the wage gap is occupational segregation. The jobs in which women dominate have traditionally been poorly paid. Because women work in a narrow range of occupations, the issue of pay inequality will not be solved solely by requiring employers to pay equally individuals doing the same job. But since even in these jobs, male employees earn higher salaries, much of the variation in pay is the result of discrimination. Pay discrimination has been illegal in the United States since the 1964 Civil Rights Act, and in Canada since 1977, when it became written into the Human Rights Act. These Acts legislate against overt acts of discrimination. They do little to change the countless ways employers have different expectations of, and assign different responsibilities to

men and women employees. Often these are done with no intent to discriminate. Employment practices that result in different job futures for men and women are generally referred to as *systemic discrimination* for they are built into organizational structures and cultures. Effective legislation depends on identifying structural constraints and uncovering hidden barriers. Recently, the focus of pay equity has shifted to making demands for equal pay for jobs of *comparable worth*. Comparable worth is based on equalizing rewards based on job components. In other words, equal pay for work of equal value.

During the postwar period, women's earnings have increasingly become a necessary part of family income. In North America, wives contribute approximately 30% of family income. This situation creates a double jeopardy for women. They enter a segregated labour force to work in a job for which they receive low pay relative to men. Their wages augment their husbands' wages but are insufficient to enable them to be self-supporting. So, although women make a concrete economic contribution to the household, universal pay differentials make it very difficult for most women to have economic independence without experiencing a comparably lower standard of living.

Balancing Marriage, Children, and Employment

Given that most women marry, most women become mothers, and most women are gainfully employed, we can envision a number of alternate scenarios facing young women today. They may remain single (with or without children); marry but remain childless; marry, have children, and work outside the home; or, marry and be full-time housewives.

For some women career options provide an alternative to marital economic dependence. Better educated women in highly paid jobs are less likely to marry and if they marry will do so later in life. They are also more likely to remain childless. The general availability of contraception means that women have far more control over fertility than they ever had in the past. Clearly there is a reciprocal relationship between fertility and paid employment, as there is between marriage and paid employment. Fewer children enable women to participate more actively in paid employment. The possibility of meaningful, reasonably well-paid work will influence the number of children women desire. As average family size shrinks and laboursaving devices become common, the benefits of paid employment rise with an increase in "real wages" (wages, taking into account inflation), and these have increased for both men and women.

In sociology the study of the relationship between family life and paid employment has undergone a gradual shift in emphasis over the last three decades (Chow and Berheide, 1988). In the past, studies of paid work focused on men; studies of family on women and children. In the 1960s when increased numbers of married women entered the labour force, soci-

ologists began to ask about the effects of maternal employment on marital or family stability and the effects of nonmaternal care on children. More recently the focus has shifted again to the interdependence between family and work and the barriers that make combining the two difficult. Initially, dual career couples were considered models; now it is clear that they are exceptions. They are in the unique position of having sufficient money to buy market substitutes for many housekeeping and childcare needs and thereby to maintain a relatively equal division of labour. Coping mechanisms will vary for different racial and ethnic groups, across social classes, and for different family types. However, most women agree that the unequal burden of domestic responsibility is the key barrier.

Despite the introduction of laboursaving devices and the entry of women to the paid labour force, the allocation of housework has remained remarkably unchanged in the last one hundred years. Women, then as now, were responsible for meal preparation, laundering, cleaning, shopping, cooking, childcare, and care of the sick and elderly. Technical innovations and the availability of substitutes (i.e., fast food) have changed the nature of the work, but it remains a time-consuming responsibility for women. While the amount of time required to perform such tasks as washing has decreased, time spent shopping has increased. Housewives and mothers spend considerable energy creating a comfortable and stress-free environment for family members; shopping for and preparing special meals, car-pooling children to various lessons and recreational activities, and so on.

One important contribution of feminist sociology has been the analysis of housework. Some have treated housework as an occupation and asked questions about its economic value, the prestige of housework, and the amount of time spent doing various tasks. According to one estimate, the value of work performed in the home, by women, without pay, constitutes 35–40% of the Gross National Product (Wilson, 1986: 65). Beginning from a different point of view, Marxist Feminists have

Chapter 6 / Susannah J. Wilson

analyzed the productive value of work women do in the home. From this point of view, women make a concrete economic contribution by sustaining the current labour force, reproducing the next generation of workers, and socializing them appropriately.

Nevertheless, much of what women do under the heading of housework eludes quantitative analysis, for it is not task oriented. It does not fall into time series or Marxist categories. There are no market substitutes for much of what women do out of love and feelings of responsibility for their families. Childcare (beyond attending to physical needs) is a good example.

Findings of various North American studies are consistent. Full-time housewives spend approximately 55 hours a week doing housework. Gainfully employed wives do 35 hours a week in addition to their paid labour; but their husbands do little more than the husbands of full-time homemakers—about ten hours a week. It is an understatement to say that men have been slow to respond to women's increased labour force participation by increasing their involvement in housework and childcare. While attitude surveys show they support women's entry to the labour force, they have not been as ready to accept domestic responsibility. This is not surprising, for while women have much to gain in terms of discretionary time by men's involvement in housework and childcare, men have much to lose. Furthermore, husbands generally create more housework than they contribute (Hartmann, 1981: 383). Some better educated and younger husbands do more, but women still organize and manage it. On the other hand, some women are reluctant to give up their control in this one area of dominance (Gerstel and Gross, 1987: 157), although in many households, pressure to share the responsibility is a major source of tension (Cowan, 1987: 172).

Because of these constraints a large number of employed women work part time. In North America, approximately one-quarter of employed women work part time. Mothers of young children are only slightly less likely to work part time, in both Canada and the US. For some, part time work represents a reasonable compromise, but many women work part-time because full-time work is unavailable, or because they cannot find suitable childcare (Women in Canada, 1985).

By the end of the century only about 25% of married women will be full-time homemakers. As the Hunts (1982) predict, we can expect to see an increased economic discrepancy between family-centred and career-centred households in future. More importantly, full-time homemakers are particularly vulnerable in the case of marriage breakdown or death. This group, referred to as *displaced homemakers*, experience a much reduced standard of living when their marriages end, particularly if they have been married homemakers for a number of years. As Bergmann (1987: 218) points out, the problem of displaced homemakers affects married women also, since they and their husbands know in the case of marriage breakdown, her social and economic position will be far more negatively affected than his. This awareness gives husbands an added dimension of interpersonal power.

Given patterns of labour force participation and of marital breakdown and the lack of policy support in these areas, men and women are left to negotiate individual solutions to problems of integrating family and employment. The key to social reform in family policy is gaining a voice in decision-making bodies.

Public Life

Women cannot initiate policy change without a stronger voice in formal political structures. For the Suffragettes, this meant first to gain the right to vote. This First-Wave of the Women's Movement started in the United States in the 1840s, in England in the 1850s, in France and Germany in the 1860s, and in the Scandinavian countries in the 1870s and 1880s (Dahlerup, 1986: 3). Full federal franchise and the right to run in Federal elections was "granted" women in Canada in 1918. Provincial voting rights were in most cases established in the two previous years, although Quebec women were not able to vote in provincial elections until 1940. In 1929, following the battle over "The Person's Case," Canadian women officially became persons under the law and thus eligible for Senate appointments. This brief indication of the landmarks hides the extent of resistance the suffragettes met in Canada and in every other society where voting rights were being determined. When we consider that less than seventy years ago, women in most Western societies could not vote or hold office, and their property rights and access to education were limited, it is clear that much has been accomplished in a short period of time. When these are compared to the equality gaps, the job ahead remains formidable.

It has generally been observed that women's political representation decreases with each level of political activity. As the level of responsibility and power increases, the number of women representatives decreases. This pyramid shape is a universal phenomenon.

In Canada, there are more women elected representatives in municipal politics than at either provincial or federal levels. One reason for this is that in Canada, municipal politics is formally divorced from party politics. Municipal nominations do not come from party associations, nor are candidates constrained by established party policies. For this reason municipal politics is less likely to be a stepping stone to provincial or federal involvement than may be the case in other countries (Brodie and Vickers, 1982). Another important reason for greater involvement at this level is that local politics requires less time and travel, so women are better able to combine political involvement and family responsibilities.

The number of women candidates has increased with each election, and the rate of increase has been much greater in the last fifteen years. Nevertheless, elected women are a very small proportion of the total. In Canadian federal elections up to 1980, a total of 34 women were elected to the House of Commons. In 1980, 5% of the House members were women. In 1984, 27 women won seats, and an unprecedented six of these were appointed to Cabinet.

Cross-cultural analysis of women's political involvement finds that there is no simple relationship between either a country's political ideology or its level of economic well-being and the political involvement of women, in either elected or appointed offices. It does seem that women are most active politically in countries where they are most active economically. This relationship holds across most of Eastern and Western Europe and in the USSR. Italy (where many employed women work in "home work") and Japan (where traditional attitudes to women remain strong) are exceptions. Lovenduski and Hills (1981) argue that one of the factors accounting for cross-cultural differences is the traditional social definition of women's domesticity. Changes in the structure of family life will therefore create or inhibit opportunities for participation. The increased number of single-parent female-headed families in the United States, Canada, Britain, Sweden, and Finland may be reflected in lower political involvement. On the other hand, the increased numbers of childless women in some countries may allow more time for political participation. However, as the authors point out, these demographic changes are recent, and their effects, speculative.

Family responsibilities make it difficult for most women to have an active political career. Women describe time, money, distance, and risks to job and housing as the major constraints to greater political involvement (Vickers, 1986). When these are coupled with difficulties of accessing the male dominated field of formal politics, the barriers are formidable. There is among women a tradition of political involvement on another and equally important level. As with other aspects of our history, much of women's public activity at the community level has gone unrecognized. Women are available to participate at the local level in part because they have created flexible group structures which take into account the realities of their lives.

Summary

It has been assumed in this chapter that recent increases in the labour force participation of women, particularly mothers of pre-school children, have been at the root of important changes in women's family lives, and these in turn have had consequences for the lives of husbands and children. It is evident that recent changes in paid employment, and in educational and political spheres, have created new opportunities for many women. Yet despite the changes, social definitions of women's roles have been slow to alter. Women's opportunities in the labour force are restricted by universal assumptions about priority given to domestic over economic roles and the real constraints of the double day for women. The observation is frequently made that when women enter the labour force they do not change jobs, they simply add paid work to their domestic tasks. Furthermore, when they do work, it is in one of a limited number of jobs, for which they receive less pay than equally qualified and experienced men. Feminists sociologists have raised a number of issues previously ignored by mainstream sociology. They have sought explanations for labour force inequalities and an understanding of the mutual effects of paid and unpaid work.

The women's movement has done a great deal to draw public attention to such issues as day care, family violence, and equal pay. These concerns have only recently been publicly addressed by politicians, the great majority of whom are men. Cross-cultural comparisons of women's political representation show that few women become either elected or appointed to public office. Social attitudes and family commitments continue to restrict opportunities for political participation.

It is tempting to assume that as societies become more industrialized and as standards of living increase, the relative position of women will improve. That the evidence does not support this assumption indicates that we can not simply wait for these problems to "work themselves out." Addressing the universal issue of sexual inequality has meant a reconsideration of fundamental beliefs about family and work life. Furthermore, it is a challenge we all face, whether in our own relationships, in our jobs, or in our more public roles as responsible citizens.

TECHNICAL TERMS

SYSTEMIC DISCRIMINATION— Employment practices and structural constraints which implicitly, if not intentionally, result in the unequal treatment of certain groups of women.

DISPLACED HOMEMAKERS—Divorced, separated or widowed housewives with little or no labour force experience.

FEMINIZATION OF POVERTY—Women make up an increasing proportion of the low income population.

OCCUPATIONAL SEGREGATION—The universal phenomenon that employed women work in a limited number of occupations in which most employees are women.

COMPARABLE WORTH—A programme to equalize pay differentials between men and women by requiring "equal pay for work of equal value."

ANTIFEMINISM—A backlash movement which supports a traditional patriarchal family structure, and opposes measures to give women economic equality or reproductive control.

QUESTIONS

1. Why is the American divorce rate so high? Why is divorce more common in Australia or Great Britain than in Canada?

2. Does antifeminism represent a genuine threat to the women's movement?

3. An increasing number of highly educated professional women have decided not to have children. Do you predict this trend will continue in the future?

4. Account for the unequal representation of women on the faculty at your university or college. What evidence do you find of systemic discrimination?

5. Ask students in your class about the division of labour in their families of orientation. In what ways do they anticipate changing areas of responsibility in their families of procreation? How do men and women differ in their expectations?

6. What factors account for the low representation of women in all levels of politics? Why do we not see higher involvement in Canada and the United States, when one-third of representatives in the National Assembly in Mexico are women?

Reverse: Family scene.
18th Century

Chapter 6 / Susannah J. Wilson

THE SOCIALIZATION PROCESS

GENDER ROLE SOCIALIZATION

Charlene Thacker
University of Winnipeg

Gender Role Socialization: An Overview

Gender role socialization is an aspect of socialization in general. It refers to the processes by which boys and girls, and men and women, become what we expect them to become in particular cultures; how they come to establish culturally acceptable identities and to behave in culturally accepted ways according to their sex. Gender identity refers to the identification of oneself as masculine or feminine in a particular culture. This includes acceptance of the identity and a degree of comfortableness with it. The establishment of gender identity and gender role occurs largely within the family context and is influenced by the relationship of the family to the society of which it is a part. Sustained and profound impacts of gender on the individual are generally thought to derive from childhood socialization.

In this chapter, much of our discussion focuses on family and work roles. This is because the roles of men and women have diverged significantly in these two arenas of social life. In other areas, such as political and military life, men have so dominated that we are discussing for the most part a male phenomenon. In addition, much of the theory linking social status to gender role relates to the historical structure of the family and the economy.

Gender Stereotypes

It is important to note that preconceived ideas about what men and women innately are—their relatively unalterable characteristics—condition what people think they can and should become. While it is true that nur-ture acts on nature, nurture also acts upon what the agents of socialization think nature to be.

Social scientists have found that people do think that the characteristics of men and women are different (Kagan, 1971: 19–21; Ruble, 1983; and Cantor and Meyerowitz, 1984). When asked to describe men, people see them as independent, aggressive, objective, competitive, active, adventurous, and ambitious. Women, on the other hand, are thought to be passive, subjective, dependent, gentle, warm, weak, and patient (see Rosenkrantz, et al., 1968 ; Broverman, et al., 1972; and McClelland, 1965). In a thirty-nation study, Williams and Best (1982) showed that many of these sex-trait stereotypes are adhered to cross-culturally. Gender role socialization practices, such as encouraging competitive sports for boys and domestic play for girls, are built upon these stereotypical ideas about what the sexes are and therefore what they should become.

Effectiveness of Gender Role Socialization

Gender role socialization is effective, because it controls motivation (Freeman, 1974: 24). As d'Andrade (1966: 201) remarks, "Usually individuals learn to *want* to occupy the sex status they are assigned..." (italics mine). Indeed, the system of gender roles might be much more conflict-ridden than it is now, or simply might not work at all, if gender role socialization were not effective.

A recent Australian study found that even very young children (seven- and ten-year-olds) had traditional sex-typed plans for themselves when they grew up. A high proportion of the girls aspired to marriage and family life, while most of the boys answered in terms of paid occupations (Russell and Smith, 1979). In a US study of four- to eight-year-olds, children demonstrated traditional career choices for themselves, as well as for others of the opposite sex (Zuckerman and Sayre, 1982). Black preschool children in the US were found to vary in achievement motivation, depending upon whether they had been exposed to traditional or nontraditional gender role socialization practices (Carr and Mednick, 1988). Traditional socialization appears to effect higher achievement motivation in boys, whereas nontraditional socialization appears to lead to higher achievement motivation in girls.

Another recent study, this time in Canada, examined the vision of the future held by 15- to 19-year-olds (Baker, 1985). These young people were asked to describe what a typical weekday might be like for them at age thirty. About 93% of the young men and about 68% of the young women expected to be working full time at age thirty (p. 78). However, it was obvious from the young women's responses that they saw housework as mainly the responsibility of the wife (p. 163). Most high school seniors in a US national sample thought that mothers should stay home with preschool children and that anything less than full-time work for husbands was undesirable (Herzog et al., 1983).

Sources of Gender Role Socialization

The family is a major agent of socialization cross-culturally, and it is usually the first agent in the young child's life. The media and school, however, are important gender role socializers in modern Western societies, but not among such groups as the early aboriginal peoples of Australia or the Yanamamo of Brazil. Generally speaking, agencies of socialization outside the family, the tribe, or cultural group as a whole, and the peer group, assume importance only with modernization.

Cross-Cultural Evidence

One of the most important sources of gender role learning in more primitive societies is through role models within the group. Since primitive societies are generally small, there is a great deal of opportunity for imitation and face-to-face interaction from infancy through all the life stages. Berndt and Berndt (1972: 127), commenting on socialization in Australian aboriginal societies, state that one of the most important models was the "straightforward sex-linked division of labor that permeated all major enterprises, from hunting and food-gathering to religious rituals." Aboriginal children learned through observation of adults that they knew, what roles they themselves would be expected to perform. They were also free to ask questions of adults.

More formal means of gender role socialization for primitive groups frequently comes in the form of initiation rites. For the Australian aboriginals, as for many other such groups, the main objective of the rites for boys was to induct them into the company of the men and to symbolically separate them from the women (Berndt and Berndt, 1972: 127). Boys were to become men, involved in the roles appropriate to their sex. These rites are physically memorable in many groups, involving such practices as circumcision and the pulling out of finger-nails. In these non-modern societies, we also find more elaborate and public ceremonies associated with becoming a "man" than with becoming a "woman," an indicator perhaps of different cultural evaluation placed on male and female roles or of the more public nature of men's roles.

An early cross-cultural survey by Barry, Bacon and Child (1957) used anthropological studies of 110 cultures to see if there were any consistent differences in the way in which male and female infants and boys and girls were socialized. They reported little difference in the way in which infants were treated, but significant differences by sex in some aspects of childhood socialization. There was generally more pressure on boys towards achievement and self-reliance, whereas for girls, the pressure was towards nurturance, obedience, and responsibility. The authors suggest that differences in socialization by sex are related to the future economic roles of men and women. Women in these cultures were more frequently assigned routine tasks, such as cooking and carrying water, which would keep them close to home. Men, on the other hand, were more likely to take up tasks such as hunting, which required a higher level of skill and which took them further from home. This research also suggests that differences in socialization by sex will be greatest in those societies which place a high premium on the strength and physical skills of the male in economic activities.

When we look at cross-cultural studies of gender roles and traits, we find that some sex differences are practically universal. For example, ethnographic studies indicate that girls are more likely to be cooperative, sociable, responsive, affectionate, and succorant; while boys are more likely to be aggressive and conflict-oriented (d'Andrade, 1966). Margaret Mead's work in New Guinea, however, shows us how the culture moulds sex differences. Among the head-hunting Tchambuli, it was the women who displayed dominance, robustness, and a willingness to initiate sexual relationships (Mead, 1935: 288). The Tchambuli men were generally graceful, charming, and coquettish (p. 264). Among the cannibalistic Mundugumor, both men and women tended to be aggressive and punishing (pp. 176–213). The Arapesh, on the other hand, were a gentle, cooperative society in which the traits of men and women were not essentially different, even though their roles were (pp. 14–15). Mead describes the social influences that mould personality in these very different tribes. Although scholars like Mead have amassed quite an impressive collection of cross-cultural and historical data on gender roles, we know relatively little about the relationship of actual sex-differentiated socialization practices to the achievement of culturally approved gender roles. Mead's work, as well as that of other early anthropologists, has been criticized on these and other methodological grounds (La Fontaine, 1986: 10–17).

Whiting and Whiting (1975) studied the social behaviour of children in six cultures: Taira (a community on the island of Okinawa in the Pacific); Tarong (in the Philippines); Khalapur (in northern India); the Nyansongo (of Kenya);

Indians living in the barrio of Santo Domingo in Juxtlahuaca (in Mexico); and a section of a small New England town in the United States (Orchard Town). They concluded that the culture does indeed influence the social behaviour of children because it affects the learning environment. Children in the simpler cultures (Nyansongo, Juxtlahuaca, and Tarong) were expected to perform more tasks for the economic well-being of the family at a younger age than were children in the more complex cultures (Taira, Khalapur, and Orchard Town) (p. 94). Children in the simpler cultures were also assigned more responsibility for younger children. The authors found these children to be more nurturant and responsible, whereas children from the more complex cultures were more dependent and dominant (p. 70). Thus, the research strongly suggests that cultural differences in socializing environments produces differences in people.

The same research also suggests that *within* cultures, there are differences in the learning environments experienced by boys and girls. This was the case in all of the cultures studied. Girls were more likely to be assigned tasks which kept them close to home. They were more involved with the preparation of food and cleaning and with the care of infants, and were more likely to be under the direct supervision of their mothers. One would expect this learning environment to foster nurturance, responsibility, and obedience. Whiting and Whiting did find the girls in the six cultures to exhibit these kinds of behaviours more than boys. Boys, on the other hand, were more likely to have chores taking them further from home, for example, herding. They were less likely to be under direct adult supervision and were more likely to interact with their peers. Whiting and Whiting found that boys in the six cultures were more likely to be aggressive and to seek dominance and attention. The greatest sex differences in behavioural tendencies occurred at younger ages (3–6) rather than at older ages (7–10), a fact which d'Andrade (1966: 191) says may suggest the operation of innate tendencies.

Parents

Since the family is considered to be the primary socialization agent, many studies have focused on parent behaviours in regard to their male and female children. Both Block (1983) and Maccoby and Jacklin (1974) have summarized the results of these studies. Maccoby and Jacklin note a great deal of similarity in the socialization of the sexes and lack of any firm evidence supporting a consistent "shaping" process linked to our traditional sex stereotypes. However, they admit that the data are frequently inadequate. They do comment on a number of themes emerging from the various studies. Boys appear to receive more attention than girls, both negative, in the way of punishment, and probably positive, in the way of encouragement and praise. Boys are also more pressured against engaging in behaviour thought to be inappropriate to their sex (p. 348). Block cites the need for further research to confirm in a more convincing fashion what the earlier studies indicate; however, there is substantial evidence that sons and daughters are treated differently (Block, 1983: 1343).

Especially important in recent research has been the inclusion of fathers as socializing agents. Fathers, more than mothers, appear to interact differently with their sons and daughters (Block, 1983: 1342 and Maccoby, 1980: 240–42). When teaching daughters, fathers tend to emphasize interpersonal aspects of the situation. They joke more, as well as give more encouragement and support to their daughters than to their sons. With sons, however, there tends to be more stress on achievement and the cognitive dimensions of the task at hand (Block, 1983: 1342–43). Mothers also treat boys and girls differently. For example, mothers of girls are more likely to give help in solving problems than are mothers of boys (Rothbart and Rothbart, 1976). In general, the studies indicate that both men and women, but particularly men, act in ways which emphasize mastery of tasks and achievement of goals with boy children, and in ways which encourage dependency and expressiveness, rather than achievement, with girl children (Block, 1983: 1343). Snow, Jacklin, and Maccoby's re-

search (1983) on the treatment of one-year-old boys and girls by fathers reveals that fathers are more likely to hold their daughters, but are more likely to prohibit their sons verbally and physically. Boys are also more likely to behave in such a way as to evoke prohibitions (p. 230). Other recent research (Roopnarine, 1986) shows little difference in the involvement of mothers and fathers in the socialization of their male and female infants and very young children.

A number of studies indicate that even in infancy, boy and girl children are treated differently by their parents. Boy babies are handled more vigorously (Moss, 1967 and Lewis, 1972). Evidence also suggests that parents are more attentive and responsive to the activities initiated by boy babies (Lewis and Freedle, 1973 and Parke and Sawin, 1976), although Yarrow et al. (1975: 48) note that it is difficult to come to any firm conclusions about differences in the overall environments of male and female infants.

School

After the parents and the home environment, perhaps the educational system, including the curriculum, the teachers, and the opportunity to interact with one's own age group in this setting, is the next most important socializing agent. Preparation for gender-stereotyped roles through offering different subjects to boys and girls has been the traditional fare of the school system (Levy, 1972). There was not much doubt that women were being prepared for domestic roles or for work roles related to their sex in nineteenth-century schools. Those girls who did attend secondary schools were unabashedly prepared in the arts of the home and etiquette. The one career considered appropriate for girls was that of schoolteacher, and primary schoolteacher at that (L'Esperance, 1982: 6–7). Turn of the century attempts by women to enter universities and professional schools, although finally successful, met with strong opposition and arguments about the proper place of woman in society.

Today such blatant gender role socialization by the schools would be labelled discriminatory. However, we still see that women are segregated into sex-typed occupational roles. Women's lack of representation as employers and managers and in skilled manual work has been directly related to their lack of managerial, scientific, and technical preparation, and this in turn has been related to schooling.

A recent action/research program developed for use in a number of secondary schools in the Greater Manchester area in Britain indicates that a number of factors within the schools are related to girls' nonscientific course options. Most of these factors are directly connected to the way in which the school acts as a socializing agent. First of all, the role models—the science teachers—are mainly men, and the peer group—the students in the science and technical classes—are mainly boys. Moreover, these boys are not neutral in regard to the presence of girls. In fact, the male peer group provides a somewhat hostile environment for girls. Another factor is that the way in which science subjects are taught is related to typical male interests. For instance, the examples used tend to relate to football and the military, instead of to the environment and aesthetics (Whyte, 1985). Finally, teachers themselves frequently believe that girls are inherently less capable of learning science and mathematics, or that it is not worth their while to pursue these subjects, since they will be unrelated to the girls' future roles as wives and mothers (p. 195).

As other research has shown, boys demand and get more teacher attention (Cherry, 1975 and Serbin et al., 1973). Boys are more likely to get both positive feedback and reprimands than are girls. Serbin et al. (1973: 803) note that girls tend to get attention only when they are very near the teacher.

There is some evidence that even modern guidance counsellors may be influenced by gender role stereotypes. When asked to provide an appropriate occupation for six sex-neutral case studies, 300 counsellors tended to choose more supervised, less highly paid occupations requiring lower levels of education when the cases were labelled female (Donahue and Costar, 1977: 483). The problem appears to be less related to girls' motivation in choosing school subjects than to the external expectations and attitudes which structure girls' choices.

Media

The media, particularly television, is an important socializing agent in modern societies (Courtney and Whipple, 1983: 45–60). The "TV" is an important piece of household furniture, frequently occupying a prominent position in the living room or recreational room. It has been estimated that by the age of eighteen, children will have spent more time watching television than they have doing any other thing, except sleeping (Barnouw, 1972 cited in Greenglass, 1982: 67). The content of television programs and advertising tends to reinforce gender role stereotypes (Greenglass, 1982: 68–71; Courtney and Whipple, 1983: 14–26; Singer, 1986: 104–109); and children who watch a great deal of TV (25 hours or more per week) appear to be more traditional in their sex-role development (Frueh and McGhee, 1975). Although studies indicate that the role of TV is to reinforce gender stereotypes, parents and the school appear to have a strong mediating influence on the effect of television viewing by children (Courtney and Whipple, 1983: 51–53).

Books

Children also learn about appropriate gender roles through textbooks that they use in school and through their recreational reading. Numerous studies of the content of children's picture books, fairy tales, and school readers lead us to four conclusions (Greenglass, 1982: 59–64). First, there are many more boys and men represented in these books than girls and women, so much so that Greenglass refers to the female character as being "invisible" (p. 59). Even when the gender of characters in picture books was indeterminate, mothers talking to their young children labelled 95% of these gender-neutral characters male (DeLoache et al., 1987). Second, males in these books are active agents in their worlds, while females tend to be passive victims, frequently waiting to be rescued (by a male). Third, females are found in serving roles, often domestic, while men and boys have all the fun and adventure. And finally, these books tend to reinforce stereotypical gender traits—competence, independence, and competitiveness for males and incompetence, fearfulness, and dependency for females. The male traits are the socially valued ones, whereas the female traits are not the ones that most people would like to have.

There have been a number of non-sexist children's books published in recent years, and they do portray nurturant males and independent females (Davis, 1984). However, one has only to scan the display cases of children's bookstores, the shelves of the children's section of the local library, and the text selections of local schools to see that many of the gender role messages in books that modern children read are quite traditional.

Toys

Parents not only interact with children directly, they also provide a home environment replete with sex-differentiated playthings and sometimes even appropriate bedroom decorations. Parents' input is particularly dominant at the younger ages. Rheingold and Cook (1975) studied the contents of almost 100 young (one month to six years) boys' and girls' rooms. Boys' rooms contained toys relating them to the world outside the home, for example, sports equipment, machines, vehicles, and military toys. Girls' rooms were filled with "domestic" toys such as dolls and doll houses. Research indicates that parents are more likely to give toys stereotyped for boys to young girls than to give "girl" toys to young boys, and that very young boys are more likely to request toys that are stereotyped for their sex (Robinson and Morris, 1986).

A number of experimental studies have shown that when parents are asked to interact with babies arbitrarily labelled boys or girls, they tend to offer sex-stereotyped toys to the infants (Will et al., 1976; Frisch, 1977; Smith

and Lloyd, 1978; and Culp et al., 1983). However, Bell and Carver (1980) found that among women not believing much in sex differences, the stereotypical presentation of toys was more strongly associated with the infant's behaviour than with the gender label.

Examination of toy stores, toy catalogues, and interviews with both toy executives and other adults and children suggest that girls' toys are viewed as more passive, solitary, and simple than either neutral or boys' toys. Boys' toys are seen as more active, social and complex than girls' toys. Boys' toys also tend to be more expensive and varied (Lyon, 1974: 404, reporting research by Goodman and Lever). The kinds of toys with which boys play, for example, cars, blocks, and building sets, frequently enhance their spatial skills; whereas typical girls' toys, such as dolls and tea sets, foster caring and serving behaviours (Greenglass, 1982: 84 and Tracy, 1987). A number of major toy companies have recently promoted boy dolls. The long-term market for these dolls and who plays with them remains to be seen.

The packaging and advertising of toys frequently leave little doubt as to their sex appropriateness. Pictures of boys tend to predominate on sports equipment packaging and even the names of products, like "Handy Andy" tool kits, tell children (and adults) who should be using them (Pogrebin, 1974: 411–12). Try to find a toy kitchen set, replete with dishpan, broom, and dustpan, with a picture of a little boy displayed as "mother's helper." Salespersons have also been found to exercise pressure toward gender-stereotyped toy choices when asked for advice (Ungar, 1982).

Theories of Gender Differentiation

What are the sources of gender role differences? A number of answers to this question have been given, from a variety of perspectives. We shall discuss the biological explanation, theories of psychosexual identity development, social learning, and cognitive developmental perspectives.

Chapter 7 / Charlene Thacker

Biologically Based Theories

One answer to the question of gender role differences is that men and women are born different. However, what can be attributed solely to nature and what is the result of social influences is far from being resolved. This is called the nature-nurture debate. Research on sex differences in physical make-up, innate cognitive abilities, and hormone-related aggression levels does indeed show that men and women are different, but it also shows that they are remarkably similar (see Maccoby and Jacklin, 1974: 349–74). Besides this, when we examine the variation of abilities, traits, and behaviours within one sex, the diversity within one sex is even more striking than the differences between the sexes (Richmond-Abbott, 1983: 79). Furthermore, innate sex differences in abilities, traits, and behaviours are extremely difficult to isolate because of the early influence of gender socialization.

Maccoby and Jacklin (1974), who have done extensive research in the area and who have carefully examined research done by others, conclude that there are only four rather firmly supported research findings regarding sex-related differences. These are that males are more aggressive, a difference which shows up at about age 2; girls' verbal ability is greater after about age 11; and beginning in adolescence, boys demonstrate greater mathematical and visual-spatial ability (pp. 351–52). Although a sex-linked recessive gene, more likely to be present in boys, has been associated with visual-spatial ability (p. 121), it is not at all clear that this is the sole cause of this sex difference or that the other observed differences are genetically based. Obviously, much more research is needed before we can come to any clear conclusions concerning the nature-nurture debate.

Social Elaboration of Biology Theories

Another explanation of the source of gender role differences has to do with the social elaboration of a biological phenomenon, women's reproductive capacities. Since only females can bear and nurse children, and since human beings have a limited supply of time and energy, women are not as free as men to engage in production and defense activities. Thus a division of sex roles related to social survival emerges. This division gives men a significant advantage in controlling the resources of the society (Sanday, 1974: 189–90) and in the exercise of physical force. Control of these domains gives men the basis for power or the exercise of effective decision-making in the community. We must note, however, that women have in the past and still do engage in significant economic activities, without which social survival would be impossible. Thus the theory refers to the relative contributions of men and women to production.

The Psychoanalytic Perspective

The psychoanalytic perspective on the development of gender identity originated with Sigmund Freud (1856–1939) (Freud, 1905 and 1940). His emphasis on psychosexual development and the unconscious in this process has produced a number of important insights, too numerous to detail here, which have built on and modified his theories. (See, for example, Deutsch, 1944–45 and Erikson, 1968.) Freud proposed that the sexual energies of the child had different focuses at each developmental stage. The baby's mouth and lips are the first focus of sexual pleasure. This is called the oral stage. During the second or anal stage, sensuality is centered on the functioning of the bowels and on aggression. Thus far, the development of boys and girls does not differ significantly. It is during the third or phallic stage, when the genitals become a focus of sexual energy and pleasure, that the gender identity development of boys and girls diverges. This occurs from about ages 3 through 6. Both boys and girls experience the Oedipus complex, so named for the figure in a Greek tragedy who, without realizing it, killed his father and married his mother. However, because of their different anatomies and possibilities for identification, boys and girls experience and resolve this complex quite differently. The following is a brief, thus necessarily oversimplified, explanation of this stage.

Boys are motivated to renounce their sexual desires for their mothers in deference to their fathers. This resolution of the Oedipal complex is occasioned by the fear of castration. At this point, the boy is aware that some persons (girls) do not have the organ that can give him, through masturbation, such pleasure. Thus, the possibility of losing the penis seems real. Through repression of the jealousy he experiences toward his father and the sublimation of his desires for his mother, the Oedipus complex is resolved. Through this resolution, the boy comes to identify with the father. Thus, gender identity is achieved.

Freud thought that the psychosexual development of girls was more complex and problematic than that of boys. At the phallic stage, girls also derive sexual pleasure through masturbation. The girl comes to compare her object of sexual pleasure, the clitoris, with the penis possessed by boys. She feels that her sexual anatomy is inferior and falls into penis envy. She finally comes to believe that she has been castrated. The girl enters into the Oedipal stage, turning to her father as love object. It is the father who can give her a child to substitute for the penis which has been lost. As the girl gradually realizes that this will not occur and because she does not want to lose her mother's love, she begins to identify with the mother. However, the fear of castration is not the strong motive for her that it is for a boy, because she feels that she has already been castrated. She may never fully resolve the Oedipus complex. Freud thought that this tortuous developmental process resulted in certain so-called "feminine" traits—jealousy, vanity, and lack of a strong superego.

Relationship With Caregiver: An Adaptation of Psychoanalytic Theory

Chodorow (1974 and 1978), operating largely out of psychoanalytic theory, suggests that gender identity is transmitted to the individual on the unconscious, developmental level. The child internalizes and incorporates into personality organization certain highly salient characteristics of the social structure. Family relationships are key in this development.

The experience of the social environment, particularly the mother-child relationship, is different for boys and girls. The earliest experience of the infant is one of dependency on and identification with the caregiver. The fact that the caregiver is almost always a woman (probably because of lactation) means that the primary attachment and identity of the child is with a female. A key developmental task in the early years is developing a sense of self separate from the identification with the mother. Chodorow suggests that mothers are more likely to encourage and abet this differentiation in boy children. Because of their own identification with their girl children, they are less likely to help them achieve separation and individuation. This is one of a complex relationship of factors which helps to account for relational and dependent personalities in many women and the fact that many insecure men are unable to form adequate interpersonal relationships.

These early developmental processes rest upon the structure of social relationships within families, and along with more conscious socialization practices, result in "masculine" and "feminine" personality and the ready assumption of appropriate gender roles by men and women. The incorporation of the psychoanalytic perspective is valuable in our understanding of gender identification because it helps to explain how gender becomes a deeply valued and emotionally central aspect of the self (Chodorow, 1974: 43).

Social Learning Theory

Another important theory of gender role differences is social learning. The central notion here is that the child, and later the adult, learns from external agents the behaviours and attitudes appropriate to his or her sex. The way in which the child learns is through reward and punishment, which reinforces sex differences, and through imitation of role models. Role modelling implies that boys and girls imitate the behaviour of the same-sex parent and others held up as appropriate gender models.

Many of the gender role socialization practices that were discussed earlier, for example, learning through parents and the provision of different learning environments for boys and girls, involve both reinforcement and imitation of role models if they are to be effective. The difficulty is in assessing just how effective these practices are, that is, in discovering to what extent gender becomes a part of a person's identity through social learning.

Cognitive-Developmental Theory

Cognitive-developmental theory, as it applies to gender role socialization, is also about the process of learning gender roles. However, the child learns that role which is in accordance with his or her labelling of self. Kohlberg (1966) suggests that gender identity is learned early—between 18 and 36 months— and that it is very difficult to change. The knowledge of being a boy or a girl prompts the child to learn appropriate behaviours, attitudes, and values from the same-sex role model. Social learning, then, builds upon cognitive development. Gender roles are learned, but the stress is on the internal self-development of the child and the possibility of self-selection of appropriate models, as opposed to imposition of gender roles by external agents.

When we examine the theories regarding gender role and gender identity differences, we see that they approach the question from different, but not necessarily competing, perspectives. We do not yet have either extensive enough or sophisticated enough research to say that one or the other provides us with the key to understanding sex-related differences. What is mostly agreed upon by researchers in the field is that biology, social learning, psychosexual and cognitive development all have a part to play, but that we have not yet put the pieces of the puzzle together in a satisfactory way.

Gender Roles and Social Stratification

Women have sometimes been called a minority group, as well as the "second sex" (de Beauvoir, 1952). These terms refer to their position in the sex-stratification structure. Although a numerical majority in the Western world (see United Nations, 1983: 144), women's status in relationship to men worldwide is generally secondary from a social point of view. What accounts for women's secondary or minority position in the stratification structure? One important answer has to do with their respective roles in the sexual division of labour. Women's roles have generally been associated with less power, lower prestige, and fewer material rewards than those roles taken on by men.

There are cross-cultural differences in women's power and authority, as well as in their prestige and share of the goods and services produced by the society. Iroquois women, under some circumstances, could sit in judgement on the chiefs, although it must be noted that the chiefs were male. Murdock (1934: 302) suggests that Iroquois society comes closest to the type we call a matriarchate, or one dominated by women. However, the overwhelming evidence cross-culturally is that societies are male-dominated, and that this is related to gender roles (Rosaldo and Lamphere, 1974: 3).

The key to understanding the status of women's gender roles may well lie in the distinction between the public and private spheres. Men's roles tend to lie in the public arena, in work outside the household in modern industrial settings or in work more directly relating the household to the outside world in premodern societies. Military and political roles tend to be male domains as well. On the other hand, women in practically every setting have roles linking them closely to the domestic or home sphere.

Economic Development and Gender Stratification

An important thesis regarding the status of women has to do with the changing structure of the family in relationship to the economy. This perspective suggests that men and women in the relatively simple economic structures of hunting and gathering societies and of horticultural societies are fairly equal. Here women usually have as important a place in production as men, even though men may do more of the hunting, and women more of the gathering. In these societies, there is greater likelihood that decision making will be communal in nature, at least to some extent, and that the status of women will be relatively high.

Sanday (1973) describes the female solidarity groups that arise in this kind of setting. Yoruba women, who operate as independent African traders controlling their own produce, also supervise their own trade guilds and have a voice in the political affairs of the community. Iroquois women controlled agricultural production, a situation perhaps occasioned by the absences of men engaged in trading and war. Iroquois women could even refuse supplies for warfare, thus preventing the formation of a war party (Sanday, 1974: 202–203).

In agrarian societies, on the other hand, women have a lesser role to play in production. This may be due to the heavy nature of the work involved in ploughing, along with the necessity of being away from the home for extended periods of time. The latter requirement, it is speculated, interferes with the demands of nursing and child rearing (Martin and Voorhies, 1975: 276–86). In addition, the great demands for childbearing in agrarian societies such as Egypt, Bangladesh, and parts of Mexico confine women's activities to the home and severely limit their participation in political life. In this kind of economic setting, the extended family form headed by the male predominates. Thus, women's status becomes lowered and their influence severely curtailed. According to this perspective, women have greater opportunities to enhance their status in modern, developed countries than in agrarian societies (Giele, 1977: 27).

One of the key differences between the pre-industrial and industrial family pertains to the way in which the family unit relates to production. In preindustrial systems, the family *is* the unit of production, that is, all the family members, except for the very youngest or the disabled, work in order to supply the family's basic needs. Although male authority may still predominate in this system, the woman's role

in production gives her a certain amount of status. This would be the case for agricultural family production units, as well as for the cottage industries which were a part of the early industrial revolution.

The segregation of work and family life which was characteristic of the later stages of industrialization profoundly affected the status of women because they lost a productive role. Of course, many women outside of families and many poor women in families worked outside the home, in the factories of the eighteenth, nineteenth, and early twentieth centuries as well as in domestic service, as seamstresses, laundresses, teachers and in other occupations. But the ideal and the model followed by the upper classes and the growing middle classes was the segregation of male and female roles. Men were to work (outside the home) and women were to keep the house and tend to the physical and emotional needs of the family. It was only during and after the Second World War that women began to enter the paid labour force in large numbers. As we shall discuss below, this did not mean that men took on a domestic role.

Occupational Roles and Gender Stratification in Industrial Societies

An important factor affecting the economic and social status of women who work outside the home in industrial societies is the type of job that they have and the income that they receive. Numerous studies indicate that the occupational structure tends to be sex-segregated. For example, women are concentrated in sales and service occupations, as well as in lower status white collar occupations (secretaries and clerks). They also tend to work in what are considered to be the "caring" professions (welfare workers, teachers and nurses) (OECD, 1980: 24). The helping, caring, nurturant, assisting character of women's occupations outside the home parallels the stereotypes associated with their roles in the home. As Tilly (1985: 210) points out for France, the sex-typing of occupations is related to the division of labour by sex in the household.

In general, "women's work" is not paid as well as "men's" work, perhaps because it is culturally defined as women's work and therefore is considered to be less valuable (Darling, 1975: 62–63). There is considerable evidence that actual sex discrimination in the form of paying women less than men to do the same job has also been practiced (Darling, 1975: 61–62 and OECD, 1980: 71). The paid occupations dominated by women tend to have generally low social status, except for the occupations of teaching and nursing (Armstrong and Armstrong, 1984: 49–51). Although there is variation by country in the proportion of women who are working in the paid labour force, Stockard and Johnson (1980: 76) comment and go on to document that "in all countries, however, capitalist or socialist, west or east, with or without specific nondiscriminatory policies, the labour force is segregated by sex and men as a whole earn more than women do."

Paid Work: An Expansion of Women's Roles

Gender roles are changing, although the extensiveness of the change and the factors affecting the shifts are not altogether clear. In modern industrial societies, the idea that woman's rightful place is in the home has been increasingly contradicted by the growing numbers of women entering the labour force. (See Darling, 1975: 11 and OECD, 1980: 22.) In fact, in most of the 24 member countries of OECD (Organisation for Economic Co-Operation and Development) the non-earning wife and the working husband is no longer the typical pattern (OECD, 1980: 29). That a growing proportion of married women with dependent children are also entering the work force (OECD, 1980: 21) alerts us to the fact that the social situation, if not the ideology, is changing. Some research has indicated, at least by implication, that this has not seriously affected gender roles, since women who work do so mainly in sex-segregated occupations (Darling, 1975; and Tilly, 1985). Furthermore, other research indicates that women who work outside the home still maintain their traditional roles in the household (Scanzoni and Fox,

1980: 751; Meissner et al., 1975; and Clark and Harvey, 1976). Even in socialist societies, like China and the USSR, where the labour force participation of women is quite high, women are still considered to have the primary responsibility for housework and childcare (Stockard and Johnson, 1980: 87; Diamond, 1975: 386).

Time-use studies in twelve different countries (Belgium, Bulgaria, Czechoslovakia, France, Federal Republic of Germany, German Democratic Republic, Hungary, Peru, Poland, USA, USSR, and Yugoslavia) demonstrate that the employed woman has one to two hours less free time a day than either the employed man or the traditional housewife (Robinson et al., 1972: 119). On weekend days, the discrepancies are even more striking. While employed men and housewives tend to increase their leisure activities on their "days off," employed women about double the time they spend on housework (p. 121). Additional American data indicate that childcare and housework remain the chief responsibility of the wife, even when she is employed full-time, with the husband "helping out" when there is a particular need (for example, playing with the children while his wife is cleaning up after supper) (Berk and Berk, 1979: 232).

Social Honour and Gender Role Egalitarianism

The fact that most men have not been socialized to think of themselves as primary care givers may make that task difficult for many of them. Besides this, there is evidence that men in nontraditional roles experience some social disapproval. In fact, 32% of the fathers sharing care-giving in Russell's study (1983) said that what they disliked the most about their new family role was the loss of status that comes with not being fully employed in the labour force. Women, on the other hand, appear to maintain a certain status from pursuing traditional sex roles in the home. Both Bose (1980) and Eichler (1977) found that the occupation "housewife" had a mid-level prestige rating out of the approximately 100 occupations that they studied. In fact, housewife was an equivalent or more prestigious occupation than the leading 25 occupations that engaged Canadian women in paid employment in 1971, with the exception of teaching and nursing. A male "housewife," on the other hand, had a very low prestige rating (eighth lowest) (Eichler, 1977: 156–58).

Although most paid "female" occupations tend to have relatively low social status (Armstrong and Armstrong, 1984: 49–51), women in them appear to gain more prestige than men who are engaged in these female-dominated occupations (Guppy and Siltanen, 1977, and Powell and Jacobs, 1984). Likewise, women in male-dominated occupations (for example, truck driver, electrical engineer, minister) appear to have less prestige than their male counterparts (Powell and Jacobs, 1984). This evidence suggests that persons making occupational choices that are considered inappropriate to their sex suffer a prestige penalty (p. 188).

The conferral and withholding of social honour and approval is a form of social control. It is likely that the aspirations of young men and women in regard to work roles and family roles are influenced by the honour accorded and withheld from them for making certain role choices.

The Interplay of Social Change and Socialization

It is unclear what part socialization plays in changing gender roles. It is something of a chicken-and-egg question. Which comes first? It is likely that gender role socialization practices respond to the structure of social relationships and as these change, so does the content of socialization. On the other hand, there is a dynamic interaction between the social structure and socialization, and changing socialization patterns result in still more change in the social structure.

Evidence indicates that girls whose mothers work outside the home are more likely to expect to do the same (Baker, 1985: 164) and that young girls with working mothers are less sex-typed in their concepts of masculinity and femininity (Urberg, 1982: 664). The socializing

impact of the female role model is a likely explanation for this phenomenon. Research also indicates that men in families in which the education of the wife is high are more likely to share in the care of children (Russell, 1983: 74 and Ericksen et al., 1979). It is possible that highly educated mothers have been socialized in a less traditional manner, or that their early socialization was modified by their formal education, or that socialization simply did not "take." Thus, they were less willing to devote themselves solely to childcare. These women may be in a better position, because of their education, to bargain with their husbands concerning the division of labour in the household (Russell, 1983: 75).

Scanzoni and Szinovacz (1980: 28–31) suggest that educational level is a tangible resource affecting decision making in the home, but that it operates in conjunction with job status and the amount of money earned. Thus, a woman with a relatively high level of education is more likely to have a high-status job that pays well. This tends to increase her "power" in the household. A survey of Canadian husbands in two-career families found that the greater the wife's income contribution to the household, the more likely the husband was to participate in cooking and cleaning (Harrell, 1986).

Attitudes do appear to be changing. A US study over the 1975–1980 period revealed significantly less traditional gender role orientations in 1980, especially among women (McBroom, 1987). As well, a three-generational study of American women showed that younger women were more profeminist than older women (Slevin and Wingrove, 1983). In a recent study of the changing patterns of participation in the labour force by US women, Oppenheimer (1982: 30) concludes that changes in sex-role attitudes, as represented by the feminist movement, have been brought about by the actual labour force behaviour of women, rather than the reverse. Thus, the changing structure of the labour force (women's increasing participation) has led to more egalitarian sex-role attitudes. On the other hand, research indicates that women with more egalitarian sex-role attitudes are more likely to enter the labour force, have a consistent work pattern, and earn more (Scanzoni and Szinovacz, 1980: 30).

Outlook for the Future

A recent study of Canadian high school girls indicates that they expect a high level of support for careers from their future husbands (Baker, 1985). If this is to be tangible, as opposed to merely moral support, it will have to come in the form of modified gender roles. Certainly more women are working outside the home than ever before. We also know, however, that the increased time men devote to housework and childcare when wives do work outside the home is minimal (Walker and Woods, 1976: 257; Meissner et al., 1975; and Juillard, 1976: 121). This indicates little change for men in traditional gender roles, but the taking on of an additional role for women. This may well lead to a higher level of tension between the sexes in family situations.

What then is the future for changed gender roles in the family? An Australian study is suggestive in this regard. Of twenty-seven Australian families involved in patterns of shared caregiving, eleven (41%) had returned to the more traditional lifestyle of the mother being the primary caregiver after only two years. The more traditional families in the study had remained much the same over the two-year period (Russell,1983: 184–85). These findings may indicate the difficulty of maintaining a different gender role arrangement in the family without adequate cultural and structural supports. For example, two of the eleven families decided to have a baby and did not intend to return to a shared caregiving situation in future. Presumably, the traditional arrangement seemed more practical to them with a baby in the house. Five families had gone into the new arrangement because the father was out of work. They returned to the traditional arrangement when the employment and economic status of the man improved. In three of the families, the fathers just couldn't seem to take it anymore and expressed relief at getting back to their tradi-

tional roles. The final couple had gone into the arrangement with the idea of meeting personal career goals of both the mother and the father, and after these were met, returned to the traditional arrangement.

While we cannot generalize from eleven cases, the findings are illustrative of the reasons that people change life styles and the reasons that they return to traditional life styles. Perhaps if better daycare were available earlier in a child's life or if women's economic opportunities were equal to or better than men's, we would find men and women responding by rearranging gender roles. The increased participation of fathers in childcare is dependent on a number of changes—changes at the level of employment, education, and social policy, as well as changes in people's beliefs and attitudes about what are proper roles for men and women.

Summary

Gender role socialization occurs largely in the context of the family, although there are important external influences on the socialization process, especially in modern societies. In modern societies, for example, the school and the media appear to play an early and important part in socialization.

Cross-cultural studies indicate that culture molds gender differences. These studies demonstrate both the variety of gender role possibilities and the similarities in gender roles cross-culturally. Within cultures, it is evident that boys and girls experience different learning environments and this appears to produce gendered individuals. Research on parent interaction with children, the school environment, books, and toys all indicate that gender role messages to boys and girls are quite different.

Although it is evident that gender roles do exist and that there are a great many sex-differentiated socialization practices, the actual connection between these practices and the establishment of culturally approved gender identities and roles is unclear. A number of perspectives have been used to explain how gender identity and role differences emerge.

The explanations discussed in this chapter were varieties of the biological perspective, theories of psychosexual identity development, social learning, and the cognitive developmental perspective.

The familial and work roles of men and women are not only different; women's roles appear to be associated with less social power, lower prestige, and fewer material rewards. Women's domestic roles have tended to keep them in the private sphere, while men's roles have been heavily linked to the public sphere. The economic roles of women have changed historically, and this has occasioned changes in their status relative to men. The modern occupational roles of women have tended to be less prestigious and less well-paid than those of men.

Gender roles do appear to be changing. More women world-wide are taking on paid occupational roles. Some domestic accommodation in the form of changed gender roles in the family might be predicted. However, there is not much evidence that men are taking on a significant domestic role. Some families have rearranged gender roles. Preliminary evidence indicates that significant change in this regard is difficult to maintain, probably because of lack of structural supports and non-supportive beliefs and attitudes.

Thus, we can see that there are strong social supports for traditional gender roles, even in modern societies. These come especially in the form of social approval and disapproval, differential employment and economic opportunities for men and women, and lack of provision for adequate childcare arrangements outside the family. In addition, we have seen that gender role socialization is still strongly slanted toward promoting traditional gender roles.

TECHNICAL TERMS

AGENTS OF SOCIALIZATION—Those institutions, individuals, and things which participate in the social learning processes involved in socializing the individual. For example, the family, members of the peer group, and television are all socializing agents in modern gender role socialization.

GENDER IDENTITY—The identification of oneself as masculine or feminine in a particular cultural context. This leads one to perform certain sex-appropriate roles and to behave in typically "masculine" or "feminine" ways.

GENDER ROLE—A set of prescribed behaviours based on the fact that one is male or female.

GENDER ROLE SOCIALIZATION—The processes of social learning through which individuals acquire the attitudes, values, and identities, as well as the knowledge of appropriate roles and behaviours, associated with being masculine or feminine.

GENDER STEREOTYPES—Exaggerated generalizations about the traits of either the typical male or the typical female.

HORTICULTURAL SOCIETY—Societies which rely upon gardening as a major means of producing their food supply. These societies use the hoe or the digging stick, in contrast to agrarian societies, which employ the plow and farm more extensively.

INITIATION RITE—A ceremonial practice designed to mark an individual's entrance into a social group or into a new social status within the group. The transition from boy to man and from girl to woman has been marked by initiation rites in many primitive groups.

MATRIARCHATE—A society dominated by women. It is doubtful that any such societies have existed.

NATURE-NURTURE DEBATE—A controversy concerning the source of human behaviour. In regard to the social and psychological differences observed between men and women, some maintain that the chief source of the differences is biological constitution (nature), while others hold that the chief source is social (nurture).

OCCUPATIONAL SEX-SEGREGATION—The concentration of men and women in different paid occupations.

OEDIPUS COMPLEX—A multifaceted set of events, emotions, psychological attachments, and identifications, elaborated by Sigmund Freud, which result in the establishment of heterosexuality for boys and girls.

PEER GROUP—A group of approximate social equals who interact with one another. Adolescent peer groups are thought to have a strong socializing influence on boys and girls.

ROLE MODEL—An individual whose performance in a role serves as a standard for others.

SEXUAL DIVISION OF LABOUR—The way in which tasks are divided between the sexes, so that some tasks are thought to be properly males' responsibility, while others are thought to be the proper responsibility of women.

SOCIAL STRATIFICATION—The structure of economic power and social status which results in inequalities between groups.

SOLIDARITY GROUP—A group within which there is cooperation and collective striving to achieve common goals.

QUESTIONS

1. What is meant by a gender role? Give several examples.

2. What are the major agencies of gender role socialization in modern societies?

3. Describe some of the differences in gender role socialization in modern societies.

4. How does the school act as a gender role socializer?

5. Explain the sources of gender role differences according to the major theories.

6. Why is it important to look at women's role in paid labour when we consider possible changes in traditional gender roles?

7. Go through the toy section of some department store catalogues (or the toy sections of a few stores). Describe the toys directed at boys and those directed at girls? Are the differences obvious? How could you tell which were the boys' toys and which were the girls' toys? How many gender-neutral toys were there relative to those that were gender-stereotyped?

8. Do a content analysis of the gender roles portrayed on children's television programs.

9. Discuss gender roles in your family or in a family of your acquaintance. How could these gender roles be modified to correspond to the changes that we have discussed? What social factors would prevent this modification?

10. Enlist the aid of family members and/or friends to plan and carry out an experiment in gender role reversal. Report the results, taking care to note what was different about your behaviour and activities based on the reversal.

FILMS

- *The Pinks and the Blues* (57 min. colour)

  Demonstrates the reinforcement of gender stereotypes in North American society, "from the moment the parents wrap a newborn baby in either a pink or a blue blanket." The film shows that the socialization process may be so subtle that parents and teachers deny that distinctions are being made.

- *Sex-Role Development* (1974) (23 min. colour)

  Examines the influence of sex-roles and stereotypes on many aspects of people's lives.

SUGGESTION READINGS

- Herbert Barry, III, et al. "A Cross-Cultural Survey of Some Sex Differences in Socialization." *Journal of Abnormal and Social Psychology* 55 (1957): 327–32.

  This is a basic reference in the analysis of cross-cultural gender role socialization practices. Barry, Bacon and Child analyse ethnographic reports of 110 cultures. The study is important in pointing out cultural variability in sex differences and gender role socialization.

- Jeanne H. Block. "Differential Premises Arising from Differential Socialization of the Sexes: Some Conjectures." *Child Development* 54 (1983): 1335–54.

  Block provides a detailed review of sex-differentiated socialization practices, with an emphasis on parental roles. She concludes the article with a discussion of the implications of sex-differentiated socialization for the cognitive development of the sexes.

- Esther R. Greenglass. *A World of Difference: Gender Roles in Perspective.* Toronto: John Wiley & Sons, 1982.

  Greenglass attempts to account for the social and psychological bases of inequality between the sexes. She begins by reviewing gender role socialization in childhood and then discusses the implications of differential socialization practices for human sexuality, family life, employment and psychopathology. Greenglass concludes with a brief discussion of future prospects for gender roles. The book concentrates on the North American experience.

- Chris Henshall and Jacqueline McGuire. "Gender development." In *Children of Social Worlds: Development in a Social Context,* ed. by Martin Richards and Paul Light, 135–166. Cambridge: Harvard University Press, 1986.

  Henshall and McGuire provide an up-to-date overview of some of the major themes informing research on gender development in Western Europe and North America. Their work is particularly useful in drawing attention to the conceptual and methodological difficulties inherent in much of this research.

- Eleanor E. Maccoby, ed. *The Development of Sex Differences.* Stanford: Stanford University Press, 1966.

  This book is a collection of writings. It begins with a discussion by Hamburg and Lunde of the role of sex hormones in the development of sex differences in behaviour. Maccoby follows by reviewing the variations in intellectual functioning between the sexes. Mischel elaborates a social-learning perspective on sex differences in behaviour, while the article by Kohlberg does the same for the cognitive-developmental perspective. D'Andrade describes the cultural bases of sex-differentiated behaviour. Dornsbusch concludes by summarizing the material, urging the necessity of increasing our knowledge in the area of sex differences.

- Eleanor E. Maccoby and Carol Nagy Jacklin. *The Psychology of Sex Differences.* Stanford: Stanford University Press, 1974.

  This book is a comprehensive effort by the authors to document the differences between the sexes. In the first two parts, the authors discuss differences in achievement, intellect, and social behaviour. In the third section of the book, Maccoby and Jacklin attempt to explain the origins of these sex differences, reviewing the major theories. Also included is an extensive annotated bibliography of the psychological literature on sex differences.

- Marlene Mackie. *Exploring Gender Relations: A Canadian Perspective.* Toronto: Butterworths, 1983.

  Mackie asks what it means to be male or female in contemporary Canadian

Chapter 7 / Charlene Thacker

society, while at the same time providing a general introduction to gender relations. Mackie utilizes a social psychological approach, although she introduces the reader to interdisciplinary material. She reviews male/female similarities and differences, and analyzes biological and social-psychological explanations of them. Mackie then discusses gender role socialization, as well as the social-structural bases of gender relations. She concludes with a discussion of future trends and prospects for gender relations in Canada.

- Jean Stockard and Miriam M. Johnson. *Sex Roles: Sex Inequality and Sex Role Development*. Englewood Cliffs, NJ: Prentice-Hall, 1980.

The authors assert that sex roles cannot be examined without reference to sex inequalities. In the first part of the book, Stockard and Johnson review the cultural, economic, political, and educational bases of sex inequalities, integrating historical and cultural data. In the second part of the book, they discuss biological, psychological, and psychoanalytic explanations of sex differences. They conclude with a brief analysis of the prospects for sex role equality.

An Italian family.

SOCIALIZATION BEYOND CHILDHOOD

Frank A. Fasick
University of Waterloo

This chapter is about the ways people are socialized as they move through age-appropriate social roles. Although the emphasis will be on modern urban-industrial societies, such as Canada, some attention will be given to the experiences of persons who spend their lives in traditional agricultural societies.

The discussion of socialization in this chapter begins with adolescence, then continues through young adulthood and middle age to the later years. These four phases in the life course represent major transitions in the lives of most persons.

Families as Mediators of the Life Course

Many of the influences that bear on the phases of the life course are mediated through families. The family is a central focus in the organization of the life course in all societies—including modern industrial societies. Family structures may differ greatly from one society to another, but the important role they play in organizing the lives of family members is universal.

Socialization in Adolescence: Finding Oneself

In childhood young people are most often defined, both in the minds of others and in their own minds, as children of their parents. This circumstance fits with children's social and emotional dependence on their families.

In modern societies the beginning of adolescence ushers in that phase in the life course when young people are encouraged to achieve an identity as autonomous individuals distinct from their parents and family. This process has been described by analysts, such as Erik H. Erikson. In his theory of developmental crises that mark the progression of individuals through the life course, he proposed the development of an ego identity as the central crisis during adolescence (Erikson, 1963,1968).

Weaning oneself from one's family and establishing in one's own mind, and in the minds of others, the kind of person one is, can be a painful and lonely effort. The relatively high incidence of mental illness and suicide among adolescents in urban-industrial societies attests to the great stress that may occasionally mark the struggle to obtain an acceptable sense of oneself (cf. Grueling and DeBlassie, 1980).

Fortunately, most young people everywhere engage in the explorations of self that make up much of adolescence without experiencing severe trauma. They approach this task with a hopefulness that helps to carry them through the ups and downs of self-discovery and receive enough positive responses from others to feel reasonably content with the kind of person they believe they are becoming.

The need to establish an identity is characteristic of adolescents in all societies. The need to establish oneself as a distinctly separate individual, however, is more characteristic of urban-industrial societies, such as Canada and the United States, than of many more traditional agricultural or peasant societies. In the traditional Chinese peasant family, for example, children were brought up to obey and respect their parents throughout their parents' lives as an expression of filial piety (Chao, 1983: 71–100). The concern of parents and other adults was not so much that the young develop a sense of personal and social independence as it was that they identify with their duty to the kin group.

The Expanding Social World of Adolescence

An important factor contributing to the development of an autonomous social identity among adolescents in modern-day Canada is the expansion of meaningful emotional relationships outside the family (Fasick, 1984). In childhood, close emotional attachments are concentrated almost exclusively on parents and important extended family members, such as grandparents. Friendships with playmates very seldom reflect a strong emotional bond.

Development of Relationships with Peers

With the advent of adolescence, friendships with people of one's age become much more emotionally charged. Young people are beginning their first real effort to establish an independent social life of their own.

Adolescents' relationships with peers are far less institutionalized than their relationships with their parents. Their emotional ties with the latter are prescribed by well understood social definitions. As children, they are expected to love their parents and their parents are expected to love them. In contrast to parental love, adolescents' friendships with persons of their own age reflect their attractiveness to others who have no obligation to share friendship with them. These friendships are the first major test of the capacity for meaningful social relationships outside the family setting.

In all societies the efforts of early adolescents to build meaningful social relationships with their contemporaries are typically fraught with insecurity. In modern-day North America this lack of self-assurance is reflected in the often nearly slavish conformity of early adolescents to their contemporaries' styles in clothing, language, music, cultural heroes, etc. As young people become more sure of themselves in the later years of adolescence, conformity to peer influence tends to decline (Berndt, 1978).

Another indication of the uncertainty young adolescents feel is the marked tendency for their friends to be of the same sex. Most often friendships in early adolescence center on common activities and interests, especially among boys (Gallatin, 1975: 126). These relationships also tend to be relatively unstable. By late adolescence friendships with persons of the same sex have usually become more emotionally satisfying and more enduring (Skorepa, Horrocks and Thompson, 1963).

Development of Heterosexual Relationships

There is remarkable variability from one society to another in the way heterosexual relationships develop among adolescents. In many traditional societies, such as in some regions of India, the opportunity for relatively free association between the sexes after childhood is limited, and marriages are often arranged by parents (cf. Mace and Mace, 1959: 130–131).

Unlike many more traditional societies, the social life of adolescents in modern-day North America undergoes a fundamental change when they begin forming romantic (or at least potentially romantic) relationships with the opposite sex. These relationships ordinarily begin sometime during mid-adolescence with the start of dating (Hansen, 1977). The introduction during adolescence of passion and romance into boy-girl relationships represents a restructuring of the relationships between the sexes. Feelings of sexual attractiveness and the ability to form romantic attachments become important to nearly everyone by late adolescence and remain important for most, if not all, of their adult lives.

In North America the teenage years are a time when adolescents can explore the meaning of romantic love and gain a sense of their sexuality without being expected to make a firm commitment leading to marriage. In fact, such a commitment is ordinarily considered inappropriate. Teenage marriages do occur, but marriage in the teens is relatively rare.

Only 17.8% of young people in the last of their teen years (i.e. 19) were married at the time of the 1981 Census in Canada (Herold, 1984: 124).

Freedom of Movement and Social Participation

In addition to adolescents' expanding social relationships they gain greater freedom of movement and social participation. Pre-adolescent children ordinarily are quite restricted in their movements outside the neighbourhood in which they live and in their access to public places, such as theatres and amusement centres. Their daily lives at home and at school are, in most instances, closely supervised. When children are not under the immediate supervision of their parents or other adults, they are ordinarily expected to account for their activities. During the adolescent years this situation changes. In early adolescence, the vast majority of young people acquire the knowledge, sophistication, and finances to make effective use of most public facilities. They still live in a restricted world but its boundaries lie far beyond those of their childhood years.

Important legal rights and privileges granted to young people in Canada around mid-adolescence greatly expand their freedom of action, at least potentially. Two of the most important legal changes are the right to leave school and to take on regular full-time employment, both of which are granted in most Canadian provinces at age sixteen. Many provinces also permit young persons at this age to live apart from their parents without their parents' consent, although relatively few adolescents do so. In nearly all provinces, adolescents are permitted to obtain a driver's licence at sixteen (Fasick, 1979). This latter privilege can greatly increase adolescents' freedom of movement. Money earned from employment often provides the finances necessary to take advantage of this increased freedom.

By the end of adolescence at eighteen or nineteen, North American young people have essentially full access to the activities of adults in the sense that they are permitted to participate in these activities. It ordinarily takes a number of years, however, before these new young adults become fully incorporated into the adult world.

In many agricultural societies, the social world of adolescents does not expand to the extent that it does for young North Americans, nor is the freedom of movement as great. In particular, relationships with kin, especially parents, throughout adolescence and young adulthood are of great importance. It is, after all, the parents or kin group who ordinarily hold the land which is the basis of livelihood for most persons in the society. The consequence is that most adolescents' lives are circumscribed by work in the family enterprise and by the local village. Traditional China is one of the most frequently noted examples of such an agricultural society (cf. Yang, 1959). Even in modern-day North America young people who grow up in agricultural regions ordinarily do not experience an expansion of their social world in adolescence to the same degree as their urban peers. Partly for this reason, urban adolescents and young adults often think of young people from rural areas as naïve.

Whether living in the narrow confines of a peasant agricultural village or in the youth culture of a North American city, the main focus of socialization during adolescence is self-discovery as a physical, moral, and social being with a culturally established, and yet unique, identity. This self-conception is an important foundation upon which young people begin to build their adult lives.

Socialization in Young Adulthood: Finding One's Place in the World

As young people everywhere move from adolescence into young adulthood, they are faced with the task of establishing themselves within the fabric of the society as fully fledged adult members. In many regions of the world, they have already become important productive members of the society and have often begun raising families of their own. Full adult status is typically not granted, however, until somewhere around the second decade of life and in peasant societies, where adulthood is often associated with ownership of land, it may be granted even later (cf. Clayton 1979).

In most North American communities there is a clear expectation that young people will leave the home of their parents sometime during their late teens or early twenties. Moving out will be associated with finding employment in some recognized occupation that provides an income considered to be adequate by community standards. There is also a generally held expectation that young people will seek a spouse, marry, and have children during their twenties, or, at latest, their early thirties. Parents and kin may help young people in their efforts to find a suitable occupation and establish families of their own, but responsibility lies essentially with the young themselves.

Work: Defining One's Place in the Economic Order

In all societies, nearly every adult has some array of tasks for which he or she is responsible. The extent to which young people may seek occupations of their own choosing is determined by social and personal circumstances. The society in which they find themselves (e.g. a peasant economy) may simply not offer a wide array of occupational opportunities. Alternatively, a modern urban-industrial society may have a complex occupational structure, but young people may find their individual occupational choices severely limited for a variety of reasons. In some European countries, educational streaming during adolescence associated with stratified educational systems does much to limit the occupational opportunities of many young adults (cf. Rubinson, 1986). In Canada and the United States, ethnic and racial prejudice continues to limit the occupational opportunities of many young people, in spite of efforts to eliminate ethnic and racial considerations in occupational placement. Throughout the world, gender role differentiation limits the occupational opportunities for women and men. Although in some regions, such as North America, ef-

forts are underway to eliminate gender discrimination in occupational placement, it still exists (cf. Tilly and Scott, 1978; Wilson, 1986).

Movement of young people into an occupation or career involves a socialization process that often begins in early adolescence and continues throughout their work life. Researchers on occupational decision making, such as Ginsberg, Ginsburg, Axelrod and Herma, have attempted to describe the processes by which young people come to select an occupation. They have proposed that the opportunities provided by the social environment, the sorts of education available, the emotional responses of young people, and their value commitments are crucial factors that influence the choice of an occupation (Ginsberg et al., 1951). Others, such as Super (1957), believe the emerging self-concept plays a greater role in vocational choice than proposed by many researchers.

Socialization into a specific job is described by some researchers as "adjustment." Assuming that persons are motivated to perform well in their occupations, these researchers claim the workers' degree of satisfaction is related to such factors as their effectiveness, the recognition of this effectiveness, and their sense that the job is fulfilling (Lofquist and Dawis, 1969).

The variability in specific work experiences of individuals that characterizes urban-industrial societies is carried over to their lifestyles. In taking on a particular vocation, people not only must master the skills related to the job itself, they must also come to grips with the lifestyle that goes with their occupation. This lifestyle usually reflects both the impact of the occupation and the level of formal education associated with it.

The most crucial lifestyle adjustments related to occupations in modern industrial economies are almost always in the domestic lives of the workers, especially those with families. The modern job is nearly always located outside the home with conditions of work set by the employer. Hours of work are ordinarily fixed and sometimes vary from day to day or week to week. The work may be very taxing either emotionally or physically—or both. In higher status jobs hours may be relatively flexible but very long. In many occupations from that of truck driver to company president extended travel may be required. Certainly, the pay people receive for their labours nearly always sets limits on the patterns of consumption that characterize their lifestyle. In these, as well as many other ways, the "long arm of the job" does much to shape workers' lives and to circumscribe in considerable degree the nature of the commitments they can make to their families.

The conflicts between occupational and family obligations are potentially so disruptive that the resolution of some conflicts are incorporated into the values of social groups. Members of the community or society are socialized into these values as they mature. In classical China, for example, the overriding importance of kin obligations led to extensive nepotism within the state bureaucracy. In present-day Canada this conflict is resolved very differently. Nepotism is frowned upon when not strictly forbidden. In most societies women are socialized to place commitment to the care of their children over commitment to an occupation. By contrast, men in many societies, including Canada, are socialized to believe that the job takes precedence (except in dire emergencies), because it is through their occupation that men provide for their children. In nearly all societies there are specific instances when family and kin obligations take precedence over economic activities. The most important of these are severe illness and death.

In all societies, regardless of how well integrated, there will be some tension between domestic and economic roles. In subsistence agricultural societies, however, where the whole family is involved in the task of raising food, such conflicts are likely to be muted. It is in the highly differentiated urban-industrial societies where individuals work for impersonal employers under highly structured conditions that conflicts are likely to become frequent and severe.

Forming a Family: An Investment in the Emotional Life

Family formation as an investment in the emotional life is more characteristic of urban-industrial societies, such as present-day Canada, than traditional societies. Throughout most of history, marriage has most often been an economic or political arrangement by means of which property is protected and alliances formed. In these circumstances, which involve interests of the larger kin group, marriages are usually arranged, or at least approved, by parents or other relatives (cf. Stephens, 1963: 190–200). Even today in North America there is an economic component to most marriages with the couple forming an economic partnership as well as a loving relationship.

Since both men and women can ordinarily live comfortably in modern urban-industrial societies without marrying, why do they? There is, of course, no simple explanation. Certainly, the idea that men and women should marry exists in one form or another in all societies. From early childhood young people in nearly all societies are socialized into the belief that marriage is the "normal" life for adults. Aside from the social value attached to marriage as the most appropriate domestic arrangement for adults, many young people are attracted to marriage by the belief that it will provide them with at least some measure of security in their interpersonal life. They and their spouse are morally bound and legally obligated to be concerned with each other's welfare.

Whatever the benefits of marriage in terms of financial and interpersonal security, young Canadians are socialized to believe that marriage should be founded on a love relationship. Romantic love as a basis for marriage is relatively recent historically in western culture, and the extent to which young persons in present-day North America do, in fact, marry for love is unclear (Stephens, 1963: 200–207). It is generally the case, however, that a love relationship is the avowed basis for most marriages, especially among the young.

If the young in nearly all societies are socialized to believe that marriage is the preferred form of domestic life, they are also socialized to believe that it is preferable, even the duty, of married couples to have children. In most subsistence agricultural societies there is an economic incentive for couples to have children. Although children are an economic burden in the early years, they soon become an asset through the work they perform. When the parents grow old, their children provide them with some measure of economic security.

In modern industrial societies, children are very seldom an economic asset. When children are young, parents are required to send them to school. With a few exceptions, such as a family farm or work as a professional entertainer, meaningful employment of children is prohibited by law. In parents' later years, they can look to publicly supported social welfare programs and to pension plans as the primary bases of their economic security.

Far from being a potential economic asset in countries such as Canada and the US, children are almost certain to be a major expense. Estimates of what it typically costs Canadian parents to raise children vary. One recent estimate of the outlay needed to raise a child to the age of eighteen in a family with two children and with an income of approximately $23,000 a year is roughly $106,000 in 1984 dollars (Eichler, 1988: 332–333). It seems reasonable to propose that a large proportion of parents' expenditures in most families are made with the children in mind at all but the highest income levels.

Not only do children represent a financial burden in modern industrial societies, they ordinarily require a heavy expenditure in time and effort by both parents and by the mother in particular. The transition to parenthood with the birth of the first child involves a reassessment of roles and relationships both within and outside the family (Russell, 1974).

The fact that most modern couples still have children, in spite of the considerable economic costs involved, implies that they derive emotional rewards from their children. Hoffman (1975) proposes a number of personal values that can be achieved through parenthood. These values include the validation of mature adulthood and an enhancement of social identity. In addition, the naïveté and vitality of their young children may be a source of amusement and pride to parents, which, along with the care the mother and father must lavish on them, leads to a sense of intimacy. Parents may also achieve a feeling of immortality.

The personal values of parenthood proposed by Hoffman can take on enhanced meaning in particular circumstances. Among lower-class men in some societies having children may contribute to a sense of manhood by providing a family group over which they have authority. This outlet helps to offset the inferior position they often have on the job. According to some researchers, the higher birth rates within the lower classes of industrial societies, including Canada, reflect this circumstance (cf. Blau and Duncan, 1967: 428).

Although most adults in most societies become parents, the roles of parents differ from one society to another. In many developing societies parents are enmeshed within a larger kinship group, the members of which play an active role in the parenting process. Parenting skills are defined by tradition and are not considered problematic.

In present-day North America mothers and fathers typically carry out much of their parenting without consistent overview or assistance from other kin. Daughters frequently acquire their general perspective and much of their knowledge about motherhood from their mothers, but there are also professional experts in parenting and a large body of scientific research to which both young mothers and fathers can turn for assistance (cf. Fine, 1980). The fact that theories of child rearing proposed by experts differ in their emphases may lead to confusion. Still, popular authorities on child rearing, such as Dr. Spock and Arnold Gesell, have done much to form parents' notions of proper child rearing practices in North America, especially among the better educated middle class.

The steady increase since World War II in the proportion of Canadian women in the labour force who are married and who have young children has had an impact on the socialization of both the parents and the children. By 1985 a little over 56% of women with husbands at home and whose youngest child was a preschooler were in the labour force (Women's Bureau, Labour Canada, 1987: 20). The children of working mothers are exposed on a regular basis to caregivers other than their mothers and fathers, often in a setting outside the home. Since this pattern of socialization differs from the mother-centered socialization that characterized child rearing during most of the twentieth century in North America, attempts have been made to determine its impact on children. In general, working mothers seem to have children who differ little in adjustment from the children of non-working mothers, although there may be minor adjustment problems and slightly inferior cognitive development, especially among working-class boys. The findings, however, are inconsistent. Both boys and girls tend to show less rigid gender role stereotyping when their mothers work (Eichler, 1988: 217–218).

Dual employment has an effect on both parents. Mothers have to come to terms with a reduced maternal role, and fathers are likely to be under pressure to assume a more active paternal role (Eichler, 1988: 218;314).

Although parenthood is one of the major life activities of most young women and men in Canada, it is not as frequent now as it was in the past. It is not the case that the proportion of couples who are able to have children but decide not to do so has increased much (Houseknecht, 1986: 511). One estimate is that only about five percent of all married couples are voluntarily childless (Veevers, 1980b: 546). Rather, the numbers of children that have been born to couples in Canada and in most other industrial societies have been relatively low during much of the twentieth century. (The "baby boom" after World War II represented a temporary increase in the birth rate of North America.) In 1985, the *total fertility rate* for Canada was 1.67 children (Eichler, 1988: 46). The *total fertility rate* is the number of children that would be born per woman, if she were to live

to the end of her child-bearing years and have children at each age in accord with the prevailing age-specific fertility rates. Since women must replace both themselves and the men in the society in each generation, the *total fertility rate* must be a little over 2.0 in order to replace the population in each generation. It is apparent, that if the 1985 *total fertility rate* for Canada continued long enough, there would be a decline in the native-born Canadian population.

It is clear that most young adults in modern day Canada, as in other industrial societies, seek the emotional benefits of parenthood but respond to the heavy costs in time, energy, and money parenthood entails by forming small families (cf. Wargon, 1979: 15).

Middle Age and the Reassessment of One's Identity

As men and women move into their forties, they are likely to become increasingly conscious of the ways in which their lives differ from the expectations they held in their youth. For some the prospect is satisfying; for others there is a sense of disappointment (Isopow, 1983: 216). The assessment of the life course at middle age frequently carries great weight because of the belief that it is too late to make significant changes.

One of the happenstances in many families is that parents are going through an assessment of their lives at the same time that their adolescent children are attempting to establish an identity of their own. Parents see their children just about to begin adult life at a time when they are very conscious that many of their most active years are coming to an end (cf. Rice, 1987: 467–470).

The co-existing concern with identity that many parents and their adolescent children experience can affect attempts at parental socialization in a number of ways. One possibility noted by Clifford Kirkpatrick (1955: 266–267) is that parents and their adolescent children may suffer from a "clash of inferiority complexes." The adolescents are often unsure of themselves and uncertain of their futures. The parents, on the other hand, may not be satisfied with their accomplishments in life.

They are also likely to be acutely aware of their declining attractiveness and vitality in the presence of their teenage children. Feelings of inferiority on the part of the adolescents may lead to overcompensation in the form of aggressiveness toward their parents and demands for autonomy. Parents are likely to respond by being aggressively authoritarian in return. The consequences are almost certain to be unsatisfactory parent-adolescent relationships, at least in the short run.

Parents may react to perceived lack of achievement in their lives by displacing their ambitions onto their children. Alternatively, parents who have found their lives to be richly rewarding may pressure their children to follow in their footsteps. In either case, the norm in modern industrial societies that young people should make their own lives is violated. This violation frequently leads to strain in the relationship between parents and their children.

In contrast, parental reactions to an assessment of their lives in middle age may lead to increased support for their children. Recognizing that the most active years of their lives are relatively few in number, parents may react by devoting more of their attention and resources to their children. They may make considerable sacrifices in order to help their children achieve their goals in life.

Another characteristic of middle-aged parent-adolescent relationships in modern industrial societies has been described by Peters (1985). A number of topics that receive much public attention, such as sports, films, popular music, youth, drug use, and sexuality, are either incorporated within the youth culture of many adolescents or are topics discussed in school. Consequently, adolescents are often more knowledgeable about current perspectives on these matters than their parents. This circumstance promotes two-way socialization between parents and their adolescent children. The parents provide much socialization regarding values and perspectives relevant to adult life. Their adolescent children, in turn, assist their parents in acquiring an understanding of current perspectives on topics with which the adolescents have become familiar through participation in youth culture or through school.

In addition to the patterns of socialization related to middle-aged parents and their children, middle-aged men and women in present day North America are likely to find themselves involved in socialization experiences that were less common a few decades ago. The increasing divorce rate has meant that many people, especially women, have had to adjust to the single life as their children leave home. Whole families have had to negotiate a complex set of relationships when divorce has created blended families, which persist throughout the lives of the family members.

Increased employment opportunities for women has meant that re-entering the labour force is much more acceptable for middle-aged women than a generation ago. This change has resulted in more alternatives for women faced with the so-called empty nest syndrome than was formerly the case. Middle-aged women who re-enter the labour force must undergo resocialization to the world of outside employment, and their husbands must adapt to a changed domestic environment.

Increasing longevity means that greater numbers of middle-aged men and women must learn the skills required to assist their aging parents, either as primary caregivers or as those responsible for their parents' care. There is little in the way of formal preparation provided to adult children who find themselves responsible for parents in need of assistance. The adult children must ordinarily work out the issues related to the care of their aged parents on their own or with professional help on a case by case basis.

Changing social conditions, such as those noted above, have made the experiences of middle age potentially more complex and more problematic than they were a quarter of a century ago. At the same time, most men and women face middle age with greater economic, social, and personal resources than did previous generations.

Chapter 8 / Frank A. Fasick

Socialization in Later Life: Adaptation to a Narrowing Social World

The potential life span of humans has changed little, if at all, during the last several hundred years. In every society the very old survived into their nineties centuries ago, much as they do today. The differences between non-industrial and urban-industrial societies lie in the proportions of persons who live into old age and in how old they live to be. There are some vigorous older adults and a few very old persons in every major society, but the proportions of persons who live through these experiences is greatest in modern urban-industrial societies. In fact, old age as a normal part of life through which most people can expect to pass is a twentieth century phenomenon limited to the societies which are the most technologically advanced.

It is difficult to define when middle age ends and the later years of life begin. Certainly one important landmark in modern industrial societies among employed persons is retirement. Even in these societies, however, formal retirement as a normal part of the life span is relatively new. Until this century many workers did not live to retirement age and those who did usually had to retire on their savings or rely on their kin (especially children) to provide for them. In Canada, the Canada Pension Plan, designed to provide a universal basis for formal retirement among employed workers, was not established until 1966 (Marsh, 1985: 264).

Retirement in an industrial society, such as Canada, can occur at very different ages for persons depending on such things as type of occupation, employer policies, finances, and health. People in physically demanding occupations (e.g. firemen, police officers, the military) very often retire when they are about fifty years of age. Most workers are likely to retire sometime between ages sixty and sixty-five.

For most individuals in industrial societies, retirement from a job means giving up a major role, yet there is often very little in the way of anticipatory socialization for retirement in most societies, Canada included (McPherson, 1983: 382). Anticipatory socialization refers to acquiring information and developing perspectives that facilitate the transition from one social role to another. In North America, most persons do little in the way of individual preparation for retirement, and there are relatively few formal retirement preparation programmes, although these are growing in number (Atchley, 1988: 189).

In spite of the presumably inadequate preparation most workers obtain prior to retirement, the vast majority seem to adjust well to retirement with approximately 70 to 90% of retirees reporting few problems (McPherson, 1983: 388). Successful retirement seems to be related to such considerations as a sufficient income, support of family members, and the opportunity to continue social activities that the retirees find satisfying (McPherson, 1983: 388–389).

Maintaining a relatively high level of participation in informal social activities throughout the later years can contribute to a sense of well-being (Longino and Kart, 1982). On the other hand, many older persons seem to go through a process of disengagement that involves a gradual relinquishment of responsibilities within the family and community, as well as a loosening of interpersonal relationships. In the view of some scholars, disengagement is voluntary for many older persons and does not result in great emotional distress (McPherson, 1983: 138).

Physical capability declines in the later years, but the decline is not likely to have much social importance for most people in urban-industrial societies until they are in their late sixties or seventies. The structure of daily activities in modern societies is such that physical strength and agility are not necessary in order to perform most of them satisfactorily. Consequently, the majority of persons are able to carry on the daily round of their lives all through their sixties and frequently well beyond. Some researchers, however, do claim that a decline in energy sufficient to have a noticeable affect on work performance may occur around age sixty (Atchley, 1988: 189).

One potential source of emotional stress for some persons is that the role of retiree does not have any clearly defined responsibilities associated with it. This situation means that many older people must rely heavily on their ability to negotiate with others the nature of their relationship with them. They must often engage in these negotiations when their financial resources may be limited and when their potential contributions to relationships may not be highly valued.

Among the most important relationships that older persons negotiate are those with their grown children. In structuring their relationships with their children, who typically have families of their own, older persons usually benefit from their children's affection, gratitude, and sense of obligation. Sons are likely to be particularly responsive to the financial needs of their parents and daughters to their need for personal attention (Horowitz, 1981).

One way in which older parents often contribute to the welfare of their grown children and their families is through the provision of personal services. In cases such as illness or childbirth, the parents (especially the mother) may provide valuable care and assistance. Relationships of grandparents with their grandchildren are often beneficial to all concerned. The importance of grandparenting in the lives of older persons is likely to be greater the closer older persons live to their children's families. In some cases older people deliberately move so that they will be near their children.

However active older people may be during most of their later years, there will almost certainly be a decline in the scope of activities with increasing age. This decline is likely to be relative, persons who were very active may experience a considerable decline in activity and still be more active than others who were not very active in the first place. Decreased activity is related to a general narrowing of the social world as persons reach advanced ages. This narrowing is associated with the decline in mobility when one ceases driving, an increasing likelihood of physical infirmity, the death or incapacity of friends, and a general decline in vitality that makes it more difficult

to carry on with activities one previously enjoyed.

As the aged experience a decline in their social world that is related to reduced contacts and abilities, their position in modern industrial societies is likely to be defined as a form of undesirable dependency. They have "outlived their usefulness." This situation contrasts sharply with the dependency of children in modern industrial societies which is deemed appropriate and is usually accepted, in varying degrees, at least through adolescence and often into young adulthood.

In many traditional agricultural societies the aged continue to have relatively high status even though they are not "useful." Their status frequently derives from their position of patriarch or matriarch who represents the continuity of the family as a kin group over the generations.

Summary

Four important transitions after childhood in the life course of persons who live in modern industrial societies are: (a) adolescence, (b) young adulthood, (c) middle age, and (d) the later years.

During adolescence young persons are attempting to establish the kind of person they are, both in their own mind and in the mind of others. Adolescents' physical, intellectual, and moral development all play an important role in their efforts to define themselves.

In industrial societies most young adults face the tasks of finding a place for themselves in the world of work and of forming a family of their own. Since most people work in bureaucratic organizations, there is considerable potential for conflict between family responsibilities and responsibilities on the job. Because of the heavy economic burden child rearing imposes on parents, the motivations for having children must be primarily emotional, rather than economic, in modern industrial societies.

Middle age brings with it a reassessment of one's life for many people. Frequently, expectations held when young have not been fulfilled. Because of the timing of generations, middle-aged parents are often going through an identity crisis at the same time as their adolescent children. This situation may lead to a disruption in parent-adolescent relationships, although it may also result in parents offering increased support to their adolescents. Because of changing social conditions, such as increasing divorce, greater employment opportunities for women, and increased longevity, socialization experiences among the middle-aged tend to be more complex than they were in the recent past.

In the later years, some people may continue to be very active in a variety of ways even though they have retired. Others may begin a process of disengagement from social relationships and activities. Because retirement does not carry with it any clear socially defined obligations, retirees must usually negotiate with others what the nature of their relationship will be. This process can be particularly important when it comes to relationships with children and their families. With increasing age, the social world of older people tends to narrow as a consequence of declining social contacts and diminishing capabilities.

TECHNICAL TERMS

IDENTITY—A sense of self as an autonomous individual, distinct from one's parents and family, as well as the sense of self as belonging to a group and having a place in the world.

TOTAL FERTILITY RATE—The number of children that would be born per woman, if she were to live to the end of her child-bearing years and have children at each age in accord with the prevailing age-specific fertility rates.

PEER GROUP—The group of people in the same social context as a person, as for example, those of approximately the same age, education level, or economic status.

"CLASH OF THE INFERIORITY COMPLEXES"—A conflict arising between adolescents and their parents because both suffer from feelings of inadequacy in relation to the other. The adolescents are unsure of themselves and their futures; the parents are aware of declining attractiveness and vitality. Their interactions are prone to conflict and aggressiveness toward each other.

FILIAL PIETY—Respect for and obedience to one's parents and grandparents.

ANTICIPATORY SOCIALIZATION—Acquiring information and developing perspectives that facilitate the transition from one social role to another.

ARRANGED MARRIAGE—The selection of marriage partners arranged by persons other than the partners themselves, typically by parents of the partners or other elders.

DISENGAGEMENT —The process of removing oneself from social obligations and relationships, often associated with old age.

QUESTIONS

1. In what fundamental respect do adolescents' friendships with peers differ from their relationships with parents? What are the implications of this difference for adolescent development?

2. What are some of the ways in which freedom of movement and social participation increases during adolescence in North America? What factors contribute to this expansion of the adolescent's social world. How do the experiences of most North American adolescents compare with the experiences of adolescents in many agricultural societies?

3. How do peer relationships of younger adolescents in present-day North America tend to change as they reach middle or late adolescence? What is the focus of relationships during the younger adolescent years?

4. What is the importance of the heterosexual relationships that develop

during middle and late adolescence in North America?

5. How is the taking on of an occupation likely to differ in traditional agricultural societies compared with present-day industrial societies? What are the important economic characteristics of these types of societies that help to explain the differing patterns of occupational placement?

6. How is "the long arm of the job" manifested in modern industrial societies? Which characteristics of work in industrial societies are likely to promote tension between responsibilities on the job and at home?

7. How do the motives of couples to rear children differ in subsistence agricultural societies and in urban industrial societies? What effect do these differing motivations have on birth rates?

8. How are the "identity crises" of adolescents and their middle-aged parents related? Under what conditions do parents' assessment of their lives lead to a deterioration in the quality of parenting?

9. What sorts of behaviours characterize "disengagement" in the later years?

10. How are the relationships between parents and their grown children typically worked out in the later years. What are some of the exchanges that tend to characterize the relationships of parents with their grown sons and daughters?

SUGGESTED READINGS

- Erik H. Erikson. *Identity: Youth and Crisis.* New York: W.W. Norton & Company, 1968.

  Erikson's thought-provoking and wide-ranging analysis of adolescence as a struggle for identity.

- Tamara K. Hareven, ed. *Transitions: The Family and the Life Course in Historical Perspective.* New York: Academic Press, 1978.

  A collection of papers, both empirical and theoretical, that examine families and the life course from a variety of perspectives. Most of the empirical papers deal with 19th century New England.

- Edward S. Herold. *Sexual Behaviour of Canadian Young People.* Markham, ON: Fitzhenry & Whiteside, 1984.

  A well-written account of current knowledge covering such topics as sexual behaviour, contraception, abortion and child bearing among adolescents in Canada.

- Joseph F. Kett. *Rites of Passage: Adolescence in America 1790 to the Present.* New York: Basic Books, 1977.

  This book describes the changing patterns in the experience of adolescence by American youths from the turn of the 19th century to the middle of the 20th century.

- Barry D. McPherson. *Aging as a Social Process: An Introduction to Individual and Population Aging.* Toronto: Butterworths, 1983.

  This volume is a scholarly and thoroughly documented account of aging in the modern world. The author describes the factors that contribute to an aging population in industrial societies and details what is known about the way individuals in these societies experience aging.

- Gail Sheehy. *Passages: Predictable Crises of Adult Life.* New York: E. P. Dutton, 1976.

  A popular best-seller that offers a readable, entertaining and insightful analysis of the various crises that are likely to confront men and women as they move through the life course.

One of the earliest family representations is the relief, ca. 1350 B.C., of Queen Nefertete, Pharoah Akhenaton and their children. Revealed here is a warm intimacy between the parents and their children—the father apparently kissing one child while the mother plays with and cuddles the others. Berlin Museum.

Chapter 9

LOVE AND MARRIAGE

Daniel Albas and Cheryl Mills Albas
University of Manitoba

Love and marriage are symbolic constructions that derive their meaning from the
social, cultural, and historical contexts of
which they are a part. The institution of marriage is a cultural universal, but the forms it
takes vary widely. A group of women might
share a husband (polygyny), just as a group of
husbands might share a wife (polyandry), or a
group of husbands and wives can share each
other (group marriage). Finally, the form with
which we are most familiar involves one husband and one wife who share physical intimacies only with each other (monogamy).

In our society we use the term love to mean
a wide range of behaviour involving the relationships between spouses, parents and children, siblings, and comrades-in-arms. Though
all these forms of the love relationship have
some aspects in common, such as caring and
identification, there are also differences. Perhaps the most important difference is the erotic
component involved in the love between
spouses. Indeed, it is so pronounced that
"making love" has come to be synonymous
with coitus. Our concern in this chapter is with
erotic heterosexual love. Since no existing definition of love is fully satisfactory, we rely on
the one most widely used. Goode (1959: 49)
defines love as "a strong emotional attachment, a cathexis, between adolescents or
adults of opposite sexes, with at least the components of sex desire and tenderness."

Many social scientists believe that the potential for love between spouses is universal.
However, its appearance, and the role it plays
in marital life vary widely across cultures and
through time. Contrary to the popular old
song, love and marriage need not "go together
like a horse and carriage." Marriage, in societies both contemporary and past, is and was
often valued more for its pragmatic virtues
than for its psycho-erotic aspects. Romantic
love is a relatively recent social invention that
evolved gradually over centuries in Western
Civilization. Like all other emotions, romantic
love is a complex mixture of feelings and ideas.
Since feelings acquire their meanings only in
relation to the ideas associated with specific
social and historical contexts, it is important to
look at the past and examine the social conditions which existed prior to the emergence of
the concept of romantic love.

We can begin our discussion of romantic
love by first considering love in ancient Greece
and Rome and then discussing the role of love
in early Christianity. We trace the reaction of
the aristocrats during the Middle Ages to the
early Christian anti-sensual and other-worldly
conception of love, and describe the introduction of the courtly model of love which provides the foundation for our contemporary
conception of romantic love. The discussion
then considers how the process of industrialization laid the groundwork for the middle,
and later the lower classes, to experience romantic love. Most importantly, we discuss the
connection of romantic love to marriage and
mate selection. After considering the macro-
structural changes associated with the emergence of romantic love, we focus on the
microsocial issues of who falls in love with
whom, when, where, and especially why.

[1] The authors wish to thank D. Rennie and E. Nett for their comments on an earlier draft of this paper.

HISTORICAL SUMMARY OF LOVE IN WESTERN SOCIETY

The Ancient Greek Concept of Love

One of the earliest conceptions of love in Western society is found in Plato's writings about the Greek upper classes in the 5th century B.C. To Plato, love was the highest form of human virtue. It inspired people to be honourable, kind, and wise. However, this noblest form of love did not go hand in hand with marriage. Love was found in passionate comradeship between men, or more precisely, between an adult and adolescent male. This conception of love grew out of the Greek military tradition. The most formidable army would be one composed of pairs of male lovers inspiring each other to deeds of heroism and sacrifice.

This Greek ideal of love came to underline the whole system of Hellenic education. It was the duty of the older lover to teach and inspire his beloved, while the younger partner was to expend every effort to become worthy of the senior's affection. In the process they would inspire each other to achieve greater perfection (Marrou, 1956). Such a relationship of love gave priority to the elements of rationality and intellectualism and was distinguished from relationships based on mere sensual desire. Plato termed the form of love which advanced Greek educational ideals, *Agape*. Ideally, Agape was exemplified in a person who loved another selflessly without expecting anything in return. Plato distinguished Agape from its less exalted form, *Eros*, which stressed physical pleasure above mental and spiritual growth. Love, in the form of Eros could be either homosexual or heterosexual. Plato's influence on our western conception of love is evident in the term "Platonic love" which, even now, still means love without eroticism. Hunt (1959: 16) noted that: "It is paradoxical that modern love began with Greek love and owes so much to it, although the forms and ideals of Greek love are considered immoral and, to a large extent, illegal in modern society."

Several aspects of Greek society contributed to the prevalence of homosexual love relations. While there was much emphasis on the moral and intellectual development of men, the same did not apply to women. Athenian society did not permit education for women of the nobility, and they were required to spend most of the time secluded in their apartments. Also, men were most frequently in their mid-forties before they married whereas their wives were mostly in their mid-teens. These disparities, plus the fact that women were considered unworthy objects of Agape did little to spark love relationships between spouses. Wives were most often foisted upon husbands by heads of families who desired a line of male heirs. Women were considered fit to bear and look after babies but not for much more; the responsibility for childcare passed out of the mother's hands by the time the child reached approximately seven years of age. The desire to marry was so low that consideration was given to passing laws that would force males to marry as part of their duty to the state. Indeed, the status differences were so great that "if a man energetically wooed women, he was regarded as effeminate, since only an effeminate person would want to spend time with such inferior creatures" (Murstein, 1974b: 57–58).

Times have changed so greatly that it is difficult for us to imagine the conditions just described. It is obvious though, that the manifestation of homosexuality during Greek times was quite different from today. Another major difference between Greek times and modern times is the change in the status of women. In ancient Greece, women could never be worthy objects of a higher form of love, because their status was so low. If high status makes people attractive, then Greek males would be more attractive to other males than would women. In contemporary society, it is possible for men and women to be equal socially and intellectually, so that "Agape" between them is very possible. In other words, the conditions exist such that each can become a worthy object of passion for the other.

The Concept of Love in Ancient Rome

Six hundred years after the times of ancient Greece, the Roman writer Ovid described the upper-class Roman conception of love in his work entitled *The Art of Love*. By this time the status of upper-class women had improved. In contrast to their earlier Greek counterparts, Roman women were often well educated and experienced in matters of the world; they also engaged in public life. Being more socially and intellectually equal and being more available for interaction made Roman women attractive to men and resulted in a very different form of male-female relationship than occurred in ancient Greece. Love relationships in ancient Rome were primarily heterosexual in orientation, but they were not yet inextricably associated with marriage. Marriage partners were selected by heads of extended family units for their social, economic, and political advantages rather than for motives of love. Consequently, most love relationships took the form of affairs outside of the conjugal union.

These affairs were to be enjoyed as pleasant pastimes and were not expected to be either profound or all-encompassing experiences. Ovid termed these relationships *amor ludens*—love as a game. As in all games, there were rules. A primary rule was not to take the relationship seriously or become dependent on a particular beloved. Only lighthearted flirtation and frivolous encounters were expected. Also, as in all games, strategy was important. Ovid, in *The Art of Love*, writes at length about strategies to entice and seduce desired members of the opposite sex. One vital ingredient in the process was physical attractiveness. This is some of the advice he had to offer on how people could make themselves more attractive (*The Art of Love*, 1957, Book 3, lines 255–276).

> "Faults of the face or physique call for attempts at disguise.
> If you are short, sit down, lest, standing, you seem to be sitting…
> If you're the lanky type, wear some billowy garments,
> Loosely let the robe fall from the shoulders down.
> If you're inclined to be pale, wear stripes of scarlet or crimson,
> If you're inclined to be dark, white is an absolute must…
> Have you a bust too flat? Bandages ought to fix that…
> Eat a lozenge or two if you think your breath

is offensive,
> If you have something to say, speak from some distance away."

Besides advice on how to advertise oneself in an open love-market, Ovid also offered strategies on how to carry on affairs when other people—including spouses—were present. It was risky to initiate and maintain these secret affairs because the consequences of being discovered were severe; men could be heavily fined by the cuckolded husband, while women could be put to death.

Ovid's view of *amor ludens* lacks Plato's concept of heavenly love or Agape, but it does emphasize the sensual aspects, as does Eros. However, there are important differences between them. Eros is built on the basis of genuine attraction to, and intense sexual yearning for, another person. By contrast, Ovid's *amor ludens* suggests love is a game and its pleasure comes from playing well. The sexual dimension plays a rather incidental role. Love and sexuality are more recreational pursuits than they are a part of serious relationships. The early Christian movement, which was beginning to emerge about this point in time (1 A.D.), condemned this sensual nonserious approach to love, and it was suppressed until the Renaissance when it reappeared in aspects of the courtly model of love.

The Early Christian Concept of Love

The next great historical influence on the conception of romantic love came with the emergence of Christianity. The early Christians reacted to the prevalent conception of love among upper-class Romans by denouncing all forms of sensuality. While Plato's Agape was oriented to eternal forms or ideas, early Christians decreed that love was to be directed towards their leader and the community He founded.

The early Christian conception of love was decidedly non-sexual; and the early Christians were, in some measure, antimarriage. Faithful followers were expected to leave their spouses and family duties and to devote their lives to the movement. In one instance, Jesus meets a follower who requests that, before he leaves, he be allowed to "first go and bury my father." Jesus responds: "Let the dead bury the dead; but go thou and preach the Kingdom of God." Another follower says to Jesus "Lord, I will follow thee; but let me first go bid them farewell, which are at home at my house." Jesus, once again, responded saying: "No man, having put his hand to the plow, and looking back, is fit for the Kingdom of God" (*Luke* 9: 59–62, Quoted in Murstein, 1974b: 87).

Sexual desires (Eros) were considered to be base, and even in marriage they were suspect. On the subject of marriage, St. Paul indicates: "For I would that all men were even as I myself. But every man hath his proper gift of God, one after this manner, and another after that. I say therefore that the unmarried and widows, it is good for them if they abide even as I. But if they cannot contain, let them marry: for it is better to marry than to burn" (I *Corinthians* 7: 7–9, Quoted in Murstein, 1974b: 88).

As the influence of Christianity spread, virginity became an exalted state. A celibate priesthood emerged and remains to this day in the Roman Catholic church. Nuns were also required to remain celibate and were considered spouses of Christ. On one hand, these patterns promoted the idealization of women and culminated in the doctrine of the Immaculate Conception and the veneration of the Virgin Mary. At the same time, however, these changes worked to stigmatize women who showed an interest in things sexual. Such women were compared to the lustful Eve, the ancient symbol of the witch, who stood opposed to the Virgin Mary and all that was good and ideal (Hunt, 1959).

As the erotic component of love was deemphasized, its aspects of Agape were stressed. In particular, the faithful were encouraged to devote themselves entirely to the spiritual community. We can understand this emphasis from a sociological perspective by realizing that the early Christians comprised a radical and persecuted sect; they were financially poor, low in social status, and without powerful connections. If they were to survive, their members would have to devote themselves completely—even to the point of sacrificing their lives for the community. Many early Christians participated in the ultimate expression of love as Agape by becoming martyrs. De-emphasizing the erotic component of love weakened spousal bonds and also made it easier for faithful members to give of themselves more completely to the community. That is to say, when the community asked its members for the ultimate sacrifice, they found it easier to comply because traditional sources of role competition and role conflict were lessened. Also emphasis on the life thereafter made it easier for persons to leave this life if their attachments here were already weakened.

Courtly Love

Even though the Christian church represented a part of the established order of feudal society, its conception of love was challenged by many of the powerful nobility of the time. The new form of love which emerged combined the code of chivalry—with its ideas of courtesy, valour, and skill at arms—and the idealization of women into a courtly model of love. Andreas Capellanus' work, *The Treatise on Love*, written at this time documents the definition and properties of love. His definition contains many romantic notions:

> Love is a certain in-born suffering derived from the sight of and excessive meditation upon the beauty of the opposite sex, which causes each one to wish above all things the embraces of the other and by common desire to carry out all of love's precepts in the other's embrace (Capellanus, 1959: 18).

He also documented thirty-one rules of love, many of which survive as romantic ideas today. The following is a small example: everyone (of the upper classes) is entitled to fall in love; no one can be in love with two persons at the same time; lovers are always jealous and jealousy stimulates love; frustration stimulates love; when lovers catch sight of each other, they turn pale and their hearts palpitate; and lovers constantly have their beloveds on their minds. Supposedly these rules came from the court of King Arthur, but it is more likely that they emerged from the numerous courts which were held regularly by the knights' ladies to debate what the rules of love ought to be.

The romantic movement originated in Southern France in the eleventh century. The Crusades brought extensive contact with unfamiliar ways of life and served to loosen somewhat the rigidities of medieval life. At the same time, Europe was experiencing a revival of interest in the ancient writings of Greece (Plato) and Rome (Ovid). Troubadours combined ideas from both of these traditions into their poems and songs of love. In the tradition of Plato, they stressed the ennobling power of love that could hit like a thunderbolt to transform an otherwise crude and insensitive clod into one who is gentle, courteous, and might even thirst for learning. Like Ovid, the troubadours stressed the sensual dimensions of a love relationship.

The "love courts" eventually came to the conclusion that "real love, could not exist in a legitimate marital relationship, because the married man and women were legally constrained to belong to each other. Real love, they declared, could not exist except when the man and women could freely and voluntarily commit themselves to one another" (Safilios-Rothschild 1977: 16). Marriages of this time continued to have little to do with love and were arranged for economic and political reasons. Hunt (1959: 190) describes how marriages were like business propositions where the "average Renaissance husband looked upon his wife with eyes which appraised rather than adored." Consequently, spouses looked elsewhere for love. These secretive relationships were similar in many respects to the ones Ovid described during Roman times. The major difference, however, was that ideally, courtly love relationships were to remain sexually unfulfilled. This dictate takes into account the Christian proscription against adultery (and merges the two traditions of *amor ludens* and Christian love). The courtly code of honour was sometimes put to extreme tests by allowing the couple to go to bed together, nude, and allowing them to caress each other but requiring that

they stop short of coitus (Bell, 1971). One of the most significant changes of this era was the social elevating of women beyond the purely religious domain. A knight's devotion to his lady shared many elements with the religious devotion to the Virgin Mary. In essence, courtly love introduced the novel idea that love could be a mutual relationship based on respect as well as passion.

Emerging Industrialization and the Concept of Love

In Medieval society, economic, political, educational, and protective functions were accomplished entirely within extended family units. For example, a master of a craft presided over a "family" which consisted not only of his wife, children, and whatever blood relatives happened to share his household, but also a number of journeymen, servants, and apprentices. Thus his functions as husband, parent, uncle, educator, employer, and businessman were essentially fused. Eventually, the domination by extended family networks began to be eroded, and the ground work was laid for integrating love with marriage. One of the most influential processes which occurred at that time and which had a profound effect on the family was institutional differentiation; that is, functions formerly performed by one institution (the family) began to be distributed among several institutions. For example, as the work place became increasingly separate from the family, educational institutions emerged to train the young for positions in a specialized world (Berger, et al., 1975).

As other institutions began to absorb many of its traditional functions, the family moved to meet new demands placed upon it by the changing nature of the industrializing society. The most important of these new responsibilities was in the emotional realm. It focused on the highly complex, demanding interaction between spouses and was extended to include their children. This new emotional environment was not only conducive to the emergence of conjugal love, it was also in accordance with the economic interests of the urban middle class of the fourteenth and fifteenth centuries.

Chapter 9 / Daniel Albas and Cheryl Mills Albas

Since families of this period tended to focus their interests on the accumulation of capital, this encouraged bonds of friendship, cooperation, and love between mates.

While the rising urban middle classes were influenced by the upper-class ideal of courtly love, they rejected the notion that the object of one's love must be found outside marriage. As a result, they became "carriers" of the revolutionary idea that love and marriage go together. This notion spread to other strata of society, both higher and lower, and reached the working class by the end of the 19th century (Berger et al., 1975). However, the connection of love with marriage initially applied only after the marriage itself, and not during courtship, and certainly not to mate choice. Parents continued to choose their children's mates. Many more changes were to occur before love became a prerequisite for marriage.

As institutional differentiation became more entrenched, parents could no longer guarantee economic opportunities for their children. The combination of economic independence and freedom of mobility encouraged individualism; a way of conceptualizing the world in which the person rather than a collectivity is at the center of the universe. As an ideology, individualism includes a set of assumptions, one of which is that when interests conflict the individual's has priority over the group's (e.g., the family). This philosophy was encouraged not only by capitalism but also by Protestantism which stressed the spiritual importance of a direct relation between the individual and God rather than one mediated by a collectivity such as the church, as in Catholicism or Judaism.

The increasing emphasis on individualism and parents' loss of control over the economic futures of their children resulted in a decline of parental authority. When children reached marriageable age, they began to press for the right to choose their own mates rather than submit to an arrangement negotiated by their parents. However, this process did not immediately result in love becoming the basis for the choice of a marriage partner. As we shall see,

"participant choice" may have little to do with romance.

Colonists in North America discontinued the practice of arranged marriages long before their Southern and Eastern European counterparts, and by the early seventeenth century, the inhabitants of New France and New England were free to choose their own mates. However, "because of the harsh realities of pioneer life, which required everyone to have a spouse, because of the short supply of women, and because of the high death rate and frequently, short marriage span, the choice was usually based on considerations other than emotional ones" (Nett, 1983: 275). Young people continued to evaluate potential spouses in ways their parents had done previously. Priority was given to requisites such as being a good provider, being healthy, and having good moral character and respectable social background. At first, freedom of marital choice meant only that when there was disagreement about the weighing of the above criteria, children's preferences were given priority. Even as late as the mid 1800s, in Western Europe and in North America, love was not considered to be a prerequisite for marriage. As Buckingham (1867) [Quoted in Duberman, 1974: 80] notes: "Love among American people appears to be regarded rather as an affair of judgement, than of the heart; its expression seems to spring from a sense of duty rather than from a sentiment of feeling." In essence, love was expected to develop, after marriage, as a function of the relationship itself, the similarity in social backgrounds of the couple, and their good moral characters, rather than something that emerged from "sex appeal."

A major factor impeding the emergence of love as a criterion for marriage was the society's unequal evaluation of the sexes. By the second half of the nineteenth century the practice of women bringing dowries to marriage had disappeared, and there was a sharp rise in their status. Economic conditions were becoming more favourable, and leisure time was increasing. Longer courtships became the rule; the romance entered into courting relationships. By the 1870s, couples were still choosing mates on the basis of role requisites, but it was becoming socially unacceptable to enter marriage without loving the other person. The dating process had become entrenched as a part of the courtship practices of young North Americans by the 1930s. Young people began looking for prospective mates on the basis of personally appealing individual traits rather than role requisites. The essentially private emotion of love came to assume public significance, and marriage was viewed as the culmination of love. Thus, the elements considered contradictory by the medieval courtly model of love were reconciled. Further, romantic love was no longer the preserve of the upper or even middle classes but could potentially be attained by everyone, making the twentieth century, the century of the love marriage (Hunt, 1959).

A Contemporary Conceptualization of Love

Perhaps the best way to understand the concept of love is to discuss it in relation to it companion concept, liking. Both Davis (1985) and Rubin (1973) have attempted to relate and differentiate these terms empirically. While they acknowledge that liking and loving have much in common, they hesitate to equate the two: "People often express liking for a person whom they would not claim to love in the least. In other instances they may declare their love for someone who they cannot reasonably be said to like very well" (Rubin: 1973: 215). Rubin (1973) postulates that liking is associated with either affection or respect, or both. Affection has its basis in mutual interacting characterized by pleasant and warm relations, while respect is a cooler relation based on another's admirable characteristics outside the interpersonal domain, for example, competence and intelligence. Affection and respect tend to go together but a liked person may be more highly evaluated on one than on the other. While liking is postulated to form the basis for love, love is not only more than liking, love is qualitatively different.

Rubin (1973) postulates three components that distinguish love from liking. They are attachment, caring, and intimacy. Attachment has a strong sexual component, and it consists of a strong desire to be in the presence of the other person. It corresponds "to what the Greeks called Eros" (Rubin, 1973: 213). Caring is really the other side of attachment. In caring, the emphasis is not so much on meeting one's own personal needs for closeness, sexual union, and so on, as it is on giving to the other person. "Love as giving corresponds to what the Greeks called Agape... and is emphasized in the New Testament, epitomized by St. John's declaration 'God is love'" (Rubin, 1973: 213). Intimacy is derived from the combination of attachment (need-fulfillment) and caring and is essentially a relation of rapport and self-disclosure. While attachment and caring are individual characteristics, intimacy is the bond between the couple. It is interactional and transcends them.

Davis takes a somewhat different approach to differentiate and relate love and liking. First, he employs the technique of "paradigm case formulation" to isolate the essential elements associated with liking and loving. The researcher begins by describing an actual case of friendship or love. A characteristic perceived to be essential to either friendship or love is *mentally* replaced by another concept, and questions are then raised as to whether the resulting relationship would still qualify as a genuine case of one or the other. If the change results in a redefinition of the relationship, the characteristic is considered central to the concept (of liking or love); if it does not, it is discarded. For example, trust is vital to friendship, but a small degree of distrust, limited to a narrow segment of the relationship, might still be allowed. However, if it expands to other areas, the friendship would no longer be possible. Trust, then, has boundary points which, if crossed, means that the relationship can no longer be recognized as a genuine friendship. The same procedure is then repeated for all characteristics believed to be associated with friendship and love. The end result is the development of a relationship rating form.

Chapter 9 / Daniel Albas and Cheryl Mills Albas

Davis argues that love relationships, with their greater intensity, generate a greater potential, than do friendships, for distress as well as enjoyment. For example, the exclusive nature of love relationships generates ambivalence, because no matter how appealing other people may be they must be forsaken. Also, the openness of love relationships permits greater mutual criticism. All of these factors combine to make love a profound and transforming experience.

STYLES OF LOVING

People vary greatly in the manner in which they express romantic love. While some emphasize the sexual dimension, others emphasize caring, and yet others focus on its pragmatic aspects. These variations have led social scientists to develop typologies of love. One of the more recent and inclusive attempts is presented by Lee (1974). Lee relies for his information on over 4,000 published accounts of love—from ancient Greece to the present—and personal interviews with 122 people. As a result of his work, he was able to elaborate six major styles of loving. Lee uses the analogy of the colour wheel to generate his categories. Just as all colours are composed of the three primary colours of red, yellow, and blue, so three primary types of love give rise to three others which are combinations of the primary types.

Lee's three *primary types* of love are as follows:

(1) Eros—a style of love characterized by strong and immediate feelings of physical attraction and sexual desire (love at first sight). This form of passionate love was first documented by the Ancient Greeks.

(2) Ludus—a playful noninvolved style of love, first described by Ovid in the 1st century A.D. This type of love is exemplified by the male in the movie *Finian's Rainbow*. When he was not near the girl he loved, he loved the girl he was near!

(3) Storge (pronounced stor-gay)—a Greek term meaning a lifelong friendship. Lee employs this term to designate love relationships that develop slowly as a result of sharing similar interests and activities. It is a companionate not a passionate form of love, and sexual interest tends to develop late in the relationship.

Lee's three *derived types* of love are:

(1) Mania—a compound of eros and ludus. This style of love is obsessive, jealous, possessive, and dependent. It is characterized by rapid and extreme mood swings.

(2) Pragma—a compound of storage and ludus. This is love with a shopping list. The person is very much aware of his or her market value and searches for someone who is compatible and a "good deal."

(3) Agape—[it] tends to be a compound of storge and Eros. A style of love that has its origins in the Ancient Greek and early Christian communities. It is exemplified in a person who loves another selflessly, without expecting anything in return. However, as Lee (1974: 50) noted: "I found no saints in my sample. I have yet to interview an unqualified example of Agape."

Since these styles of loving are ideal constructs, probably no one person will fit entirely into any one type. Furthermore, it is possible for a relationship to begin with one style—for example, passionate or erotic—and then to change and mature into another style, for example companionate or storge. It is interesting to note that Lassewell and Lobsenz (1980) found that the greater the differences between two people in their styles of loving, the more difficulty they experienced in relating to each other.

Chapter 9 / Daniel Albas and Cheryl Mills Albas

THE INSTITUTIONALIZATION OF
LOVE IN MARRIAGE:
A CONTINUUM

Goode (1959) states that when we distinguish between societies regarding the role of romantic love in marriage, we need to do so in terms of a continuum rather than as a dichotomy. At one extreme of this continuum, romantic love is negatively sanctioned. It is viewed as laughable or at least tragic for the persons involved. Examples of societies that fall close to this almost nonexistent view of romantic love are often Oriental, particularly traditional China and Japan. Over the centuries, as the idea of romantic love was developing in Western societies, no equivalent process occurred in these Oriental societies. However, traditional patterns are breaking down, and romantic love as the basis for mate selection is very much on the increase (Landis, 1965).

Approximately midway along the love continuum are found what Goode (1959) terms "love patterns," where love is permissible and even expected, but it is not strongly approved of or desired as a basis for courtship and marriage. Love patterns are relatively common across the societies of the world. In the Orient, India could be considered a society symbolizing "love patterns." Although as in Japan or China, marriages are arranged, Hinduism stressed the unity of religion, love, and sex. Evidence comes from the erotic sculpture on the temples of Kajuraho, and also from the Kama Sutra,—a book that describes how to enjoy sexuality and how to express love through equality. The love of God was described by Sanskrit poets and artists in terms of the erotic yearnings of lovers for each other. Ideally, spouses were to grow to love each other after marriage. Contrast this notion with the respect expected by spouses in traditional Japan and China. In India, allowances were made for the possibility that a couple might fall in love and want to marry; but, of the eight known forms of marriage, a love marriage ranked sixth in terms of desirability and did not qualify, as did the first four, as a means to bring "purification" to ancestors. Thus, ancient Indian society can be said to fall within the love pattern because love, as a basis for marriage, was permitted, but not positively sanctioned.

Some contemporary African societies' approach to love would also fall within the range of the love pattern. Vanderwiele and Philbrick (1983: 917) indicate that Ugandanese and Senegalese youth aged 18–22 years score as high as do young American college students on a standardized romantic love scale. They trace the increasingly romantic orientation to "Western forms of romantic idealism [transmitted] through popular literature and the film industry and the popular and excessively romantic "Hindu" films lavished on the Ugandan [and Senegalese] public." Although the young romanticize feelings of love, a combination of the societal conditions of economic insecurity and the dominance of kinship lines mean that "most youth would rather trust their reason and their parents to make the best choice for them when it come to marriage" (D'Hondt and Vandewiele, 1983: 620). Once again, these two societies recognize romantic love and their people experience it, but they do not encourage its link to marriage; and so for purposes of classification they fit within the love pattern.

Toward the positive end of the love continuum we find that Goode (1950) terms the "romantic love complex." Love as a basis for marriage is not only recognized but is strongly approved. He indicates that Polynesian societies fit into this classification. Mead (1928) found that in Samoa courting couples devote considerable effort to affairs of the heart. They write love letters to each other, they create and sing love songs, and they spend considerable time in each other's company. However, these relationships often are not as enduring or as intense as the ones we expect in Western societies: "Samoans rate romantic fidelity in terms of days or weeks at most and tend to scoff at tales of life long devotion (they greeted the story of Romeo and Juliet with incredulous contempt)" (Mead, 1928: 155–156). In Western society, it is expected that love will form the basis of a lifelong relationship and that the bonds between the couple will be deep and intense. This concept of the romantic love complex is becoming increasingly prevalent across the societies of the world. The next question that needs to be answered, then, is what causes love?

EXPLANATIONS OF THE ROLE OF ROMANTIC LOVE

Kinship Patterns and the Emergence of Love

Before romantic love can occur, a society must have a concept of it and must allow leeway for its development. Parsons (1949) emphasizes that the declining role of kinship is the most important basis for the emergence of love. Goode (1959) supplements this thesis by noting the role that stratification patterns play in the dynamics of love. As we noted earlier, to the degree that unmarried people of the opposite sex are free to interact with each other, love is a potential outcome. Because love may lead to marriage, the kinship group and its concerns become involved. Wherever kinship ties are strong, priority will be given to group norms rather than to the individual's desires. Mace and Mace (1959: 121) detail why romantic love did not simultaneously emerge along parallel lines in <u>Eastern and Western</u> societies.

It is a rigid principle of Eastern life that the stability of the family and the maintenance of the social order always came before the happiness of the individual. Romantic love is an unruly emotion, which, out of control, can do as much damage as uncontrolled anger.

Kinship groups seek to maintain themselves and their way of life (values, norms, and beliefs) over time. This aim is best accomplished by avoiding intimate contact with others who do not share similar orientations. As a consequence, the emphasis is on endogamy; that is, marrying others who share similar social and cultural backgrounds. The practice is stressed among the higher classes as a means of maintaining wealth, power, and prestige. The end result of the process is the maintenance of the existing social structure.

Goode (1959) suggests five ways in which societies attempt to control love and thereby avoid upsetting the existing social structure: (1) child marriage; (2) the narrowing of the pool of eligible mates; (3) isolation of the sexes; (4) chaperonage; and (5) indirect controls.

The first strategy is child marriage. It is an efficient way of controlling love, because children are married off before they are old enough to interact in any meaningful way with other potential spouses. Sometimes the kin group attempts to generate affectionate bonds between the young pair by ensuring that as they grow up, they play together. This pattern existed in India where the bride went at a young age to live with her husband's family. The children were often betrothed at birth and married by the time they were nine or ten, but the marriage was not physically consummated until much later (Stephens, 1963). Child betrothal is also practiced in other societies such as Toda, Trobriand, Siwai, Lesu, Murngin, and Reindeer Chukchee.

Another related form of control is the limiting of the pool of eligible mates until the number is so small that there is virtually no choice left. For example, among Bedouin Arabs, a young man must marry his father's brother's daughter.

A third strategy is to isolate the sexes to prevent contact with potentially inappropriate mates. This practice occurs in the harem system of traditional Islam and, in the Western world, when upper-class families send their children to private schools.

Chaperonage is a fourth type of control. Young couples are not allowed any form of privacy, and so it becomes more difficult to interact in ways that might result in intimate lovemaking. This tactic was widely practiced in Western societies and still occurs in many Latin American countries. Among the peasants of the Arabic Islam traditions, young women are not only chaperoned but also insulated by a veil. It is very difficult to fall in love with a person one has never seen!

A fifth strategy societies use to control love before marriage is to create the illusion of free mate choice while, at the same time, exercising indirect controls. One way in which this practice occurs is by socializing children to be comfortable only with certain styles of interaction (lifestyle), and reinforcing the patterns by ensuring that children live in areas and play at leisure activities where they meet others like themselves (i.e. eligible mates).

Love can be effectively controlled by the larger kin group only to the degree that the group's influence is felt in the everyday lives of its young members—that is, in the impact of economic and residential ties as well as in affective bonds developed during frequent interaction. However, as Parsons (1949) notes, industrialization is associated with a weakening of kin ties, because employment opportunities now depend less on them and more on individual initiative. Also, the nature of the employment world is such that workers must move to where the jobs are, and consequently many couples now live in different communities from those of their families of orientation. Economically independent households also make for a decline in rates of kin interaction. The result is that husband and wife are free to focus attention on each other, and children learn this as the normal pattern of socialization.

Parsons also indicates that industrialization is related to the rise of the youth culture. Its values are independence from family ties, having fun, and having lots of interaction with members of the opposite sex. These values downplay the importance of endogamy and lead to an emphasis on the emotions generated in the give-and-take of social interactions with other young people, not necessarily like themselves. In this instance, Goode's first four institutional strategies to control love lose much of their significance, and parents can resort only to increasingly indirect controls over their children's love lives. It becomes clear, then, that any explanation of the influence of romantic love in mate selection as we know it must focus on emotions and face-to-face interactions which, of course, are played out against a backdrop of the macro-structures of society.

The Two-Component Theory of Love

Earlier in this chapter it was said that love differs in fundamental ways from, and is founded on different principles from, liking. Research indicates that we like others who are consistently pleasant in their behaviour and who reward us positively. While these principles also apply to most love relationships, there are exceptions. People sometimes fall in love with others who injure them mentally, physically, and socially. For example, in cases exemplifying the "Stockholm Syndrome," female hostages "fall in love" with their abductors and vice versa. Sometimes when people learn that their loved one has been unfaithful, the result is an increase of passionate feelings for that person. Hence, on occasion, love emerges from conditions which seem more conducive to hatred or aggression.

We need a theory to explain why both intensely positive and intensely negative (and presumably unrewarding) experiences generate love. Berscheid and Walster (1978) suggest the applicability of Schachter's (1964) two-component theory of emotion to explain sudden intense feelings of love—what Lee (1974) calls erotic and manic styles of loving, and what Berscheid and Walster themselves refer to as passionate love.

Schachter presents a new paradigm for understanding human emotions. In essence, any emotion requires a "feeling" or physiological arousal (which is fundamentally the same for all emotions) and an accompanying interpretation or label to identify which emotion we are experiencing. Schachter and Singer (1962) tested this theory in a rather complicated experiment. Some subjects received injections of adrenaline which increased heart beat rate and breathing and caused facial flush. These subjects were categorized as physiologically aroused. A second group was injected with a placebo and was categorized "unaroused." Some subjects were informed, others were misinformed, and the rest were told nothing about what physiological experiences they might expect. All subjects were then placed in a situation designed to provoke either anger (in a room with an angry person) or euphoria (a room where paper airplanes were being tossed about). The results were as expected; highly physiologically aroused subjects who lacked an accurate explanation as to what they ought to experience reacted more intensely, by exhibiting very strong euphoria or anger depending on the room to which they were assigned. Thus Schachter argues that when we are aroused but really do not know why, we look to our environment for clues to tell us how we should feel. We then organize this information into an emotional label which, in turn, influences how we do feel.

If Schachter is correct, if a cognitive label is a necessary part of an emotion, then the larger social and cultural setting will have a strong impact on whether, when, and with whom people experience love. In order to experience romantic love, such a cognitive label must exist in the vocabulary of the culture. For example, anthropologists who describe romantic experiences typical of our society to people who have no concept of romantic love report that the response is often one of incredulity. These people have no sense that others would think that way, and they often wonder whether we are mad! (Wilkinson, 1978).

While the concept of romantic love is now found in most industrialized societies, it may have reached its zenith in North America. Not only do we have a concept of romantic love, but we encourage it in numerous ways. Even before children are old enough to read, they hear the fairy tales of Cinderella, Snow White, and Sleeping Beauty where there is "always beauty, always obstructions, always love, always a class barrier.... always married bliss. The unsaid last line of every story is 'someday this may happen to you.' Parents set the proper example for their children by relating to the child their own prince-and-beauty story. 'Why did you marry Daddy?' 'Because we fell in love'" (Udry, 1971: 163).

Young children are often teased about having a boyfriend or girlfriend and about being in love. They soon learn the distinction between an opposite sex companion who is a friend rather than a boyfriend or girlfriend. At the same time they are bombarded by commercial symbols of romantic love. For example, girls often play with teenage-looking dolls which come equipped with attractive wardrobes. They learn to "doll up" to make themselves more "fall-in-lovable." The mass media adds to this barrage of romantic symbols. Television shows, especially soap operas, and films play a major role in perpetuating ideas about romantic love. Over 90% of popular songs in 1957 focused on the theme of romantic love (Horton, 1957); a review of "Columbia's Top 100 of the Eighties" (1985) suggests that the proportion of love songs remains much the same.

In essence, North American society provides adolescents with an abundance of love labels; many opportunities to interact freely with members of the opposite sex; privacy—especially in the form of the automobile; and systematically socializes them to fall in love. In North America, the institutionalization of love is so pervasive that "only those who are very obtuse, emotionally incapacitated, or perversely reared will be deprived of the experience of love" (Udry, 1971: 162).[1] By the late teen years, more than 90% of American men and women have fallen love—often more than once.

Having established that in North American society there is a very clear cognitive label for romantic love, the next step is to identify the

---

[1] Why is there so much emphasis on romantic love in Western, particularly North American, culture? Greenfield (1969) indicates that industrial societies must socialize their members to be rationally oriented. On the other hand, getting married and having children cannot be rationally justified in economic terms, but they are necessary if the society is to survive. A strongly developed conception of romantic love encourages people to marry. The effectiveness of romantic love as an inducement to marry is demonstrated by Theodorsen (1965). Students from the US, Singapore, China, Burma, and India completed a "romanticism scale" and indicated their desire to marry. The intensity of romanticism varied directly with the desire to marry. The American students scored highest, followed by students from Singapore, China, Burma, and finally India. Larson (1976) administered the same questionnaire to Canadian students and found their scores very similar to those of the Americans.

connection between the label and its basis in physiological arousal. If a person is in the presence of a suitable other of the opposite sex and experiences things such as a rapid heart beat, the person "knows" these are symptoms of falling in love. "In this way," Nett (1988: 206) indicates, "young persons manage their emotions so that they fit the scripts they have learned from fairy tales, from love stories in books, TV programs and movies, as well as from their peers." It is important to note that the variations in heart beat, sweaty palms, and shaky knees we associate with arousal for love are the same as those for fear. Given these underlying physical commonalities, it is not surprising that people sometimes confuse the two. For example, Dutton and Aron (1974) compared reactions of males to an attractive female in a fear-provoking and a non-fear-provoking situation. In the first instance they met her as they finished crossing a 5 ft. wide, 450 ft. long suspension bridge anchored 230 ft. above a ravine. In the second case, they had just crossed a firmly constructed, firmly anchored bridge over a small stream. Dutton and Aron found that men re-labelled inner feelings of fear at least partly as sexual arousal or romantic attraction. White, Fishbein, and Rutstein (1981) also found support for this idea.

Thus we can make sense of the Stockholm Syndrome where hostages fall in love with their captors. We can also now make sense of Ovid's advice in *The Art of Love* to would-be lovers in Ancient Rome. He suggests that a good way to arouse a woman's passion is to take her to the arena to see the gladiators disembowel one another! Ovid does not offer an explanation for his advice but according to the two-component theory of love the physiological arousal caused by the grisly scene in the arena could easily be misinterpreted as intense attraction to her mate. Over the centuries

things have not really changed all that much, and the same type of information still circulates among adolescent males. It is widely known that the most "mood-provoking" settings for dates are also the most frightening— namely horror movies, demolition derby, roller coasters, and the like.

The next step is to explain why, even though we may frequently experience intense feelings of physiological arousal, we do not constantly fall in love. We also need an explanation for the persistence of love in a relationship. That is, how it is possible for love to continue when physiological arousal abates. One possible answer to both of these questions is found in the feeling rules, feeling work, and labels of society.

Feeling Rules, Feeling Work and Labels

It is not merely a matter of personal whim that we label feelings of physiological arousal as love. On the contrary, love labels are structured by the micro context within which they occur as well as the larger social and cultural worlds. Every society has a general set of "feeling rules" (Hochschild, 1983; 1979; 1975) and more specific "love rules" which define an acceptable "field of eligibles" (Winch, 1958). In Western culture the "field of eligibles" consists of partners who are of the opposite sex, single, similar in age (although love relationships between older men and younger women are more acceptable than vice versa), and similar in other social background characteristics. The "love rules" of our society also favour young, physically attractive people.[1] As Berschied and Walster (1978: 161) note: "If persons admit that they are sexually attracted to a hunchback,

---

[1] The movie *The Graduate* provides an example of a "love" relationship that is not in accord with Western love rules. A young college graduate is wooed by a married woman who is old enough to be his mother. They eventually meet in a hotel where she tries to seduce him. Evidence that members of the movie audience had internalized the rules of our culture surfaced with their groans and looks of disgust just at the point where the young man placed his hand over her bare breast! However, all is well that ends well, and our hero finally shows that he has internalized the love rules by rejecting the mother in favour of her daughter—a more "natural" partner.

to an octogenarian, or to someone with no nose, they are branded as sick or perverse."

The classic lovers Romeo and Juliet experienced love at first sight. In Schachter's terms we can say they experienced physiological arousal which was quickly labelled love. However, the label was not randomly manufactured. It was in accordance (almost) with the "love rules" of the society. Romeo and Juliet were of opposite sexes, physically attractive, of similar age, and similar social class and ethnic backgrounds. The only problem for them was that their families were engaged in a long-standing feud! In most relationships, though, love is not so "automatic."

In some measure, feeling rules, the guidelines which dictate how we ought to feel, differ for males and females. More specifically, in traditional marriages males are the breadwinners, and females are dependent on them for economic support and status. Waller (1938: 243) describes the situation in blunt terms: "There is this difference between the man and the woman in the pattern of bourgeoisie family life: a man, when he marries, chooses a companion and perhaps a helpmate [feeling rule], but a woman chooses a companion and at the same time a standard of living. It is necessary for a woman to be mercenary" [feeling rule]. Thus it is easier for males to label their feelings as love while women must be more cautious about assigning a love label, because it will also include their eventual social and economic well-being. Love involves more than physiological arousal, which is codified in accordance with cultural understandings. Love must also be managed; that is, would-be lovers must engage in "feeling work" to bring their emotions in line with the "feeling rules" (Hochschild, 1983; 1979; 1975).

Not only do the feeling rules regulating love differ between the sexes, but they also differ in the amount of "feeing work" they do (Hochschild, 1983; 1975). We can define "feeling work" as the effort a person makes to attempt to change the degree or quality of an emotion. One way in which this difference can be noted is to examine how long it takes for people to decide they are in love. Kanin et al.,

(1970) noted that women took longer than did men to decide whether they loved the other person, and once that commitment was made, they worked harder than did men to communicate their emotions. Another interesting difference between the sexes in the amount of "feeling work" they are willing to do to maintain a relationship is evident in Kephart's (1967) study of college students. He asked over 1,000 college students the following question: "If a boy(girl) had all the qualities you desired would you marry this person even if you were not in love with him(her)?" Very few (4% of women and 12% of men) answered yes. But consistent with Hochschild's feeling rules for the sexes, 72% of women and only 24% of men were too pragmatic to answer "no," and opted for the "uncertain" option instead. Consistent with the feeling work hypothesis, females focused on what work they might do to make their feelings consistent with cultural dictates. For example, one respondent notes: "If a boy had all the qualities I desired, and I was not in love with him—well, I think I could talk myself into falling in love."

Also females work harder than do males to discourage themselves from loving someone who does not fit into their field of eligible mates. The following illustration concerns a young woman who finds herself "in love" with a Catholic priest who is twenty years her senior: "I started trying to make myself dislike him...When I was with him I did like him, but then I'd go home and write in my journal how much I couldn't stand him. I kept changing my feelings." She finally was able to work through her tangled emotions and convince herself that she did not really love him after all.

Another interesting difference between males and females in the amount of feeling work they do occurs in relation to premarital coitus. Reiss (1981) states that even though the "double standard" of sexual behaviour for males and females is weakening, it nevertheless remains. Females who engage in premarital coitus work harder than do males to convince themselves that they really love the other person and thereby legitimate their actions. In sum, then, the two-component theory of love states that people must experience physiological arousal and then be able to label it as love before they can "fall in love." The label is not indiscriminately attached but rather falls within the feeling rules and love rules of the larger society. As Hochschild notes, women especially work hard at evoking the proper emotions to fit the proper label. This information suggests that love is something that tends to emerge and become stronger (or weaker) as part of an interactional process. Reiss (1960) offers a theory of love which focuses more directly on the process of interaction and so complements Hochschild's work. It is also possible to integrate part of Schachter's two-component theory of love into Reiss' model. The next section, then, attempts to describe some other possible interrelations and connections.

The Wheel Theory of Love

A classic study of engaged and married couples noted that about three-fourths of them were not intensely attracted to each other when they first met (Burgess and Wallin, 1953). In Lee's terms discussed earlier, then, most couples fall into the sturgaic rather than erotic style of loving. In essence, love appears to be something that grows out of interaction over a period of time. Reiss' wheel theory of love conceives of love as something composed of weightings along four interpersonal processes or spokes of a wheel which can turn either up or down. These "spokes" include rapport, self-revelation, interdependency, and basic need fulfillment. Love feelings can vary in intensity from zero to one hundred percent. How intense a relationship must be before it can be labelled love varies across subcultures. For example, the high school subculture defines the necessary intensity levels in a manner which allows love to occur frequently.

The first stage of Reiss's model is labelled a feeling of rapport. When couples first meet, they enter into casual conversation and exchange superficial biographical information. Similarity of backgrounds and interests can foster the development of rapport. However, if one person feels ill at ease the relationship will most likely end. Thus, ease of communication is the first step in the development of intimacy.

If a couple feels comfortable with and attracted to each other, they will want to know more about the other person. In this process, they engage in Reiss's second stage, termed self-revelation. There is an attempt to discover on which issues differences and similarities exist and what their significance is for the relationship. The aim is to explore whether the respective social worlds are close enough so as eventually to be able to sustain them in a viable relationship as a couple. These growing feelings of rapport provide the fund of trust necessary for further self-disclosures and eventually lead to intimacy. Although Reiss focuses on verbal disclosures, we also communicate through body movements and eye contact, as well as through the distance we maintain from each other. All of these factors combine to operate as an integrated set, sometimes substituting for, sometimes complementing, and sometimes amplifying each other (Altman and Taylor, 1973). This is probably why Davis (1985) did not find differences in the amount of verbal disclosure between best friends and lovers. He neglected the fact that the nonverbal medium is the special language of love.

Increasing physical proximity almost always accompanies a growing sense of rapport. This tendency for couples to move physically closer as intimacy develops has been experimentally demonstrated to occur as early as thirty minutes into a blind date (Bryne et al., 1970). We can see it occurring regularly in dating situations where couples travel in automobiles equipped with bench, not bucket, seats. Early in the evening the female is more likely to sit near the door on her side of the car. As feelings of rapport develop and the process of self-revelation begins, the tendency is for her to decrease the distance somewhat by moving opposite the glove compartment, then the radio, and finally, not atypically, to end the evening in the "twin-headed driver" position. Couples disclose more about themselves by going "space in space together," and at the same time, they also obtain (implicit) permission to physically touch, press, and compress each other (Davis, 1973). Another important nonverbal factor which signals an increase in intimacy between couples is eye contact. As we noted earlier, Rubin (1973) found that the intensity of reported feeling between couples is directly related to their amount of mutual gazing. Of all the "organs of love," the eyes are frequently considered to be the most important (Simmel, 1921; Soloman, 1981).

As the process of self-revelation continues and trust increases, couples dare to reveal even more about themselves. They often invite the other person into their private environments where it is more likely that potentially unsavoury information will be revealed. At the same time, there is a tendency to increase the range of body areas that are available for contact and exploration. The act of coitus is an ultimate symbol of self-revelation. It involves the most dramatic removal of the physical and psychological barriers that separate people. This desire to be physically close, to touch, to bare one's body and soul to another person requires an explanation—the most reasonable one in our culture is love.[1]

After self-revelation, comes Reiss's third stage, which he labels mutual dependence. When couples come to realize how mutually dependent they have become for meeting basic personality needs (his fourth stage), then the pressures to label themselves as being in love become almost overwhelming. By this point couples are accustomed to doing things that require the presence of the other person. The absence of one means that activities which require joint participation are no longer possible, and also that one no longer has an audience with whom to share emotional intimacies. A couple's joint realization that they are in love requires the making of serious commitments—most frequently to marriage.

The relation of love feelings to the length of the marriage is an interesting one. Berschied and Walster (1978) believe that in marriage the intensity of passionate love feelings (Lee's erotic and manic styles of loving) are in a fight against time. The longer a couple is married, the lower they tend to score on Rubin's love scale (Cimbalo, Falling, and Mousaw, 1976). To this point we have emphasized a clockwise forward rotation of Reiss's love wheel and increased loadings on each of the spokes (i.e. rapport, self-revelation, mutual dependency, and personality need fulfillment). However, the love wheel can also reverse itself. Couples tend to be most similar in their social and psychological characteristics and orientations during the processes of dating and courtship. This closeness facilitates the forward rotation of the love wheel, but with time couples often change their orientations. These changes do not necessarily occur at the same rate or in the same direction for both parties. Whitehurst and Booth (1980: 78) state that often after marriage men switch their focus to the "next operation...success...or venture...his job" so for them marriage becomes "a peripheral activity while for women marriage remains quite central." Not surprisingly Dizard (1968) found that the more effort men invested in their careers and in increasing their incomes, the less happy were their marriages for their wives and for themselves. Another factor which requires considerable expense both in time and in energy in marriage is children. As Whitehurst and Booth (1980: 78) note, more demands fall on women who are required to rearrange their "role priorities...involvement with children as first, maintaining the house as second, and their partnership with their husband as third." As role priorities and interests diverge, couples tend to feel less rapport and so they decrease the amount of self-revelation. The less intimacy they feel, the less the need for coitus. As a result they become less mutually depen-

---

[1] This is consistent with Bem's (1972) "self-perception theory". Social scientists usually consider underlying attitudes to be the major determinants of behaviour. Bem assumes the exact opposite. To the extent that couples behave in ways consistent with being in love (e.g., spending long periods of time together and high amounts of verbal and non-verbal disclosure) then the logical inference is that they are in love (i.e., behaviour determines attitude).

dent on each other and rely less on each other for basic personality need fulfillment.

However, the wheel of love need not reverse itself. The crucial factor appears to be whether or not couples continue self-revelation even when their worlds are very different. Pineo (1961) found that divergence of interests and activities over time affected marital adjustment scores only to the degree that it impaired the process of self-revelation. Murstein (1974b: 393) reviewed the empirical literature relevant to this point and noted that marriages are unsatisfactory only to the degree that a member "stops confiding in his or her spouse, is insufficiently involved in trying to settle differences, stops kissing the spouse, decreases markedly the frequency of sexual relations, and in short, ceases to react to his or her partner with much positive expression." Munro and Adams (1978) reinforce these notions. Their study of couples married twenty years or more revealed that many still retained their romantic beliefs and sentiments.

In sum, then, the interactional theories of love just reviewed share much in common. They agree that the larger social context plays a vital role in structuring relationships, and that love is a matter of personal and social definition. There are also rather basic differences between them. While the two-component theory of love can explain the appearance of sudden intense feelings (somewhat akin to Lee's erotic and manic styles of loving), it is deficient as an explanation of the maintenance of love. Reiss's wheel theory of love views love growing from repeated interactions between members of the opposite sex and so offers a potential explanation for Lee's conception of a storgaic style of loving. Reiss's wheel theory, though, is not as well equipped to deal with situations of intense "love at first sight." For a discussion of some additional limitations and an attempt to rectify them, readers may wish to note our discussion of the pulley alternative for the wheel theory of the development of love (Albas and Albas, 1987).

SUMMARY

In this chapter we attempted to discuss historically and cross-culturally the concept of love and its relation to marriage. A brief historical summary of the conception of love in Ancient Greece, in Roman times, during the Middle Ages, among the early Christians, and during the Industrial era in Europe was followed by a discussion of love in contemporary society. Links between liking and loving in contemporary society were also addressed. The next section summarized Lee's (1974) typology of the various styles of loving. This was followed by a discussion of the institutionalization of romantic love in marriage and how we may understand the relationship in terms of a continuum rather than as a dichotomy. The remainder of the chapter described various explanations for the emergence and maintenance of love, the relation of kinship patterns to the emergence of love, and then Schachter's two-component theory, Hochschild's feeling rules, feeling work, and labels, and finally Reiss's wheel theory of love.

TECHNICAL TERMS

AGAPE—A style of love that has its origins in the ancient Greek and early Christian communities. It is exemplified in a person who loves another selflessly, without expecting anything in return.

FEELING RULES—That set of rules which exists in every society and that govern how we ought to feel in particular situations.

FEELING WORK—The work we must do to bring our emotions into line with the "feeling rules" of a particular situation.

EROS—A form of passionate love first documented by the ancient Greeks.

MANIA—A style of love that is obsessive, jealous, possessive, and dependent.

PRAGMA—This is love "with shopping list." The person is very much aware of his or her market value, and searches for someone who is compatible and a "good deal."

STORGE—A Greek term meaning a lifelong friendship; a companion of love.

QUESTIONS

1. Explain how the importance of the military combined with the education, age, and status differences between men and women contributed to the homosexual ideal of love in Greece during Plato's time.

2. Show clearly what the connections were between love, sex, and marriage in Classic Greek, Roman, Early Christian and Medieval times.

3. Suggest a sociological explanation for the fact that the early Christians de-emphasized the erotic component of love.

4. What part did industrialization play in forging the linkage between love, sex, and marriage? How did industrialization change the patterns of mate selection?

5. Show how the two component theory of love is better adapted to explain "love at first sight" rather than the gradual maturing of a deep love sentiment. Show how the wheel theory of the development of love works in the opposite way.

6. What is meant by the terms "feeling (i.e., love) rules" and "feeling work"? What role do they play in "falling in" and "falling out" of love?

The Babylonian Marriage Market, by Edwin Long.
Royal Holloway College, Egham, Surrey, England.

Chapter 10

SEXUALITY AND MARRIAGE

Daniel Albas and Cheryl Mills Albas
University of Manitoba

Sexuality is one of the few cultural universals.[1] Unlike romantic love, which may or may not be institutionalized in a given society, sexuality is a universally institutionalized component of human experience. It is very difficult to define the concept of human sexuality because it encompasses aspects of the psychological, social, and cultural, as well as reproductive biological, processes. Generally though, sexuality refers to the thoughts, feelings, and actions of humans who have learned a pattern of cues designed to evoke erotic arousal. We also learn the conditions in which these thoughts, feelings, and actions are appropriate. Sexuality includes a wide range of overt behaviours like sexual intercourse, masturbation, giving birth, and breast feeding as well as touching, caressing, and talking affectionately. We experience a more covert aspect of sexuality in our feelings, thoughts, attitudes, and values.

The Evolution of Marriage as a Regulator of Sexuality

Although our evolutionary past favoured us with large brain capacity, in the process we were left, at least in terms of sexual regulation, biologically incomplete. Compared to our humanoid ancestors, we lack internal sexual controls which come with the oestrus cycle. That is, an oestrus female becomes sexually attractive to males only during the few hours of the month when she is most likely to conceive. Once conception occurs she ceases to be receptive to or attractive to males.

In humans, the oestrus cycle was replaced by a menstrual cycle which allows females to be continually receptive to males and attractive for mating. At the same time, humans evolved into bipedal creatures with a narrowed pelvis and a consequently smaller birth passage than in other female hominids. As a result, compared to other primates, human infants are born in a relatively more immature and therefore more dependent state. Accordingly, the three developments: 1) the menstrual (monthly) cycle rather than oestrus (seasonal); 2) the helplessness of the newborn human; and 3) the replacement of parental instinct by weaker cultural constraints combine to produce disadvantageous consequences for the newborn. Namely, the nursing mother may be tempted away to form another union and temporarily or permanently abandon the child (Nett, 1988).

Societal survival, then, is best assured by relatively stable and permanent unions between parents who assume joint responsibility for each other and their offspring. Since this is the case, societies make rules to prohibit conception outside of a legal relationship. Indeed, a primary function of marriage is to license parenthood and to legitimate children. In no society is sexuality regarded as a natural, inevitable response like eating, breathing, or sweating. It is universally regulated by the institu-

[1] The authors with to thank D. Rennie and E. Nett for their comments on an earlier draft of this paper.

tion of marriage.[1] Many societies prohibit premarital sexual relations; most societies prohibit extra-marital sexual relations (at least for women); and in all societies there are rules to prohibit sexual relations between immediate family members. While the incest taboo prohibits sexual regulations between particular categories of people, marriage, the other side of the coin, specifies rules to establish who is an acceptable mate.

At a very general level, then, we can assume that in all societies sexuality is a very closely regulated form of activity and that it is clearly linked to family life. The remainder of this chapter focuses specifically on sexuality as a human activity. There is a discussion of the polar theories—biological and sociological— to explain human sexuality and a presentation of salient findings on the variations in sexuality within our own society and across other societies.

MODELS OF SEXUALITY

The Biological Model

Three basic interpretive models have evolved to explain human sexuality. Freud is the best-known representative of the first, which is biologically based. The biological model he proposed has dominated much of the work on human sexual behaviour for the past half-century. According to Freud, humans are born with a powerful sexual drive (libido) which ensures species procreation. The sexual drive is so strong it plays a causal role not only in the domain of gender roles (viz., "anatomy is destiny"), but also has a major impact on the larger institutions of society. In essence, the very foundations of society are continually threatened because the universal sexual drive of humans continually seeks expression in ways inimical to the cultural prescriptions. Society attempts to protect itself by elaborating institutions which dictate that sexuality is to be repressed, inhibited, and channelled. Indeed, the need to control the potentially powerful and disruptive effects of sexuality becomes a basic explanation for the universality of the family as an institution. Variations in the strength of the sex drive over the human life cycle and between males and females are in large part due to variations in individual hormonal levels and the effectiveness of repression or other societal forms of inhibition. In essence, humans are viewed as possessing biologically determined sexual natures. A social world may shape, but does not initiate, the sexual process.

The Social Script Model

This sociological model has its origins in the work of Ford and Beach (1951) and stresses the social basis of human sexuality. In essence, the content of human sexuality is created by culture. To understand just how much of human sexual behaviour is a learned social product, we will look to the work of Gagnon and Simon (1973). They offer a social script model of sexuality in which actors in erotic situations are guided by cultural scripts similar in many ways to the scripts that guide actors on the stage. These scripts specify what we are to consider sexually attractive or stimulating, where or when it is appropriate to engage in sexual expression, and how often and especially why we engage in sexual interaction.

Since these scripts are societally composed, people of different historical periods and cultures, and those in different social classes in the same culture will develop somewhat different patterns of acceptable sexual expression. Contrary to the biological model, sexual interaction according to this view is not something that "comes naturally" but rather something that must be learned in "a social environment."

As Gagnon and Simon (1973: 108) state: "Sex is really just like everything else...there is no

---

[1] "Marriage is a socially legitimate sexual union, begun with a public announcement and undertaken with some idea of permanence; it is assumed with a more or less explicit marriage contract, which spells out reciprocal rights and obligations between spouses, and between spouses and their future children" (Stephens, 1963: 5).

natural man struggling against the pressures of civilization." In contrast to the Freudian drive model of sexuality, the social script model views society not merely as a regulatory body to handle or control a biological constant, but as something which plays a creative role in the basic sexual nature of humans. Sexuality, like any other object, is viewed as a social construction and our so-called "sex drive" is something we *learn*.[1] If we are given the opportunity to learn, we become sexually interested. Our degree of interest depends on how important our socio-cultural environment considers sexuality to be and on our unique learning experiences. A lack of sexual interest is not the result of repression of a biological constant but rather is interpreted as a lack of opportunity to learn. In essence, through learning the socio-cultural guidelines on how to become sexually aroused and how and when to respond, we "create or invent the capacity for sexual behaviour." In effect, unlike the lower animals whose sexuality is species-specific, human sexuality is culture-specific. For brevity we shall refer to the social script for sexual behaviour as the sexual script.

A Psychological Theory: Object-Relations Theory

This paradigm is less fully developed than either the biological or the social script model. It builds on Freud's psychological (as distinct from his biological) theory of sexuality and object-relations theory, and places the learning of sexuality into a developmental, motivational context. The focus is upon the way in which sexuality is integrated into personality. The motivational basis of sexuality comes, not from a biological drive, but from a psychological record of sensual experiences people acquire in interaction with others. The role of the socio-cultural world in the experience of sexuality is mediated through psychological processes. This theory builds on Freud's notion that "sensual pleasure is the shared factor in different sexual experiences, both infantile and adult, nongenital and genital" (Person, 1980: 614). Initially pleasure comes from the stimulation of "dermal surfaces" as infants interact with their mothers (or surrogates). This process continues as children move through the psycho-sexual stages of development. The eventual accumulated record of these experiences plays a definite role in personality formation and leaves an imprint on later sexual life. Sexuality plays a decisive role in personality formation by mediating gender and sex prints—the unique characteristics of sexuality in every person somewhat analogous to fingerprints. The psychological realization that one is either male or female plays a decisive role in the Oedipal drama, as well as in how we experience sexuality and the fantasies we attach to it. The contribution of this paradigm is that it provides a broad view of sexuality as sensuality and focuses on its developmental aspects, particularly in children and adolescents.

In this chapter, where we emphasize the *marriage relationship* as the major source of sexual regulation and regular sexual outlet for most adults, we will describe the cross-cultural variations in sexuality, and so stress will be on the social script model.

CROSS-CULTURAL DIFFERENCES IN SEXUAL SCRIPTS

Since sexual scripts are learned in the give-and-take of everyday interaction, we are frequently unable to distance ourselves from and understand the role they play in our lives. One way to accomplish the task is to examine some cross-cultural variations in the what, where, and when, as well as the how and why of sexual behaviour. It is hoped that such an examination will make clear the nature and importance of sexual scripts and their impact on human behaviour.

---

[1] As we discussed in the previous chapter, physiological (sexual) arousal must be labelled before it is meaningfully experienced (Schachter and Singer, 1962).

The What and Why of Sexuality

Standards of Beauty

Much of what we know about human sexuality throughout the world is based on Ford and Beach's (1951) review of anthropological reports from 190 societies. We focus first on the *what* and, in some measure on the *why* of sexuality. In all societies, physical appearance is an important aspect of sexual attractiveness. Male attractiveness, however, tends to be based more on skill and prowess than on facial appearance. For women, physical beauty is a more important factor. Across societies there may be tremendous variation in what constitutes a sexually attractive person; that is, what is considered by one society to be a desirable characteristic, such as slimness, may be considered repulsive to members of other cultures. For example, in most cultures plump women are considered to be preferable to slim ones. In old Hawaii, for instance, what we in North America classify as extreme obesity in women and are taught to think of as negatively seductive, was considered to be highly erotic. In a few cultures breasts are an important criterion of sexual attractiveness—sometimes small upright ones are preferred while at other times and places the most desirable form is long and pendulous. Sometimes and in some places people make themselves sexually attractive by intentionally deforming their ears, noses, or lips. Personal cleanliness and youthfulness are widely considered as adding to a person's attractiveness.

Behaviour That is Sexualized and Arousing

The types of behaviour which are sexualized also vary markedly from one society to the next. Conduct which is considered to be either lewd or highly erotic in one society may be totally unrelated to sexuality in another. For example, in some cultures offering food to another person may be an act charged with sexual meaning. Only married couples or lovers may eat in each other's presence. All other men and women must carefully avoid the sight of each other when they eat (Davenport, 1977; 1965). Everywhere, the sight of the sex organ is considered to have the potential for arousing sexual desire; yet, in many cultures, complete nakedness is experienced as anti-erotic. In many societies, kissing or some variant as the "oceanic kiss," is used to arouse sex partners. The oceanic kiss consists of gently touching cheek to cheek or nose to nose while at the same time inhaling deeply so as to sense the other's odour. Among the peoples of Oceania it is an invariable component of the sexual embrace—they consider the European way of kissing disgusting (Davenport, 1977).

While both manual and oral stimulation of a partner's genitals is widely practiced, it is taboo in a few cultures such as the Tikopia and the Wageo. Behaviours such as biting, scratching, hair-pulling, or otherwise causing pain are prescribed ways to express and enhance sexual excitement in other societies.

Responses to Arousal

Just as there are variations in scripted ways of expressing sexual arousal, there are also variations in the associated scripted emotions. For example, among the Gusii of southwestern Kenya, sexual arousal occurs only in conjunction with feelings of antagonism and hostility. The sex roles enjoin men to be virile and demanding while women are expected to resist excessive male demands. Consequently, coitus between husband and wife is viewed as an act in which men affirm their masculinity by overcoming women's resistance, inflicting physical pain, and possibly humiliation. Women are expected to frustrate men physically and, at the same time, deride their sexual abilities. Men admit to heightened sexual gratification during intercourse when their partners cry and protest. Normal intercourse becomes a kind of ritualized rape (Davenport, 1977). At the other end of the sex role continuum, the men of New Britain Island—a territory of New Guinea—associate the sex act with fear; they are the ones who worry about being raped (Rubin, 1975). Manus women do not associate sexual arousal with either hostility and antagonism or fear, but they do associate it with deep feelings of disgust (Davenport, 1977). Adolescent males in North American society tend to associate coitus with feelings of achievement and conquest, whereas females associate it with feelings of solidarity (Udry, 1971).

The Where and When of Sexuality

To this point, we have emphasized the what and, in some measure, the why of sexual interaction. However, the *where* and *when* are also important parts of sexual scripts. The same location may be prescribed by some and proscribed by other cultural groups for coitus. Consider the case of two tribes who live in New Guinea; one views coitus as unclean and prohibits it in gardens for fear it will blight the crops, while the other prescribes the garden as a favoured location in the belief that it will stimulate plant growth (Friedl, 1975). In a wide variety of cultures people prefer a private location for sexual intercourse. North American society ranks high on this dimension. Not only do parents tend to have separate sleeping quarters (master bedroom), but the room is likely to have a lock. In affluent societies such as ours we can afford to create suitable private areas indoors, so that is where most acts of coitus occur. In societies where private places are not available, couples frequently meet during the night and use the cover of darkness to create whatever privacy they can. For example, in many villages in northern India men and women occupy separate sleeping quarters. A man who wishes to have coitus with his wife gets up during the night and goes to the women's quarters where they engage in coitus in the presence of many other sleeping women and children. The North American Crow and Kwakiutl Indians consider the only proper time for coitus is night with its accompanying darkness. Conversely, Yap society expresses a strong preference for coitus only during daylight hours, while the Chenchu of India believe that children conceived in the dark will be blind.

There are widespread limitations on when it is permissible for people to engage in coitus. Many cultures prohibit coitus during menstruation, pregnancy, or prior to the weaning of infants. Orthodox Jews proscribe coitus dur-

ing menstruation and for seven days thereafter. Some other groups prohibit acts of coitus up to 260 days out of the year. Throughout the world, some period of postpartum sexual abstinence is common; amongst the Dani of New Guinea the time of abstinence is four or more years, while it has been reported that the Cheyenne Indians of North America abstained from intercourse for as long as ten years (Heider, 1970). In some cultures it is the norm that anyone who is ill must refrain from coitus; this proscription may also extend to all of the sick person's relatives.

The polygamous form of marriage presents additional complications in terms of scheduling coitus. For example, among the Siriono of eastern Bolivia, a dutiful husband, in order to prevent conflict, follows a rotating schedule and makes himself sexually available to each wife in turn. This rotation system is not just a matter of tact on his part; the rights of his wives are often supported by local law. These practices also exist in other cultures. For example, in Madagascar, if a husband spends a day with one wife which rightfully "belongs" to another wife, it is legally defined as adultery and the injured wife can demand a divorce and alimony (Barnouw, 1982).

Frequency of Coitus: The Case of Three Societies

Beyond the who, what, why, where, and when of sexual behaviour, there are also scripted variations in how frequently couples in different societies engage in coitus. Variations are a consequence of the degree to which a society values sexual pleasure, culturally elaborates the sexual dimension, and provides its members with opportunities to learn about and become interested and active in sex. It is possible to represent these variations on a continuum ranging from very high to very low, and to discuss them using three societies as illustrations.

The Mangaians

At the extreme high end of the continuum are the Mangaians of the Cook Islands in the South Pacific Ocean. Here sexuality is viewed in a positive manner, and both sexes are encouraged to engage in frequent intercourse. For example, just as in Arab society where camels form an important component of daily life and so there are many words to describe their various forms and uses, so also in Mangaia there is a variety of words to describe coitus, the sexual organs, and sexual activities. The term for orgasm is the same as that for the achievement of perfection, pleasure, and comfort (Marshall, 1972: 26). Young Mangaians of both sexes are encouraged to show an early interest in sex. Up until about ten years of age, both sexes engage in regular masturbation. At this point boys undergo superincision, symbolizing manhood. Soon after, the young males are introduced into sexual intercourse by older women who teach them coital techniques, cunnilingus, and how to bring a girl to orgasm several times before they have their own. As Marshall (1972: 24) states: "Managaians say that a woman must 'learn' orgasm and that 'the good man' teaches her to have it." It appears as if the process is successful, because there is no word in their language to describe frigidity. While it is assumed that sexuality is a stronger drive in males, women are still expected to be eager and active partners.

The adolescent "subculture" of the Mangaians also encourages frequent sexual expression. In their lives, the sexual dimension is highly salient and free of emotional entanglements so that "a flick of the eye, a raised eyebrow in a crowd, can lead to copulation—without a word. There is no social contact between the sexes, no rendezvous, that does not lead to coitus—copulation is the only imaginable outcome of heterosexual contact" (Marshall, 1972: 23). Males are greatly concerned as to how they are evaluated by their partners. The focus of the concern is on ensuring "that the female will pass along his 'good' name" (Marshall, 1972: 24). Boys compete with their rivals to see how many orgasms they can achieve.

The Mangaian cultural emphasis on sexual expression extends into adulthood. Consequently, the frequency of sexual intercourse between husbands and wives is extremely high. Males are expected to reach orgasm at least once each night and their partners expect each episode to last at least fifteen minutes. Marshall's (1972: 29) informants reached consensus on the probable frequency of orgasms for males aged eighteen to forty eight years: for the group aged approximately eighteen to twenty-eight years, the average number of orgasms per night was three, and the average number of nights per week was seven. Corresponding rates for males twenty-eight to thirty-eight were two orgasms, on average, per night for approximately five to six nights per week. The rates for males aged thirty-eight and over declined to once per night approximately three to four times a week and eventually to two to three times a week. In essence, then, Mangaian society certainly ranks very high in terms of the value placed on sexual pleasure, its cultural elaboration of the sexual dimension, and provisions for its members to learn about and become active in sexual affairs.

India

Indian society ranks as less sexually oriented and is the one chosen to represent a more moderate variation in the dimensions listed above. Westerners often assume, on the basis of some of the ancient elaborate Kama-Sutra sex manuals, erotic temple sculptures, and the high level of fertility and population growth, that Indian society is highly sexually oriented. However, one way in which we can understand their considerably more moderate attitude toward sexual activity is to consider the mean coital frequency per week of married women. Maximum coital frequency for Indians occurs in the twenty to twenty-nine year age group who average approximately two to two and one half times per week (Nag, 1972: 235). Not only are figures for Indian women much lower than for women in Mangaian society, they are also lower than for North American women as we shall see later in this chapter.

The question we must address is why these variations occur and why there are also variations between Hindu and Muslim groups within India. Hindu rates are lower than corresponding rates for the Muslim population. Among Hindus there is a widespread belief that semen is a source of strength and should not be squandered:

> Everyone knew that semen was not easily formed; it takes forty days, and forty drops of blood, to make one drop of semen...Everyone was agreed on one point, that the semen is ultimately stored in a reservoir in the head, whose capacity is twenty *tolas* (6.8 ounces).... Celibacy was the first requirement of true fitness, because every sexual orgasm meant the loss of a quantity of semen, laboriously formed (Carstairs, 1967; quoted in Nag, 1972: 235).

Hindu men often complain of general weakness, believing they have lost too much semen and consequently suffer from *jiryan* (spermatorrhoea). This concept also exists in milder form among Muslim men. It is reasonable to suggest that the belief in the possibility of spermatorrhoea serves to dampen sexual appetites. In Hindu scriptures and philosophy, sexuality is not considered sinful, but moderation is emphasized as a part of moral virtue, and popular leaders such as Ghandi tried to uphold the ideal that the only purpose for coitus is procreation. One possible reason for a higher rate of sexual activity among Muslims lies in their belief that the pleasures of the flesh are god-given and therefore meant to be enjoyed. As Nag (1972: 236) states: "The lack of stress on moderation of sex in Islam is perhaps the reason for the higher frequency of coitus among the Moslems than among the Hindus." On the other hand, Mangaian males have no concern about spermatorrhoea and go beyond both Hindus and Muslims in placing a value on the pleasures of the flesh. Mangaian males are also expected to demonstrate, through frequent intercourse, the limits of their virility.

Another factor which moderates rates of coitus among Muslim and Hindu men is a relative lack of privacy. Unlike Mangaians, Indians do not indulge in coitus outside of their houses; many live in extended family networks and, as we noted earlier, husband and wives may well sleep in separate quarters. This situation tends to exert a moderating influence on Indian coital frequency rates. Differential organization of sex roles in the sexual domain may also contribute to the lower rates of coital frequency among Indians. Indian women are expected to be passive in sexual relationships and to engage in coitus mainly for the pleasure of the man (Nag, 1972). A passive orientation is not conducive to achieving sexual pleasure or, by implication, to encouraging pleasure in a partner. By contrast, in Mangaia, both men and women are expected to be sexually active, and they are provided with almost unlimited opportunities to do so.

Dugan Dani

On the extreme low end of the coital frequency continuum are the Dugan Dani, a Papuan culture in the highlands of West New Guinea. Here sexuality, as a cultural pattern, is minimally elaborated. Unlike the situation in Mangaia, in Dani language, coitus is not given a disproportionate number of names nor does it play a vital role in the lives and identities of the people. While the Dani do not believe, as do Hindus, that coitus is dangerous or that it might weaken men physically or spiritually, they are, in the words of their ethnographer, "genuinely casual and unconcerned about sex" (Heider, 1970: 75). Heider does not provide quantitative data but indicates the frequency of coitus is unusually low. Premarital sexuality is minimal, even though weddings in Dani society take place only every four to five years. Few children are born out of wedlock or "prematurely." Even after marriage, one indicator of the Dani's low coital frequency rate is the low birth rate. Dani couples are also expected to observe an "extra-ordinarily long period of sexual abstinence after the birth of a child...about four to six years" (Heider, 1970: 74). It appears that the ideal is adhered to, because family genealogies consistently show that children are spaced five or more years apart.

This somewhat casual, almost unconcerned Dani orientation toward sex is contrary to Freud's drive model of sexuality. Freud's model would suggest that theoretically such low coital frequency rates would be possible only in the presence of an extremely strong control system. However, Heider (1970: 75) addresses the issue by stating that "with the Dani not only is there no apparent legal mechanism but there seems to be neither concern not anxiety about it [sex]." He concludes "the observations of the anthropologist come into direct conflict with the assumption of a basic human sexual drive." Since the sexual dimension is not socially and culturally elaborated—either positively, as in Mangaia, or somewhat negatively, as among the Hindus—if Heider's evidence is reliable, the social script model would indicate that sexuality does not play a great role in the life of the Dani. The script model dictates that if sex is not considered a major concern at the socio-cultural level, little will be made of it at the personality level.

Learning Sexual Scripts in North American Society

For our characterization of North American society, we rely on the Kinsey surveys (1948; 1953), as well as the more recent national surveys of Westoff (1974) and Hunt (1974). Before we examine the sexual frequency rates more closely, we must lay the groundwork by detailing how males and females in North America learn the sexual scripts that govern sexual behaviour in marriage.

The acquisition of a sexual culture, the learning to become sexual, is pivotal to the sociological model of sexuality. In our society there are marked differences between male and female patterns of sexuality. Women are biologically equipped to have multiple orgasms (Masters and Johnson, 1970) and so could potentially derive more pleasure than men from coitus. However, men think and talk more than do women about sexuality, men experience more orgasms per sexual episode, per month, per whatever measure. This difference plays a vital role in North American marital sexuality and so needs to be explained.

To understand why the sexes differ so greatly, we rely extensively on Gagnon and Simon's (1973) discussion of the social script model and, where appropriate, we draw comparisons to the biological model of sexuality.

In the course of the discussion we attempt to elucidate both models and, at the same time, provide a theoretical foundation to understand marital sexuality in North American society.

Freud's drive model closely links the concepts of sex and gender and views sex as the major determinant of gender. The social script model strongly differentiates sex from gender and views gender as the major factor structuring behaviour. Sex becomes but one manifestation of the more basic processes of gender role learning. Sex is ascribed on the basis of biology; it refers to being born as recognizably either male or female. On the other hand, gender is something that is achieved and refers to our learning of societal conceptions of masculinity and femininity. In other words, gender becomes linked to the body (sex) through socially learned meanings. In terms of sexual functioning, even though the body is associated with an undefined capacity for arousal, we must learn the sexual scripts and then tie them to bodily sensations before we can meaningfully experience sexual sensations. The discussion which follows is an attempt to detail the process of gender role learning and its implications for male and female patterns of sexuality.

While newborn male and female infants have very similar characteristics, our society differentiates male from female behaviour very early in life. Little boys soon learn that to be masculine means that they are to value achievement. Increasingly they find that they are valued for what they do, or potentially can do, whereas girls are more likely to be appreciated for being pretty or just being there. Since femininity is something girls already have, they, unlike boys, do not have to eliminate previously acquired behaviours. As boys make the transition to a non-familiar role, they segregate themselves from girls and disavow their links to the past. The emerging male peer group calls for its members to repudiate girls as playmates and to scorn their activities. Many aggressive acts against girls during the elementary school years can be understood in terms of peer group norms. Here boys are provided with the opportunity to reinforce their emerging sense of masculinity and to demonstrate their distance from girlish things (Udry, 1971).

One well-documented difference between male and female peer groups is the value boys place on learning a "forbidden" sexual vocabulary—the type found on lavatory walls—which, in turn, allows them to trade bits of sexual information. One way to achieve status is to be "knowledgeable" in the sexual domain. Most boys learn about masturbation from other boys. They may even engage in group masturbation contests ("circle jerk") to see who can "come" the fastest. Sexually oriented behaviour becomes, especially for working-class boys, a device for confirming one's status among other males. By age twelve, 21% of males have masturbated as compared to about 12% of females (Kinsey, 1953). Hunt (1974) notes that the rates for young adolescent males were approximately 66% as compared to approximately 33⅓% for females. Among females, there is little talk about masturbation so that those who do engage have tended to make the discovery on their own, and the experience is often unconnected with their behaviour in other domains. A relative lack of development of the sexual dimension in the female preadolescent world leads to their being less interested than boys in things sexual. According to the social script model, this occurs not because of "repression of some biologically based pre-existent sexuality but because sexuality is not valued in their social world and few opportunities are available to learn how to be sexual. Preadolescent males, on the other hand, are socially encouraged to develop a sex drive, but it remains a sex drive and not a heterosexual drive" (Udry, 1971: 98).

Male adolescence is associated with an increased involvement with sexuality and an increasingly heterosexual focus. By age 15, 85% of males are masturbating as compared to 10% of females (Kinsey, 1953). More recent surveys show some increase in rates for females, but the difference between males and females continues to be great (Gagnon and Simon, 1973). For males, adolescence brings a change in the mental component associated with masturbation. While at earlier ages it was a purely physical experience detached from any image, with adolescence, fantasies about the opposite sex increasingly become part of the masturbation experience. This greater increase in sexual activity for males, as compared to females, can be accounted for in terms of the interaction between hormonal and anatomical factors, and socio-cultural demands.

In humans, sex hormones do not influence sexual expression directly; their effects are mediated by the interpretations and meanings we attribute to their manifestations. In males, more of their attention is drawn to their genitals during puberty because their increased hormonal activity results in frequent erections even when they are not thinking sexual thoughts. At the same time, the social demands for achievement, aggressiveness, and potency we associate with the masculine role also encourage experimentation. The result is high sexual activity. On the other hand, even though females also experience hormonal changes, both their subcultural environment and, it might be argued, their anatomy make it easier for them to ignore their genitals and the sexually related effects of their hormones. In the female adolescent subculture, genital-related talk is not as pervasive as it is among males. As a consequence, females are provided with less of an opportunity to learn about the physical signs of sexual arousal. Even today, many young women still refer to the genital area as "down there." Males, conversely, have many words—none of which are vague—to refer to their genitals. Furthermore, female genital anatomy makes it more likely that signs of sexual arousal will either escape attention or be misinterpreted. In males, erections are obvious and more easily interpretable as signs of sexual arousal. What we are attempting to say, then, is that differential male and female involvement in masturbation is mainly due to our ability to learn the signs of sexual arousal and the fact that subcultural worlds vary in the emphasis they place on sexual expression. According to Gagnon and Simon (1973), differential involvement with masturbation plays a vital role in the development of the different sexual natures of men and women.

Puberty is a biological phase; adolescence, on the other hand, is a social status. It is during adolescence that our society acknowledges for the first time that young people have a sexual capacity and that they are expected to direct it toward the opposite sex. However, it is not a universal dictate that this sexual capacity be undividedly directed towards the opposite sex. For example, among adolescents in East Bay, in the South Pacific, the sexual script dictates that unmarried adolescent males focus their sexual attentions on other males. Homosexuality is encouraged until marriage. After marriage, the script dictates that they be exclusively heterosexual (Davenport, 1977).

In our society, the dating process, which occurs at adolescence, serves to introduce males and females to each other's world view and to reinforce earlier learned attitudes towards sexuality. Young males pursue young females, but the significant audience is other males. What is critical in the male world view is not so much affection or romantic meanings but rather the utilitarian, predatory, "body centered" aspects of dating as a means to confirm their status among their peers. For females, as for males, there are many continuities between the worlds of childhood and adolescence. The female world view and its emphasis in our society of furthering the reality of marriage, of becoming wives and mothers, leads them to enter the dating process and marriage with a "person centered" or sex-with-affection approach to sexuality (Reiss, 1980).

In dating, males and females learn not only each other's world view but also the societal script for sexual arousal. The script moves from "hugging and kissing, to petting above the waist, to hand-genital contacts (sometimes mouth-genital contacts) and finally to coitus" (Gagnon and Simon, 1973: 22). However, our arousal stems from the learned meanings we attach to the sights, sounds, and sensations of the sexual process rather than from the process itself. For example, during medical examinations, females breasts and genitals are often touched and manipulated without any accom-panying arousal because we do not define the situation as sexual. Similarly, there is nothing inherent in kissing that produces arousal. Prior to adolescence, males view it as a "sissified" form of action, while females may view it as desirable but not necessarily sexual. Over time, both sexes learn to define these behaviours as sexual and mentally to connect inner body stirrings to the scripted sequences of outer actions to produce joint feelings of sexual arousal. Likewise, to a large extent, we learn which parts of the body are erogenous.

For mutually satisfactory sexual relations in marriage, couples must learn to synchronize their rates of arousal. Since women are exposed to fewer learning opportunities, their bodies may be so vaguely eroticized that when they first engage in the socially scripted sequence of petting behaviours the inner stirrings they become aware of may be misread as signs of an "imminent bowel movement" (Gagnon and Simon, 1973: 74). Males, on the other hand, have much more intense exposure to a sexual culture and often initially face the problem of "over-eroticization" which leads to premature climax.

MARITAL SEXUAL BEHAVIOUR IN NORTH AMERICAN SOCIETY

Kinsey's Studies: Sexual Scripts at Mid-Century

Freud made the study of sexuality a legitimate area of scientific psychological investigation. His in-depth studies of the sexual lives of individuals are penetrating and insightful, but they do not tell us much about the sexual lives of communities and how their behaviour relates to the larger structures of society, like education, religious affiliation, or social class. Kinsey, more than anyone else, established an empirically oriented sociological approach to the study of human sexual behaviour.

Kinsey's information is based on large sample sizes—5,300 white males and later 5,940 white females. The interview techniques of Kinsey and his associates have been widely praised. Language was modified to suit the level of the respondents; the interviews moved briskly; and, sensitive questions were inserted at the point interviewers felt the mood was optimal to elicit a valid response. However, his sampling methods are inadequate and his respondents are not representative. There is a disproportionate number of mid-westerners and prison inmates, while blacks, rural residents, and the poorly educated are underrepresented. Since all of his subjects were volunteers, the data may reflect a sexually liberal bias. Despite these shortcomings, the "Kinsey data remain today the fullest and most reliable sampling of human sexual behaviour" (Brecher, 1971: 112). They marked a new era in the systematic study of sexual behavior and provide a valuable historical benchmark to which more recent large-scale studies, such as those by Westoff (1974) and Hunt (1974), can be compared. One inadequacy of large-scale surveys is that they focus almost exclusively on what people say they do; they leave out the meanings people attribute to their actions and the manner in which these actions are connected to the rest of their lives.

Given the generally greater emphasis on sexuality by males, it is not surprising to find that, before marriage, they experience orgasm approximately six times more frequently than do females (Kinsey, 1953). Since females are socialized to associate sex with affection, we would expect marriage to make a greater difference in their sexual lives than in the sexual lives of males. This is very much the case. Marriage increases female orgasmic rate by 560% while the corresponding rate for males is 63% (Kinsey, 1953).

Marriage not only legitimates sexuality but encourages its expression. Consequently, married people engage in more sexual intercourse than unmarried people at all points in the life cycle (Kinsey, 1953). Perhaps the most striking conclusion to be derived from the data is a decline in frequency of coitus by age. Married couples in their teenage years engage in coitus at a median frequency of about three times per week; during their twenties, two to three times a week; in their thirties almost two times a week; and in their forties about once a week.

Earlier in this chapter we noted a similar pattern of declining coital rates among the Mangaians and the Indians. While, at first, these similarities across cultures might suggest a biological basis for the decline in sexual activity, a recent study by Adams and Turner (1985) shows that some men and a substantial minority of women actually experience more intense sexual lives at older ages than they did when they were younger. The decline Kinsey notes is also too early in life to be attributed to biological causes. Masters and Johnson (1970) indicate the biological changes which might affect sexual interest often appear only when we reach our sixties.

A comparison of Mangaian and Indian rates of coitus with those of North America reveals the cultural factors associated with the decline in sexual activity through the life cycle. A forty-year-old male in Mangaian society engages in more acts of coitus than the average North American male half that age and supposedly at the peak of his sexual activity. In turn, the average forty-year-old North American male more than doubles the coital rate of his Hindu Indian counterpart. Since the variations in these rates cannot be attributed to biology because it is a constant, culture becomes the major explanatory variable. Social factors also play a role. In North American society, the frequency of coitus declines more rapidly among lower-class couples than among middle class ones (Kinsey, 1953). Gagnon and Simon (1973) explain the difference by indicating that after lower-class males have been married for several years, they no longer receive the same prestige they once did for engaging in more frequent coitus. Furthermore, they lack training in how to introduce imaginative ways to heighten sexual interest through romantic settings, erotic conversations, or erotic fantasies. As a consequence, their sexual appetites moderate over time, because the sheer novelty of coitus is extinguished and they lack ways of rekindling their interest.

More psychological factors also play a role in declining coital frequency over time. We noted in the earlier description of the social script model that potency is a vital component of masculine identity. For a husband who initiates a sexual encounter and then finds he is unable to achieve or maintain an erection sufficient for coitus, the result can be traumatic. One way to cope is to avoid starting something he may not be able to finish. Even though he may desire coitus more frequently, he exercises caution, and the result is a lower rate of sexual activity. As we noted earlier, physical attractiveness also plays an important role in sexual arousal. However, as couples age, they may pay less attention to their appearance; they may put on weight or allow their bodies to get out of shape. As a result they may feel they lack the energy necessary to complete the act. Whatever the reason for the decline in frequency of coitus for any particular couple, the cultural script prescribes a decline in sexual interaction over the years.

Another interesting regularity in coital frequency rates is a decline for those women born after the turn of the century. For example, 16–20-year-old wives born before 1900, engaged in coitus with an average frequency of 3.2 times per week; the rate drops to 2.6 for that age group of wives born between 1900–1909. This pattern is consistent for all age groups. One way to account for these changes is to look at the changing sexual scripts for women and men. Women born before 1900 lived under the influence of Victorian ideals. Only men were expected to be interested in sexual matters. Coitus was a husband's right and a wife's duty. After the turn of the century, however, women's rights slowly started to become an issue. Increasingly, husbands were expected to adjust their sexual appetites to fit their wife's expectations so that coitus could become more mutually enjoyable. But since women did not have the same opportunities as did men to learn to become sexual, the result of the "adjustment" was a decline in coital rates.

Although women born after 1900 engaged in coitus less frequently than those born before that date, a greater percentage of them experienced orgasm. Much of this change can be traced to a rise in the status of women. The societal change in gender expectations emerged gradually with the process of indus-

trialization and was accelerated by the two World Wars. During the process of industrialization, fathers left the home to go to work, and the result was a decline in patriarchy. Both adolescent males and females began to spend more time in educational institutions to prepare themselves for positions in the industrial economy. World War I brought a great influx of women in the work force. As more women entered the work force, it became increasingly apparent that there were ways in which they could exist independently of male economic support. Winning the right to vote in 1920 symbolized the giant strides Canadian women were making in the workplace and in education. One change directly pertinent to the change in sexual attitudes occurred in the area of women's fashions. Highly restrictive clothing, such as the whalebone corset, was discarded and replaced by the girdle which, in turn, has been largely replaced since the 1960s by pantyhose. During the 1920s the length of women's skirts moved from just a few inches off the ground to a height where the knee is exposed. Slacks, a further symbol of change in women's sex roles, also became an acceptable mode of dress. These changes and others like them led increasingly to a mixing of the sexes in work and educational settings. When combined with an increase in leisure time also made possible by industrialization, the ground was laid for the sexes to socialize each other to their world views on love and sexuality.

Women not only became more active in all public spheres of life, they also had greater opportunity to learn to become more interested and active in sexual matters. Thus, the increased rates of orgasm for those women born after 1900 and who entered marriage during the "roaring twenties" and thereafter, can be made sense of in terms of larger societal transformations.

In addition to these broad societal changes which influenced women's sexual scripts, it is also important to remember that much sexual learning occurs during marriage. Thus, as we might expect, rates of orgasm increase the longer a woman has been married. In contrast to other sexual indices of marriage which decline over time, this one actually increases.

While premarital coital rates (discussed in other chapters) are strongly influenced by social background factors such as education, religiosity and social class, such is not the case for marital coital rates. It seems as if the social relationship of marriage has such a powerful influence on coital rates, other social factors which might influence them are pushed to the background. However, we do know that the educational level of both partners is positively related to the wife's ability to achieve orgasm. Social class has a substantial effect on how coitus is carried out, how much time is spent in foreplay, and how much time is spent in coitus itself. For example, among couples with lower levels of education there are fewer preliminaries, less kissing, and less fondling. The fact that we live in a pluralistic sexual world becomes especially evident in the fact that what one social class considers "normal" another social class considers "perverted." Kinsey was fond of repeating a discussion he had with a campus policeman who had no more than an eighth grade education (classified as working class). The policeman complained that university students (classified middle class) were mostly "perverts." "They would lie under the trees in pairs and just pet and pet. Sexual intercourse the policeman could understand; but this interminable petting must be some form of perversion!" (Brecher, 1971: 106). Lower- and working-class partners are also more likely to prefer coitus in the dark, while middle and upper classes prefer some light in the room. Higher-class couples prefer more nudity than do lower-class couples; and both middle and upper classes were more likely than lower classes to have engaged in oral sex.

Recent Changes in Sexual Scripts

More than a generation has passed since the Kinsey studies were published. Our society continues to change in ways that suggest a continuation of the earlier changes in sexual scripts. Trends in premarital and marital sexual attitudes and behaviours which began in the 1920s, continued into the 1930s, and finally stabilized in the 1940s. They remained more or less constant for about twenty years and then changed suddenly again during the late 1960s and into the early 1970s. This latter period was a time of social upheaval in the United States, associated with an unpopular war abroad and widespread discontent among minority groups at home. The women's movement agitated for greater equality between women and men in the areas of sexual and social life. The result was a reduction in the old "double standard" of sexual behaviour. The proportion of women who experienced premarital sexual intercourse doubled, while, for men, the rates increased only slightly. Another result was that for the first time more than 50% of wives of working age were now involved in the labour force (Eichler, 1983).

Eroticization

Along with these changes in gender roles has come a greater societal acceptability of sexual feelings. Indeed, since the late 1960s, this general acceptance has blossomed into an "eroticization" of North American culture. In most circles, sexuality no longer needs to win grudging acceptance. The pendulum has swung so far the other way that it is now considered almost "unnatural" not to have a "sexual appetite" most of the time. As Petras (1973: 16) indicates, "sexuality has come to be defined as one of the few remaining individualizing experiences in mass society ... [it] represents one form of the search for intrinsic meanings and gratifications." An avalanche of magazines, books, and films speak to both men and women with an openness that would have offended public sensibilities only a few decades ago. David Ruben's (1969) *Everything You Always Wanted to Know About Sex—(but were afraid to ask)* and Alex Comfort's (1972) *The Joy of Sex* became best sellers.

The rise in the social status of women, the eroticization of the larger culture, and improvement in contraceptive methods would lead us to expect an increase in female sexual activity. Indeed, such seems to be the case. Contemporary marriages involve higher coital frequency rates than marriages of a generation ago. The changes are consistent for all age levels and for both sexes. While the median coital frequency rates per week for the youngest category (16–25 years) of wives during the 1940s was 2.45, it rose to 3.25 by 1972. During the same time period, the rates for the oldest category (56–60 years) of wives doubled from 0.5 to once a week (Hunt, 1974).

At first glance these changes appear dramatic, but it is wise to add a note of caution when interpreting Hunt's data. The rate of respondents refusing to participate is extremely high. More specifically, the information was collected from twenty-four urban areas chosen to represent the diversity of American cities. Random samples were chosen from telephone directories, and respondents were contacted by telephone. They were asked to participate anonymously in discussions about sexual behavior. Only about 20% of the respondents agreed to participate, which means that his conclusions do not include information from 80% of his projected sample size.

Changing Practices

Not only are married couples engaging in coitus more frequently than they were a generation ago, they are also engaging in sexual practices indicative of change in the role structure of sexual relations. Kinsey's studies showed that a generation ago, intercourse itself was quite perfunctory and circumspectly carried out within tight guidelines. Sexual scripts were imposed on and accepted by couples, and there was little room for personal interpretation or modification. Current evidence suggests that sexual scripts are loosening. They take on the character of general proposals for action, and there is considerable room for interpretation and exploration.

Hunt (1974: 195) states that a "dramatic and historic change" has occurred "not only are today's married Americans having intercourse more frequently, but they seem to be doing so more imaginatively, voluptuously, and playfully than their counterparts of a generation ago." This change is consistent with the transformation in the basis on which families are

held together. As Burgess, Locke, and Thomes (1963) indicate, "the family in historical times has been in transition from an institution with family behaviour controlled by mores, public opinion and law, to a companionship with family behaviour arising from mutual affection and consensus of its members." In essence, then, our discussion suggests that today coitus is less governed by institutional dictates and more by shared agreement between couples as to what is acceptable and pleasurable.

The increasingly open climate regarding sexual matters and the increased emphasis on women's equal participation in coitus have resulted in greater freedom and pleasure for both males and females. However these changes have also created some new tensions. Since roles are reciprocal, when the expectations for one actor change, there must be a corresponding change on the part of the other actor. In the case of coital relations in marriage, wives are now entitled to the pleasures of the act so husbands must take an active role in ensuring that these pleasures occur. However, these efforts may not always be viewed as positive, especially in the case of lower-class women. For example, Rubin (1976) found that many of her sample of married, lower-class women experienced their husband's concern with their achievement of orgasm as but another chore imposed on them in a life already filled with chores. As the following thirty-five-year-old women who works part time, takes care of the house, husband, six children, and an aging father, indicates:

> It feels like somebody's always wanting something from me. Either one of the kids is hanging on to me or my father needs something. And if it's not them, then Tom's always coming after me with that gleam in his eye. Then, it's not enough if I just let him have it, because if I don't have a climax, he's not happy. I get so tired of everybody wanting something from me all the time. I sometimes think I hate sex (Rubin, 1976: 151).

Some of these wives experienced the changing sexual conception of women as a form of oppression. They became preoccupied with achieving orgasm during coitus, not so much for themselves, but because they did not want to disappoint their husbands and especially to validate his sense of being a good "man and husband."

> I rarely have climaxes. But if it didn't bother my husband, it wouldn't bother me. I keep trying to tell him that I know it's not his fault, that he's really a good lover. I keep telling him it's something the matter with me, not with him (Rubin, 1976: 152).

The increased emphasis on achieving orgasm during coitus, as reflected in the larger society and particularly through the media, for these women becomes another standard they feel they must meet. They have little control over their own lives to begin with, and this new expectation imposed on them may be experienced as an ultimate form of encroachment. One exasperated woman, after she had read about women's capability to achieve multiple orgasms, wondered just what her husband would expect of her next:

> It's really important for him that I reach a climax, and I try to every time. He says it just doesn't make him feel good if I don't. But it's hard enough to do it once! What'll happen if he finds out about those women who have lots of climaxes (Rubin: 1976: 153).

An additional anxiety for these women comes from worrying about whether their husbands might prefer someone more responsive than they are. Rubin (1976), like Hunt, found that similar proportions of working-class and middle-class couples engaged in the same variety of precoital and coital techniques. However, in-depth interviews revealed considerably more reservations among working-class than middle-class wives about the appropriateness of such experimentation in sexual activities. Working-class wives also experienced more discomfort when they experimented with new techniques. Given the fact that sexuality has been defined as a masculine, "body centered," pursuit, it is not surprising that most lower-class husbands respond more favourably than do their wives to the changing sexual climate. These differences give rise to incompatible definitions of appropriate sexual scripts. As one working-class husband complained:

> I think sex should be that you enjoy each other's bodies. Judy doesn't care for touching and feeling each other though. She thinks there's just one right position and one right way—in the dark, with her eyes closed tight. Anything that varies from that makes her feel upset (Rubin, 1976: 136).

This couple clearly had a conflict over the "why" of sex (sex for pleasure), the "how" (only one right way), and the "where" (in the bedroom and in the dark).

The emergence of new erotic expectations does not mean that the old ones have completely disappeared. Even in marriage it is not always easy for spouses to free themselves from the standards they internalized as children. This is especially true when the two scripts and their incompatible expectations continue to exist in an uneasy relation to each other.

> The media tell us that the double standard of sexual morality is dead. But with good reason, women don't believe it. They know from experience that it is alive and well, that it exists side by side with the new ideology that heralds their liberation. They know all about who are the "bad girls" in school, in the neighbourhood; who are the good girls. Everybody knows! (Rubin, 1976: 136–137).

Wives know about these contradictory standards, and they experience a tension between "letting go" and being "sexy" or restraining themselves and being "proper." The tension remains, because even though husbands encourage them, these women sense that their husbands also share many of these ambivalent feelings about the elaboration of the sexual act. Much of the tension centres around oral sex, where the taboo has been strongest. One twenty-eight-year-old mother of three, married for ten years explains:

> I always feel like its not quite right, no matter what Pete says. I guess its not the way I was brought up, and its hard to get over that. He keeps telling me it's okay if it's between us, that anything we do is okay. But I'm not sure about that. How do I know in the end he won't think I'm cheap (Rubin,1976: 141).

Thus, at least for many working-class wives, the new sexual freedoms can be experienced as a mixed blessing and for some, a new kind of oppression.

There are some problems, even for middle-class wives who have not experienced such dramatic changes in sexual scripts. While Rubin (1976) found middle-class wives more relaxed and accepting in their attitudes toward sexuality, many felt guilty about their inability to overcome their inhibitions and live up to their own "liberal" standards. At the same time that working-class wives wished their husbands would be less solicitous, their middle-class counterparts were more likely to blame themselves for their inhibitions and worry about being neurotic.

The contradictions associated with the new sexual climate cannot all be explained by lingering Victorianism. Paradoxically, the very freedoms associated with the loosening of sexual scripts may have decreased some people's enjoyment of coitus by raising the standards for satisfaction. People who experience difficulties in meeting the new standards may find a relative lack of sexual desire to be a major problem. Contrary to Freud's drive model of sexuality, the loosening of sexual controls is not associated with an unleashing of wild and intense instinctual forces, but rather with feelings of relative deprivation. For example, Shaver and Freedman (1976) in their survey of young adults, found that more than one-half of the men and one-third of the women were dissatisfied with their own sexual lives and believed that other's sexual lives were better. For them, sexual satisfaction became the victim of a revolution of rising expectations.

One way in which some couples attempt to increase their sexual pleasure is to turn to sexual manuals for advice. Interestingly enough, Lewis and Brissett's (1967) analysis of these types of books suggests that instead of helping the readers enjoy sexual play more, they subtly transform coitus into a kind of work. Emphasis is on "studying" the "techniques," instructions relate to "production schedules," and coitus becomes an achievement, a "good" rather than a process of sexual expression, pleasure, and communication.

Coitus and the Quality of Marriage

Sexual adjustment is an important part of a couple's life-long relationship, but it is not synonymous with overall marital adjustment. It is possible for couples to be satisfied with their sexual life and yet not be happily married, just as the possibility exists for happy marriage to coexist with lower degrees of sexual satisfaction. While these possibilities do exist, researchers from Kinsey onwards have found an overall relationship between sexual adjustment and marital adjustment. Ard (1977) reports that the sexual component continues to be important even after twenty (or more) years of marriage. In her review of relevant literature, Nett (1988: 241) concludes, the view that "a good sex life (both the amount and quality) is central to a good overall relationship is fairly well substantiated."

Since the quality of coitus is becoming a more important part of married life and love, we would expect the relationship between love and sexuality to be getting stronger. Hunt's (1974) study lends support to this contention. He notes that marital coitus is 50% more frequent in emotionally close, as compared to emotionally distant, marriages. This finding represents quite a change from a generation ago. Terman (1938) found coital rates were only slightly higher among happily married than unhappily married couples. Hunt also notes that emotionally close couples find coitus more pleasurable than do emotionally distant couples. However, the relationship is much stronger for females than it is for males. Sixty-five percent of women in emotionally distant relationships experienced coitus as not pleasurable, as compared to forty-one percent of their male counterparts. Patton and Waring (1985: 181) also state that "the wife's degree of sexual fulfillment is more closely associated with her perception of marital intimacy." This information makes sense in terms of our earlier discussion which indicates that females are socialized to a "relationship" or "person centered" view of sexuality, whereas males are socialized to view it as "body centered." Because females more strongly equate coitus with love, if love is absent, then coitus has little basis for justification and is less likely to be pleasurable. On the other hand, since sexual potency is intricately bound to the notion of masculinity, males are more likely to engage in coitus and find it meaningful, even in the absence of emotional closeness. As Patton and Warring (1985: 181) state: "Husbands are more likely to see their sexual relationship as a separate component of their marital relationship."

The absolute frequency of coitus is not as important to marital adjustment as is the agreement of desired frequency between husband and wife. Although most marriages include coitus, some do not. A representative Canadian sample found that 4% of husbands did not have sexual relations with their wives (Report of the Committee on the Operation of the Abortion Law, 1977: 329). Blazer (1964) and Friedman (1962) carried out in-depth investigations as to why people remain "married virgins." Kinsey (1953) noted that in some marriages coitus occurred only once or twice a year, and yet the couple felt affection for each other and were considered "happily married"; they simply considered it to be an extremely unimportant area of their life together. As long as both partners have little or no interest in coitus, sexual adjustment may be almost perfect. Such cases, however, are very much the exception.

It is more often the case that couples must find some way to adjust to their differing levels of desire for coitus. The socialization patterns for males and females result in different expectations for frequency, especially in the early years of marriage. Hunt (1974) found approximately 80% of husbands desired more frequent coitus than they actually experienced. However this difference is in accordance with traditional sexual scripts and may result in less potential for conflict than if it were the woman who desired more frequent coitus. Emerging sexual scripts encourage women to be as sexual as men and have as much right to sexual fulfillment. Accordingly, some women will surpass their husbands in desire for coitus. Hunt found that about one-third of the wives in his sample desired more frequent sexual relations with their husbands. Not only do these women feel deprived, their husbands also come under pressure because sexual potency is closely linked to masculinity.

Extramarital Relations

As marital strain increases, the frequency of marital coitus tends to decline and "as the latter becomes more infrequent [due to marital dissatisfaction] the more likely is extramarital involvement to occur" (Edwards and Booth, 1976: 73). However Glass and Wright (1977), Edwards and Booth (1976), and Johnson (1970) found that the relationship between extramarital relations and dissatisfaction with marriage and coitus hold more strongly and consistently for males than for females. Generally, males are more likely than are females to be unfaithful to their spouses. Kinsey (1948, 1953) found that 26% of married women as compared to 50% of married men had engaged in extramarital intercourse; similarly, Hunt's (1974) figures were 18% and 41% respectively. Edwards and Booth study of Toronto couples found corresponding rates of 5% for married women and 22% for married men. These data on extramarital relations seem very compatible with and reinforce the female sexual script of our society which prescribes that love, marriage, and sex go together and ought not to be separated, whereas for males, the linkages in the sexual script are much looser.

With the present AIDS scare it is probable that the extent of marital infidelity will be considerably lessened. Where earlier, spouses may not have hesitated before engaging in extramarital relationships, they will probably now think twice—first, in fear of their own lives in the event that they may become infected and second, in fear of causing the infection of and possible death of their spouse.

SUMMARY

In this chapter we attempted to discuss cross-culturally the concept of sexuality and its relation to marriage. First, there is a discussion of the evolution of marriage as a regulator of sexuality. This was followed by a discussion of three models of sexuality; the biological model of Freud, the social script model suggested by Gagnon and Simon, and object-relations theory. Emphasis was placed on cross-cultural differences in learning cultural scripts. The what and why of sexuality were addressed in terms of standards of beauty; behaviour that is sexualized and arousing; and responses to arousal. The where and when of sexuality were described in terms of a continuum, and case studies of three societies were presented. This was followed by a section on learning sexual scripts in North American society and finally, a discussion of marital sexual behaviour in North America, along with some recent changes in sexual scripts.

TECHNICAL TERMS

COITUS—Refers exclusively and explicitly to the penetration by the male penis of the female vagina. It does not include other forms of sexual intercourse such as, for example, anal penetration.

GENDER—Is something that is achieved. It refers to our learning of societal conceptions of masculinity and femininity.

INCEST TABOO—A usually unspoken rule that universally prohibits at least immediate family members from having sexual relations with one another.

SEX—Is ascribed on the basis of biology. It refers to being born as recognizably either male or female.

SEXUALITY—Refers to the thoughts, feelings, and actions of humans who have learned a pattern of cues designed to evoke erotic arousal. We also learn the conditions in which these thoughts, feelings, and actions are appropriate.

DRIVE MODEL OF SEXUALITY—People are born with a strong sexual drive which is discharged, sublimated, or transformed into neurosis.

SOCIAL SCRIPT MODEL—People learn and internalize the cultural rules or scripts regulating the what, where, when, how and why of sexual matters. The content of sexuality is formed by culture.

LOOSE SCRIPTS—The cultural guidelines take on the character of general proposals for action; actors are given considerable leeway for interpretation and negotiation.

TIGHT SCRIPTS—The cultural guidelines are strictly imposed upon and more or less directly received by actors; there is little room for improvisation.

QUESTIONS

1. Compare the social script for sexuality of males and females. How have they changed over time?

2. Detail how the biological developments of the replacement of the oestrus cycle with the menstrual cycle, the narrowing of the female pelvis and the longer period of helplessness of the newborn human baby conspired to make the survival of the human infant and society as a whole problematic.

3. Compare the social script model of sexuality with the biological drive model.

4. What have been the major changes in marital sexuality since the time Kinsey carried out his studies?

Reverse: A wedding in Pakistan.

Chapter 11

PATTERNS OF MATE SELECTION

G. N. Ramu
University of Manitoba

The patterns of mate selection differ from one society to another, and these differences are based upon a given society's emphasis on individual freedom, romantic love, or maintenance of kinship and/or group identity among other considerations. For example, in North America, it is customary for a person to select his/her spouse through a more or less extended courtship process. Parents and kinship groups (where the latter exist) play a minor or relatively insignificant role in courtship. Consequently, mate selection in North America is based on "free choice." Both cultural and institutional mechanisms (e.g. dating) support, if not promote, personal freedom in matrimonial arrangements.

By contrast, "arranged marriages" are quite common in most non-Western societies. For example, in the Kolar Gold Field (KGF), a mining town in South India, the lower caste gold miners usually marry (or have a claim on) their mother's brother's daughter or father's sister's daughter (Ramu, 1977). Such "cross-cousin marriages" are not only preferred, but also encouraged as part of cultural expectations, in what has been termed a "preferential mating system." In the same town, the younger members of the trading community (*Marwaris*) not only expect their elders to choose spouses for them as a matter of course, but prefer that they do so. The bride and groom do not normally meet until the day of marriage and, in most cases, have not even seen pictures of one another. The family and kinship groups arrange marriage taking into account the status of the family of the prospective spouse,

dowry, personal characteristics, and other considerations (Ramu, 1973).

In another Asian society, Japan, instead of parents, experienced matchmakers, the *nakodo*, arrange the majority of marriages at the request of parents of the prospective brides and grooms (Blood, 1967). These matchmakers are often friends and relatives, or even supervisors at work. The matchmakers are usually rewarded, and such rewards are calculated as a proportion of the total expenses of the marriage. They normally investigate the qualifications (for example, socio-economic position, lineage, health of potential spouses, and other cultural attributes specific to Japanese society) of both families before establishing the suitability of the alliance.

Apart from individuals, as in North America, parents, as in India, and professional matchmakers, as in Japan, various commercial agencies such as computer and video dating services, and newspapers and magazines (classified advertisements) offer methods of selecting partners in a number of societies. For example, Wiebe and Ramu (1971) note that matrimonial advertisements in English language newspapers in India are used as means of seeking alliances. Similar practices prevail in the United States (Jedlicka, 1980; Bhargava, 1988) and Israel (Peres and Meivar, 1986). However, use of mass media for the selection of one's future partner is a minority practice in most societies.

Not all traditional societies subscribe to arranged marriages. In some societies, individuals, especially men, take the initiative in establishing premarital relationships. Among the Tepoztlan in Mexico, a love letter, written by the young man (or written on his behalf by others, if the young man is illiterate) to a young woman he is interested in marrying, begins the courtship process (Stephens, 1963: 188). When the girl receives the letter and responds favourably, a meeting is arranged between them. If she refuses to respond, then the young man will have to start all over again with someone else.

Similarly, courtship among the Ibans of Borneo Island is also initiated by young men. A young man who is interested in a young woman enters her house during the night when everyone is asleep. He wakes her up and offers her a roll of betel nut ingredients wrapped in a leaf. If she accepts the roll and chews it, it is understood that the young man's visit is acceptable, and he may stay and speak to her. But instead, if she beckons him to light the lamp, it is an indication that she has refused the offer, and the young man should exit. Following weeks of such nightly visits, and if the parents of the girl consider the match acceptable, the nightly courtship continues until the couple are formally united. It should be noted that the couple normally do not engage in sexual relations during their nightly meetings, for it is deemed immoral to do so, and the girl will earn a bad reputation. This would reduce her chances of getting a good husband (Stephens, 1963: 189–190). Although the young men take the initiative in courtship matters, the approval of parents and other kin is essential for their marriage.

Why do some groups, such as the *Marwaris*, arrange marriages of their children and others, such as those in North America, appear to be somewhat indifferent to their children's marital choices? How can such cross-cultural differences be explained sociologically? What are the implications of such diverse practices for family systems and wider social organization? The following discussion attempts to address these questions.

MATE SELECTION AND SOCIAL ORDER

In the vast majority of societies, whether Western or non-Western, various groups strive to preserve their distinctive social and cultural attributes, and such efforts eventually lead to a diverse social order. Thus the *Marwaris* in the Kolar Gold Fields in South India strenuously attempt to retain their religious, linguistic, caste, and economic status, just as the Hutterites in western Canada or the Amish in the United States seek to retain their ethnic and religious identity. The preservation of distinct identity depends not only on the desire on the part of a given group, but also on the development of appropriate institutionalized mechanisms, i.e. patterned practices and a normative structure. One critical area for implementing cultural integrity (whether in society as a whole or in sub-groups, including class) is mate selection and the degree of control over the choice of partners by younger members. Whether strictly or loosely regulated, some form of control is evident in virtually all societies, regardless of their level of technological development. For example, Stephens (1963: 198) found that in 33 of the 39 societies surveyed, extended family or kinship groups played a key role in controlling marriage markets, and choice was based on the aforementioned criteria. Even in societies where parents or kinship groups do not arrange marriages, individuals themselves show their concern for the maintenance of socio-economic status by choosing as partners only those who have characteristics comparable to their own. This tendency among those with similar social characteristics to marry has been termed *endogamy,* from the Greek roots *endo* (within) and *gamos* (marriage). The term endogamy refers to conformity to the rule that a person marry someone with similar salient social characteristics which, depending on specific situations, might include race, religion, ethnicity, and social class. Besides endogamy, other important considerations in the selection of one's partner include personal and socio-psychological attributes. The term *heterogamy* refers to marriage outside one's racial, ethnic, or religious group. Various forces, including individualism, secularism, and geographic mobility, have contributed to the tendency among some individuals to marry outside the group.

Endogamy exists in varying degrees in almost all societies. For example, in North America, race, ethnicity, and social class, among other factors, play crucial roles in mate selection. In another part of the world (Hindu India), caste continues to be an important basis of social organization, and informal attempts to preserve it include control of mate selection and caste endogamy, with inter-caste marriages being an exception rather than typical. Marriage between kin, such as cross-cousin marriages, or within one's caste and subcaste are arranged by parents or marriage brokers. When a desired match cannot be arranged by these means, parents advertise for a suitable bride/groom in newspapers. The most frequently stipulated condition in such classified matrimonial advertisements is the caste or subcaste (*jati*) of the prospective candidates (Wiebe and Ramu, 1971).

Societies or sub-groups which stress endogamy as a means of maintaining their integrity are likely to de-emphasize romantic love and choice in favour of arranged marriages (Goode, 1959). This is because these societies believe that free choice based on personal motives, such as love, can be potentially disruptive of the social organization and especially social stratification. "Kinfolk or immediate family can disregard the question of who marries whom, only if marriage is not seen as a link between lines, only if no property, power, lineage, honour, totemic relations and the like are believed to flow from kin lines through the spouses to their offspring" (Goode, 1959: 42).

By contrast, in Western societies, love is actually encouraged and is a commonly expected element in mate choice. In these societies, the cultural imperative is that one is free to fall in love with a person of his/her choice, and it is a widely held belief that it is "…mildly shameful to marry without being in love with one's intended spouse" (Goode, 1959: 41). Besides romantic love, numerous personal considerations such as companionship, communi-

cation, sexual adjustment, common values, and aspirations determine the choice of one's mate. It is because individuals retain freedom in these spheres that the western mate selection system is perceived as based on "free choice." Ideally, freedom in the choice of one's partner encourages the homogenization of socially and culturally divergent groups. But there are some limitations in this respect that should be noted.

In North America, a combination of free choice and restrictiveness prevails and affects the successive phases of one's selection of a marital partner. Since marriages are not arranged by elders or kinship groups, virtually any single person of appropriate age is a potential mate. However, the process of selection is not as random as it appears, because the "universe" from which the partners are drawn is generally limited with respect to small clusters of people in school, work, or neighbourhood. As Goode (1982: 54) notes in his discussion of social selection in the North American marriage system,

> Since the marriageable population in the United States (and increasingly as well in other countries) is gradually segregated into pools of eligibles with similar social class backgrounds, even a free dating pattern with some encouragement to fall in love does not threaten the stratification system: That is, people fall in love with the "right" kind of people.

The degree to which one conforms to the norms of endogamy depends on the size of the pool of eligible mates and the social setting in which the selection occurs. If the pool is large, one can be more selective, and thus criteria used in selection are likely to be somewhat stringent. In contrast, under conditions of scarcity, e.g. not enough males or females, few beautiful or accomplished people, etc., individuals tend to be somewhat flexible and less demanding. The social setting is equally important because it provides differential opportunities for meeting prospective spouses. For example, in a study of 1800 persons in Philadelphia, Erickson (1981) found that about a quarter of respondents had met their future partners in stores, buses, restaurants, and even in elevators. The rest had married those they knew from their school days, at work, or in the neighbourhood. What Erickson's study highlights is that even impersonal or transient urban settings (buses, elevators, etc.) provide opportunities for one to meet a prospective mate.

It would be incorrect, however, to infer that the selective marriage market in North America is consciously developed, as it is, for example, among certain groups in India. Rather, it is basically a concomitant of social structure and residential patterns. In most cases, individuals are not aware of the constraints that influence their choice, mainly because mate selection is a long process (about eight to ten years of dating and courtship) that involves several partners. Consequently, although mate selection in North America is formally free, it is affected by impersonal forces, and this is evident from the general tendency toward endogamy.

PROCESSES OF MATE SELECTION IN NORTH AMERICA

Historical Patterns in Mate Selection

Although dating, romantic love, and premarital sexual relations have emerged as the key elements of mate selection in contemporary North America, historical information suggests that some form of arranged marriages were prevalent in the seventeenth and eighteenth centuries. Demographic considerations, as well as strict cultural rules, often dictated the nature of mate selection in colonial and rural North America in the seventeenth and eighteenth centuries. For example, the French immigrants to New France (Quebec) in the early years of settlement were overwhelmingly males and experienced a shortage of brides. Some cohabited with Native women and others had to "import" brides from France. Upon the request of French subjects in New France, the King of France persuaded some 1,000 eligible women to migrate to New France and offered them lavish gifts and incentives (Elkin, 1964). In a marriage market where

the demand far exceeded the supply, there appeared to be little scope for dating and courtship. People tended to marry whoever was available despite the fact that parents and kin (especially the upper strata) tried to exert control over the marriage of their children. The question was often not whom one would marry, but whether one would marry at all.

Among the entrepreneurs in New England, and in other parts of the US, marriage alliances were quite often entered into for business reasons (Farber, 1972; Hall, 1978; Marcus, 1980). Marriage involving two wealthy families meant the pooling of capital, maximization of profit, and the production of heirs. Such practices reveal not only the endogamous nature of marriage and family control of mate selection, but also the absence of a courtship system in which prospective spouses are key decision-makers. Furthermore, some ethnic groups, such as the East European Jews in the early 1900s, employed "match-makers" to find suitable partners for their children (Hurvitz, 1975), a practice which prevails among some groups in New York even today.

While parents exercised some influence over the mate selection process in colonial America, it was seldom an institutionalized function of either the extended family or kinship system, mainly because these were uncommon. Unlike the French-Canadians (Garigue, 1956; Piddington, 1976), the American immigrants did not attempt to institutionalize the extended family and kinship systems. Consequently, if parents participated in the mate selection process, it was mainly because the opportunities for eligible persons to make their own choices were limited.

The forerunner of contemporary dating was "bundling," practiced by many during the frontier years. This practice entailed permission given to courting couples to share a bed for the night on the condition that they remained fully clothed, bundled themselves with blankets, or kept boards between them so as to preclude sexual activity. It seems to have originated in North European countries and was transplanted to New England by the immigrants (Reiss, 1980). Bundling was practiced mainly during winter months. Also, the couples that bundled probably were closer to marriage and not merely casual acquaintances.

Although bundling was expected to be an honours system in which sexual intimacies were prohibited, the increase in sexual activity resulting in premarital pregnancies contributed to its decline and eventual abandonment (Smith and Hindus, 1976: 561; Calhoun, 1945: 133) by about the nineteenth century. Another reason for its demise was the transition of America from a colonial and mercantile society to a farming, and later, industrial society. Even after bundling disappeared, parents continued to play an important role in the courtship process. For example, as Cox (1981: 113) notes, in rural America parents often introduced marriageable young men and women to each other so that they could get acquainted, and, if all went well, become engaged and married. Parental involvement was also facilitated because, before the turn of the century, there were simply few opportunities for young men and women to interact outside the home. Schools (apart from the very early grades) were not co-educational. Other than in church or in stores of various kinds, there were few public places where eligible partners could meet.

In later years, urbanization and industrialization of America, expansion of mass education at high school and college levels, increasing leisure, the introduction of ice cream parlours, movie houses, and automobiles, and the absence of social and familial pressure on adolescents to be in the work force created conditions for teenagers to meet without parental supervision (Hollingshead, 1975: 310–23) and led to the emergence of and institutionalization of dating.

Dating: The Path to Courtship

Dating, as part of mate selection, first appeared at the turn of the century and referred to a specific date, time, and place of meeting. To "date" in the early 1900s would have simply meant to meet someone of the opposite sex at a mutually agreed upon place and time and engage in conversation. Gradually, and coin-

ciding with changes in the norms and values governing heterosexual relations between the unmarried and the introduction of the automobile on a mass basis, the term developed wider connotations. Gordon (1981) suggests that dating (as a regular activity) in the US began after the World War I, became widespread in the 1920s and 1930s, and was common among high school students in the 1940s and 1950s. During the 1950s, dating became essentially a filtering process in that one dated many partners before settling on one person who seemed to meet the specifications of an ideal mate. Only then did serious "courting" begin, with marriage in mind.

There is consensus among sociologists that dating in contemporary North America is no longer what it was prior to 1965 (e.g. Murstein, 1980: 78). The traditional dating pattern in which the male called the female in advance, picked her up at her home or dormitory, took her to a restaurant, concert, or movie, and then dropped her back at her residence, is generally considered to be a thing of the past. The contemporary practice is for youngsters to casually get together in groups, organize parties at home to listen to music and dance, or go out for a pizza or even for a stroll in shopping malls, etc. Such group encounters provide opportunities for two persons of the opposite sex to be attracted to each other, and, subsequently, they "pair off" and withdraw from the group. The emergent pattern is much more casual and flexible than traditional dating. Also, the stress seems to be on "going Dutch" which, in part, seeks to reduce the exploitation of girls by boys who in the past expected sexual favours in return for the money spent on dating. Furthermore, contemporary youth are financially more independent than their counterparts in previous generations because of the availability of part-time jobs, and this allows them to share the expenses. Young women, influenced by egalitarian values, are reluctant to have their dating expenses paid by their male equals.

The young people of today have not only changed the dating script but also the terminology, referring to various stages such as casual dating, steady dating, and engagement. For example, the term "dating" is generally viewed as passé. One seldom says that "I have a date tonight," because it sounds too formal and old-fashioned. Instead, for example, in the university where the author teaches, one prefers to say that she/he is "going out with...," which is comparable to casual dating. If a person says that "I am going around with...," the reference is to a more steady relationship (similar to steady dating in earlier decades), which also entails "making out," implying sexual intimacies. Further, at the end of the "going around with" stage, a couple may live together, become engaged, marry, or break up.

While the term "dating" might be outdated, the practice continues in various forms. True, for many young people, dating and living together have become part of a heterosexual relationship prior to marriage. But a careful analysis of patterns of dating among the young today suggests that the basic stages and functions have not disappeared altogether. What appears to have happened is that dating behaviour has changed consistent with changes in other aspects of social life, including social roles.

The traditional dating continuum, which included the casual dating, steady dating, and engagement phases, seems, in many cases, to have been extended by the inclusion of additional stages. Such an extension has resulted from an increasing tendency among the adolescents to start dating at an earlier age. Although some form of friendship and pairing off develops in the early years of junior high school, real dating seems to begin in senior high school where dancing, music, parties, and sports-related activities provide opportunities for heterosexual interaction. Consequently, given that the average age at marriage is about 25 years, an average North American dates and courts for over 10 years. During this period he/she is likely to date as many as 14 different individuals (Bell and Coughly, 1977: 354).

The long duration of dating and the involvement with numerous partners have contributed to certain modifications in the dating con-

tinuum. One such change, which has already been alluded to, is "group dating" as the initial phase of a rather long dating career. Compared to previous generations, contemporary youth begin their heterosexual interaction earlier and thus lack competence and skills to initiate and sustain "paired" relationships that formerly characterized the casual dating stage. The informality of group dating provides the participant with sufficient time and opportunities to develop necessary interactional skills and confidence to enter into paired relationships. By the time adolescents enter senior high school, they are most likely to begin "pairing off," and this phase is somewhat comparable to casual dating. Experiences acquired during group dating allow them to manage their couple relationships without the awkwardness and other problems attributed to casual dating in the 1940s and 1950s.

As noted earlier, the "going around" phase is comparable to the traditional steady dating and is characterized by intense mutual dependence, love, sex, and the desire to make the relationship more permanent. Such a desire may lead to the exchange of rings or some other symbolic and public acknowledgement of exclusive commitment. When a couple go steady, it marks the beginning of courtship, since the objective of going out is not recreation but a desire to further explore each other's qualities with a view to making the relationship more permanent.

By the time they complete senior high school, most students would have gone steady at least once. The probability of continuing their relationship beyond senior high school is high if the couple enter college together or are in an environment conducive to maintaining their bond. In such instances, couples are likely to be engaged or live together before their formal marriage. Those who terminate steady relationships with senior high school sweethearts are most likely to start all over again either in college or elsewhere. But they are less likely to date as many as they did in their high school years and typically date only those who appear to have the attributes of an ideal mate.

Chapter 11 / G. N. Ramu

Courtship Cohabitation

Living together (or non-marital cohabitation) is hardly a new phenomenon and historically has always existed, primarily among the lower classes or other marginal groups. In recent decades, however, it has drawn the attention of researchers and social commentators because of its increasing incidence among the college students, and urban middle classes. Reiss (1980: 106–107) classifies living together into two categories: courtship cohabitation, and non-legal marital cohabitation. The latter is often called, the common-law marriage. In this section, we will focus mainly on the courtship cohabitation.

The courtship cohabitation is seen by some scholars as an extension of the traditional dating continuum (Newcomb and Bentler, 1980; Macklin, 1978; Gwartney-Gibbs, 1986). It is generally a temporary alliance, serving as either an alternative or an adjunct to steady dating and engagement. As Gwartney-Gibbs (1986: 423) notes, courtship cohabitation is becoming "a new normative step leading to marriage."

Danzinger (1976) suggests that premarital cohabitation serves as a screening mechanism so that prospective couples try out their ability to adjust and be compatible. The increasing incidence of courtship cohabitation among the urban middle classes and college students has been due to the changing sexual norms, availability of contraceptives, peer group support, decline in parental authority, and economic necessity.

More important, courtship cohabitation is viewed as a "trial marriage." That is, couples who are interested in getting married prefer to live together in order to test their interpersonal and sexual adjustment capabilities. However, Moeller and Sherlock (1981) and Markowski and Johnston (1980) have found that cohabitation prior to marriage has had little influence on marital adjustment. Furthermore, Demaris and Leslie (1984), Watson (1983), and Watson and DeMeo (1987) report that premarital cohabitation does not necessarily ensure the choice of a right partner or a high level of marital satisfaction. Instead, they found that

couples who had lived together prior to their marriage reported low levels of marital satisfaction. And yet, many studies report an increase in the numbers of those who live together.

For example, Trost (1981), reporting on the patterns of cohabitation in Scandinavian countries, suggests that in Sweden about 20% of all households consisted of non-marital unions, whereas in the 1950s, only 1% were non-marital unions. He also found that nearly all newly married couples had been living together prior to their marriage. In the United States, according to the Bureau of the Census in 1986, over two million households included an adult male and female who were unrelated (US Bureau of Census, 1986: 2). This does not imply that all of these couples were cohabiting, because the Census does not maintain information on the kind of relationship maintained. To wit, a resident female nurse caring for a disabled man is included in the category, as is a widower renting a room to a female student. Nonetheless, Glick and Norton (1977) speculate that since most of these cohabiting persons are concentrated in comparable age groups, they may be living together.

The data on the patterns of non-marital cohabitation in Canada suggest an increase although the proportion is still very small. The 1981 Census found 352,000 couples living together as common-law partners, which represented only 6% of all couples, twice as many as in 1971. By 1986, the numbers rose to 487,000 (or 8%), which constitutes a 38% increase from 1981 (Statistics Canada, Daily, July 9, 1987). In short, one in 12 Canadian couples in 1986 was living together.

One of the major problems of the Census data on non-marital cohabitation is that they do not distinguish the courtship cohabitants from the non-legal marital cohabitants. Consequently, one cannot confidently conclude that living together is simply a prelude to marriage. Nevertheless, based on a survey of about 15,000 Canadian men and women between the ages of 18 and 65, Burch (1985: 13–15) notes that common-law relations reflect neither instability nor promiscuity, and, in most cases, they are as much a prelude to marriage as a substitute for it.

Functions of Dating

The meaning and functions of dating are, to a large extent, dependent on age, sex, and the stages of one's dating career. Skipper and Nass (1966) summarize the purposes of dating in terms of recreation, socialization, status grading and achievement, and courtship leading to marriage. In a study of dating patterns among the males at Harvard University, Vreeland (1972) found that dating served companionship, instrumental, and traditional functions. These Harvard men viewed dating as a means of friendship, sexual satisfaction, recreation (instrumental), and marriage (traditional). Likewise, Gordon (1981) notes that friendship and companionship are basically what most persons are seeking in dating members of the opposite sex. Waller (1937), in his pioneering analysis of dating patterns on a college campus during the late 1930s, held that dating differs from courtship in that it is mainly concerned with casual fun and excitement (recreation) rather than marriage.

Socialization

The socialization function of dating is relevant for those who are in the early stages of dating, especially high school students. It is a competitive situation in which one's skills of communication, attraction, and talents of various sorts with respect to opposite sex are tested and honed on a one-to-one basis. Group dating and subsequent paired relationships provide opportunities to adolescents to learn the necessary techniques to impress and entertain their dates as well as to build self-confidence (needless to say this does not always occur).

Recreation

In considering the recreational function of dating, a distinction should be made between adolescent and adult patterns, because the former stresses recreation while the latter typically involves courtship. The conception of dating in terms of "fun and thrill seeking" (c.f.

Waller, 1937; Gorer, 1964; Hollingshead, 1975) probably corresponded with the realities of the 1930s and 1950s. Dating behaviour in that period foreshadowed the double standard and male dominance that were likely to follow in marriage. Recent studies, however, suggest that college dating in the 1970s was a more serious and marriage-directed affair (see Gordon (1981) for a review).

Status Achievement

The view that dating is a means of status achievement and grading (i.e. ranking) emerges from Waller's (1937) study, which suggested that individuals attempt to date those persons rated as the most "desirable" on the campus in order to enhance their own status and prestige within the peer group. For example, dating an exceptionally attractive girl elevated the male's standing in his peer group, just as the girl's status rose if she dated a wealthy boy or star athlete. Also, a person who dated a member of a fraternity or sorority who was equal to or above his/her own status enjoyed higher prestige than those who did not. While this may have been true during the late 1930s, the changing values governing sex roles and the importance attached to qualities other than beauty, athletic talent, or other attributes that are generally in short supply have had the effect of reducing the importance of prestige-seeking in dating among the contemporary youth.

Mate Selection

Finally, dating is still a salient stage for mate selection in North America. The absence of extended kin groups and their inability to control resources and jobs (except in the upper classes), the decline of parental authority, rapid economic changes, and the celebration of the individual vis-a-vis the group have effectively undermined the kinds of control on mate selection by elders that are typical in traditional cultures, such as those found in much of Asia, Africa, or India. Initially, dating brings together persons so that they may become acquainted for recreational and romantic purposes. A series of such casual relationships generate knowledge and experience regarding members of the opposite sex. This experience in turn helps younger men and women in their efforts to find a marriage partner.

Freedom Versus Control in Marital Choice

It was noted earlier that although the general perception is that North Americans freely choose their own marriage partners, in reality such a freedom is restricted, because there is an indirect sorting of individuals according to their social class, race, ethnicity, religion, residence, and other such attributes. There are at least two ways in which free choice is moderated. First, an individual is socialized into a family culture that influences preferences for the kind of person who is likely to be viewed as a desirable and compatible mate. This is evident from the high degree of conformity to norms of endogamy, a point which will be discussed later.

Second, neighbourhood, schools, colleges, and places of work and leisure are usually the settings in which eligible men and women meet, date, and court. As was seen earlier, these are organized in terms of various criteria of social stratification. Consequently, in the potential universe of mates, only certain people are eligible to participate. It is within this universe, therefore, that decisions are made.

Despite such indirect controls, prospective mates in North America still exhibit a considerably higher degree of freedom than their counterparts in many non-Western societies. For example, in many traditional societies, even though the bride-to-be is willing to marry within her group, she has no freedom to choose from within the pool of eligible men. The specific choice, as a rule, is made by her parents, and the marriage is not only endogamous but arranged. By contrast, most North Americans, while conforming to endogamy in varying degrees, retain the freedom to choose the most desirable person from the pool of available mates. Such pools are loosely organized around race, ethnicity, social class, and similar characteristics.

Race

Race is a salient part of social structure, and consequently, racial endogamy remains the norm for most people. In fact, the social concern for the preservation of racial segregation was so severe that until recently 16 states in the United States had anti-miscegenation statutes with penalties of up to $10,000. If a key purpose and consequence of endogamy is the preservation of specific values and practices of a group, the persistence of racial endogamy in the absence of legal restrictions underscores the importance attached to certain status considerations in marriage. Even after the repeal of laws prohibiting interracial marriages, interracial dating and marriages continue to be socially and statistically insignificant. For example, only about 1.5% (or 719,000 couples) of 50.7 million married couples in the US in 1983 were racially mixed (Scanzoni and Scanzoni, 1988: 81). The most restricted form of intermarriage is between blacks and whites, reflecting the historical tension and distance between these two groups.

There have been gradual changes in attitudes and behaviour regarding racial intermarriages. Gallup Polls conducted in 1968 and 1983 indicate that the proportion of those who approve of marriage between whites and non-whites rose from 20% to 43% between those years (Gallup, 1984: 16).

Although there is a more tolerant view of interracial marriages in recent years in certain circles, such marriages are still not widely accepted or contracted. Where they do take place, the pattern is for black men to marry white women (Heer, 1974; Monahan, 1970, 1976). Black males who marry white women are often upwardly mobile, both spouses are older at marriage (at least one of them usually having been married before), and they tend to be voluntarily childless because of the fear of prejudice and discrimination against their children.

There are a number of explanations for racial endogamy. Adams (1980: 238) argues that *visibility* and *salience* of race in North America make it difficult for persons to marry across racial lines. Unlike religion or ethnicity, racial identity is much too conspicuous and thus constrains many individuals from choosing their mates from another racial group. Salience refers to the continuing importance attached to one's racial background and the resultant prejudice and discrimination built into North American society.

Religion

Religion, like race, plays a dominant role in mate-selection, although its influence is not as restrictive. Traditionally all three religions in America—Catholicism, Protestantism, and Judaism—have opposed interreligious marriage. This position is based on the assumption that interfaith marriages undermine religious commitments and are likely to disrupt normal family functions deemed unique to each religious group. As a result, Christian and Jewish religious organizations are fairly active in trying to promote marriages between members of their own group.

The Roman Catholic church and Jewish religious bodies have set stringent conditions for their members who desire to marry outside their religions. Sometimes the conditions are so severe as to force the couple to call off their marriage or abandon their church or synagogue. For example, historically, the Roman Catholic church excommunicated those who married non-Catholics. In recent years, the Church has become slightly more flexible in that permission is given if a pre-marital agreement is signed by the non-Catholic partner pledging a commitment to a Catholic way of life and the raising of children as Catholics. Since 1970, the rules have been further relaxed after Pope Paul IV accepted the recommendations made in this regard by the Ecumenical Council (Leslie and Leslie, 1980: 138–39).

Jews have historically regarded marriage to non-Jews as unacceptable, basing their opposition on the concern for the survival of Jews as a distinct people. Given that they are only a fraction of the population (3% in the US and 1% in Canada in 1981), liberal marriage policies are viewed as a serious threat to Jewish identity and culture. The three branches of Judaism—Orthodox, Conservative, and Re-

form—differ in their attitudes and approaches toward interreligious marriages, with the Reform rabbis being the most flexible (Leslie and Leslie, 1980: 139–41).

Like other religious groups, Protestants oppose intermarriages. Given their numerous denominations and the absence of a centralized ecclesiastic hierarchy, the enforcement of norms of endogamy is rather difficult for Protestants.

The positions of the religious organizations concerning intermarriage has clearly influenced the marital patterns in North America, as the data on intermarriage suggest. For example, Carter and Glick (1976) have noted that in the US, 91% of Protestants (66% of the population), 78% of Catholics (26% of the population), and 93% of Jews (3% of the population) marry among themselves. The attitudes of Americans, however, are more liberal than their marital practices, as a 1983 Gallup poll suggests—79% of Americans approved of interreligious marriages (Gallup, 1984: 98).

Changes in the proportion of religious intermarriages in Canada have been gradual. Heer (1962) and Heer and Hubey (1976) found that the percentage of interreligious marriages rose from 5.8% in 1927 to 21.4% in 1972. There are, as in the US, differences in the flexibility demonstrated by the three major religious groups. Of those who married outside their own faith in 1972, 22.7% were Protestants, 20.5% were Catholics, and 15% were Jews.

Such variation is partially explained by the size of the group relative to others in a particular area. For example, the larger the size of the city, the less the chance of intermarriage taking place, because there will be a greater supply of eligible mates in a given religion (Latowksy, 1971; Chimbos, 1983; Friederes et al., 1971).

In general, those who marry across religious boundaries tend to be older at their first marriage, of higher socio-economic status, and from family backgrounds that placed less emphasis on religion and church-related activities. Also, research suggests that intermarriages, depending on age at marriage and social class, are prone to divorce (Monahan,

1973; Rosenthal, 1970; Bumpass and Sweet, 1972).

Ethnicity

In courtship and mate selection, ethnicity is not as critical as race or religion, but it is still important, especially in Canada, where the maintenance of ethnic culture and identity are encouraged by governmental policies and programs. Analysis of previous research has shown (Tavuchis, 1979; Mindel, 1976; Ishwaran, 1980) that promotion of ethnic identity and ties is an important function of the family and in most cases is accomplished by socializing children into ethnic culture.

Canadian data on interethnic marriages suggest that there is a continuing conformity to ethnic endogamy. The proportion of interethnic marriages rose from 11.6% of all marriages in 1921 to 24.4% in 1971 (Kalbach, 1983). Driedger (1983) found that the university students he studied maintained liberal attitudes toward interethnic dating and marriages but generally conformed to ethnic endogamy when actual marital choices were made. Chimbos (1983) suggests that the Greek parents in his study did not disapprove of their children marrying across ethnic lines as long as their mates were of the same religion.

Social Class

Although there are differences of opinion on valid and reliable measures of social class, sociologists agree that at a minimum such composite measures as education, occupation, and income cumulatively give a good indication of an individual's or family's standing in the social hierarchy (e.g. lower, middle, or upper class). Membership in a social class group shapes one's attitudes, values, and approach to life, and, more importantly, it determines whether one has access to the means necessary to realize one's aspirations in life. For these reasons, people with similar social class backgrounds tend to share common interests and goals, which are the bases for marital decisions.

While there are instances of class-discrepant marriages (e.g. a noble and commoner), it is common for North Americans to marry someone from about the same social class level as themselves. Marriage is a means by which class distinctions are maintained, and this is true especially of the upper classes. Goode (1973: 258-9) suggests that upper classes expend more efforts to control the mate selection of their children than other classes, because they have more to lose if their children marry social inferiors, as do their children if they do not accede to their parents' wishes. Eshleman and Hunt (1965) have shown that there is a tendency for those who court and marry to have parents with similar backgrounds, especially occupational.

Education is another indicator of social class. The similar educational status of spouses positively contributes to marital adjustment, since the couples are likely to have comparable values, goals, interests, and outlooks on life. In the US, as in Canada, most people tend to marry those with similar levels of education. Nearly three-fourths of those who married in the US were in the same or next adjacent level of education, although the gap in educational levels of spouses has increased recently (Rockwell, 1976).

Age

The difference of age at first marriage between the husband and wife in North America is gradually declining in this century although the tendency still seems to be for husbands to be slightly older than their wives. For example, in Canada, the mean age at first marriage in 1941 was 26.3 years for males and 23 for females, and by 1985, the difference had slightly declined—25.6 and 23.7 years for males and females respectively. Similar trends have been noted in the US.

In 1900, the difference between the median age at which men and women got married for the first time was about four years; by 1930, the difference was reduced to three years; and by 1979, the median age of men marrying for the first time (24.4) was about two and one-half years older than the women they marry (Melville, 1983: 53).

An implication of increasing equality in age is the emerging egalitarian character of marriage. Age in most cultures is associated with knowledge, experience, and deference, which command power and authority. If the husband, is say, 10 years older than his wife (which is quite common in countries like India), he has a greater base for exercising authority and power in marital relations.

Personal Qualities in Marital Choice

Factors such as race, religion, ethnicity, and social class assist only in an initial screening of eligible couples. It is from within the selected pool of potential mates that an individual chooses his or her partner. The personal qualities of potential partners play an important role in narrowing the choice. These qualities include physical appearance, sexual adjustment, communication skills, values and aspirations regarding marriage, family, and occupation, among others. In what follows, we provide a discussion of attractiveness and companionship as illustrations of personal qualities which are critical in the selection of marital partners.

Attractiveness

In mate selection, as a study by Stroebe et al., (1971) concluded, individuals generally seek mates whose attractiveness is roughly equivalent to their own. Furthermore, in matters of physical appearance, there are some sex differences. It has been reported that women tend to stress intelligence, ambition, and drive in males, while men value beauty in their future wives (Coombs and Kenkel, 1966). Female beauty is valued not only in North America, but in other societies as well. A case in point is the relationship between the amount of dowry and physical appearance of a bride in India. It is customary, although not legal, for the parents of a girl to give a handsome dowry to their future son-in-law. The amount corresponds to the educational and occupational status of the groom—the higher the status, the larger the dowry. In the Kolar Gold Fields in South India, it was observed that grooms tended to reduce the amount of dowry in cases of brides who were physically attractive, especially those who had a fair complexion (Ramu, 1977). North American studies have shown that a woman's appearance enhances her chances of upward mobility through marriage. A physically attractive woman has a greater chance of marrying some one above her own social class (Elder, 1969).

Companionship

Demographic estimates suggest that those who marry in the 1980s are likely to be married to the same person, unless death or divorce intervene, for over half a century. Such a long marital life and the importance attached to emotional relationships in North America make companionship a critical factor in mate selection. A person, in choosing his/her mate, usually takes into account the future partner's ability to be a good companion in terms of mutual friendship, support, understanding, tolerance, dependence, and the capacity to function as a two-person team. At least two personal attributes contribute to companionship: communication and sexual adjustment.

Genuine communication depends, among other things, upon intellectual habits, sensitivity, and empathy. It is a method by which a couple exchanges their views, their attitudes, and their feelings toward each other. More important, communication is critical for the resolution of interpersonal differences and conflicts. The quality of companionship is enhanced when the couple can successfully engage each other's attention and enjoy their conversations. In essence, a couple's communication skills are crucial for their marital solidarity and satisfaction.

The issue of sexual adjustment between spouses is extremely complex and depends upon such considerations as sex-based conceptions of sexual competence and permissiveness, social class, and salience of sexual relations in marriage (see Spanier and Lewis, 1979; Himeloch and Fava, 1955). Also, sexual adjustment has become increasingly important in light of increased expectations on the part of women. During the dating and courtship stages of their relations, most couples experiment sexually and narrow their choice to those whom they perceive as capable of satisfying most, if not all, of their sexual needs. One should, nevertheless, be cautious in inferring that sexual adjustment plays a greater role than other criteria. A satisfactory sexual adjustment depends, in most cases, on non-sexual matters, such as expressed romantic love, communication, friendship, mutual dependence, and economic security.

SUMMARY

Most societies consider that marriage is too important an affair to be left to the total discretion of young men and women. As long as societies continue to stress structural differences, some form of control on mate selection will prevail. In North America, there is a strong emphasis on a differentiated social order, based on such criteria as race, religion, and ethnicity, that would be threatened if total freedom in mate choice prevailed. The norms of endogamy generally restrict the range of choices that are available to participants in the marriage market. In this sense, mate selection is structurally controlled, thus ensuring an orderly perpetuation of critical social differences. Although mixed marriages are neither legally prohibited nor unknown, they are not commonplace enough to posit a homogenizing trend in Canada and the United States.

Nevertheless, relative to most non-Western societies, North Americans "freely" choose their spouses and "arrange their own marriages." Dating, or its contemporary equivalent, permits opportunities for a series of heterosexual encounters for nearly a decade in the life of most young men and women. Such experiences permit individuals to narrow their choices to one person and court that person for a considerable time before a final decision to marry is made. In short, the freedom of choice that one enjoys exists within certain structural limits.

QUESTIONS

1. State the reasons why some societies stress arranged marriages while others permit "free choice."

2. Discuss how and why endogamous marriages continue to be a dominant pattern in North America.

3. How have patterns of dating changed in recent years? Outline various stages of dating or its equivalent on your college campus.

4. Examine in detail various factors in mate selection. Do you consider that one can still freely choose a mate in North American society?

SUGGESTED READINGS

- Bert N. Adams. "Mate Selection in the United States: a theoretical summarization." In *Contemporary Theories About the Family*. Vol. 1., ed. Wesley Burr. New York: Free Press, 1979.

- William J. Goode. "The Theoretical Importance of Love." *American Sociological Review* 24 (1959): 38–47.

  An analysis of links between various aspects of social stratification and mate selection. Goode argues that those societies which stress property, prestige, kinship and the like are likely to control the expression of romantic love and arrange the marriages of younger members. Free choice based on love is likely to prevail in societies which have low emphasis on continuity of social hierarchy.

- Michael Gordon. "Was Waller Ever Right? The rating and dating complex revisited." *Journal of Marriage and the Family*. 43 (1981): 67–76.

  The validity of some of the conclusions of Willard Waller's pioneering research on dating patterns on a college campus is examined in detail. The author "seriously questions" the historical accuracy of what has become to benchmark study in the area of dating and mate selection.

- Bernard L. Murstein. "Mate Selection in the 1980s." *Journal of Marriage and the Family.* 42 (1980): 777–792.

  A critical assessment of the significant of dating and mate selection in the 1970s.

The comprehensive list of references will be valuable for those interested in further understanding of this topic.

Well-wishers beam upon a shy bride and bearded groom at a Sikh wedding. Here the woman's veil has been removed and she and her husband-to-be see each other for the first time. With relatives and friends, they face the priest's dais in a Delhi home, ready for the ceremony to begin. Sikh religion, founded by Guru Nanak, a dissenter from Hinduism, forbids divorce.

MATE SELECTION
A Theoretical Perspective

Jarmila L.A. Horna
University of Calgary

The issue of mate selection is one of the most interesting, most discussed, and most complex in all of family study (Adams, 1979). The determinants of mate choice have differed from historical era to historical era and from society to society. In the preceding chapter, the empirical data on multiple factors that contribute to an individual's choice of his or her marital partner have been reviewed. Such an overwhelming amount of empirical evidence needs to be systematically organized and theoretically interpreted; to achieve this goal, the present chapter will look at the research findings through a prism of theoretical and conceptual frameworks. Before proceeding to these theories, it is important to emphasize that the North American findings, based most frequently on samples drawn from the middle class population of college students, cannot always be generalized beyond the confines of North American countries. While the findings may be applicable to most social groups in Canada, the United States, or other industrialized countries, the world as a whole seems to move toward the idea of free choice in marriage, sometimes referred to as love marriages, at a slower pace (Murstein, 1980).

Cross-Cultural Patterns of Mate Selection

Some norms or rules governing who can marry whom or who has the final decision-making power in choosing a mate are cultural universals. Likewise, the criteria of desirability and eligibility in any marriage market or system, as well as the rules which circumscribe the field of eligible mates in terms of preferences and prohibitions, are found in every society (Sueng Gyu Moon, 1979). The criteria, however, differ from one society to the other. Similarly, the method of choosing a mate varies from one society to the other and is dependent upon societal concern for the preservation of social differences. In systems with a minimal interest in preserving rigid barriers, or where the elders do not extend authority or power, individuals are likely to choose their own mates—of course, still within certain limits (Goode, 1959, 1963; Larson, 1976; Marsh and O'Hara, 1961; Stephens, 1963; Strauss, 1946; Zimmerman, 1947).

The assortative pattern of mate selection (under which potential mates are sorted or selected rather than randomly chosen) is characteristic of pre-industrial, traditional societies, while random mating is a distinctive feature of urban-industrial, modern societies. In the latter societies, an emphasis on individualism as opposed to familism, and an increased use of person-centered criteria in mate selection with the view that marriage is a personal matter, is prevalent. Complementing this is greater freedom from parental control with a minimum of parental interference, and an emphasis on romantic love as an institutionalized basis of selection.

Generally, a wide range of societal patterns exists across different societies, from families having little involvement in the selection of a spouse, to societies where families select the individual's spouse with little or no involvement by that individual in the decision-making process (Freeman, 1974; Hutter, 1981). Typically, one of the four forms of social mate choice, i.e. (1) arranged marriage, (2) free choice of mate, subject to parental approval, (3) free choice of mate, not subject to parental approval, and (4) societies in which both arranged marriage and free choice of mate is practiced, is found in a particular society (Goode, 1963; Hutter, 1981; Stephens, 1963).

In accordance with the degree of protection needed by the kin, the responsibility for marital choice can be taken away from the potential spouses (Cerroni-Long, 1984; Shibutani and Kwan, 1965). In turn, it may be assigned to parents or elders whose experience can guarantee the creation of a union that best serves the interests of the family, group, or society. Romantic love may be singled out as the most important element which distinguishes the free choice system from the arranged marriage system (Sueng Gyu Moon, 1979). Since love attachments may occur in any society and become potentially disruptive of lineages and the social stratification system, love must be controlled or channelled in some way (Goode, 1959). Thus, in arranged marriage systems such customs as child marriage, segregation of potential mates, and chaperonage are frequently used for controlling love relationships. By contrast, the free choice system permits or encourages love relationships, with the source of control internalized in the person and supported by peers, parents, or others—after exogamy and endogamy have extended their influence.

To illustrate these points, let us explore marriage in a Muslim society. Muslims consider marriage to be the joining of two families and a possible extension of the extended kin group (Korson and Sabzwari, 1984). Although the consent of the principals is required by religious law, the wishes of the principals are not necessarily considered to be the most important. Moreover, it is highly unlikely that an unattached woman would live alone, because this would be improper and unseemly. In urban areas, girls may be perceived to be an even greater burden because of the limited number of employment opportunities available to women. Her marriage, then, may be viewed as a relief from an economic burden and, indeed, a family achievement.

Another Muslim cultural factor makes free marital choice practically impossible and contributes to the desire for an early marriage for women—the concept of *Izzat* or family honour (Korson and Sabzwari, 1984). Since almost all marriages are arranged by the families of the principals, the burden of maintaining the family's honour rests with the women. Because the men of the family might be considered the protectors, if not the enforcers, of the normative behaviour of married as well as unmarried women, the earlier a girl is married, the sooner the major responsibility for her behaviour is removed from her parental family.

Different stages of societal development are typically linked with different patterns of mate selection. The contemporary pattern differs from the mate selection patterns of other historical periods (McCall, 1966; Scanzoni and Scanzoni, 1981). While under the "traditional pattern," parents and kin groups did the marriage bargaining; under the "intermediary pattern," both the parents and the young persons themselves were involved. In both cases the bargaining concentrated on marriage as the end goal, whether it was conducted primarily by the kin or the courting couple.

The rate of advance toward free mate selection seems to be related to the country's rate of industrialization (Murstein, 1980). A brief look at various countries shows that, for example in Turkey, three-quarters of the marriages were still arranged in the 1960s and 1970s. Likewise, a number of factors retarding the change toward a wider acceptance of free choice are found in India, which is progressing toward modernity. Among them, a belief that there is only one predestined mate who is to share reincarnated lives creates a situation under which supervision by parents is essential in order to avoid mistakes. The result is a compromise and an increasing number of "semi-arranged" marriages. A similar pattern is found in Japan, where many continue to prefer a matchmaker to arrange their marriage, at least ceremonially, in spite of Japan's rapid industrialization.

The impact of modernization on marriage can be observed by comparing India and China. While India generally still remains strongly affected by conservative traditions restricting contact between the sexes and favouring arranged marriages, the urban population is increasingly moving away from this attitude (Kurian, 1979). Similarly Chinese society, traditionally oriented toward arranged marriage, is undergoing change. Traditional values have been substantially undermined in mainland China by the influence of the Communist Party, which supports equality of the sexes and concern for society rather than for the family. People are encouraged to marry, not for personal compatibility, but preferably for political compatibility in the approved socialist ideology. In practice, however, some degree of arranged marriage which reflects neither personality nor political compatibility lingers on (Murstein, 1980), especially in the countryside in both India and China, making a free mate selection norm a thing of the future.

At the other end of the spectrum are societies where individual love is a central point of a person's marital choice. A typical West European shift is toward basing marriage on husband-wife affection, and already the number of consensual unions based on such affection is growing (Festy, 1980). In Scandinavian countries and Iceland, childbearing is often part of these unions and does not significantly affect marriage likelihood or its timing when it does occur. In European socialist countries, for example in Czechoslovakia, the Soviet Union, or Poland, love, too, is the primary motive for marriage for both sexes in spite of an ideology similar to that in China (Horna, 1986; Lobodzinska, 1975; Murstein, 1980).

A particular combination of free choice and matchmaking is found in Israel (Peres, Meisels, and Frank, 1980). Matchmaking, which has a long and noteworthy history among European Jews, has been revived in Israel. The matchmaking exchange system, including commercial matchmaking, offers a second opportunity to those who failed to find their mate through the methods prescribed by the norm of romantic love. Even then, one still needs to put oneself into the emotional state of being in love in order to make a favourable decision about a prospective mate.

North American Variations

Numerous differences in mate selection patterns among various ethnic or racial groups have been amply documented in both Canada and the United States. For example, mate selection differentials between whites and blacks in the United States have frequently been observed. Because of the greater excess of women among blacks than among whites during the years in which mate selection and first marriage typically occur, the demographic necessity creates a more restricted field of marriage eligibles for black women than for white women (Spanier and Glick, 1980). Consequently, the marriage squeeze experienced by young marriageable black women may affect courtship and entrance into marriage. Furthermore, blacks in the United States seem to have developed a set of norms that successfully delays the entrance of their adolescents into the institution of dating (Dornbusch et al., 1984). Black families exert more control in this specific area than any other group, most likely because of the black parents' perception of a threatening social environment within which their children develop heterosexual attachments.

Not all ethnic or racial groups favour intermarriages equally (Gurak and Fitzpatrick, 1982). Even in New York, where high rates of ethnic intermarriages are rather common and the rates of out-group marriage either with other major Hispanics groups or non-Hispanics are high, particularly for the second generation Hispanics, Puerto Ricans have a low rate of out-group marriage in both generations. It is suggested that it is the Puerto Ricans' residential and occupational segregation and institutional completeness that most likely override the impact of factors responsible for intermarriage of other Hispanic groups. Likewise, the data on intermarriage in the 125 largest American metropolitan areas indicate that it is a city's degree of heterogeneity and a group's relative size which affect the proportion of a group's members who are "outmarried" (Blau, Blum and Schwartz, 1982). The heterogeneity in national origins, mother tongue, birth region, industrial sector, and occupation increase intermarriage rates, but racial heterogeneity does not have this effect.

Similar to the US variations, Canadian immigrants and their attitudes toward their children's interethnic marriages also differ (Chimbos, 1983; Ishwaran, 1983; Larson, 1976; Ramu, 1983). Several Canadian surveys show that, in spite of their common experience of immigration, each of the immigrant-ethnic groups adheres to different attitudes, and changes them at a different rate. For example, among the Dutch, Greek, and Slovak immigrants, the Dutch immigrants showed more favourable attitudes toward intermarriage than did the Slovaks or the Greeks (Chimbos, 1983).

Not only ethnic and racial differences, but belonging to a specific age cohort may affect mate selection (Jedlicka, 1978, 1980). Thus, findings about mate selection among young adults cannot be generalized as applicable to courtship and marriage in later life ((Dressel, 1980). Particularly, older women are consistently disadvantaged; most of those in the older age groups will have to remain unmarried after widowhood, whether they want to or not (Jedlicka, 1978). Not only do men have more freedom in determining their marital status,' but women also face a double standard of preferential mating which means that men express preference for younger women and women for older men. Likewise, possessing traits which are viewed as undesirable in usual face-to-face contacts can influence mate selection.

Whether influenced by age or other traits, such situations may lead to the use of formal mate selection networks such as personal ads or computer dating. These networks foster an atmosphere of acceptance; however, they can hardly be viewed as equivalents of a free choice process.

The preceding examination of mate selection diversity points out that the general patterns of mate selection processes may only apply to different groups to different degrees. Thus the scope of generalizations is necessarily restricted; the theoretical perspectives to be presented in the next part are applicable to those social groups or societies that are rather similar in their socio-economic, ethno-racial, and other characteristics (Adams, 1979). Only those theories that have attracted most attention are selected, somewhat arbitrarily, for the following review; some of them have been widely accepted while others have met with criticism for their inadequacies or because they could not be successfully replicated and verified by other researchers.

Complementary Needs Theory

Perhaps no other theory of mate selection has generated so much interest, controversy, and criticism as the complementary needs theory (Udry, 1963, 1965; Winch, 1958). This theory starts with the observation that marital selection has been shown by earlier studies to be predominantly homogamous with regard to age, race, religion, social class, education, residence, and previous marital status. Since these variables merely specify the field of eligible spouses but do not account for the actual selection within the field of eligibles, Winch sought an answer to the question of how mate selection takes place within a field of eligibles who share common interests. He inaugurated a study to test his theory of complementary needs in mate selection in 1950, and eventually developed the following fourfold typology of complements: husband-nurturant/wife-receptive; husband-receptive/wife nurturant; husband-dominant/wife-submissive; husband-submissive/wife-dominant.

Winch proposed that: "In mate-selection each individual seeks within his or her field of eligibles for that person who gives the greatest promise of providing him or her with maximum need gratification" (1971: 488). The two types of complementariness are Type I, whereby both spouses possess the same need but to a differing degree—if one spouse is high on one need, the other spouse would be low on that need, and Type II, whereby spouses posses different needs—if one spouse is high on the need to be dominant, the other would be high on the need to give deference.

Ever since Winch published his theory of complementary needs, there have been numerous attempts to replicate, extend, or refute this theory. One of the family sociologists who presents a thorough critique of Winch's propositions is Richard R. Clayton (1979). He follows criticisms first voiced by Rosow (1957) that (1) it is not clear whether the needs are operative at the overt behaviourial level or at the covert or even subconscious levels; (2) Winch's theory does not take into account the possibility that these needs are gratified outside of the marital dyad; (3) the theory does not explicitly provide criteria for deciding which needs are complementary and when; and (4) in many cases similarity of need and intensity of the same need may be as functional to the marriage as complementary needs.

Another critic of Winch's theory is Ira L. Reiss. While Reiss accepts that any need satisfaction will contribute to becoming attached emotionally to another person, he points out that some particular needs may be the key element in the development of a heterosexual love relationship. This particular type of need is an intimate relationship in which there is a high degree of self-revelation, especially of those aspects of oneself that are not generally revealed to acquaintances, for example, basic hopes, fears, or self-feelings. Winch's dominance-submissiveness may be related to love, but mainly because it triggers off different degrees of intimate self-revelations.

Reiss also points out that marital role expectations are important factors in the development of a love relationship. Furthermore, some types of traits do not go well with homogamy, whereas others do. For example, having a bad temper is something best left to only one person in a marriage, whereas a need for nurturance would seem perfectly suitable for both mates to posses (Reiss, 1976: 103). Another of Reiss's criticisms stems from the fact that in contemporary societies, there are ways of satisfying various needs by interacting with a wide number of other people outside the love relationship.

Parental-Image Hypothesis

The basic proposition of the parental-image hypothesis is that men and women seek partners who are substitutes for their parents of the opposite sex in physical appearance and temperament. In Richard Clayton's assessment (1979), this hypothesis grew out of psychoanalytic literature, with its base in the Oedipus and Electra complexes of Freud, probably combined with American folklore. Clayton agrees with Bruce Eckland (1968) that, while it admittedly would seem reasonable to expect parent images to either encourage or discourage a person marrying someone like his/her parent, no clear evidence has been produced to support this hypothesis.

Amidst such scepticism directed toward the parental-image hypothesis, Davor Jedlicka (1980) uses new evidence collected from brides and grooms of mixed ethnic parentage in Hawaii. His data seem to support the parental-image hypothesis for both sexes. Reportedly, no single indicator is likely to be equally relevant, as some subjects may place greater importance on parent's religion, occupation, age, or some other aspect of personality or ethnicity, while others may consider the type of parent-child interaction.

Filter Theory

Alan Kerckhoff and Keith Davis (1962) propose that the potential partners' characteristics that influence the mate selection process are scrutinized through a series of filters. These filters might operate at different stages of the courtship process. The initial filter, functioning early in the relationship, considers such attributes as race, religion, age, and social class. This filter is likely to limit people's choices before they begin dating—although this limitation is not necessarily conscious and may well be influenced by residential location or parents.

When the couples have already limited their field of eligibles by using such attributes as age, religion, and social class, and if the relationship continues, partners are further screened through new filters: first, the value consensus; then, complementarity of their needs. Thus, while social attributes presumably operate at an early stage, values and needs become crucial later on. Kerckhoff and Davis posit that for those couples who survive, despite lack of value consensus, need complementarity seems to be the cohesive that holds them together.

Commitment-Wheel Model

Richard R. Clayton (1979) sees mate selection as a process by which two people with many opportunities for choosing mates move from a point of no commitment to a state where both are mutually committed. The increasing degree of involvement is also expressed through a physical commitment to the other. Few, if any, couples marry who have not had an opportunity to establish rapport and find out if they consider each other stimulating physically, socially, and emotionally. An essential first step toward rapport with stimulating potential mates is related to the fact that people are almost forced to choose from among persons who are living in close proximity, who share similar characteristics, and are relatively equal in physical and social attractiveness. If their early dating experiences are satisfying and rapport continues to develop through mutual self-disclosure, the chances are fairly good that both persons will recognize and note how many similarities exist between them. In particular, this stage will facilitate an exchange of beliefs, attitude and value orientations, interests, preferences, and aspirations. The potential marital partners who make it beyond this stage will have experienced the value homogamy comparisons suggested by Murstein (1970), Kerckhoff and Davis (1962), and Winch (1958, 1967).

During the next stage, the two persons recognize a feeling of mutual dependency and are willing to reject alternative commitments. This is the engaged-to-be-engaged stage during which both partners begin to delve more deeply into the extent to which they are mutu-

ally similar in values and goals. In the last stage of the process, partners reach a mutual recognition that each is capable of satisfying the other's needs and begin the process of anticipatory marital role playing. As the couple has gathered enough data, the partners make public their commitment and intentions to get married.

Premarital Dyadic Formation Theory

According to Robert A. Lewis' (1973) proposition, there exist six pair processes through which couples progressively proceed during their dating and courtship careers. The success of a couple's growing dyadic formation depends upon a successful achievement of a stage immediately preceding the current one. Although all six processes may operate to some degree during the entire successful relationship, there is an optimal period for introduction of each variable. These processes consist of:

A. The achievement by pairs of perceiving similarities in each other's: (1) Socio-cultural background, (2) Values, (3) Interests, (4) Personality.

B. The achievement of pair rapport, as evidenced in a pair's: (1) Ease of communication, (2) Positive evaluation of the other, (3) Satisfaction with pair relationships, (4) Validation of self by the other.

C. The achievement of openness between partners through a mutual self-disclosure.

D. The achievement of role-taking accuracy.

E. The achievement of interpersonal role-fit, as evidenced by a pair's: (1) Observed similarity of personalities, (2) Role complementarity, (3) Need complementarity.

F. The achievement of dyadic crystallization, as evidenced by a pair's: (1) Progressive involvement, (2) Functioning as a dyad, (3) Boundary establishment, (4) Commitment to each other.

(5) Identity as a couple (Lewis, 1973: 23).

There are, however, questions regarding the hypothesized sequence, specifically why the achievement of pair rapport should precede the development of role-taking accuracy, rather than vice-versa (Rubin and Levinger, 1974; Murstein, 1980). In spite of these critical questions, Lewis can be credited with a positive move "away from monolithic, single principle approaches, such as those of homogamy and complementary needs, to a belief in multi-determined factors in marital choice" (Murstein, 1980: 788).

Instrumental Theory

At the heart of the instrumental theory, developed by Richard Centres in 1975, is the proposition that

> in the intersexual dyad formation each person seeks, among his circle of acquaintances, within the compass of his self-acknowledged compeers, to form a relationship with that person or those persons whose behaviourial and other resources provide (or are perceived to provide) maximum gratification and minimum punification for his needs (Centres, 1975: 63).

It is assumed that some of these needs are more important than others, and some are more important for one gender than for the other. For example, male dominance has high attractiveness value for females, but female dominance has less attractiveness value for males. In turn, female nurturance has high attractiveness value for males, but male's nurturance has less attractiveness for females (Centres, 1975: 75).

Centres' thinking does represent an advance over the monolithic complementary need theory of Winch. His instrumental theory, however, has been criticized, namely, because it reeks of sexism, as women are perceived to fulfil their own identity by finding a male with stronger drives than their own (Murstein, 1980: 788).

Barriers/Attractions—Alternative Attractions Model

A novel developmental theoretical approach interprets mate selection as a process of responding to attractions and overcoming barriers (Adams, 1979, 1980; Levinger, 1965). The term barriers relates to both beginning a relationship or getting out of a relationship. The process of choosing a specific person for a marriage partner progresses through a series of stages. After getting over barriers to a beginning, such as certain factors that limit the field of eligible people (e.g. incest taboo and non-propinquity), a person reaches the stage of early attraction. This early attraction between the sexes may be based on many of the same factors as any other form of friendship; however, the most likely stimulus is physical appearance and attractiveness.

Following, or parallel with, an initial attraction may come alternative attractions. The alternative is not always another human being; it could be going to school, taking a new job, or even a single lifestyle. Beyond the immediate attractions of the relationship itself loom barriers to breakup. Instead of falling prey to an alternative attraction, a given relationship may be moved toward marriage by the conscious or unconscious feeling that this person is "right for me." Another barrier to breakup occurs when the relationship begins to take on a life of its own. Not only is there a positive interest in perpetuation, but the obverse side of the coin is the cost of breaking a long-term relationship (Adams, 1979: 263). When these barriers to breakup occur, the relationship continues and leads toward the next step, i.e. marriage itself.

Social Exchange Theory

At the macrosociological level, exchange theory is frequently applied in the analysis of the societal division of labour, social stratification, or organization studies. From the mate selection point of view, it suggests that a person capable of the possible greatest reward for the lowest cost to a potential partner will be selected from prospective mates (Knox, 1985;

Nye, 1980). It has been proposed that many people might feel reluctant to admit that an exchange of rewards occurs in love, because such a notion somehow devalues the ideal of love as selfless, and as being without expectations of return (Emerson, 1976; Scanzoni and Scanzoni, 1981). However,

> To speak of love is to speak of the expressive rewards persons seek from a marriage partner—rewards such as companionship (someone to do things with, go places with, spend leisure hours with), empathy (someone to talk things over with, someone to bring reinforcement of one's self-concept, someone to understand and care), and physical affection (hugging, kissing, the squeeze of a hand, caressing, sexual gratifications). Prior to marriage, these same three elements in one degree or another are sought after as valued rewards in a developing relationship (Scanzoni and Scanzoni, 1981: 173).

Among the assets considered critically important in a date or a mate may be: providing security in the relationship while at the same time respecting the partner's individuality and freedom, sharing in day-to-day household and financial responsibilities, sharing the load of decision-making, and being appreciative.

Another proposition from an exchange perspective examines bargaining which takes place within relationships. The two individuals agree to exchange only with one another, at least until such time as the balance of trade becomes unfavourable in terms of broader market considerations. They agree to exchange exclusively for so long as the rewards in this involvement exceed the cost of continuing it in the face of chances for other rewards elsewhere (McCall, 1966: 197). Thus all courtship systems resemble market or exchange systems; they differ from one another with respect to who does the buying and selling, which characteristics are more or less valuable in that market, and how open or explicit the bargaining is (Goode, 1971). As with the traditional pattern of mate selection, where bargaining about the terms of exchange is carried out between the kin groups involved, the basic objective to try to strike the best bargain possible has not changed under modern arrangements when two young people themselves make a decision to marry (Bell, 1983).

People enter marriage because they believe it to be a rewarding situation that includes both the instrumental and expressive sides of life as each partner tries to find ways of giving and receiving both expressively and instrumentally (Scanzoni and Scanzoni, 1981). What prospective partners seek is the satisfaction of each one's expectations as well as the overall benefit of the relationship. Once a person identifies that other person who can offer the equivalent of what one has to exchange, other bargains are made about the conditions for continuing the relationship (Knox, 1985). Thus, for the sake of equity, people judge what is fair or unfair in a situation or relationship; they feel most comfortable when getting exactly what they feel they deserve in a relationship. An inequitable relationship makes everyone feel uneasy, including the overbenefited mates who feel guilty and fearful of losing their favoured position (Walster and Walster, 1978; Walster, Walster, and Berscheid, 1978). Individuals tend to pair with someone whose perceived capacity to reward them is approximately equal to their own perceived rewardability. Equity of reward is not necessarily identical to similarity because individuals may be equitably matched though dissimilar (Murstein, 1980).

One of the types of exchange conceptualization is represented by Murstein's stimulus-value-role theory, first proposed in the 1970s. The major aspects of Murstein's S-V-R perspective include:

> The stimulus stage concerns factors which draw the individuals to each other, and involves appreciation of the other's physical, social, mental, or reputational attributes. Individuals are drawn to each other on the basis of equity of the weighted amalgam of stimulus attributes. If they move on to the value stage, they assess their value compatibility (attitudes toward life, sex roles, marriage, etc). Though some individuals marry only on the basis of stimulus or stimulus plus value compatibility, the majority of persons move on to the role stage. For them, value similarity is necessary but not sufficient. It is necessary to function in compatible roles. Roles comprise the expecta-

tions vis-a-vis the self and partner and the perceived fulfillment of these expectations. Successful passage through the three stages generally leads to some degree of permanence in the relationship (cohabitation, marriage) (Murstein, 1980: 786).

The weighting of these factors is not identical. An equity position and role compatibility appear to be more important than similarity. Furthermore, the degree of perceived similarity to the partner is a function of self-acceptance, and only individuals with numerous interpersonal assets and few liabilities really choose each other while those with fewer assets and more liabilities often settle for each other (Murstein, 1980). If the potential mates find themselves in an unequal position, they may still continue their involvement in a relationship as long as they derive more profit from that relationship than from any other available to them (Lloyd et al., 1984). If they have no alternative relationship, they may still continue relationships where the costs exceed the rewards and choose to suffer in an unhappy relationship rather than to be alone. For example, when someone is seeking a marital partner in order to escape singlehood or one's parents, then the feeling that a particular prospective mate is "the best I can get" may prevail and overcome other factors in the mate selection process (Adams, 1980). Typically, the person who has the least interest in continuing the relationship can control that relationship (Knox, 1985; Waller and Hill, 1951). This "principle of least interest" is illustrated by the woman who said, "He wants to date me more than I want to date him so we end up going where I want to go and doing what I want to do." Any proper exchange between prospective mates may, however, become further complicated because people tend to offer idealized images of themselves and largely to accept the idealized image of the other throughout the whole period of courtship (Karp and Yoels, 1985).

Prevailing stereotypes about romantic women to the contrary, men rate the "desire to fall in love" as a significantly more important reason for entering the relationship than do

women, and second, a substantial number of breakups are precipitated by women, perhaps due to their economic situation. Since in most marriages the wife's status, income, and life chances are far more dependent upon her husband's than vice versa, parents in almost all societies have been more concerned with finding appropriate mates for their daughters than for their sons. In "free choice" systems of mate selection, the woman must be especially discriminating. Men, on the other hand, can afford the luxury of being romantic. The fact that a woman's years of marriageability tend to be more limited than a man's also contributes to her need to be selective. Furthermore, because of women's greater interpersonal sensitivity and discrimination, their criteria for falling in love—and for staying in love—may be higher than men's, and they may reevaluate their relationships more carefully (Hill, Rubin, and Peplau, 1977).

To complicate the process further, mate selection may be influenced not only by a present match, but by the marriage type contemplated by an individual for the future. Such factors as value consensus, personality fit, and so on may well be important when the expected marital pattern is interaction, but these factors will less likely affect the choice of a spouse when the expected marital pattern is parallel. This anticipatory process may have an impact on people's perception of equity in their choice of marital partner.

If two persons are in a relationship that turns out to be inequitable, they will experience distress and will try to relieve that distress in one of three ways: they may try to do something to restore equity to the relationship, or they may try to convince themselves that the relationship is equitable even though it isn't (so that equity exists in their heads if not in actuality). Or, third, they may simply decide to break up (Walster and Walster, 1978: Walster, Walster, and Berscheid, 1978; Scanzoni and Scanzoni, 1981).

The propositions regarding exchange, equity, and the principle of least interest can be supported from an opposite direction, that is, from those couples who break up before marriage. Even when a relationship is to be discontinued, there are two sides to every breakup; very few breakups are truly mutual, with both parties deciding at more or less the same time that they would like to end their relationship. In the large majority of cases there are two distinct and unequal roles, "breaker-upper" (the rejecting lover) and "broken-up-with" (the rejected lover) (Hill, Rubin, and Peplau, 1977: 323).

Fixed-Sequence and Circular-Causal Theoretical Perspectives

The theories of mate selection and the development of couple relationships overviewed on preceding pages can be broadly divided into two types: "fixed-sequence and "circular-causal" models of relationship development (Levinger, 1983; Stephen, 1985). Fixed-sequence models have focused on identifying psychological and demographic factors that serve as filtering or matching criteria in the selection of a partner for a committed, long-term relationship. Partners have a tendency to match according to their race, religion, age, ethnic background, education, and socioeconomic status, as well as such features as physical attractiveness, height, weight, and hair colour. Additional similarities may involve the use of drugs and stimulants including alcohol, tobacco, and coffee or tea (Price and Vandenberg, 1980), or similarities in beliefs, attitudes, and values (Byrne and Blaylock, 1963; Corsini, 1956; Katz, 1965; Levinger and Breedlove, 1966; Murstein, 1972; Newcomb and Svehla, 1937). Repeated findings of this sort have formed the basis for fixed-sequence filter theories of partner selection (Kerckhoff and Davis, 1962; Lewis, 1973; Murstein; 1970, 1976, 1980). Fixed-sequence theories postulate sequenced stages of selective filtering for premarital relationships. Stages tend to be marked by individuals' increased awareness of their partners' psychological orientations or behaviourial patterns. New information about the partner is scrutinized consciously or unconsciously at each stage to determine whether or not the partner remains an attractive candidate for a long-term relationship. If

the partner is considered acceptable, the relationship continues; if not, the relationship is terminated, and the partners regain their status as singles and sample again from the pool of eligibles. Such studies that have attempted to predict relationship development based upon matching of these characteristics have yielded inconclusive results or results that later research has not successfully replicated (Centres, 1975; Keckhoff and Davis, 1962; Levinger at al., 1970; Rubin and Levinger, 1974; Stephen, 1985).

An alternative, circular-causal perspective holds that being in a relationship may change the way an individual views the world (Berger and Kellner, 1964; Bolton, 1961; Reiss, 1960; Stephen, 1984; Davis, 1973; Kreckel, 1982; Levinger, 1980; Newcomb and Bentler, 1978; Pearce and Cronen, 1980; Price et al., 1981). Circular-causal models of relationship development emphasize the transformational power of relationships, and the importance of emergent commitments and knowledge shared by couple members. The progress of a relationship is seen as an outcome of initial matching or filtering as well as of communication processes. Communication increases dyadic interdependence by creating emergent meaning structures that may influence the beliefs and behaviour of relationship partners.

Circular-causal conceptions distinguish themselves from filter models of relationship development in their emphasis that cognition is dynamic and subject to redefinition in conversation. In both sets of models, the passage of time is marked by progressively deeper disclosure. While in fixed-sequence models, disclosed information provides a basis for selective filtering, in circular-causal models, beliefs, attitudes, values, and individuals' frameworks for interpreting reality are reworked to accommodate divergent views. This process gradually generates a joint "micro-culture" (Berger and Kellner, 1964; Fine, 1979), which helps to orient couple members with regard to each other and aspects of the world beyond their relationship.

Furthermore, in contrast to the position forwarded by the filter models, Stephen (1984,

1985) and several other theorists (Berger and Kellner, 1964; Bolton, 1961; Davis 1973; Kreckel, 1982; Levinger, 1980; Newcomb and Bentler, 1978; Pearce and Cronen, 1980; Reiss, 1960) argue that communication between couple members may shape their perceptions and may evoke commitments that determine a relationship's development. Since almost any contact between different cognitive systems leads to mutual contamination and the development of interdependence, it may be as much the communication exchange between partners that determines the progress of their relationship as the background factors themselves. Moreover, partners sharing similar experiences might alter their perceptions in a like fashion. If other researchers (Kelley, 1955) found no evidence for convergence over time, it may be because they began their measurements after the point at which the subjects had formally announced their engagement, or because they often relied on measures related to global issues, for example the "nature of man" (Stephen, 1985) instead of beliefs and attitudes that pertain directly to intimate relationships (Stephen and Markman, 1983).

Summary

For decades, the mystery and intricacies of the choice of one's marital partner have puzzled both people who make their own choosing, and researchers who study the mate selection process. There have been numerous attempts to describe empirically and analyze theoretically the factors and the dynamics of the mate selection process at both individual and societal levels. At first, most of these attempts addressed primarily the individual or psychological aspects of mate selection, or represented the "old cultural stand-bys of demographic nose-counting of rate of homogamy in religion, socioeconomic status, education, etc." (Murstein, 1980: 789).

The last few decades have been witness to the gradual shift from examining the correlates of marital choice toward analyzing the causes and dynamics of the mate selection process throughout its development from singlehood to marital or nonmarital cohabitation. There

has also been a greater recognition that most of the factors entering the process of mate selection correlate among themselves and within the socio-economic contextual factors.

In this chapter, we have examined those theories that have had the greatest impact in family sociology in the area of mate selection. We have seen how the theory of complementary needs posits that in mate selection each individual seeks a partner who will provide complementariness to himself or herself. This complementariness may mean that both partners possess the same need but to a differing degree, or that each partner possesses different needs; in either situation, the partners complement one another.

The parental image theory proposes that men and women seek partners who are substitutes for their parents of the opposite sex. The main argument of the filter theory is that the potential partner's attributes and characteristics are scrutinized through a series of filters that operate at different stages of the relationship. The premarital dyadic formation theory suggests that there exist six pair processes through which couples progressively proceed during their dating and courtship careers.

Another, developmental view of mate selection is presented as a process of responding to attractions of a prospective mate, overcoming barriers, and refuting or accepting alternative attractions. Thus, mate selection is a process of choosing a specific person for a marriage partner within a series of stages through which relationship passes on its way to marriage or is discontinued.

As applied to mate selection, the social exchange theory posits that prospective partners choose one another on the basis of exchange of rewards and costs associated with them. These rewards may consist of expressive rewards, physical attraction and affection, shared responsibilities, social status or economic gain, and the like. According to exchange theorists, an individual will select someone who can offer the greatest rewards at the lowest cost. The relationship will continue as long as exchange between partners remains equitable.

Chapter 12 / Jarmila L.A. Horna

The development of mate selection theories has proceeded from examining the monolithic, single-factor to the complex, multi-dimensional approaches, from the unidirectional to reciprocal and interactive perspectives, from static to developmental approaches, from theories which only pay attention to mates who successfully proceed toward marriage, to theories which also consider discontinued relationships, and from the linear fixed-sequence models to circular-causal models. The multitude and variety of mate selection theories document both lack of consensus among family sociologists with regard to the most adequate perspective, and a continuing struggle to bring forward a theory which will provide the greatest explanatory power.

TECHNICAL TERMS

ASSORTATIVE MATING—Potential mates are sorted or selected rather than chosen at random.

COMPLEMENTARITY—Gratification of other partner's needs when (a) both partners possess different needs or (b) when both partners possess the same need but to a differing degree.

DYADIC FORMATION—The process through which two people become a dyad (couple).

FILTERS—In mate selection, partners are screened through a series of filters: (a) such attributes as race, ethnicity, religion, age, social class; (b) value consensus; and (c) complementarity of their needs.

RESOURCE —An ability, possession, or other attribute allowing a person to reward or punish another person; any ability possessed by one person is a resource only in relations with specific other persons who value it.

SOCIAL EXCHANGE IN MATE SELECTION—Person capable of the possible greatest reward for the lowest cost to a potential partner will be selected from prospective mates.

QUESTIONS

1. Explain the theory of complementary needs, and suggest why this theory generated so much criticism.

2. Summarize social exchange theory in its application to mate selection; characterize and illustrate rewards, costs, and equity in choosing one's partner.

3. Distinguish among the following: filter theory, commitment wheel model, and barriers-attraction-alternative attraction model of mate selection.

4. Explain the process and dynamics of the premarital dyadic formation.

5. Outline and discuss theories of mate selection according to classification by the fixed-sequence/circular-causal perspective.

SUGGESTED READINGS

- Bert N. Adams. "Mate selection in the United States: a theoretical summarization." In *Contemporary Theories about the Family*, Vol. 1, ed. Wesley R. Burr et al., 259–267. Glencoe, IL: Free Press, 1979.

   An overview of theories of mate selection. Includes Adams' own theoretical model of the process of choosing a specific mate; this model consists of nineteen theoretical propositions based on the theories under his review.

- David A. Karp and William C. Yoels. "From strangers to intimates." In *Marriage and Family in a Changing Society*, 2d ed., ed. James M. Henslin. Glencoe, IL: Free Press, 1985, 188–197.

   Succinct overview of the process during which strangers become intimates through rapport, self-revelation, mutual dependency, and need fulfillment. A good summary of some mate selection theories is supplemented with interesting illustrations from the real life.

Chapter 12 / Jarmila L.A. Horna

- Bernard I. Murstein. "Mate selection in the 1970s." *Journal of Marriage and the Family* 42 (1980): 777–792.

  This entire journal issue is devoted to the decade review of the developments in family studies. Murstein's article summarizes research in the United States, cross-cultural currents, some other research and earlier theories, but concentrates mostly on three theories first proposed in the 1970s: stimulus-value-role theory, dyadic formation theory, and instrumental theory.

- G. N. Ramu. "Courtship and marriage." In *The Canadian Family*, ed. K. Ishwaran, 246–262. Toronto: Gage, 1983.

  Brings together various findings on Canadian mate selection and marriage, and delineates the social forces that encourage conformity to traditional patterns or are conducive to change.

- Timothy D. Stephen. "Fixed-sequence and circular-causal models of relationship development: divergent views on the role of communication in intimacy." *Journal of Marriage and the Family* 47 (1985): 955–963.

  Before presenting results of his study which show that (after controlling for changes in relationship commitment and satisfaction) couples become significantly more similar in their beliefs, attitude, and values, Stephen reviews current theories of partner selection and relationship development.

- Robert F. Winch. *Mate-Selection: A Study of Complementary Needs.* New York: Harper and Row, 1958.

  The original study which proposed the theory of complementary needs, and created considerable interest, generated a lot of controversy, and gave rise to much criticism.

Reverse: An emotional moment during a wedding in France. Pierre Belzeaux, France

PART IV

THE MARITAL SYSTEM

A Finnish wedding in Northern Scandinavia.
Fred Bruemmer

MARRIAGE
A Developing Process

James M. White
University of British Columbia

Most people reading this book are either presently married or have been married or will be married in the future. The marriage rates for developed countries continue to remind us that from 70% to 95% will marry at least once in their lifetime. However, the very way in which we categorize marital status as either "married, divorced, separated, widowed, or single" reinforces a view of marriage as a relatively fixed outcome rather than a developing process. For example, research, as well as the popular press, often tends to emphasize getting into or getting out of a marriage rather than the more subtle processes which occur during the life of a marriage. This chapter emphasizes these processes which are taking place in contemporary marriages.

Defining Marriage

At the outset it is important to have some notion of what we mean by the term "marriage." On the surface, it would seem we all know what a marriage is since our parents are married, our friends are married; in fact, we are surrounded by this phenomenon. However, the fact that we are surrounded by marriages can just as easily give us a myopic view of marriage based on our particular culture and background. If we look at the many things to which the term "marriage" refers, we get some idea of the complexities which reside in our use of the term. For example, "marriage" can refer to a particular form of relationship between two people, yet it is a current debate in North America whether the two people should necessarily be of opposite genders. A second example is that "marriage" can refer to a formal institution established by the laws of a society. But, what then of the Kaingang, a Brazilian tribal society, who have no formal laws in this respect (Henry, 1964)? "Marriage" can also refer to the social institution of marriage whether it is formalized in laws or not. "Marriage" may mean one thing to a member of a particular religion and something different to non-members. For example, in most Christian denominations "marriage" is considered a holy sacrament. These diverse meanings for the term "marriage" can confuse any discussion of the subject since it is quite easy to switch meanings inadvertently during a discussion.

To what does the term "marriage" refer? The following captures much of what we mean by this term:

A marriage is a group (usually a dyad) which is regulated by formal and/or informal institutional social norms governing mating.

This definition needs some further explanation. An institution is a set of social norms regulating a relatively well defined area of social life. Some social institutions commonly found in most societies are religious, political, economic, and the social institutions of family and marriage. It is this last institution which contains the norms regulating marriage.

Levels of Analysis

In order to gain a clear notion of what we mean by the term "marriage," it is necessary to introduce some analytic concepts which will help us in this task. These concepts are all part

TABLE 13-1: LEVELS OF ANALYSIS

Level of Analysis	Units of Observation	Measures & Concepts
Individual	individuals as subjects	marital status, marital quality
Relationships	minimum unit is the dyad (e.g. cohabitation).	agreement, communication
Group	minimum unit is a relationship regulated by social norms (e.g. marriage or family)	cohesion, stability
Institution	unit is aggregate behavior (e.g. marriages)	institutional norms regulating marriages

of a general picture which we can call *levels of analysis*. A level of analysis refers to the set of possible objects or units which may be appropriately studied and about which generalizations can be properly made. There are four levels of analysis with which we will be concerned in this chapter. They are the individual level, the relationship level, the group level, and the institutional level. Corresponding to each level of analysis are units of observation, which may be appropriately studied at each level, and concepts and measures which are appropriate. Table 13–1 may help in making these ideas more clear.

Table 13–1 summarizes some complex issues. The problem is that different aspects of marriage may be emphasized, depending on which level of analysis one chooses. If we wish to study the physical health of individuals who are married compared with individuals who are not married, then a definition of marriage would probably be only a legal one (i.e. formal norms). If, on the other hand, we suspect that being in a living-together relationship affects one's physical health, then we might not bother with marital status but be interested in the presence or absence of a living-together relationship (relationship level). If we change questions and decide we are interested in whether or not married couples agree with each other's attitudes about politics to a greater extent than randomly paired individuals of opposite genders, then we would want a definition of marriage appropriate for the group level of analysis. Each level of analysis and research question demands a different orientation toward "marriage."

This complex situation is further complicated by the fact that most marriages are found in the context of the family. For instance, in 1985 about 72% of white and black households in the United States were categorized as families (US Bureau of the Census, 1986), and in Canada about 84% of the population resided in families (Minister of Supply and Services, 1987). Of course, some of these families are single-parent families. For example, in Canada about 12% of all families are single-parent families, and the number is similar for white families in the United States.

When a marriage is part of a family, it becomes one of the many dyadic relationships (relationship level) within the family group, such as sibling dyads, parent-child dyads, and the marital dyad. For most people, marriage is a prelude to family. However, with delays in marriage and delays in childbirth, we might suspect a corresponding rise in childless marriages. For instance, in Canada in 1961 only 40% of the women between the ages of twenty to twenty-four were single, in 1981 there were 51% who were single, and in 1986 there were 60% who were single (Minister of Supply and Services, 1987). Burch (1985) reports that about

75% of females were married at least once, and 67% raised at least one natural child. This finding indicates that the number of childless marriages is still less than 10%, especially when one considers adoption (2.5%) and step-children (2.1%). Given these statistics, increases in childlessness due to delayed marriage and female labour force participation do not seem as likely a response to delayed marriage as decreases in fertility and family size. For most marriages, the course of marriage will begin as a dyadic group, become a family relationship when children are present, and later return to the status of a dyad when the children leave home.

It is not possible to discuss processes or changes in marriage without specifying the level of analysis. For example, if we say that "marriage is changing," we need to know whether we are referring to the *institution* of marriage or marriage as a *relationship*. If we refer to the institution of marriage, then we are claiming that the social norms which regulate the group are changing. On the other hand, if that statement refers to "marriage" as a relationship, then it could mean, for example, that the nonverbal communication between husbands and wives is changing. So, in order to understand processes of change, we must be clear about the level or levels on which change is taking place. As well, we must be clear about what we mean by "change."

Developmental Change in Marriage

The previous section made the point that in order to discuss family change and development in a meaningful way, we must specify the level of analysis and exactly what is changing (i.e. norms, roles, attitudes, etc.). In this section, the discussion focuses on both *what* is changing and *how* it changes. This section identifies some of the different stages and events in marriage and the processes contained in our concept of change.

Developmental change in marriage takes place when a marriage shifts from one qualitatively distinct stage to another stage of marital life (Duvall, 1971; Hill and Rodgers, 1964; Rodgers, 1973; Aldous, 1978). These qualitatively distinct periods in the life of a marriage are called *marital stages*. It is an imposing task indeed to attempt to enumerate all of the possible stages in married life since there are a great many. Each stage is bounded by transition events which mark the end of the previous stage and the beginning of the next stage. For instance, the wedding day is a transition event which ends the engagement stage and begins the early years of marriage. The birth of the first child ends the early years of the marriage as a non-family group and begins the marriage as a relationship within the family group.

The process of development in a marriage is not a strictly determined march through specific stages and events but is, rather, a process where individual choice, economic variables, political variables and many other variables play a role. Hence, it is best to describe this process as a probabilistic or stochastic process. An example will make this idea clearer. Imagine all the many possible events and stages for marriages such as divorce, separation, remarriage, wedding day, early marriage, cohabitation, to mention but a few. Now, imagine a marriage in one particular stage, such as the early years of marriage. The possible transitions to a next stage are several. The couple could separate or divorce or have a first child or one spouse could die. The notion of developmental change does not tell us what any one marriage will do next, but it does tell us that the longer the couple remains in the early childless married stage the probabilities for various next stages change. This is what Featherman (1985) implies in his definition of developmental change as where the probability of a transition to the next stage is dependent on both the present stage and the duration of time spent in the present stage. For example, the probability for having a first child changes with the duration of marriage. The very early months of marriage have a relatively low probability which then increases up to about 12 months and then decreases fairly rapidly to about 42 months, after which it tends to level off (Teachman and Polonko, 1985).

At the institutional level, the theory of family development is concerned with changes in norms which govern marital stage transitions. For example, we all learn rules about the proper way in which to sequence marital and family events. This socialization into the institutional norms of marriage and family is often pervasive and subtle, as with the rope skipping rhyme "...first comes love, then comes marriage, then comes Susie with a baby carriage." This represents the normative sequence of stages for marriage as part of family life. These sequencing and timing norms regulate stage transitions at the group and relationship levels (Neugarten, Moore, Lowe, 1965). Thus, although there are many possible marital stages, socialization into particular patterns of transitions makes certain stages much more preferred, and, therefore, more probable than other marital stages.

Developmental change should not be confused with *adaptive change* in marriage. Adaptive change indicates a process similar to the process analyzed in ecology. In ecology, the environment places pressures on a population to adapt to changes or vanish. The same is true for marriages. Marriages must continually adapt to changes in the world that surrounds them, changes, for example, in the economy, war, and disease. There are ample illustrations of research on family adaptations such as adaptation to the work world (Rallings and Nye, 1979) and adaptation to stressor events (Hansen and Johnson, 1979).

INDIVIDUAL PROCESSES IN MARRIAGE

Assessing Marital Quality

One of the areas in the study of marriage which has received the greatest scholarly attention is the assessment of how happy, satisfied, or well adjusted spouses are in their marriage. Throughout the fifty-year-long history of this interest in marital assessment, various scales and measures have been devised, with the major result being an abundance of such measures. The result of such a profusion of

scales of marital satisfaction, happiness, and adjustment has been some confusion as to what exactly is being measured by all these measures. This situation was partially cleared up by the factor analytic study by Spanier (1976), which showed four major dimensions from a pool of such measures. From this analysis came the Dyadic Adjustment Scale (Spanier, 1976), one of the most popular of current measures. Most recently, the Dyadic Adjustment Scale has been criticized because of its multi-dimensionality, and many scholars have focused on finding a one-dimensional scale to measure marital quality (Norton, 1983; Fincham and Bradbury, 1987).

If all this is confusing, then some understanding of the situation has no doubt been gained. Such confusion did not go unnoticed by scholars. Gottman in his book *Marital Interaction* (1979) reviews the various correlations between diverse measures of marital satisfaction, happiness, and adjustment. He concludes that since these diverse measures of marital satisfaction, marital happiness, and marital adjustment are so highly correlated with one another, they are all measuring the same dimension or construct. Lewis and Spanier (1979) identified the construct which unifies all these diverse measures as being "marital quality." Lewis and Spanier (1979), in their review of empirical findings, reach a conclusion similar to Gottman's, that all these measures are highly correlated. They then argue convincingly that all these diverse measures are actually measuring the same thing, and that is "marital quality." Given Gottman's point regarding the strong correlation of these measures and the fact that similar questions appear in several scales, Lewis and Spanier's concept of "marital quality" is now commonly accepted by family scholars as unifying the diverse literature on marital satisfaction, happiness, and adjustment.

The single most important fact to keep in mind regarding any discussion of marital quality is that it is measured by an individual spouse's response to a scale. The importance of this point is that marital quality is a measure of the individual's assessment of his or her

TABLE 13-2 SELECTED COVARIATES OF MARITAL QUALITY[*]

Independent Variables	Direction of Association	Dependent Variable
Husband's Occupational Status	+	
Wife's Satisfaction with her Employment	+	
Size of friendship network	+	
Perceived similarity with spouse	+	
Expression of affection	+	MARITAL QUALITY
Number of shared activities	+	
Role complementarity	+	
Education level	+	
Religiosity	+	
Parental level of marital quality	+	

[*] Lewis and Spanier (1979).

marriage. Thus, it is quite possible that one spouse in a marriage would be very satisfied while the other spouse is much less satisfied.

The question of greatest interest to scholars is "What are the factors which lead to a person evaluating his or her marriage as being of high quality?" Indeed, many of the factors contributing to the assessment of marital quality have been identified. (See Table 13–2.) However, this relatively simple question has a complex answer since so many of the factors interact with one another. For example, we know that the greater the religiosity of the individual, the more likely that person is to evaluate his or her marriage in a favourable way. We also know that favourable assessments are directly related to higher education level. However, we seldom know the effect for a low score on religiosity combined with high level of education on the individual's assessment of his or her marriage. More importantly, we have little understanding of how these covariates change over the life course for the average marriage.

The best estimate we have of the process affecting the individual assessment of marital quality is from the research on how marital quality changes with stages of the family. Although this research is clearly concerned with developmental changes in marriage, most of the methodology has been cross-sectional in design and, therefore, constrains any conclusions regarding changes in marriages. What we do know is that marital quality does vary according to family stage. This finding was first noted by Rollins and Feldman (1970) and is now referred to as the "U" shaped relationship between marital quality and family stage. Although different researchers have used slightly different family stages, the relationship has largely been substantiated not only

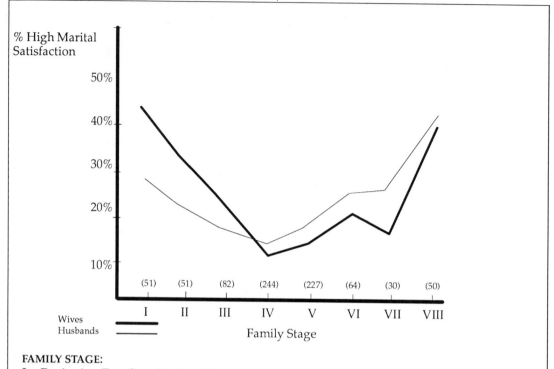

FAMILY STAGE:
I = Beginning Families; II = Families with infants; III = Families with preschoolers;
IV = Families with school age children; V = Families with teenagers; VI = Launching;
VII = Empty nest; VIII = Retirement

FIGURE 13–1: MARITAL QUALITY BY FAMILY STAGE
SOURCE: Adapted from Rollins and Feldman (1970), Figure 1, p. 25.

for samples in the United States but in Canada as well (Frideres and Lupri, 1981). Anderson, Russell, and Schumm (1983) found that the "U" shaped relationship was not simply due to greater conventionality among older people in their sample. (See Figure 13–1.)

In conclusion, we know quite a few of the factors affecting an individual's assessment of marital quality. What we don't know is how these many factors interact. The research on marital quality and family stage gives a relatively clear though methodologically limited picture of changes in marital quality. The "U" shaped curve indicates that people find they are most satisfied and happy with marriage at the beginning, before romantic idealization of the spouse and the relationship has been tar-

nished by experience. With the addition of children and the diminishing of marital roles compared to parental roles, comes less marital satisfaction. As early child bearing and the responsibilities of small children pass and are supplanted, once again, by greater amounts of time for the marital roles, the assessment of marital quality begins to rise. Finally, when children leave home and there is a return to marital as opposed to parental roles, marital quality is comparatively high. This process is clearly a developmental process. That is, marital quality is dependent on the stage one occupies. However, there are undoubtedly adaptations which are associated with high marital quality, but many of these are at the dyadic rather than individual level of analysis.

Chapter 13 / James M. White

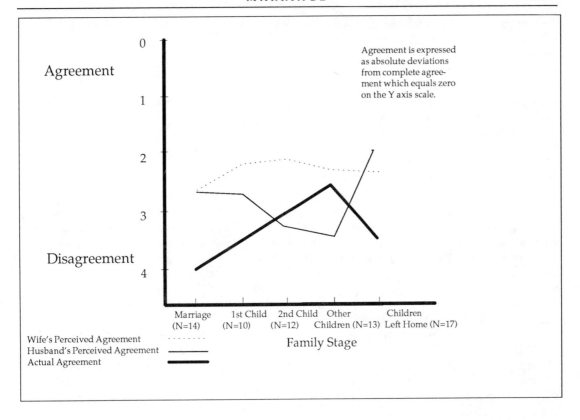

FIGURE 13–2: ACTUAL DYADIC AGREEMENT AND INDIVIDUAL PERCEIVED AGREEMENT BY FAMILY STAGE

SOURCE: Adapted from White (1987), Figure 1, p 53.

DYADIC PROCESSES IN MARRIAGE

There are two major areas which receive scholarly attention at the dyadic or relationship level of analysis. Both of these areas provide measures which can be used to measure properties of the dyad rather than the individual. These two areas are the area of interpersonal agreement and the area of marital communication.

Spousal Agreement in Marriage

The area of marital agreement receives scholarly attention from a diverse range of scholars: for example, Larson (1974) and Kirkpatrick and Hobart (1955) in Sociology; Laing, Phillipson and Lee (1966) in Psychiatry; Kelly

and his associates (1983) in Psychology; and, Niemi (1974) in Political Science. The study of agreement in marriage is of great interest for several reasons. We suspect that a couple who have high levels of disagreement will not be happy. Therefore, we expect the level of agreement in marriage to be associated with marital stability. Another reason for the study of marital agreement is that it allows us to focus on the processes which contribute or detract from agreement such as negotiating skills and social skills. Thus, this area has been of concern to academic and therapist alike.

What is dyadic agreement? A couple's agreement can be measured in several ways. One way is simply to ask the husband and wife each a question independently of each other and compare the two responses. A more complex comparison is possible if we ask each spouse if the other spouse agrees or not with their attitude. This is an individual level measure called "perceived agreement" and if we refer back to Table 13–2 we find that it is positively related to an individual's assessment of his or her marital quality. However, as we shall see shortly, the individual may believe there to be high levels of agreement in the marriage when such is not actually the case.

The research on marital agreement shows that the greater the level of agreement in a marriage, then the greater is the marital stability (Laing, Phillipson and Lee, 1966). Riskin and Faunce (1972), in their review of interactional research, concluded that the ratio of agreements to disagreements in a couple's interaction is the best single factor discriminating the couple's level of marital distress. Gottman (1979) observed both clinical and non-clinical couples interact and used a ratio of the number of agreements between spouses, divided by the number of agreements plus disagreements. He found, consistent with the conclusions of Riskin and Faunce (1972), that this measure of agreement in the couples' interaction discriminated between distressed and non-distressed couples. It appears that this measure of agreements to disagreements is one of the best ways to discriminate normal couples from couples seeking clinical assistance for their marriages.

The process by which marital agreement is achieved is not a simple one. For example, some degree of agreement in marriage is due to the selection of a partner similar to oneself (Lewis and Spanier, 1979). Selecting a mate who comes from the same socio-economic background, religious background, and education level establishes many areas of similarity and agreement even before the wedding date. So, certainly part of the process is premarital. However, there is a considerable degree of marital agreement which is established during the course of the marriage. Some of this is naturally established when two people share the same experiences, such as children and household. McLain and Weigert (1979) refer to

this as a process of "biographical fusion." Other aspects of agreement are reached in the daily struggles toward not only a tolerable relationship but a rewarding one. These processes will be examined shortly as dyadic processes of communication.

The little information we have about the process of spousal agreement over the course of the relationship points out that dyadic agreement is not always recognized by the individuals in the relationship. Figure 13–2, for example, shows that across family stages dyadic agreement improves at times when the tasks and demands of children at home require that couples coordinate their activities. Coordination requires agreement on methods and goals. Figure 13–2 also shows that when actual agreement is the greatest, a number of individual spouses do not recognize or perceive agreement in their relationships. This finding raises questions about the accuracy of individual assessments of a marriage. Furthermore, this finding has implications for the study of spousal communication since it is often assumed that effective communication results in accurate perceptions of the relationship.

Communication in Marriage

Walk down almost any row of popular magazines and you will see at least some articles claiming "Save your marriage: thirteen tips on how to improve communication." In fact, communication has become somewhat of a universal panacea for what ails today's marriages. There is, as we shall see, both truth and myth to these claims.

In order to examine the findings about marriage and communication, it is convenient to organize this area into two parts. One part deals with verbal communication in marriage and the other with nonverbal. Basic to all communication is the characteristic that one person influences another. In technical terms, communication takes place when the probability for a behavior is conditional on an other's actions (Shannon and Weaver, 1949). Verbal communication occurs when spoken language is used, and nonverbal communication refers to all those gestures and utterances which may employ sound and gesture but not language.

The research on verbal communication in marriage points out that there is a strong relationship between the quality of communication and marital quality (e.g. Blood and Wolfe, 1960; Navran, 1967; Kahn, 1969; Murphy and Mendelson, 1973). However, an uncritical acceptance of these findings could lead to some unwarranted conclusions in regard to the importance of verbal communication. Raush et al., (1973) report that couples avoiding communications on some issues are as well adjusted as other couples. As well, the research correlating communication with marital quality suffers from the methodological problem of a lack of independence between the measures for each area. That is, there are questions about communication which measure agreement and questions about marital quality which measure agreement. The resulting high correlations are at least in part due to this overlap between the measures. Mishler and Waxler (1968) found several communication differences between normal families and families where one member was a diagnosed schizophrenic. Their conclusion is instructive for us. They concluded that although there were communication differences, they could not with confidence say whether the communication pattern developed as a cause of the disease or as a consequent adjustment to having a family member with the disease. In terms of verbal communication, we know that the number of verbal disagreements is associated with low marital quality (Gottman,1979), but we do not know whether this is cause or symptom. It could be that some other factor such as marital commitment is causally linked to both disagreements and marital quality. In light of these findings and problem areas, the only conclusion warranted in regard to the quality of marriage and verbal communication is that there is a positive relationship, but this relationship might be due to methodological flaws or spurious attributions of cause.

Research into nonverbal communication suggests that it is a more important factor in marriage than is verbal communication. Non-verbal communication is considered to be the gestures, body movements, facial expressions, eye contact, and non-language sounds (e.g. whines, groans) occurring in interaction, whether intentional or not. In nonverbal research, it has long been observed that one cannot "not communicate" since even silence sends a message. Gottman (1979), in his observational study of couple interaction, found that nonverbal measures discriminated better between couples seeking clinical help for their marriages and non-clinical couples than did either the verbal measures or the ratio of agreements to agreements plus disagreements. He concludes that nonverbal behavior is a better discriminator of marital distress than verbal behavior. Noller (1984) reports that couples low in marital quality misunderstand one another's messages more than high marital quality couples. Furthermore, at least one study suggests that the ability to understand the other spouse's nonverbal messages is related to marital quality (Gottman and Porterfield, 1981). Gottman and Porterfield (1981) used video-taped messages from one spouse to test the ability of the other spouse to understand the nonverbal message better than a stranger. They found that the wife's marital satisfaction was highly correlated with the husbands score on a nonverbal marital communication scale (M.C.S.II). More importantly, they found that for satisfied couples, husbands were better at reading the nonverbal messages of their spouses than were the strangers, but for dissatisfied marriages, there was no difference between the husband's ability to decode his wife's nonverbal messages and the ability of a stranger to decode the wife's nonverbal messages. This study suggests that in distressed marriages, husbands may be poor at reading and interpreting the nonverbal messages of their wives.

Research into the nonverbal behavior of married partners suggests that nonverbal behavior may be more important in predicting marital distress than is verbal behavior. One interpretation of this research is that nonverbal communication tends to carry more emotional content than does verbal communication.

After all, a caress or physical closeness carries a much stronger message of liking than does the verbal message "I like you" unaccompanied by such nonverbal affection. It is obvious, however, that sending the same message both verbally and nonverbally insures that the message is both strong and consistent.

There is a strong correlation between communication and marital quality. However, caution is necessary since no causal relation has been shown to exist. Furthermore, any discussion of communication in marriage should examine nonverbal as well as verbal forms of communication. Undoubtedly, communication effectiveness changes over the course of the marriage. At this point, we do not know if communication skills are at a high point in dating and then deteriorate as marriages age or if communication continues to become more accurate and effective as the marriage traverses its course.

THE CHANGING INSTITUTION OF MARRIAGE

Marriage as an institution is quite different from marriage as a relationship. Marriage as an institution refers to the social rules or norms which regulate social life in the area of marriage and family. These norms are of two basic types. First, there are norms which regulate such things as the roles of husband and wife, division of labour in the household, and division of property. Many of these norms are formalized in law such as "the degrees of consanguinity," dictating with whom one can mate, or the laws regulating division of matrimonial property in the event of a divorce. There is a second set of norms which are unlike the first set. This second set of norms regulate the timing and sequencing of marital and family events (Neugarten, Moore, Lowe, 1965). These norms are processual norms which regulate the developmental processes in marriage. For example, we all know that those who have premarital births deviate from the timing and sequencing norms in North America. We have learned that the timing and sequencing of these events should follow a particular order

of love, marriage, and then births. These are processual family norms.

The processual norms within one institution such as marriage and family are, in turn, buttressed by the processual norms in other institutions such as work and education. The processual norms across all the different social institutions have to articulate with each other and work smoothly with each other. For example, imagine a different type of society from ours where at the age of eighteen one is expected to leave one's family, get married, have a child, start working, start university, and buy a house. Clearly, if this were even possible, the stress load on the individual and couple would be crippling. Rather, most societies organize these events by means of age-graded norms and processual norms. Thus, one is expected to finish education before starting a full-time job, get a full-time job before getting married, and get married before having children.

The consequences for not following these normative sequences have been well documented. For instance, Morgan and Rindfuss (1985) studied the effects on marital disruption for various sequences for the events of conception, marriage, and birth for a sample of US females. Their research showed that sequences with premarital births had a negative effect on later marital stability. Hogan (1978, 1980) found that American men who traversed sequences other than the normative sequence of finishing education, starting a first job, and then marriage had significantly higher rates of marital instability. White (1987b) found that non-normative sequences for the events of first job, marriage, and first child are related to later life work interruptions for females in a Canadian sample. Thus, it appears that one consequence of not following normative institutional sequences is a lack of inter- and intra-institutional articulation later in the life course.

The institutional norms regulating the timing and sequencing of events are changing. Some of these changes come about because of adaptation to the norms of other institutions. For example, fertility and desired family size are decreasing because of a complex of norms in work and education, which suggest more education and job consolidation before marriage for both males and females. As a result, both childbirth and marriage are delayed, while new norms emerge to regulate cohabitation as a processual step between dating and marriage. As marriage is delayed, there is less and less time for females to have children. As well, dual careers and rising expectations regarding parental roles make it less likely that large families can be accommodated in busy schedules. The end result of these normative shifts for marriage is that we spend more time than previously in the conjugal unit as husband and wife, rather than as mother and father. One impact of fewer children is that the last child leaves the home while parents are comparatively young, so that we spend greater amounts of time in marriage after the children have left (Rodgers and Witney, 1982). This change suggests that one outcome of smaller families is to place an even greater emphasis on marriage as a rewarding and important social institution.

CROSS-CULTURAL PROCESSES

The changes in the institution of marriage and the family and other social institutions can be better understood in light of the processes of adaptation and development which are taking place in the world. One can safely say that there are no societies whose changes are totally explained by internal social development. Rather, the internal development of most societies is now linked to adaptations which are needed to survive in a competitive world. The direction of adaptations the institution of marriage makes are surprisingly uniform across cultures. What varies are the rates at which each culture's institutions adapt to the world environment. For example, rates of adaptation in traditional cultures are slowed by norms which are distinctly different and distant from those required in the world today.

Kumagai (1984) shows an amazing convergence in the timing of marital and family events for the United States, Canada, and Japan (Figure 13–3). The rapid adjustments for

Japan are due to two factors. First, females have much longer life expectancies today, and second, children are spaced much more closely together than in the past. These two factors are also present for the United States and Canada but are much more pronounced in Japan. The overall trend encountered in Figure 13–3 can be summarized as the trend that marriage will be increasingly important as children are fewer and leave the home earlier, leaving the post-parental years to be spent in the conjugal unit. The delay of marriage and childbirth will only change this slightly since longevity has made a proportionately larger increase in time spent in marriage relative to delayed fertility.

The world-wide trend is for greater amounts of time to be spent in the post-parental marriage. Some might say that the institution of marriage is not constructed to stay together for such a lengthy time without the glue of children to hold it together. They cite the high divorce rates in the United States as evidence of this structural instability of the institution of marriage. However, the Canadian divorce rates are about half that of the United States, yet Canadians with their longer life span spend more time in marriage than do couples in the United States. One conclusion is that there are some norms which reside in the Canadian institution of marriage which promote stability and that are not found in the United States institution. Such cross-cultural variability is nonetheless within the range of adaptations required for both cultures.

The adaptations required for all cultures can be summarized as adaptations to a post-industrial, information-based world economy, to greater emphasis on individual gratification rather than the group, and to the greater longevity of individuals. The adaptations required of the institution of marriage are several:

1. Marriage will be delayed so that prolonged education can be accommodated.

2. Marriage will be delayed and childbirth will be delayed so that women can enter the labour force.

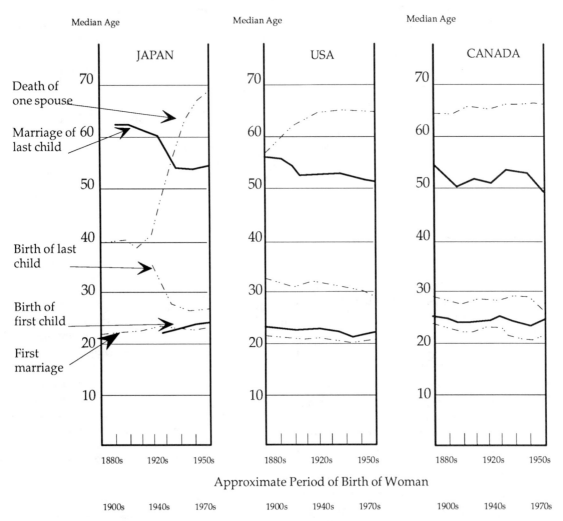

Median Age — JAPAN
Median Age — USA
Median Age — CANADA

Death of one spouse
Marriage of last child
Birth of last child
Birth of first child
First marriage

1880s 1920s 1950s   1880s 1920s 1950s   1880s 1920s 1950s

Approximate Period of Birth of Woman

1900s 1940s 1970s   1900s 1940s 1970s   1900s 1940s 1970s

Approximate Period of First Marriage

SOURCES: Japanese Bureau of Statistics, Imperial Cabinet, 1887–1939; Japanese Statistics Bureau of the Prime Minister's Office, 1949–1981; Center for Population Studies, Ministry of Health and Welfare, 1981; Glick, 1977: Table 1; Rogers and Witney, 1981: Table 1. *From Kumagai (1984), Figure 3, p. 200*

FIGURE 13–3:
MEDIAN AGE OF MOTHERS AT THE BEGINNING OF SELECTED STAGES OF THE FAMILY LIFE CYCLE: JAPAN, UNITED STATES, AND CANADA.

3. Fertility will be restricted because: (a) children are costly, (b) standards of child rearing are higher, (c) due to work and education, women will have fewer years for childbearing and will desire to continue in the labour force.

4. Marriage must become more companionate due to the increased longevity of marriages and emphasis on personal gratification.

5. Marriage must maintain the individual's commitment to the institution of marriage despite emphasis on individual gratification.

CONCLUSION

A marriage, as we have discovered, may refer to several different things: for example, a two-person group regulated by social norms, a legal unit, or a dyadic relationship within a family. Even though we defined a marriage as "a group (usually a dyad) which is regulated by formal and/or informal institutional social norms governing mating," this definition does not resolve all the difficulties. Some of these difficulties are a product of varying levels of analysis used in the study of marriage. At the individual level of analysis, we are often interested in the subjective assessment of marital quality. At the dyadic level of analysis, interest is often focused upon the interaction within the relationship. At the group level of analysis, attention is directed to the cohesion and stability of the marriage. This stability of the marriage as a group is often related to the social norms toward fidelity, monogamy, and divorce. At the institutional level of analysis, both the norms regulating a particular stage of married life (static) and the norms regulating the sequencing of stages of marriage (process) become the areas of concentration.

Communication does appear to be an important ingredient in marriage. There is, however, much which we do not as yet comprehend about how and why communication is important. For example, the relative importance of nonverbal as opposed to verbal com-

munication is just starting to be understood. It has been suggested that the relative efficacy of nonverbal communication comes from the fact that nonverbal communication carries a greater emotional and affective component than does verbal communication.

The institution of marriage and the family must adapt to changes in the normative structure of other institutions, such as work and education. Moreover, all social institutions within a given society continually adapt to the changes in the world economic, social, and political system. The changes in this world system are characterized by increasing emphasis on an information-based economy, individual gratification, and the increasing longevity of people. The results of these world trends for each society are somewhat different since the starting points for each society are different. However, for the developed world, these trends affect work and educational institutions by emphasizing the need for extended educations to deal with a technologically complex world, later entry into jobs, and, female participation in the labour force as a form of personal gratification. The result of these changes in the institutions of work and education is that all social institutions must gradually reorganize their processual norms. If, within each society, marriage as an institution structures its norms to optimize relationships that are characterized by both companionship and commitment, then marriage should have a secure future in the twenty-first century.

TECHNICAL TERMS

NORM—A social rule that forbids, permits or requires an action for a specific social position (or category of social actors).

ROLE—A social role is composed of all the norms related to a specific position, for example, the role of wife. (Note that the position of wife is structurally defined as "a married female" whereas the role of wife is defined by the expected actions (norms) which are appropriate for someone in that position.)

RELATIONSHIP—A dyad or larger unit (triad, etc.) that is engaged in social interaction whether that interaction is regulated by norms or not.

GROUP—A group is at least one relationship that is regulated by the norms of a social institution.

INSTITUTION—A social institution is composed of all those norms, formal and informal, regulating a relatively well defined area of social life, such as the family, work, or religion.

MARRIAGE—A marriage is a group (usually a dyad) which is regulated by formal and/or informal institutional norms governing mating.

FAMILY—A social group containing at minimum one parent-child relationship and regulated by institutional norms.

STAGE—A marital or family stage is defined as a qualitatively distinct set of institutional norms and roles in the life course of the group. The beginning and end of a stage is marked by a transition event such as a wedding ceremony marks the transition from engagement to marriage, or the event of the birth of the first child marks the transition from early marriage to young family.

QUESTIONS

1. According to the definitions of marriage and the family are the following relationships marriages, families or neither? A homosexual relationship? A single parent with one child? People in a commune sharing a common domicile and engaging in sexual relations? A cohabiting couple? Why did you answer each of these in the way you did?

2. Relate the "U" shaped curve for marital quality (Figure 13–1.) to the curve for actual agreement in marriage (Figure 13–2.). What might this imply about marital communication over the life course of a marriage?

3. How do you explain Gottman's (1979) findings that measures of non-verbal communication discriminate distressed from non-distressed marriages better than verbal communication measures?

4. Identify the factors which might cause divorce rates to climb in the coming decade and the factors which might contribute to a decline or stabilization of divorce rates in the next decade.

5. Marriage as an institution must adapt to changes in other institutions. Some of these changes are tied to longer periods of education, females continuing to enter the labour force, and delay of marriage. What sequencing norms could change in order to accommodate these other changes? (Hint: What "stage" could be added to the stages of "dating," "engagement" and "marriage" which might accommodate these changes?).

SUGGESTED READINGS

• R. A. Lewis and G. B. Spanier. "Theorizing about the quality and stability of marriage." In *Contemporary Theories About The Family*, ed. Wesley Burr et al., vol. 1. New York: Free Press, 1979.

This essay is still the best overview of the research on the subject of marital quality. This paper summarizes the massive amount of research in the area of marital quality and attempts to construct an empirically based theory accounting for the findings. This essay represents a good starting point for any student interested in marital quality.

• F. D. Fincham and T. N. Bradbury. "The assessment of marital quality: A reevaluation." *Journal of Marriage and the Family* 49 (1987): 797–810.

This is a fairly technical article but useful to develop a sophisticated view of measurement problems in the assessment of marital quality. It may be helpful to read the essay by Lewis and Spanier (1979) first.

- P. Noller. *Nonverbal Communication and Marital Interaction*. New York: Pergamon Press, 1984.

  A detailed and technical review of the research on nonverbal communication in marriage, with an account of the results of studies over the last three decades.

- J. Aldous. *Family Careers*. New York: Wiley, 1978.

  This book is a good introduction to the developmental approach. There are lengthy discussions on the "marital career" throughout the book and chapters six through ten deal solely with changes in marriage over the life course. This is a very readable book and should offer no problems to the undergraduate student.

- C. Ahrons and R. H. Rodgers. *Divorced Families* New York: Norton, 1987.

  This work focuses on families where at least one marriage is a second one and children are present. These families have been variously called "blended families," "reconstituted families," or, as in this book, "binuclear families." This work is very readable and addresses the important issues in remarriage and step parenting.

SUGGESTED FILMS AND STUDY

- *Who's Afraid of Virginia Woolf?* from the play by Edward Albee staring Richard Burton and Elizabeth Taylor.

  In conjunction with this film the student might wish to read the analysis of this film in the classic work by P. Watzlawick et al., *The Pragmatics of Human Communication*. New York: Norton, 1967.

Reverse: A couple in Kenya.

POWER AND AUTHORITY IN THE FAMILY

M.B. Brinkerhoff and Eugen Lupri
University of Calgary

This chapter is about family power and family authority, a topic that has fascinated experts and the lay public alike. We begin with the sociologists' definition of power and authority.

Defining Family Power and Authority

Power is an attribute of every social group, including the modern companionate family. Because marriage consists of two partners who must make collective decisions, it meets the minimal conditions for the development of power relations (Simmel, 1904, 1955). Power may be seen as the imposition of the will of actor A (who may be either an individual, such as a husband, a wife, or a parent, or a collectivity, such as an organization, state, or organized religion) upon actor B, even in spite of B's resistance, so that A dominates B. Power may be conceptualized as a resource at the disposal of individuals or of a collectivity, and used for their benefit and advantage.

Many family sociologists have relied on Weber's classical definition of power: "Power is the probability that one actor within a social relationship will be in a position to carry out his own will despite resistance, regardless of the basis on which this probability rests" (1949: 152). Power is a concept of *potential* behaviour in a *social relationship*; it allows for variation from time to time between one behaviourial domain and another. An individual may have the potential for exercising his or her power, but may choose not to activate or use it. Activated power involves the actual exertion of control, which may initiate, change, or modify the actions of another individual or collectivity (Straus, 1964). The converse may also occur: when constancy is desired, power can be used to effect no change.

The concept of power must be distinguished from the concept of authority. Again we rely on Weber's classical distinction: authority is legitimated power. That is, if actor A has power over B, both perceive this ability as A's right. A's power over B is accepted as both legitimate and proper, so that B has an obligation to comply with A's decisions. Thus authority relations entail two complementary properties: domination and submission. Accordingly, Weber states, "...patriarchalism means authority of the father, the senior of the house, the sib elder over the members of the household, the rule of the master over the slave" (Gerth and Mills, 1958: 195–196).

Simmel, too, argues that authority consists of superordination and subordination. An individual may come "to enjoy prerogative decision making...because the family or other social institutions confer authority of decisions in a given area upon him" (Simmel, 1961: 541).

The exercise of authority as a form of legitimated power is based on widely accepted social norms and social values.[1] Christian values, for example, have traditionally included the authority of the husband over his wife and the

---

[1] Weber's threefold classification of "legal" authority, "traditional" authority, and "charismatic" authority stipulates different grounds for exacting obedience based on socially legitimated power.

authority of the father over his children. In his letters to the Colossians, Paul is quite explicit about the "proper" and legitimate power relations within the family:

Wives submit yourselves unto your own husbands, as it is fit in the Lord. Husbands, love your wives and be not bitter against them. Children, obey your parents in all things: for this is well pleasing unto the Lord. Fathers, provoke not your children to anger, lest they be discouraged. Servants, obey in all things your masters according to the flesh...(Colossians 3: 18–23).

This precept of male supremacy is by no means limited to Judaeo-Christian thought as the following quote shows:

Men have authority over women because Allah has made the one superior to the other and because they spend their wealth to maintain them. (The Koran)

Although the source of authority in each of these examples is not human beings, and the obligations are fulfilled not for women and men but for a supreme being, the impact of Christianity and the Islamic faith on the distribution of power within the traditional family has been and still is of great magnitude.

The law or the state as a source of authority represents another type of accepted legitimate power. In Quebec, under the Civil Code of 1886, married women had no legal status whatever. The State delegated the husband's authority over his wife. The Civil Code of 1886 states:

Woman is our property. She bears our children...the wife is his property just as the first tree is the property of the gardener...to women belong beauty, grace and the art of seduction...her obligations are dependency and subjection (Kircheisen, 1929: 153–54).

In this case the husband's authority over his wife is legitimated power because it is justified on the grounds that the state, through its laws, holds him responsible for the behaviour of his wife and children.

The delegation of authority to one individual or collectivity may change, however. The Ontario Family Law Reform Act of 1978 is a case in point.

Every spouse has an obligation to provide support for himself or herself and for the other spouse...and every child who is not a minor has an obligation to provide support for his or her parent...(selected from Part Two, Sections 14 through 18 of the Act).

The traditional concept of the wife's dependence on her husband has become obsolete. The wife's economic contribution to her husband and to their children has been recognized fully in that the husband is no longer bound to maintain his wife. Spousal reciprocity prevails: each spouse is obligated to provide support for the other.

In our illustrations of authority supported by religion and the State, the belief in male authority is characteristically buttressed by a gender *ideology*—a set of beliefs about the human condition that supplies a rationale for the required behaviour. Prescribed authority patterns change, however, because of changes in the ideological bases on which they are built.

Historical Studies of Family Power and Authority

As early as 1855, the French sociologist Frederic Le Play reported a change in family authority patterns in his famous *Les Ouvriers Européens*, which is considered to be the first sociological study of the family based on systematic research. As European society shifted from an agrarian economy to an industrial system, Le Play observed a rapid decline of the patriarchal peasant family, accompanied by a lack of stability in the worker's family. This change alarmed La Play, and he recommended to the French government of his time a set of policies that would favour the formation of "stem" families (*familles souches*), in which authority was vested in the father and property was held in common under the patriarch.

In the *Natural History of Folk Society as a Basis for German Social Policy*, the German philosopher Wilhelm Heinrich Riehl (1835) proclaimed categorically that the husband's authority over his wife and his children represented self-evident natural law. The differentiation of the sexes was understood to be a genuine expression of the natural inequality

Chapter 14 / M.B. Brinkerhoff and Eugen Lupri

of men and women. As Riehl stated it: "In creating male and female, our Lord has put inequality and dependence as a fundamental condition of all human evolution" (1855: 3). To Riehl, inequality between the sexes was an eternal law of nature, and the male's authority was simply the consequence of this natural order. Like Le Play, Riehl was concerned about the decline of paternal authority in the family, because patriarchalism guaranteed the stability of household and society.

In contrast to the idea of patriarchalism as the natural form of the family, the Swiss philosopher Johann Jakob Bachofen contested male supremacy in his *Mutterrecht* (1861). He claimed that patriarchy was preceded by a stage of original promiscuity and, with it, the supremacy of women, which resulted in the development of maternal succession of property rights and (at times) in the formation of matriarchal, matrilineal societies. Bachofen's theory is of questionable validity because maternal succession does not necessarily imply maternal domination.

Another important work on the distribution of power between the sexes is Friedrich Engels' *The Origin of the Family, Private Property, and the State* (1884), in which he described the family as the most exploitative institution in society:

The first-class antagonism appearing in history coincides with the development of the antagonism of man and wife in monogamy, and the first-class oppression with that of the female by the male sex (1902: 79).

Before the publication of this famous work, Marx and Engels had jointly conducted empirical studies into the life circumstances of the English working-class family (1845), which was characterized and shaped by the forced paid employment of women and children in the factories of the textile industry. Although Engels generally bemoaned the conditions under which women and children were forced to work and the way in which their work outside the home undermined the family's solidarity, he also recognized a positive aspect to this development. He argued at length that through paid work, women and children become economically independent from their husbands and fathers and thereby laid the groundwork for their own emancipation. He saw the decline of paternal authority and male dominance as the result of the changing economic position of women and children in family and in society.

In *The Family: From Institution to Companionship*, Burgess and Locke (1945) responded primarily to those scholars (e.g. Sorokin, Zimmerman, Westermark) who tended to equate basic family changes, including the decline of paternal authority, with family demoralization and disintegration. Burgess and Locke admitted that from an historical point of view the modern family was indeed undergoing a fundamental transformation; this process of change, however, would lead not to disintegration but rather to family *reorganization*. Reorganization meant a reshaping through the redefining of basic personal attitudes and family values by both husband and wife and by parents and children. The reorganizing process would eventually stabilize family interaction and culminate in the companionate family, in which personal happiness and companionship would prevail.

On the basis of a meticulous analysis of available comparative data, Goode (1963) concluded that everywhere in the world a trend toward some type of conjugal family system is now under way. This trend is due at least in part to industrialization and urbanization, although other factors, such as values and ideologies, also contribute independently to the change. In *World Revolution and Family Patterns* Goode (1963) traced the changing position of women in society at large, and showed how their paid work and their participation in public life have gradually eroded the supremacy of the male in the family. Goode maintained that the changing status of women rests on changing values. To him the crystallizing variable—the necessary but not the sufficient cause of improvement in women's position—was "ideological":

...the gradual, logical, philosophical extension to women of originally Protestant notions about the rights and responsibilities of the *individual* undermined the traditional idea of "woman's proper place" Goode, 1963: 56 (emphasis in original).

Thus the emerging ideology of the conjugal family is not only a powerful but also a radical source of change, which is destroying older traditions, such as paternal authority, in almost every society.

Finally, in their intriguing book *The Symmetrical Family*, (1975), Michael Young and Peter Willmott observed that the family has undergone three major changes in the past two hundred years, and that the future family and work roles of couples will gradually become symmetrical in structure and functioning. These British sociologists based their predictions on a careful scrutiny of historical source material and on findings from sample surveys of about 2000 women and men, representing the adult population of the London Metropolitan Region.

In the emerging symmetrical family, Young and Willmott predicted that male authority will decline and power will be divided equally between the sexes. The division of responsibilities between men and women is becoming egalitarian, and their traditionally separate worlds are merging. Like the companionate family, the symmetrical family of the future will embrace a strong egalitarian ethos.

From our brief historical review we can identify at least four structural conditions associated with the decline of paternal authority in favour of greater equality between the sexes. First, when women gain some sort of economic independence from men, the distribution of family power tends to shift. This factor appears to be a necessary, although not sufficient, condition for the development of an equal division of family power. Second, the move toward an egalitarian pattern in the family is reinforced by changes in the public domain. For more than a half a century, women everywhere have sought equality in the public domains of law, religion, politics, and the economy. Third, women and men must be committed to a gender ideology that supports the realization of egalitarian norms both in public and in private. And finally, this egalitar-

ian ethos must be translated into behaviour within the private arena of the family. Women's equal sharing of economic tasks outside the home must be paralleled by men's equal sharing of household and child-rearing tasks. The extent to which all these conditions prevail, and, in contemporary society, under what circumstances, constitutes the structural context within which family power and family authority must be examined conceptually and empirically.

In the next section we will examine how family sociologists have used power, both conceptually and theoretically. This discussion will be followed by a section on recent empirical studies of family power and its correlates.

THEORIES OF FAMILY POWER AND AUTHORITY

Although a great deal of confusion attends the epistemological foundation of power in family sociology, recent research has been guided by three interrelated theoretical orientations: exchange theory, normative resource theory, and structural power theory. We will discuss each in turn.

Social Exchange Theory

The exchange of work, gifts, ideas, affection, or thoughts is an ubiquitous social fact. Exchange implies reciprocation: when we work, we expect something in return, even though the nature of the return is not always specified clearly. Exchange theory is based on the view of social behaviour as exchange (Blau, 1964).

Social exchange theory is applicable to the study of family life, because much of family interaction can be viewed in terms of costs and benefits. Interaction between family members, for example, can be characterized as attempts to maximize rewards (both material and non-material) and to reduce costs (both material and nonmaterial). Family members have an infinite number of choices, and will choose the best available outcome based on their perception of costs and rewards. Family interaction is sustained over time because family members find interaction rewarding—for whatever reasons (Thibaut and Kelly, 1959; Nye, 1978, 1979; Blau, 1964; Homans, 1951, 1974; Chadwick-Jones, 1976).

An important dimension of exchange is the "norm of reciprocity," which underlies much of social interaction, including family interaction. The norm of reciprocity dictates that favours received must be repaid. Without reciprocity, family life could not exist. Even though reciprocity is an important property of social exchange, Blau (1964) argues that reciprocal behaviour may often be unequal; one party may gain more from the exchange than the other. This inequality causes the asymmetry of many family relationships, in which, for example, the children are more dependent on their parents or the wife is more dependent on the husband than the reverse. This asymmetry may become exploitation by the more powerful, which may lead subsequently to negative exchanges, with conflict, opposition, and retaliation (Chadwick-Jones, 1974).

According to social-exchange theory, then, power is derived from imbalance in the social exchange, and imbalance is brought about by the unequal distribution of resources. Thus, availability and control of resources are the most important determinants of power in marriage.

Many, if not most, studies have sought to explain power differences within couples by the use of social-exchange theory. More than thirty-five years ago, in a pioneering attempt to explore dating relationships, Waller (1951) derived the *principle of least interest* from an exchange model of behaviour. He observed that imbalance or unequal interest existed within the dating couples in his sample. More important, the party that was less interested in maintaining the relationship tended to dominate or to have more power over the party that showed greater commitment and emotional involvement. As we will show later, however, emotional power is also a kind of resource.

The social-exchange model continues to be applied to the study of family power. The *normative resource theory*, in turn, is a derivative of this theory, and has gained a wide international application.

Normative Resource Theory

The classic study by Blood and Wolfe (1960) showed that a husband's power within the marriage tended to increase in proportion to the resources he could muster: education, income, prestige, social status, and so on. Blood and Wolfe also found that the husband's power was associated with the stage of the family life cycle and with the presence of children. In addition, wives who worked for pay had more power than wives who were not gainfully employed.

This study led to the formulation of what is called internationally the "resource theory of marital power." It constitutes an alternative to, or a modification of, what Blood and Wolfe called the ideological theory, which postulates that tradition is the major base of family power. If tradition makes little difference in authority patterns, asked Blood and Wolfe, what other alternatives exist? They believe that resources are the main alternatives to tradition as a source of family power, i.e. authority.

> The power to make decisions stems primarily from the resources which the individual can provide to meet the needs of his or her marriage partner (1960: 14).

This resource theory of marital power has been challenged on many grounds. Heer (1963) argued that the resource theory of marital power failed to distinguish conceptually between power and authority. Not only do husbands have more resources than wives, but legal, political, and religious systems delegate more power to them, and widespread social norms dictate that they should have more legitimate power, i.e. authority.

When the resource theory was applied to the study of marital power in different countries, the findings were inconsistent. Research results about decision making from the United States, France, West Germany, and Belgium showed a positive association between the husband's power and socioeconomic resources, such as education, social status, income, and occupation.[1] Findings from Greece and Yugoslavia, however, revealed a negative association between the husband's power and his socioeconomic status.[2] Furthermore, on closer inspection of those studies that reported an overall positive association, there were indicated curvilinear tendencies in the data and weak relationships that lacked statistical significance.[3]

These divergent findings, produced by the application of resource theory to various societies, led Rodman (1967, 1972) to formulate a "theory of marital power in cultural context." He postulated that egalitarian norms are not distributed equally throughout the societies that were examined, but that in certain modernizing societies, the middle and upper-status groups are the first to accept the ideology of gender equity. Thus the institutionalization of egalitarian gender norms varies from society to society, influencing the effect of resources on the distribution of marital power. In other words, the effect of resources on the husband's power must be seen in the normative context from which emerge the cultural or subcultural expectations about the distribution of marital power.

The most comprehensive theoretical synthesis is to be found in *Power in Families*, edited by Cromwell and Olson (1975). They identify three power domains: power *bases*, power *processes*, and power *outcome*. Power bases involve the kind of resources discussed above, as well as the knowledge or rewards that the family members possess. These resources form the basis of their control over one another. Power processes refer to the network of family interaction. They involve making judgements about the quality of family activity, complying with someone's wish, settling of differences, or clocking family events. Power outcomes include determining who makes decisions on

various family issues and which spouse is more influential in the final decision. Cromwell and Olson's classification is useful because these three domains of power-bases, processes, and outcomes—address respectively the *determinants*, the *nature*, and the *effects* of power, (Scanzoni, 1979: 299–302).

Safilios-Rothschild (1970, 1976), who has criticized normative resource theory for its neglect of "relative love and need" as power resources, conceptualizes power in terms of "orchestration power" and "implementation power." According to this analysis, spouses who have orchestration power have the power to make infrequent but important decisions that determine the lifestyle and the crucial characteristics of family life. The spouse with orchestration power can delegate unimportant and time-consuming decisions to the other spouse, who thus acquires "implementation power." A Canadian study found that wives have power in domains not considered very important either by themselves or by their partners (Brinkerhoff and Lupri, 1978, 1983). In other words, wives are more likely than husbands to have implementation power.

Safilios-Rothschild (1976) maintains that love is a more important resource for women who have no access to higher levels of socioeconomic resources. Love has an exchange value in the struggle for marital power, but in their conceptualization of power, family sociologists have ignored it as a viable resource. Building on Waller's "principle of least interest"—that the less involved person has more power because he or she has less to lose if the relationship is discontinued—Safilios-Rothschild showed empirically that the spouse who is "more in love" has less orchestration power and, more likely, greater implementation power. Those couples who perceived themselves as being equally in love revealed a

---

[1] See for the United States: Blood and Wolfe (1960), Kandel and Lesser (1972); for West Germany: Lamousé (1969), Lupri (1969, 1965); for Belgium: Laplae, 1968; for France: Michel (1967).

[2] See Safilios-Rothschild (1967) for Greece, and Buric and Zecevic (1967) for Yugoslavia. A subsequent study in Canada (Brinkerhoff and Lupri, 1978, 1983) also found a negative association.

[3] Reported for Greece by Safilios-Rothschild (1970), and, subsequently, for Canada by Brinkerhoff and Lupri (1978, 1983).

more egalitarian distribution of power in their marriage.

Both the normative theory of marital power and the social-exchange theory have come under close scrutiny in recent years (Scanzoni, 1979; Held, 1980; Burr, 1976; MacDonald, 1980; Gray-Little and Burks, 1983). We will highlight the major lines of criticism in the final section of this chapter, but now let us discuss briefly the third theoretical effort to explain marital power.

Structural Theory: Power Deference

Critics of both the social-exchange theory and the normative theory argue that decision making is an invalid measure of marital power and that resources represent *personal* qualities that favour men rather than women. Thus an exchange built on the accessibility of resources ignores the different structural location of women and men in the larger institutional complex. Women's access to legal, political, and religious power is extremely limited when compared with men's; thus, the replies to decision-making questions, on which the resource theory is built, reflect not conjugal power but "normative and cultural expectations" (Brinkerhoff and Lupri, 1983: 211). In other words, they reflect what we defined earlier as legitimated power —that is, authority. Some critics and feminist scholars have referred to this phenomenon as *deference power* (Gillespie, 1970; Bell and Newby, 1976).

The notion of deference power may be derived from Simmel (1973), for whom all forms of social interaction are inherently dialectical. Exchange *is* interaction, not a theory of interaction (Bell and Newby, 1976: 156). According to Blau, the most widely recognized expert of social-exchange theory:

> Differences in informal rank arise in social processes in which instrumental services are *exchanged for deference* (1959: 60) (Our emphasis).

Bell and Newby pose this crucial question: What is the going rate of exchange and how is it arrived at? They believe it is deference, which is derived from power. Deference involves exchange, but it is important to know how the norms of exchange are established or imposed. The resource-exchange model fails to specify clearly the nature of the resources that are exchanged and how they operate in the interaction between husband and wife. Do resources such as income, occupational prestige, or education actually direct exchanges in the interaction process or enhance an individual's legitimate power in exchanges?

The "deferential dialectic," as Bell and Newby call it, helps us to understand the dynamics in the distribution of power between husband and wife and, more important, how power domains remain stable and durable. Family conflict theorists, such as Sprey (1969, 1979) and Gillespie (1971), have long maintained that family life is based on institutionalized principles that give rise to internal contradictions, often latent and unrecognized. Legitimate power or authority is essential to the maintenance of structural stability and functionality of all human groups, including the family. At the same time, however, the abuse of authority and power generates conflict and tension, which can threaten the disruption of groups, including the family. Thus, according to Bell and Newby, deference, not exchange, is the specific dialectic in the struggle for and over marital power. The inherent tensions in the deferential dialectic can be managed, at least in principle, by this superordinate (Simmel) patriarch, who derives his power from authority.

For these reasons, we contend, women are blocked structurally by social, legal, and psychological barriers from potential power-based resources, and thus from gaining as much power as their husbands (Gillespie, 1971). In today's marriages, traditional forms of authority form a persistent barrier to an equal distribution of power between husband and wife. This gender inequity persists because control over important resources is largely determined not by personal factors but by structural conditions and by the overall gender ideology that prevails in a society at any given time. The crucial variable in a power relationship is dependency, feminists main-

Chapter 14 / M.B. Brinkerhoff and Eugen Lupri

because dependency represents a form of powerlessness (Eichler, 1981).

The extent to which equality prevails in today's marriage has been a topic of perpetual dispute. In the next section we will present some recent empirical findings on the distribution of power and its correlates in contemporary families.

EMPIRICAL STUDIES OF MARITAL AND FAMILY POWER

In a previous section we discussed several historical studies which showed that the contemporary family has evolved from a paternalistic to a more egalitarian form. Scanzoni (1979b: 26–36) has traced this evolution in terms of four ideal types.[1] Let us look at these marriage arrangements in turn.

Marriage Types and Bargaining Power

The first arrangement, called the *owner-property* type of marriage, existed before and during the eighteenth century. In the preindustrial era, the family was a unit of production but the wife had virtually no formal rights. By law and custom, she was the property of her owner-husband. To secure its survival, however, the family operated as a collective economic enterprise to which both the wife and the children contributed economically by working in the home and in the fields. Thus women in the eighteenth century did possess a limited but important resource: their labour power. Their bargaining position, however, was restricted severely by formidable legal and social restraints.

In the nineteenth century the owner-property type was replaced gradually by what Scanzoni calls the *head-complement* marriage arrangement. Prevailing family norms were changing, and as a result, an expressive dimension was added to the existing instrumental realm of marriage. Friendship, companionship, complementarity, and affective ties between husband and wife emerged as reciprocal marriage obligations. As head of the household, the man continued to possess greater power and control over the instrumental dimension of marriage. As complement, the woman's involvement in expressive domains strengthened her bargaining position in family affairs when compared to the owner-property arrangement.

The third marriage type, the *senior-partner/junior-partner* arrangement, is a much more recent development than the owner-property and head-complement types. The wife now becomes a junior partner to her husband in the sense that she had independent access to the marketplace. According to Scanzoni, the rapidly expanding economy after the Second World War drew masses of women into factories, offices, and schools, and provided wives with earning power that historically few women had enjoyed. Women's power began to be based on the production of resources, primarily income and higher educational attainment, that were independent of the husband's. Thus this newly emerging junior-partner arrangement contrasts sharply with earlier farm enterprises and small shops, where men controlled capital though wives helped earn it.

In the junior-partner marriage, high reciprocal expectations exist with regard to emotional, sexual, and personal gratification. These high expectations, coupled with the new economic opportunities for women and changing divorce laws may help account for the rising divorce rates observed in most industrialized nations.

The feminist movement has contributed greatly to the development and emergence of a fourth marriage type: the *dual-career* marriage, or, as Scanzoni calls it, the *co-provider*

---

[1] According to Max Weber (1949), "ideal types" are concepts created by taking several characteristics typical of a phenomenon and accentuating those characteristics to their logical maximum or reducing them to their logical minimum. They are not ideal in the normative sense; neither are they accurate descriptions of reality. As a heuristic device, ideal types represent logical exaggerations of reality against which reality may be measured to facilitate comparison.

arrangement. In this arrangement the wife is no longer a junior partner but both spouses contribute equally to the economic needs of the household. The equal-partner arrangement is similar to what we called earlier the *symmetrical* family, in which instrumental and expressive roles are no longer gender-based, but are filled by both husband and wife. This role interchangeability distinguishes the co-provider wife from the junior-partner wife; in the co-provider marriage, the partners alternately perform the same roles and share more equally in both domestic and paid work. The co-provider marriage, therefore, embraces a strong egalitarian ethos. Power is distributed more equally as both partners bargain from an equal base of strength. Compared with the three other types, the co-provider marriage marks the beginning of a very different marital and familial life style. In this arrangement the potential for personal fulfillment and emotional gratification is quite high, but so is the potential for marital dissolution.

The four marriage types described by Scanzoni do not represent reality or concrete situations, but rather an objectively probable course of development. This course of development is not uniform but uneven, and it varies within and between societies. The four types represent a unified conceptual framework and may be used as a measure or model in examining the distribution of power between men and women in the contemporary family. They will help us to place current survey results about conjugal decision making in historical and comparative perspectives. These empirical findings will be discussed in the following subsections.

Decision Making and Conjugal Power

In their attempt to measure conjugal power on the basis of decision-making items, family sociologists around the world have relied heavily on Blood and Wolfe's (1960) classic study. In this study the researchers asked a sample of respondents how final decisions were made in areas deemed important in any marriage. Marital power is defined as belonging to the spouse who makes the final decision in each of the areas listed in a questionnaire or read out by the interviewer in a personal interview.

Measuring Decision Making

On the basis of the literature and our own research we have constructed several scales and composite measures of marital power, composed of the following items:[1]

"WHO USUALLY MAKES THE FINAL DECISION ABOUT...?"

1. What car to buy?

2. What house or apartment to live in?

3. What job the husband should take?

4. Where to go on vacation?

5. When to call a doctor?

6. What job the wife should take?

7. How much money to spend on food?

8. Which friends to entertain?

9. Which relatives to entertain?

10. What appliances to buy?

11. What to do evenings and on weekends?

"IF CHILDREN ARE AT HOME..."

12. How much spending money should the children have?

13. When should children be disciplined?

14. What clothes should children wear?

15. What time should children be home at night?

---

[1] The answers to retrospective questions are not without methodological pitfalls. The most obvious limitation arises from the fact that the respondents' recall may be faulty and be coloured strongly by their current emotional state. Another weakness of the retrospective question is that respondents may recall events selectively.

Table 14-1:

DECISION-MAKING SCALE FOR MARITAL POWER BASED ON FOUR AREAS FOR CANADA (1980), FEDERAL REPUBLIC OF GERMANY (1978),[a] AND MEXICO (1977): PERCENTAGES AND POWER SCORES[b] BY GENDER ROLE

WHO DECIDES?[c]	AS REPORTED BY[d]	HUSBAND'S JOB			WIFE'S JOB			HOUSE/APARTMENT			CHOOSING DOCTOR		
		Canada	Germany	Mexico	Canada	Germany	Mexico	Canada	Germany	Mexico	Canada	Germany	Mexico
Husband always	WIFE	18.4%	68.0%	70.2%	1.2%	1.3%	21.4%	2.6%	2.3%	36.8%	1.3%	2.1%	21.3%
	HUSBAND	29.2	69.7	78.6	10.0	0.3	64.3	2.6	2.6	38.1	1.7	3.9	21.3
Husband more often than wife	WIFE	31.2	8.6	5.5	5.0	0.3	4.2	6.4	3.4	2.7	3.7	2.3	4.4
	HUSBAND	39.7	8.0	4.7	20.3	0.3	3.6	7.6	4.4	4.3	7.2	3.4	2.9
Both the same	WIFE	47.6	18.5	18.8	40.2	18.3	29.0	79.3	89.3	34.5	48.6	59.9	39.8
	HUSBAND	29.9	18.3	10.9	52.1	18.8	17.3	73.8	86.5	28.8	49.5	62.8	43.4
Wife more often than husband	WIFE	2.3	0.3	1.2	28.7	16.9	4.2	9.3	2.3	4.6	36.7	5.7	4.0
	HUSBAND	1.1	0.3	1.2	9.2	21.4	2.4	14.4	2.6	4.3	35.9	4.9	4.9
Wife always	WIFE	0.6	0.5	4.3	25.0	59.4	41.2	2.4	1.0	21.5	9.7	10.4	30.5
	HUSBAND	0.0	0.3	4.7	8.4	54.9	12.4	1.7	0.5	24.5	5.7	6.5	27.5
Family's Mean Power	WIFE	3.6	4.5	4.4	2.3	1.6	2.6	3.0	3.0	3.2	2.5	2.7	2.8
	HUSBAND	4.0	4.5	4.5	3.1	1.6	4.1	2.9	3.1	3.3	2.6	2.9	2.9

Family's Overall Power Score[e]:

	Canada	Germany	Mexico
WIFE	2.8	3.0	3.3
HUSBAND	3.2	3.0	3.7
COUPLES	3.0	3.0	3.5

[a] Percentages for FRG do not equal 100% due to presenting a "No Answer" response.
[b] The higher the score, the greater the husband's power.
[c] Response categories for each decision are weighted as follows: Husband always = 5; husband more than wife = 4; both the same = 3; wife more than husband = 2; wife always = 1.
[d] N's for Canada range from 522 to 543; for FRG, 237 to 365; and for Mexico, 249 to 261. The variation is due to non-response.
[e] Based on the averages for the four decisions.

We measured each decision-making item on a five-point scale where a numerical value of 5 is assigned to the answer "Husband always makes the final decision," a value of 4 to "Husband makes decision more often than the wife," a 3 to "Both make the decision jointly," a 2 to "Wife makes decision more often than husband," and 1 where the "Wife always makes the final decision." We calculated total scores separately for husbands and wives by summing the respondents' answers to a given number of family decision-making items and dividing each total by the number of items to which they responded. We call this the "Total Mean Power Score." We also calculated "Mean Power Scores" for each individual item. The possible scores range from 5.00, when the husband always makes the decision, to 1.00, when the wife always decides.

To illustrate these measuring procedures, Table 14–1 shows four basic decision-making items for which comparable results are available from Canada, the Federal Republic of Germany, and Mexico. The answers to these four items and the calculated power scores are presented for each country and separately for husbands and wives. As can be seen from an inspection of percentages and the Family's Mean Power Scores, decision making varies significantly by country. What job the husband should take is more likely to be a joint decision for Canadian couples than for either West German or Mexican couples. The majority of West German and Mexican husbands and wives reported that the husband always decides what job he should take; thus the German and Mexican mean power scores for this decision are higher than those shown for the Canadian respondents, reflecting more power by the husbands in relation to their wives.

Deciding what job the wife should take appears to be more complex, as it varies both by country and by who is reporting, husband or wife. The German family's mean power scores of 1.6 are identical and considerably lower than those calculated for the Canadian and Mexican respondents. This means that German wives have more power than their husbands in deciding what job they (the wives) should take. The Canadian mean power scores reflect a greater equality of decision making in this area as well as a greater "say" on the part of Canadian wives, as indicated by the percentages shown for the categories of "wife more often than husband" and "wife always." Note the differences between what Canadian wives report and what their husbands say. Among the Mexican respondents we find even more pronounced spousal differences in reporting what job the wife should take. Almost two out of three (64.3%) Mexican husbands report that they always make the decision in this area as compared to one of five (21.4%) Mexican wives, who are more likely than their husbands to report that they themselves always decide what job they should take; the respective percentages are 41.2 and 12.4. The calculated mean power scores, 2.6 for Mexican women and 4.0 for Mexican men, clearly reflect these spousal perceptual differences. The data lend further support to the notion that in marriage there exist two conjugal power realities, one perceived by the wife and one perceived by the husband. These incongruencies, however, are not as marked in the decision-making areas of "what house or apartment to live in" and "when to call a doctor."

Although we have examined comparative reports on only four decision-making areas, it is apparent that marital power is complex and most difficult to measure empirically. Problems of conceptual equivalence, validity, and reliability abound. Spousal incongruency increases the complexity.

Authority Types

As we have seen, some decisions are more likely to be made by the wife, some are more likely to be made by the husband, and some are more likely to be made jointly. This is an evolving pattern of decision making, and it is often based on primary interest, presumed competence, and tradition. Wolfe (1959) has argued that within every family the husband has a range of authority, the wife also has a range of authority, and a residual range is shared between them. In addition, domains

TABLE 14-2:

THE DISTRIBUTION OF CONJUGAL POWER IN CANADIAN MARRIAGES AND THE PRESENCE/NON-PRESENCE OF CHILDREN IN THE HOME[a]: REPORTED BY HUSBANDS AND WIVES IN 1981 AND 1975

AUTHORITY TYPE		ALL COUPLES[b]			WIVES' REPORT			HUSBANDS' REPORT		
		No Children	No Children under 17	Children	No Children	No Children under 17	Children	No Children	No Children under 17	Children
Syncratic	1981	49.5%	54.5%	58.4%	48.1%	58.1%	60.0%	50.9%	51.1%	57.8%
	1975	30.4	33.3	50.1	31.5	42.9	53.5	29.3	25.9	46.5
Autonomic	1981	45.8	34.9	34.8	48.1	31.5	31.3	43.4	38.2	38.4
	1975	65.2	54.2	45.3	65.2	49.2	41.3	65.2	58.0	49.5
Wife-Dominant	1981	1.4	8.2	6.1	1.9	9.7	8.0	0.9	6.9	4.1
	1975	1.1	9.0	2.9	0.0	1.6	3.5	2.2	14.8	2.2
Husband-Dominant	1981	3.3	2.4	0.7	1.9	0.8	0.7	4.7	3.8	0.7
	1975	3.3	3.5	1.8	3.4	6.3	1.7	3.3	1.2	1.8
Total N's	1981	212	255	594	106	124	300	106	131	294
	1975	181	144	561	89	63	288	92	81	273

[a] "No children" means never having had children; "no children under 17" means no young children at home; "children" means children ages 16 and under in the home.
[b] "All couples" reflects average percentage points of wives' and husbands' reports.

may exist in which neither husband nor wife has authority over the other.

According to Wolfe, authority relations may differ in two basic ways: the extent of the range of authority of husband and wife and the extent of the shared range of authority. Figure 14–1 illustrates this conceptualization of the conjugal power distribution and the following four types of authority:

1. *Wife Dominant*: the wife's range of authority, at least on the 11 or 15 items (if children are present), is considerably larger than the husband's.

2. *Syncratic*: there is nearly a balance of relative authority, and the shared range is equal to or greater than the combined ranges of husband and wife.

3. *Autonomic*: the relative authority is nearly equal, but the husband's and wife's ranges together are greater than the shared range.

4. *Husband Dominant*: the husband's range of authority is considerably larger than the wife's.[1]

We analyzed available 1975 and 1981 survey data from random samples of about 500 couples living in Calgary, Canada, according to Wolfe's conceptualization of authority patterns.[2] The results are presented in Table 14–2, which shows the distribution of four types of authority as reported by husbands and wives in 1975 and 1981, and controlled for by the presence of children in the home.

As can be seen, the largest proportion of both Canadian husbands and wives reported in 1981 that their marriage was of the syncratic type, where couples make decisions equally and jointly. The results indicate that the presence of children in the home does have an effect on the prevalence of this type of authority. Couples with children in the home were somewhat more likely than couples with children living away from home to report syncratic marriages (58.4%, 54.5%, respectively). Childless couples were least likely to report syncratic decision making. About one of two (49.5%) couples without children had such marriages in 1981.

Conceivably, the presence of young children in the home both promotes and requires greater sharing and the pursuit of joint activities by all family members.

The second most commonly reported type of authority in 1981 was the autonomic marriage, in which the husbands and wives exercise equal but independent decision-making power. Childless couples reported this relationship somewhat more frequently than couples with children; the percentages were about 45 and 35, respectively.

Reportedly, both husband-dominant and wife-dominant marriages are exceedingly rare; less than 10% of all respondents reported such types. Even so, a careful inspection of the percentages for the 1981 study reveals that wife dominance was reported much more frequently than husband dominance, by both women and men, particularly by couples whose children were over 17 years of age and

---

[1] Using all 15 decision-making items, which include those involving children, family power scores were derived as follows: Respondents who did not answer at least 75% of the items were eliminated from the analysis. Recall that scores are assigned by giving a value of "5" when the husband always makes the final decision, a "4" when he more often makes it than his wife, a "3" when both decide jointly, a "2" when the wife makes the decision more than the husband, and a "1" when she always makes the final decision. Consequently, the 15–item scale has potential scores ranging from 15 to 75. Using the same proportions as Wolfe (1959), and Center, Raven and Rodriques (1971) for determining the categories, respondents with scores less than 36 are termed "Wife Dominant," while those with scores greater then 54 are "Husband Dominant." The remaining, more egalitarian, respondents with scores ranging from 36 through 54, are separated into two groups depending on the number of decisions "made jointly"—if more than seven are joint decisions, then the family power type is "Syncratic," or shared. If seven or less are shared, the power type is termed "Autonomic."

[2] A description of the 1975 survey is to be found in Brinkerhoff and Lupri, 1978 and 1983; a detailed account of the 1981 study can be found in Lupri and Mills, 1985.

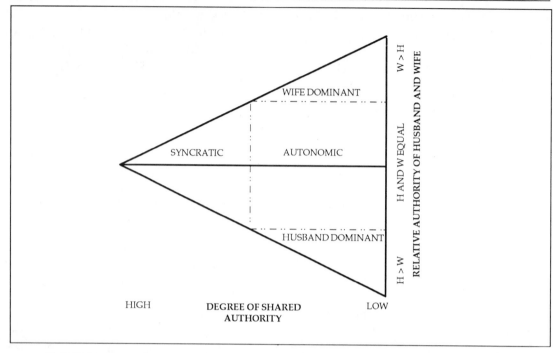

FIGURE 14-1: THE THEORETICAL DISTRIBUTION OF CONJUGAL POWER

The higher the degree of Shared Authority the more equal the Relative Authority of the husband and wife. The broken lines divide the distribution into four authority types: Wife Dominant, Syncratic, Autonomic, and Husband Dominant. Adapted from Wolfe, 1959: 105.

had left the home. The relatively high incidence of wife dominance among the latter is more likely to be related to the couples' advanced age and their position in the life course than to simply having children.

Perhaps the most interesting and consistent finding of our analysis is the impressive effect of time on the distribution of marital power in Canadian marriages. A comparison of the 1981 and 1975 data in Table 14-2 shows a dramatic decline of autonomic decision making in favour of syncratic patterns. This trend is remarkably consistent across all three comparison groups and is reflected consistently in both the wives' and the husbands' reports. Furthermore, there appears to be an increase in the proportion of wife-dominant marriages and a decrease in husband-dominant marriages, although a few reversals exist in the husbands' reports. Clearly, the distribution of power in Canadian marriages is not static but evolving.

Working Wives and Authority Patterns

Earlier in this chapter we argued on the basis of historical evidence that when women gain some sort of economic independence from men, a development toward a more equal division of conjugal power can be observed. Thus we would hypothesize that wives who work for pay become less dependent on their spouses for economic support and tend to participate more in *syncratic* decision making than their nonemployed counterparts. We have sought the effect of Canadian wives' employment status on the distribution of conjugal power. The results, based on couples' reports and controlled for by the presence of children, appear in Table 14–3.

The wife's employment status *per se* does not significantly affect the extent of syncratic marriages in our 1981 sample of respondents. The data shown for the total sample in the right-hand column of Table 14–3 indicate that cou-

TABLE 14-3:

DISTRIBUTION OF CONJUGAL POWER IN CANADIAN MARRIAGES AS REPORTED BY COUPLES
ACCORDING TO THE PRESENCE OF CHILDREN AND WIFE'S EMPLOYMENT STATUS, 1981

AUTHORITY TYPE	NO CHILDREN		NO CHILDREN UNDER 17[a]		CHILDREN UNDER 17[a]		TOTAL SAMPLE	
	Employed Full time	Not Employed	Employed Full time	Not Employed	Employed Full time	Not Employed	Employed Full time	Not Employed
Syncratic	45.5%	55.0%	54.7%	51.5%	61.6%	58.7%	54.5%	56.0%
Autonomic	49.7	35.0	34.9	35.9	32.2	34.2	39.0	34.9
Wife-Dominant	1.8	0.0	9.3	9.7	5.2	6.0	4.7	6.8
Husband-Dominant	3.0	10.0	1.2	2.9	0.9	1.1	1.7	2.3
Total Percent	100.0	100.0	100.1	100.0	99.9	100.0	99.9	100.0
N's	167	20	86	103	211	184	464	307

[a] "No children" means never having had children; "no children under 17" means no young children at home; and "children" means children ages 16 and under in the home.

Chapter 14 / M.B. Brinkerhoff and Eugen Lupri

ples where the wife is not gainfully employed are as likely to report syncratic decision making as are couples where the wife works for pay.

Controlling for children, i.e. parenthood, tends to generate a weak relationship between the wife's employment status and the extent of syncratic marriages among Canadian couples. As shown in Table 14–3, among couples with children—either under 17 years of age living at home or over 17 years of age living away from home—the proportions of reported syncratic marriages in which the wife works full-time for pay are larger than among couples in which the wife does not work outside the home: 54.7% vs. 51.5% and 61.6% vs. 58.7% respectively. In contrast, among the childless couples in which the wife is employed, only 45.5% report syncratic relationships, compared with 55.0% of the childless couples in which the wife does not work for pay outside the home. Indeed, couples without children and in which the wife works are somewhat more likely to practice autonomic decision making (49.7%) than syncratic decision making (45.5%). This finding shows that the effect of women's employment on the marital power structure is not uniform but rather depends on whether or not the couple has children. Among childless couples the wife's employment is likely to lead to autonomic marriages, in which both partners are equal but each possesses a great amount of independent decision-making power. Among couples with children, the wife's outside work also leads to greater equality in marriage, but the authority relations are more likely to be of the syncratic type, in which both partners make most vital decisions jointly.

Two other features in Table 14–3 deserve comment. One is the relatively high proportion (10%) of reported husband-dominant marriages among the childless couples in which wives are homemakers. The other noteworthy pattern corroborates earlier results: nearly one of ten marriages among couples with older children are of the wife-dominant type. The wife's employment status has no effect on the prevalence of this type, because the percentages for the couples with older children living away from home and in which the wife is employed are similar to those in which the wife is not employed: 9.3 and 9.7, respectively.

Authority Types and Marital Happiness

The high incidence of divorce in almost all industrialized countries, including Canada, may reflect marital strain in the conjugal relationship. But measuring the magnitude of marital strain, happiness, or satisfaction is much less precise than determining the incidence of divorce at any time. Perceptions of marital happiness and satisfaction with one's marriage are highly subjective by nature and subject to several compounding factors.

To assess the respondents' degree of perceived marital satisfaction we asked the respondents to rate their marriage on a scale of one through seven, where 1 represented "very dissatisfied" and 7 "very satisfied." When given this choice, 41.8% of the total sample of respondents rated their marriage as "very satisfactory" (Table 14–4). This subsample of 444 respondents, or 222 couples, yielded three comparison groups: 87 *childless* respondents, 132 respondents with *no* children under 17 years of age in the home, and 225 *with* children under 17 in the home.

As can be seen at the bottom of Table 14–4, 41.2% of all childless couples rated their marriage as very satisfactory, or about the same percentage as the total sample of 444 respondents (41.8%). Slightly more than half (52.8%) of older couples—those with children over 17 living away from home—reported their marriage as very satisfactory. Couples with children under 17 in the home were least likely to do so: 38%. These data indicate that marital satisfaction is related to the couples' stage in the family life cycle. This finding corroborates Canadian results obtained by Rhyne (1981) and by Lupri and Frideres (1981).

The basic question posed by our analysis, however, is: do power relations within a marriage affect marital satisfaction? Table 14–4 shows that they do.

Chapter 14 / M.B. Brinkerhoff and Eugen Lupri

TABLE 14–4:
THE PERCENTAGE OF CANADIAN MARRIAGES RATED AS "VERY SATISFACTORY" ACCORDING TO COUPLES' REPORTS, BY TYPE OF AUTHORITY AND THE PRESENCE OF CHILDREN, 1981

AUTHORITY TYPE	Percent Reporting "Very Satisfactory" Marriage			
	Total Sample*	Childless Couples	No children under 17 in the home	Children under 17 in the home
Syncratic	50.9	50.0	62.5	45.1
Autonomic	32.4	33.0	39.1	28.5
Wife-Dominant	42.3	66.7	52.4	25.7
Husband-Dominant	25.2	14.3	33.3	25.0
Total Percent	41.8	41.2	52.8	38.0
Number of Cases	444	87	132	225

* Averaged responses of husbands and wives.

The greatest proportion of all Canadian couples who rated their marriage as "very satisfactory" belonged to the category of syncratic decision-making couples (50.9%). Syncratic relationships, in which power is shared equally by spouses, appears to be most conducive to perceived marital satisfaction. Wife-dominant couples ranked second in prevalence, with 42.3% rating their marriage as "very satisfactory"; autonomic couples (32.4%) ranked third, and husband-dominant couples (25.2%) were least prevalent.

Controlling for the presence of children changes the order of prevalence appreciably. As shown in Table 14–4, the greatest percentage of *childless* couples who rated their marriage as "very satisfactory" was found among the wife-dominant couples (66.7%), syncratic couples ranked second (50.0%) in prevalence. In contrast, the greatest percentage of couples with *no* children under 17 in the home who reported their marriage as very satisfactory was classified as syncratic (62.5%), with wife-dominant couples (52.4%) in second place. Yet another order of prevalence can be observed

among couples *with* children under 17 in the home who reported very satisfactory marriages. Although the greatest percentage also belonged to the syncratic category (45.1%), the autonomic type (28.5%) was found to be second most prevalent, followed closely by wife-dominant (25.7%) and husband-dominant (25.0%) couples.

To establish a relationship between authority type and marital satisfaction is less difficult than to explain the relationship. Among couples with children, mutual discussion and equal decision making are highly conducive to marital happiness. Among the childless couples, wife-dominant marriages produced greater marital satisfaction. In all three comparison groups, husband dominance was associated with the least marital satisfaction.

In conclusion, the causal ordering of the presented data needs to be clarified. Although it appears that there is an association between conjugal power and perceived marital satisfaction, our cross-sectional data cannot tell us which one of the two comes first. We suspect that certain power constellations in a marriage

lead to conjugal relationships that are perceived to be satisfactory or unsatisfactory, but
the reverse possibility cannot be rejected.
Happy marriages may be much more conducive than unhappy marriages to the development of syncratic or autonomic power relations, or unhappy marriages may breed
husband dominance. Only data from carefully
designed longitudinal studies can shed light
on the causal ordering of the association between conjugal power and marital satisfaction.

Authority Types and Socioeconomic Status

Social status is an important influence on
family life in general, and on the distribution
of conjugal power in particular. Cross-national
studies on the relationship between various
indicators of social status and authority patterns have produced divergent findings, as we
showed earlier in our discussion of the "theory
of marital power in cultural context." According to this theory, egalitarian norms are not
distributed equally throughout societies, and
paternalism is more likely to survive in societies that are least developed. In advanced industrialized societies such as the United States,
France, and West Germany that favour an egalitarian ideology, higher-status husbands hold
greater conjugal power (Rodman, 1972). In developing nations such as Greece and Yugoslavia where strong patriarchal norms prevail,
highly educated, higher-status husbands are
more likely than lower-status husbands to
hold egalitarian views and to grant wives
more power (Safilios-Rothschild, 1970; Rodman, 1972). Recent Canadian findings add yet
another variation to the complex interconnec-
tions between the amount of power, the cultural or normative context, and the specific
tangible and intangible resources that affect
the distribution of marital power. Brinkerhoff
and Lupri (1983) found no support for the
alleged positive relationship between the
husband's socioeconomic status and his
power. The Canadian data tend to point toward a *curvilinear* association: husband domi-

nance appears to be more prevalent among
couples of both the lower and the upper socio-
economic status groups, but the differences
between these two groups and the middle-sta-
tus group are not statistically significant.

How is socioeconomic status related to authority type? When socioeconomic status is
operationalized in terms of husband's education, occupation, and income, the findings all
point consistently in the same direction: husbands with a low socioeconomic status are
much more likely than their counterparts with
high socioeconomic status to report that their
marriage was of the syncratic type, where couples make decisions equally and jointly (Table
14–5). Autonomic marriages, in which husbands and wives have equal but independent
decision-making power, are much more prevalent among couples with higher socioeconomic status. The percentage differences between "low" and "high" socioeconomic status
groups across the three empirical indicators
for each of the two authority types point uniformly in the same direction, are of considerable magnitude, and represent statistically significant relationships. As we would expect, the
incidence of husband-dominant and wife-
dominant marriages is relatively low and does
not vary by husband's socioeconomic status.

Although both syncratic and autonomic
marriages represent egalitarian relations, their
power sources differ. When controlling for the
wife's employment status, it was found that
working-class wives were not only more likely
to work for pay, but their proportionate share
of the total family income was significantly
greater than that of their corresponding counterparts in the middle and upper status
groups. Thus working-class wives' greater relative economic contribution translates into
their increased bargaining power and their
greater equal sharing in vital decision-making
areas. Decisions in working-class families are
more likely to be made jointly than in middle
and upper-class families, where we find a
highly egalitarian distribution of power, most
commonly with each spouse having large allocations of autonomy in decision making.

TABLE 14-5: AUTHORITY TYPE AND SOCIOECONOMIC STATUS OF HUSBAND AMONG CANADIAN COUPLES, IN PERCENT, 1981

SOCIOECONOMIC STATUS INDICATORS

AUTHORITY TYPE	Education[1]			Occupation[2]			Income[3]		
	Low	Medium	High	Low	Medium	Upper	Low	Medium	High
Syncratic	69.5	62.0	50.0	69.9	61.0	50.9	70.0	65.5	53.5
Autonomic	25.7	34.0	45.6	25.8	34.9	44.9	26.1	29.5	42.3
Wife-Dominant	1.3	1.6	0.7	1.6	1.0	1.2	0.8	1.4	1.4
Husband-Dominant	3.3	3.7	3.7	2.7	3.1	3.0	3.1	3.6	2.8
Total Percent	100.0	100.0	100.0	100.0	100.0	100.0	100.0	100.0	100.0
Number of Cases	151	250	134	182	195	165	130	139	217

[1] Husband's education "less than high school degree" is "Low," "high school degree, technical, vocational and some university" are categorized "Medium," and "university degree and graduate degrees" are "High."

[2] Occupations are classified by the Blishen-McRoberts (1976) scale with "Lower" being less than 45, "Middle" ranging from 45 to 64, and "Upper" being scores 65 and over.

[3] Husband's income was classified with less than $18,000 annually as being "Low," from $18,000 through $24,999 as "Medium," and over $25,000 as "High."

TABLE 14-6:
AUTHORITY TYPE AND DURATION OF MARRIAGE AMONG CANADIAN COUPLES, IN PERCENT, 1981

AUTHORITY TYPE	TOTAL SAMPLE*	DURATION OF MARRIAGE IN YEARS				
		Up to 3	4 to 7	8 to 15	15 to 30	30 & longer
Syncratic	55.6	54.9	59.6	57.0	52.4	55.1
Autonomic	37.2	41.2	36.1	36.6	38.2	31.5
Wife-Dominant	5.6	1.7	3.2	5.8	7.1	11.0
Husband-Dominant	1.6	2.2	1.1	0.6	2.3	2.4
Total Percent	100.0	100.0	100.0	100.0	100.0	100.0
Number of Cases	1052	175	213	240	298	127

* The number of cases in the total sample is less than shown in Table 14-3 because of varying non-response rates.

Conjugal Power Across the Life Course

In this final section we will examine whether the length of marriage has an effect on power arrangements. As you will recall, our sample consisted of newlyweds, young couples, middle-aged couples, and older couples. Are the elderly as syncratic or autonomic in their decision making as younger couples? Are husband-dominant or wife-dominant relationships related to specific life events or stages in the family life cycle? Because power is fluid and subject to change, we would expect some variation in the distribution of authority types across the life course.

The answer to these questions can be found in Table 14–6, which presents data on conjugal power according to duration of marriage. As Table 14–6 shows clearly, syncratic decision making (hence equality) is a dominant feature in marriage at any stage in the family life cycle. It peaks somewhat in the group married four to seven years, declines slightly in middle-aged couples, and then rises again among the elderly couples. The autonomic patterns, in which each partner takes the major responsibility for decisions in the areas in which each is considered to possess superior skills and

knowledge, decline over the life course. This decline may be a function of the life cycle in later life, as children leave the home, but our sample of couples is too small to permit a detailed analysis.

Perhaps the most noteworthy pattern in Table 14–6 pertains to wife dominance across the life course. Wife-dominant couples are more than three times as prevalent as husband-dominant couples, but both are found to be rare role patterns (5.6% and 1.6% respectively). As is evident in Table 14–6, wife dominance increases consistently as the duration of marriage increases. It peaks in the group married 30 years or longer with an incidence of 11%, which is twice the proportion shown for the total sample and more than six times the proportion for the newlyweds. We suspect that part of this enhanced power resides in the relative physical strength of the partners. The superior vigour of older women is supported by both comparative and gerontological research and is captured in Townsend's (1975: 78) description of English elderly couples on an outing: "The women clearly had more bounce." This evidence for the "matriarchy of later life," however, must be seen within the total familial context, as wife-dominant marriages among the old represent still a minority when compared with both syncratic and autonomic couples.

The data reported here stem from a cross-sectional study of Canadian couples of all ages. Therefore we do not know whether time, as expressed in length of marriage, has had an effect on conjugal power relationships or whether these observed changes are the result of different cultural expectations and socialization experiences of the younger and older couples. As in almost all family research, the fear of committing the *generational fallacy* looms large in this study.

Decision Making and Power: A Critique

Several lines of criticism can be levelled at decision making as a measure of marital power. First, sociologists (including the authors) have tended to underestimate the complexity as well as the multidimensional nature of power. Decision making is only one dimension of power. To equate the two not only raises problems of validity and reliability but seriously undercuts the theoretical importance of the concept of power in family research.

A second criticism focuses on the number and type of decisions that researchers have used to measure marital and familial power. The balance and distribution of power are influenced heavily by what items and how many items are used to measure power.

A third line of criticism centres around the common-sense observation that not all items are equally important or frequent. Yet assigning an equal numerical value to every item, as we have done, assumes that all the items we used and described earlier are indeed equally important. Summing the scores and dividing the sum by the number of items in order to obtain a Mean Power Score, as we have done, also assumes that all decisions are made with equal frequency.[1]

A fourth criticism concerns the sample of respondents used in family power studies. Earlier research almost always obtained information on family life and circumstances, including power data, from females only, a research practice that Safilios-Rothschild (1969) called appropriately "wives' family sociology." A major methodological weakness in past and present research was and (still is) that information was collected on *individual* males and females, and the subsequent inference was made to the marital unit of husbands and wives. This is a serious limitation because it takes at least two individuals to have a power arrangement and because female/male variations provide incomplete and often misleading information about the couple. The common practice of merely aggregating the responses of men and women obscures social reality; in power studies it obscures pair and family interaction patterns.

The fifth criticism directed at decision making as a measure of power follows directly from the previous one. Each marriage partner views the same power arrangement from a different perspective. In this report and elsewhere (Brinkerhoff and Lupri, 1983), we have shown that a considerable discrepancy exists between husbands' and wives' reports of their respective roles in the decision-making process. Indeed, two highly interwoven power realities, his and hers, may exist in most marriages. Spousal incongruency, therefore, can be both a methodological dilemma and a fact of daily family interaction.

Finally, by its very nature, the emphasis on decision making that takes place within the confines of the conjugal unit neglects to view

---

[1]   Elsewhere the authors have documented that the relative salience and frequency of each item are highly significant for determining the balance of power in marriage (Brinkerhoff and Lupri, 1978; 1983). Canadian wives acquired most of their power from items not considered very important either by themselves or by their partners. For decisions that ranked as highly important, the husband was culturally expected to have the "final say." According to decision-making scales, wives appeared to be equal to their husbands or even more powerful; but in reality, wives made decisions only in areas in which it was traditionally expected—areas of lesser importance (Brinkerhoff and Lupri, 1978: 219). This finding illustrates vividly the need to weight decision-making items by their overall importance to the respondents.

marriage relations, including power arrangements, within the structural context of the larger society. Earlier in the chapter we stressed the distinction between power and authority, a distinction to which family sociologists pay lip service but which they fail to operationalize when they use decision-making items as a measurement of power. In other words, decision-making power, particularly the way in which it is operationalized, ignores what we identified earlier as deference power. Decision making as a measure of power, then, fails to come to grips with the inherently dialectical nature of social life.

SUMMARY

Family relations are hierarchical, and power is an attribute of group structure, including small groups. Power relations are asymmetrical and entail inequality of access to resources. Authority is legitimated power and involves voluntary obedience governed by certain systems of belief. The power and authority of the male over the female have traditionally been buttressed by a gender ideology; power and authority change, however, as their ideological bases erode. Family power incorporates the interactions of all household members, whereas marital power refers to behaviours between couples.

Sociologists studying family power have been guided by three interrelated orientations: exchange theory, normative resource theory, and structural power theory.

A study of decision making generated four authority types: wife-dominant, husband-dominant, syncratic, and autonomic. The largest proportion of couples reported syncratic power relations, in which wives and husbands had joint and equal power in decision making. Next most frequent were autonomic marriages, in which husbands and wives had equal but independent decision-making power. Wife-dominant and husband-dominant marriages were found to be rare, but wife dominance was most commonly reported by couples with children.

Women's monetary contribution through paid work affects the distribution of power in Canadian marriages. We found a strong association between syncratic marriages and reported degree of marital happiness. The passage of time also affects the power distribution in Canadian marriages. Wife dominance tended to increase over the life course, and peaked among elderly couples.

Clearly, decision making as a measure of familial or conjugal power raises serious questions about the validity of findings from previous studies, including ours.

TECHNICAL TERMS

AUTHORITY—Legitimate power that is institutionalized (see also legitimate power)

AUTONOMIC MARRIAGE—Marriage in which each partner has equal but independent decision-making power

CHARISMATIC AUTHORITY—Based on the belief that some persons have exceptional personal appeal

COERCIVE POWER—Based on the fear that the partner will punish the other

DEFERENCE POWER THEORY—Model based on the assumption that role prescriptions give males the right to demand compliance from women.

EGALITARIAN MARRIAGE—Form of authority structure in which power and decision making are shared equally between partners (see syncratic and autonomic marriages)

EXCHANGE THEORY—Model based on the assumption that family life, including family power, can be viewed in terms of costs and benefits

EXPERT POWER—Based on the belief that the other person has greater knowledge

HUSBAND-DOMINANT
MARRIAGE—Marriage in which the husband makes most of the major decisions

LEGAL AUTHORITY—Delegated power to the state, courts, etc. on the basis of rational rules

LEGITIMATE POWER—(Authority) based on the acceptance of roles giving the other person the right to demand compliance

MATRIARCHY—Form of family authority structure in which females or mothers exercise the greatest power

NORMATIVE RESOURCE
THEORY—Model based on the assumption that conjugal or familial power is based on the accessibility of resources such as money, education, prestige, occupation, etc.

PATERNALISM—A milder form of patriarchalism in which the husband-father is the final authority

PATRIARCHY—Form of authority structure in which fathers or males exercise the greatest power

POWER—The capacity to control of influence the actions of others, regardless of consent

PRINCIPLE OF LEAST
INTEREST—Situation in which the partner with the least interest in continuing the relationship has the most power

REWARD POWER—Based on the belief that the other person will do something in return for agreement

SYNCRATIC MARRIAGE—Marriage in which both partners share equally in all major decisions

TRADITIONAL AUTHORITY—Authority that is conferred by custom and accepted practice

WIFE-DOMINANT MARRIAGE—Marriage in which the wife makes most of the major decisions

SUGGESTED READINGS

- Peter M. Blau. *Exchange and Power in Social Life.* New York: John Wiley, 1964.

  This is one of the pioneering works on exchange and power assuming that persons and groups behave as they do in order to gain rewards and avoid costs.

- Merlin Brinkerhoff and Eugen Lupri. "Conjugal Power and Family Relationships: Some Theoretical and Methodological Issues." In *The Canadian Family*, ed. K. Ishwaran, 202–233. Toronto: Gage, 1983.

  A critical assessment of decision making as a measure of conjugal power on the basis of 464 Canadian couples.

- R. E. Cromwell and D. H. Olson, eds. *Power in Families.* New York: John Wiley, 1975.

  Covers power and authority in family life, problems of concept formation and measurement.

- John Scanzoni. "Social Process and Power in Families." In *Contemporary Theories About Families*, ed. Wesley Burr et al., 525–668. New York: The Free Press, 1979.

  A useful overview of theorizing and research in family power and authority.

- John Scanzoni and Maximiliane E. Szinovacz. *Family Decision-Making: A Developmental Sex Role Model.* Beverly Hills, CA: Sage, 1980.

  Two experts examine family decision-making processes over the life course.

- Jetse Sprey. "Family Power and Process: Toward a Conceptual Integration." In *Power in Families*, ed. R. E. Cromwell and D. H. Olson, 61–79. New York: John Wiley & Sons, 1975.

  An excellent critique of current research on family power with an attempt to integrate different conceptual approaches.

- Maximiliane E. Szinovacz. "Family Power." In *Handbook of Marriage and the Family*, ed. Marvin B. Sussman and Suzanne K. Steinmetz, 651–693. New York: Plenum Press, 1985.

  The most up-to-date and comprehensive review of family power by an expert in the field.

- M. Young and P. Willmott. *The Symmetrical Family*. London: Penguin, 1975.

  Written by two British sociologists, this book shows that the family has undergone three major changes in the past 200 years, and that future family and work roles of both husband and wife will gradually become symmetrical in structure and function.

Chapter 15

MARITAL ROLES IN TRANSITION

Nancy Mandell
York University

Studies from around the world indicate that marital relationships are in transition. Yet there is no consensus on either the direction or pace of this change. North American and European data indicate a broad movement from less traditional to more egalitarian marital interactions concomitant with the general process of industrialization. In contrast, research from less industrialized nations depicts a more stable, patriarchal family structure with men performing the economic role of provider and women maintaining primary responsibility for home and children (Ramu, 1988). Even within North America, feminist sociologists insist that despite the general trend of the past few decades toward an egalitarian marriage ideal, women are still subject to traditional role expectations and behaviour (Berardo, Shehan and Leslie, 1987; Coverman and Sheley, 1986). Central to this critique are analyses of marital power relations and the division of labour within the household.

In this chapter, these critiques and discrepant portrayals of changes in spousal interaction are reviewed by examining Canadian and cross-cultural data. In the first section, two models of marital-role interactions are presented which capture the factors precipitating change. Subsequent sections assess current family structures focusing on role changes and their effects on marital power relations. The chapter concludes with an evaluation of equity issues and speculates on future trends.

Marital-Role Models

Existing literature portrays two ideal typical forms of marital interaction, the traditional and the egalitarian. The traditional model portrays male/female worlds as separate but parallel, each reigning in his or her gender-prescribed area of expertise. Egalitarian marriages portray male/female worlds as equal and integrated, with involvement in tasks being determined by desirability, availability, capability, and turntaking. Each model defines marital relationships as sets of historical, socioeconomic, and legal responsibilities specifying the rights, duties, and privileges of spouses. Basic to each model are certain ideological notions of universal and appropriate experiences of family life.

Traditional marital roles are grounded in a rigid, sex-differentiated, economic division of labour. Parsons's and Bales's (1955) theory of role differentiation assigned husbands and wives supposedly equal and complementary functions with men in instrumental roles as breadwinners and women in expressive roles as homemakers. Considerable power and privilege flow from this male domination of the economic role. As sole providers, men are assumed to be the head of the household. The scheduling of daily family routines, the location of the family home, and the relationship of the wife and children to the husband all revolve around the husband's work commitments. Husbands assume a benign but firm control over the family authority structure. Often the use of physical force to ensure obedience is tacitly accepted as a husband's legitimate right. Sexual relations are initiated by husbands, who are expected to be moderate in their demands and faithful to their compliant wives. With the children, husbands are to be firm but affectionate, loving but distant.

Rigid adherence to sex roles prescribes a sex-segregated division of labour with husband's participation in household activities consisting of traditional male chores of repair and maintenance. Husbands are careful not to interfere in their wives' daily household management and child care. Any male participation in these tasks is viewed as "helping out" their wives. As non-economic contributors, wives are at best "junior partners" (Scanzoni, 1978) who perform socially necessary but invisible labour. Since women's domestic labour is unpaid and outside the market economy, their work is considered of lesser significance than male wage earning. Even if women's domestic labour is seen as important, domestic activities are viewed as personal services, labours of love, willingly performed for others (Luxton, 1980). A "good" traditional wife takes proper care of her children, husband, and house, allows her husband freedom to work uninterrupted, and is demure and self-effacing. While subject to their husbands' ultimate authority, women make most household and childcare decisions and exercise considerable influence over other areas as well.

Egalitarian marriages are based on contemporary views of sex-role equality and shared roles. Gender-role behaviour does not guide marital-role enactment. Rather, husbands and wives are guided by presumably androgynous norms of professional behaviour and ideal depictions of parenting in a child-centered society. Responsibility for earning money, caring for the children, and looking after the house is split equally between spouses. Both share equitably in decision making and control over family resources. Residence takes into account the work commitments of both spouses. Sex is jointly initiated for mutual enjoyment. The marriage specializes in providing emotional intimacy, support, and companionship. This emotional interdependence leads to greater flexibility and interchangeability in marital roles.

Even though neither model seems to depict accurately the Canadian family, both constructs do provide ideal typical ways in which to understand marital roles as both ideological constructions and as historical, economic, and social relationships (Barrett and McIntosh, 1982). Each model describes a particular family form characteristic of distinct historical periods. Traditional marriages were more common in North America fifty years ago in the middle years of advanced capitalism. They are still prevalent in industrializing nations like the Philippines, Africa, and India. The closest approximation to egalitarian models is found in the Western dual-career marriage. Each model then legitimates what already exists normatively.

Each model is characterized by a distinct ideological bias. Traditional models are what Eichler (1988) calls monolithic and conservative, treating the family as a uniform structure, ignoring change and violence. Even when researchers agree first and second generation ethnic families are traditional, such as the Greek (Chimbos, 1980), Portuguese (Anderson and Higgs, 1976), Arab (Abu-Lanan, 1980), Polish (Radecki and Haydenkorn, 1976), Hutterite (Peter, 1983), and Dutch (Ishwaran, 1983: 189–199) considerable variation in marital-role enactment occurs. In contrast, egalitarian models are constructed ideologically as enlightened, humanitarian, and democratic. They are grounded in values of individualism which have arisen out of the human potential and women's liberation movements of the past twenty years. Yet, in their own way, egalitarian models are similarly monolithic, glossing over elements of class, race, and gender which affect marital interaction. Middle-class marriages, for example, are reputed to be more egalitarian in decision making than are either upper- or working-class families. Yet this distinction appears more ideological than real (Coverman and Sheley, 1986). Black American role relationships differ significantly from Canadian black families in that the latter are more patriarchal, yet literature rarely distinguishes between types of black families. Moreover, despite ethnic differences in marital relationships, most studies show that by the third generation, marriage and family patterns closely approximate those of the ideal typical English Canadian family (Larson, 1976: 352).

While researchers from around the world concur that egalitarian marriage relationships are rare, studies suggest marital roles are becoming increasingly symmetrical as we move toward an egalitarian marital ideal (Pollack, 1981). Visualized as a continuum, marital roles are viewed as moving linearly from a highly differentiated division of labour, segregated on the basis of sex role, toward a flexible, negotiative sharing of wage and domestic labour that transcends sex role (Szinovacz, 1984). Those who do not view the change as moving toward increased role sharing suggest that societal fores have had the effect of reinforcing male/female asymmetry by expanding women's roles while men's remain the same (Yogev, 1981; Hunt and Hunt, 1977).

This latter view seems more representative of Canadian marital roles. Data (Meissner, 1985; Brinkerhoff and Lupri, 1978) indicate that most Canadian marriages do not fit neatly into either the traditional or the egalitarian model. Rather, Western marital scripts appear neotraditional, or what is sometimes called quasi or pseudoegalitarian (Coleman, 1984: 310). These relationships are basically asymmetrical and husband-dominated, while still espousing egalitarian ideals. Even though both the husband and wife earn money, the husband is still viewed as primarily responsible for wages, and his work comes first in terms of the amount earned and his influence on decision making. Full-time employed wives contribute about 28% of the total family income (Statistics Canada 1986) in Canadian marriages, and yet they continue to conform to traditional role expectations as homemakers, caretakers, and sexual companions.

Within neotraditional marriages, the husband's role has become less authoritarian and more companionate, leading researchers

(Pollack, 1981; Scanzoni, 1988) to see the long-term historical trend as moving toward egalitarianism. The ideology of the contemporary marriage relationship stresses intense personal involvement and open communication between spouses. Based on romantic love, the ideal relationship stresses role flexibility, equality, the sharing of responsibility and the development of intimacy within a context of commitment and exclusivity. Within this companionate relationship, women are viewed as equal partners and friends, both contributing to and gaining from the psychic security of the home.

However, what characterizes these relationships as pseudoegalitarian is their inequity and role asymmetry. Given the traditionally lower wages women receive, wives continue to need their husband's economic support. The continuing five-year decline in real economic growth erodes wages, requiring husbands to rely increasingly on their wives' income. Yet women's employment is still treated by many employers and husbands as optional, not obligatory. The strong correlation between income and power is reflected in the husband's continued dominance of the household.

With the exception of egalitarian American black middle-class families (Willie, 1981), the vast majority of Canadian and American couples are neotraditional. Also, quasi-egalitarianism characterizes marital relationships in contemporary Russia (Shlapentokh, 1984), China (Walstedt, 1978), Sweden (Haas, 1981), Australia (Herbst, 1952), Eastern Europe (Szalai, 1972), Belgium (Silverman and Hill, 1967), the upper middle-class of West Africa (Little, 1979b), and the Caribbean (Henry and Wilson, 1975). Within these societies, the majority of families follow the pattern of choosing their marriage partner on the basis of romantic love, having children, establishing a permanent heterosexual union, and residing in a home of their own.

Ideological Pushes Toward Quasi-Egalitarianism

The social and political recognition of women's rights in the past twenty years has provided basic ideological support for egalitarian roles. A 1981 American poll indicated that in one generation, norms concerning whether women should work outside the home had altered. Another 1981 American poll by the Connecticut Mutual Life Insurance company concluded that a large cross-section of the American population eschews traditional sex roles as old-fashioned. Instead, Americans say they support the new marital ideology of egalitarian sex roles, emphasizing shared child rearing, housework, and wage earning. Similarly in Canada, 1981 and 1984 Gallop polls indicate increased acceptance of role sharing.

These results compare with an earlier, 1978 poll of thirty-one of the largest urban centres in Canada in which over 60% of the respondents preferred a traditional legal marriage with children and wife as homemaker. Only 23% wanted a dual-career marriage with children. As the social and economic reality of married life has altered, ideologies have also shifted.

The majority of employed married women today, in all countries for which there are data, report their desire for egalitarian roles. Their husbands however, have largely resisted these pushes. Men, like any other dominant group, are more aware of their own burdens and responsibilities than they are conscious of their unearned profit in power, property, and prestige. Thus, they are likely to view even small losses of these advantages as large threats (Goode, 1982: 137). Husbands and wives still live in separate political, economic, and professional worlds, reflected in their attitudes to power, self-esteem, and actual time allocated to family work. Despite liberalized divorce laws, married women's economic contributions, and societal acceptance of working women, neither family life nor social institutions are yet synchronized with an egalitarian ideology (Kimball, 1983). The continuing discrepancy between the espousal of symmetrical roles and the reality of sex discrimination within families and the workplace suggest marital roles are still in transition, heading slowly toward a new arrangement.

Economic Pushes Toward Quasi-Egalitarianism

In all cultures, economic patterns shape family forms. Within Canada, there has never been one traditional family form, but rather family structures have varied according to ethnic, regional, and social class influences. Yet regardless of this diversity, one dramatic economic change has affected most families in western, industrialized nations. In the last twenty years we have witnessed an enormous increase in the rates of female labour force participation. Currently, the majority, 56% of Canadian wives are employed either full- or part-time (Statistics Canada, 1986). This results in dual-earner families being the modal form. In the United States, the increase has been even more astonishing with only about 12% of American families now fitting the traditional model of two parents with a breadwinner husband and a full-time wife-mother at home (Thorne with Yalom, 1982: 5).

What is unusual about the past few decades is the entry of married women, particularly those with small children, into the labour market. In some countries, this trend occurred earlier than in Canada. In 1970, for example, 82% of Soviet women of working age were employed (Shlapentokh 1984: 174) compared with 42% of American women. In Canada, between 1967 and 1973, there was an increase of 73% in mothers with preschoolers working for wages. By 1984, 53.6% of Canadian mothers of preschoolers and 59.1% of Canadian mothers with children under 16 had entered the labour force (Statistics Canada, 1986).

Historically, labour force statistics indicate that during periods of high unemployment, wars, and periods of increased divorce, both married and single women enter the labour markets out of economic necessity, rather than as a result of ideological changes in sex roles. The unstable and inflationary world economy of the past twenty years certainly qualifies as an economic crisis. Moreover, economists do not foresee a significant upturn in the near future. Given the length of this continuing crisis, both husbands and wives currently married and the young contemplating marriage are in the unique historical position of experiencing a form of marriage unlike their birth families. Norms of marital interaction, expectations of spouses, and the actual behaviour encountered are in transition from the traditional one-wage-earner family structure predominant forty years ago to the two-wage-earner family.

HOW HAVE MARITAL ROLES CHANGED?

Attitudes Toward Marital-Role Sharing

Most attitudinal sex-role studies demonstrate a clear trend toward more egalitarian perceptions of gender roles (Stein, 1984). Thornton, Alwin, and Camburn (1983), in their longitudinal analysis of women and their children, found sons and daughters more egalitarian than their mothers, indicating endorsement of more flexible role expectations. While attitudes about the roles of women and men in general have become less traditional (Cherlin and Walters, 1981), specific aspects of marital roles are more impervious to change. North Americans, for example, endorse the married women's right to expand her traditional role to include wage earning, but are considerably more equivocal about enlarging married men's roles to include domestic labour (Meissner, 1985). Only between 10 and 40% of respondents in various studies believe that men should perform more housework and child care (Stein, 1984: 145). Where substantial attitudinal endorsement of egalitarian marital roles has occurred, change appears among younger, better educated, and employed women (Acock and Edwards, 1982) and among all classes of black women. Women who espouse feminist sex-role attitudes are least likely to conform to traditional role definitions and more likely to obtain high status jobs (Acock and Edwards, 1982).

Husbands' sex-role attitudes continue to affect wives' domestic and wage-earning roles (Spitze and Waite, 1981). In a recent survey of 489 midwestern couples, Hiller and Philliber (1986) found that perceptions of partners' expectations, even when incorrect, strongly influence spouses' behaviour. Moreover, the husband's expectations and prerogatives, and the wife's perception of these expectations, continue to have a more pronounced impact on marital-role bargains than do other variables, such as wife's employment status.

In all countries, women acknowledge that having a supportive husband substantially contributes to their work satisfaction and to the success of their two-earner marriage. Supportive or cooperative is defined by Holmstrom (1972) as husbands who have positive attitudes toward their wife's career, take their wife's work seriously, actively help their wife, do not complain about the inconvenience of two-earner families and do not feel hindered by their wife's career.

When attitudes are measured directly, more recent studies have produced contradictory results. On the one hand, some studies find that couples with traditional sex-role attitudes tend to have more traditional relationships in the home (Huber and Spitze, 1983). Male acceptance of feminist ideology in New Zealand predicts nontraditional task expectations (Koopman-Boyden and Abbott, 1985). A belief system which supports egalitarian interaction stimulates egalitarian family behaviour for Cuban exiles living in the United States (Richmond, 1976). Male adherence to feminist ideology correlates with husbands' reported sharing of family tasks (Bird, Bird and Scruggs, 1984) and with fathers' solo participation in child care (Levant, Slattery and Loiselle, 1987).

On the other hand, other studies find little relationship between husbands' sex-role attitudes and the amount of housework they do (Geerken and Gove, 1983). Coverman (1985) even discovered that husbands with nontraditional sex-role attitudes are slightly less likely to perform household chores. Despite changing attitudes about sharing household tasks, married women, even those who are employed, retain day-to-day responsibility for housework and child care (Hiller and Philliber, 1986).

Chapter 15 / Nancy Mandell

The Relationship of Attitudes to Behaviour

Even though sex-role attitudes are becoming more liberal, emphasizing interchangeable rather than specialized roles as the preferred norms for spousal behaviour, actual marital behaviour has altered very little. Husbands still retain major responsibility for wage earning, contributing 72% of the total family income when their wives are employed and 60% of the total family income if their wives are employed full-time (Pryor, 1984). Husbands, rather than wives in dual-earner families, work on weekends more often, start their jobs earlier and end them later, work more hours and more days per week, and more often hold second jobs. In all respects except shiftwork, husbands more often than wives work schedules which are potentially detrimental to their participation in family life (Staines and Pleck, 1983).

Wives, both non-employed and employed, across couple types, spend considerably more time doing housework than husbands, performing about 79% of all the housework done in their homes (Berardo, Shehan and Leslie, 1987). Dual-career couples were not found to be more egalitarian than other couple forms. Even though employed wives contribute less to the family income, their family workday (Nock and Kingston, 1984), the combined number of hours that a couple works each day, equals their husbands.

Female employment has altered males' traditional sex-role attitudes while not affecting substantially men's participation in domestic labour. Women's roles seem to have expanded while men's have remained the same, supporting the contention that most marital roles are quasi-egalitarian, not egalitarian. In fact, the lack of democratization in the face of widespread female employment indicates further dichotomization of male/female lifestyles (Hunt and Hunt, 1977, 1982; Chafetz, 1986).

Marital Power Relations

Most studies of family power have attempted both to measure accurately and to explain marital-role changes within a func-

tionalist frame. The functionalist view of sex roles (Parsons and Bales, 1955) continues to emphasize separate spheres for women and men. In the gender-based division of labour, women are seen as chiefly responsible for child-rearing, familial and domestic tasks regardless of their other work, and men are seen as responsible for non-domestic tasks in the economy, polity, and other social and cultural institutions. This gender division of tasks is seen by feminists as the root of gender-based power differences (Chafetz, 1986). This division of labour produces power inequalities between the sexes because the public world of the economy and the polity, rather than the private world of the family, constitute the central institutions in our society.

Functionalists have used the concept of separate spheres as the basis on which to build and measure theories of family power. Beginning with the work of Blood and Wolfe (1960), resource theorists have argued that the decision-making power of each spouse is directly dependent upon the extent to which that spouse contributes valued resources to the marriage (Warner, Lee and Lee, 1986). Valued resources typically include "anything one partner may make available to the other helping the latter satisfy his needs or attain his goals (Blood and Wolfe, 1960: 12). Attributes acquired in the public sphere, such as knowledge, income, education, and occupational prestige, are brought into the secluded, private family. Since husbands historically have greater access to external resources, resource theorists maintain husbands have relatively more power than wives.

Cross-cultural application of resource theory has revealed that cultural norms influence marital power (Rodman, 1967, 1972). Rodman has differentiated between patriarchal, modified patriarchal, and egalitarian cultures. In Greece and Yugoslavia, where norms remain markedly patriarchal, husbands dominate decision making by virtue of being male, regardless of their resources. Yet in Canada, the United States, France, Belgium, Denmark, Germany, Ghana, Mexico, and Turkey, where patriarchal norms are being replaced with more egalitarian marital ideals, decision making between spouses is becoming more flexible and negotiable. In these countries, control over valued resources more likely determines a spouse's decision-making power than sex per se.

If the resource theory of marital power is accurate, the emergence of the two-earner family should increase wives' decision making and control, and decrease that of their husbands. Some studies have argued that the massive movement of women into the paid labour force since the early 1970s has accelerated a push toward greater egalitarianism in marriage. As married women take on employment, power relationships between husbands and wives inevitably democratize. Wives' employment, it is argued, helps equalize the balance of power in marriage for three reasons. Money provides women with financial independence and bargaining power. Employment experience confers on women a sense of self-worth and confidence which they bring back to the marriage. Finally, husbands understand and respect paid employment, its stresses, competition, and achievements (Crosby and Herek, 1986).

Recent evidence does not confirm a trend toward greater egalitarianism in wives' decision making or household and childcare work loads. Rather, husband-dominant trends exist in both these areas for dual-career and dual-earner wives.

North American data show a trend toward egalitarian decision-making patterns with the husband's authority intact. Dyer (1979) in the United States found 84.5% of families had egalitarian power relations. Brinkerhoff and Lupri (1978) in Canada report a high degree of equality. Overall, Canadian wives are slightly more powerful than their husbands but in areas considered unimportant such as household and child care. Other studies indicate that employed wives, regardless of their income, have attained a greater role than nonemployed wives in only one area, financial decision making (Piotrkowski and Repetti, 1984). This increase in power among employed wives appears cross-culturally as well (Bahr 1974;

Rodman 1972). Employed wives are especially likely to acquire more power regarding major economic decisions, with less power in internal household areas. The effect of female employment on housekeeping, recreation, child care, and socialization roles appears minimal. Neither dual-earner nor dual-career professional wives, women whose careers most closely resemble their husbands in terms of education, commitment, prestige, income, and pressure, have achieved decision-making power commensurate with their husbands. Patriarchal norms espousing a sex-segregated division of labour and power still account for much of the husband's authority.

While most of our focus has been on changing societies, we should keep in mind that there are numerous countries for which traditional husband-dominant forms of power relationships still exist. The Hindus in India (Gupta, 1979; Ishwaran, 1977), the Muslims of Pakistan (Korson, 1979), and the Berbers in Morocco (Joseph, 1979) are patriarchal, patrilineal, and patrilocal societies. In these areas, women and men never ask "Why marriage?" but instead accept that it is only through marriage that they can achieve maturity, recognition, and meaningful social roles. Arranged marriages with the children's consent are still common. Romantic love is considered a weak basis on which to build a socio-economic union between two families. Formal marriage contracts specifying rights and obligations of spouses and bride dowries are still negotiated. In India, even though dowries are outlawed, in-laws maintain the tradition by presenting the groom's family with luxurious and scarce consumer items, cars, and property as wedding gifts. Within Canada, these traditions persist in first and second generation immigrant families. By the third generation, family patterns closely approximate the Western ideal.

Household and Childcare Roles

Despite the fact that 72% of Canadian men and women state housework should be shared by both husbands and wives (Gallop Poll, 1981), most men married to employed wives do no more domestic work than men married to housewives.[1] The domestic role is considered shared if neither spouse performs less than 40% or more than 60% of the following tasks: cooking, after-meal cleanup, planning meals, grocery shopping, vacuuming, scrubbing floors, and laundry. Child care is considered shared if neither spouse did less than 40% or more than 60% of the childcare and socialization tasks in routine care, child's development, emotional support, and child's entertainment (Smith and Reid, 1986). Across all couple types, wives spend considerably more time in housework than husbands, performing 79% of all the housework done (Berardo, Shehan and Leslie, 1987). Berardo, Shehan and Leslie (1987: 388) discovered that husbands' actual number of hours in housework ranged between four and six hours, about 14% of the total amount of time spent in housework. The same authors report that while dual-career husbands' proportional contributions (24%) were much higher than the average husband, dual-career husbands still only contributed 5.75 hours/week, three times less than their wives. As Ross (1987: 818) notes, husbands of employed wives do a larger proportion of the housework than husbands of nonemployed wives, mainly because the wives do less overall.

Employed women in general spend much less time in housework than homemakers do, averaging 17 hours/week rather than 35 hours/week (Berardo, Shehan and Leslie, 1987; Atkinson, 1987; Marat and Finlay, 1984). Married women with children increase their weekly workload by fifty percent when they take on full-time employment without any corresponding shift in their husband's workload. Time budget studies from numerous countries demonstrate employed women with household responsibilities work approximately seventy hours a week. In households with two parents with at least one child under the age of twelve, the median number of hours spent on housework is 41.8 (Beckett and Smith, 1981). If husbands and wives were sharing both wage and domestic labour, then we would see spouses spending similar amounts of time performing chores.

In no country for which we have evidence is this the case (Eshleman, 1985). Employed women actually reduce their weekly housekeeping from fifty to twenty-eight hours per week while their husbands maintain a steady four hours a week in housekeeping and an additional four hours in traditional male activities of repair and maintenance. Stein (1984) estimates that men do between 21 and 32% of total family work in the United States. Other American data are less sanguine (Atkinson, 1987; Berardo, Shehan and Leslie, 1987; Marat and Finlay, 1984). In Canada, a recent study conducted in East York, Toronto, shows women doing almost all the domestic and network maintenance work, with men married to working wives doing no more domestic work than those who are married to housewives (Wellman, 1985). Michelson's (1985: 72) data, based on a large Toronto survey confirms that the total daily work load of the employed mother is very high compared to others. Without significant help from either family members or outsiders, she has less time for virtually all nonemployment related activities.

Evidence from Russia indicates that only one-third of men are active in their households, with women spending twice the amount of time in domestic tasks (Shlapentokh, 1984). In both 1926 and 1970, 51% of the Russian work force were women. By 1985, about 71% of women were in the labour force. In all time periods, women did far more housework, about three times as much as men, and had far less free time than men. Although Eastern European countries have much higher rates of female labour force par-

---

[1] Discrepancies in reports on spousal participation in housework and childcare result from the use of different measurement techniques. As Atkinson (1987: 9) notes, studies focusing on *time* spent in housework show that employed wives spend much less time in housework than homemakers do, but that husbands of employed wives spend no more time in housework than husbands of homemakers do. But, studies focusing on the *frequency* with which tasks are done indicate that the more hours wives are employed, the less involved wives are and the more involved husbands are in housework.

ticipation, studies show no indication of men's greater participation in household chores (Szalai, 1972). In Russia, although women have had virtually equal opportunity to work, the effect has not been to equalize opportunity and pay, or alter male dominance of the domestic scene (Adams, 1980: 55). In fact, the scarcity of Russian men results from deaths due to world wars and from Stalin's purges. This paucity both accounts for the high level of female involvement in the labour force and the continued privilege and domination accorded the relatively small population of men.

Even in countries where sex roles are deemphasized and egalitarian relationships are encouraged, wives perform traditional tasks. In China, women who are workers, which includes almost all able-bodied women, still have the major responsibility for child care, family care, and housework (Hare-Mustin, 1988). In Israel, traditional roles are reemerging (Tiger and Shepher, 1975). Even on the kibbutz, most of the men are in agricultural and industrial roles, and the women are in service or educational roles (Eshleman, 1985: 106). Sweden, Finland, New Zealand, and Australia show similar patterns. Norwegian couples who have both chosen to work part-time do not equally share housework or child care. Sweden, socially and politically progressive in legislating paternity leaves and flex hours for husbands, has found men have been slow to take advantage of these schemes (Morgenthaler, 1979). Similarly, American data indicate men do not use paternity leaves when available nor do they use flextime to spend it with their families (Friedman, 1985).

Considerable disparity exists then between espoused egalitarian ideals and actual household and parental roles. Even in marriages where roles are presumed to be shared, women end up working at least 25% more than the men (Bernard, 1976). In these quasiegalitarian relationships, husbands and children do minimally increase their involvement in household chores but along sexually traditional lines. Wives and daughters still perform the female tasks of cooking, cleaning, dishwashing, shopping, and laundry (Atkinson, 1987;

Cogle and Tasker, 1982). Two-thirds of women in dual-earner families retain sole responsibility for grocery shopping, cooking, and washing clothes, while less than half maintain sole responsibility for child care, washing dishes, and cleaning house (Maret and Finlay, 1984: 360). Husbands and sons maintain and repair cars, mow the lawn and rake the leaves, and attend to the house (White and Brinkerhoff, 1981). These latter tasks are seasonal, random, and can often by put off until time and inclination coincide (Atkinson, 1987).

Surprisingly little change in this traditional division of responsibility is evident between 1975 and 1979 in the United States. The vast majority of household labour was and is still done by wives. Berheide (1984) estimates that in North America between 74% and 92% of the tasks in eight major areas—meal preparation, cleaning the kitchen, laundry, straightening, ironing, outside errands, child care, and other household tasks—are performed by the women in the house. Any reduction of time spent on household labour comes from lowering standards, buying help, or assistance from friends or neighbours rather than help from the family. It seems fair to say that employed wives hold down two full-time jobs while their husbands have one. This situation has been ironically referred to by Kay (1965) as the "triple-career family."

Pleck (1979: 487) suggests the "non-trivial" increments in husbands' family work associated with wives' employment represents the beginning of a major shift in men's family roles. When husbands increase their participation in the household, they tend to become involved with the more rewarding job of child care. Fathers tend to play more with their children but rarely take part in their daily, demanding, physical care.

A recent study of men in dual-career families confirms this trend. Gilbert (1985) asked his male respondents to indicate who took primary responsibility for household and parental roles. Three types of husbands were identified: traditional husbands, whose spouses took responsibility for both household duties and parenting; participant husbands whose spouses took responsibility for household duties but generally shared the parenting; and, role-sharing husbands who said they shared both household and parental roles. Not surprisingly, these three types differed in their perceptions of how a two-earner family affects their own lifestyle. From "their position of detachment," traditional husbands have few complaints and are pleased with their spouses' mothering and professional achievements. Participant and role-sharing husbands cited scheduling and coordinating as the most frequent problems. Interestingly, participant husbands, that modal pseudoegalitarian group, perceived more difficulties than role-sharing husbands. This, Gilbert suggests, reflects their awareness of certain inconsistencies in their marriages when they share parenting but not household tasks. As one of Gilbert's respondents commented, "It's totally unfair and unreasonable, but she does everything."

This slow but steady growth in father involvement in parenting has profoundly positive effects for mothers and children. Studies (Lamb, 1981; Parke and Sawin, 1976; Levant, Slattery and Loiselle, 1987) have demonstrated that fathers are as sensitive, affective, nurturant, and responsive to infants as are their mothers. Mothers perform better in their parenting role when they have the help and support of their husbands (Pederson, 1976). Couples who share childcare responsibilities equally report greater personal happiness, less marital strife, and improved family relationships (Defrain, 1979; Kimball, 1983).

Which Men Do More and Why?

Given the personal and marital happiness role-sharing couples report, why do husbands not participate more in domestic labour? Employed wives certainly want their husbands to do more. Goode (1982), Stein (1984) and Gilbert (1985) suggest a number of structural and social psychological reasons why men resist. Institutionally men do not receive external support for increased home involvement. Other than Sweden, husbands are not encouraged to acquire domestic skills, to take paternity leave, or rearrange their work schedules

to accommodate childcare responsibilities. In fact, professional careers are predicated on their participants' ability to work long, uninterrupted hours. Ideologically, professional work has always been portrayed as so demanding that little time or energy is left over for anything else. The demands of professional occupations are seen as structurally incompatible with involvement in family tasks. Yet studies of class patterns of husbands' participation in domestic labour are notoriously contradictory. What little data we have on working-class men suggest when their wives are employed, they perform approximately 19% of household chores as compared with 6% for husbands with incomes above the median (Model, 1981).

It is not the type of job which determines husband's involvement, but the number of hours worked per week (Coverman and Sheley, 1986; Staines and Pleck, 1983). Education, income, and occupation appear less strong as predictors of men's domestic activities than time spent in paid work, whether at one professional career or at one or more working-class jobs. Men likely to be involved in domestic activities tend to be younger, with children and employed wives and jobs that do not require long work hours (Coverman, 1985).

Men's lack of participation is not, however, indicative of the salience of their family role. In Cohen's (1987) small sample of 30 working and middle-class Boston area men, 90% defined their marital and/or parental roles as their most important social roles and most complained that their jobs made unreasonable demands upon them personally and unwelcome intrusions into their family lives.

Following resource theory, studies continue to demonstrate that husbands' participation in domestic activities is greatest when spousal income differentials are smallest (Stein, 1984; Bird, Bird and Scruggs, 1984; Model, 1981). Bird, Bird and Scruggs (1984) report that as wives' income rose, they reported increased participation by husbands in meal preparation and cleaning tasks. This finding that it is the wife's *relative* economic contribution which determines her power and domestic responsibilities (Maret and Finlay, 1984) leads researchers to suggest that as women and men approximate equality in the workplace, they will move toward a more egalitarian sharing of domestic responsibilities. Yet, other studies directly refute this resource-based conclusion by noting that the ratio of husband's earnings to wife's earnings does not significantly alter participation in domestic activities, thus concluding there is no evidence that the relative power of husbands and wives affects the domestic division of labour (Farkas, 1976; Huber and Spitze, 1983; Coverman, 1985). Rather, time spent in paid labour and men's adherence to feminist or nontraditional gender roles (Spitze and Huber, 1981; Seccombe, 1986) seem to have the most impact on spousal allocation of family work.

When confronted with the unequal allocation of family work, husbands typically underestimate their wives' involvement in the house and children and overestimate their own. Repeatedly, studies show that husbands think they are "helping out" at home far more than their wives thought they were, that husbands tend to see their participation as positive while their wives judge their results as less satisfactory or negative, and that generally husbands grossly underestimate their employed wives' role overload and stress (Smith and Reid, 1986; Hertz, 1986; Michelson, 1985).

The structural incompatibility of integrating work and family demands and men's lack of feminist peer support constrain men's domestic activities. Men obtain little moral support and logistical help in performing tasks around the house (Lein, 1979). Men rarely draw on their social networks for help with child care and housework (Lein, 1979). Women tend to call on neighbours, families and friends for help, while men's friends, typically drawn from work, are often practically unhelpful.

Men also have personally little to gain from increased participation in household management. Domestic labour studies (Berheide 1984; Ferree, 1980) report women feel negative or ambivalent about housework. Household tasks are described as repetitive, unrewarding, and time consuming. There is little intrinsic incentive to pursue these tasks. Not only is housework unappealing but, ideologically, it has long been trivialized as women's work, as their labour of love (Luxton, 1980).

Since most women have been raised with traditional sex roles, relinquishing domestic activities, especially child care, threatens notions of self-esteem and identity (Yogev, 1981). Without clear role models or cultural rules for combining the traditional female role of mother and wife with the new one of career woman (Yogev, 1981), these women are "caught in the middle" between an old dream and a new reality (Hertz, 1986).

MARITAL SATISFACTION

The traditional model of segregated sex roles implies spouses lead separate but parallel lives, each deriving satisfaction from the successful enactment of their traditional roles. In the sex-role transcendent model, marital satisfaction is derived from the affection, intimacy, and emotional support of the companionate relationship. Companionship is the norm for marital interaction. This means husbands and wives seek from marriage a friend, a lover, and a confidante. Such intense and intimate involvement between spouses helps integrate rather than segregate the worlds of men and women.

The gradual redefinition of marital success and adequate role performance according to the companionship ideal has resulted in two contradictory trends in the literature. The ideology of marriage as a relationship between equal companions accounts largely for the democratization bias to find equal and harmonious marital relationships. At odds with this are studies demonstrating considerable inequity in work loads, decision making, and time allocated for family work and leisure pursuits. How can spouses who are expected to be loving, concerned, and united as friends rationalize their unequal relationship?

Gilbert (1985: 71), and Yogev and Brett (1985: 610) explain that crucial to marital satisfaction is a sense of fairness or equity about family and professional roles. Actual distribution of duties and power is insignificant. Rather, satisfaction results from perceptions of equity or proportional returns in the exchange of personal and economic resources. Even though employed wives are busier than nonemployed wives and husbands, they seem to accept this work distribution as reasonable (Duffy, Mandell and Pupo, 1989). Men and women in dual-earner families perceive what they should give and get out of their married lives differently (Yogev and Brett, 1985).

Overall, men of all social classes seem to be happier and derive greater benefits from marriage than women. Yet traditional wives have less marital satisfaction than employed wives. But both employed and nonemployed wives report marital frustration, dissatisfaction, regret, and problems more often than husbands (Bernard, 1973). A 1984 Canadian Gallop poll confirms these trends. The poll asked a cross-section of Canadians "Who do you think gains more from marriage, the man or the woman?" Woman feel that men gain more from marriage, and men agree this is so. When this data was compared with similar data from 1974, 1964, and 1954, trends remained the same.

Throughout the marriage, sexual relations, money and employment, in-laws, child rearing, different intimacy needs, and time management cause marital conflict and dissatisfaction. Both husbands and wives of all social classes report considerable marital unhappiness when they judge their income to be insufficient. Husbands who actively participate in household and childcare tasks appear most satisfied while traditional husbands report slightly higher levels of depression (Kessler and McRae, 1982). It is not increased work loads which depress husbands but their inability to accept their wives as co-providers.

In general, there is no simple relationship between wives' employment status and their marital satisfaction (Locksley, 1980). The exception appears only in lower income families where employed wives continue to report poorer marital relations than fulltime housewives (Wright, 1978).

For the rest of working wives, employment confers both rewards and hardships. Women from all social classes suffer from role overload. They complain of having too much to do and too little time to do it (Catalyst, 1981). Also, career and family cycling difficulties, prioritizing commitments, and work-family-personal scheduling conflicts are common sources of strain (Dyk, 1987). Not only do spouses have less intimate time together, but also women virtually give up personal activities (Michelson, 1985). Time budget studies from North American and abroad indicate that employed wives renounce substantial proportions of their leisure activities such as gardening, visiting with friends and relatives, watching television, and even eating and sleeping, while their husbands do not reduce their time expenditures in any of these areas (Broderick, 1984: 200; Michelson, 1985). While both husbands and wives suffer role overload in dual-earner families, employed wives experience significantly more work/family role strain than their husbands (Keith and Schafer, 1980; Hall and Hall, 1980; Skinner 1982; Piotrkowski and Repetti, 1984). Attempts to compare men's and women's total work day have begun to conceptualize work-/family-role strain as a composite measure of the total number of hours individuals labour in both domestic and wage-earning jobs. Such a measure identifies the interface of work and family roles, noting both the positive and negative spillover effects from one domain to the next.

Despite their role overload, compared with nonemployed wives, employed women are physically and emotionally healthier, report higher self-esteem, competency and morale, have fewer feelings of social isolation, and have a stronger sense of identity, personal growth, and autonomy (Kessler and McRae, 1982). Congruent with these positive benefits, a recent Canadian study suggests employed wives are more likely to be "very satisfied" with their marriages than are housewives (Lupri and Frideres, 1981).

Even though most Canadians report they enjoy being married (Rhyne, 1984), spousal violence remains a pervasive feature of many marriages. Establishing wife battering statistics remains problematic, but our best estimates maintain that 25% of all Canadian wives are severely beaten during the course of their marriage and that wife assault will occur at least once during two-thirds of all marriages (Sinclair, 1985: 18). Clear evidence has been found of women using violence against their husbands (Strauss and Gelles, 1975, 1985), yet most of this violence is self-defense or retaliation. Wife battering is a more common occurrence affecting over *one million* Canadian women each year (MacLeod, 1987). According to MacLeod (1987), wife battering includes psychological, sexual, physical, verbal, and economic violence repeatedly aimed at women. The persistence of the violence and the concomitant loss of dignity, control, and safety and the feelings of powerlessness and entrapment experienced by women establish this violence as battering (MacLeod, 1987: 16).

Wife abuse is strongly linked with marital dependency. Wives who feel they have no economic or lifestyle alternatives are more likely to remain in abusive relationships (Kalmuss and Straus, 1982). As expected, wife abuse occurs in approximately 20% of the marriages in which the husband is dominant, as opposed to 5% in more democratic or egalitarian marriages. Movement toward egalitarian marital roles suggests a future decrease in spousal violence. Certainly within North America, domestic violence has received public visibility. Spousal violence leads to divorce, negatively affects women and children, and results in an economic loss in the United States of several billion dollars each year due to abuse-related absenteeism on the job (Emery, 1982; Coleman and Cressey, 1984).

Conclusions

Are marital roles in transition from a traditional to an egalitarian norm? Some studies (Ramu, 1988; Marat and Finlay, 1984) suggest that male and female role changes, when measured against a traditional, patriarchal norm, have become substantially more egalitarian. Others (Ross, 1987; Berardo, Shehan and Leslie, 1987; Hiller and Philliber, 1986; Coverman

and Sheley, 1986; Michelson, 1985) argue there has been neither sweeping nor dramatic evidence of movement toward role sharing (Miller and Garrison, 1984). Despite the fact that women have taken on the financial role of co-provider, the traditional division of labour and dominant role of the male "head-of-household" is still very much in evidence (Hiller and Philliber, 1986).

Canadian marital roles seem to be quasi or pseudoegalitarian, meaning that while husbands and wives profess a desire for egalitarianism, marital relationships are asymmetrical and husband-dominated. Even though both spouses earn money, the husband is still viewed as primarily responsible for wage earning, and the wife is seen as responsible for child care and domestic activities. In their large survey, Hiller and Philliber (1986) found, for example, that even though many couples agree that child rearing and managing money should be equally shared, nearly one-third felt that housework is the wife's job and 43% agreed income earning is the husband's job. Women and men are not relinquishing traditional roles and obligations but rather expanding and adding new roles to the old ones (Yogev, 1981). Given that around 21% (Ross, 1987) of married, employed women enjoy an equal division of labour in the home, women's marital roles seem to have expanded to take on more marital work, and thus they enjoy less leisure than their partners. Toronto estimates suggest employed wives continue to spend around 4.8 hours a day in family work while their husbands spend about 1.6 hours a day (Michelson, 1985). When husbands spend time doing routine household tasks, it is because practical circumstances, such as wives at work or wives busy with other household duties, prevent their wives from performing these chores (Berk, 1985). When added to their wage-earning roles is women's perpetual responsibility for these two areas of housework and child care extreme role overload is created. This double burden ensures women's continued segregation in low paying female job ghettos and limited mobility within professional and managerial jobs.

Chapter 15 / Nancy Mandell

TECHNICAL WORDS

MARITAL ROLES—Sets of sociohistorical, economic and legal responsibilities specifying the rights, duties and privileges of spouses.

TRADITIONAL MARITAL ROLES—Based on a rigid, sex-segregated, economic division of labour with men and women performing supposedly equal and complementary functions with men in instrumental roles as breadwinners and women in expressive roles as homemakers.

EGALITARIAN MARRIAGES—Portray male/female worlds as equal and integrated with involvement in tasks determined by desirability, availability, capability and turntaking. The domestic and childcare role is considered shared if neither spouse performed less than 40% or more than 60% of the tasks.

PSEUDOEGALITARIAN MARITAL ROLES—Basically asymmetrical and husband dominated relationships in which the husband and wife earn money but the wife is viewed as primarily responsible for domestic activities and the husband for earning money and his work comes first in terms of the amount earned and his influence on decision making.

QUESTIONS

1. Compare and contrast the traditional, egalitarian and quasiegalitarian marital role models in three areas of the marital relationship.

2. Outline the ways in which female and male marital roles have altered in the past 30 years.

3. Define the resource theory of marital power. Discuss how useful it is in explaining contemporary spousal relationships.

4. Marital satisfaction seems linked to the democratization of marital roles. Discuss male and female perceptions of marital satisfaction in contemporary marriages.

5. Why do men not share domestic responsibilities with their wives when the women take on paid employment?

SUGGESTED READINGS

- Margrit Eichler. *Families in Canada today*, 2d. ed., Toronto: Gage, 1988.

- William Michelson. *From sun to sun: Daily obligations and community structure in the lives of employed women and their families.* NJ: Rowman and Allanheld, 1985.

- Audrey D. Smith and William J. Reid. *Role-sharing marriage.* New York: Columbia University Press, 1986.

- Rosanna Hertz. *More equal than others.* Berkeley: University of California Press, 1956.

FILMS

- *The Masculine Mystique*. National Film Board. 1984. 86 min.

  A story of four men and their relationships with men, women and feminism.

- *Class of Promise*. National Film Board. 1986 42 min.

  Explores the difficulties women face in entering traditionally male areas of business by following a new cohort of business administration students at the University of Western Ontario.

- *No Way! Not Me*. National Film Board. 1988. 30 min.

  History of women's lives in the past century in Canada focusing on the economic and social consequences of their traditional choices.

- *The Next Step*. National Film Board. 1986.

  A series of three, 28 minute films focusing on the need for services for battered women. The situation of women in urban, rural, northern and native settings is examined.

A large family, Gee's Bend, Alabama, 1937.

PART V

FAMILIAL DISORGANIZATION AND REORGANIZATION

Reverse: "The Angry Wife" by Meckenam.

DIVORCE

John F. Peters
Wilfrid Laurier University

Divorce is commonly seen as the end result of two heterosexual people in a marriage relationship who could not "get along." From the perspective of the sociologist, the topic of divorce is much more extensive and complex. Marriage breakup and divorce is the product of an institution known as marriage and family. Every society appears to have a keen interest in the permanence and perpetuation of the institution of the family. Political and economic systems reinforce the family, and therefore, laws are construed in the interest of the family, as well as the interest of the individual members: sometimes a web of seeming contradictions. At the same time virtually all societies have some means of socially or legally dissolving marriage.

Each country and each era has its own gatekeepers who wield power and make judgement in moral matters. Laws of divorce are dependent upon dominant values held with regards to marriage, childhood, adult and state responsibilities. With the purpose of alleviating the exploitation of women in marriage the Soviet Union loosened divorce laws after 1917 (Rheinstein, 1972). Nevertheless, laws of marriage and divorce in that country have been changed several times since, reflecting either failure or success of earlier legislature, or a realignment of law for a different perception of family and/or production ends. People who hold the view that a marriage is a sacred institution in which a couple is bonded for life "in sickness and in health, in riches and in poverty," will reluctantly yield to any pressure suggesting the termination of the marriage bond or "yoke."

Canada's first move toward a modern divorce law took place in 1968. Grounds for divorce were seen as (a) a marital offense, which included adultery, physical cruelty, and mental cruelty, or as (b) marriage breakdown. Separation for not less than three years, addiction to drugs or alcohol, and desertion were grounds for the latter category. Through its 18-year history, separation or adultery were used as grounds about 30% each for all divorces granted (Peters, 1987, 144–147).

The Divorce Act, 1986, considerably simplifies procedures for Canadians. Spouses separated for a twelve-month period are eligible for divorce, and this is the means most couples use. In addition, adultery and physical or mental cruelty still continue as options for divorce applicants.

Countries such as Spain, Malta, Argentina, Brazil, Chile, Columbia, Paraguay, the Philippines, Italy, and Portugal contain laws which show the sacramental nature of marriage in the Roman Catholic Church and the indissolubility of this institution. Secular law has conformed to the dogma of the church. Rheinstein presents an interesting history of law and divorce in Italy (1972: 158–193). In France, Napoleon secularized marriage in 1795, but after his rule, the unpopular law was broken (Rheinstein, 1972: 194–221). Ireland does not permit divorce.

In modern times, in societies where mate choice is left to the individual, where conjugal family living is common, and where personal happiness is a normal expectation, marriage dissolution in the form of divorce is expected to be high. The Swedish government does not wish to interfere with the freedom of the individual in the family. Swedish law relating to marriage, divorce, and remarriage reflect this ideology.

Italy had no divorce until recently, but it is estimated that by 1964 there were some 2,300,000 separated persons. Judicial separation accounts for about one-half of this number (Camera dei Deputati, 1969). Marriage annulments are also common in Italy, and generally favour the wealthy (Rheinstein, 1972: 174).

In polygynous societies, marriage tension can be camouflaged by the husband ignoring one of the wives. Another alternative is some form of concubinage, as was commonly found in Old Testament times. Until recently, when divorce was not permitted in Italy, many men simply lived with other women. In Brazil, a mistress relationship is common. In many regions of the world, including Western countries, common law living has been widespread both before marriage and after a marriage was dissolved. Because the partners are not legally married in a common law relationship, it allows for greater fluidity in heterosexual relationships. Some married couples separate on a trial basis. Still others keep a social front of marriage while choosing to live separately in the same dwelling. It should therefore be clearly evident that divorce statistics in themselves are not an adequate measure or gauge of a society's marriage stability.

The purpose of this chapter is to present an up-to-date account of marriage dissolution in modern society. First, we shall address statistical measurements and make some cross-cultural comparisons. This will be followed by a brief discussion of marriage annulment. A discussion of social change relevant to divorce is presented. Some perspectives on the social activity of the once-married are also highlighted. The chapter then presents research on the topic of the children of the divorced. Finally, remarriage is discussed in the latter part of the chapter.

Statistics

The quantitative measures we use for divorce are commonly government statistics. These measures are often reliable, accurately indicating the number of annual legal divorces. Some countries more efficiently collect and publish family statistics. These statistics should always be observed over a period longer than one year. A three- to five-year period generally shows relevant trends of increase, stability, or decline.

Statistics within a country will also vary considerably. Using Canada as an example, Newfoundland's divorce rate in 1985 was .97, while Alberta's rate was three and a half times that figure (3.45) (Table 16–1). In the United States, the divorce rate is the lowest in the northeast (Massachusetts: 2.9) and highest in the Pacific West (Nevada: 13.7, New Mexico: 7.9).

There are often rural/urban differences or variations due to religious affiliation or ethnic identity. Some regions may have a younger population than other regions, thus affecting the frequency of marriage and divorce. Many countries have geographical centres where divorces are more readily processed or where laws are more lenient, such as in Reno, Nevada. Canada has divorce laws which are federal, whereas in the United States divorce laws are legislated by each of the 50 states.

In some countries, laws are such that divorce is easy to obtain and quick to process. In Sweden, should both members of a marriage wish to terminate their relationship, they may file for divorce and finalize the process in less than a month. Should they have children, the process may be completed within a three-month period. In most countries divorcing couples must show the specific reason for marriage breakdown, and these reasons must comply with the legal grounds for divorce. A mutual agreement to terminate the relation is seldom seen as acceptable grounds. It has often been stated that a couple is able to marry with relative ease, but must go through considerable stress to separate. In Brazil, where divorce was first permissable in the 1970s, one may not divorce a second time.

Divorce statistics are sometimes erroneously used as a country's measure of marital happiness (Pike, 1975). Divorce statistics do not measure the satisfaction of marital relationships or heterosexually bonded people. Every society has the institution of marriage, and every society has couples who choose to live apart be-

TABLE 16-1:
DIVORCE BY RATE PER 100,000 POPULATION AND PER 100,000 MARRIED WOMEN 15 YEARS AND OVER BY COUNTRY AND PROVINCE, 1985

Area	Number	Rate per 100,000 Population	Rate per 100,000 married women 15+
Canada	61,980	244.4	1,003.5
Newfoundland	561	96.6	430.9
Prince Edward Island	213	167.6	722.0
Nova Scotia	2,337	265.4	1,122.5
New Brunswick	1,360	189.1	801.9
Quebec	15,814	240.3	1,035.1
Ontario	20,854	230.0	909.7
Manitoba	2,314	216.3	897.6
Saskatchewan	1,927	189.0	784.0
Alberta	8,102	344.9	1,431.4
British Columbia	8,330	288.0	1,134.4
Yukon & N.W.T.	168	228.0	1,120.0

Marriage and Divorces, Vital Statistics, Vol. 11, 1985, Table 10, pp. 16, 17.

cause of marital tension or disagreement. To date, there is no accurate measurement of this phenomenon, and there is no proof that separate living is more common in countries with conservative divorce laws as compared to liberal divorce laws. One needs to recognize that expectations in marriage change, and therefore societies which have liberal divorce laws may have higher expectations of a heterosexual union than do societies that are much more traditional. We assume those separated in a society with liberal divorce laws are much more likely to seek a legal divorce. Their separated status is generally only temporary.

Divorce statistics show the rate as per 1,000 population (Table 16–2). The divorce rate might range from 5.0 in the United States to .2 in Italy. A more sophisticated divorce rate would be one calculated on the base of 100,000 married women over 15 years of age. Such a

statistic would be more accurate, because the proportion of the population under 16 years of age would not affect the actual divorce calculation.

Another way to look at divorce is by making a comparison with the rate of marriage in the population. This appears appropriate, since only married persons can divorce. One would find such contrasts as: 555 for Sweden to 164 for Israel or 42 for Italy (1983). However, one serious shortcoming is that the rate of marriage or divorce is still not known. A low marriage rate, as in Sweden (4.3) could critically affect this measure. At the same time a low divorce and marriage rate, as in Italy, could also affect the rate. Two columns showing a country's marriage and divorce rates followed by a third showing the rate of divorce compared to marriage would solve this dilemma (see Table 16–2). There is a further problem in

TABLE 16-2:
COMPARATIVE MARRIAGE AND DIVORCE RATES FOR
SOME SELECTED COUNTRIES, 1986

Country	Rate Per 1,000 Population	
	Marriages	Divorces
Australia	7.2	2.5
Belgium	5.8	1.9
Canada	7.3	2.6
Czechoslovakia	7.7	2.5
Denmark	5.7	2.8
German Democratic Republic	7.9	3.1
Federal Republic of Germany	6.0	2.1
Finland	5.3	2.0
France	4.9	2.0
Greece	6.4	0.8
Hungary	6.9	2.8
Israel	6.9	1.2
Italy	5.2	0.3
Japan	6.1	1.4
Netherlands	5.7	2.4
New Zealand	7.6	2.6
Northern Ireland	6.6	1.0
Norway	5.0	2.0
Poland	7.2	1.3
Scotland	7.1	2.6
Sweden	4.6	2.4
Switzerland	6.0	1.8
United States	10.1	5.0
U.S.S.R.	9.8	3.4

Demographic Yearbook, 1986, pp. 470-473.

using the annual divorce and marriage rates. These are two very different populations. Those who marry are often previously single and usually in the 20–28 age range. The divorced population come from that group with the status of married, with a higher frequency in the 28 to 40 age cohort.

Another helpful statistic is that of duration of marriage before divorce. In the United States this figure has a mean of 7 years, and in

Canada it is 11 years. The grounds for divorce significantly affect this Canadian statistic. Because 30% of Canadians who divorced prior to 1986 used the grounds of the three-year separation, the average duration of marriage at divorce would have been affected by approximately a year. The time it takes to obtain a divorce through the courts will also affect the duration of marriage. This process may take as little as 30 days (Sweden) to three years.

One might also wish to compare the proportion of divorces in cohort years for the duration of marriage. In Canada 16, 30, and 22% of all divorces are obtained by those in the 0–4, 5–9 and 10–14 cohort duration years of marriage.

One finds some interesting cross-cultural comparisons among those divorcing within one year of marriage. This group represents 32% of all divorces in Egypt and only .2% of all divorces in Canada. The mean age for divorcing men is 32 in England and Wales, about 33 in the United States, and 36.5 in Canada. For women it is 33, 30, and 34 respectively. Age at marriage for those divorcing is also often documented in government statistics. In western societies divorce is more frequent among those marrying more than a year below the mean marriage age.

As divorce becomes more socially acceptable the rate of remarriage also increases. Divorce statistics often show the marital status of those divorcing. In Canada, almost 11% of those divorcing have been previously divorced. Among those divorcing in England and Wales, 20% were couples who had both previously been divorced, and an additional 11% were couples in which one member had previously been divorced.

In using marriage statistics one may note the percentage who enter marriage with the status of divorced. In most western countries the marriage of spinsters and bachelors is declining, while the percentage and absolute number of divorcées who are marrying is climbing. The population of the divorced has risen in the last decade. Many are remarrying. In Canada, currently 17% of all brides and 19% of all bridegrooms had previously been divorced. This percentage is climbing.

Marriage Annulment

Divorce as we know it today is a relatively recent practice. Public sentiment and law do affect the divorce grounds and the divorce process established by legislature. However desertion, separation, and empty marriages have always existed. The Roman Catholic Church has always permitted annulment. The Church of England granted marriage annulments until 1857. This declaration considers the marriage to be null and void from the time of its inception because of premarital impediments. In other words, the marriage is considered never to have existed. Children from such a union are however considered legitimate, because they were born in an "assumed" marriage. Those persons issued an annulment are free to marry (again).

Given the Catholic Church's view of marriage, annulment might be understood as follows. Marriage is viewed as a sacrament (a point Luther disagreed with at the time of the Reformation). Marriage is seen theologically as necessary because of the loneliness of man and for procreation. Fidelity is expected. Parents carry the responsibility of teaching values to their children. The family, in a sense, is the domestic church where Christian life is lived out in a very special way. However, the clergy recognize that this ideal is not always met. The alternative to the malfunctioning marriage, in which these sacred goals are not met, is annulment.

It appears that annulment in many cases is not much different from divorce. Two people cohabit, have children, and terminate their relationship. The real distinction pertains to the time of the cause of difficulty (Kephart, 1981: 472). The cause or reason for an annulment is viewed as preceding the actual marriage, whereas in divorce it occurs presumably after the marriage. Fraud is one of the most common grounds for an annulment (Rheinstein, 1972: 174). Such misrepresentation may be in relation to pregnancy at the time of marriage (by another man), or a premarital history of prostitution or homosexuality. Annulments have been granted for misrepresentation in salary, virginity, or character defects of the husband prior to marriage. In more recent years, a lack of mental capability or understanding at the time of marriage is commonly used as grounds for annulment.

We need to be reminded that the Roman Catholic Church in western cultures is not a monolithic church. In some dioceses, annulment rarely occurs, while in other areas it is frequent. Applications are made to the Marriage Tribunal through the parish priest. Whereas the annulment process once took up to seven years, it may now take 18 months. Catholics who have obtained an annulment and are thinking of marriage (remarriage?) are advised to seek a divorce so as to comply with requirements of the law.

Social Change

Family instability and marital dissolution is closely related to social change. The city of Beijing in the People's Republic of China is a prime example of the effect of rapid political and social change on the divorce rate. This city's rate doubled in five years (Burton, 1988). In most western countries, divorce rates increased dramatically during World War II, then declined a half dozen years later. In Scanzoni's (1970) research, marriage dissolution and urbanization are associated. In the urban community, one is exposed to a heterogeneous society, and heterosexual interaction may be common. With a decline in a society's religious values, there is often a rise in divorce. Parental attitudes toward a child's potential partner are less important. Families have fewer children. All family members have greater independence from both nuclear and extended family members. There is greater sexual freedom. Virginity for either the male or the female is rare at marriage. Cohabitation is increasing. And divorce itself is now seen as socially acceptable. Expectations of marriage have changed in the modern world. Few women find a marriage rewarding that simply involves keeping house, raising children and complementing their husband's interest and activities. More fathers participate in parenting, some even help in housecleaning and cooking. There are new expectations of family

recreation and of emotional bondedness. At the same time, married persons seek some autonomy, some independence.

Social change in the specific form of the feminist movement has had a direct effect upon traditional family practices. Gender roles and positions of power in marriage are being altered. Marriage expectations and child socialization are changing. Some would prefer to identify this movement as a phenomenon of liberation to both men and women, freeing both sexes from cultural and social constraints. Men have in fact had an undisputed advantage in economic and political power. Years of discrimination in sex roles, including that found in dating behaviour (Peters et al., 1978), has reinforced male dominance. Now, many women are insisting that equality be enforced, rather than merely discussed. Women who give evidence of their own skill and ability are frequently considered aggressive by men. The movement toward equality is sensitizing both men and women toward the importance of personhood, understanding, and personal growth. To some married women this has already meant that hidden dreams and personal potential can be realized, rather than be stifled through social myths and constraints.

In some cases, married women with feminist views react strongly against the system, the marriage institution, and anyone, including husbands who have contributed to these perceived and real restrictions. In other instances, attempts are made to alter restrictions, so that self-actualization can take place. Women under 35 are most hopeful. Older women face greater ambivalence as they are caught between loyalty to a traditional marriage and an often unbending husband. Frequently, husbands become frustrated during this process (Miller, 1971). Many men do not empathize with their wives. However, increasingly, when they see the commitment and persistence of their wives, husbands will make attempts to understand the issues involved. Male preoccupations have traditionally focused upon work or occupational status. The emphasis on equality of the sexes redirects the husband's focus from the workplace to his wife and family

(Bernard, 1981). Many men feel threatened by this new concern. Most do not know how to handle it, nor even how to verbalize the frustration. Traditional family patterns have been indelibly imprinted. The rationale for the continuance of the traditional role of male dominance, as voiced by the confused husband, is becoming increasingly unsupportable. Some middle-aged married men are beginning to alter their stance.

The middle-class, married woman, aged 35 and over, with teenage children, may opt for the economic security provided by her husband, preferring to keep the family intact, even if her personal needs are not met in the marriage. On the other hand, some married women will choose divorce, seeing it as the only recourse. In each case there is a price to be paid.

The social changes we have experienced in North America over the last half century may not all be viewed as destructive to family relationships. A second adult income (the wife's) has resulted in improved lifestyles in many homes and has also increased economic and social opportunities for family members. For many, the change, even if leading to and through divorce, has eventually led to greater personal freedom and self-fulfillment.

Activity and Stages found Among the Separated

Separation and divorce radically alters one's social life. Social engagements will depend upon one's age, sex, extended family stigma, custodial care and age of children, economic resources and community reaction. In general, the couple-oriented social network ends and one is "declassed" by divorce (Arendall, 1986, 36). With divorce many friendships terminate. In heterosexual and married couple social groupings, a single member may consider himself or herself as the "fifth wheel." Conversations which once dealt with activities relating to a heterosexual dyad, socially affirmed through the institution of marriage, become inappropriate. In some cases, the spouse of an intact marriage of the same sex may feel threatened: "my husband may become too intimate with her." In many cases the divorced person feels isolated, precisely at the time when meaningful friendships would be most helpful and desirable.

Several social groups with a local or national constituency have been formed to respond to the needs of the recently separated. Group members empathize and support one another emotionally. In Raschke's 1973 Minneapolis study of 277 single parents, social participation reached a peak for both males and females in the 13–24 month period after physical separation from their spouse (1977). The female's social participation was always lower than that of the male's. Raschke claims that the male's greater social participation is due to his greater opportunity for making social contacts, and the fact that he is less likely to have custody of the children. At the same time, some women find the presence of their children very rewarding—a substitute for social engagements. The study also shows that social participation alleviates stress for both the male and the female (Raschke, 1977).

Bernard's earlier work has shown that there is a male and a female perspective to marriage (1972). In marriage, men benefit more than women do and show a greater satisfaction with marriage than do women. Baker shows divorce also has a different meaning for females compared to males (1984). Research in Finland suggests that women who live alone after divorce are more satisfied with their life situations than those women who remarry. The opposite trend was true for men, but not to any level of significance (Niemala, Myyra & Lento, 1985, 20).

The author has developed a typology of the recently divorced and separated. The first of the five types is the divorced person who withdraws from society. This person is identified as the *isolate* and chooses to avoid "normal" social functions. The second type is that of the *sex-seeker*. Sex is an attempt to attain personal fulfillment and social acceptance, possibly a sense of freedom.

The third type is the *career-oriented*. This category is comprised mostly of women. Many in the middle or lower classes have spent some years in home and child-rearing activity, not in gainful employment. With divorce, they have been forced to become financially self-suffi-cient, and many spend several years in train-ing for preparation in a career or profession of their liking.

The *family-oriented* divorced persons focus upon and expend most of their energy on the child(ren). One female appropriately stated that her child gave her purpose in life (Schlesinger, 1974: 144). Frequently it is the financially stable single-parent group that can afford this type of support which might in-volve much time in parent-child relationships. The family-oriented divorced enjoy seeing growth and increasing life satisfaction in the development of their offspring from child-hood to youth.

The fifth type is that of the *companion-seeker*. The prime concern of this person is to find a companion who will emotionally complement one's interests and expectation. Usually this person exercises considerable caution to avoid an intimate relationship with a mate perceived as having the same personality characteristics as the ex-spouse. Financial and emotional se-curity are generally part of the search. Those with child(ren) give consideration to a good "second" parent.

The sixth and last type is the *I'm o.k.* person. They feel good about themselves, even if stig-matized. They have a reasonably good self-identity, and their goals are fairly clearly estab-lished.

These six types are not permanent or static types. Individuals may shift from one to the other. Possibly, the very recently divorced will tend to be isolates, or the sex-seekers. The fam-ily-oriented type may be comprised of those with more than one child between 6 and 16 years of age. These children have developing personalities, and the single parent may seek to maximize the goals and pursuits of the off-spring. It is also possible that some types are combined such as spouse seeker and the fam-ily oriented, or the sex seeker and career ori-ented.

The separating process can be seen as having several distinct stages. Gershenfeld's first stage is called Disillusionment. At this early stage the shroud of the romantic fiction is dropped. The person's awareness increases. The spouse is seen as not meeting the idea expectations. Attraction and trust between the partners begins to decline. The irritation grows. The second stage is one of Erosion. Stage one deteriorates and verbal assaults aug-ment. There is fierce competition in terms of general contribution to home, children, mar-riage, and social responsibilities. Disrespectful remarks about one another are purposefully made in the midst of friends—nasty, cutting, critical, and malicious remarks. Sometimes there is fighting. New habits are learned with-out one being conscious that they are being internalized. One begins to flirt, to criticize and condemn the spouse, to become very defen-sive, and perhaps, to become brutal.

The third stage is one of Detachment. This is the mental separation stage. There is little to talk about between the partners. Boredom sets in. The couple avoids sex and avoids touching each other. Each participates in his/her own activities: reading, T.V., art, sewing, gardening, carpentry. They realize that confrontation only leads to conflict and that conflict offers no resolution. They slowly switch to a future ori-entation. The woman may wonder about her appeal to the other sex. She may begin to figure out her financial situation. Each may begin to accumulate some money for use in future goals. Throughout this time, there may be pe-riodic brief vacillations between love and hate, between appreciation and despising. But in general purposeful avoidance of one another takes place.

The fourth stage is that of Marital Separa-tion. This is the actual physical separation and is without doubt the worst stage. People feel betrayed and ashamed; the whole family is hit. It is the least understood stage (Weiss, 1975). Stress is at its maximum. The individual now senses that the most intimate person in life is gone! Even relatives and friends do not under-stand. They are alone! But in a sense, they are still connected. They are eager to hear any information about the spouse: Where was he seen? What did he wear? Who was he with?

Chapter 16 / John F. Peters

They listen with great interest to any bit of information. And upon occasion the couple may come together: to chat, to have sex, to try to make things work one more time. In the middle-class sample of Arendell, 1/3 shared some sexual activity in the first year after divorce (1987).

During this stage there is a gross distortion of time. Time moves too slowly, then too quickly. One seeks to avoid silence, because it is a reminder of being alone. In a group they are desperate to hear someone talk. There is much indecisiveness. Every incident seems to show the person as loser. All evidence suggests that this stage of marital separation is the worst.

The fifth stage is that of Mourning. At this point, the person is very irritable, is seeking a perfect world, and becomes extremely frustrated, even angered, because the perfect world is not realized. There is a desire for vengeance. There are memory traces of the past: birthdays, anniversaries, vacations, gifts of appreciation, etc. The person goes through severe depression.

The next stage is that of Second Adolescence. This stage can be compared to the experiences of adolescence: separation from parents, search for freedom, individualism, gaudy clothes. At this stage, there is a new search for one's identity. In this pursuit the person gets a new hair-do, a new wardrobe, possibly associations with new groups or people. The person may become involved in a wide variety of activities: photography, yoga, Transcendental Meditation, dance, travel tours, hobbies. All this is an attempt to ward off depression and to find one's new identity.

The final stage is that of Exploration and hard work. This is the resolution after the second adolescence. It is a shift from passiveness to constructive activism. The person begins to sort out him/herself. There is a determination to make things work. There is a "I'm going to make it" commitment. It is the antithesis of previous stages (3–5) where the person only saw despair and had a "loser" mentality. Relationships with the husband, children, relatives, in-laws and friends are looked at and

resolved in a manner congruent to the rather strained situation. Despite the difficulty there is a strong resolution to make the best of the circumstances, and to come to terms with issues which impede the person's self-identity and personal goals.

Individuals go through these stages at different rates, and with varied degrees of intensity. In a few cases, some problems are never resolved. Help does come from friends, counsellors, support groups, and neighbours. Throughout this separating period, particularly in the early stages, new habits are learned to cope with the intra-spouse relationship. When these behavioral patterns (defensiveness, manipulation, retaliation, distrust) are carried over into the second marriage, they can again be destructive to the new relationship and marriage cohesiveness. This pattern helps explain the reason for a higher divorce rate in second marriages.

There is a small but growing number of the separated and divorced who are amiable with one another. People often wonder why they separated if they can remain friendly! These individuals continue to respect one another as adult persons, do not want the separation to be destructive to their children, but feel the bonded relation incompatible to their own interests, goals, and personal growth. When relations are amicable as described above, and both live geographically close to one another, joint custody of the children might be a reasonable option.

Children

Though divorce is primarily considered the concern of the wedded couple, children cannot be overlooked. Divorce is a marriage affair as well as a family affair. Adults choose divorce, children do not. Most parents who divorce are particularly concerned about effects upon their children. Often extended family members, teachers, the community in which they live, and the court also show concern. In countries which have a relatively high divorce rate, it is estimated that approximately one-third of all children will see their parents divorce before age 16. On the average one-parent families

TABLE 16-3:
DIVORCES BY 0, 1 AND 2 DEPENDENT CHILDREN IN
PERCENT OF TOTAL DIVORCES

Country	Year	Number of Children by Percent of Divorces		
		0	1	2
Canada	1981	48.1	22.8	20.6
Egypt	1978	74.3	12.6	6.1
Hungary	1981	38.2	36.1	21.2
Japan	1981	31.2	28.7	30.0
Poland	1981	35.6	43.6	16.4
Sweden	1981	33.8	29.3	28.7
U.S.A.	1979	43.6	25.0	19.3

Demographic Yearbook, Marriage and Divorce Statistics, 1982.

last about four and one-half years. Given the prevalence of children from divorced parents, Commaille feels such families should not be considered as rare or deviant (1983: 102).

There is considerable variation by country in number of children of those divorcing. Table 16–3 shows selected countries and those divorcing with 0, 1, or 2 children. In Japan, 31% of those annually divorcing have no children, while in Sweden, the number is 34%, in the United States, 44%, and in Canada, 48%. Egypt shows 74%. In North America about 60% of all divorces involve children under 18 years of age. The majority have either one or two children.

Characteristics of the modern nuclear family present peculiar problems for the children of the divorced. In the extended family found in an earlier era, children in the care of one parent were readily absorbed into the larger network (Davis, 1939). The small nuclear family unit often fosters parent-child relations which may be deeply personal. Our custody procedures sometimes force a child to evaluate or rank each parent. However, most North Americans feel that children are better off with one parent than in a strife-ridden, two-parent family.

The children of the divorced are not a homogeneous group. Factors which play an important part in affecting these children are the age of the child and events prior to and following the divorce. The custodial parent is often preoccupied with the disintegration of the marriage and therefore is unable to address the needs of the children adequately. It is good for children to have contact with another adult, possibly within the extended family.

Two recent works which have studied the child's long-term adjustment are worth noting. Hetherington (1980) found marked improvements among divorced parents and their preschool children over a two-year period. The longitudinal five-year study by Wallenstein and Kelly (1980) is not as optimistic. The children were found to be separated into three fairly equal groups: those who were psychologically well adjusted, those in the middle range of mental health, and those children who were intensely unhappy and dissatisfied. Twenty-five percent of the entire sample complained of loneliness.

Hetherington has coined the time following separation or divorce as a "chaotic lifestyle" which might last for an entire year. "Adults and children in the separated families were more likely to eat pickup meals at irregular times, the children's bedtimes were erratic, the children were more likely to arrive late at school, and so forth" (1978). In this period the ambivalence about separation, the increased anxiety, the occasional depressions, and the personal disorganization are bound to have some effect on children. In most cases, a reorganization of their lives begins within a year. A stable identity and a new life situation may take a few more years.

With regard to the children of the divorced we conclude that: (1) almost all children experience an initial period of great emotional upset following a parental separation; (2) most return to normal development within one or two years following the separation; and (3) a minority of children experience some long-term psychological problems as a result of the separation (Cherlin, 1981: 79). The more recent US research of Glenn and Kramer shows that white children of the divorced have a statistically significant "lower commitment to marriage." Children of the divorced tend to marry at a younger age. The research suggests that divorce tends to run in families (1987).

It must be recognized that single parents encounter an unusually difficult task. They experience responsibility overload in having to make all decisions and provide all the family needs. They experience task overload with working, housekeeping, and parenting. They experience emotional overload, giving emotional support to their children with depleted emotional resources of their own (Weiss, 1979). Children have no preparation for divorce. Most mature markedly within the first two years. They acquire greater independence and often become emotionally close to the custodial parent.

Universally mothers gain custody of their children more often than fathers: 67% in Canada, 75% in the United States, and 85% in Sweden. The balance of custodial care goes to the father, relatives, or in a few instances, the state. In France, while 44% of all non-custodial parents regularly visit their children, 30% do not visit at all (Commaille 1983: 105). A recent US study shows more custodial fathers to be of three types: regular, occasional and never. In the study, fathers saw their children less than five times the first twelve months following the divorce. Visits are less frequent with very young children and teenage children (Arendall, 1987). Though wage earning fathers are legally obligated to help support the children financially, in the United States only 43 percent do. Most single parent mothers find it difficult to have this law enforced. Child support is a crucial concern to many single mothers, recognizing that a disproportional number of these mothers receive government aid. It is not that these women come from the lower class in large numbers, but rather that the fathers do not pay child support (Ambert, 1980: 155, 156). Some seemingly concerned citizens seem to decry the absence of the father in the home. What appears more acute is the absence of the income of the male wage earner. Some European countries such as Sweden meet this need by making available more financial aid to single mothers. In Hungary government housing is more readily available for single parents.

As in divorce, remarriage is a process in which the child has little direct choice. How do children fare in this radically different life style? There is no one measure of success, but research points to two specific considerations: the type of courtship by the parent and the consequences of living with a stepparent. Most adults are satisfied in remarriage and find it superior to their previous marriage. Though new social norms have not been well defined for the reconstituted or blended family, and though adjustments are wrought with complexity, as the financial situation improves, a new set of kin supplement some fractured extended family bonds, and there is one more parent to supply affection and emotional support (Cherlin, 1981: 91). Often the daily routine of life becomes more stable. Other siblings and relatives do have an effect upon children. One new problem that does arise is the lack of well defined incest taboos between step brothers and sisters. Generally accepted guidelines will become established as the number of reconstituted families increases. In general remarriage is seen as a plus from the perspective of the child. Bernard states that the child receives a "reservoir of resiliency" (1972). A new parent is a salvaging force.

TABLE 16-4:
REMARRIAGE AND COHABITATION AFTER TWO YEARS OF DIVORCE
IN SWEDEN, HUNGARY, NORWAY AND POLAND, 1980

Country	Remarried		Cohabiting		Total	
	Female	Male	Female	Male	Female	Male
Sweden[1]	9	14	22	26	30	40
Hungary	21	33	12	14	33	47
Norway	9	7	20	44	29	55
Poland[2]	--	--	--	--	29	33

[1] Figures include only those with dependent children.
[2] Specific remarried and cohabiting data not available.
"Remarriage," J. Trost, *The Aftermath of Divorce*, 1985, pp. 51–74.

Remarriage

Folk wisdom suggests that a divorced person will never again enter marriage. After all did marriage not prove to be disastrous? And yet should remarriage take place common wisdom suggests that the union would be happy and permanent. Have they not learned what not to do in the first marriage? Both the above "logical" arguments are faulty.

In France 65 percent of all divorced men and 60 percent of all divorced women remarry (Cammaille, 1983: 98). An American study shows that five out of every six men and three out of every four women become remarried after divorce before they reached the age of 75 years. Countries like Canada, Denmark, Hungary, the Netherlands, Norway, Sweden and the USA show that men are more likely to remarry than women (Trost, 1985). It has been estimated that at least one of the divorcing partners has another intimate friend of the opposite sex in 25 percent of all divorces. In 1969, 50 percent of all males and females divorcing remarried within 12 and 14 months of the divorce respectively (US Dept. of Health, Education and Welfare, 1973: 13). The larger percentage of remarriages occur within three years of the divorce. The divorcée has a greater likelihood of remarriage when compared with their same aged single or widowed sex counterpart. A research in Finland shows that "re-

marriage can be used as a defensive strategy against all these painful working-out processes" (Niemela et al., 1985).

Taking remarriage statistics for the type of marriage form of the formerly divorced is deceptive. Research in Sweden of those who had been divorced and with dependent children in 1978, found that two years later 22 percent of the women and 26 percent of the men were cohabiting (Table 16–4) (Trost, 1985, 54: 55). About one-half that proportion were legally remarried. The proportion cohabiting over remarrying was even larger in Norway. Hungary and Poland also have a large proportion who cohabit after the divorce. In North America it is not uncommon for the separated to cohabit for a period of time until the legal divorce process is terminated. In the Netherlands the widowed or divorced may "Live Apart Together," a social and legal term indicating coresidence with an intimate friend (1985, 55–56). The purpose of this living arrangement may be alimony, social support benefits, convenience and some continued social and emotional independence.

Research of those who remarry show several distinct patterns. The younger the age at divorce, the greater the likelihood of marriage. Divorced men with custody of children tend to become remarried sooner. Besides being more affluent, custodial fathers feel a need for a

TABLE 16-5:
PROPORTION (IN PERCENT) OF ALL MARRIAGES INVOLVING THE DIVORCED,
CANADA, 1985 AND THE UNITED STATES, 1984

	Marriages with at least one Divorced	Groom only Divorced	Bride only Divorced	Both Divorced
Canada	27.2	9.8	8.2	9.1
United States	45.6	11.6	10.5	23.5

Marriage and Divorces, Vital Statistics, Vol. 11, 1985, Table 5, p.8, Ottawa, 1986, Statistics Canada.

partner to help with the rearing of their children.

The highly employed divorced male is a preferred mate because he is economically able to support a financially dependent wife. His prospective wife may consider financial stability a prime criterion for remarriage. The divorced woman with no income is therefore more prone to remarry than the divorced woman with a steady moderate income. This characteristic was also found in Finland (Niemela et al., 1985). The older remarrying male is likely to choose a woman who will fill the traditional role of wife. In most cases divorced women over age 40 have had a traditional marriage. However, during the months or years after divorce they have learned new skills and gained competency in handling a range of activities themselves. Most wish to choose a marriage life style of equality.

Remarriage amongst the divorced in Canada is not as high as in the US for at least two reasons. First, Canada's divorce rate is considerably lower and therefore the divorced population is smaller. Second, Canada has a higher proportion of Roman Catholics. Roman Catholics have a more conservative view of both divorce and remarriage. Remarriages which include only one divorced person are comparable in the United States and Canada (about 10% each), but remarriages in which both partners have previously been divorced is much higher in the United States (23% vs 9%).

Statistically divorced persons who marry have a higher rate of divorce when compared with first marriages. There are a number of reasons for this social fact. Those who divorce a second time already understand the divorce process. They are familiar with the judicial process. Similarly they have already felt the social stigma and discrimination of the once married. The fear of public reaction to a dissolved marriage has already been encountered with relatives and friends. These factors are no longer strong barriers to divorce in the second marriage.

The First and Second Marriage Compared

There are numerous differences between the first and second marriage which almost make any comparison unrealistic. By the time of the second marriage individuals have had more life experience in interpersonal relations, in the work place, sexually and in some cases in parenting. Often career or professional aspirations have been partially achieved or at least more clearly focused. Coping mechanisms and tolerance levels, one would assume, have expanded. There are more weighty financial obligations and responsibilities, as well as estate matters to address in the second marriage. Most first marrieds begin with few financial assets. Furthermore one finds fewer joint bank accounts among the remarried than among first marrieds. Some female divorcees report "stashing away" a bit of money just in case the second marriage does not work out. Many

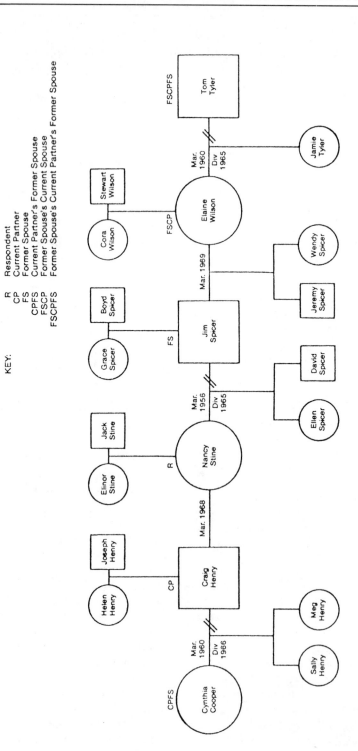

KEY:

R	Respondent
CP	Current Partner
FS	Former Spouse
CPFS	Current Partner's Former Spouse
FSCP	Former Spouse's Current Spouse
FSCPFS	Former Spouse's Current Partner's Former Spouse

FIGURE 16-1: DIAGRAM OF BINUCLEAR FAMILY

From C. R. Ahrons and R. H. Rodgers, *Divorced Families* (New York: Norton, 1987).

second marriages have children from a previous marriage, a situation most unlikely in the first marriage. Plus, there is the memory of the first marriage; flashes of reflection some of which echo the vibrations of fear within subsequent marriages. Trost has found that remarriage in America, England, France, Hungary and Sweden has less homogeny in re-marriages when compared with first marriages (1985, 58). This is particularly evident in education and age.

Some remarriages fail because there has been insufficient time between the termination of the former relationship and that of the new. Disengaging takes time. Few intimate relationships terminate without strain, anger and trauma. These wounds heal slowly. The divorced require adjustment and adaptation, first to a single life, then possibly to a new couple life style. Too frequently, in the desperate need of solace and companionship new friendships are developed at an unnatural pace. However, many women do not remarry because of increasing opportunities in the labour market, allowing them to be economically self-sufficient. Messinger found that remarrieds began with high hopes and were surprised and unprepared for the difficulties which followed, particularly in the step-parent role. Most were caught in a power struggle between three parents, the custodial, non-custodial and the step-parent. Furthermore, heightened sexuality of the new couple with teenage children sometimes created embarrassment and difficulty for the children (1984).

Despite the higher rate of divorce in post first marriages many are very satisfactory. Some research recognizes step parent/step child relations as a key component to happiness in the second marriage (Ahrons and Rodgers, 1987, 165). Many remarrieds wish to dispel the myth that they are doomed to failure. Some individuals make every effort to prove to themselves and others that they are capable of living with a wedded partner in an enduring relationship. Most feel that the earlier marriage deteriorated to the place where rebuilding was impossible. The new relationship spells faith, hope and love.

The reconstituted family is a social group in which at least one partner was previously married and brings custodial children into the union. Ahrons and Rodgers stress the unique family system as binuclear because the social and psychological function of its members operate with two centres, though understandably with unequal emphasis. The actual function of the family remains the same even though the structure has dramatically changed (1987: 201).

The potential complexity of relationships can be readily seen in Figure 16–1. New roles and relationships in the reconstituted family take time to develop. How does a male of 8 interact with an "instant" sister of 7 who may be in the same domestic family, or who may be living in her father's household across town? Often sibling rivalry, considered stressful in "normal" families is intensified in the reconstituted family.

The step parent role is highly ambiguous in our society, especially the step mother role. Some prefer children to use terms such as "aunt" or "adult friend." Many teenage children address their step parents by their first name. Teenagers may find the age gap between themselves and their step mother considerably reduced compared to the age of their mother. Ambert's research shows that most relationships with step-in-laws such as the child and the non-custodial parent's parents uncles and aunts are generally terminated after divorce (1988). Because the binuclear family, now considered deviant, will out number the nuclear family in North America by 1990, Ahrons and Rodgers find it necessary to consider both family forms as normal (1987).

Summary

Divorce or some form of marital dissolution is found in every society. The social stigma and frequency of the practice varies considerably. In most societies women generally encounter more difficulty than men.

The frequency and acceptance of marriage annulment has increased amongst Roman Catholics. Annulment focuses upon the events which predate the marriage whereas in divorce, events which postdate the marriage are important.

Divorce statistics are quantifiable and are, especially useful for intra-societal, cross-cultural and international comparisons. Statistics force the social scientist to research the social reasons for variation. Canadian provinces and the US states show considerable variation. There is also a marked contrast between such countries as the USSR and Israel. Religion, urbanization, age at marriage, kinship cohesion and social tolerance are only some of the social factors affecting the divorce rate. At the same time government statistics do not accurately portray a society's degree of marital satisfaction and harmony. Couples may be separated but not legally divorced. Or couples may live in the same household but live in a state of emotional divorce.

Theoretical contributions focusing upon attraction and barrier forces, levels of involvement and role theory are a few helpful ways of explaining divorce. A typology of the recently divorced was also presented. The seven stages for the separating is a further useful means to describe the process of separation.

Feminism is closely linked to changing attitudes toward marriage and divorce. New norms of marital expectations have not been clearly defined, and once defined may vary through the family cycle. Should a middle-aged divorced woman from a traditional marriage wish to remarry, she will likely choose a relationship of greater equality, that is a relationship void of chauvinism.

Children do not go through their parents' divorce unscathed. They often sense insecurity or inattentiveness and experience a chaotic or erratic life style. Many recover after a year. Close relations often develop between the custodial parent and the child. In North America about one half of all divorces include dependent children.

The majority of the divorced remarry, particularly those under age 40. Men have a higher rate of remarriage than do women. The second event usually occurs within three years of the divorce. Many choose a partner who similarly has gone through a divorce experience. Chil-

dren usually experience greater stability with their custodial parent's remarriage. Relationship roles within the reconstituted or blended family are not yet crystallized.

TECHNICAL TERMS

ANNULMENT—A pronouncement by the Roman Catholic Church that the marriage is void.

BLENDED FAMILY—The blending of two families through marriage.

CONCUBINE—Historically a woman who cohabits with a man without being married to him.

POLYGYNY—The marriage of one husband to several wives.

RECONSTITUTED FAMILY—See "Blended Family."

QUESTIONS

1. Show how divorce is a personal, social, economic, political and legal event.

2. Discuss the Roman Catholic practice of marriage annulment.

3. Discuss the topic of divorced children.

4. Identify and explain the seven stages in the process of separating.

5. Clearly identify the differences between the first marriage and remarriage.

SUGGESTED READINGS

- C. R. Ahrons and R. H. Rodgers. *Divorced Families*. New York: Norton, 1987.

  A holistic sociological and humanistic well researched book.

- Anne-Marie Ambert. *Divorce in Canada*. Toronto: Academic, 1980.

  A good overview of the subject.

- Margrit Eichler. *Families in Canada Today*, 2d. ed. Toronto: Gage, 1988.

  Chapter 10, Legal Policies, addresses law in relation to marriage and divorce, property settlements and adoption.

- Howard H. Irving. *Divorce Mediation*. Toronto: Personal Library Publishers, 1980.

  Mediation is presented as a viable and rational alternative to the adversarial system. Other topics include the lawyer's role, custody and shared parenting.

- Fredrick Capaldi and Barbara McRae. *Step-families*, New York: New Viewpoints/Vision Books, 1979.

  An applied book on step-families.

- D. C. McKie et al. *Divorce: Law and the Family in Canada*. Ottawa: Minister of Supply and Services, 1983.

  A thorough historical study of divorce in Canada.

FILMS

In 1987 TV Ontario produced three half hour movies on divorce in the series of 10 dramas for the television course, *Family Matters*.

- *Shattered Images* (Program 7) depicts a couple's ambivalence and confusion about marriage, as well as an unsuccessful attempt at reconciliation.

- *Children of Divorce* (Program 8) depicts two separated parents use of children in their disagreements, then finally a more mature and realistic resolution.

- *Out from Under* (Program 9). A single mother of two children struggles with a social worker, her new husband, limited economic resources and a new way of life.

- *Kramer vs. Kramer.*

VIOLENCE IN THE FAMILY

Peter Chimbos
Brescia College, University of Western Ontario

The family, we are told, is a group committed to the individual's social and psychological well-being. It is in the family where the individual is supposed to find affection, gentleness, love, and security. This ideology not only encourages people to marry and to stay married, but also perpetuates the social myth of family non-violence. The facts, however, suggest that physical violence between family members is a common occurrence and can be said to be almost universal (Steinmetz and Straus, 1974). This chapter examines the predominant patterns of family violence, including wife beating, child battering, and the abuse of the elderly. Family violence refers to the use of physical force by one family member against another with the intention to cause pain, injury, or death. Common violent interactions between family members include hitting, kicking, shoving, throwing things, and even assaulting with a deadly weapon.

Some forms of family violence have been viewed as legitimate when used in situations approved by the norms of society. The spanking of a child to control or modify his behaviour is often sanctioned and expected in many societies. Studies in England and the USA show that between 84 and 97% of all parents use physical punishment at some point in the child's life (Steinmetz and Straus, 1974). In these studies about 50% of the parents either used physical punishment or threatened to hit their children even during the senior year in high school.

In certain societies and historical periods, the killing of one family member by another has been considered a socially sanctioned behaviour. Examples of such lethal acts include female infanticide among the people of Tibet and traditional China, gerontocide among the Eskimos, and the killing of a child or wife by the early Roman father who possessed strong patriarchal powers (Chimbos; 1978: 5). Even in Colonial America, an 1846 law gave parents the right to put to death ungovernable children (Brenner, 1970: 37). Such practices, however, can hardly be justified on moral or "legal" grounds since it is the powerful individuals who make the social rules and use the most extreme form of violence to control or destroy the lives of the powerless and nonproductive members of society.

Cross-Cultural Studies of Family Violence

Since the late 1960s many forms of family violence have attracted a great deal of attention among social scientists, medical doctors, politicians, and advocates of children's rights and of women's liberation. Exploratory research on the extent and patterns of family violence has been conducted in several countries but most extensively in the United States. There is agreement among many social scientists and political decision-makers that one of the most serious of all family problems is violence. When a husband, for example, intentionally inflicts injury and suffering on his wife, some measure of co-operation, trust, and affection is interrupted or destroyed (Goode: 1969). The end result of this may be the complete dissolution of the marital relationship, with negative consequences on both partners and their children.

Family violence is a phenomenon practised in varying degrees throughout history and in most of the world's societies (Levinson, 1988: 443). Straus's cross-cultural analysis of family violence suggests that for many societies a high proportion of homicides and other forms of violence occur within the family. Although family violence is common in urban-industrial, agrarian, and preliterate societies, the highest rates occur in societies that have high violence rates in other institutional spheres (Straus; 1977: 714–730). Even tribal societies are similar to civic societies in that the vast majority of victims of killers are intimates (Nettler; 1982: 107–120). According to a homicide study of seven African tribes, the vast majority of victims were relatives of killers (Bohannan, 1960: 106). In some cultural groups, however, such as the Sherpa tribes of Nepal, family violence is virtually unknown.

Available data indicate that about 50% of the homicides in Western countries involve people who are related to each other (Nettler; 1982: 107). In Canada, for example, at least 40% of homicide victims are closely related to the slayer; 57% of these being husband or wife to the slayer. According to American data, intrafamilial homicides account for between 20 and 40% of all murders (Gelles & Petrick-Cornell, 1986: 67). Other forms of violence, such as wife beating, child battering, and assaults between siblings, occur so often that it would be hard to find a group or an institution in North American society in which violence is more prevalent than it is within the family (Steinmetz and Straus; 1973).

In the Soviet Union, frequently the victims of homicide are relatives, especially spouses, both legal and common law. In one study, 42% of the victims of premeditated murder were relatives of the offender. According to another study, 24% of the victims were wives of the offender (Borodin; 1974). One may argue then that patterns of family violence observed in the Soviet Union may not differ markedly from those of North America and other modern industrial societies.

Violence also occurs during the courtship period. An exploratory study by Makepeace (1983: 174–177), at a midwestern state university (USA), shows that 21% of the responding students had direct personal experience of courtship violence. At least 61% of them had personally known someone who had been involved in such a violent interaction. Common types of courtship violence include pushing, slapping, punching, and striking with objects. As with marital violence in general, the female partner in this study was more likely to be victimized, or at least to feel victimized, than was the male.

Laner's study (1983: 287) of premarital violence on American college campuses concluded that physical abuse is more likely to occur in serious rather than casual dating relationships. This violent interaction, Laner argues, occurs more often between serious courting partners because they, like married couples, have greater intensity of emotional involvement, an implied right to influence one another, and an extensive knowledge of one another's social biographies, which include vulnerabilities and fears.

Common-law marriages tend to be more violent than legal marriages. According to Canadian data, common-law husbands and wives are far more likely to be killed than their legally married counterparts. The presence of stepchildren, the spontaneous and fragile nature of common-law relationships, and the allocation of resources to children of previous marriages increase the chances for conflict and consequently elevate the risk of spousal homicide (Chimbos, 1978: 38; Wilson and Daly, 1987: 220–221).

If family violence is so common, why is it generally unrecognized and under-reported? Why is it, for example, that family violence, which is as old as the human family, was not adequately investigated and discussed by social scientists prior to the 1960s. The inattention to family violence finds its roots in the idealized depiction of the family as a group, wherein the individual finds love, cooperation, and affectionate care. Such a picture of family life has been described by Steinmetz and Straus (1974) as both a social myth and a crucial ideology which encourages people to

Chapter 17 / Peter Chimbos

get and stay married. Other factors may include society's acceptance of some family violence, such as the right and moral obligation of parents to use physical force as means of controlling the child's behaviour, and the privacy of the home, which often makes some aspects of family violence strictly a private matter.

Fear of stigmatization and reprisal also prevent the victim from reporting assaults to police or other agencies. The battered wife, for example, "may be afraid of endangering her children or any neighbour that may become involved. She sees only one alternative—sacrificing herself" (Hunter, 1981: 412). It is not surprising then to see law enforcement agencies having difficulty getting the cooperation they need to arrest and prosecute wife beaters and child abusers.

Wife Battering

Deliberate assault by the husband against his legal or common-law wife is probably one of the most common of all forms of violence, but one that has been much under-reported by the victims and law enforcement agencies. According to one Canadian study, fear of revenge by the husband, and the perceived social stigma of being the victim of interpersonal violence keeps many women afraid to report assaults to the police (Canadian Urban Victimization Survey, 1985: 5). A report on wife battering in Canada estimated that one in ten women (approximately 500,000 women) who are married or in a relationship with a live-in lover are battered each year. One-third of the women surveyed were beaten weekly or daily, and another 26% were beaten at least once a month. An investigating committee on wife battering in Ontario "has listened to women who have lost teeth, sustained eye injuries, and suffered miscarriages as a result of their husbands' attacks..." For women once battered, the fear of another assault is ever present (Standing Committee on Social Development, 1982: 4). Many wives have been permanently disabled from attacks by their husbands; others have endured brutal death (Canadian Advisory Council on the Status of Women, 1980: 1–3).

About 25% of the subjects, in an American survey, admitted that there has been violence between spouses at some time in their marriages. Nearly two million American women are severely attacked by their husbands each year (Straus et al, 1979). In 1984, about half (48%) of the 4,408 intrafamilial homicides in the US were between spouses. Of these interspousal homicides, the majority of the victims were women killed by their husbands (Browne, 1987: 275). There is a growing belief among investigators that husband-wife violence is actually greater than reported in surveys, and may occur in 50% of marriages. Even in a country like Norway, where the liberation of women has made much progress, wife battering still takes place (Gould, 1978: 60).

The American survey of Straus, Gelles, and Steinmetz (1974) has shown that wives are just as likely to attack their husbands as men are to attack their wives. However, women are much more likely to get the worst of it.[1] In other words, wives do considerably less damage than husbands in fights that do not involve weapons. This is because (a) wives on the average are smaller and physically weaker than husbands, (b) women are less likely to be trained in the use of physical force, and (c) in many instances, the wives involved are pregnant and almost completely unable to defend themselves adequately. In one survey, one in four women who were victims of violence were hit when pregnant (Gelles, 1972: 145). It is not surprising then to see that "miscarriages are five times more common among battered women than among those who are not battered" (Strong et al., 1983: 406).

Gelles (1983: 186) also observes that many women attack their husbands to protect themselves from potential harm or other degrading or humiliating experiences. A number of wives use what Gelles calls "protective reaction violence." This means that " a wife may strike first (and hard) to protect herself from her husband if she believes she is about to be abused again."

---

[1] In Canada, for example, 75% of the spouse-killers are men and 25% are women; a ratio of four to one.

Many of the female spouse killers are women who have been terrified of their husbands. Totman (1978: 94), in her study of female murderers concludes:

> women murder mates when their relationship with the mate is felt to be directly and overtly destructive to them and their sense of identity as a women...and when they have exhausted all other alternative sources of action either actually or in fantasy and find them not viable.

Reports from the Soviet Union also indicate that the killing of husbands by wives is often preceded by ill-treatment. Furthermore, wives in the USA are more likely to kill their spouses in self-defense. Husbands and wives, for example, kill one another with equal frequency, but wives are seven times more likely than husbands to murder in self-defense (e.g. defending themselves from physical or sexual attacks by their husbands). The following comments made by a wife who killed her common-law husband recapitulate such altercations (Chimbos, 1978: 55):

> Both my common-law husband and I were out drinking that night. I suggested that we should go home early. He refused and stayed at the bar with his friends. Then I left him there and came home. After a while he came back home drunk and an argument started. He first started hitting me with his fist and then with a shoe. He kept coming on me. I went into the kitchen, took the knife and stabbed him. I had to do it. He had beaten me up so many times that I had no feelings left. I couldn't face other people. I'd been in the hospital six times because of him beating me up.

Most wives who are physically abused by their husbands do not abandon marriage and many do not seek intervention. According to Gelles (1976: 659–668), there are three major variables affecting the wife's decision to either stay with an abusive husband or to seek intervention:

1. Severity and frequency of violence. The less severe and less frequent the violence, the more a woman will remain with her abusive husband and not seek intervention;

2. Violence a wife experiences as a child. The more she was struck by her parents, the more inclined she is to stay with her abusive husband. This means that victimization as a child raises the wife's tolerance as an adult;

3. Education and employment. Wives who do not seek intervention are less likely to have completed high school and more likely to be unemployed. Thus, the fewer resources a woman has the less power she has, and the more entrapped she is in a violent marital relationship. According to Gelles (1983: 187): "Violence is most common among young families where women have young children. These women are less likely to be earning an income outside the home to protect themselves. Many battered wives are trapped in violent marriages. Their only viable resource may be to hit their husbands to defend themselves."

The Ontario Standing Committee on Social Development (1982) has arrived at the following conclusions regarding the economic dependence on battered wives:

> The economic dependence of some victims on their husbands perpetuates conditions under which the battering can continue. The victim may feel that financially her only option is to remain in the home. From a psychological perspective, a state of "learned helplessness" may be blocking any attempt to leave the batterer.

Martin (1976) reports, moreover, that there are additional factors which help us to understand why battered women are kept captives in a violent marriage. Such factors include: (a) social norms legitimizing the husband's right to hit his wife; (b) outsiders blaming the wife for precipitating violence and therefore she feels guilty about her behaviour; (c) hope on the part of the wife that the husband will change and "grow up" emotionally ; and (d) the myth that staying married is always best for the children.

Another factor which contributes to the wife's staying with an abusive husband is the lack of shelters for battered women in the community. Many battered women have nowhere to go to escape the brutality of their husbands. Through the support of community services, battered wives find viable alternatives to a violent home and access to legal advice and counselling.

Ann Seiden of the Illinois Mental Health Department describes a pattern that indicates psychological problems making certain women compliant to physical brutality by their husbands. The abused women, Seiden argues, are pathetically oriented to "being good girls." If someone tells them what to do they will comply. That is partly what makes these women appear as "good girls" to the outside world, and partly why they put up with the abusive husbands (Meyers, 1983: 349). Lack of assertiveness, low self-esteem, and emotional acceptance of guilt for the husband's behaviour are also characteristics commonly observed among battered wives.

The emotional consequences for battered women are many. They live in paralysing terror; they are overwhelmingly passive and unable to act on their own; and they experience a feeling of helplessness and despair (US Commission on Civil Rights, 1978: 527–531). Wives who are struck by their husbands are also more likely to strike their children. According to one investigator "the battered women were eight times more likely to batter their children when living with a batterer than with a non-batterer" (Walker, 1984: 1). The more violent the parent is to the child, the more violent the child is towards brothers and sisters (Straus et al., 1979).

Explanations of Marital Violence

One of the most rewarding approaches to marital violence is social learning theory, which suggests that violent behaviour is learned in interaction with others, especially intimates. Individuals who assault their spouses fulfil patterns of behaviour learned in childhood from other violent models. The forms of learning include: (a) role modelling during the early years of socialization. The child, for example, observes his parents assaulting each other and then imitates their vi-

olent behaviour as an adult; (b) being a victim of violence at the hands of parents or guardians, especially in early life. This leads to acceptance of violence as a means of dealing with interpersonal conflicts.

Thus, the more violence the child experiences in early life, the more likely he is to internalize violent behaviour and apply it in adult life when confronted with threatening situations. Various studies on marital violence have supported the social learning theory (Gelles, 1976; Chimbos, 1978; Straus et al., 1979, Canadian Advisory Council on the Status of Women, 1980; Browne, 1988: 271–287).

The "general systems theory proposed by Straus (1973: 111–113) is another useful approach to understanding marital violence, which is more or less a crystallization of Goode's (1971) resource theory. According to this theory, it is the power structure of marital relationships which is conducive to husband-wife violence. When the husband lacks the resources (economic, educational) to fulfil his leadership role, the wife becomes dominant in decisions. When this occurs, the following processes develop: a) dissatisfaction with marriage; b) the use of physical force by the husband to maintain his dominance and ; c) counterviolence by the wife.

A study by O'Brien (1971: 697) supports this theoretical view. According to his data, violence between spouses was more common where the husbands were under-achievers in their work-earner role and where the husband demonstrated status characteristics lower than those of his wife. Gelles' (1972) data also indicated that violence between spouses was most likely to occur when husbands were unemployed or had lower educational and occupational statuses than their wives. It would appear then that violence between spouses occurs more often in those marriages where the authority of traditionally oriented husbands is being questioned by under-achievement in their occupational roles on one hand, and an emerging leadership role by the wife on the other. It is the males of the lower socioeconomic classes who are most fearful of the emerging leadership role of women, accompanied by increased equality between the sexes (Whitehurst, 1974: 75–81).

While there is some evidence to support the proposition that husbands who lack resources are likely to use violence in marital relationships, more research is needed to verify the theory. More conclusive testing of the theory awaits better data which would control for variables such as experience with violence in early life, subjective definition of "lacking resources," patriarchal attitudes of "spouses," and attachment to social networks (Chimbos, 1978: 14). Furthermore, a general systems theory may be biased if it can be employed to implicate the battered woman or to excuse the abusive husband because he lacks resources (Bograd, 1984: 561).

An additional perspective introduced to the study of marital violence is social control theory, which proposes that spouses are more likely to become involved in violent behaviour when: (a) meaningful relationships (e.g. attachments to kinship and friendship networks) are absent as absorbers of conflict and crisis; and (b) others are not present to intervene at the time of the incident. This suggests that friendship, family, and kinship networks may serve as social support systems and family control mechanisms. It is therefore hypothesized that spouses of nuclear families who are socially isolated from relatives, friends, neighbours, and other local reference groups have higher risks of resorting to violence in coping with marital problems.

The social control hypothesis is supported by Gelles' research (1973: 241), which indicates that "violent families are characterized by isolation from their neighbours." In attempting to explain this, Gelles proposed that such isolation cuts families off from needed social "resources." Such deprivation "may contribute to an escalation of family problems, stresses, conflict and ultimate violence." Likewise, a study on marital homicide found that spouse killers and their spouses had been socially isolated

from close relatives such as parents, in-laws, siblings, and even their own children. At least 94% of the spouse killers describe their relationships with relatives during the six months prior to the homicidal act as cool and distant (Chimbos, 1978: 58).

One final explanation for violence against women is the sexist ideology deeply rooted in cultural norms and patriarchal family systems (Eshleman, 1988: 574). Men have devised a framework of rules based on the concept of women as being subordinate, inferior, dependent, and subject to physical and social control by men.[1] Such rules, structured by the unequal distribution of power based on gender, have become part of a cultural tradition passed on from one generation to the next.

As the dominant class, men have differential access to important material and symbolic resources, while women are devalued as secondary and inferior. Violence (such as rape or battering) is the most overt and visible form of control wielded by men as a class over women (Bograd, 1984).

Ancient Roman husbands, for example, had the legal right to beat their wives for "misbehaviour" such as drinking wine, walking outdoors with their faces uncovered, or attending public games without permission (Dobash and Dobash, 1979). The use of physical force by husbands to control their wives' behaviour continued to be a common practice through the Middle Ages and into modern times (Siegel, 1983: 288). Through the Middle Ages, wife beating was openly encouraged in the Christian, Jewish, and Muslim regions and in countries across Europe. Husbands could kill their wives for adultery without fear of punishment, and wives were expected to give absolute obedience to their husbands (MacLeod, 1980: 27).

In many Middle Eastern societies "husbands have traditionally had the legal right to punish their wives physically" (Coleman and Cressey, 1984: 140). The use of the whip by the husband

---

[1] Cross-cultural studies indicate that in most societies wife beating is provoked by sexual jealousy, adultery, failure to meet household responsibilities, and disobedience by the wife, all indicating the husband's determination to control the wife (Levinson, 1988: 437).

to deal with a disobedient wife was an established tradition in sixteenth-century Russia. The Domostroy, which embodied the Russian moral code, stated that "if a wife refused to obey and does not attend to what her husband tells her, it is advisable to beat her with a whip according to the measure of her guilt" (Mace and Mace, 1963: 94).

Manifestations of male superiority and machismo (maleness), observed among men in certain societies, are also cultural norms conducive to violence against wives. The crudest examples can be found among Mexico's poorly educated peasants and slum-dwellers where wife-beating is widespread (Hutter, 1981: 403). Wife beating in rural Mediterranean (Cyprus, Greece, Sicily, and Portugal) can also be traced to value orientations that emphasize male dominance over females and male honour (Lozios, 1978). These norms are learned through the process of socialization and carried on from one generation to the next.[1]

Each of the foregoing theories is partial and must be considered with caution. However, the integration of two or more theories can be very useful in obtaining a better understanding of wife battering and family violence in general. One study based on a value-added perspective, for example, has provided us with useful information on the conditions and processes under which marital homicide is likely to occur. According to the finding, marital homicide is the result of an interactive process in which the offender's negative socialization experience in early life (e.g. being a victim of violence) and situational factors (e.g. being isolated from kin and friendship networks, and lack of viable alternatives to deal with threats presented to the offender by the victim), come together in such a way that lethal assault against the spouse becomes more and more likely (Chimbos, 1978).

The value-added perspective is an alternative to the psycho-pathological model which suggests that individuals who seriously assault or kill their spouses suffer from some psychopathological disease such as sadomasochistic complexes (Kurland et al., 1955), pathological jealousies (Guttmacher, 1955) and psychological inter-lockages (Cormier, 1961). This model has serious limitations as it posits a single causal variable (mental aberration or disease) and ignores other variables, which can be at least as important in explaining marital violence.

Are wife abusers any different from non-abusers? Researchers (Newman, 1979; Gelles, 1980; Hornong, 1981) have identified the following characteristics of American men who inflict violence upon their wives:

1. Men who have failed as providers and are under economic stress (e.g. those with incomes below the poverty line) are more likely to abuse their wives.

2. Men who have experienced violent and abusive childhoods are more likely to use physical force against their wives.

3. Abusive husbands tend to be "loners" who have no close friends or confidants. Also they are highly dependent on their wives and that is why they are particularly dangerous when a woman threatens or tries to leave home. Like their husbands, abused wives tend to be emotionally dependent on their mates and isolated from other human contacts.

4. Abusive husbands have an obsession with their wives' behaviour, such as the kinds of friends she has and the kinds of people she talks with on the telephone.

5. The presence of alcohol is very common among men who assault their wives. In other words, excessive alcohol use may turn otherwise docile husbands into wife assaulters.

---

[1] Helplessness, a characteristic commonly observed among battered women, also, results from early childhood sex-role training which encourages girls to be more passive and dependent, as it can develop from the adult abusive relationship (Walker, 1984: 5).

Although wife abuse is found in all social groups, it is not equally distributed; highest rates are found among couples living in large urban communities, minority racial groups, people with some high school education, blue-collar workers, families with low incomes and people under 30 years of age (Gelles, 1983: 187). The higher frequency of wife abuse among lower-class couples is partly due to under-reporting of incidents by couples coming from middle and upper classes. Furthermore, middle-class and upper-class couples have more viable alternatives to cope with stressful situations. They have greater financial resources, more access to marital counsellors, and perhaps better communication skills in solving marital conflicts.

How can we break the cycle of wife abuse? There are certain strategies that can be used to cope with the problem:

1. Temporary removal of the husband from the home. An arrest will give a clear message to the husband who batters his wife. Arrest is only one of the strategies to handle abusive husbands and, according to some observers, it works in most cases.

2. Family consultant intervention in cooperation with law enforcement agencies. Counsellors who are trained in family crisis intervention may intervene in marital disputes and prevent further violence. They can help spouses by easing tension (without direct police intervention) and referring them to appropriate social agencies in the community.

3. Shelters. Through shelters, abused wives have access to legal advice, counselling and protection. Unfortunately 45% of Canadians live in areas where there is no shelter for battered wives. Governments ought to provide shelters and other support services which are designed to meet the special needs of aboriginal, immigrant, rural, disabled, teenaged, or older

women who are battered (MacLeod, 1987: 131).

4. Courts ought to protect women from their abusive husbands, especially during the process of separation and divorce. Courts can issue civil protection orders to protect wives from abusive husbands. A judge, for example, can order a wife abuser to: (a) abstain from abuse, (b) move out of the residence shared by the victim, (c) attend counselling sessions, (d) pay support and restitution, and (e) stay away from the wife and children.

5. Treatment for abusers. Abusive husbands can learn that they are responsible for their own violent behaviour and that there are viable alternatives to cope with stressful situations.

6. A style of child-rearing that emphasizes the learning of empathy, respect for women, and egalitarian relationships between spouses rather than the domination and exploitation of women. Such aspects of socialization should be emphasized not only in the family but in other institutional spheres such as the school. The Standing Committee on Social Development (1982: 44) in Ontario has recommended that:

The school system should develop an awareness among young people of the crime of wife battering. Classes should investigate its possible causes and look at society's responses to the violence. The issue should be studied in the context of male-female relationships in the family and in society in general.

Child Abuse

Another aspect of family violence which has emerged as a social problem is child abuse—the intentional physical injury inflicted on a child by his or her parents, guardians, or caretakers. It includes kicking, belting, burns, serious bruising, broken bones, and sexual molestation. Child abuse, however, may include lack of love and physical and emotional neglect. David Gil (1970: 6) defines child abuse as the "intentional, non-accidental use of physical force, or intentional, non-accidental acts of omission on the part of a parent or other caretakers at hurting, injuring or destroying the child."

Definitions and perceptions of child abuse differ from one country to another. Some countries, for example, recognize child abuse as a separate, identifiable, and distinctive problem. Other countries perceive child abuse as a minor problem that warrants no special policies and programs (Kamerman, 1975: 34–35). It should also be noted that the normally "acceptable" child abuse and neglect observed in North America and other Western cultures is relatively rare in small-scale, non-western cultures (Korbin, 1981).

Child abuse is not a new phenomenon—it is as old as the institution of the family. Throughout history, parents and guardians practised various kinds of assaults against children, including infanticide. Common reasons for infanticide include population control, maintenance of a physically healthy population, and avoiding shame and ostracism of unmarried mothers (Hutter, 1981: 420–421). Radhill (1974: 173) suggests that the beating of children "has been justified for many centuries by the belief that physical punishment was necessary either to maintain discipline, to transmit educational ideals, to please certain gods, or to expel evil spirits." He also argues that children today are typically exposed to less violence from their parents and guardians than in the past.

The actual incidence of child abuse is unknown because: (a) many non-accidental injuries are not reported and (b) there is no clear line between "acceptable" punishment and abusive behaviour of parents or guardians. On the basis of their data, investigators have estimated that over two million American children a year (almost 4% of all children from three to seventeen) are victims of parental abuse and at least 2,000 die as a result (Schuman, 1984: 176). According to a Canadian inquiry, at least 250 children are injured in a non-accidental manner for every million population in urban areas. About 3% of these children will be killed each year and about 30% of the younger ones will receive permanent physical injury or brain damage (Perspectives Canada, 1980: 24). Another estimate is that in 1979 about 60,000 Canadian children were physically abused by 35,0000 parents (Hagedorn,1983: 363).

In England more than 3,000 children are severely injured non-accidentally each year and six of them die each week as a result. Each year more than 40,000 English children experience injuries, ranging from the severe to mild (Gould, 1978: 60). Child abuse and neglect has become a concern to social scientists and medical practitioners in other countries, including Greece (Agathonos et al., 1982), West Indies, Arab States, and India (Kamerman, 1976). Laws and social services for the protection of children from parental abuse in these countries are inadequate or ineffective.

Do mothers show a higher incidence of child abuse than fathers? Straus et al., (1980) argue that the incidence of child abuse by mothers is 75% higher than by fathers, because mothers are more likely than fathers to be involved in the childcare role. Furthermore, child abuse is more often found in single (female) parent homes in which the mother is working. The fact that the mother has to earn the entire family income and, at the same time, care for the children without assistance, creates a stressful situation that may lead to child abuse (Gelles and Hargreaves, 1978). This also suggests that child abuse will increase with the growing frequency of single-parent (female) families who often lack assistance from kin networks and the community.

Stepparenting is another important factor for consideration. According to Wilson and Daily (1987: 229–230) "children living with one natural and one stepparent are much likelier to be physically abused or killed than children with two natural parents." The high risk of maltreatment of children by their stepparents, these investigators argue, support a Darwinian evolutionary theory, which identifies fundamental conflicts of interest within the stepfamily.

Why do parents abuse their children? The psychopathological research suggests that child abusers suffer from personality problems, including impulsiveness, immaturity, depression, sado-masochistic complexes, poor emotional control, psychopathy, and even psychoses. These characteristics are deeply rooted in the parents' early childhood experiences, such as physical punishment, and emotional and psychological abandonment (Coles, 1964; Goldstein, 1965; Wasserman, 1967). Negative childhood experiences, therefore, create pathological states which cause parents to abuse their children.

The psychopathological model which has dominated the literature of child abuse is too narrow. Gelles (1974: 193–94) has indicated four major problems with the psychopathological approach to child abuse.

1. Most of the research findings on child abuse are inconsistent and contradictory. Investigators contradict themselves by first stating that the abusive parent suffers from a personality problem and then stating that the child abuser is no different from the rest of the population.

2. There is little agreement among researchers as to the pathological personality traits of child abusers.

3. The analysis of the abusive parents' behaviour takes place after the fact, and therefore little understanding of the causes of the behaviour is offered. "Analyzed after the fact it is obvious that a parent who beats his child almost to the point of death has poor emotional control and reacts with uncontrolled aggression."

4. Studies of psychopathology are based on nonrepresentative samples and without the consideration of comparative groups of child abusers from the rest of the population.

Sociological variables are also associated with child abuse. Gelles (1978: 580–592), in his US research, found that the incidence of child abuse and neglect are more common in the lower socioeconomic classes. Another study in Athens, Greece, suggests that parents of abusive children referred to the Institute of Child Health, had experienced a multiplicity of problems such as unemployment, ill health, and poverty. Most of these parents belonged to the lower social class and were socially isolated from their families of origin (Agathonos et al., 1982: 307–310). The lower-class parent, social scientists argue, has fewer resources with which to perform familiar roles and responsibilities. More specifically, "he has less prestige, money and power so that his sense of frustration and bitterness is greater than a member of the middle class" (Goode, 1969: 967). Whereas it is probably the case that middle- and upper-class parents are more likely to cope better with stress because they have greater financial resources and greater access to abortion, contraception, and family therapists.

While parents may be held legally and socially responsible for violent acts against their children, societal pressures are partly to blame. Roberta Kulmar (1977: IV), in her analysis of child abuse in the USA, writes:

> Society too must bear part of the blame for child abuse. This is so in part because ours is a society which is prone to violence and exploiting the powerless and because ours is a society which does not adequately meet the needs of minorities, unemployed, the emotionally ill or the mentally retarded.

Which perspective is the most promising in helping us to understand the phenomenon of child abuse? Gelles (1983: 200–201) suggests a sociopsychological model of the causes of child abuse which includes psychological, cultural, social situational factors. Such a model, therefore, would consider socialization experience, psychopathic states, social position of parents, class and community values regarding violence, sources of family stress, and immediate precipitating factors. A sociopsychological model also includes categories of children who have a high risk of being abused by parents or guardians. Such categories include mentally retarded children, restless children, children of unplanned pregnancies, adopted children, and stepchildren.

What are the consequences of child abuse? The abused children of today are likely to become the abusive parents and spouses of the future (Gelles & Pedrick-Cornell, 1986: 74; Browne, 1987: 27). A child who observes violence in the home and is the victim of parental violence is 1,000 times more likely than a child raised in a nonviolent home to grow up and use violence against a child or spouse. Gelles (1983: 188) comments:

> Violence and the threat of violence are the messages people grow up with. It is not surprising that children who experience harsh punishment at home are the most ardent supporters of capital punishment. At the bottom of the tangled web of violence is the truism that violence does indeed beget violence. Each generation of children brought up on violence is another generation of potential child-, wife-, and, yes, husband-beaters.

Battered children also have a high risk of death or permanent injuries. According to Rosenblatt and Greenland (1974: 1), "Once a child has been severely abused by his parents the chances are one in five that he will be injured again. Child victims of such repeated abuse are also likely to sustain permanent crippling injuries or risk dying at an early age." Walker (1984: 1) further indicates that:

> Children who live in abusive homes are at a high risk to become adjudicated as delinquent; often accused of burglary, arson, forgery, prostitution, running away, drug charges and other assaults. Research also show that between 50% to 80% or more of incarcerated women have been battered. They are typically found guilty of property crimes, drug offenses, child abuse and homicide.

The harsh discipline to socialize children in certain societies may also be reflected in violent behaviour against minority groups. According to Bellak and Antell (1975), the Nazi leaders, who were responsible for the killings of millions of innocent people, were cruelly mistreated as children at the hands of their parents or guardians. Hostility to children in Germany is widely accepted, as 60% of the parents surveyed believe in beating, not slapping or spanking, their children (Hakell and Yablonsky, 1982: 297).

What can be done to prevent or at least reduce child abuse? The following strategies can help to protect children and assist and strengthen their families:

1. Community counselling services for abusive parents. Some authorities believe that most abusive parents can learn to stop battering their children if they receive effective counselling. Such services should be offered through hospitals, community mental health centres, family services, and social service agencies. Special treatment should be given to those abusive parents (less than 10% of the total) who suffer from severe mental disorders. Among such mental conditions are schizophrenia, serious post-partum or other types of depression, chronic alcoholism, significant sexual perversion, and serious antisocial violent behaviour (Steele, 1974: 3).

2. Non-credit family courses in hospitals and public schools to teach people how to cope with children and family stress. Parents and potential parents can learn what to expect of children as they develop physically and psychologically and how to discipline them in non-violent ways.

3. The consideration of long-term programs that may require changes in our institutions, values, and life styles. These may include: (a) providing economic and occupational security for parents; (b) exploring means of establishing supportive social networks for violent families; (c) encouraging a style of child-rearing that is free of violence and psychological neglect; and (d) reassessing cultural norms that legitimize the right of parents, guardians, and teachers to use physical force to train and control the child. As

Gelles (1983: 188) suggests: "Reject violence as a normal part of family life and you will begin to see that it is possible to raise a healthy, happy and well-behaved generation that does not see the fist as the solution."

Elder Abuse

The abuse of the elderly by their grown children (or grandchildren) and institutional caretakers is another form of family abuse which is attracting a great deal of attention by social scientists and the mass media. This behaviour may range from verbal threats to physical attacks. The English first labelled this practice as "granny-bashing" and more recently as "granslamming." Elder abuse became an issue of concern early in the 1980s primarily because (a) a growing proportion of the population is elderly and (b) exploratory research on family violence has discovered a significant number of elderly victims (Pedrick-Cornell and Gelles, 1983).

Information on the prevalence of elder abuse is limited by the fact that research is based on small nonrepresentative samples (Pedrick-Cornell and Gelles, 1983: 191). Furthermore, much elder abuse goes unnoticed and unreported. Elders often fail to report abuse because of being confined to bed or a wheelchair, fear of retaliation, lack of alternative shelter, and the shame and stigma of having to admit that they reared such a child (Steinmetz, 1981: 259). It is estimated, however, that over one million elders per year are abused, neglected, or exploited by their own children in the United States (Eastman, 1984: 30; Pedrick and Gelles, 1983: 191). Many other elders are said to encounter mistreatment in nursing homes and other institutions.

Although it is difficult to get accurate information on the amount of elder abuse, the available data offer some tentative insight into characteristics of the individuals involved and the abusive situation. Pedrick-Cornell and Gelles (1983: 192), who have reviewed the available research on elder abuse in the United States, report the following:

a) The abuser is thought to be a middle-aged female and typically the offspring (daughter) of the victim. The middle-aged children, especially the daughters, are emotionally and financially unprepared and often unable to assume responsibility for elder parents. Such caretaking responsibilities "often coincide with the launching of their own children, a period of university or wedding expenses, as well as a time when women are looking forward to fulfilling their own educational and occupational plans" (Steinmetz, 1981: 258).

b) Older individuals with physical or mental impairments run a greater risk of being abused than those of similar age who do not suffer from major impairments.

c) The responsibility for caring for a dependent, aging parent can lead to a stressful situation for the caregiver as well as the entire family.

Steinmetz (1981: 257–260) argues that the economic dependency of the elderly is an important factor in situations of abuse. Like the battered child, the battered parent relies on the caretaker for basic survival needs. This is why battered parents often refuse to report the abuse for fear of retaliation. Lacking economic resources and physical strength, the battered parents are often trapped in situations where they can not find viable alternatives. The phenomenon of elder abuse then is most likely to occur in societies where nonproductive elders are assigned low social status and prestige.

Investigators have observed at least three conditions which are related to abuse of parents by adolescent children: (1) Parents' failure to assume authority in the home. In other words, the parents do not provide a firm structure to guide the youngster's behaviour; (2) History of violence. There is a direct relationship between child abuse and parent abuse. The more the child is struck by his parents, the more likely he will be to abuse his dependent parents later on; (3) Drugs also contribute to the Battered Parent Syndrome. Drugs, however, must be viewed as facilitators of parent abuse rather than a cause (Yudell, 1984: 178–180).

More research is needed before we can draw any reliable conclusions on elder abuse. Some suggestions for future research, presented by Pedrick-Cornell and Gelles (1983: 194), include: (a) self-reported surveys on elder abuse from subjects in nonclinical settings; (b) the use of comparative groups (economic status, ethnicity, and kinship support systems); (c) studies which are designed to test theoretical propositions, and (d) precise, measurable, and scientifically valid definitions of elder abuse.

Until scientific knowledge is developed, a number of steps can be taken to deal with abused elders. First, practitioners should be aware that the elderly are abused by family members, and not hesitate to ask sensitive questions surrounding the appearance of bruises, fractures, or other injuries to an elderly patient or client. Second, the community must use existing domestic violence services (e.g. battered wife shelters) for female victims of elder abuse, and abusers should be made aware of community services which assist those who care for elderly relatives (Pedrick-Cornell and Gelles, 1983: 194). Furthermore, professionals who work with elders (doctors, nurses, and dentists) ought to report cases of suspected elder abuse to the police or investigators involved in family crises intervention.

Summary

Family violence is a very common occurrence in almost all human societies and may range from a simple assault to a lethal act. In certain societies and historical periods, some manifestations of family violence have been viewed as normal and legitimate. However, many social scientists, medical doctors, and politicians agree that one of the most serious of all family problems today is violence. According to recent studies, violence is also common during the courtship period, and the female is most likely to be victimized. Such violent interaction occurs more often in serious dating relationships characterized by strong emotional involvement.

Family violence is generally unrecognized and under-reported. There are several reasons for this including: (a) the idealized depiction of the family as a group of love and affection; (b) the acceptance of some violence as legitimate; (c) fear of stigmatization and; (d) reprisals.

Wife battering is the most common manifestation of family violence, but one that has been much overlooked. Many women are battered and humiliated at the hands of their husbands and lovers. Although wives are just as likely to attack their husbands, they are more likely to get the worst of it. However, women tend to attack their husbands first to protect themselves from potential harm. There are certain variables affecting the wife's decision to either stay with an abusive husband or seek outside help including: (a) severity and frequency of violence; (b) violence the wife experienced as a child; (c) education and employment; (d) societal reaction; and, (e) lack of shelters in the community. Personality factors such as lack of assertiveness, low self-esteem, and being pathetically good also contribute to women's captivity in a violent marriage.

Various theoretical perspectives have been applied to the understanding of marital violence. Some of these include social learning theory, general systems theory, social control theory, and sexist ideologies, deeply rooted in the cultural values and institutions of society. A value-added perspective, however, which includes both early life experiences and situational elements, can provide us with a better understanding of marital violence. Although wife abuse is found in all social classes, it is frequently higher among lower-class couples with fewer economic and social resources. Generally, abusive husbands are underachievers in their occupational roles, have been victims of violence in the hands of parents or guardians, are isolated from friends, have an obsession with their wives' behaviour, and view women as being subordinate, inferior, and subject to domination by men.

The problem of wife abuse can be confronted with special social action. Suggestions include the removal of the husband from the home, family consultant intervention, shelters for battered women, protection of wives by courts, treatment of abusive husbands, and child-rearing practices emphasizing respect for women and egalitarian relationships.

Child abuse is another form of family violence which has received the attention of social scientists and medical practitioners in many countries. Violence against children has been a common practice throughout history and has been justified on disciplinary, moral, and educational grounds. Although both parents use physical force to control the child's behaviour, the parents who are most likely involved in the childcare role show the highest incidence of child abuse.

The psychopathological model views abusive behaviour towards children as abnormal and deeply rooted in the parents' negative childhood experiences. This perspective, however, has been criticized for its monistic view and methodological limitations. The sociopsychological model, which includes psychological, cultural, and situational factors is more promising and dominates the literature on child abuse.

The negative consequences of child abuse are many, including the learning of violent behaviour, development of poor self-image, and self-destructive attitudes on the part of the child. The abuse of children can be prevented, or at least reduced, by making counselling services available to abusive parents, teaching parents and potential parents how to socialize and discipline children in non-violent ways, and reassessing social institutions, values, and life styles which are conducive to violent behaviour.

The abuse of the elderly has become an issue of interest as a result of exploratory research in family violence. The extent of this form of violence is difficult to determine, as much of elderly abuse goes unnoticed or unreported. Fear of retaliation by the abusers, lack of physical strength on the part of the elderly, and lack of alternative shelters in the community contribute much to the silence of the problem.

Abusers of the elderly tend to be their middle-aged children, who are emotionally and financially unprepared to cope with new responsibilities. In many instances these adult abusers had been battered as children by their parents. The battered parents, on the other hand, tend to be individuals who lack the economic resources and physical strength for independence. More research is needed, however, before we can develop reliable theoretical models of the causes and consequences of abuse of the elderly. In the meantime, much effort is needed by practitioners and professionals to detect elderly abuse and refer the victims to community social services.

TECHNICAL TERMS

CHILD ABUSE—The intentional physical injury inflicted on a child by his or her parents, guardians, or caretakers.

ELDER ABUSE—The intentional verbal threats or physical attacks against elderly persons by their children, grandchildren, or institutional caretakers.

INFANTICIDE—The intentional killing of an infant by a parent, guardian, or caretaker.

INTRAFAMILIAL HOMICIDE—The intentional killing of one family member by another.

FAMILY CONSULTANT—A counselor, trained in family crisis intervention, who may intervene in family disputes and prevent further violence.

FAMILY VIOLENCE—The use of physical force by one family member against another with the intention to cause pain, injury, or death.

PRELITERATE SOCIETIES—Cultures that have no written language, a relatively simple technology and division of labour, relative cultural homogeneity, and relative isolation from modern industrial societies.

POST-PARTUM DEPRESSION—A mental condition of a woman resulting from numerous physiological and psychological changes after giving birth to a child.

PSYCHOPATHOLOGICAL MODEL—A perspective which suggests that personality problems deeply rooted in early childhood experiences are important factors contributing to deviant behaviour (e.g. wife battering, child abuse) in later life.

SADO-MASOCHISTIC COMPLEX—A symbiotic relationship in which one person obtains sexual gratification by inflicting physical pain on another person, and the other person obtains sexual pleasure from experiencing the physical pain.

SCHIZOPHRENIA—A type of mental disorder characterized by inability to make appropriate emotional responses, a loss of contact with social reality, and often the presence of hallucinations.

SEXUAL PERVERSION—A pathological deviation from normal sex habits.

SPOUSAL HOMICIDE—The intentional killing of a person by his/her legal or common-law spouse.

VALUE-ADDED PERSPECTIVE—A theoretical orientation which considers a multitude of factors accumulating consecutively over the person's lifetime without which the deviant behaviour (e.g. marital homicide) could not be elicited.

WIFE BATTERING—Recurrent and deliberate assault by the husband against his legal or common-law wife.

QUESTIONS

1. If family violence is so common, why is it generally unrecognized and under-reported?

2. Discuss some of the variables affecting the wife's decision to either stay with an abusive husband or to seek intervention by the police and other agencies.

3. According to Murray Straus's "general systems theory," what kinds of marital relationships are conducive to husband-wife violence? Are there any studies to support the theory?

4. Discuss how sexist ideologies and values may contribute to physical abuse and control of women by men. Give some historical examples.

5. Discuss some of the social and psychological characteristics of men who inflict violence upon their wives.

6. Outline some of the strategies that can be used to break the cycle of wife battering.

7. How does the psychopathological perspective explain child abuse? According to Gelles, what are the major problems with the psychopathological model to child abuse?

8. What can be done to prevent or reduce child abuse? Outline some of the short-term and long-term programs that may be introduced in our communities.

9. Discuss the demographic and social characteristics of individuals who abuse their elderly parents.

10. According to Suzanne Steinmetz, what factors contribute to the abuse of the elderly? What can be done to prevent or reduce abuse of the elderly in our society?

SUGGESTED READINGS

- Frank Bolton and Susan Bolton. *Working With Violent Families*. Beverly Hills: Sage, 1987.

  This book provides clinical and legal practitioners with substantial body of knowledge from which to conduct professional activities with violent families.

- Peter D. Chimbos. *Marital Violence: A Study of Interspouse Homicide*. San Francisco: R. and E. Research Associates Inc., 1978.

  An exploratory study of marital murder based on personal interviews with spouse killers. The study examines the social conditions and processes which lead to lethal violence between spouses.

- John Eekelaar and Sanford N. Katz, eds. *Family Violence : An International and Interdisciplinary Study*. Toronto: Butterworths, 1978.

  Presents evidence of family violence in its many different forms from different parts of the world. It also demonstrates how the social and legal systems of various countries have reacted to it.

- Richard Gelles and Claire Pedrick-Cornell. *Intimate Violence in Families*. Beverly Hills: Sage, 1986.

  The authors discuss some of the myths of family violence, victims of family violence, theories explaining violence within the home and programs for prevention and treatment.

- Linda MacLeod. *Battered But Not Beaten*. Ottawa: Canadian Advisory Council on the Status of Women, 1987.

  Based on interviews with battered women in Canada, the author examines the meaning of wife battering for victims and survivors, the socioeconomic characteristics of battered women, the social costs of wife battering and a realistic model for prevention.

- J. P. Martin ed. *Violence and the Family*. New York: John Wiley, 1978.

  Presentation of case studies, research and theories on family violence with emphasis on sociological and historical perspectives. Issues of law enforcement and the role of social services in preventing family violence are also examined.

- Claire Pedrick-Cornell and Richard Gelles. "Elder Abuse: The Status of Current Knowledge" In *Marriage and Family* ed. Ollie Pocs and Robert Walsh. Guilford, CT:Dushkin, 1983.

  This paper assesses the state of knowledge of elderly abuse and examines the limitations of current research on the patterns and causes of elderly abuse.

- Standing Committee on Social Development. *Violence: Wife Battering*. First Report on Family Violence.

Toronto: Government of Ontario, Queens Park, 1982.

A provincial government report on wife battering in Ontario. Special emphasis is given to demographic aspects of the victims, police and court responses to wife battering and prospects for prevention.

- Suzanne K. Steinmetz. *The Cycle of Violence, Assertive, Aggressive and Abusive Family Interaction*. New York: Praeger Publishers, 1977.

  Based on a study of 57 families, the author shows how patterns of intrafamily conflict resolution are passed on from parents to children, what conditions escalate the use of physical force of one family member against another, and how families deal with the stresses of marriage.

- Vincent B. Van Hasselt et al. *Handbook of Family Violence*. New York: Plenum Press, 1988.

  Examines various perspectives to the study of family violence, forms of family violence including wife battering, child abuse, neurological factors in family violence, alcoholism and family violence and family violence in cross-cultural perspective are discussed in this book.

FILMS

- *Loved, Honoured and Bruised* National Film Board of Canada. 25 minutes.

  Jeannie, married 16 years, left her husband because he physically and mentally abused her. The film shows the various stages in this process.

- *To Have and to Hold*. National Film Board of Canada. 20 minutes.

  A documentary about men who batter women. In this film, men who have used physical violence as a means of controlling or dominating their wives or lovers discuss why they inflicted injury on those nearest to them.

Chapter 17 / Peter Chimbos

- *Twelve and a Half Cents* Canadian Broadcasting Corp. 49 minutes.

  A powerful drama reflecting the frightening realities of life in big city poverty ghettos, this is the poignant story of a cycle of child-beating that ends in disaster.

- *Children in Peril* International Tele-Film Enterprises Ltd. 24 minutes.

  An NBC News documentary of child abuse through interviews with professionals.

- *Child Abuse: The People Next Door* National Film Board of Canada. 20 minutes.

  A realistic dramatization of the causes and consequences of child abuse. The film looks at the demands of parenting and provides useful information about the resources and support networks that exist in many cities.

Reverse: "The Wedding Dance" by J.B.S. Chardin

FAMILY AND LEISURE

Jarmila L.A. Horna
University of Calgary

Everyday experiences offer many opportunities to observe how leisure within the family circle can have both positive and negative effects on the family relationships. Sociologists who study the family and leisure life domains emphasize that family leisure is a complex, multidimensional, interwoven, and dynamic phenomenon. When we approach family leisure from the family perspective, we can see that leisure may function either as a bonding factor in the family, or as a divisive element of the family life. Leisure may be not only a source of opportunity for family togetherness, but also a centrifugal force encouraging family members to pursue their interests independently (Hantrais, 1983, 1984). There exists the negative and debilitating possibility that family leisure can potentially be an arena of conflict and have dysfunctional consequences. Thus leisure can work in two ways: on the one hand, it brings out family conflicts; on the other hand, it can help to deal with, and perhaps eradicate, those conflicts.

Approached from the opposite—leisure—perspective, the family can be both an enabling and an constraining factor of leisure. The family functions as a context of leisure activities in terms of space, time, and material conditions, as well as a source group of co-participants in leisure pursuits. Moreover, the family contributes to the leisure socialization and can influence the leisure domain in terms of allowing free choice and personal development or by forcing constraints upon the family members' leisure.

Both domains, the family and leisure, as well as the specific family leisure, develop and dynamically change over the stages of the family life cycle. Family leisure can expand or compress during these individual stages and may become a more or less bonding element between the spouses or parents and their children. It can enhance or lower the quality of marital and familial relationships and the degree of marital satisfaction. Individual family members' preoccupations, interests, and activities develop in response to the events of marriage, childbirth, and all subsequent critical transitions as children develop and eventually leave home (Rapoport and Rapoport, 1978).

Leisure from an Historical Perspective

While the family as a social institution has lived in one form or another from the dawn of existence of human societies, the same cannot be said about leisure. In simple social systems, life appears to flow without clear boundaries among activities such as production of goods, family life, child-rearing, music and dance, and affective expression of relationships. In the primary or face-to-face community, life seems relatively seamless or undifferentiated. For example, in the traditional life in Samoa, a day passed as some kind of tidal ebb and flow of life in which elements of the necessity we call work, and the freedom we call leisure, were integrated rather than segmented. There, in time, place, mode of behavior, companions, and even mood, the clear divisions between work and play, home and workplace, duty and choice, almost disappeared (Mead, 1928; Kelly, 1982). Even in contemporary, simple societies, not the production-scheduled machine, but the schedule and rhythm of the seasons, of planting and harvest, are the rules of the time framework. Consequently, pre-industrial leisure also tends to be either integrated into the work and survival patterns of life or to be related to special events, for example "holy days" in which people would gather for customary celebrations. The gathering itself might provide the possibility of games, play, spectacles, and various forms of social interaction. The slack periods of agricultural production allow for far more holiday periods than is ordinarily permitted by an economy in which production requires that the machines be tended and running (Kelly, 1982). For example, in early eighteenth-century France there were 84 saint's days per year, to which some 80 days a year when work was impossible (due to sickness, frost etc.) should be added. Peasants and artisans, who made up approximately 95% of the French labour force, were idle for 164 days per year, mostly because of religious observances or lack of work (Dumazedier, 1974).

As in medieval Europe, the settlers' leisure in North America included pursuits from circuses to courting, from crowds to solitary wilderness treks, from sober meetings to wild and violent debauches (Kelly, 1982). The leisure of people living in towns was enriched by the availability of neighbours, regular social interchange on the streets, around school and church, and ease of visiting. Community events were a regular and expected part of the weekly round. People in the country, however, were forced to find most of their leisure within the family and in such survival-related activities in the natural environment as fishing and hunting. A considerable influence was exerted by the Puritans who maintained that any distraction from the seriousness of prayer, worship, and other sober enterprises was evil. Even sport was accepted rather as discipline and training than purely for enjoyment. Moreover, the large illiterate population was cut off from many kinds of activity taken for granted by the elite.

Another specifically North American phenomenon influencing earlier leisure patterns was the high sex ratio of males to females. On the frontier, in mining boom towns, and open range cattle country, the ratio was as high as 100 to 1. Thus in the earlier days of settlement, whether the economic base was ranching, farming, mining, or trading, the chances of marriage were small for most men. In such a man's world, many of the means of entertainment did not require any companions but other men, so the commercial entertainment of the town tended to be for men. A good deal of leisure was related to work and involved making some kind of game of the tasks around the ranch: for example, breaking horses was a hard and dangerous work, but it could also be a contest (Kelly, 1982).

Those who came to the West as family units had to develop their own leisure opportunities. For them, the role of a social or leisure event might have been played by such activities as making games of some chores, teasing and interaction of brothers and sisters, helping parents with their work, learning to play some musical instrument, and taking advantage of opportunities of the area by caring for animals, fishing, and exploring, dancing and music, or such kinds of events as branding, driving cattle to market, a wedding, a funeral, a revival, or a hanging.

In the early industrial city, where the social timetable was no longer based on the cycles of planting and harvest crops, nor on the milking of cows, life for many was reshaped by the rigid requirements for attention of the machine. The long work week and overpowering conditions in mines, factories, and most shops dominated non-work time. Workers were exhausted, frustrated, and, in many cases, ill. The tensions and fatigue did lead many to use the break in the work monotony to try to forget, perhaps escape to the neighbourhood bar, especially when the tenement was crowded. There were no parks, playing fields, or other recreation areas near those tenements. Women had even fewer places to go; most of them had to make do with the space of their rooms and front steps (Kelly, 1982).

Thus, until comparatively recently, there was no such thing as family recreation; what little leisure men and women had was spent chiefly in the company of their own sex. If a man desired female companionship, he could hardly obtain it from his wife, since she lived in a different world. Most societies were male-dominated, and women were too submissive to achieve the equality which companionship requires (Blood and Wolfe, 1960; Parker, 1976). It is only in about the last century that members of the family unit have spent their recreation time together. In the nineteenth century a great variety of relatively new leisure activities was added to the experience of most families. It is quite possible that today's family produces more of its own recreation than did the family of fifty or a hundred years ago, and that probably the family function of "consuming" recreation is today greater than ever (Parker, 1976).

Furthermore, particular forms of leisure activity have been closely associated at various periods with the design, layout, and equipment of the family home. For example, the nineteenth century extension of literacy through universal education provided the setting for the popularity of reading, especially serialized novels, often aloud to a whole family. Aloud, because many drawing rooms were lit only by one good lamp, and the reader would sit under it, a practice doomed by the introduction of the first practical incandescent gas mantle in 1887. For the well-to-do Victorian, lawn mowers and heavy iron rollers, invented in the 1830s, permitted trim lawns, making new lawn-based pastimes possible (Cherry, 184). The non-working class Victorian entertainment, extravagant wining and dining, called for large dining and reception rooms and an army of servant labour. From the family leisure viewpoint, the segregation of children in such households had its implications not only for the house design, but also for the family leisure forms, so different from the later twentieth century's integrated family unit and its leisure.

Unlike its earlier counterpart, the contemporary family home typically accommodates a variety of leisure demands, for example, individual and communal activity, or several activities which may occur simultaneously for different members of the household, each with their own requirements for space. Consequently, the leisure opportunities and constraints posed by the physical characteristics of the home and its immediate surroundings affect the quality of leisure of its occupants. The family home remains the dominant setting for relaxation, in spite of a vast array of clubs, sports centres, parks, and commercial entertainments which are available to attract people away from home comforts (Glyptis and Chambers, 1982).

In an increasingly fragmented and specialized world of work that makes it difficult for people to find their meaning and self-identity through jobs, a privatized leisure becomes an alternative. Consumerism influences private leisure, and community life is being displaced by the immediate family as a social context for leisure. Family life itself, however, also grows fragmented in favour of individual life and leisure styles (Goldman and Dickens, 1984). Thus the contemporary commercialization can split up the family and encourage different leisure activities for men, women, and children.

Leisure in Non-Western Cultures

So far we have examined leisure and the family in the Western world. It is interesting to learn that, for example, in the Muslim world, family leisure as we know it, is not widely present even today. Although Islam never sanctified time nor frowned on leisure activities, the segregation of the sexes and the lack of urban open space still curtail the rise of recreation (Ibrahim, 1982). The typical resident of an Islamic country may have annually eight religious days off: three for fitr, four for adha, one for Mohammed's birthday, and a month for Ramadan which is a month of half-day workdays, but still only one-day weekends:

The Muslim world is a segregated world where men and women are separated in their social lives. While in some urban centres the picture is changing, the coffee houses have always been the domain of men. For the common man in the Middle East, it is his recreation centre. After a six to eight hour workday, men go home, have a meal and a nap, then proceed to the coffee house. Here they have after-meal coffee or tea and play some table games. Women stay at home, watch children, and enjoy the modern conveniences like television. Television also keeps the men at home, but the coffee houses still have enough appeal to lure them out (Ibrahim, 1982: 208).

In accordance with their religion, Muslims teach their children swimming, shooting, and horseback riding. Sport has been accepted in Islam, but for men only. Recreation activities residual from those practised by the early Muslims are still seen in poetry, song, music, and dancing, as well as in table games. When some new activities appear, these are mainly modern sports, watching television, and attending the movies. While in the Western countries, gardens and parks became public and are often used by families in their leisure time, nothing like that has happened in the Islamic countries as yet.

Unlike in Islamic countries, most married couples in Israel share their leisure activities. The typical Israeli family is viewed as one with strong familial ties and considerable amount of joint activities. There are, however, marked differences between husbands and wives in the range and level of their physical activity. Although access to active recreational sports is not outside the life boundaries of married women in Israel, they still are considerably less involved than their husbands (Shamir and Ruskin, 1983).

Family Leisure Roles

Leisure and family life are thoroughly interwoven. The family is the milieu in which most of us first learn to play, and two-thirds of all leisure interests we ever develop are initially practised with other family members (Roberts, 1981). It is almost impossible to draw clear boundaries between leisure and other family activities. If industrialism separated work and leisure, as we have described in the historical overview in this chapter, it never divided the family from leisure and recreation. In spite of this close correlation, however, it appears to be rather difficult to establish a cause-effect relationship between family and leisure. Similarly, it is not easy to find out whether engaging in joint recreation builds family solidarity or, on the contrary, family solidarity facilitates joint recreation.

Patterns of leisure are not uniform; they vary greatly between traditional and non-traditional marriages. In the traditional marriage, the world of the man is extra-domestic; all his interests and pursuits, his primary allegiance, and all his leisure activities are carried out within this world. The basic gender-role segregation forces the wife/homemaker into leisure which is domestic, unindividuated, occurs in the home, and is virtually undifferentiated from the ordinary round of life. For the wife participating in the labour force, leisure in any form may be totally lacking due to the pressure of her commitments. In contrast, the non-traditional marriage and family is characterized by the absence of rigid gender-role definitions. Such joint marital organization does not simply make time available for leisure, especially women's, it also supplies the structure of values which make individual leisure a part of the self-image of marital partners (Bell and Healey, 1973).

Leisure activities are not all likely to have the same influence on a marriage. Even though leisure is associated with a pleasurable definition of the situation and discretionary time, these conditions can be derived either alone or with others, with one's spouse, and with little or no interaction, despite the presence of others (Orthner, 1975). Thus, it is possible to distinguish among three leisure activity patterns: (1) individual activities that require no communication with others, and may actually discourage interaction; (2) joint activities that require a high degree of interaction for successful completion of the activity, and tend to open communication and encourage role interchange; and, (3) parallel activities that are little more than individual activities in group settings, allowing a minimum of interaction among the participants. Although persons usually participate in each of these types of leisure to a greater or lesser degree, in a particular marital relationship the interactional consequences may be quite different if one pattern dominates the others. In the course of the marital career, when

> a particular activity pattern, i.e., individual, parallel, or joint, becomes a dominant pattern, other activities are reduced and this has interactional consequences that may be positive or negative for the relationship (Orthner, 1975: 99).

Thus, if the family is moving toward companionship as a source of marital solidarity, the leisure factor is of critical importance. However, it cannot be said that leisure activities are the prime movers in marital interaction. Rather, the process of selecting activities appears to be somewhat circular, with persons or groups choosing activities that reinforce their relational definitions; the leisure activities, in turn, reinforce these definitions (Orthner, 1976).

An insightful typology is proposed by Colette Carisse (1975) who posits that each family will develop one of possible patterns which will be preferred according to the family's environment. These patterns, namely togetherness, similarity, closeness, and individuality, can be described as:

A. The couples have the same leisure interests and like to do things together as much as possible;

B. These couples have many interests in common but physical propinquity is not specifically searched for;

C. Physical closeness is highly valued, but doing different things while together is considered normal;

D. These couples value individuality: each individual has its own interests and pursue them according to their own time schedule (1975: 196).

These four patterns representing couple's preferred values may be actualized in completely different lifestyles. Although togetherness is usually thought of as the one behaviour indicative of family cohesion, a family can have a high cohesion while, for example, autonomy, expressed in series of individual pursuits, is also highly valued. Carisse suggests that any increase in free time and opportunity for new activities will be used according to rules already developed in the family system. In other words, leisure activity is but one among other activities in the family life schedule, and it will likely follow the same general pattern.

Similar to other marital roles, the conjugal or familial leisure and recreational role is also normatively defined and reinforced by sanctions, by the spouses. Research data document that only a small minority views this role as equally the duty of husband and wife, while a majority of women and a plurality of men think that it is optional (Nye, 1976). The opinion seems to be that someone should organize and promote recreation for family members, but it does not matter whether it is the husband or the wife who assumes this responsibility—it is not especially centred in either the wife/mother or husband/father position. Furthermore, since only a minority of either gender would feel strong disapproval of a spouse who failed to enact this role, sanctions to enforce the recreational role are comparatively weak. However, even if the recreational role is viewed as less crucial than other family roles, "recreation, not previously conceptualized as a duty, appears to be increasing in importance. If that direction continues, it may rank with older, established roles in importance" (Nye, 1976: 154).

Empirical Findings

Most of the earlier studies addressing the family and its leisure issues have been descriptive in nature, and focused primarily on specific types of family leisure and recreation activities. Other studies examined the factors affecting those activities, or they analyzed family leisure and recreation, and their effects on marital satisfaction. Some researchers found a positive relationship between family solidarity and outdoor recreation (West and Merriam, 1969). Others hypothesized that the participation of individuals in particular leisure activities is related to the overall adjustment process in marriage (Orthner, 1975), and that the generalized perception of desiring to share one's leisure time with the spouse is related to overall relational satisfaction.

Among the more recent research projects, John R. Kelly's (1983) study of leisure roles in three different communities in the United States discovers that adults seemed to value most the leisure which was defined as least free from role constraints. From the family leisure perspective, Kelly's finding that relational leisure is chosen by an individual primarily because of the interaction and not the form or the locale of the activity, is important. Marriage, family, and friendship associations appear to have a greater influence on the use of non-work time, particularly informal and everyday kinds of activities, than the more traditional social variables. For example, leisure locales and companions are not related to work but to the family for most adults; leisure, family, and friends are one realm of life space, employment is another. Leisure, however, is not dualistic and thus completely separate from other roles and meanings. Rather,

> leisure, family and friends as companions, community resources, the environment both indoors and out, and varied cultural media are all part of the non-work world. An almost infinite number of activities may be leisure in a vast range of settings. However, for the most part, leisure roles are intertwined with other non-work roles, especially familial (Kelly, 1978c: 326).

Interestingly, even though freedom has been stressed as the central element of the meaning of leisure, leisure with higher perceived constraint ranks higher in importance to adults than relatively unconstrained unconditional leisure: "It is not that we disvalue freedom, but that family interaction even with somewhat less freedom—is valued highly" (Kelly, 1983: 129). Family leisure is constrained by expectations, but for most adults, the most important leisure is relational, social leisure chosen for the anticipated satisfaction. The family interaction itself, whether involving a high or low degree of intensity, whether central or residual to their life, is the dominant form of leisure for adults living in nuclear families.

The most significant factor in the meanings, motivations, and satisfactions for leisure of married men and women is the stage in the family life cycle. Both marriage and parenthood significantly alter the role expectation and contexts of most leisure pursuits. In examining the correlation between married couples' lifestyles and the stage of their life cycle, several researchers found that the early and middle years of active parenting tend to be distinctive in the leisure lives of most people. Children and the home are positive centres of interest. Because of the constraints faced, particularly by parents of young children, such leisure activity as there is tends to take place around the home (Rapoport, Rapoport, and Strelitz, 1977). Specifically, such factors during the early years of parenting as typically tight financial conditions, and the fact that husbands and wives tend to be stretched physically to meet occupational and child-rearing demands lead to a decrease of activities outside the home, and a withdrawal into the home, first among women, then men; however this does not necessarily mean an increase in joint activities. Whatever the resulting pattern may be, daytime leisure with small children can create considerable tension, and if parents have to take their children with them when visiting in the evenings, they may feel that the main purpose of their outing is defeated. The transition to parenthood has a powerful effect on young couples' recreation patterns, particularly curtailing women's leisure activities (Rapoport, Rapoport, and Strelitz, 1977).

In leisure, the number of years married or marital career stage is a significant variable. Research findings document more similarity between joint and parallel participation during the middle life stage than during the first stage. This indicates that shared experiences per se, even if parallel, may be as valuable to the older couples as highly interactive experiences were to the younger couples. Contrary to the popular beliefs that leisure patterns spill over into other life domains, Orthner's (1976) data suggest that increased leisure interaction is more likely to influence communication than other role sharing.

Chapter 18 / Jarmila L.A. Horna

Family Leisure Activities

Up to this point, we have examined leisure concepts and family leisure roles and learned that the family leisure types as known today are a rather recent phenomenon found mostly in industrial societies. To place the family and leisure, both individual and familial, into the context of one's life experience, Horna (1983) proposes a multidimensional approach whereby the two life domains—the family and leisure—are visualized as two triangles partially overlapping, thus creating a third triangle in their middle. Within this scheme of two partially overlapping triangles, the first triangle represents the family roles and obligations; the second triangle represents leisure in general, and may include any potentially leisureable activity. The middle, overlapping triangle represents family leisure. From this perspective, family leisure is conceptualized as those leisure activities or inactivities in which individuals participate with their partner and/or children regardless of the place or time. By analyzing all three triangles, especially the middle one, representing family leisure, and by examining the nature and frequency of activities, the composition of participating groups who share activities, and the reasons for participation or satisfaction derived from it, it becomes possible to visualize family leisure in proportion to other life domains.

We shall now turn to the content and extent of family leisure itself, as represented by the above schematic overlapping triangle of family leisure, to take a closer look at leisure activities and people who co-participate in them. Of course, these factors should not be examined in isolation from other life domains. All factors within both the family and leisure triangles, as well as in the work domain, variably enhance or impinge upon one's life at different stages and, thus, in the final instance shape family leisure as well.

Daily Time Expenditures of Married People

Considerable research documentation of daily casual observations of family life can be found. For example, Martin Meissner's and his research collaborators's (1975) examination of the division of domestic labour and the distribution of daily activities of married couples in Vancouver, Canada, shows differences between the hours which husbands and wives contribute to housework, as well as differences in the husband's or wife's total workload, which includes outside employment of both spouses. As the wives' job hours increase, their hours of regular housework decline, while the husbands' housework remains virtually at the same low level, so men always work less than women. Most employed women have less time for sleep and meals, while men's times remain the same throughout. When husbands contribute to domestic work, they are usually found in activities which often approximate a state of leisure, for example, repairs and maintenance, sundry services such as animal care, small errands, and work related to leisure activities, where discretion is greater. Most married women, on the other hand, do the regular, necessary, and most time-consuming work in the household every day.

In terms of average hours spent on leisure, gardening, visiting, and watching television stand out most prominently. However the "time which women have for each is consistently reduced under the pressure of mounting obligations, particularly on a workday. The leisure experience of men in these three most popular activities is oblivious to rising household requirements" (Meissner et al., 1975: 433).

More empirical evidence on the time distribution in men's and women's lives comes from the data collected in Canada by Petherick and Sametz (1984). Their findings, too, leave no doubt that married women commit most of their time to the family and household obligations, but they are allotted less free time in comparisons with their husbands.

Similarly, Horna's (1983) study of married and cohabiting couples in a western Canadian city documents that performance of various family and household tasks and duties is in most instances divided between the spouses, but the allocation of the tasks is not symmetrical. It follows the traditional pattern along gender lines, i.e. women are responsible for the family and child-related matters and the household chores including shopping, while men mostly do repairs and maintenance or take care of such occasional larger purchases as an automobile. There are not many tasks shared equally by both spouses, since it is "usually the wife" who prepares meals or cleans the house, and it is "usually the husband" who takes the garbage out or repairs things around the house. Their greater task and time loads notwithstanding, women get little cooperation from other family members in performing "their" tasks.

The results of an American study also confirm the above patterns. Geerken and Gove (1983) report huge differences between the time husband spends on housework compared with the wife, even if the wife is employed. The husband's total time spent in labour, i.e. work and housework, is about the same whether or not the wife works. The wife working outside the home remains primarily responsible for the four tasks traditionally assigned to the wife, namely cleaning, cooking, dishes, and caring for the children: she receives no help, especially not from her husband. Her children are most likely to pitch in by cleaning house, though this may be simply cleaning up after themselves. Furthermore, if the wife reduces time spent in housework, there is only a relatively small change in task responsibility after her entry into the labour force. The presence, number, and ages of children may reduce the wife's responsibility for housework, but they decrease her leisure time.

An interesting observation related to the husband's contribution to the household chores, or lack of it, is made by Richard A. Berk and Sarah Berk (1979). They report that the wife's employment status does not influence husbands in the early morning hours. Whatever contribution the husbands make, it usually occurs in the evening. The Berks observe that the significant number of husbands who do contribute are married to employed wives who leave for work shortly after dinner. "The timing of the employment becomes all the more critical if one examines which household chores husbands initiate: clearing the table, putting dishes in the sink, washing dishes,

putting dishes away, and other chores associated with the period immediately after dinner" (1979: 231). Similarly, if husbands take care of their children, they are most likely to do it immediately after dinner, when the wife is tied up in the post-dinner chores, and the child care activities are somewhat less onerous ("play with children," "talk with children").

The above illustrations represent just a small sample of numerous findings that all point in the same direction, i.e. the discrepancy in the amount of women's and men's obligations vis-a-vis their leisure. In spite of the above overwhelming evidence, there may be an exception to such prevalent patterns. When Joan Vanek (1980) reports the results of her earlier study of farm households in the United States, she finds important similarities in the leisure of husbands and wives on the farm. Vanek argues that the nature of work, whereby both spouses produce goods and neither works for a salary or wage, is such that both are able to integrate leisure and family life with work. Consequently, a great deal of leisure is shared. Although husbands and wives also have separate activities, these appear to be symmetrical, meaning that each spouse spends roughly the same amount of time in reading, in informal contact, in organizational participation, as well as the same amount of time off the farm.

Types of Leisure Activities

What, then, do married people do in their leisure, how are they involved with their spouses and children? More than 25 years ago Erwin Scheuch (1960) described the prevailing pattern of spending leisure time as staying inside the home, whether pursuing solitary activities or interacting with family members, while outside activities were much rarer and were likewise predominantly familial in character. Furthermore, the family was relatively more important for leisure during weekends than on working days. Scheuch, however, argued that such focus on the family did not mean a lack of outside contacts. All evidence at Scheuch's disposal led him to the conclusion that leisure within the family is preferred and not forced upon the participants.

The patterns of leisure styles and behaviour in the United States are presented in John R. Kelly's (1978a) study of three communities. Regardless of the community type, marriage intimacy, reading, and family activity lead all activity rankings. Only in the "new town," are family outings, visiting family and friends, watching television, and religious worship ranked lower than in the other two communities, perhaps because the newtowners were uprooted from childhood communities, associations, and kin networks. Other data, that originated from questionnaires completed by persons camping at eastern-coast seashore camp sites in the US, allowed Wallace Dynes (1977) to examine patterns of fathers' free time activities at the residence and away from it. Contrary to a frequent assumption that fathers exclude their family from outside activities, Dynes documents that the fathers interact relatively more with their families outside than inside the home. Therefore, he urges distinguishing between location and family participation because of the marked preference for excursions compared to home activities and the family's tendency to participate, relatively speaking, more often in excursion than in home activity.

A brief look at Australian families in G.T. Caldwell's (1977) study shows that families elsewhere are also devoted to their homes and residential blocks. It is the home where most Australians spend most of their leisure time, caring for the home, listening to the radio, reading or pursuing hobbies, with television viewing being by far the most time-consuming of all free-time activities, for all gender and employment categories, both on weekdays and weekends. Saturday mornings are reported to be ritually given to shopping, the afternoon to sport, mostly by men, and the nights to an evening out. Sundays, on the other hand, are for the home and family, mostly attending to home chores, visiting or receiving relatives and friends (Caldwell, 1977: 428).

Horna's (1983) already mentioned western Canadian survey of leisure behaviour of married or cohabiting couples shows that reading for relaxation and recreation ranks among the most frequent leisure activities although it is more of a workday leisure activity than a weekend pastime. Similarly, individual and team sports and physical exercise take place preferably on workdays. Hobbies, crafts, and gardening are more popular among women, and take place on all days of the week. Unlike men, only a few women are interested in spectator sports, including sport on TV. In addition to their higher participation rates, men watch sports for longer periods. Television viewing is the most prevalent activity, even when sport programs are excluded from the count. Also listening to the radio, records, and tapes, while doing nothing else, is more frequent among men than women in general; however, commercial entertainment, movies, and theatre is primarily a joint activity. Thus, there is considerable family participation, whether joint or parallel; it is found most frequently in sports, hobbies, TV viewing, and commercial entertainment (including movies, particularly among respondents with young children at home). Leisure activities with consistently high participation rates and large time expenditures can be broadly characterized as sociability, social interaction, or companionate. They represent a variety of forms and involve a variety of other participants: visits at the respondent's home or someone else's home, talking with friends and relatives on the telephone, games with children, and relaxation with one's spouse. These social or interactive activities take place on all days of the week but are more frequent on weekends than workdays.

The unequal male-female distribution of leisure time and differences in leisure behaviour are further associated with different types of interference with an individual's leisure participation. When interference with women's leisure is reported, it results most of all from their children's needs. If men report interference with their leisure at all, it comes primarily from their work and much less from their children. Also the frequency of interference of the family and household with free time and leisure is greater for women than for men.

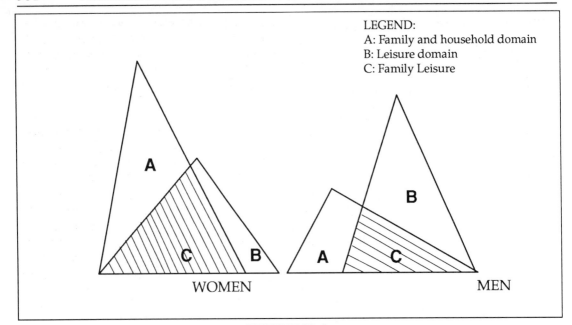

FIGURE 18–1:
SCHEMATIC REPRESENTATION OF WOMEN'S AND MEN'S DIFFERENTIAL INVOLEMENT IN LIFE DOMAINS AND FAMILY LEISURE
SOURCE: Data derrived from Horna, 1983

In addition to the above discussed male-female differences in time allocations and leisure participation, there are also male-female differences in perceptions and definitions of specific activities. Susan Shaw (1984) in her research in Halifax, Nova Scotia, asked her respondents which of their activities would be defined "leisure," "work," a "mixture of work and leisure," or "neither work nor leisure." Shaw reports that some activities, such as cooking, home chores, shopping, child care, and travel, are much more frequently defined as leisure by males than by females. In addition, a few activities, such as gardening and social events, get higher leisure ratings by females compared to males. On the other hand, there is only a small gender difference in the definition of free time activities. Shaw argues that this is probably because men, in general, do feel less obligation and more freedom of choice with respect to these activities than do women.

As illustrated by the graph, there is no mirror-like pattern of life or leisure domains for men and women. Men tend to take more time for their individual leisure pursuits, especially spectator and active sports, while women spend more time on hobbies, crafts, and gardening, socialize more on the phone, and play more with their children than their husbands do. Consequently, the married men's and women's overlap of the family and leisure domains varies. There are variations by gender in (a) time allocated to leisure in general, and to specific activities in particular, (b) the frequency of participation on leisure activities, (c) the number and composition of other participants engaged in activities with the wife or husband, and (d) the reasons why the overlap increases or decreases during the lifetime.

As Figure 18–1 schematically presents, the originally proposed model of universally overlapping triangles requires revision: there are two unequal types of the family and leisure domain triangles—one type for men, the other for women. Consequently, their overlap, signifying family leisure, assumes a gender differentiated form too.

Summary

Until comparatively recently, and in some societies even today, there was no such activity as family leisure. The leisure patterns known to us in contemporary Western societies are not found in simple, preindustrial societies nor in such culturally different societies as Muslim countries of the Middle East. In earlier societies, all aspects of life blended into one undifferentiated rhythmic flow, guided by the natural cycle and change of the seasons, or days and nights. This life had no clear-cut division between work and leisure; its rhythm was only occasionally interrupted by breaks, songs, games, and ceremonies. What little free time people had was spent in the company of their own sex and age group. Only in the last century or so has the leisure life of the family unit taken place within it.

Contemporary family leisure participation takes place within the context of other obligations which must be fulfilled by all family members. The forms of family leisure, the types of family and leisure relationships, the emphasis on joint, parallel, or individual activities—all develop and change over the stages of the family life cycle. They are sensitive to the "domestic age" consisting of the age, gender, marital status, and parenthood variables. Women's access to free time for leisure pursuits is more seriously impinged upon by their domestic and employment obligations than is the case of their husbands. Among the most frequently reported leisure activities are television viewing, hobbies, sports (perhaps more frequently spectator than active), and reading, all of which are most likely individual or parallel than genuinely joint pursuits. Moreover, there is a high rate of participation in those activities which can be broadly characterized as sociability, social interaction, or companionate: relaxation with one's spouse, games with the children, visiting, and talking with friends and relatives on the telephone.

The family and leisure relationships and family leisure itself can be approached from either the family or leisure perspective. When viewed from the family vantage point, we can see that family leisure may function as a bonding factor in the family life: participation by the family members in their joint leisure pursuits can strengthen the family unit, and contribute to its togetherness and well-being. Family leisure can, however, have an opposite, negative effect on the family life. It may become a divisive and centrifugal force which would prompt family members to pursue their leisure interests primarily independently. Instead of building togetherness, family members can find themselves in an arena of conflict.

An examination of family leisure from the leisure perspective reveals that the family can have a multitude of roles in the leisure domain. They may be found in socialization as well as in terms of time, space, and material conditions allocated to leisure by the family. Moreover, the family group is found to be the primary source of leisure companions and co-participants.

TECHNICAL TERMS

LEISURE—Activity that is chosen primarily for its own sake. The choice is perceived as real by the participants even though there may be a number of limiting or constraining factors involved (Kelly, 1982: 23).

PSYCHOLOGICAL CONCEPT OF LEISURE—Leisure conceived of as a state of mind or experience. The primary dimension of leisure is perceived freedom (Neulinger, 1981: 29-30).

FAMILY LEISURE—Leisure activities in which individuals participate with their partner and/or children regardless of the place or time.

THREE LEISURE ACTIVITY PATTERNS:
INDIVIDUAL— Require no communication with others and may actually discourage interaction.
JOINT—Require a high degree of interaction for successful completion of the activity.
PARALLEL—Little more than individual activities in group settings, allowing a minimum of interaction among the participants.

QUESTIONS

1. Outline the differences between simple and complex industrial societies in terms of their life and leisure patterns.

2. Discuss the impact of Islam on leisure activities in Muslim countries of the Middle East.

3. Summarize the major historical points in the development of leisure patterns, especially family leisure, in Europe and North America.

4. Explain how leisure can be either a bonding or divisive factor in the family life.

5. Characterize the difference between approaching family leisure from (a) the family perspective, and (b) the leisure perspective.

6. List and discuss leisure activities, participation, and constraints in the lives of married women and men.

SUGGESTED READINGS

- John R. Kelly. *Leisure*. Englewood Cliffs, NJ: Prentice-Hall, 1982.

  It is a comprehensive textbook which integrates discussions on leisure and its various aspects from the fields of history, philosophy, economics, sociology, psychology, political science, and commercial leisure services. Includes considerable material on leisure history, and on leisure throughout the life course and its concomitant search for identity.

- Stanley R. Parker. *The Sociology of Leisure*. London: Allen and Unwin, 1976.

  One of the most widely quoted books on the topic of leisure. Includes an historical overview of leisure, and a separate chapter on the family and leisure.

- Rhona Rapoport and Robert N. Rapoport. *Leisure and the Family Life Cycle*. London: Routledge and Kegan Paul, 1978.

  Since its first publication in 1975, this book became an instant classic as a pioneering contribution to the fields of both family and leisure studies. There is a wealth of detailed, original empirical material collected in the form of in-depth biographical case studies.

- Alexander Szalai, ed. *The Use of Time: Daily Activities of Urban and Suburban Populations in Twelve Countries*. The Hague: Mouton, 1972.

  Not up to date anymore, this book is still unsurpassed in its wealth of comprehensive data on men's and women's lives, division of labour in their families, and their participation in leisure activities.

A slum in Mexico City (1960s).

FAMILIES IN POVERTY

Carol Agócs
University of Western Ontario

It has been confirmed by the research of generations of sociologists, economists, psychologists, anthropologists, and historians that poverty robs family members of opportunities for individual achievement and for fulfilling social interaction. Yet families have shown resourcefulness and strength in coping with the rigours of poverty over the course of human history. Despite widely differing interpretations of the impact of poverty on the family and despite large variations among the world's cultures in the definition and meaning of poverty, impoverished economic conditions profoundly affect the lives of families in every part of the world today.

Production, Consumption, and Families

The concept of poverty is related to the systems of production and distribution of economic resources in and among societies. When total socio-economic systems are compared, differences are found in levels of productivity and standards of living from one society to another, as measured by such indicators as per capita income. A social system may be viewed as "poor" in comparison with other societies if it provides for most families only a minimal standard of living, reflected in high rates of infant mortality and low life expectancy (Eames and Goode, 1973: 17).

When a single social system is considered, the concept of poverty refers to differences in standards of living that arise from the unequal distribution of economic resources within that society. Here, poverty is a social definition associated with the living conditions of that segment of the population with the fewest resources. The family is an economic unit—both a unit of production and a unit of consumption. The relationship of a particular family to the structures and social processes of production and consumption that characterize its society places the family within the social hierarchy.

In pre-industrial societies in which the primary productive activities are hunting and gathering or subsistence agriculture, the kin or family group is usually the basic unit of production, in the sense that family members work cooperatively to produce what is needed for life. In societies based upon hunting and gathering, systems of distribution tend to be egalitarian, and there is no sense of relative deprivation and no social concept of poverty (Eames and Good, 1973: Ch. 2). In societies based upon subsistence agriculture, social inequality may be pronounced and acknowledged, but here too, the family is generally the basic unit of production. Normally, the agricultural community is able to produce enough food and goods to meet the basic needs of most of its families, but natural disasters, war, depletion of the environment, or rapid population growth may disrupt the local economy and even drive people from the land. In several countries of contemporary Africa, the collapse of traditional subsistence agriculture as a result of drought, war, and the concentration of economic resources in more affluent parts of the world has led to starvation and homelessness—the most dire manifestations of poverty.

In industrial and post-industrial societies, most economic functions that are socially defined as productive pass to bureaucratically organized institutions in centralized locations to which workers must travel to earn a cash income, on which the family's livelihood depends. During the early period of industrialization in Britain and North America, fathers, mothers, and children frequently went together to the factory, especially in textile towns (Hareven, 1975; Tilly and Scott, 1978). But with the gradual entrenchment of bureaucratic patterns of work, home and work became separate spheres, and the productive activity of men, women, and children became both spatially segregated and differentially ranked within the hierarchy of society.

The economic activities in which family members cooperated increasingly involved consumption: the purchase of goods and experiences made possible by the wage labour of individuals. The family's productive functions became limited to the production of new workers for the economy and the physical and emotional sustenance of its members who worked outside the home. These services, which include the preparation of food, maintenance of the home, and care of the young, old, and sick, have typically been provided without pay by the homemaker or working wife in the family.

As the family became a unit of consumption, its connection to the wage system and the levels and patterns of consumption that the wage provides came to define the family's relationship to the distribution of economic and social resources. To be poor in a pre-industrial society is to be unable to produce the family's basic necessities, but in an industrial or post-industrial society, to be poor is to fall below the level of consumption deemed acceptable in that society, primarily because adult family members are marginal to or excluded from the occupational structure.

This chapter focuses upon poverty among families in societies in which the family is primarily a unit of consumption. It deals with the impact of poverty upon families in which children are present and leaves aside the special considerations raised by the impoverishment of the elderly and of individuals not living in family settings.

Working Definitions of Poverty

Even when we confine discussion to stratified urban and urbanizing societies, we can apply no universal definition of poverty, since the organization of production and levels of consumption vary greatly from one society and historical era to another. Poverty is a relativistic concept in societies whose levels of productivity have moved above the bare level needed for survival because of changing and differing perceptions of what constitutes deprivation. The prevailing concept of an adequate standard of living for families exceeds, to some degree, the basic minimum needed for survival. In such societies, poor families may have access to enough resources for survival, but not for what is socially defined as a decent or acceptable standard of living.

Within a stratified society, the various meanings or operating definitions of the concept of poverty may be reflected in differing official definitions of the "poverty line" adopted by government and social agencies. Such definitions are usually formulated with reference to patterns of expenditures for minimum basic needs of families of differing sizes living in communities of varying sizes. In Canada, the "low income cut-off" used by Statistics Canada is different from the "poverty line" specified by the Canadian Council on Social Development, and from the definitions used to administer provincial social welfare programs. For example, estimates for 1988 for a family of four living in a large Canadian city placed the low income cut-off at $23,521 (before taxes), according to the National Council of Welfare, and at $25,667 if Canadian Council on Social Development criteria were used (National Council of Welfare, 1988a: 9; 14). Public opinion, judging from a 1987 Gallup poll, considered $407 per week to be the "least amount of money" such a family required to "get along," while the average weekly poverty level for a family of that size was only $383 (National Council of Welfare, 1988a: 5). The small differences among these various definitions are far less important than the fact that the poverty line for a family of four is less than half the average income of families that size (National Council of Welfare, 1988a: 7). Indeed, most poor families live on incomes that are substantially lower than these poverty lines, since the poverty line is an upper limit.

In 1986, 16% of Canadian families with one child and 21.5% of those with three or more children were living on incomes below the poverty level (National Council of Welfare, 1988b: 24). If all Canadian families were ranked according to their income levels, and we examined the bottom 20% of families, we would find that they received only about 6% of the total income of all families, while the top 20% received 39% of that income (National Council of Welfare, 1988: 105). These proportions, which have not changed over the past thirty-five years, show the relative lack of economic resources available to poor families in Canada, and the concentration of income in the highest stratum. A reduction in poverty can only be achieved, then, by moving toward a more equitable distribution of income among families.

Working definitions of poverty, such as those used by Canadian social agencies, may not seem meaningful or relevant in less affluent countries where poverty has the elemental meaning of starvation, thirst, and death. Yet, most people living in stratified societies would probably understand poverty to mean consumption below a standard accepted in the society. Poverty, then, is likely to be associated with malnutrition and hunger, shelter that does not provide adequate protection, poor health and a shortened lifespan, and lack of access to the cultural amenities that give meaning to the lives of the majority of members of society. These are indeed the consequences of low income, and they represent a relative lack of access to economic and social resources. For example, zero order correlations between per capita income and various indicators of family well-being for 36 countries were found to be as follows: infant mortality, −0.53; energy consumption, 0.97; literacy ratio, 0.45; school enrolment, 0.70; life expectancy, 0.61 (Hawley,

1981: 332). It is clear that "people with persistently low incomes do not simply live scaled-down versions of the lifestyle of middle-income people; they are in fact required to lead markedly different lives" (Canadian Council on Social Development, 1984: 11).

Who Are the Poor?

In the world's industrial and post-industrial societies, such as Canada, the United States, the USSR, and countries of the European Economic Community, the incidence of poverty tends to be related to several demographic attributes of families. In general, families consisting of a woman with dependent children, those whose members are elderly or otherwise excluded from opportunities to earn income, families that are members of ethnic or racial minority groups, families with many children, and families residing in rural areas are especially likely to be living in poverty. Families having more than one of these attributes are at still greater risk.

In Canada, 56% of poor families are headed by adults who are in the labour force (National Council of Welfare, 1988b: 55). Most poor families headed by adults younger than retirement age, then, are members of the "working poor," whose poverty most often results from low earnings because of low wages, layoffs, intermittent work, and extended unemployment. The full-time worker earning a minimum wage would take home the equivalent of only 68% of the poverty line income for Halifax in 1988, for example (National Council of Welfare, 1988a: 6). Among the working poor, living in families, persons with low levels of education and skill, young family heads, the self-employed, seasonal and service workers, farmers, fishermen, and female wage earners are overrepresented (Osberg, 1981: 59). However, female-headed families in which the woman has earnings from her work have twice as much income, on average, as similar families that must depend on welfare (National Council of Welfare, 1988b: 90). Research in several countries confirms that the majority of poor families are supported by people whose employment opportunities are limited to unstable and poorly paid jobs with no opportunity for advancement (Eames and Goode, 1974: 115, 138).

In North America and Europe, the two-breadwinner family has become the norm, and the single income family is at a relative disadvantage. The National Council of Welfare has estimated that the number of low-income families in Canada would nearly double if women in two-income marriages were not working for pay. Female-headed single-parent families are especially likely to be poor in Canada. Marital breakdown, parenthood in the absence of marriage, and the failure of fathers to meet their obligations to support their children are the typical events that result in a family's dependence on one female breadwinner. Family responsibilities and wage and job discrimination against women combine to create conditions of poverty for a large proportion of families led by women.

In Canada, 56% of families headed by women are living on incomes below the poverty line, compared with 23% of single fathers (National Council of Welfare, 1988: 2, 33). Female-headed families, on average, make do with half the income present in two-parent families in Canada. Although 60% of poor children in Canada live in two-parent families (National Council of Welfare, 1988b: 29), a growing proportion of Canada's poor families are headed by women.

The difficulties of rearing children alone and in poverty are clear in the story of a twenty-two-year-old woman from Newfoundland, a single mother of two children, ages five and three. Alice had quit school at grade 10, and was pregnant and married at the age of 15. Less than two years later, a victim of domestic violence, she was supporting her children alone with no financial support from her former husband. Alice managed to complete high school by taking night courses, as well as a year of clerical training. To support her family, she has since combined social assistance with income from cleaning and babysitting jobs, as well as clerical work. But Alice must still wash her family's clothes by hand and purchase only second-hand clothing, and she cannot afford

to buy nutritious food for her children (Canadian Council on Social Development, 1984: 21).

Among the families of the working poor, rural-to-urban migrants are numerous in many parts of the world, especially in countries undergoing rapid urbanization and high rates of population growth, combined with low rates of industrialization. In the Third World, the large urban settlements that have been magnets to the rural poor typically developed as centres of colonial administration rather than industrial production. These cities have become the focus of political and administrative power and symbols of the culture and products of the contemporary international economy. However, those tantalizing products are out of the reach of the majority, and in general, the city offers far too few stable job opportunities to meet the needs of its burgeoning population. A large proportion of adults earn a bare subsistence income from casual labour, collecting and selling junk, peddling, and domestic work. Others eke out a living in family-based handicraft, trade, service or industrial enterprises requiring very low capital investment (Lloyd, 1979: Ch. 6).

Despite lack of opportunity to earn stable incomes, migrant families often consider themselves economically better off than they were in the rural village, which they were forced to leave by population pressure, lack of any economic opportunity for the next generation, or even starvation. Migrants often resettle in the city with no more tangible prospects than the vague belief that the family's prestige and economic position will improve: the city is the promised land, while the future on the land is bleak or hopeless.

But in large cities of the developing world such as Accra, Casablanca, Bogota and Lusaka, and even on the peripheries of European capitals such as Paris and Rome, poor families live in shanty towns (Sinclair, 1978: 16; Blair, 1874: 126; Morosini, 1962). These illegal settlements are known by various names—barrios, favelas, or ranchos in Latin America, bidonvilles in Paris and North Africa, bustees in India, and borgate in Italy. The shanty towns have been created by migrant families who, lacking other housing alternatives, build themselves shacks on vacant land from scraps of wood and metal, mud bricks or concrete blocks, and other cast-off materials. Many squatter settlements are on the outskirts of the city far from job opportunities and lacking in public services such as water, sewers, electricity, transportation, or schools. The families who live there are marginal to the economic, cultural, and political life of the city. They have no resources but their own labour, for which there is virtually no demand, and the assistance of neighbours and kin.

The life of a shanty town family is vividly described in the diary of Carolina Maria de Jesus (1962), an unmarried woman supporting three children in the slums of São Paolo. Carolina moved to the city from the rural interior, alone, with no job waiting, and a baby on the way. She built a shack of boards scavenged from a construction site, flattened tin cans and cardboard, and spent her days, the child strapped to her back, searching through trash for bits of food and old clothes, as well as cans and paper bags which she sold. Two more children were born; their fathers contributed nothing to their support.

She had received only two years of schooling, but as an escape from her troubles Carolina wrote a diary on notebooks recovered from garbage. Her writings were scorned by the neighbours, but her diary was eventually published and became a literary sensation. Her earnings as a writer allowed her to leave the slum and to buy a house for herself and her children.

An entry in Carolina's diary describes the misery and hopelessness of family life in the shanty town:

July 15, 1955. The birthday of my daughter Vera Eunice. I wanted to buy a pair of shoes for her, but the price of food keeps us from realizing our desires. Actually we are slaves to the cost of living. I found a pair of shoes in the garbage, washed them, and patched them for her to wear. I didn't have one cent to buy bread. So I washed three bottles and traded them to Arnaldo. He kept the bottles and gave me bread. Then I went to sell my paper. I received 65 cruzeiros. I spent 20 cruzeiros for

meat. I got one kilo of ham and one kilo of sugar and spent six cruzeiros on cheese. And the money was gone...

I was ill all day. I thought I had a cold. At night my chest pained me. I started to cough. I decided not to go out at night to look for paper...

I washed the children, put them to bed, then washed myself and went to bed. I waited until 11:00 for a certain someone. He didn't come. I took an aspirin and laid down again. When I awoke the sun was sliding in space. My daughter Vera Eunice said: "Go get some water, Mother!"

July 16. I got up and obeyed Vera Eunice. I went to get the water... [Later] I went to Señor Manuel, carrying some cans to sell. He gave me 13 cruzeiros. I kept thinking that I had to buy bread, soap and milk for Vera Eunice. The 13 cruzeiros wouldn't make it. I returned home, or rather to my shack, nervous and exhausted. I thought of the worrisome life that I led. Carrying paper, washing clothes for the children, staying in the street all day long. Yet I'm always lacking things, Vera doesn't have shoes and she doesn't like to go barefoot... (de Jesus, 1962: 17–18).

The Burden of Poverty: Effects of Poverty on Children and on Family Structure and Relationships

The social class position of parents accounts for a considerable proportion of the variation in the occupations and incomes of their children (Jencks, 1979: 81, 214). The child born to a poor family begins life with many relative disadvantages that depress his or her chances of achieving a significantly higher standard of living. The difficulties faced by children growing up in poverty are well documented and begin with lower life expectancy at birth, and tendencies toward premature birth and below average birth weight (Blaxter, 1981: 74; National Council of Welfare, 1975: 10–11).

The ability of the child growing up in poverty to acquire the education necessary to gain access to steady employment is further hampered by a complex of social factors. There is evidence that poor children in Canada, Britain, and the United States are more likely than others to be absent from school because of illness or accidents and to have hearing or speech impairments or behaviour problems that hinder school success (National Council of Welfare, 1975: 11–13; Blaxter, 1981: 90–100; 134). While poor parents often place a high value on education (Lewis, 1961), children growing up in low-income families are far less likely than middle class youth to complete high school or to attend university, even if they had achieved high scores on tests of mental ability (McRoberts, 1974). Research evidence has quite consistently demonstrated that the school achievement of children is more strongly related to the family's social class background than to intelligence or to quality of the educational resources available to the child (e.g. Coleman, 1966; Jencks, 1972).

The strains of poverty impact not only upon the life chances of children, but also upon the relationships of family members. Patrick Burman observed that, at its best, the family "sustains and confirms the identity of its members, and offers love and the opportunity to love." However, it is also true that "the family can inflict abuse and reinforce inequality in a more thorough and intimate way than any other institution" (Burman, 1988: 165).

Research in the United States has shown that unemployment significantly increases the likelihood of divorce (Osberg, 1981; Wilson, 1987), that marital stability is directly related to socioeconomic status (Glick and Norton, 1980), and that economic stress appears to precede and contribute to family dissolution (Schiller, 1976: 96–98). Broken marriages, in turn, create single-parent families, usually headed by women, and these families run a high risk of living in poverty.

Economic pressures can create increasing levels of stress in a couple's relationship as their family responsibilities grow. The couple may marry or set up a household while both are young, and because both partners bring low educational attainment and few skills to the marriage, their job opportunities are poor and their family income low. Children may begin to arrive early in the relationship, and their mother finds it necessary to leave the labour force and care for them full time since she cannot earn enough to pay for child care.

Her partner finds it increasingly difficult to provide for the growing family on his limited income. Unemployment may create a burden of strain on the relationship of husband and wife and make life unbearable. The couple's ability to cope is further undermined by the prevailing ideology that blames the victims of unemployment and poverty rather than the economic and social conditions that create these difficulties (Ryan, 1971). The couple begin to blame themselves and one another for their inability to meet the family's needs. The man's feeling of worth as a provider is threatened, while the woman is taken to task for nagging and for being unable to stretch the family's meagre resources to cover its needs. Wife and child battering, alcoholism, infidelity, abandonment of the family, depression, or physical ailments may follow as the strain increases. Under such assaults, it is perhaps surprising, not that many poor families experience dissolution, but that so many remain intact (for descriptions of these realities see Rubin, 1976; Ch. 5).

The impact of economic stress on the social psychology of family relationships can be viewed in terms of exchange theory, wherein marriage is seen as a balancing of costs and benefits to the partners (Scanzoni, 1972). The couple's relationship might be viewed as a bargain involving the exchange of rewards such as love, respect, companionship, services, and material support. Men who enjoy well paid jobs and high social status have considerable bargaining power in the family, while men who lack these resources command less respect and emotional commitment from family members on the basis of their relationship to the economic system. Men whose employment-based bargaining power is low may attempt to claim respect on the basis of traditional patriarchal norms of male power and authority. Family members may not consider these claims entirely legitimate, and their resentment may lead to withdrawal of emotional support from the husband and father at the time he needs it most, for example, while he is unemployed. From the woman's point of view, the man may have proved to be an unreliable supporter and an inconsiderate partner and, therefore, a poor emotional investment in the long term. The bonds of affection and mutual respect that may have sustained the couple in hard times become strained to the breaking point as each individual comes to see few rewards in maintaining the bargain that their relationship represents to them.

The experience of a mother rearing children in poverty typically reflects both the class-based and the patriarchal structure of everyday social reality. No matter what their income level, employed mothers carry the burden of the "double day" of paid work and responsibility for the care of children and the home. This burden weighs most heavily under conditions of poverty, whether or not the children's father is present in the home. A sense of entrapment and exhaustion seems virtually inevitable when a mother's days (and often nights) consist of long hours of physically demanding and poorly paid work, during which she is preoccupied with anxieties about her children's welfare and the adequacy of the childcare arrangement (if any) she is able to afford (Gannagé, 1986). The mother who stays at home with her children while her husband is employed often finds herself cast in a powerless and confining domestic role, in which she is the dependent and subordinate servant of her husband and children, while struggling to stretch her husband's wage (Luxton, 1980; Burman, 1988; Ch. 9). For the women raising her children on public assistance, there is the added burden of social stigma and isolation, and a diminished sense of self-esteem and competence.

The Matrifocal Family Structure

Economic conditions not only contribute to marital dissolution, but may also favour the mother-led household as an adaptation to the structural conditions of poverty. Mother-led or matrifocal families are usually understood to be households in which the strongest and most enduring bond is between a mother and her children. No male is regularly present in the home in the role of husband and/or father, although consensual unions may be estab-

lished and the roles occupied for temporary periods. Such households may include the woman's mother or other kin.

A case study of a Native community in Canada's Yukon illustrates factors conducive to the emergence of the mother-led household as a response to poverty under some social and economic conditions (Cruikshank, 1976). Traditionally, this Native community lived by hunting, trapping, and fishing, but the contemporary economy is based upon wage labour from mining and government services. The traditional subsistence skills of Native males have become redundant and most jobs are filled by technically trained single men who come north for a few years from the urban south. Native men are generally unable to earn enough income to support their families which must depend upon government assistance.

From the perspective of the Native woman, the Native man is rarely a dependable supporter. But job opportunities as domestics, waitresses, and cooks are available to Native women, who are thereby able to be more economically independent than are men. While the woman may earn enough to provide for herself and her children, she would have difficulty supporting a man as well. Moreover, as a family head she may be eligible for public assistance, which constitutes the most reliable support for the family when employment income is inadequate. While the well-paid white workers might appear attractive mates, until 1985, Canada's Indian Act specified that an Indian woman who married someone who was not a registered Indian lost her right to live on her reserve and to take advantage of federal benefits available to Indians.

Thus, for both the man and the woman there are many disincentives to marriage or the establishment of a permanent relationship. Factors built into the economic and political systems, which poor people are powerless to influence, make it reasonable for both to enjoy one another's company without making long-term commitments, which would be unrealistic, burdensome, and doomed to failure in many cases. The "matrifocal" family structure, then, is best seen not as an ideal or typical form that corresponds to a cultural norm but a realistic adaptation to economic marginality.

Prior to the late 1960s, American scholars tended to generalize about family structure among the poor primarily on the basis of observations in the Caribbean and in black communities in large American cities. Some theorists hypothesized that the matrifocal family was an instance of cultural transmission from Africa (e.g. Herskovits, 1941) or a legacy of slavery (e.g. Myrdal, 1944), while others (Liebow, 1967; Moynihan, 1965) tended to associate this form of the family with the black American experience in the industrial city. Many of these writers described family relationships among the poor as frail and ephemeral, characterized by failure, abandonment, social disorganization, and an absence of social support.

But more recent research has cast serious doubts upon these earlier speculations, both by broadening the base of historical and comparative observation and by developing analyses of the effects of specific characteristics of social and economic structures on family patterns. In the late nineteenth and early twentieth centuries, the two-parent nuclear family structure was predominant among American blacks (Gutman, 1977). On the other hand, mother-led families have been observed among the poor in Puerto Rico, Colombia, Venezuela and other parts of Latin America, South Africa, Singapore, Java, Tahiti, some Native communities in the United States and Canada, and among urban whites in the United States (Eames and Goode, 1973: 182–85; Blumberg and Garcia, 1977: 102, 123, 135). Comparative research has demonstrated that economic deprivation, and in particular, male unemployment, not race, is at the root of the mother-led family structure as an adaptation to poverty among significant segments of some urban communities (see Blumberg and Garcia, 1977; Wilson, 1987).

Although these hypotheses await confirmation by comparative research incorporating careful controls, it can be tentatively suggested that a matrifocal family structure may be a prevalent adaptation to poverty when the following conditions are present. First, economic conditions are so marginal in the community that there is no property or marketable skill or knowledge that can be inherited by children from their parents. Second, families are dependent for their livelihood on a wage economy in which the individual, not the family, is the productive unit. The matrifocal family structure is generally not found in traditional societies in which the family is the basic unit of production (Blumberg and Garcia, 1977: 109). Third, the adult male is marginal to the economy and has very few opportunities to obtain steady employment at a wage high enough to support a family throughout the year. Fourth, viable economic opportunities are more accessible to women than to men, through employment, charity, or welfare assistance available to women who are heads of families. These subsistence opportunities are compatible with the woman's childcare responsibilities, and the income they produce is not significantly less than the family would receive if a male supporter were present (Blumberg and Garcia, 1977: 109). The lack of welfare programs in poor countries may limit the prevalence of the matrifocal structure in those settings (Blumberg and Garcia, 1977: 117). A fifth factor, whose impact needs to be examined, is the influence of a history of colonial oppression, whereby a people's indigenous institutions and lifestyle have been destroyed or controlled by a dominant group of another culture.

It must be kept in mind that the matrifocal family structure has not been observed among the very poor in many parts of the world and in no community has it been found to be the only form of family life. In many poor communities the conventional nuclear family is virtually universal, while the extended family is common in some, and variants on both these patterns have been observed.

Is the Poor Family Disorganized?

Some scholars have pointed out that the prevailing concept of the matrifocal family structure is simplistic and biased. While there is evidence that the mother-led family may be more prevalent among the very poor in some societies than among the middle class, because it represents a rational strategy for coping with economic marginality, it is only a perspective based on a presumption that the middle-class lifestyle is the only acceptable model—or that only men can be adequate heads of families— that leads to the characterization of such families as disorganized or as failures.

Carol Stack, an American anthropologist, lived with her pre-school son in a poor black community and conducted field observations over a three-year period. Stack (1974) described complex patterns of cooperation and mutual aid within and between families, and large kin networks which spanned several households. These stable kin networks and the collective patterns of self-help and exchange within them constituted a resourceful strategy for coping with poverty and racial oppression. For example, the practice of exchanging children among kin and friends in the community—known as "child-keeping"—was both a symbol of trust and a way of sharing limited resources. Often the female relatives of the child's father contributed to the child's support and upbringing whether or not the relationship between the child's parents was still active. Many households consisted of three generations and stable networks of blood relatives and affines were enlarged through fictive kinship, the practice of incorporating friends into the family circle by defining them as cousins, sisters, brothers, or daddies. Ties of social support were further cemented through the exchange of money, food, clothing, and other goods and services. Trading enabled families with no surplus income to cover some of their needs when their money was gone, as was frequently the case because of the high levels of unemployment and the low incomes in the community. The activity of daily life, to a large extent, revolved around the cultivation and use of these complex and interdependent human relationships.

A 1979 survey of Native households in Winnipeg found that 58% contained single-parent rather than two-parent family groups (Peters, 1984). Most of the single-parent households received welfare, while in the two-parent households, the male worked full time in a majority of instances, although unemployment was endemic among Winnipeg's Natives. A follow-up study found that most of the households experienced some fluctuation in their membership during the previous months, and had had overnight guests for an average of five days each month (Peters, 1984: 16). Temporary residents who received public assistance or unemployment benefits, or who worked, shared their income with the household, and some visitors without incomes contributed by babysitting or caring for the sick. Survey respondents indicated that their guests were welcome, and that they had received aid from them as well as extending accommodation and food.

Peters' study, like Stack's work, suggests that the structure of families in poor communities is described by neither the conventional nuclear family model, nor by the concept of the matrifocal household. One difficulty is that the household and the family, as a group of individuals who interact as kin, are not coincident. Both Stack and Peters found elastic extended family groups whose membership expanded and contracted as the need arose, and whose boundaries spanned several households. In the case of Natives, these households were many miles apart, as they included the reserve and urban contingents of the kin group. Within these flexible family groups, sharing and exchange of resources and social support was continuous. Valentine (1968) has suggested that a family structure based on household units and characterized by consensual relationships and a strong mother-child bond is a flexible adaptation to uncertain and fluctuating economic circumstances, and is therefore viable and constructive rather than a negative or problematic social pattern.

Explaining Poverty in Relation to Status, Class and Power

Max Weber analyzed the system of social stratification in societies by using the concepts of status, class, and power (Gerth and Mills, 1958). Each of these central dimensions of social inequality provides a perspective from which to view the causes and impacts of poverty in families. We begin with the view that the poor are essentially a status group with a distinctive lifestyle.

Status Group Analysis: The Culture of Poverty

In terms of the concept of status, poverty is a question of social honour or prestige and of the way of life or subculture associated with a given rank in the social hierarchy. Occupations are important not merely because of the level of income they command but because of the relative prestige they symbolize and the lifestyle they appear to represent. Canadians tend to view the occupations of judge or doctor as having high prestige, while hunters and trappers, waitresses and welfare recipients rank near the bottom of the social hierarchy. The judge and the doctor not only earn vastly more income than the hunter or the waitress, but their families will tend to have different ways of life and views of the world. Occupational status and the social prestige and economic opportunity associated with it, then, tends to differentiate families into class-based subcultures.

The urban anthropologist Oscar Lewis is among the most influential of those who have argued that poverty can be viewed as a culture with its own distinctive values and behaviour patterns that is found in societies around the world and that is passed down from generation to generation (Lewis, 1966). The most important characteristics of this culture are: (a) a matrifocal family structure in which women and children constitute the basic family unit, while men are present intermittently; (b) a lack of participation in the organized life of society, including steady employment, churches, voluntary associations, labour unions, and the political system; (c) attitudes of fatalism, dependence, hopelessness, and resignation to one's perceived fate in life; and, (d) a tendency to prefer gratification in the present, to saving and planning for an uncertain future.

Lewis' analysis of the culture of poverty grew out of field work in the slums of Mexico City, San Juan, and New York City (1966 and 1959). Lewis believed that the behaviour patterns he observed in these families had developed in the past as responses to the deprived material circumstances in which they had lived. But, in time, these patterns crystallized into a cultural system that took on a life of its own and became an influence upon behaviour, independent of the material conditions of poverty. The implication was that it was the values and lifestyle of poor families that blocked their escape from poverty by locking them into patterns of behaviour incompatible with upward mobility in an urban environment. This notion reinforced the already prevalent belief that the victims of poverty are to blame for their own misfortunes (Eames and Goode, 1973: 9; Ryan, 1971).

The culture-of-poverty analysis has been widely criticized on several grounds. First, this analysis has been said to misconstrue the relationship of cultural patterns to material deprivation. For example, our analysis of matrifocal family structure in the Indian community of the Yukon suggests that this behaviour does not arise from values, preferences, or traditional culture passed down from one generation to the next. After all, the two-parent structure is the norm among poor families in traditional Native communities, as well as for blacks in the US. The matrifocal family structure is best understood as an adaptation to a particular configuration of economic and social conditions (listed on previously).

To pursue this argument a step farther, it does not make sense to argue that the poor are impoverished because they are fatalistic; insofar as they do manifest this outlook, it is a consequence of prolonged and unrelieved material deprivation and lack of access to opportunity to improve their lives. The poor, then, are not poor because of their "culture." Instead, their ways of life—to the extent that there is an identifiable pattern of behaviour shared by many poor families—are adaptations to the social and economic structure that has deprived them of a decent standard of living, power, a place in society, and a future for their children.

Chapter 19 / Carol Agócs

Another count against the culture of poverty perspective is that it is not a valid representation of the lifestyles of poor families. Where Lewis saw social disorganization, pathology, cultural deprivation, and alienation from social relationships, other researchers such as Stack (1974) have found complex social relationships and mutual assistance behaviour in slum communities.

The type of family structure in which the mother-child bond is the most enduring relationship and whose boundaries are elastic enough to encompass several households, three generations, and various kin, fictive kin, and friends, is not a "broken," disorganized family. This family form is simply one of several structural variants. As a social form that humans have developed to adapt to and master their environment, it has as much claim to legitimacy and social acceptance as the nuclear family model, which evolved among the middle and working classes but which does not meet the needs of the poor under certain conditions.

While this discussion has tended to emphasize continuities and uniform social patterns among the poor in many parts of the world, as does the culture of poverty analysis, the poor are as variable a social category as any other. The prevalence of patterns attributed to the poor, such as the family structure based on the mother-child bond, has not been demonstrated and systematic comparative research is needed to reveal circumstances in which such adaptations may develop. For example, closer inspection would undoubtedly reveal significant differences among ethnic groups in family structures and patterns of behaviour of the poor. Irelan's study (1969) of 1000 black, Mexican-American and Anglo-American families in California, for example, found that the values Lewis claimed were characteristic of the culture of poverty were most likely to be held by Mexican-Americans whether they were poor or not. Irelan suggested that, since Lewis studied primarily Latin American families, he was basing his conclusions about the culture of the poor in general on data that described only one ethnic group.

Class Analysis: The Dual Labour Market

Those who view the poor through the lens of class are likely to see the socio-economic structures and processes that oppress poor families and create the conditions that give rise to their survival and coping strategies. Class analysis, in a sense, widens the lens so that the observer focuses not just on the poor family, but on the entire social and economic system of which that family is a part. Class analysis calls attention to world-wide social and economic forces that create poverty, and views poor families as exploited victims. One similarity between class analysis and the culture-of-poverty perspective is that both see the poor as an undifferentiated group that is affected by and reacts to poverty in relatively uniform ways, regardless of ethnic variations.

A major focus of class analysis is the relationship of the poor to the economic structure in a capitalistic society in which the family is a unit of consumption and must depend upon the income its breadwinners are able to provide. In such a society one frequently observes what some analysts have called a dual labour market consisting of primary and secondary segments (e.g. Gordon, 1972; Gordon, Edwards and Reich, 1982). The primary labour market includes those jobs that are relatively secure and reasonably well-paid and that offer some opportunities for advancement and often union representation for workers. The secondary labour market consists of jobs that offer poor working conditions, low pay, little or no security, no opportunities for advancement, and generally, no union protection. The kinds of jobs generally available to shanty-town dwellers in the Third World (described on pages 310–311) fall into the secondary labour market. So do many jobs held by wage workers in industrial and post-industrial economies, such as farm labourers, unskilled construction workers, dishwashers, domestic workers, and seasonal employees.

The secondary labour market constitutes a "reserve army of labour" that absorbs the shocks of business cycles and changes in demand and in the technology of production—a labour force that employers are free to mobilize as needed and then cast off when convenient. If we examine the social characteristics of workers who hold part-time, insecure, and unpleasant jobs, we find an over-representation of women, youth, the unskilled and poorly educated, recent migrants and immigrants, and ethnic and racial minority groups. It is no coincidence that these are also the social characteristics that are associated with poverty. Indeed, the working poor—the majority of the poor in modern and developing societies—are attempting, against great odds, to support their families on the paltry and uncertain incomes provided by precisely those jobs that constitute the secondary labour market. It is the dependence of these families upon the vagaries of the secondary labour market that gives rise to coping strategies such as a family structure centred on the mother-child bond.

From the perspective of class analysis, poor families are trapped in poverty, not by cultural forms they themselves prefer and perpetuate, but by economic and social exploitation and gender, racial, and ethnic discrimination. The poor are unable to escape dependence on the secondary labour market because they lack the skills, educational credentials, and social characteristics that are the price of entry into the primary labour market. They lack these attributes because of discrimination and because the schools and other institutions of society operate to safeguard the privileges of those with wealth and power who control these organizations in their own interests. One of those interests is the continued existence of the secondary labour market which buffers employers and the primary labour market from fluctuations in the demand for labour and which provides a low cost labour force for the performance of labour intensive functions, thus keeping the costs of producing some consumer goods artificially low. Finally, it is in the interest of employers to maintain an impoverished underclass as a form of social control upon the primary labour force. For workers in that sector who have families to support, the threat of sliding into poverty creates resignation to low wages, poor working conditions, and regimentation in the workplace that might not otherwise be tolerated.

Power Analysis: Poor Families as Clients

Those who view poverty as fundamentally a state of powerlessness emphasize the interference of large bureaucratic structures, both corporate and governmental, in the lives of poor families (e.g. Donzelot, 1979; Piven and Cloward, 1971). The family as an institution has been affected by the growth of large bureaucracies such as hospitals, schools, and social agencies, which have taken on many of the functions performed by the traditional family. As bureaucratic experts increasingly absorb what were once family responsibilities, the relative power of families over their own affairs tends to decrease or, perhaps more accurately, to be shared with these organizations instead of with the extended kin network.

In affluent societies, poor families can turn to social agencies and various programs of public assistance as a last resort, but the price of dependency on bureaucratic assistance is social stigma, and the paternalistic interference of these organizations, with their rules and mechanisms of control, in the life of the family, and the family's resulting loss of control over the many decisions (Burman, 1988: ch. 5).

Poor families that must turn to public or charitable agencies for income and services frequently find that, as clients, they become dependents and sometimes even wards of bureaucratic institutions, whose expert helpers are cast in the role of decision-makers and providers for the family. David Stymeist (1975) points to the irony that it is the presence of an impoverished class of clients that provides white collar professional employment for many workers in the welfare and criminal justice systems. In the small northern community in which Stymeist did field work, which had a large Native population and little industry, agencies that provided health and welfare services to impoverished Indian families were major employers of the white, middle-class population and the primary source of income in the community (Stymeist, 1975: 83).

Chapter 19 / Carol Agócs

The poor are distinguished by their lack of control over the circumstances of their lives and by their lack of choices. They are marginal to the economic system, while the state intervenes in their affairs as a "judging and intruding presence" (Burman, 1988: 77). Because their labour is not in demand, they must take whatever jobs and income they can get. The economic, social, and political institutions of society operate according to rules established by those with wealth and power and represent their interests. The poor lack the resources to force society's institutions to meet their needs; consequently, they are most often the victims or the powerless clients of these institutions.

Poor Families and Public Policy

We have discussed three interpretations of the causes of poverty and its impact upon families: the culture of poverty perspective; class analysis; and, the view that powerlessness is a critical dimension of the family lives of the poor. Each of these perspectives implies a different orientation for public policy and social action to deal with poverty. We conclude this chapter with comments on policy implications of these three interpretations. It will become clear that the diagnosis one makes of the causes and implications of poverty for family life is crucial, since recommendations for action follow from this analysis. Conducting research and theorizing about the causes and impacts of poverty, then, is not just an academic exercise.

The culture of poverty analysis holds that the values and behaviours of the poor constitute a cohesive and self-perpetuating system that interferes with the ability of the poor to respond constructively to opportunities for upward mobility (Lewis, 1966: xiv). The implication of this interpretation is that the poor themselves must change (Ryan, 1981). To this end, society must provide programs of socialization or resocialization to teach middle-class values and behaviour patterns to the poor.

The culture of poverty analysis, as we have seen, has little empirical support and is therefore a misleading and inappropriate guide to policy. It misplaces the emphasis upon the symptoms of poverty and the coping strategies of the poor rather than upon the causes of poverty. Moreover, poor families are still waiting for the opportunities that they are alleged to be unable to take advantage of to present themselves. Yet this perspective has strongly influenced the formulation and implementation of social programs, including those designed to compensate preschool children for the learning opportunities they have missed or to teach work habits, family planning, or new patterns of parenting. These efforts to resocialize the poor do nothing to alter the material conditions of their poverty.

Class analysis implies that the lives of poor families and the futures of their children can be improved only by creating economic opportunity so that these families can provide for their own needs, or by redistributing wealth so that they share in the standard of living deemed acceptable in their society. It is the affluent that must change, not the poor. It is assumed that if families have a reliable supply of sufficient income to meet their needs, they will have a choice as to whether to adopt such social patterns as the matrifocal family structure or attitudes such as fatalism and inability to delay gratification, since these behaviours are strategies for coping with poverty and are not valued as ends in themselves. Unfortunately, because no social system in which these behaviours have been systematically observed has succeeded in eliminating poverty, there has been no empirical test of this assumption. But ultimately, the family patterns of the poor are not at issue since they do not "cause" poverty and because the poor have as much right to pursue family life as they choose as do other members of society.

The implication of class analysis is that, if the social system as a whole is impoverished, as in many developing countries, its standard of living must be raised by an infusion of wealth from the developed countries. In affluent societies, in which a minority of the population can be considered poor, wealth must be redistributed from the rich to the poor by means of the system of taxation, for example, by providing a guaranteed annual income to all families.

Failing reforms that could bring about such redistribution, some advocates of the class interpretation would argue for the necessity for revolution to end extreme inequality.

Summary

In a contemporary urban or urbanizing society, poverty is a state of relative material deprivation that arises from a lack of income from employment or other sources. In such societies, a majority of poor adults of working age are in the labour market but are unable to earn a wage adequate to their families' needs. In addition to the families of the "working poor," those supported by women, families living in rural areas, members of ethnic and racial minorities, and migrants to the city are heavily represented among the poor.

The effects of poverty on families are profound. The life chances of children are affected by higher rates of infant and child mortality, and the incidence of health problems is higher among the poor than among higher income groups. The escape of poor children from poverty is further hindered by the failure of the educational system to meet their needs.

Poverty also strains the relationship between parents, as evidenced in higher rates of marital dissolution than are found among higher income groups. Households consisting of a woman supporting children are highly likely to live in poverty.

The question of household composition and family structure among the poor has long been highly contentious since it raises issues central to the theory and methodology of family studies and has implications for conflicting political and social ideologies. The controversy has focused around two problems. First, what is the nature of family structure among the poor? Second, what is the appropriate interpretation of the reality that the matrifocal household is more prevalent among the poor than among other social strata?

Until about two decades ago, American scholars who studied the structure of families in poverty tended to focus on the mother-led family as a distinctive type. Many discussions compared this structure with the nuclear family prototype familiar to the middle class, with the implication that the mother-led family was a deviant, "broken," socially disorganized form. This view was often rooted in the argument that the mother-led family was part of a complex of social behaviours that constituted a coherent culture of poverty. The implication of this interpretation was that strategies for social reform should seek to change the life-styles of the poor to make them similar to those alleged to be characteristic of the middle class. This approach, however, does nothing to change the access of the poor to economic opportunity and thus does not address the cause of poverty: material deprivation.

During the past twenty years, the culture of poverty analysis has been vigorously challenged on theoretical and ethical grounds, as well as from the standpoint of new perspectives afforded by recent research. The concept of the matrifocal family structure has been criticized in several ways. First, while some poor families may live in mother-child households, at least temporarily, research evidence suggests that such units are often embedded in a network of linked households of kin and quasi-kin, among whom assistance and support are regularly exchanged. Second, the mother-led family constitutes a viable adaptation to a specific set of social and economic conditions with which the nuclear model is not compatible. Third, the mother-led family is only one type of family structure among the poor and comparative research is needed to examine the conditions under which it is prevalent.

From the perspective of class analysis, family patterns in poor communities can be seen as adaptations to economic marginality and lack of access to income. Hence, solutions to the social problems of poverty necessitate change in the distribution of social and economic resources.

Poor families in general represent neither a tower of strength nor a tangle of pathology. Contemporary scholars of the family are moving toward an acknowledgement that the family is a complex and pluralistic institution among the poor as it is among other social strata.

TECHNICAL TERMS

POVERTY—A state of relative material deprivation arising from a lack of income.

MATRIFOCAL FAMILY STRUCTURE—Social pattern consisting of households in which the strongest and most enduring bond is between a mother and her children, and no male is regularly present in the role of husband and/or father.

CULTURE OF POVERTY—A concept that holds that poverty is a culture with distinctive values and behaviour patterns, that is international, and that is transmitted from one generation to the next.

DUAL LABOUR MARKET—A concept that views the labour market as consisting of a primary and a secondary segment. In the primary sector, jobs are relatively secure, well-paid, and offer some opportunity for advancement. The secondary sector consists of jobs characterized by poor working conditions, low pay, and little or no security or opportunity.

QUESTIONS

1. How does poverty affect families and family relationships?

2. How is poverty defined?

3. What social and economic conditions are associated with the matrifocal family structure?

4. Compare the culture of poverty, dual labour market, and power analyses of the causes and remedies for poverty.

5. What is the practical importance of theories and research about the causes and effects of poverty?

SUGGESTED READINGS

- Patrick Burman. *Killing Time, Losing Ground: Experiences of Unemployment.* Toronto: Wall & Thompson, 1988.

  A moving account of the actual experiences, thoughts, and feelings of unemployed people. Based on interviews done in London, Ontario.

"The Family." A sculpture by Gustave Vigeland.
Vigeland Sculpture Park, Oslo, Norway.

POSTSCRIPT

Chapter 20

THE FAMILY OF TODAY AND TOMORROW

Paul C. Glick
Arizona State University

So much is known about recent trends in family life, and so little is known with confidence about the future of the family, therefore, attention will be focused in this chapter primarily on changes that have occurred during the last few decades which provide clues about what seems most likely to happen during the next few decades. In keeping with my years of experience in tracing and interpreting family changes from the demographic perspective, that approach has been adopted for the present analysis.

The major sections of this chapter deal with changes and variations in three phases of family demographics, namely, marriage, fertility, and living arrangements. However, unlike most of my previous research, this presentation features not only conditions in the United States but also comparisons among a dozen or more countries of special interest mainly in Western Society, always including the United States, Canada, and some other English-speaking countries. Many countries that might otherwise have been selected did not have readily available information on certain key subjects over a period of years, or the inclusion of many of them would have required too much space. Most of the statistics shown in the tables were obtained from the United Nations Demographic Yearbooks.

Although India and China are not listed in the tables, they are discussed in regard to the strong efforts that are being exerted to limit family size. Many of the countries with high birth rates in Latin America, Oceania, and Africa do not collect regularly very extensive

family statistics, although the World Fertility Survey that was conducted mostly during the 1970s, and which will be mentioned again below, did assemble much valuable information about family life for many of the less developed countries for the first time.

Marriage

Soon after the end of World War II most of the countries of Western Culture experienced a baby boom. Among other things, improving economic conditions gave young couples the courage to enter into marriage at an earlier age than during the Great Depression of the 1930s and World War II, and more of them chose to have at least one or two children rather than none, while others had one more child during the 1950s than they might otherwise have had (Westoff, 1978). But this "Golden Age" of marriage and childbearing was followed by a delay in marriage, an upsurge in divorce, and a sharp decline in childbearing (Festy, 1980). Despite these changes, there was an increase in marriages during the 1960s and 1970s, but the increase in the number of unmarried young adults was even faster in the United States and many other countries.

Under these circumstances the marriage rate declined between 1965 and 1980 in most of the countries listed in Table 20–1. During this period the marriage rate among the fifteen countries went down on the average by more than ten percent. But there were wide and increasing variations in the amount of change in the marriage rate, with two of the countries actually showing an increase. In both 1965 and

1980 the marriage rates in the English-speaking countries and Israel were higher than the average for the entire group (about 55 per thousand unmarried women in 1965 and 45 in 1980). On the other hand, relatively low marriage rates were found consistently for the Germanic, French, and Scandinavian countries. These differences reflect dissimilar conditions among the countries with respect to such variables as average age at marriage, level of economic prosperity, and traditions related to marital behavior including the extent to which cohabitation outside marriage was becoming increasingly accepted as at least a temporary alternative to marriage, especially before the arrival of children.

Decline in Marriage

Many interacting factors have been responsible for the decline in the marriage rate during the last two decades. Liberalizing social changes have given young adults more options in regard to their marital behavior. Women have been increasingly accepted as co-workers in occupations that were once regarded as the province for men only, and employment opportunities for women in the service industries have grown rapidly (Thornton and Freedman, 1983). These developments have been facilitated by the greater increase in the education of women than men and by the concurrent decline in the birth rate (Glick and Norton, 1979). As more women have been working and doing so longer, they have been postponing marriage. In the United States over half again as large a proportion of women in their twenties in 1985 as in 1970 had never been married (US Bureau of the Census, 1985b).

Norms relating to marriage and childbearing traditionally sanctioned by religious organizations have gradually given way to more recent emphases on personal achievement and happiness as the basic goals for adults (Anderson, 1983). Having smaller families has made housekeeping less of a full-time job for women, and the husband is less often the only breadwinner. Accordingly, with the decline in the division of labour between the home for women and the work place for men, there has

been a reduction in the gain associated with marriage (Espenshade, 1985).

A "marriage squeeze" that developed as a consequence of the baby boom is a hard demographic factor in the decline of marriage opportunities for young women during the last two decades and was anticipated over two decades ago by Glick, Beresford, and Heer (1963). When the birth rate was rising during the baby boom, the girls born during a given year were more numerous than the boys born two or three years earlier when the birth rate was lower, and those were the boys who would be their prospective marital partners later on. Therefore, during much of the 1960s and 1970s there was an excess of women in the usual ages for first marriage, and that situation helped to lower the marriage rate for women (Guttentag and Secord, 1983; Baldwin and Nord, 1984). Now that children born during the baby bust (after the baby boom) are entering the usual ages for first marriage, a reversal of the marriage squeeze will be in effect for the rest of the twentieth century and should be a factor contributing to an increase in the marriage rate for women in the United States and in other countries that have had similar wide fluctuations in the birth rate since the end of World War II.

Some Consequences of the Decline

Before the recent decline in marriage began, the first marriage rate among young adults had been unusually high. Then as their cohort became older, there were relatively few persons eligible to marry at ages older than usual, because most of the cohort had already married, and that contributed to the decline in the marriage rate for unmarried persons of all ages combined. But many adults who have delayed marriage for reasons other than the marriage squeeze may begin deciding to marry—at the same time that younger adults may be entering marriage at the usual ages. As a consequence, the first marriage rate during the next decade or two may rise again—unless other factors have a counteracting effect. For example, just as those who delay having children seldom make up for it later on, so also the chances are

TABLE 20–1: MARRIAGE, DIVORCE, AND REMARRIAGE RATES FOR FIFTEEN DEVELOPED COUNTRIES: NEAR 1965 AND 1980

Country	Marriage Rate per 1,000 Unmarried Women		Divorce Rate per 1,000 Married Women		Remarriage Rate per 1,000 Divorced Women	
	1965	1980	1965	1980	1965	1980
Canada	61	52	2.3	10.9	169	90
United States	75	60	11.2	21.3	111	92
Israel	93	100	4.2	5.0	100	N/A
Japan	60	47	3.5	3.0	77	67
Austria	42	32	5.3	7.9	45	45
Hungary	60	28	7.7	9.8	91	53
German Democratic Republic	41	42	5.5	10.9	51	26
Germany, Fed. Rep. of	48	31	4.0	7.3	63	55
France	45	36	3.0	4.8	38	44
Netherlands	64	39	2.3	8.3	57	43
Norway	47	33	3.0	7.4	55	37
Sweden	49	23	5.1	11.8	45	29
England and Wales	67	53	3.1	11.8	108	92
Australia	62	61	3.8	19.5	110	121
New Zealand	72	46	3.5	7.5	126	142

N/A = Not available.

SOURCE: United Nations, *Demographic Yearbook, 1967*, 1968; United Nations, *Demographic Yearbook, 1968*, 1969; United Nations, *Demographic Yearbook, 1982*, 1984; U.S. National Center for Health Statistics, "Advance Report of Final Divorce Statistics, 1983," *Monthly Vital Statistics Report*, 1985, vol. 34, no. 9, supplement; U.S. National Center for Health Statistics, "Advance Report of Final Marriage Statistics, 1983," *Monthly Vital Statistics Report*, 1986, vol. 35, no. 1, supplement.

that many of those who delay marriage will become adjusted to that lifestyle and decide never to marry at all.

Those women who were the most likely to delay marriage were well educated and had a preference for becoming established in their careers before they "married and settled down." However, most of the attractive partners for these women were already married by that time and intended to remain married. Thus, well-educated women in their thirties who have never married are especially likely

never to marry. Projections made by Norton and Moorman (1987) indicate that about ten percent of the young adults in the United States today are not expected ever to marry. The corresponding level was only one-half that high among members of their parents' cohort.

A delay of marriage tends to be associated with an older average age at marriage and a relatively low birth rate. In fact, a delay of marriage has historically been a practice in many countries to limit childbearing to the number the parents wanted. But in Asia the median age at marriage is rising and the birth rate is falling, according to results of the World Fertility Survey reported by Lightbourne et al. (1982). At least in half of the countries in the survey a delay of marriage until 20 or 21 years of age lowered the women's fertility rates. Other research about entry into marriage in Asia by Rindfuss et al. (1983) led to the conclusion that where virginity at the time of marriage is prized, the average age at marriage tends to be relatively young. But in more developed countries where effective means of birth control are extensively used, first marriages are being increasingly delayed, and that has contributed to the recent decline in the marriage rate.

The foregoing discussion of marriage rates displayed in Table 20–1 has referred primarily to first marriages, because they constitute the preponderance of marriages covered in the first two columns of the table. The rates in the table are not limited to first marriages because historical changes for many of the countries could not be presented in the absence of the desired controls by age. The treatment of remarriage in a later section is likewise presented with no control on age, but at least the base for those rates excludes widows, and that focuses the analysis of recent changes in remarriage directly on those who marry after divorce.

Divorce

Probably as far back as divorce statistics are available in most of the developed countries, there has been a gradual increase in divorce rates, with some fluctuations associated with depressions, wars, and changes in divorce laws. In the United States the divorce rate dropped to a low point during the Great Depression of the 1930s, hit a peak after World War II, and fell again during the baby boom. In 1958 the rate reached a low level of 2.1 per 1,000 population and thereafter rose slowly to 2.5 by 1965, the year commonly regarded as the end of the baby boom. Then an upsurge in divorce resulted in a doubling of the rate during the next decade, climbing to 5.0 by 1976. Thereaf-

ter, the rate went up more slowly, reaching peaks of 5.3 per 1,000 population in both 1979 and 1981. After that, it declined somewhat to 4.9 in 1984 and then edged upward again to 5.0 in 1985, where it still stood at the time of this writing in mid-1986 (Glick, 1986; US National Center for Health Statistics, 1986b). Thus, the US divorce rate appears to have at least temporarily stabilized not far below the crest that was reached near 1980. A similar pattern was followed in Canada but at a much lower level. Its divorce rate reached a peak in 1980 (United Nations, 1984).

These introductory remarks about the long-time trend and recent levels of the divorce rate are based on simple rates per 1,000 population, because more refined rates are not available for many of the countries shown in Table 20–1 for long periods into the past, and even in the countries with the most advanced statistics, refined rates are usually not published until after two or three years. The more refined divorce rates per 1,000 married women are presented in Table 20–1 for fifteen countries in about 1965 and 1980.

Increase in Divorce

The divorce rate went up between 1965 and 1980 in almost all of the countries, and for half of the countries the rate more than doubled. The average of the rates went up from 4.5 per 1,000 married women in 1965 to 9.9 in 1980. Six of the countries had divorce rates above 9.9 in 1980; these countries were Canada, United States, German Democratic Republic, Sweden, England and Wales, and Australia, most of them being English-speaking. High divorce rates tend to be associated with high overall marriage rates because remarriages after divorce are important contributors to the level of the overall rates. Moreover, research conducted by Balakrishnan et al. (1986) and Bennett et al. (1986) show that in Canada and Sweden, respectively, the variable found to produce the highest risk of ending a marriage in divorce was teenage marriage, closely followed by cohabitation prior to marriage.

Over the last hundred years many industrial and social changes have contributed to the

Chapter 20 / Paul C. Glick

weakening of family ties. Fewer husbands and wives share the responsibility of operating a family farm or shop. The expansion of service industries during recent decades have created opportunities for women to become employed outside the home where they work side by side with men other than their husbands. The declining birth rate made it easier for women to accept offers of employment, and an unprecedented increase in the education of women prepared them for assuming more responsible positions. Therefore, as more wives achieved enough economic independence, more of those whose marriages had become intolerable sought a divorce and maintained separate homes for themselves and their children, if any. For highly educated wives the period between marriage and divorce became shortened (Bennett et al., 1986). More husbands whose marriages had deteriorated separated from their wives. If the wives had few, if any, children and if they were economically self-sufficient, the husbands had relatively little sense of guilt in "walking out."

The increase in divorce has occurred in a growing atmosphere of liberalism of laws and attitudes about divorce and a significant lowering of the level of tolerance of marital disharmony (Carmichael and McDonald, 1986). Traditional attitudes about what is normative behavior for married couples, grounded in religious sanctions, have been increasingly replaced by attitudes regarded as more realistic and practical. With fewer children involved, modern marriages are more often held together to the extent that mutual attraction between the husband and wife remain strong. Moreover, when death rates used to be higher, many of the unhappily married persons were relieved by the passing of one of the spouses.

Some Consequences of the Increase

The upsurge in divorce in various countries has been so rapid that it may be followed by a temporary decline before becoming stabilized or rising once again, in the view of Roussel and Festy (1979). During a period of rapid change in divorce, the number of eligibles for divorce diminishes until a younger group of eligibles

emerges. Norton and Moorman (1987) made projections of lifetime probabilities that women in the United States would end their first marriage in divorce. Their study, based on data from the Census Bureau's Current Population Survey for June 1985, showed that women 35 to 39 years old at that time were likely to have the largest proportion ending their first marriage in divorce, as compared with those who were older and those who were younger: 24% for those 55 to 59 years old, 36% for those 45 to 49, 56% for those 35 to 39, and 54% for those 25 to 29. Women in their thirties in 1985 were in the vanguard of children born during the baby boom and were in their twenties in 1975 at the height of the upsurge in divorce. Additional support for their conclusion is the fact that the US divorce rate has already started to decline and is levelling off.

The no-fault divorce laws that were legislated in the United States during the 1970s largely legalized an already established trend toward making divorce easier and less acrimonious than it had been. But many women who had little or no work experience prior to divorce received very unsatisfactory settlements under the new system because they were convinced to agree to minimal property settlements or support payments in exchange for custody of their children (Weitzman, 1985). After the passage of the new Divorce Act in Canada in 1969, the divorce rate doubled within a decade from 12 per 1,000 population in 1969 to 24 per 1,000 in 1978, although there was considerable immigration of young adults during this period (McKie et al., 1983). After the 1975 Family Law Act was passed in Australia, a larger proportion of divorces have been occurring within a short period after marriage, under five years, presumably implying that marriages which fail to meet expectations very early on should be abandoned without delay (Carmichael and McDonald, 1986).

The disturbing effect of divorce on the children involved is perhaps the most serious consequence of divorce from the standpoint of the state. In a given year close to two percent of all the children under 18 years of age in the United

States are involved in their parents' divorce, many for the second or third time. Therefore, between one-third and one-fourth of all US children may be expected to experience parental divorce at least once before their eighteenth birthday (Glick, 1986). Most people would agree that the best environment for growing children is a home with well-adjusted and harmonious parents. However, living with a well-adjusted single parent may usually be a better place for young children than one with poorly-adjusted married parents who have come to dislike each other intensely. Then again, the worst scenario may be the child with a maladjusted and poor parent.

Remarriage after Divorce

For several decades before 1960 the rate of remarriage after divorce followed the same general trend of the divorce rate in the United States. Both rates were low during the 1930s, both reached high levels during the late 1940s, and both reached low levels again during the 1950s. But by the mid-1960s remarriage rates went up to record high levels and then declined sharply until the early 1980s, while the divorce rate rose continuously to record high levels near 1980 and then declined slightly. By the mid-1980s there were indications that both the divorce and remarriage rates were in the process of stabilizing (Glick and Lin, 1987).

The divergence of the divorce and remarriage trends after the mid-1960s was a consequence of a growing tendency for divorced persons to delay remarrying longer than previously or perhaps never to remarry. Accordingly, the number of divorced persons who had not remarried continued to rise, thereby increasing the base of the remarriage rate, while the number of divorced persons who remarried was declining, thereby decreasing the numerator of the remarriage rate. These two opposing trends accentuated the lowering of the remarriage rate.

In the fourteen countries for which remarriage rates are shown in Table 20–1, there was a general tendency for the rates to decline between 1965 and 1980. The average decline was about 15% from 88 to 66 remarriages per 1,000

divorced women, but in Canada the remarriage rate fell by nearly one-half because of an unusually rapid increase in divorce and delayed remarriage (McKie et al., 1983). Meantime, however, the remarriage rate actually rose by about ten percent in Australia and New Zealand. An intensive analysis of the remarriage rates in New Zealand by Carmichael (1985: 94) concluded that "the rise in the female unstandardized remarriage rate commencing in the late 1960s was almost entirely the product of the increasing youthfulness of female divorcees." Young adults increased rapidly in number after 1960 as a consequence of the earlier baby boom and an increase in immigration. Also, first marriage and divorce were occurring sooner, thereby making remarriage possible to occur at a relatively young age. Carmichael cites a study which found evidence that the falling American remarriage rate is more likely to have resulted from a lengthening of the gap between divorce and remarriage than from a decrease in the proportion of divorced persons who will ever remarry. The especially low rates of remarriage among divorced women in Scandinavia, France, and some other European countries is no doubt closely related to the growing practice of cohabitation outside marriage as an alternative to remarriage. In fact, the remarriage pattern among most European countries are quite similar. It is the English-speaking countries that have the highest remarriage rates.

In the United States, as elsewhere, the remarriage rates vary according to the social and demographic characteristics of divorced persons. Men have higher remarriage rates than women, therefore it is possible that fewer divorced women than men are anxious to remarry. Other findings show that remarriage rates are generally higher than first marriage rates, young persons have higher rates than older persons, those with less education have higher rates than those with more education, and divorced persons have higher remarriage rates than widowed persons (Glick, 1984b).

When women remarry they generally hope that the status of the second husband will be equal to or higher than that of the first husband. However, a recent study by Jacobs and Furstenberg (1986) revealed that most of the difference between the two husbands can be accounted for, on the average, by (1) the passage of time between the two marriages, so that the first husband should have elevated his career position toward the corresponding level of the second husband and (2) the second husband tends to be three years still older than the wife than the first husband was, and he should therefore be expected to have advanced farther in his career. But the husband and wife in the second marriage tend to have more dissimilar characteristics in such respects as previous marital status, age, and education than the husband and wife in the first marriage (Dean and Gurak, 1978). In other words, this research implies that persons who remarry are less likely to have a homogamous marriage than persons who marry for the first time.

The wider age gap between the spouses in remarriage may reflect the premium the man places on having a relatively youthful wife, whereas the woman may place a premium on an older man who has a relatively high income. Divorced women who remarry tend to do so more quickly if they have children than if they are childless, but there is evidence that divorced women with children have more difficulty than childless divorced women in becoming remarried (Glick and Lin, 1987). Nonetheless, there is other evidence that childless divorced women had been remaining divorced for a longer time in 1980 than in 1975 (Glick and Lin, 1986b). Perhaps it is easier for a childless divorced woman than a divorced mother with custody of children to find an agreeable partner with whom to cohabit.

A large majority of divorced persons in the United States eventually remarry, but because of the recent decline in the remarriage rate, the proportion doing so has been decreasing. Using 1980 Current Population Survey data, Glick (1984b) found that five-sixths of the divorced men and three-fourths of the divorced women had remarried by the time they were 65 to 74 years old. Using more recent data, Norton and Moorman (1987) concluded that

the proportion of divorced women who eventually remarry may fall to about 70%. Despite the decline in remarriage, the proportion of all marriages in the United States that involved either the bride or the groom in remarriage increased from 31% in 1970 to 45% during the early 1980s and appears to have stabilized (US National Center for Health Statistics, 1986a). The median interval between divorce and remarriage fell from 3.2 years in 1975 to 2.2 years in 1980 and has remained at about that level. The median age at remarriage after divorce has remained at near 32 years for men and 29 years for women (Glick, 1986).

After remarriage comes redivorce for about one-half of the married couples involved. Projections of lifetime chances of ending a first marriage in divorce is about one-half for young adults at the time of the US Current Population Survey in 1980 (Glick, 1984b). Using the 1980 data, Glick also showed that 54% of remarried women and 61% of remarried men were likely to end their second marriage in redivorce. Norton and Moorman (1987) used 1985 CPS data to make projections that implied that about 56% of the first marriages of women in their late thirties may end in divorce and that there has apparently been a decline in the difference between the chances of divorce after first marriage and after the second marriage.

In countries with high divorce rates, the vast majority of remarriages occur after divorce rather than widowhood. However, the relatively small number of persons who become widowed during their twenties are just about as likely to remarry as divorced persons of the same age (US Bureau of the Census, 1977).

Fertility

Throughout the Western World, the birth rate has followed a longtime downward trend. A primarily rural economy was giving way to a primarily urban economy, and improvements in public health caused the death rate to fall. The population was becoming more literate and less bound by traditional attitudes about the value of a large family. Thus, the interaction among these and other factors con-

TABLE 20–2: FERTILITY, ABORTION, AND STERILIZATION IN SIXTEEN DEVELOPED COUNTRIES: NEAR SELECTED DATES

Country	Total Fertility Rate			Percent of Births to Unmarried Women		Total Abortion Rate[1]	Percent of Contra- ceptors Sterilized[2]
	1960	1970	1983	1964	1980		
Canada	3.9	2.3	1.7	6	12	.3	48
United States	3.7	2.5	1.8	7	17	.9	33
Israel	4.0	4.0	3.0	.3	2.5	.9	N/A
Japan	2.0	2.1	1.8	1	1	2.5	N/A
Austria	2.6	2.3	1.5	11	18	3	N/A
Hungary	2.0	2.0	1.7	5	7	1.1	2
German Democratic Republic	2.3	2.2	1.8	9	23	.7	N/A
Germany, Fed. Rep. of	2.4	2.0	1.8	5	8	.3	N/A
France	2.7	2.5	1.8	6	11	.4	5
Netherlands	3.1	2.6	1.4	2	3	.2	6
Norway	2.8	2.5	1.7	4	15	.5	9
Sweden	2.2	1.9	1.7	13	40	.6	N/A
England and Wales	2.6	2.4	1.8	7	11	.4	21
Australia	3.4	2.9	1.9	7	12	.4	N/A
New Zealand	4.0	3.2	1.9	10	21	.3	N/A
U.S.S.R.	2.8	2.5	2.4	N/A	N/A	5.4	N/A

[1] Japan, 1975; Israel, 1982; U.S.S.R., 1970; other countries, 1980.
[2] Variable dates, 1973 to 1981, except Canada, 1984, and United States, 1982.
N/A = Not available.

SOURCE: Leon F. Bouvier, "Planet Earth 1984–2034: A Demographic Vision." *Population Bulletin*, 1984, vol., 39, no. l; Tomas Frejka, "Induced Abortion and Fertility." *Family Planning Perspectives*, 1985, vol. 17, no. 5; Mary Kent and Carl Haub, "1986 World Population Data Sheet." Population Reference Bureau, 1986; Robert J. Lightbourne and Sushula Singh with Cynthia P. Green, "The World Fertility Survey: Charting Global Childbearing." *Population Bulletin*, 1982, vol. 37, no. l; United Nations, *Demographic Yearbook, 1967*, 1968; United Nations, *Demographic Yearbook, 1982*, 1984; and communication with Jean van der Tak, June 1986.

tributed to the development of a climate of opinion favouring a declining birth rate (Roussel and Festy, 1979). Young children were being perceived as less of an asset, fewer children were needed to assume that some would live long enough to support their parents in old age, and the growing secularization of social life was reducing the time spent with close family ties. Instead, adult attention was being centered more on the acquisition of consumer goods that were meant largely for the satisfaction of adults in or out of a family. The resulting downward trend in the birth rate was accentuated by the Great Depression of the 1930s and was held in check during World War II. After that came the baby boom from the mid-1940s until the mid-1960s in the United States and other countries. The baby boom was entirely unprecedented and now seems quite unlikely to be repeated during the foreseeable future.

The peak of the baby boom was reached in the United States and Canada during the mid-1950s and somewhat later in most of the other countries for which various measures relating to childbearing are presented in Table 20–2. The first measure is the total fertility rate (TFR). This rate shows how many children an average woman would have in her lifetime if she were to have the same birth rates at each age as women were having during the given year. A TFR of 2.1 children is needed in the countries shown in Table 20–2 to reproduce the population without any immigration from other countries. All of the countries except Japan and Hungary had TFRs above 2.1 children in 1960, but by 1980 only Israel and the USSR had rates above 2.1.

Accordingly, almost all of the countries listed in Table 20–2 would eventually have a declining population if their TFRs did not rise and if they had insufficient compensatory immigration in future years. In fact, already by the late 1970s deaths were outnumbering births in Austria and in East and West Germany. By the early 1980s, net immigration and the higher fertility rates of the immigrants were not enough to keep several other Western European countries from having a declining population, including France, the United Kingdom, and Hungary (Bouvier, 1984). The most recent information shows that the world population is growing by 1.7% per year through natural increase (excess of births over deaths), with 0.6% in developed countries, 2.0% in less developed countries, and 2.4% for less developed countries excluding China, where the comparable figure is 1.1% (Kent and Haub, 1986).

Birth Incentives and Disincentives

The birth dearth that developed after the baby boom caused concern among the governments of many countries about the consequences that would be associated with a declining population. In France, the prospect of entering a period of no population growth has been regarded as a threat to the national pride and as a danger to the national security (Westoff, 1978). In Sweden and Canada, family allowances were instituted not so much to increase the birth rate but to give children a better start in life. In several Eastern European countries, family allowances, birth payments, and paid leave associated with childbirth were instituted in the 1960s primarily to keep the fertility rates from falling below the replacement level (David, 1982). The effects of these pronatalist incentives were often temporary and disappointing, with the consequence most often being earlier first or second births rather than the addition of more third and higher order births. The costs tend to exceed the benefits in areas where economic measures are used to stimulate the birth rate.

By contrast, the two most populous countries, India and China, have been making strong efforts to reduce their population growth. Beginning in the 1950s, the family planning program in India has gone through a number of phases of governmental promotion with some success but far less than was expected, partly because of the scattered rural areas being hard to reach effectively and because of reactions against the program during some periods (Visaria and Visaria, 1981). China has had far greater success in lowering its birth rate, as indicated by the reduction of the rate by one-half between 1970 and 1980, when the one-child-per-family campaign was in full force (Tien, 1983). But barriers to this campaign have included the high cost of the inducements offered and the persisting preference for male children. In areas where a rapid decline in the birth rate occurs and where there is no effective social security program, serious problems are eventually created for the support of elderly family members who were born when birth rates were much higher.

Births to Unmarried Women

Bearing children outside marriage has been on the increase in developed countries since the mid-1960s at the same time that the total fertility rate was on the decline (Table 20–2). This means that married fertility was falling more rapidly than total fertility. During this period, almost every country shown experienced a sharp increase in the percent of births to unmarried mothers, with the rate much more than doubling in several countries, notably Sweden where the practice of cohabitation outside marriage has become the most extensive. In this period of increasingly delayed first marriages and climbing divorce rates, more of the young unmarried adults were engaging in marriage-like behavior (Westoff, et al., 1983). Many of the participants were baby boomers who were unable to find employment, and some consisted of the excess women of marriageable age who were caught in the marriage squeeze without a husband but with access to men. More of the premarital pregnancies were resulting in premarital births; this tendency to prefer having "illegitimate" births to becoming married merely to make the births legitimate was increasing "everywhere" in Western Europe (Roussel and Festy, 1979).

By 1984, the proportion of births in the United States to unmarried women rose to 21% for women of all races, 13% for white women, and 59% for black women (US National Center for Health Statistics, 1986c). O'Connell and Rogers (1984) have shown that among women in the United States who first married between 1950 and 1974, the proportion who separated from their husbands within five years was 24% for those who had out-of-wedlock births as compared with 17% for those who had been in their first pregnancy at the time of marriage, and only 12% for those who had not been pregnant before marriage (or whose premarital pregnancies, if any, had ended in abortion). A study by Jones et al. (1985) demonstrated that the United States had a much higher adolescent pregnancy rate than several other countries with similar cultural backgrounds and economic development (Canada, England and Wales, France, the Netherlands, and Swe-

den). The authors sensed that there was greater concern in the United States about reducing adolescent sexuality than about reducing adolescent pregnancy. They recommended the adoption of such measures as more comprehensive sex education as well as free access for adolescents to contraceptives regardless of family income and to other fertility related activities that health care facilities provide.

Legal Abortion

If it had not been for a substantial increase in legal abortion in most of the developed countries during the last decade or two, the extent of childbearing out of wedlock would probably have been still high. A study by Frejka (1985) concludes that the total fertility rate would have been at least 20% higher in these countries, on the average, if no abortions had been performed. As the total (legal) abortion rates in Table 20–2 indicate, the countries vary widely according to how extensively abortion is used to prevent unwanted births. A total abortion rate is the average number of abortions a woman would have during her lifetime if the current age-specific abortion rates were to continue. Thus, the rate for the United States in 1980 was 0.9, or nearly one abortion per woman before the age of 45 years, whereas the rate for Canada was 0.3, or only one-third as large. Even though the Supreme Court did not decide that abortions were legal under most circumstances in the United States until 1973, the US rate has become one of the highest, as a reflection of the liberalization of attitudes about family planning practices that also increased divorce and cohabitation rates.

In some countries, including Hungary and Japan, where the abortion rate has been quite high for several decades, the rate has been declining as other effective means of limiting family size have been increasingly adopted. In several Eastern European countries, there have been extreme fluctuations in abortion rates since 1950 primarily as a consequence of alternately raising and lowering restrictions on the availability of abortion as a birth control technique (David, 1982).

Chapter 20 / Paul C. Glick

In the United States the abortion ratio (abortions per 1,000 live births plus abortions) reached a peak of 300 in 1980 after which it remained extremely high at 299 in 1981 and 1982 then declined to 294 in 1983 and 287 in 1984 (Henshaw et al., 1984; Henshaw, 1986). About three-fourths of abortion seekers in the United States are unmarried, but the largest numbers in Eastern Europe are married women over 25 years of age (David, 1982). Even where abortion is resorted to extensively, it seldom inhibits fertility as much as other "fertility determinants"—contraception, late marriage, and infertility for a period after childbirth (Frejka, 1985). During recent years, declines in abortion have occurred where sterilization has been on the increase.

Sterilization

Throughout those parts of the world where contraception is practised by most women, there is a strong trend toward more use of sterilization by couples who have had all the children they want. Although information for various countries is scant, among those shown in Table 20–2, Canada and the United States have clearly the highest proportions of all contraceptors of reproductive age who have adopted sterilization—Canada with 48% and the United States with 33%. For currently married women the corresponding figures are much higher, 59% and 41%, respectively (Balakrishnan, et al., 1985); Bachrach, 1984). In Canada more than three-fourths of the married persons who have become sterilized are women, whereas the proportion in the United States is close to two-thirds. Among Canadian wives in 1984 who were 40 to 44 years old, fully 83% of the contraceptors depended on sterilization of themselves or their husbands to prevent pregnancy.

A study by Pratt et al. (1984) found that among the 18% of American married couples in 1965 intending to have no more children, one or both spouses were sterilized. Corresponding figures rose to 36% in 1973 and to 61% in 1982. A large part of the change during the last decade was a result of a sharp decline in the use of the pill, from 36% in 1973 to 20%

in 1982. The proportions for other methods in 1982 were 41% for sterilization, 7% for the IUD (intrauterine device), 7% for diaphragm, 14% for condom, 3% for foam, 5% for periodic abstinence, 2% for withdrawal, and 2% for other methods. Breastfeeding of infants, which also reduces the risk of pregnancy, is a practice that has increased sharply among American women since the early 1970s and by 1982 reached a high level of 73% for college-educated mothers and 51% of the college educated who nursed their children for three months or more (Pratt et al., 1984).

A global survey of the use of sterilization for contraceptive purposes in developing countries arrived at the conclusion that this is an important method in many Asian and Latin American countries but not in the predominantly Muslim countries and in most of Africa (Khoo, 1985). Although the rate of increase in the use of this method has slowed down, an increasing proportion of the acceptors are relatively young and have few children. Those who have resorted to sterilization are generally persons who have previously used such effective means of contraception as the pill, the diaphragm, or the IUD. More couples who have completed their family building are coming to realize that by adopting sterilization they greatly increase their opportunity to enjoy intimate personal relations with their spouse or partner with no risk of an unwanted pregnancy.

Living Arrangements

The changes in social conditions that have so radically changed the patterns of marriage and fertility have brought about extensive changes in the household structure of the population. Smaller proportions of the people live in families consisting of two parents and children, and more live in one-parent families, in one-person households, and in households of unmarried couples. But because a majority of the lone parents remarry, and because many of those living alone or as unmarried couples also marry, the proportion of the population in the United States that currently resides in married-couple households still accounts for about

TABLE 20–3: NUMBER OF PERSONS IN THE HOUSEHOLD
FOR FOURTEEN COUNTRIES: 1972–1981

Country	Year	Average Number	Persons in the Household (percent)				
			Total	1	2	3	4+
Canada	1976	3.1	100	17	28	17	28
United States	1980	2.7	100	23	31	17	29
Egypt	1976	5.2	100	6	11	12	71
Israel	1972	3.8	100	12	22	18	48
Japan	1980	3.2	100	20	17	18	45
Philippines	1975	5.9	100	2	7	11	80
Hungary	1980	2.8	100	20	28	22	30
Poland	1978	3.1	100	17	22	23	38
Norway	1980	2.7	100	28	26	16	30
Sweden	1975	2.4	100	30	31	17	22
France	1975	2.9	100	22	28	19	31
England	1981	2.7	100	22	32	17	29
Australia	1976	3.1	100	16	28	17	39
New Zealand	1981	3.0	100	18	29	16	37

SOURCE: United Nations, *Demographic Yearbook, 21982*, 1984.

three-fourths of the entire household population. In 1983 nearly one-half (46%) of the US population lived in homes comprising a married couple with children under 18, while over one-fourth (27%) lived in homes of married couples with no young children (Glick, 1984). Between 1960 and 1983, the proportion of the population living in one-parent households doubled (from 4% to 8%), the proportion living alone likewise doubled (from 4% to 8%), the proportion in unmarried-couple households doubled (from 1% to 2%), and the remaining proportion nearly doubled (from 5% to 9%). Thus, all of these substantial increases in the smaller types of household population caused the proportion living in married-couple households to decline only from 86% to 73%.

For international comparisons of household composition, Table 20–3 is introduced. This table is based on a recent United Nations publication, but no earlier publication provided comparable data, and that precludes an international analysis of recent changes in this variable. Moreover, since corresponding data for several of the countries shown in Tables 20–1 and 20–2 were not available, information for some other countries are presented in their place in Table 20–3.

By the late 1970s or early 1980s, most of the developed countries shown in Table 20–3 had average household sizes near three persons. The other countries include Israel, with nearly four persons per household, and Egypt and the Philippines with more than five per household; each of these countries had high to very high fertility rates and consequently the smallest proportions of households consisting of only one person as well as the largest proportions with four or more persons. Countries with relatively large proportions of households maintained by only one adult usually have relatively large proportions of the population in old age, or in young adult ages but living as noncustodial divorced persons or as never-married young people who have left their parental homes to live alone in an apartment.

Declining Size of Household

Among the countries shown in Table 20–3, the typical household consists of two persons, except for the few where the majority of households have four or more members. Countries with relatively large households usually have an above-average number of young children in the home. This variable is correlated with religious and cultural values relating to family life, and in countries without an effective social security system it reflects a need for enough children to provide for the parents during their old age. Also, in countries with severe housing shortages the household may consist of more than one family.

The average size of household in the United States has been declining ever since the early colonial era. Of special interest, however, is the speeding up of the decline during recent years. Thus, it took thirty years, from 1940 to 1970, for the average size to decrease by one-half person, from 3.67 to 3.14 persons, but only fifteen years, from 1970 to 1985, to decrease by another one-half person, from 3.14 to 2.69 persons (Sternlieb and Hughes, 1986). That last decade and a half was the period when the numbers of one-parent households, one-person households, and cohabiting couples were skyrocketing in the United States and in many other developed countries as well. And yet, it was a period when an increasing proportion of baby boomers were still, or once again, living in the homes of their parents (Glick and Lin, 1986a). Among the reasons were difficulty in finding jobs, attendance at local colleges, marital disruption, or premarital childbearing.

Lone Parenting

One-parent households represented eight percent of all households in the United States in 1984 (US Bureau of the Census, 1985a). A little over one-tenth of the lone parents were men, and this proportion has not changed much since 1960. Two of every three lone parents in 1983 were separated or divorced and one-fourth had never married (Glick, 1984a).

Racial differences in lone parenting are very great. Thus, black families in the United States are four times as likely as white families to have only one parent in the home and four times as likely to have a never-married mother as the parent. Partly because black parents more often than white parents are not high school graduates, lone custodial parents are half again as likely as married parents to have terminated their education without graduating from high school. However, the situation is changing. The number of lone parents with some college education increased three times as rapidly since 1970 as the number of other lone parents (Norton and Glick, 1986). With only one earner in most one-parent families, the average income per family member in the United States in 1984 was only 56% as large for mother-child families as for all families, however, it was 119% as large for father-child families as for all families.

Under these circumstances it is not surprising that 34% of all mother-child families in the United States in 1983 were recipients of Aid to Families with Dependent Children (AFDC) as compared with only six% of father-child families. Expenshade (1985) cited several studies that show a close relation between the rapid increase in the number of AFDC recipients after 1965 and the increase in births to unmarried women as well as the decline in marriage among unmarried mothers. Another reason for the big increase in the number of mother-child families is the excess of young women of marriageable age because of the marriage squeeze. Many of these women became mothers without becoming wives. AFDC benefits are given to women in the United States who pass a means test. In many other developed countries child support provisions are universal or are granted as supplements to low earning families along with work incentives.

During future years before the end of the century, there is likely to be little change in the proportion of households that are maintained by one parent, according to projections prepared at the US Bureau of the Census (Grymes and Hernandez, 1986). However, an increasing proportion of the growth is expected in households that are occupied by one person living entirely alone, either as elderly persons or as young noncustodial parents whose former spouse maintains a one-parent household.

Cohabitation Outside Marriage

Recently the type of household with the most rapid growth in North America and Northern Europe has occurred among the still small numbers of unmarried persons of opposite sex who are living together. This practice began to pick up momentum as a new way of life for "yuppies" (young upwardly mobile professional persons) in large cities or close-in suburbs but has diffused to other increasingly sophisticated young adults who are delaying marriage or remarriage (Sternlieb and Hughes, 1986). In the United States the number of cohabiting couples was four times as large in 1985 as in 1970 (two million versus one-half million), with the most rapid gain during the last half of the 1970s (US Bureau of the Census, 1985b). During that period annual increases in these twosomes were close to 20% (Glick, 1984a), but after 1980 the increments dwindled until there was no significant change between 1984 and 1985. By that time four percent of all couples maintaining households were cohabiting informally. This level was small as compared with that in Sweden, where the corresponding figure was 15 to 16% in 1979 (Trost, 1979), and since that time the additions have considerably slackened, according to communication with Trost.

A reasonable way to show differences in cohabitation rates among various countries is to analyze the rates for certain age groups. A Canadian survey of women 18 to 49 years old found that about three-tenths of those unmarried were cohabiting (Balakrishnan et al., 1985). Among unmarried women in their late twenties, the cohabitation rates for several countries were as follows: one-fifth for the United States in 1980 (Sweet and Bumpass, 1984); one-fourth for Norway in the late 1970s (Brumborg, 1979); and one-fourth for France in 1977 and one-third for Sweden in 1975 (Roussel and Festy, 1979). These last authors observed that the practice was still infrequent in most of the Mediterranean countries and in Ireland, Belgium, and Luxemburg. Wherever cohabitation is practised, the range of commitment between the couples involved varies widely from having a fixed wedding date to having no thought of marriage. Cohabitation commonly precedes childbirth in Sweden and Denmark but not in France, Germany, or Norway. The birth of a child in France is usually the "watershed event" that transforms an informal union into marriage (Carlson, 1986).

Much has been learned about couples who engage in cohabitation outside marriage and who are frequently referred to in the United States as POSSLQs (partners of opposite sex sharing living quarters), a term that was first used by a reporter in *Newsweek* magazine on January 7, 1980. A study in Lane County, Oregon, discovered that 53% of the couples who applied for marriage licenses in 1980 were already living at the same address, as compared with 13% in 1970 (Gwartney-Gibbs, 1986). An American national survey by Tanfer and Horn (1985) found that 30% of the never-married women in their twenties in 1983 had cohabited, including 12% who were doing so at the survey date. They also reported that never marrieds who had ever cohabited were overrepresented by blacks, metropolitan residents, and those with no college education, infrequent church attendance, little employment, and parents who were not in an intact marriage.

Several studies based on data from the US Census Bureau's Current Population Survey in 1975 or 1980 throw additional light on the characteristics of cohabitants. Glick and Norton (1979) showed that a majority of unmarried couples live together for a relatively short time (less than two years) before they marry or "split," and that cohabiting men were three times as likely to be living below the poverty line as other men of comparable age. Glick and Spanier (1980) reported that 43% of cohabiting couples with the women under 35 years of age consisted of a never-married man and a never-married woman and that more never-married women than men were living with a separated or divorced person. Using unpublished CPS data for 1980, Glick (1984a) showed that 30% of the unmarried couples had young children in the home, and that of these children about three-fourths were the woman's children, whereas about two-thirds of the remainder were the man's children, and the rest were children the couple had together. Incidentally, about five percent of all children living with one parent in the United States live in the home of a cohabiting couple.

As a final research note about cohabitation, it is of interest that recent studies are showing that premarital cohabitation is more likely than not to be associated with subsequent divorce. Balakrishnan et al. (1985) reported that a national survey in Canada found that premarital cohabitation was, in fact, one of the principal factors in marital dissolution, with a premarital birth being the only factor that more greatly increased the risk of separation or divorce. A similar study based on Swedish data found that only teenage marriage created a greater risk of marital dissolution than premarital cohabitation (Bennett et al., 1986).

Polygyny

A part of the global picture of family life includes reference to the location and extent of polygynous marriage. This marriage practice is a common feature in eastern Moslem countries and in Africa but is most prevalent in sub-Saharan Africa, where it is found among 12 to 38% of the men (Goldman and Pebley, 1986). During the nineteenth century fewer than ten percent of American Mormon men practised polygyny. In Cameroon, Senegal, and Sudan, the conditions that make possible the marriage of one man to more than one woman are the rapid growth of population, the wide average gap between the ages of men and women at first marriage, and the custom of widows marrying the brother or other close relative of their deceased husbands. As population grows the marriage squeeze causes an excess of young marriageable women as compared to the older marriageable men. But because fertility rates in these countries are likely to fall more rapidly than mortality rates during the next few decades, the potential for polygyny in sub-Saharan Africa may diminish.

Summary

After World War II, the marriage rate went up during the baby boom in most of the countries of Western Culture. But later the marriage rate fell in both the English-speaking countries with high rates and the other countries with lower rates. Liberalizing social changes gave young adults more options regarding their marital behavior. Also a marriage squeeze resulted in an excess of unmarried women in the usual ages for first marriage. Many of these unmarried women obtained more education and employment but found discrimination in the workplace that led many to join the Women's Movement.

The divorce rate reached a peak after World War II, fell sharply during the baby boom, then rose to unprecedented heights by 1980. Factors associated with the rising divorce rate included the increasing employment and financial independence of women, the declining birth rate, less gain to women from marriage, and an increase in cohabitation. Liberalizing divorce laws made it easier to end an unsatisfactory marriage, but this often operated to the disadvantage of young mothers and women in middle age with little work experience.

Most divorced persons are delaying marriage while they experiment with maintaining a one-parent household, with cohabiting, or with living alone. The English-speaking nations have the highest remarriage rates as well as very high marriage and divorce rates.

Fertility levels in most of the world have been declining as the value of a large family has diminished in the increasingly urbanized society. China has been the most successful in reducing its birth rate. In many other countries, too few births occur to avoid population decline without compensating (both helpful and troublesome) immigration. Meantime, the unmarried birth rate has been increasing while marital fertility decreased.

The use of abortion to prevent unwanted births has increased in developed countries. The birth rate in these countries during recent years has been one-fifth lower than it would have been if no abortions were performed. In countries with high abortion rates, other effective contraceptive methods have been increasingly adopted. The most rapidly expanding practice has been sterilization of the husband or wife. Canada and the United States have the highest proportions of contraceptors who have adopted sterilization. Breastfeeding is another effective way to reduce the risk of pregnancy and is being increasingly used, especially among college-educated women.

Average household size has been declining throughout most of the world. Families are having fewer children, and more persons have become divorced, after which they live in one-parent households, alone, or with a cohabiting partner. This tendency has been counteracted to some extent by more young adults living longer with their parents or returning to their parental home after divorce, unemployment, or unwed motherhood. Perhaps surprisingly, in sub-Saharan Africa, about one-sixth of the men are polygynous, but this proportion is likely to decrease.

The Family of Tomorrow

During the foreseeable future, much lower levels of change in family life seem likely to occur than those since the end of World War II, especially since the mid-1960s. Not much change in direction or in magnitude of the trends is anticipated during the next decade or two. Most of the factors that produced the recent changes have approached or reached their maximum limits. As long as the economy finds useful places for women to be employed, very few can be expected to leave their employment and return to the full-time job of raising a large family. Already the divorce, remarriage, fertility, and cohabitation rates in the modern world are tending to stabilize, and there is little reason to expect more than moderate fluctuations around the current levels.

The smaller cohort of persons born after the baby boom should find entrance into the labour market and into marriage somewhat easier in coming years. The marriage squeeze will be operating during the rest of this century in a direction opposite of that during the last two decades. This shift could contribute to a moderate increase in marriage and a similar decrease in divorce as the supply of young women of marriageable age becomes scarcer than the corresponding supply of young men. Still other developments could convince more of the unmarried adults to marry relatively early and more of the married couples to stay married. Among these other developments could be a growing fear of contracting diseases associated with sexual intimacy and a clearer recognition that divorce can create new problems as well as solve some old ones.

Students of the family generally agree that most adults, but certainly not all, will continue to find marriage, the first or second time around, the most useful way to enjoy steady intimate companionship, to rear and socialize young children, and to share in the maintenance of stable home life (Westoff, 1978; Thornton and Freedman, 1982; Davis, 1984; Kirkendall and Gravat, 1984). Although this generalization grows out of American experience and research, it seems relevant just about all over the world.

TECHNICAL TERMS

ABORTION RATIO—The number of abortions as a percentage of the number of births plus abortions in a given year.

DEMOGRAPHY—The scientific study of the growth and distribution of population; it includes family demography.

FERTILITY DETERMINANTS—These include contraception, late marriage, and infertility for a period after childbirth.

HOMOGAMOUS MARRIAGE—A husband and wife with similar characteristics, such as age, education, and religion.

MARRIAGE SQUEEZE—A factor making it relatively difficult for a woman born during the baby boom to find a man of the "right" age to marry; the man would be two or three years older and therefore would have been born earlier when the birth rate was lower than it was when she was born.

Chapter 20 / Paul C. Glick

NO-FAULT DIVORCE—A divorce based on incompatibility leading to the complete breakdown of the marriage; it involves no claim of fault by the husband or wife, and it requires the equal division of property after divorce.

POLYGYNY—That form of polygamy involving one man with more than one wife at a given time.

POSSLQ—Partners of opposite sex sharing living quarters (unrelated adults cohabiting).

REPLACEMENT LEVEL—The number of children born per women to avoid a change in the population from one generation to the next; currently a total fertility rate of about 2.1 children in developed countries.

TOTAL ABORTION RATE—The average number of abortions per woman during the entire reproductive period. The rate applies to women in a give year.

TOTAL FERTILITY RATE—The average number of children born per woman during the entire reproductive period. The rate applies to women in a given year.

QUESTIONS

1. Why has the marriage rate been declining and the divorce rate increasing during recent years in most of the countries of Western Culture?

2. What is the total fertility rate? How high must it be to replace the population from one generation to the next?

3. Why are homogamous marriages more likely than those that are not homogamous to remain intact?

4. What is "no-fault" divorce? What are its advantages and disadvantages as compared with "fault" divorce?

5. Why has the average size of household been declining throughout most of the Western countries?

6. What is the "marriage squeeze"? Discuss its cause and some of its consequences to those who are involved.

SUGGESTED READING

- Leon F. Bouvier. "Planet Earth 1984–2034: A Demographic Vision." *Population Bulletin* 39, No. 1 (1984).

  An analysis of differences among nations in fertility and immigration levels in relation to natural resources, technological level, and political structure.

- Andrew J. Cherlin. *Marriage, Divorce, Remarriage*. Cambridge: Harvard University Press, 1981.

  The causes and consequences of changes in marital status, with a concluding section on differences by race, from the perspective of a family demographer.

- Paul C. Glick and Sung-Ling Lin. "Recent changes in divorce and remarriage." *Journal of Marriage and the Family* 48: (1986) 737–747.

  Changes in rates since 1960 and extent of remarriage by duration of divorce, number of children, and education.

- Marcia Guttentag and Paul F. Secord. *Too Many Women: The Sex Ratio Question*. Beverly Hills: Sage Publications, 1983.

  A social history of the changing ration of men to women in different cultures from ancient times, with an analysis of the effects of the changes on social and political life.

- Lester A. Kirkendall and Arthur E. Gravatt, eds. *Marriage and the Family in the Year 2020*. Buffalo, NY: Prometheus Books, 1984.

  The anticipated consequences of changing social and technological conditions on interaction within the family and on the relation of the family to the social order by the year 2020.

- D. C. McKie et al. *Divorce: Law and the Family in Canada*. Ottawa: Statistics Canada, 1983.

  Recent changes in divorce placed in historic context, together with the reasons for divorce and the outcome of the divorce process in Canada.

- Edward G. Stockwell and H. Theodore Groat. *World Population: An Introduction to Demography*. New York: Franklin Watts, 1984.

  A textbook on factors in population growth in developed and underdeveloped countries, including such topics as exposure to intercourse, fertility regulation, and family planning policies and programs.

- Arland D. Thornton and Deborah Freedman. "The changing American family," *Population Bulletin* 38, No 4 (1983).

  An analysis of trends in marriage, fertility, sexual activity, roles of spouses, and living arrangements during recent decades.

- Jan Trost. *Unmarried Cohabitation*. Vasteras, Sweden: International Library, 1979.

  The history of cohabitation in Sweden and other countries under which couples live together outside marriage.

- Lenore J. Weitzman. *The Divorce Revolution: The Unexpected Social and Economic Consequences for Women and Children in America*. New York: The Free Press, 1985.

  The background and consequences of no-fault divorce, with recommendations for revision of laws to provide more equitable lifestyles for husbands and wives after divorce.

REFERENCES

Abu-Laban, Sharon. 1980. Arab-Canadian family life. In *An olive branch on the family tree: Arabs in Canada,* ed. Baha Abu-Laban. Toronto: Ministry of Supply and Services, Canada.

Acock, Alan C., and John H. Edwards. 1982. Egalitarian sex-role attitudes and female income. *Journal of Marriage and the Family* 44: 581–589.

Adams, Bert N. 1968. *Kinship in an urban setting.* Chicago: Markham Publishing.

———. 1979. Mate selection in the United States: A theoretical summarization. In *Contemporary theories about the family,* vol. 1, ed. W. R. Burr et al. Glencoe, IL: Free Press.

———. 1980. *The family: A sociological interpretation.* Boston: Houghton Mifflin.

———. 1983. *The family: A sociological interpretation,* 3d ed. Chicago: Dorsey Press.

———. 1988. Fifty years of family research. *Journal of Marriage and the Family* 50: 5–17.

Adams, I., et al. 1971. *The real poverty report.* Edmonton: Hurtig.

Agathonos, H., and N. Stathopoulou. 1982. Child abuse and neglect in Greece: Sociomedical aspects. *Child Abuse and Neglect: The International Journal* 6: 307-310.

Ahrons, Constance, and Roy Rodgers. 1987. *Divorced families.* New York: W. W. Norton.

Albas, D., and C. Albas. 1987. The pulley alternative for the wheel theory of the development of love. *International Journal of Comparative Society* 28: 3–4.

Aldous, Joan. 1977. Family interaction patterns. *Annual Review of Sociology* 3: 105–135.

———. 1978. *Family careers.* New York: Wiley.

Altman, I., and D. Taylor. 1973. *Social penetration: The development of interpersonal relationships.* New York: Holt, Rinehart and Winston.

Ambert, Anne-Marie. 1980. *Divorce in Canada.* Don Mills, ON: Academic.

———. 1984. Longitudinal changes in children's behaviour toward custodial parents. *Journal of Marriage and the Family* 46: 463–468.

———. 1988. Relationships with former in-laws after divorce. *Journal of Marriage and the Family* 50: 679–686.

Anderson, Grace, and David Higgs. 1976. *A future to inherit.* Toronto: McClelland and Stewart.

Anderson, Michael. 1971. *Family structure in nineteenth century Lancashire.* Cambridge: Cambridge University Press.

———. 1983. *What is new about the modern family: An historical perspective.* Office of Population Censuses and Surveys, British Society for Population Studies, Occasional Papers, no. 31, 1–16.

Anderson, S. A., et al. 1983. Perceived marital quality and family life-cycle categories: A further analysis. *Journal of marriage and the family.* 45: 127–139.

Arafat, Ibithaj, and Betty Yorburg. 1973. On living together without marriage. *Journal of Sex Research* 9: 97–106.

Ard, B. 1977. Sex in lasting marriages: A longitudinal study. *Journal of Sex Research* 13: 274–285.

Arendell, T. 1987. *Mothers and divorce.* Berkeley: University of California Press.

Armstrong, Pat, and Hugh Armstrong. 1984. *Canadian women and their segregated work,* rev. ed. Toronto: McClelland and Stewart.

Assaad, Marie Bassili. 1980. *Female circumcision in Egypt: Social implications, current research, and prospects of change.* The Population Council, One Dag Hammarskjold Plaza, New York, NY 10017.

Atchley, R. C. 1988. *Social forces and aging,* 5th ed. Belmont, CA: Wadsworth.

Atkinson, J. 1982. Anthropology. *Signs* 8: 236–258.

———. 1987. Gender roles in marriage and the family. *Journal of Family Issues* 8: 5–41.

Atwater, Lynn. 1979. Getting involved. *Alternative Lifestyles* 2: 33–68.

Axelrod, Morris. 1956. Urban structure and social participation. *American Sociological Review* 21: 13–18.

Bachofen, Johann Jacob. 1861. *Das Mutterrecht.* Stuttgart: Ferdinand Enke.

Bachrach, Christine A. 1984. Contraceptive practice among American women, 1973–1982. *Family Planning Perspectives* 16: 253–259.

Backett, Kathryn. 1987. The negotiation of fatherhood. In *Reassessing fatherhood,* ed. Charlie Lewis and Margaret O'Brien. London: Sage.

Bahr, S. J. 1974. Effects on power and the division of labor in the family. In *Working mothers,* ed. L. W. Hoffman and F. I. Nye. San Francisco: Jossey-Bass.

Baker, Maureen. 1984. His and her divorce research. *Journal of Comparative Family Studies* 15: 17–28.

———. 1985. *What will tomorrow bring?.... A study of the aspirations of adolescent women.* Ottawa: Canadian Advisory Council on the Status of Women.

Balakrishnan, T. R., K. V. Rao, Evelyne Lapierre-Adamcyk, and Karol J. Krotki. 1986. A hazards model analysis of the covariates of marriage dissolution in Canada. Paper presented at the annual meetings of the Population Association of America, April 3–5, San Francisco.

Balakrishnan, T. R., Karol J. Krotki, and Evelyne Lapierre-Adamcyk. 1985. Contraceptive use in Canada, 1984. *Family Planning Perspectives* 17: 209–215.

Bardis, Panos D. 1952. Family forms and variations historically considered. In *Handbook of marriage and the family*, 2d ed., vol. 1, ed. H-T Christensen. Boston: Rand McNally.

Barnouw, E. A. 1972. *A history of broadcasting in the United States*, vol. 3. New York: Oxford University Press.

Barnouw, V. 1982. *Ethology: An introduction to anthropology*, 4th ed. Georgetown, ON: Irwin-Dorsey.

Barrett, Michèle, and Mary McIntosh. 1982. *The anti-social family*. London: Verso.

Barrett, S. 1974. *Two villages on stilts: economic and family change in Nigeria*. New York: Chandler Publishing Company.

———. 1977. *The rise and fall of an African utopia*. Centre for Developing Area Studies, McGill University, Development Perspectives 1. Waterloo, ON: Wilfred Laurier University Press.

———. 1982. Sex and conflict in an African utopia. *Journal of Comparative Family Studies* 13: 19–35.

———. 1987. *Is God a racist? The right wing in Canada*, Toronto: University of Toronto Press.

Barry, Herbert, III, et al. 1957. A cross-cultural survey of some sex differences in socialization. *Journal of Abnormal and Social Psychology* 55: 327–32.

Bascom, W. 1948. West Africa and the complexity of primitive cultures. *American Anthropologist* 50: 18–22.

Becker, Howard, and H. E. Barnes, 1952. *Social thought from lore to science*, 2d ed., vol. 1. Boston: D.C. Heath.

Beckett, Joyce O., and Audrey D. Smith. 1981. Work and family roles: Egalitarian marriage in black and white families. *Social Service Review* 55: 314–326.

Beechey, Veronica. 1978. Women and production. In *Feminism and materialism*, ed. Annette Kuhn and Ann-Marie Wolpe. London: Routledge and Kegan Paul.

Bell, Colin, and Howard Newby. 1976. Husbands and wives: The dynamics of the deferential dialectic. In *Dependence and exploitation in work and marriage*, ed. L. Barker and S. Allan. London: Tavistock.

Bell, Colin, and Patrick Healey. 1973. The family and leisure. In *Leisure and society in Britain*, ed. Michael A. Smith et al. London: Allen Lane.

Bell, Nancy J., and William Carver. 1980. A reevaluation of gender label effects: Expectant mothers' responses to infants. *Child Development* 51: 925–27.

Bell, Norman. 1962. Extended family relations of disturbed and well families. *Family Process* 1: 175–193.

Bell, Norman, and E. Vogel, eds. 1960. *A modern introduction to the family*. New York: Free Press.

Bell, Robert R. 1971. *Marriage and family interaction*, 3d ed. Homewood, IL: Dorsey.

———. 1983. *Marriage and family interaction*, 6th ed. Homewood, IL: Dorsey.

Bell, Robert R., and Kathleen Coughly. 1980. Premarital sexual experiences among college females, 1958, 1968 and 1978. *Family Relations* 29: 352–7.

Bellak, Leopold, and Maxine Antel. 1975. *Human behaviour*.

Bem, D. 1972. Self-perception theory. In *Advances in experimental social psychology*, vol. 6, ed. L. Berkowtiz. New York: Academic.

Benedict, Ruth. 1954. Continuities and discontinuities in cultural conditioning. In *Readings in United Development*, ed. W. C. Stendler Martin. New York: Harcourt Brace.

Bennett, John W., and Leo Despres. 1960. Kinship and instrumental activities: A theoretical enquiry. *American Anthropologist* 52: 254–267.

Bennett, Neil G., et al. 1986. Premarital cohabitation and subsequent marital stability. Paper presented at the annual meetings of the Population Association of America, April 3–5, San Francisco.

Bennholdt-Thomsen, Veronika. 1981. Subsistence production and extended reproduction. In *Of marriage and the market*, ed. Kate Young et al. London: CSE Books.

Berardo, D. H., et al. 1987. A residue of tradition: Jobs, careers, and spouses' time in housework. *Journal of Marriage and the Family* 49: 381–390.

Berger, Brigitte, and Peter Berger. 1983. *The war over the family*. Garden City: Doubleday.

Berger, P., and H. Kellner. 1964. Marriage and the construction of reality: An exercise in the microsociology of knowledge. *Diogenes* 46: 1–24.

Bergmann, Barbara. 1987. *The Economic emergence of women*. New York: Basic Books.

Berheide, Catherine White. 1984. Women's work in the home: Seems like old times. In *Women and the family: Two decades of change*, ed. Beth B. Hess and Marion B. Sussman (*Marriage and Family Review* 7, Nos. 3/4, Fall/Winter). New York: The Haworth Press.

Berk, Richard A., and Sarah F. Berk. 1979. *Labor and leisure at home: Content and organization of the household day*. Beverly Hills: Sage.

Berk, Sarah F. 1985. *The gender factory: The apportionment of work in American households*. New York: Plenum.

Bernard, Jessie. 1964. The adjustment of married mates. In *Handbook of marriage and the family*, ed. Harold T. Christensen. Chicago: Rand McNally.

———. 1972. *Remarriage*. New York: World.

———. 1973. *The future of marriage*. New York: Bantam Books.

———. 1976. Homosociality and female depression. *Journal of Social Issues* 32: 213–238.

———. 1981. The good provider role: Its rise and fall. *American Psychologist* 36: 1–12.

Berndt, Catherine H., and Ronald M. Berndt. 1972. Aborigines. In *Socialisation in Australia*, ed. F. J. Hunt. Sydney: Angus and Robertson.

Berndt, R. 1965. Marriage and the family in north-eastern Arnhem Land. In *Comparative family systems*, ed. M. Nimkoff. Boston: Houghton Mifflin.

Berndt, T. J. 1978. Developmental changes in conformity to peers and parents. Paper presented at the annual meeting of the American Psychological Association, Toronto, August.

Berscheid, E., and E. Walster. 1978. *Interpersonal attraction*, 2d ed. Don Mills, ON: Addison-Wesley.

Beteille, A. 1964. Family and social change in India and other South Asian countries. *The Economic Weekly* 16: 237–244.

Bhargava, Guru. 1988. Seeking immigration through matrimonial alliances: A study of advertisements in an ethnic weekly. *Journal of Comparative Family Studies* 19: 245–260.

Billingsley, A. 1968. *Black families in white America*. Englewood Cliffs, NJ: Prentice-Hall.

Bird, Gloria W., et al. 1984. Determinants of family task sharing: A study of husbands and wives. *Journal of Marriage and the Family* 46: 345–355.

Blair, Thomas. 1974. *The international urban crisis*. St. Albans: Paladin.

Blanton, Judith. 1980. Communal child rearing: The Synanon experience. *Alternative Lifestyles* 13: 87–116.

Blau, P. M. 1964. *Exchange and power in social life*. New York: Wiley.

Blau, P. M., and O. D. Duncan. 1967. *The American occupational structure*. New York: Wiley.

Blau, P. M., T. C. Blum, and Janet E. Schwartz. 1982. Heterogeneity and intermarriage. *American Sociological Review* 47: 45–62.

Blaxter, Mildred. 1981. *The health of the children: A review of research on the place of health in cycles of disadvantage*. London: Heinemann.

Blazer, J. 1964. Married virgins—A study of unconsummated marriages. *Journal of Marriage and the Family* 26: 28–32.

Block, Jeanne H. 1983. Differential premises arising from differential socialization of the sexes: Some conjectures. *Child Development* 54: 1335–54.

Blood, R. 1967. *Love match and arranged marriages: A Tokyo-Detroit comparison*. New York: Free Press.

Blood, R., and D. M. Wolfe. 1960. *Husbands and wives: The dynamics of married living*. Glencoe, IL: Free Press.

Bloom, D. 1982. What's happening to the age at first birth in the United States? *Demography* 19: 351–391.

Bloom, D., and A. R. Pebley. 1982. *Voluntary childlessness: A review of the evidences and implications*. Population Research and Policy Review. Amsterdam: Elsevier.

Blumberg, Rae, and Maria Garcia. 1977. The political economy of the mother-child family: A cross-societal view. In *Beyond the nuclear family model*, ed. Luis Lenero-Otero. London: Sage.

Blumenfeld, Emily, and Susan Mann. 1980. Domestic labour and the reproduction of labour power. In *Hidden in the household*, ed. Bonnie Fox. Toronto: The Women's Press.

Blumstein, Philip, and Pepper Schwartz, 1977. Bisexuality: Some social psychological issues. *Journal of Social Issues* 33: 30–45.

———. 1983. *American couples*. New York: William Morrow.

Bograd, Michele. 1984. Family systems approaches to wife battering: A feminist critique. *American Journal of Orthopsychiatry* 54: 558–568.

Bohannan, Paul. 1960. *African homicide and suicide*. Princeton, NJ: Princeton University Press.

———. 1963. *Social anthropology*. New York: Holt, Rinehart and Winston.

Bohen, Halcyone. 1984. Gender inequality in work and family. *Journal of Family Issues* 5: 254–272.

Bolton, Charles D. 1961. Mate selection as the development of a relationship. *Marriage and Family Living* 23: 234–240.

Booth, Charles. *Life and labour of the people of London*. London, 1952.

Borodin, S. V. 1964. *Judicial procedure in murder trials*. Moscow.

Bose, Christine. 1980. Social status of the homemaker. In *Women and household labor*, ed. Sarah F. Berk. Beverly Hills: Sage.

Boserup, E. 1970. *Women's role in economic development*. New York: St. Martin's Press.

Bossard, J. H. S., and Eleanor B. Boll. 1948. Rites of passage—A contemporary study. *Social Forces* 26: 247–255.

Bouvier, Leon F. 1984. Planet earth 1984–2034: A demographic vision. *Population Bulletin* 39: 1–40.

Brecher, E. 1971. Who does what, when, and with whom—Alfred Charles Kinsey (1894–1956). In *People as partners: Individual and family relationships in today's world*, ed. J. Wiseman. San Francisco, CA: Canfield.

Brenner, Johanna, and Barbara Laslett. 1986. Social reproduction and the family. In *Sociology: From crisis to science?* vol. 2, ed. Ulf Himmelstrand. London: Sage.

Brenner, R. H., et. al. 1970. *Children and youth in America: A documentary history*. Cambridge: Harvard University Press.

Brinkerhoff, Merlin. 1980. Women, their work and families: Some continuities in studies of structural constraints. Canadian Sociology and Anthropology Association. Annual Meeting, Montreal, June.

———. 1982. Women's work in Mexico and Canada: The constraints of various dimensions of SES and family life cycle. *International Journal of Comparative Family Studies* 13: 307–328.

Brinkerhoff, Merlin, and Eugen Lupri. 1978. Theoretical and methodological issues in the use of decision-making as an indicator of conjugal power: Some Canadian observations. *The Canadian Journal of Sociology* 3: 1–20.

———. 1983. Conjugal power and family relationships: Some theoretical and methodological issues. In *The Canadian family*, ed. K. Ishwaran. Toronto: Gage.

Brinkerhoff, Merlin, Victor Castillo Vales, and James Girgulis. 1980. Barriers to the work world: The case of the married Yucatecan woman. *International Journal of the Sociology of the Family* 10: 243–263. (1981. Barreas al mundo laboral: el caso de las mujeres casadas en Yucatan. *Revista Mexicana de Sociologia* 43: 105–128).

Broderick, Carlfred. 1971. Beyond the five conceptual frameworks. *Journal of Marriage and the Family* 33: 139–159.

————. 1984. *Marriage and the family*, 2d ed. Englewood Cliffs, New Jersey: Prentice-Hall.

Broderick, Carlfred, and James Smith. 1979. The general systems approach to the family. In *Contemporary theories about the family*, ed. W. Burr et al., vol. 2. New York: Free Press.

Brodie, M. J., and J. M. Vickers. 1982. *Canadian women in politics: An overview*. The CRIAW Papers, No. 8. Ottawa: Canadian Research Institute for the Advancement of Women.

Broverman, Inge K., et al. 1972. Sex-role stereotypes: A current appraisal. *Journal of Social Issues* 28: 59–78.

Browne, Angela. 1987. *When battered women kill*. New York: Free Press.

————. 1988. Family homicide: When victimized women kill. In *Handbook of family violence*, ed. Vincent B. Van Hasselt et al. New York: Plenum.

Brumborg, Helge. 1979. *Cohabitation without marriage in Norway*. Samliv Uten Vigsel, Artikler Fra Statistik Sentralbyra, no. 16.

Bryne, D., et al. 1970. Continuity between the experimental study of attraction and "real life" computer dating. *Journal of Personality and Social Psychology* 16: 157–165.

Bumpass, Larry L., and James A. Sweet. 1972. Differential in marital instability. *American Sociological Review* 37: 751–766.

Burch, E. 1982. Marriage and divorce among the North Alaskan eskimos. In *Anthropology for the eighties*, ed. J. Cole. New York: the Free Press.

Burch, T. K. 1985. *Family history survey*. Statistics Canada, Catalogue 99–955. Ottawa, Canada.

Burch, T. K., and A. K. Madan. 1986. *Union formation and dissolution*. Statistics Canada, Catalogue 99–963. Ottawa, Canada.

Burgess, Ernest W. 1926. The family as a unity of interacting personalities. *The Family* 7: 3–9.

————, ed. 1926. *The urban community*. Chicago: University of Chicago Press.

Burgess, Ernest W., and Harvey J. Locke. 1945. *The family: From institution to companionship*. New York: American Book Company.

Burgess, Ernest W., and Leonard Cottrell. 1939. *Predicting success or failure in marriage*. New York: Prentice-Hall.

Burgess, Ernest W., and P. Wallin. 1953. *Engagement and marriage*. Philadelphia: Lippincott.

Burgess, Ernest W., Harvey J. Locke, and Mary Margaret Thomes. 1963. *The family*, 3d ed. New York: American Book Co.

Burman, Patrick. 1988. *Killing time, losing ground: Experiences of unemployment*. Toronto: Wall & Thompson.

Burnham, P. 1987. Changing themes in the analysis of African marriage. In *Transformations of African marriage*, ed. D. Parkin and D. Nyamwaya. Manchester: Manchester University Press.

Burr, Wesley. 1973. *Theory construction and the sociology of the family*. New York: Wiley.

Burr, Wesley, et al., eds. 1979. *Contemporary theories about the family*, 2 vols. New York: Free Press.

Burr, Wesley, Geoffrey Leigh, Randall Day, and John Constantine. 1979. Symbolic interaction and the family. In *Contemporary theories about the family*, vol. 2, ed. Wesley Burr et al. New York: Free Press.

Burton, S. 1988. The sexual revolution hits China. *Time* Sept. 12.

Buunk, Bram. 1980a. Extra marital sex in the Netherlands. *Alternative Lifestyles* 3: 11–39.

————. 1980b. Sexually open marriages. *Alternative Lifestyles* 3: 312–328.

Byrne, D., and B. Blaylock. 1963. Similarity and assumed similarity between husbands and wives. *Journal of Abnormal and Social Psychology* 76: 636–640.

Caldwell, G. T. 1977. Leisure. In *Australian society*, ed. A. F. Davies, et al. Cheshire: Longman.

Calhoun, Arthur W. 1945. *A Social history of the American family*. New York: Barnes and Noble.

Camera dei Deputati. V. Legislatura. 1969. N. 1–467–A (April 30), 12–13.

Campbell, John K. 1968. *Honour, family and patronage*. Oxford: Claredon Press.

Canada. Ministry of Supply and Services. 1988. *Canada Year Book 1988*. Catalogue No. 11–402E/1987.

Canada. Women's Bureau, Labour Canada. 1984. *Canadian attitudes toward women: Thirty years of change*. Ottawa: Ministry of Supply and Services, Canada.

————. 1986. *When I grow up...* Ottawa: Ministry of Supply and Services, Canada.

————. 1987. *Women in the labour force, 1986–1987*. Ottawa: Ministry of Supply and Services, Canada.

Canadian Advisory Council on the Status of Women. 1985. *Canadian urban vicitimization survey*, Bulletin No. 4, Ottawa: Ministry of the Solicitor General, Canada.

Canadian Council on Social Development. 1984. *Not enough: The meaning and measurement of poverty in Canada*, Ottawa: CCSD, Canada.

Canter, Rachelle J., and Beth E. Meyerowitz. 1984. Sex-role stereotypes: Self-reports of behavior. *Sex Roles* 10: 293–306.

Capellanus, A. 1959. *The Art of courtly love*, trans. John Jay Parry. New York: Ungar.

Carisse, Colette. 1975. Family and leisure: a set of contradictions. *Family Coordinator* 24: 191–197.

Carlson, Elwood. 1986. Couples without children: Premarital cohabitation in France. In *Contemporary marriage: Comparative perspectives on a changing institution*, ed. Kingsley Davis. New York: Russell Sage Foundation.

Carlson, John. The recreational role. 1976. In *Role structure and analysis of the family*, ed. F. Ivan Nye et al. Beverly Hills: Sage.

Carmichael, Gordon A. 1985. Remarriage among divorced persons in New Zealand. *Australian Journal of Social Issues* 20: 87–103.

Carmichael, Gordon A., and Peter F. McDonald. 1986. The rise and fall (?) of divorce in Australia 1968–1985. Paper presented at the annual meetings of the Population Association of America, San Francisco, April 3–5.

Carr, Peggy G., and Martha T. Mednick. 1988. Sex role socialization and the development of achievement motivation in black preschool children. *Sex Roles* 18: 169–180.

Carstairs. 1967. *The twice born*. Bloomington: Indiana University Press.

Carter, Hugh, and Paul C. Glick. 1976. *Marriage and divorce: A social and economic study*. Cambridge: Harvard University Press.

Catalyst. 1981, May. Preliminary results of the catalyst two-career survey. *Catalyst Career and Family Bulletin*, No. 2.

Catton, W., and R. Smircich. 1964. A comparison of mathematical models for the effect of residential propinquity on mate selection. *American Sociological Review* 29: 522–9.

Cebotarev, E. (Forthcoming). Women, human rights and the family in development theory and practice. *Canadian Journal of International Development*.

Centres, Richard. 1975. *Sexual attraction and love: An instrumental theory*.

Cerroni-Long, E. 1985. Marrying out: socio-cultural and psychological implications of intermarriage. *Journal of Comparative Family Studies* 16: 25–46.

Chadwick-Jones, J. K. 1976. *Social exchange theory*. New York: Academic Press.

Chafetz, Janet S., and Anthony G. Dworkin. 1987. In the face of threat: Organized antifeminism in comparative perspective. *Gender and Society* 1: 33–60.

Chao, P. 1983. *Chinese kinship*. London: Routledge and Kegan Paul.

Cheal, David. 1983. Intergenerational family transfers. *Journal of Marriage and the Family* 45: 805–813.

———. 1987a. "Showing them you love them": gift giving and the dialectic of intimacy. *Sociological Review* 35: 150–169.

———. 1987b. Intergenerational transfers and life course management. In *Rethinking the life cycle*, ed. Alan Bryman et al. Basingstoke: Macmillan.

———. 1988. Theoretical approaches to the study of family life. In *Marriage and the family in Canada today*, ed. G. N. Ramu. Toronto: Prentice-Hall.

Chekki, D. A. 1974. *Modernization and kin network*. Leiden: Brill.

Cherlin, A. 1981. *Marriage, divorce, remarriage*. Cambridge: Harvard University Press.

Cherlin, A., and P. B. Walters. 1981. Trends in United States' men's and women's sex role attitudes: 1972 to 1978. *American Sociological Review* 46: 453–460.

Cherry, Gordon E. 1984. Leisure and the home: A review of changing relationships. *Leisure Studies* 3: 35–52.

Cherry, Louise. 1975. The Preschool teacher-child dyad: Sex differences in verbal interaction. *Child Development* 46: 532–35.

Chimbos, Peter D. 1978. *Marital violence: A Study of interspouse homicide*. San Francisco: R. and E. Research Associates.

———. 1980. The Greek experience in Canada. Toronto: McClelland and Stewart.

———. 1983. Immigrants' attitudes toward their children's interethnic marriage. In *Marriage and Divorce in Canada*, ed. K. Ishwaran. Toronto: Methuen.

Chodorow, Nancy. 1974. Family structure and feminine personality. In *Woman, culture, and society*, ed. Michelle Zimbalist Rosaldo and Louise Lamphere. Stanford: Stanford University Press.

———. 1978. *The reproduction of mothering: Psychoanalysis and the sociology of gender*. Berkeley: University of California Press.

Chow, Esther Ngan-Ling, and Catherine Berheide. 1988. The interdependancy of family and work: A framework for family life education, policy, practice. *Family Relations* 37: 23–28.

Christensen, H. T., ed. 1964. *Handbook of marriage and the family*. Chicago: Rand McNally.

Cimbalo, R. S., V. Falling, and P. Mousaw. 1976. The course of love: A cross-sectional design. *Psychological Reports* 38: 1291–1294.

Clark, Susan, and Andrew Harvey. 1976. The sexual division of labour: The use of time. *Atlantis* 2: 46–66.

Clayton, Richard R. 1979. *The family, marriage, and social change*, 3d ed. Lexington: D. C. Heath.

Clayton, Richard R., and Harwin Voss. 1977. Shacking up: cohabitation in the 1970s. *Journal of Marriage and the Family* 39: 273–283.

Clignet, R. 1987. On dit que la polygamie est morte: Vive la polygamie! In *Transformations of African marriage*, ed. D. Parkin and D. Nyanwaya, 199–210. Manchester: Manchester University Press.

Cogle, F. L., and G. E. Tasker. 1982. Children and housework. *Family Relations* 31: 359–399.

Cohen, Theodore F. Remaking men. 1987. *Journal of Family Issues* 8: 57–77.

Cole, J. 1982. Women in Cuba: The revolution within the revolution. In *Anthropology for the eighties*, ed. J. Cole. New York: Free Press.

Coleman, James C. 1984. Intimate relationships, marriage and family. Indianapolis: Bobb-Merrill.

Coleman, James S. 1966. *Equality of educational opportunity*. Washington, DC: US Government Printing Office.

Coleman, James W., and Donald R. Cressey. 1984. *Social problems*. New York: Harper & Row.

Coles, Robert. 1964. Terror-struck children. *New Republic* 150: 11–13.

Comfort, A. 1972. *The joy of sex: A gourmet guide to lovemaking*. New York: Crown Publishers.

Commaille, Jacques. 1983. Divorce and the child's status: The evolution in France. *Journal of Comparative Family Studies* 14: 97–114.

Connelly, P. 1978. *Last hired: first fired*. Toronto: The Women's Press.

Conover, Patrick. 1975. An analysis of communes and international communities with particular attention to sexual and genderal relations. *The Family Coordinator* 24: 453–464.

Cooley, C. H. 1902. *Human nature and the social order*. New York: Scribners.

Coombs, Robert, and W. F. Kenkel. 1966. Sex differences in dating aspirations and satisfaction with computer-selected partners. *Journal of Marriage and the Family* 28: 62–66.

Coppinger, Robert M., and Paul C. Rosenblatt. 1968. Romantic love and subsistence dependence of spouses. *Southwestern Journal of Anthropology* 24: 310–19.

Cormier, Bruno M. 1961. Psychodynamics of homicide committed in marital relationships. Paper read at the Third World Congress of Psychiatry, Montreal.

Corsini, R. 1956. Understanding and similarity in marriage. *Journal of Abnormal and Social Psychology* 52: 327–332.

Cosand, B. J., L. B. Bourque, and J. F. Kraus. 1982. Suicide among adolescents in Sacramento County, California, 1950–1979. *Adolescence* 17: 917–930.

Cottrell, L. S. 1953. New orientations for research on the American family. *Social Care Work* 34: 54–60.

Coult, Alan D., and Robert V. Habenstein. 1962. Notes and commentaries on the study of extended kinship in urban society. *Sociological Quarterly* 3: 141–145.

Courtney, Alice E., and Thomas W. Whipple. 1983. *Sex stereotyping in advertising.* Lexington: D. C. Heath.

Coverman, Shelley. 1985. Explaining husbands' participation in domestic labor. *Sociological Quarterly* 26, No. 1.

Coverman, Shelley, and Joseph F. Sheley. 1986. Change in men's housework and child-care time, 1965–1975. *Journal of Marriage and the Family* 48: 413–422.

Cowan, Ruth S. 1987. Women's work, housework, and history: The historical roots of inequality in work-force participation. In *Families and work,* ed. N. Gerstel and H. Gross. Philadelphia: Temple University Press.

Coward, Rosalind. 1983. *Patriarchal precedents.* London: Routledge.

Cox, F. D. 1981. *Human intimacy: Marriage, the family and its meaning.* St. Paul: West.

Croll, David A. 1982. *Poverty in Canada: Updated poverty line.* Ottawa: Senate of Canada.

Cromwell, R. E., and D. H. Olson, eds. 1975. *Power in families.* New York: Wiley.

Crosby, Faye, and Gregonym Herek. 1986. Male sympathy with the situation of women: Does personal experience make a difference? *Journal of Social Issues* 42: 55–66.

Cruikshank, Julie. 1976. Matrifocal families in the Canadian north. In *The Canadian family,* ed. K. Ishwaran. Toronto: Holt, Rinehart and Winston.

Culp, Rex E., et al. 1983. A comparison of observed and reported adult-infant interactions: Effects of perceived sex. *Sex Roles* 9: 475–479.

Cummings, Elaine. 1963. Further thoughts on the theory of disengagement. *International Social Science Journal* 15: 377–393.

Cummings, Elaine, and William C. Henry. 1961. *Growing old: The process of disengagement.* New York: Basic Books.

Currie, Dawn. 1988. Re-thinking what we do and how we do it. *Canadian Review of Sociology and Anthropology* 25: 231–253.

d'Andrade, Roy G. 1966. Sex differences and cultural institutions. In *The development of sex differences,* ed. Eleanor E. Maccoby. Stanford: Stanford University Press.

D'Hondt, W., and M. Vanderwiele. 1983. Attitudes of West African students toward love and marriage. *Psychological Reports* 53: 615–621.

Dahl, Tove Stang, and Annika Snare. 1978. The coercion of privacy. In *Women, sexuality and social control,* ed. Carol Smart and Barry Smart. London: Routledge and Kegan Paul.

Dahlerup, Drude, ed. 1986. *The new women's movement.* Beverly Hills: Sage.

Damas, David. 1976. The problem of the Eskimo family. In *The Canadian family,* ed. K. Ishwaran. Toronto: Holt, Rinehart and Winston.

Darling, Martha. 1975. *The role of women in the economy.* Paris: Organisation for Economic Co-operation and Development.

Davenport, W. 1965. Sexual patterns and their regulation in a society of the southwest Pacific. In *Sex and behavior,* ed. F. Beach. New York: Wiley.

———. 1977. Sex in cross-cultural perspective. In *Human sexuality in four perspectives,* ed. F. Beach. Baltimore: Johns Hopkins University Press.

David, Henry P. 1982. Eastern Europe: Pronatalist policies and private behaviour. *Population Bulletin* 36: 1–48.

Davis, Albert J. 1984. Sex-differentiated behaviors in nonsexist picture books. *Sex Roles* 11: 1–16.

Davis, J. 1977. *People of the Mediterranean.* London: Routledge and Kegan Paul.

Davis, Kingsley. 1939. The forms of illegitimacy. *Social Forces* 18: 77–89.

———. 1940. The sociology of parent-youth conflict. *American Sociological Review* 5: 523–535.

———. 1950. *Human society.* New York: Macmillan.

———. 1984. Wives and work: The sex revolution and its consequences. *Population and Development Review* 10: 397–417.

———. 1985. Near and dear: Friendship and love compared. *Psychology Today.*

Davis, M. 1973. *Intimate relations.* Glencoe, IL: Free Press.

de Beauvoir, Simone. 1952. *The second sex.* Trans. H. M. Parshley. New York: Knopf.

De Jesus, Carolina Maria. 1962. *Child of the dark.* New York: Dutton.

Dean, Gillian, and Douglas T. Gurak. 1978. Marital homogamy the second time around. *Journal of Marriage and the Family* 40: 559–570.

deFrain, J. 1979. Androgynous parents tell who they are and what they need. *Family Coordinator* 28: 237–243.

Delleman, I., et al. 1975. *Motieven voor vrijivillige kinder loosheid.* Groningen: Instituut voor Algemene Psychologie.

DeLoache, Judy S., et al. 1987. The three bears are all boys: Mothers' gender labeling of neutral picture book characters. *Sex Roles* 17: 163–178.

Delphy, Christine. 1979. Sharing the same table. In *The sociology of the family,* ed. Chris Harris. Keele: University of Keele.

Demographic yearbook. 1984. *Marriage and divorce statistics, 1982.* New York: United Nations.

———. 1988. *Natality statistics, 1986,* 470–473. New York: United Nations.

Deutsch, Helene. 1944–45. *The psychology of women: A psychoanalytic interpretation,* vol. 1: 1944; vol 2: 1945. New York: Grune and Stratton.

Deutscher, Irwin. 1962. Socialization for parental life. In *Human behaviour and social processes,* ed. Arnold Rose. Houghton-Mifflin, Boston.

Diamond, Norma. 1975. Collectivization, kinship, and the status of women in rural China. In *Toward an anthropology of women,* ed. Rayna R. Reiter. New York: Monthly Review Press.

Dizard, J. 1968. *Social change in the family.* Chicago: University of Chicago.

Dobash, R. E., and Russel Dobash. 1979. *Violence against wives: A case against the patriarchy.* New York: Free Press.

Donahue, Thomas J., and James W. Costar. 1977. Counsellor discrimination against young women in career selection. *Journal of Counselling Psychology* 24: 481–86.

Donzelot, Jacques. 1979. *The policing of families.* New York: Pantheon.

Dornbusch, Sanford M., et al. 1984. Black control in adolescent mating. *Sociological Perspectives* 27: 301–323.

Dressel, P. L. 1980. Assortative mating in later life. *Journal of Family Issues* 1: 379–396.

Dressel, Paula, and W. Ray Avant. 1978. Neogamy and older persons. *Alternative Lifestyles* 1: 13–37.

Driedger, Leo. 1983. Ethnic intermarriages: Student dating and mating. In *Marriage and divorce in Canada,* ed. K. Ishwaran. Toronto: Methuen.

Duberman, L. 1974. *Marriage and Its alternatives.* New York: Praeger.

Duffy, Ann, Nancy Mandell, and Norene Pupo. 1989. *Few choices: Women, work and family.* Toronto: Garamond.

Dumazedier, Joffre. 1974. *Sociology of leisure.* Amsterdam: Elsevier.

Durkheim, Emile. [1897] *Suicide,* trans. J. A. Spaulding and G. Simpson. Glencoe, IL: Free Press, 1964.

Dutton, D., and A. Aron. 1974. Some evidence for heightened sexual attraction under conditions of high anxiety. *Journal of Personality and Social Psychology* 30: 510–517.

Duvall, E. 1971. *Family development.* Philadelphia: Lippincott.

Duvall, Evelyn, and Brent Miller. 1985. *Marriage and family development.* New York: Harper and Row.

Dyer, Everett D. 1979. *The American family: Variety and change.* New York: McGraw Hill.

Dyk, Patricia A. H. 1987. Graduate student management of family and academic roles. *Family Relations* 36: 329–332.

Dynes, Wallace. 1977. Leisure location and family centredness. *Journal of Leisure Research* 9: 281–291.

Eames, Edwin, and Judith Goode. 1973. *Urban poverty in a cultural context.* New York: Free Press.

Eastman, P. 1984. Elders under siege. *Psychology Today* January.

Eckland, Bruce K. 1968. Theories of mate selection. *Eugenics Quarterly* 15: 77–84.

Edgell, Stephen. 1980. *Middle-class couples.* London: Allen and Unwin.

Edwards, J., and A. Booth. 1976. Sexual behavior in and out of marriage: An assessment of correlates. *Journal of Marriage and the Family* 38: 73–81.

Eichler, Margrit. 1977. The prestige of the occupation housewife. In *The working sexes,* ed. Patricia Marchak. Vancouver: University of British Columbia. Institute of Industrial Relations.

———. 1981. Power, dependency, love and the sexual division of labour. *Women's Studies International Quarterly* 4: 201–219.

———. 1985a. The connection between paid and unpaid labour. In *Women's paid and unpaid work,* ed. Paula Bourne. Toronto: New Hogtown Press.

———. 1985b. And the work never ends: feminist contributions. *Canadian Review of Sociology and Anthropology* 22: 619–644.

———. 1987. Family change and social policies. In *Family matters,* ed. Karen L. Anderson et al. Toronto: Methuen.

———. 1988. *Families in Canada today: Recent changes and their policy consequences,* 2d ed. Toronto: Gage.

Elder, Glen H. 1969. Appearance and education in marriage mobility. *American Sociological Review* 34: 519–33.

———. 1977. Family history and the life course. *Journal of Family History* 2: 279–304.

———. 1984. Families, kin, and the life course. In *Review of child development research,* vol. 7, ed. Ross Parke. Chicago: University of Chicago Press.

Elkin, F. 1964. *The family in Canada.* Ottawa: Vanier Institute of the Family.

Elkin, F., and W. A. Westley. 1955. The myth of adolescent culture. *American Sociological Review* 20: 680–684.

Elliott, M. A., and Merrill, F. E. 1950. *Social disorganization.* New York: Harper.

Emerson, Richard M. 1976. Social exchange theory. In *Annual Review of Sociology* 335–362. Annual Reviews Inc.

Emery, R. E. 1982. Interpersonal conflict and the children of discord and divorce. *Psychological Bulletin* 92: 310–320.

Engels, Friedrich. [1884]. *The origin of the family, private property and the state.* New York: Pathfinder Press, 1972.

Epstein, Joseph. 1974. *Divorce in America.* New York: Dutton.

Ericksen, Julia A. 1981. Marital pickups replace cupids. *Honolulu Advertiser* May 26.

Ericksen, Julia A., et al. 1979. The division of family roles. *Journal of Marriage and the Family* 41: 301–13.

Erikson, Erik H. 1963. *Childhood and society,* 2d ed. New York: Norton.

———. 1968. *Identity: Youth and crisis.* New York: Norton.

Eshleman, J. Ross, and Chester L. Hunt. 1965. *Social class factors in the college adjustment of married students.* Kalamazoo: Western Michigan University Press.

Eshleman, Ross. 1988. *The family*. Toronto: Allyn and Bacon.

Espenshade, Thomas J. 1985. Marriage trends in America: Estimates, implications, and underlying causes. *Population and Development Review* 11: 193–245.

Etaugh, Claire. 1980. Effects of nonmaternal care on children: Research, evidence and popular views. *American Psychologist* 35: 309–311.

European Leisure and Recreation Association. 1983. ELRA Congress examines leisure today and tomorrow. *World Leisure and Recreation Association Journal* 25, No. 5: 4–6.

Farber, Bernard. 1964. *Family organizations and interactions*. Chandler.

———. 1972. *Guardians of virtue: Salem families in 1800*. New York; Basic Books.

Fasick, F. A. 1979. Acquisition of adult responsibilities and rights in adolescence. In *Childhood and adolescence in Canada*, ed. K. Ishwaran. Toronto: McGraw-Hill Ryerson.

———. 1984. Parents, peers, youth culture and autonomy in adolescence. *Adolescence* 19: 143–157.

Featherman, D. L. 1985. Individual development and aging as a population process. In *Individual development and social change: Explanatory analysis,*. ed. J. R. Nesselroade and A. Van Eye. New York: Academic.

Feldman, Harold. 1981. A comparison of international parents and internationally childless couples. *Journal of Marriage and the Family* 43: 593–600.

Ferree, M. M. 1980. Satisfaction with housework. In *Women and household labour*, ed. S. F. Berk. Beverly Hills: Sage.

———. 1984. The view from below: Women's employment and gender equality in working class families. In *Women and the family: Two decades of change*, ed. Beth B. Hess and Marvin B. Sussman. *Marriage and Family Review* 7, Nos. 3/4.

Festy, Patrick. 1980. On the new context of marriage in Western Europe. *Population and Development Review* 6: 311–315.

Finch, Janet. 1987. Family obligations and the life course. In *Rethinking the life cycle*. Alan Bryman et al. Basingstoke: Macmillan.

Fincham, F. D., and T. N. Bradbury. 1987. The assessment of marital quality: A reevaluation. *Journal of Marriage and the Family* 49: 797–810.

Fine, M. J., ed. 1980. *Handbook on parent education*. New York: Academic Press.

Finlay, H. A., ed. 1969. *Divorce, society and the law*. Melbourne: Butterworths.

Firth, R. 1965. Family in Tikopia. In *Comparative family systems*, ed. M. Nimkoff. Boston: Houghton Mifflin Company.

Firth, R., et al. 1969. *Families and their relatives*. London: Routledge and Kegan Paul.

Ford, C., and F. Beach. 1951. *Patterns of sexual behavior*. New York: Harper and Row.

Fox, Bonnie. 1988. Conceptualizing "patriarchy." *Canadian Review of Sociology and Anthropology* 25: 163–182.

Freedman, M. 1968. The Family in China, past and present. In *Comparative perspectives on marriage and the family*, ed. H. Geiger. Boston: Little, Brown and Company.

Freeman, Jo. 1974. The social construction of the second sex. In *Sexism and youth*, ed. Diane Gersoni-Stavn. New York: R. R. Bowker. Originally published, 1970, in *Roles women play*. Brooks/Cole.

Freeman, L. 1962. *Virgin wives—A study of unconsummated marriages*. Springfield, IL: Charles C. Thomas.

———. 1974. Marriage without love: mate-selection in non-Western societies. In *Selected studies in marriage and the family*, 4th ed., ed. Robert F. Winch and Graham B. Spanier. New York: Holt, Rinehart, and Winston.

Frejka, Tomas. 1985. Induced abortion and fertility. *Family Planning Perspectives* 17: 230–234.

Freud, Sigmund. [1905]. *The standard edition of the complete psychological works of Sigmund Freud*, ed. James Strachey, Vol. 7 (1901–1905) *A case of hysteria, Three essays on sexuality and Other works*. London: Hogarth, 1953.

———. [1940]. *An outline of psycho-analysis*. London: Hogarth, 1949.

Frieders, James, et al. 1971. The impact of Jewish-Gentile intermarriages in Canada: An alternative view. *Journal of Comparative Family Studies* 2: 268–275.

Friedl, E. 1975. *Women and men: An anthropologist's view*. New York: Holt, Rinehart and Winston.

Friedman, D. 1985. *Corporate financial assistance for child care*. New York: The Conference Board. Research Bulletin, No. 177.

Frisch, Hannah L. 1977. Sex stereotypes in adult-infant play. *Child Development* 48: 1671–75.

Frueh, Terry, and Paul E. McGhee. 1975. Traditional sex role development and amount of time spent watching television. *Developmental Psychology* 11: 109.

Gagnon, I., and W. Simon. 1973. *Social sources of human sexuality*. Chicago: Aldine.

Galdson, Richard. 1965. Observations of children who have been physically abused by their parents. *American Journal of Psychiatry* 122: 440–443.

Gallatin, J. E. 1975. *Adolescence and individuality: A conceptual approach to adolescent psychology*. New York: Harper & Row.

Gallup, George H. 1984. *The Gallup poll. Public opinion*. Wilmington, DE: Scholarly Resources.

Galper, Miriam. 1978. *Co-parenting: Sharing your child equally*. Philadelphia: Running Press.

Gannagé, Charlene. 1986. *Double say, double bind: Women garment workers*. Toronto: Women's Press.

Garigue, Phillippe. 1956. French Canadian kinship and urban life. *American Anthropologist* 58: 1090–1101.

Geerken, Michael, and Walter R. Gove. 1983. *At home and at work: The family's allocation of labor*. Beverly Hills: Sage.

Geiger, H. 1965. The Soviet family. In *Comparative Family Systems*, ed. M. Nimkoff. Boston: Houghton Mifflin.

———. 1968. *The family in Soviet Russia*. Cambridge, MA: Harvard University Press.

Gelles, Richard. 1972. *The violent home*. Beverly Hills: Sage.

———. 1973. The other side of the family: Conjugal violence. Durham: University of New Hampshire. Unpublished Ph.D. dissertation.

———. 1974. Child abuse as psychopathology: A sociological critique and reformation. In *Violence in the family,* ed. Suzanne K. Steinmetz and Murray A. Straus. New York: Dodd, Mead.

——. 1976. Abused wives: Why do they stay? *Journal of Marriage and the Family* 38: 659–668.

——. 1978. Violence toward children in the United States. *American Journal of Orthopsychiatry* 48: 580–592.

——. 1980. Violence in the family: A review of research in the seventies. *Journal of Marriage and the Family* 42: 873–85.

——. 1983. The myth of battered husbands. In *Marriage and the Family,* ed. Ollie Pocs and Robert Walsh. Guilford, CT: Dushkin.

Gelles, Richard, and Claire Pedrick-Cornell. 1986. *Intimate violence in families.* Beverly Hills: Sage.

Gelles, Richard, and E. F. Hargreaves. 1978. Maternal employment and violence towards children. Mimeographed.

Gerson, Kathleen. 1983. Changing family structure and the position of women: A review of the trends. *Journal of the American Planning Association* 49: 138–148.

Gerstel, Naomi, and Harriet E. Gross. 1987. *Families and work.* Philadelphia: Temple University Press.

——. 1983. Commuter marriage: Couples who live apart. In Contemporary families and alternative lifestyles, ed. Heanon Macklin and Roger Rubin, 180–193. Beverly Hills: Sage.

Gerth, Hans, and C. Wright Mills, eds. 1958. *From Max Weber: Essays in sociology.* New York: Oxford University Press.

Giele, Janet 1977. Introduction: The status of women in comparative perspective. In *Women: roles and status in eight countries,* ed. Janet Giele and Audrey Chapman Smock. New York: Wiley.

——. 1988. Gender and sex roles. In *Handbook of sociology,* ed. Neil J. Smelser. Newbury Park: Sage.

Gil, David G. 1970. *Violence Against children.* Cambridge: Harvard University Press.

Gilbert, Lucia Albino. 1985. *Men in dual-career families: Current realities and future prospects.* Hillsdale, NJ: Lawrence Erlbaum Associates.

Gillespie, Dair L. 1971. Who has the power? The marital struggle. *Journal of Marriage and the Family* 33: 415–458.

Ginsberg, E., S. W. Ginsburg, S. Axelrod, and J. L. Herma. 1951. *Occupational choice: An approach to a general theory.* New York: Columbia University Press.

Glass, S., and T. Wright. 1977. The relationship of extramarital sex, length of marriage and sex differences on marital satisfaction and romanticism: Athariasiou's data reanalyzed. *Journal of Marriage and the Family* 39: 691–703.

Glenn, N. D., and K. B. Kramer. 1987. The marriages and divorces of the children of the divorced. *Journal of Marriage and the Family* 49: 811–825.

Glick, Paul C. 1975. A demographer looks at American families. *Journal of Marriage and the Family* 37: 15–26.

——. 1984a. American household structure in transition. *Family Planning Perspectives* 16: 205–211.

——. 1984b. Marriage, divorce, and living arrangements: Prospective changes. *Journal of Family Issues* 5: 7–26.

——. 1984c. How American families are changing. *American Demographics* (January) 21–25.

——. 1988. The role of divorce in the changing family structure. In *Children of divorce: Empirical perspective on adjustment,* ed. Sharlene A. Wolchik and Paul Karoly. New York: Gardner Press.

Glick, Paul C., and Arthur J. Norton. 1979. Marrying, divorcing, and living together in the U.S. today. *Population Bulletin* 32: 1–40.

——. 1980. Marriage and married people. In *Family in transition,* ed. Arlene Skolnick and Jerome Skolnick. Boston: Little, Brown.

Glick, Paul C., and Graham B. Spanier. 1980. Married and unmarried cohabitation in the United States. *Journal of Marriage and the Family* 42: 19–30.

Glick, Paul C., and Sung-Ling Lin. 1986a. More young adults are living with their parents—who are they? *Journal of Marriage and the Family* 48: 107–112.

——. 1986b. Recent changes in divorce and remarriage. *Journal of marriage and the Family* 48: 737–747.

——. 1987. Remarriage after divorce: Recent changes and demographic variations. *Sociological Perspectives* 30: 162–179.

Glick, Paul C., David M. Heer, and John C. Beresford. 1963. Family formation and family composition: Trends and prospects. In *Sourcebook in marriage and the family,* ed. Marvin B. Sussman. Boston: Houghton Mifflin. Co.

Glueck, S., and E. Glueck. 1957. Working mothers and delinquency. *Mental Hygiene* 527–552.

Glyptis, Susan A., and Deborah A. Chambers. 1982. No place like home. *Leisure Studies* 1: 247–262.

Goldman, Noreen, and Anne R. Pebley. 1986. The demography of polygyny in sub-Saharan Africa. Paper presented at the annual meetings of the Population Association of America, San Francisco, April 3–5.

Goldman, Robert, and David R. Dickens. 1984. Leisure and legitimation. *Society and Leisure* 7: 299–323.

Goode, William J. 1959. The theoretical importance of love. *American Sociological Review* 24: 39–47.

——. 1963. *World revolution and family patterns.* New York: Free Press.

——. 1969. Violence among intimates. In *Crimes of violence,* vol. 13, ed. Donald J. Mulvihill. Washington: United States Government Printing Office.

——. 1971. Force and violence in the family. *Journal of Marriage and the Family* 33: 624–635.

——. 1971. World revolutions and family patterns. *Journal of Marriage and the Family* 33: 624–635.

——. 1973. *Explorations in social theory.* New York: Oxford University Press.

——. 1977. Family cycle and theory construction. In *The family life cycle in European societies,* Jean Cuisenier. The Hague: Mouton.

——. 1982. *The family* 2d. ed. Englewood Cliffs, NJ: Prentice Hall.

——. 1982. Why men resist. In *Rethinking the family: Some feminist questions,* ed. Barrie Thorne with Marilyn Yalom. New York: Longman.

Goode, William J., Elizabeth Hopkins, and Helen McClure. 1971. *Social systems and family patterns*. Indianapolis: Bobbs-Merrill.

Goody, E. 1962. Conjugal separation and divorce among the Gonja of northern Ghana. In *Marriage in tribal societies*. Cambridge: Cambridge University Press.

Gordon, David. 1972. *Theories of poverty and unemployment*. Lexinton: D.C. Heath.

Gordon, David, Richard Edwards, and Michael Reich. 1982. *Segmented work, divided workers*. Cambridge: Cambridge University Press.

Gordon, Michael. 1981. Was Waller ever right?. The rating and dating complex reconsidered. *Journal of Marriage and the Family* 43: 67–76.

Gorer, Geoffery. 1964. *The American people: A study in national character*. New York: Norton & Co.

Gottman, J. M. 1979. *Marital interaction: experimental investigations*. New York: Academic Press.

Gottman, J. M., and A. L. Porterfield. 1981. Communicative competence in the nonverbal behavior of married couples. *Journal of Marriage and the Family* 42: 817–824.

Gough, Kathleen. 1959. The Nayars and the definition of marriage. *Journal of the Royal Anthropological Institute* 89: 23–34.

———. 1960. Is the family universal: The Nayar case. In *A modern introduction to the family*, ed. Norman Bell and E. Vogel. New York: Free Press.

Gould, Joyce. 1978. Violence in the family. *International Council of Social Democratic Women Bulletin* No. 6.

Gray-Little, Bernadette, and Nancy Burks. 1983. Power and satisfaction in marriage: A review and critique. *Psychological Bulletin* 93: 513–538.

Greenfield, S. 1961–62. Industrialization and the family in sociological theory. *American Journal of Sociology* 67: 312–322.

———. 1969. Love and marriage in modern America: A functional analysis. *Sociological Quarterly* 6: 361–377.

Greenglass, Esther R. 1982. *A world of difference: Gender roles in perspective*. Toronto: Wiley.

Grollman, Earl, A., ed. 1969. *Explaining divorce to children*. Boston: Beacon.

Gross, Harriet Eugel. 1980. Dual-career couples who live apart: Two styles. *Journal of Marriage and the Family* 42: 567–576.

Grueling, J. W., and R. R. DeBlassie. 1980. Adolescent suicide. *Adolescence* 15: 589–601.

Grymes, Robert O., and Donald J. Hernandez. 1986. Projections of the number of households and families: 1986 to 2000. *Current Population Reports*, Series P-25, No. 986, 1–11.

Guppy, L. N., and J. L. Siltanen. 1977. A comparison of the allocation of male and female occupational prestige. *Canadian Review of Sociology and Anthropology* 14: 320–30.

Gupta, Giri Raj. 1979. Love, arranged marriage and the Indian social structure. In *Cross-cultural perspectives of mate-selection and marriage*, ed. George Kurian. Westport, Connecticut: Greenwood Press.

Gurak, Douglas T., and J. P. Fitzpatrick. 1982. Intermarriage among Hispanic ethnic groups in New York City. *American Journal of Sociology* 87: 921–934.

Gutman, Herbert. 1977. *The black family in slavery and freedom, 1750-1925*. New York: Random House.

Guttentag, Maria, and Paul F. Secord. 1983. *Too many women? The sex ratio question*. Beverly Hills: Sage.

Guttmacher, Manfred S. 1955. Criminal responsibility in certain homicide cases involving family members. In *Psychiatry and the law,* ed. Paul Hoch and Joseph Zupin. New York: Grune and Straton.

Gwartney-Gibbs, Patricia A. 1986. The institutionalization of premarital cohabitation: Estimates from marriage license applications, 1970 and 1980. *Journal of Marriage and the Family* 48: 423–434.

Haas, L. 1981. Domestic role sharing in Sweden. *Journal of Marriage and the Family,* 43: 957–967.

Hagedorn, Robert. 1983. *Sociology*. Toronto: Holt, Rinehart and Winston.

Hall, D. T. and P. S. Hall. 1980. Stress and the two-career couple. In *Current concerns in occupational stress,* ed. C. L. Cooper and R. Payne. New York: Wiley.

Hall, Peter D. 1978. Marital selection and business in Massachusetts merchant families. In *The American family in socio-historical perspective, 1700–1900,* ed. Michael Gordon. New York: St. Martin's Press.

Hansen, D. A., and V. A. Johnson. 1979. Rethinking family stress theory: Definitional aspects. In *Contemporary theories about the family,* vol. 1, ed. W. R. Burr et al. New York: Free Press.

Hansen, S. L. 1977. Dating choices of high school students. *Family Coordinator* 26: 133–138.

Hantrais, Linda. 1983. *Leisure and the family in contemporary France*. Polytechnic of North London, Papers in Leisure Studies, No. 7.

Hantrais, Linda, P. A. Clark, and Nicole Samuel. 1984. Time-space dimensions of work, family and leisure in France and Great Britain. *Leisure Studies* 3: 301–317.

Hare-Mustin, Rachel. 1988. Family change and gender differences. *Family Relations* 37: 36–41.

Hareven, Tamara. 1975. Family time and industrial time: Family and work in a planned corporation town, 1900–24. *Journal of Urban History* 1: 366–89.

Hareven, Tamara. 1977. The family cycle in historical perspective: A proposal for a developmental approach. In *The family life cycle in European societies,* ed. J. Cuisenier. The Hague: Mouton.

Harrell, W. Andrew. 1986. *Husband's involvement in housework: The effects of relative earning power and masculine orientation*. Edmonton Area Series, No. 39. Edmonton: Population Research Laboratory, University of Alberta.

Harry, Joseph, and Robert Lovely. 1979. Gay marriages and communities of sexual orientation. *Alternative Lifestyles* 2: 177–200.

Hartmann, Heidi. 1981. The family as the locus of gender, class, and political struggle. *Signs* 6: 366–394.

Haskell, Martin, and Lewis Yablonsky. 1982. *Juvenile delinquency*. Boston: Houghton Mifflin.

Hawley, Amos. 1981. *Urban society: An ecological approach.* New York: Wiley.

Hazard, John. 1939. Law and the Soviet family. *Wisconsin Law Review* 245.

Hebart, Walsh, et al. 1980. Rotational employment of Coppermine Innuit men: Effects and community perspectives. Indian and Northern Affairs Publication No. QS-8160–036–EE-A1 Escom Report No. A 1–36, Ottawa.

Heer, David. 1962. The trend of interfaith marriages in Canada. *American Sociological Review* 27: 245–50.

———. 1963. The measurement and bases of family power: An overview. *Journal of Marriage and the Family* 25: 133–144.

———. 1974. The prevalence of black-white marriage in the United States, 1960 and 1970. *Journal of Marriage and the Family* 36: 246–258.

Heer, David, and Charles A. Hubay. 1976. The trend of interfaith marriages in Canada: 1922–1972. In *The Canadian family*, K. Ishwaran. Toronto: Holt, Rinehart and Winston.

Heider, K. 1970. *The Dugan Dani: A Papuan culture in the highlands of West New Guinea.* Chicago: Aldine.

Heinrich, A. 1979. Divorce as an integrative social factor. In *Cross-cultural perspectives of mate-selection and marriage,* ed. G. Kurian. Westport, CT: Greenwood Press.

Held, Thomas. 1980. *Soziologie der ehelichen Machtverhaltnisse.* Neuwied: Luchterhand.

Henry, Francis, and Pamela Wilson. 1975. The status of women in Caribbean societies: An overview of their social economic and sexual roles. *Journal of Social and Economic Studies.*

Henry, J. 1964. *Jungle people.* New York: Vintage.

Henshaw, Stanley K. 1986. Trends in abortions, 1982–1984. *Family Planning Perspectives* 18: 34.

Henshaw, Stanley K., et al. 1984. Abortion services in the United States, 1981 and 1982. *Family Planning Perspectives* 16: 119–127.

Herbst, P. G. 1952. The measurement of family relationships. *Human Relations* 5: 3–35.

———. 1954. Family living-patterns of interaction. In *Social structure in a city,* ed. O. A. Oeser and S. B. Hammond. London: Routledge and Kegan Paul.

Herold, E. S. 1984. *Sexual behaviour of Canadian young people.* Markham, Ontario: Fitzhenry & Whiteside.

Herskovits, Melville. 1941. *The myth of the negro past.* New York: Harper.

Hertz, Rosanna. 1986. *More equal than others.* Berkeley, California: University of California Press.

Herzog, A. Regula, Jerald G. Bachman, and Lloyd D. Johnston. 1983. Paid work, child care, and housework: A national survey of high school seniors' preferences for sharing responsibilities between husband and wife. *Sex Roles* 9: 109–135.

Hetherington, Mavis E. 1978. Children and divorce. *Parent-child interaction: In Theory, research and prospect,* ed. R. Henderson. New York: Academic.

———. 1978. The aftermath of divorce. In *Mother-child, Father-child Relations,* ed. J. H. Stevens Jr. and M. Mathews. Washington.

Hill, Charles T., Zick Rubin, and Letitia Anne Peplau. 1977. Breakups before marriage: the end of 103 affairs. In *Family in transition,* 2d ed., ed. Arlene S. Skolnick and Jerome H. Skolnick. Boston: Little, Brown.

Hill, Reuben A. 1958. Sociology of marriage and family behaviour—1945–56: A trend report and bibliography. *Current Sociology* 7: 1–98.

———. 1970. *Family development in three generations.* Cambridge, MA: Schenkman.

———. 1971. Modern systems theory and the family. *Social Science Information* 10: 7–26.

———. 1977. Social theory and family development. *The Family Life Cycle in European Societies,* ed. Jean Cuisenier, 9–38. The Hague: Mouton.

Hill, Reuben A., Alvin L. Katz, and Richard L. Simpson. 1957. An inventory of research in marriage and family behaviour. *Marriage and Family and Family Living* 19: 89–92.

Hill, Reuben A., and Donald Hansen. 1960. The identification of conceptual frameworks utilized in family study. *Marriage and Family Living* 22: 299–311.

Hill, Reuben A., and Roy Rodgers. 1964. The developmental approach. In *Handbook of marriage and the family.* Chicago: Rand McNally.

Hiller, Dana V., and William W. Philliber. 1986. The division of labor in contemporary marriage: Expectations, perceptions and performance. *Social Problems* 33: 191–201.

Himmeloch, Jerome, and Silvia F. Fava, eds. 1955. *Sexual behaviour in American society.* New York: Norton.

Hitchens, Donna. 1979–1980. Social attitudes, legal standards and personal trauma in child custody cases. *Journal of Homosexuality* 5: 89–95.

Hobart, C. W. 1973. Attitudes toward parenthood among Canadian young people. *Journal of Marriage and the Family* 35: 71–81.

Hochschild, A. 1975. The sociology of feeling and emotion: Selected possibilities. In *Another voice,* ed. M. Millman and R. Kanter. Garden City, NY: Anchor.

———. 1979. Emotion work, feeling rules and social structure. *American Journal of Sociology* 85: 551–575.

———. 1983. *The managed heart: commercialization of human feeling.* Berkeley: University of California Press.

Hoffman, L. W. 1968. Effects of maternal employment on the child. In *Social book in marriage and the family,* 3d ed., ed. Marvin Sussman. Boston: Houghton Mifflin.

Hoffman, L. W., and J. D. Manis. 1979. The value of children in the United States: A new approach to the study of fertility. *Journal of Marriage and the Family* 41: 583–596.

Hogan, D. P. 1978. The variable order of events in the life course. *American Sociological Review* 43: 573–586.

———. 1981. *Transitions and social change: The early lives of American men.* New York: Academic Press.

Hollingshead, August B. 1975. *Youth and Elmtown revisited.* New York: Wiley.

Holmstrom, R. 1972. The two-career family. Cambridge: Schenkman.

Homans, G. C. 1951. *The human group*. London: Routledge and Kegan Paul.

———. 1974. *Social behaviour: Its elementary forms*, rev. ed. New York: Harcourt Brace Jovanovich.

Horna, Jarmila L. A. 1983. A multidimensional approach to the study of the family and leisure. In *Leisure, work and family*, ed. Stanley Parker. International Sociological Association, Research Committee on Leisure.

———. 1985a. Desires and preferences for leisure activities: More of the same? *World Leisure and Recreation* 27: 28–32.

———. 1985b. The social dialectic of life career and leisure: A probe into the preoccupations model. *Society and Leisure* 8, No. 2.

Horna, Jarmila L. A. 1986. The trends in marriage and child-bearing: A comparative look at Czechoslovakia and Canada. *Family Perspective* 20: 223–236.

Hornong, Carlton, et al. 1981. Status relationships in marriage: Risk factors in spouse abuse. *Journal of Marriage and the Family* 43: 675–92.

Horowitz, A. 1981. Sons and daughters as caregivers to older parents: Differences in role performance and consequences. Paper presented at the annual meeting of the Gerontological Society of America, Toronto, November.

Horton, D. 1957. The dialogue of courtship in popular songs. *American Journal of Sociology* 62: 569–578.

Houseknecht. 1986. Voluntary childlessness: Toward a theoretical integration. In *Family in transition*, 5th ed., ed. A. S. Skolnick and J. H. Skolnick. Boston: Little, Brown.

Humphrys, A. 1965. The family in Ireland. In *Comparative family systems*, ed. M. Nimkoff. Boston: Houghton Mifflin.

Hunt, J. G., and L. L. Hunt. 1977. Dilemmas and contradictions of status: The case of the dual-career family. *Social Problems* 24: 407–416.

———. 1982. The dualities of careers and families: New integrations or new polarizations? *Social Problems* 29: 499–510.

Hunt, M. 1959. *The natural history of love*. New York: Knopf.

———. 1974. Sexual behavior in the 1970's. Chicago: Playboy Press.

Hurvitz, Nathan. 1975. Courtship and arranged marriages among Eastern European Jews prior to World War I as depicted in Briefenshteller. *Journal of Marriage and the Family* 37: 422–430.

Hutter, Mark. 1981. *The changing family*. Toronto: Wiley.

Ibrahim, Hilmi. 1982. Leisure and Islam. *Leisure Studies* 1: 197–210.

Ilieva, N., and V. Oshavkova. 1977. Changes in the Bulgarian family cycle from the end of the 19th century to the present day. In *The family life cycle in European societies*, ed. J. Cuisenier. The Hague: Mouton.

Irelan, Lola, Oliver Moles, and Robert O'Shea. 1969. Ethnicity, poverty, and selected attitudes: A test of the "culture of poverty" hypothesis. *Social Forces* 47: 405–12.

Irving, Howard. 1972. *The family myth*. Toronto: Copp Clark.

Ishwaran, K. 1977. *A populist community and modernization in India*. Leiden: E. J. Brill.

———. 1977. *Family, kinship and community*. Toronto: McGraw-Hill Ryerson.

———. 1980. *Canadian families: Ethnic variations*. Toronto: McGraw-Hill Ryerson.

———. 1982. Interdependence of the elementary and extended family. In *The Indian family in transition*, ed. John S. Augustine. New Delhi: Vikas.

———. 1983. *The Canadian family*. Toronto: Gage.

Ishwaran, K., and Chan Kwok. 1979. The socialization of rural adolescents. In *Childhood and adolescence in Canada*, ed. K. Ishwaran. Toronto: McGraw-Hill Ryerson.

Jacobs, Jerry A., and Frank F. Furstenberg, Jr. 1986. Changing places: conjugal careers and women's marital mobility. *Social Forces* 64: 714–732.

Jansen, Harriet. 1980. Communes. *Alternative Lifestyles* 3: 255–277.

Jedlicka, Davor. 1978. Sex inequality, aging and innovation in preferential mate selection. *Family Coordinator* 27: 137–140.

———. 1980a. Formal mate selection networks in the United States. *Family Relations* 29: 199–203.

———. 1980b. A test of the psychoanalytic theory of mate selection. *Journal of Social Psychology* 112: 295–299.

Jencks, Christopher. 1972. *Inequality: A reassesment of the effects of family and schooling in America*. New York: Basic Books.

———. 1979. *Who gets ahead? The determinants of economic success in America*. New York: Basic Books.

Jones, Elise F., et al. 1985. Teenage pregnancy in developed countries: Determinants and policy implications. *Family Planning Perspectives* 17: 53–63.

Jong-Gierveld, Jenny de, and Monique Aalberts. 1980. Singlehood: A creative or lonely experience. *Alternative Lifestyles* 3: 350–368.

Joseph, Roger. 1979. Sexual dialectics and strategy in Berber marriage. In *Cross-cultural perspectives of mate-selection and marriage*, ed. George Kurian. Westport, CT: Greenwood Press.

Juillard, Joelle Rutherford. 1976. Women in France. In *Women in the world: A comparative study*, ed. Lynne B. Iglitzin and Ruth Ross. Santa Barbara: Clio Books.

Kagan, Jerome. 1971. *Understanding children*. New York: Harcourt Brace Jovanovich.

Kahn, M. 1970. Non-verbal communication and marital satisfaction. *Family Process* 9: 449–456.

Kalbach, Warren E. 1983. Propensities for intermarriage in Canada as reflected in ethnic origins of husbands and their wives 1961–1971. In *Marriage and divorce in Canada*, ed. K. Ishwaran. Toronto: Methuen.

Kalmar, Roberta. 1977. *Abortion: The emotional implications*. Iowa: Kendal-Hunt.

Kalmuss, D. S., and M. Straus. 1982. Wife's marital dependency and wife abuse. *Journal of Marriage and the Family* 44: 277–286.

Kamerman, S. 1975. Eight countries: Cross national perspectives on child abuse and neglect. *Children Today* 5: 34–39.

Kamiko, T. 1977. The internal structure of the three-generation household. In *The family life cycle in European societies*, ed. J. Cuisenier. The Hague: Mouton.

Kandell, Denise B., and Gerald S. Lesser. 1972. Marital decision-making in American and Danish urban families: A research note. *Journal of Marriage and the Family* 34: 134–138.

Kanin, E., et al. 1970. A research note on male-female differentials in the experience of heterosexual love. *Journal of Sex Research* 6: 64–72.

Kantor, David, and William Lehr. 1975. *Inside the family*. San Francisco: Jossey-Bass.

Kaplan, Max. 1960. Leisure in America: A Social Inquiry. New York: Wiley.

Karanja, W. 1987. "Outside wives" and "Inside wives" in Nigeria: a Study of the changing perceptions in marriage. In *Transformations of African marriage,* ed. D. Parkin and D. Nyamwaya. Manchester: Manchester University Press.

Karp, David A., and William C. Yoels. 1985. From strangers to intimates. In *Marriage and family in a changing society,* 2d ed., ed. James M. Henslin. New York: Free Press.

Katz, M. Agreement on connotative meaning in marriage. 1965. *Family Process* 4: 64–74.

Kay, Hamahill. 1965. The outside substitute for the family. In *Man and civilization: The family's search for survival,* ed. Seymour M. Farber et al. New York: McGraw-Hill.

Keith, P. M., and R. B. Schafer. 1980. Role strain and depression in two-job families. Family Relations 29: 483–488.

Keller, Bonnie B. 1979. Marriage by elopement. *African Social Research* 27: 565–585.

Kelley, E. L. 1955. Consistency of the adult personality. *American Psychologist* 10: 659–681.

Kelly, H. H., et al. 1983. *Close relationships.* New York: W. H. Freeman.

Kelly, John R. 1978a. Family leisure in three communities. *Journal of Leisure Research* 10: 47–60.

———. 1978b. Leisure styles and choices in three environments. *Pacific Sociological Review* 21: 187–207.

———. 1978c. Situational and social factors in leisure decisions. *Pacific Sociological Review* 21: 313–330.

———. 1982. *Leisure.* Englewood Cliffs, NJ: Prentice-Hall.

———. 1983. Leisure Identities and Interactions. London: Allen and Unwin.

Kent, Mary Mederios, and Carl Haub. 1986. 1986 World Population Data Sheet. Washington, DC: Population Reference Bureau, April.

Kepart, W. M. 1967. Some correlates of romantic love. *Journal of Marriage and the Family* 29: 470–474.

———. 1981. *The family, society and the individual,* 5th ed. Boston: Houghton Mifflin.

Kerckhoff, Alan. 1974. The social context of interpersonal attraction. In *Foundations of Inter-Personal Attraction,* ed. Ted L. Huston. New York: Academic.

Kerckhoff, Alan, and Keith E. Davis. 1962. Value consensus and need complementarity in mate selection. *American Sociological Review* 27: 295–303.

Kessler, R. C., and J. A. McRae. Jr. 1982. The effect of wives' employment on the mental health of married men and women. *American Sociological Review* 47: 216–227.

Khoo, Siew-Ean. 1985. Sterilization: The current situation. Paper presented at the meetings of the International Union for the Scientific Study of Population in Florence, Italy, June 5–12.

Khuri, F. 1970. Parallel cousin marriage reconsidered: A Middle Eastern practice that nullifies the effects of marriage on the intensity of family relationships. *Man* 5: 597–618.

Kimball, Gayle. 1983. *The 50–50 marriage.* Boston: Beacon Press.

Kinsey, A., W. Pomeroy, and C. Martin. 1948. *Sexual behavior in the American male.* Philadelphia: W. B. Saunders.

Kinsey, A., W. Pomeroy, C. Martin, and P. Gebhard. 1953. *Sexual behavior in the American female.* Philadelphia: W. B. Saunders.

Kircheisen, F. M. 1929. *Napolean I, Emperor of the French.* London: Hutchinson and Co.

Kirkendall, Lester A., and Arthur E. Gravatt. 1984. *Marriage and the family in the year 2020.* Buffalo: Prometheus Books.

Kirkpatrick, C. 1955. *The family as process and institution.* New York: Ronald Press.

Kirkpatrick, C., and C. Hobart. 1954. Disagreement, disagreement estimate, and non-empathic imputations for intimacy groups varying from favorite date to married. *American Sociological Review* 19: 10–19.

Knox, David. 1985. *Choices in relationships: An introduction to marriage and family.* New York: West.

Koch-Nielson, Inger. 1980. One parent families in Denmark, *Journal of Comparative Family Studies* 11: 17–29.

Kohl, Seena B. 1983. Working together: Husbands and wives in the small-scale family agricultural enterprise. In *The Canadian family,* ed. K. Ishwaran. Toronto: Gage.

Kohlberg, Lawrence. 1966. A cognitive-developmental analysis of children's sex-role concepts and attitudes. In *The development of sex differences,* ed. Eleanor E. Maccoby. Stanford: Stanford University Press.

Kolanda, P. 1968. Region, caste and family structure: A comparative study of the Indian "joint" family. In *Structure and change in Indian society,* ed. M. Yinger and S. Cohn. Chicago: Aldine.

Komarovsky, Mirra. 1967. *Blue collar marriages.* New York: Random House.

———. 1976. *Dilemmas of masculinity: A study of college youth.* New York: Norton.

Konig, René. 1976. *Die Familie der Gegenwart.* München: C. H. Beck.

Koopman-Boyden, Peggy G., and Max Abbott. 1985. Expectations for household task allocation and actual task allocation: A New Zealand study. *Journal of Marriage and the Family* 47: 211–219.

Korbin, Jill. 1981. *Child abuse and neglect: cross cultural perspectives.* Berkeley: University of California Press.

Korson, J. Henry. 1979. Endogamous marriage in a traditional Muslim society: West Pakistan. A study in intergenerational change. In *Cross-cultural perspectives of mate-selection and marriage,* ed. George Kurian. Westport, CT: Greenwood Press.

Korson, J. Henry, and M. A. Sabzwari. 1984. Age and social status at marriage, Karachi, Pakistan, 1961–64 and 1980: a comparative study. *Journal of Comparative Family Studies* 15: 257–279.

Kreckel, M. 1982. Communicative acts and shared knowledge: a conceptual framework and its empirical application. *Semiotica* 40: 45–88.

Kuhn, Annette. 1978. Structures of patriarchy and capital in the family. In *Feminism and materialism,* ed. Annette Kuhn and Ann-Marie Wolpe. London: Routledge and Kegan Paul.

Kumagai, F. 1984 The life cycle of the Japanese family. *Journal of Marriage and the Family* 46: 191–204.

Kurian, George. 1979. Marriage in transition: a comparison of India and China. *International Journal of Critical Sociology* 3: 60–69.

Kurland, Albert A., et al. 1955. A comparative study of wife murderers admitted to state psychiatric hospitals. *Journal of Social Therapy* 1: 7–14.

L'Esperance, Jeanne. 1982. *The widening sphere: Women in Canada 1870–1940. Ottawa: Ministry of Supply and Services.*

La Fontaine, Jean. 1986. An anthropological perspective on children in social worlds. In *Children of social worlds: Development in a social context,* ed. Martin Richards and Paul Light. Cambridge: Harvard University Press.

Laing, R. D., et al. 1966. *Interpersonal Perception.* New York: Springer.

Lamb, M., ed. 1981. The role of the father. In *Child Development,* 2d ed. New York: Wiley.

Lamousé, Annette. 1969. Family roles of women: A German example. *Journal of Marriage and the Family* 31: 145–152.

Lamphere, L. 1977. Anthropology. *Signs* 2: 612–627.

Landis, P. 1965. *Making the most of marriage,* 3d ed. New York: Appleton.

Laner, Mary. 1983. Premarital violence: Battering on college campuses. Report cited in *Criminology,* by Larry J. Siegal, 257. New York: West.

Laplae, Claire. 1968. Structure des taches domestiques et du pourior de decision de la dyade conjugale. In *La dyade conjugale,* ed. Pierre de Bie et al. Bruxelles: Editions Vie Ouvriere.

Larson, L. 1974. System and subsystem perception of family roles. *Journal of Marriage and the Family* 36: 123–138.

———. 1976. *The Canadian family in comparative perspective.* Scarborough, ON: Prentice-Hall.

Lasswell, M., and N. Lobsenz. 1980. *Styles of Loving.* Garden City, NY: Doubleday.

Lasswell, M., and T. E. Lasswell. 1982. *Marriage and the Family.* Lexington: Heath.

Latowsky (Kallen), Evelyn. 1971. The family life styles and Jewish culture. In *The Canadian family,* ed. K. Ishwaran. Toronto: Holt, Rinehart and Winston.

Laws, Judith Long. 1971. A feminist review of the marital adjustment literature. *Journal of Marriage and the Family* 33: 483–516.

Lazlett, P., and R. Wall, eds. 1972. *Household and family in past time,* Cambridge: Cambridge University Press.

Lee, Gary. 1980. Kinship in the seventies. *Journal of Marriage and the Family* 42: 923–934.

Lee, J. 1974. The styles of loving. *Psychology Today.*

Lein, Laura. 1979. Male participation in home life: Impact of social supports and breadwinner responsibility on the allocation of tasks. *The Family Coordinator* 28: 489–495.

Lenero-Otero, Luis., ed. 1977. *Beyond the nuclear family model.* London: Sage.

Le Play, Frederic. 1855. *Les Ouvriers Europeens.* Paris.

Leslie, Gerald. 1982. *The family in social context.* New York: Oxford University Press.

Leslie, Gerald, and Elizabeth M. Leslie. 1980. *Marriage in a changing world.* New York: Wiley.

Levaut, Ronald F., et al. 1987. Fathers' involvement in housework and child care with school-aged daughters. *Family Relations* 36: 152–157.

Le Vine, R. Political Socialization and Cultural Change. In *Old societies and new states,* ed. C. Geertz. Glencoe, IL: Free Press.

Le Vine, Sarah Ethel. 1986. The marital morality of Mexican women: an urban study. *Journal of Anthropological Research,* 42 183–201.

Levinger, George. 1965. Marital cohesiveness and dissolution: An integrative review. *Journal of Marriage and the Family* 27: 19–28.

———. 1976. A social psychological perspective on marital dissolution. *Journal of Social Issues* 32: 21–47.

———. 1979. A social exchange view on the dissolution of pair relationships. In *Social exchange in developing relationships,* ed. Robert Burgess and Ted Huston. New York: Academic Press.

———. 1983. Development and change. In *Close relationships,* ed. H. H. Kelley et al. San Francisco: Freeman.

Levinger, George, and J. Breedlove. 1966. Interpersonal attraction and agreement: a study of marriage partners. *Journal of Personality and Social Psychology* 3: 367–372.

Levinger, George, et al. 1970. Progress toward permanence in courtship: a test of the Kerckhoff-Davis hypothesis. *Sociometry* 33: 427–443.

Levinston, David. 1988. Family violence in cross-cultural perspective. In *Handbook of family violence,* ed. Vincent B. Hasselt et al. New York: Plenum Press.

Levy, B. 1972. The school's role in the sex stereotyping of girls: A feminist review of the literature. *Feminist Studies* 1: 5–23.

Levy, Joseph. 1980. Leisure and the family: towards some conceptual clarity. *Leisure Information Newsletter* 6, No. 3: 6–7.

Levy, Marion. 1949. *The family revolution in modern China.* Cambridge: Harvard University Press.

Lewis, Hylan. 1961. Child rearing among low income families. Washington Center for Metropolitan Studies, June 8, 1961.

Lewis, I. 1962. Marriage and the family in northern Somaliland. Kampala: East African Institute of Social Research.

Lewis, L., and D. Brissett. 1967. Sex as work: A study of avocational counselling. *Social Problems* 15: 8–17.

Lewis, Michael, and Roy Freedle. 1973. Mother-Infant dyad: The cradle of meaning. In *Communication and affect: language and thought,* ed. Patricia Pliner et al. New York: Academic.

Lewis, Michael. 1972. State as an infant-environmental interaction: An analysis of mother-infant interaction as a function of sex. *Merrill-Palmer Quarterly* 18: 95–121.

Lewis, Oscar. 1959. *Five families: Mexican case studies in the culture of poverty.* New York: Wiley.

———. 1966. *La vida: A Puerto Rican family in the culture of poverty—San Juan and New York.* New York: Random House.

Lewis, Robert A. 1973. A longitudinal test of a developmental framework for premarital dyadic formation. *Journal of Marriage and the Family* 35: 16–25.

Lewis, Robert A., and Graham B. Spanier. 1979. Theorizing about the quality and stability in marriage. In *Contemporary theories about the family,* vol. 1, ed. W.R. Burr et al. Glencoe, IL: Free Press.

Lewis, Robert A., and Graham Spanier. 1982. Marital quality, marital stability, and social exchange. In *Family relationships,* ed. F. Ivan Nye. Beverly Hills: Sage.

Liebow, Elliot. 1967. *Tally's corner: A study of Negro streetcorner men.* Boston: Little, Brown.

Lightbourne, Robert, Jr., and Susheela Singh with Cynthia P. Green. 1982. The world fertility survey: Charting global childbearing. *Population Bulletin* 37: 1–55.

Little, K. 1979a. A question of matrimonial strategy? A comparison of attitudes between Ghanaian and British university students. In *Cross-cultural perspectives of mate-selection and marriage,* ed. G. Kurian. Westport, CT: Greenwood.

———. 1979b Women's strategies in modern marriage in anglophone West Africa: An ideological and sociological appraisal. In *Cross-cultural perspectives of mate-selection and marriage,* ed. G. Kurian. Westport, CT: Greenwood.

Litwak, Eugene. 1959–1960. The use of extended family groups in achievement of social goals. *Social Problems* 7:177–187.

———. 1960a. Geographic mobility and extended family cohesion. *American Sociological Review* 25: 385–94.

———. 1960b. Occupational mobility and extended family cohesion. *American Sociological Review* 25: 9–21.

Litwak, Eugene, and Ivan Szelenyi. 1969. Primary group structures and their functions. *American Sociological Review* 34: 465–481.

Lloyd, P. 1966. Agnatic and cognatic descent among the Yoruba. *Man* 1: 484–500.

———. 1968. Divorce among the Yoruba. *American Anthropologist* 70: 67–81.

———. 1969. *Africa in social change,* Penguin African Library.

———. 1979. *Slums of hope? Shanty towns of the third world.* Middlesex: Penguin.

Lobodzinska, B. 1975. Love as a factor in marital decision in contemporary Poland. *Journal of Comparative Family Studies* 6: 56–73.

———. 1979. Love as a factor in marital decision in contemporary Poland. In *Cross-cultural perspectives of mate-selection and marriage,* ed. G. Kurian. Westport, CT: Greenwood.

Locksley, A. 1980. On the effects of wives' employment on marital adjustment and companionship. *Journal of Marriage and the Family* 42: 337–346.

Lofquist, L. H., and R. V. Dawis. 1969. *Adjustment to work: A psychological view of men's problems in a work-oriented society.* New York: Appleton-Century-Crofts.

Longino, C., and C. Kart. 1982. Explicating activity theory: A formal replication. *Journal of Gerontology* 37: 713–722.

Lovenduski, J., and J. Hills. 1981. *The politics of the second electorate.* London: Routledge and Kegan Paul.

Lowrey, L. 1986. Cited by Dennis Foreese. Inequalities of gender and age. In *Sociology,* ed. K. Ishwaran. Toronto: Addison-Wesley.

Lozios, P. 1978. Violence and the family: Some Mediterranean examples. In *Violence and the family,* ed. J. P. Martin. Chichester: Wiley.

Lupri, Eugen. 1965. Industrialisierung und Strukturhandlungen in der Familie: Ein interkultureller Vergleich. *European Journal of Sociology* 5: 57–76.

———. 1969. Contemporary authority patterns in the West German family: Study in cross-national validation. *Journal of Marriage and the Family* 31: 134–144.

———. 1976. Gesellschaftliche Differenzierung und familiale Autorität. In *Soziologie der Familie,* 2d ed., ed. Eugen Lupri and Günther Lüschen. Cologne: Westdeutscher Verlag.

Lupri, Eugen, and Donald L. Mills. 1987. The household division of labour in young dual-earner couples: The case of Canada. *International Review of Sociology* (New Series) 2: 33–54.

Lupri, Eugen, and James Frideres. 1981. The quality of marriage and the passage of time: Marital satisfaction over the family life cycle. *Canadian Journal of Sociology* 6: 283–305.

Luxton, Meg. 1980. *More than a labour of love.* Toronto: The Women's Press.

Lyon, Nancy. 1974. A report on children's toys and socialization to sex roles. In *Sexism and youth,* ed. Diane Gersoni-Stavn. New York: Bowker. Reprinted from *Ms.* 1 (December 1972): 6, 57.

Maccoby, Eleanor E. 1980. *Social development: Psychological growth and the parent-child relationship.* New York: Harcourt Brace Jovanovich.

Maccoby, Eleanor E., and Carol Nagy Jacklin. 1974. *The psychology of sex differences.* Stanford: Stanford University Press.

MacDonald, Gary W. 1980. Family power: The assessment of a decade of theory and research. *Journal of Marriage and the Family* 42: 111–124.

Mace, D., and V. Mace. 1959. *Marriage: East and West.* Garden City, NY: Doubleday.

———. 1963. *The Soviet family.* Garden City, NY: Doubleday.

MacKinnon, C. 1982. Feminism, marxism, method, and the state: An agenda for theory. *Signs* 7: 515–544.

Mackintosh, Maureen. 1979. Domestic labour and the household. In *Fit work for women*, ed. Sandra Burman. London: Croom Helm.

Macleod, Linda. 1980. *Wife battering in Canada: The vicious circle*. Ottawa: Minister of Supply and Services, Canada.

———. 1987. *Battered but not beaten*. Ottawa: Canadian Advisory Council on the Status of Women.

Maine, H. J. S. *Ancient Law*. New York: Dutton, not dated.

Makabe, Tomako. 1980. Provincial variations in divorce rates: A Canadian case. *Journal of Marriage and the Family* 42: 171–183.

Makepeace, James M. 1981. Courtship violence among college students. *Family Relations* (January).

Malinowski, B. 1927. *Sex and repression in savage society*. New York: Meridian.

Mao, Zedung. *Selected works*, vol. 1, London, 1954.

Marat, Elizabeth, and Barbara Finaly. 1984. The distribution of household labor among women in dual-earner families. *Journal of Marriage and the Family* 46: 357–364.

Marcus, G. 1980. Law in the development of dynastic families among American business elites: The domestication of capital capitalization of the family. *Law and Society Review* 14: 859–903.

Marrou, H. 1956. *The history of education in antiquity*. New York: Sheed and Ward.

Marsh, J. H., ed. 1985. *The Canadian encyclopedia*, 3 vols. Edmonton: Hurtig.

Marshall, Barbara. 1988. Feminist theory and critical theory. *Canadian Review of Sociology and Anthropology* 25: 208–230.

Marshall, D. 1972. Too much in Mangaia. In *Change: Readings in society and human behavior*. Del Mar, CA: CRM Books.

Martin, Del. 1976. *Battered wives*. New York: Pocket Books.

Martin, M. Kay, and Barbara Voorhies. 1975. *Female of the species*. New York: Columbia University Press.

Mason, Karen O., and Yu-Hsia Lu. 1988. Attitudes toward women's familial roles: Changes in the United States. *Gender and Society* 2: 39–57.

Masters, W., and V. Johnson. 1970. *Human sexual inadequacy*. Boston: Little, Brown.

Mattessich, Paul, and Reuben Hill. 1987. Life cycle and family development. In *Handbook of marriage and the family*, ed. Marvin Sussman and Suzanne Steinmetz. New York: Plenum.

Matthiasson, J. 1980. The Inuit family: Past, present and future. In *Canadian families: Ethnic varieties*, ed. K. Ishwaran. Toronto: McGraw-Hill Ryerson.

Maykovikh, Minako. 1976. Attitudes versus behavior in extra-marital sexual relations. *Journal of Marriage and the Family*. 38: 693–699.

———. 1980. Japanese Canadians. In *Canadian families: Ethnic varieties*, ed. K. Ishwaran. Toronto: McGraw-Hill Ryerson.

McBroom, William H. 1987. Longitudinal change in sex role orientations: Differences between men and women. *Sex Roles* 16: 439–452.

McCall, Michal M. Courtship as a social exchange. In *Kinship and family organization*, ed. Bernard Farber. Wiley.

McClelland, David C. 1965. Wanted: A new self-image for women. In *The woman in America*, ed. Robert Jay Lifton. Boston: Beacon Press.

McIntosh, Mary. 1979. The welfare state and the needs of the dependent family. In *Fit work for women*, ed. Sandra Burman. London: Croom Helm.

McKie, D. C., et al. 1983. *Divorce: Law and family in Canada*. Ottawa: Statistics Canada.

McLain, Raymond, and Andrew Weigert. 1979. Toward a phenomenological sociology of family. In *Contemporary theories about the family*, vol. 2, ed. W.R. Burr et al. Glencoe, IL: Free Press.

McPherson, B.D. 1983. *Aging as a social process*. Toronto: Butterworths.

McRoberts, Hugh. 1974. Follow-up of Grade 12 Students from the Porter-Blishen Study of Educational Aspirations. Council of Ontario Universities, June 2.

Mead, Margaret. 1928. *Coming of age in Samoa*. New York: Morrow.

———. 1935. *Sex and temperament in three primitive societies*. New York: Morrow.

Meissner, Martin. 1985. The domestic economy-half of Canada's work: Now you see it, now you don't. In *Women's worlds: From the new scholarship*, ed. M. Safiret et al. New York: Praeger.

Meissner, Martin, et al. 1975. No exit for wives: Sexual division of labour and the cumulation of household demands. *Canadian Review of Sociology and Anthropology* 12: 424–439.

Melville, Keith. 1983. *Marriage and family today*, 3d ed. New York: Random House.

Messinger, L. 1984. *Remarriage, a family affair*. New York, Plenum.

Metcalf, William. 1984. A classification of alternative lifestyle groups. *Australian and New Zealand Journal of Sociology* 20: 66–77.

Meyers, Laura. 1983. Battered wives, dead husbands. In *Family in transition*, ed. Arlene S. Skolick and Jerome H. Skolnick. Toronto: Little, Brown.

Michel, A. 1967. Comparative data concerning the interaction in French and American families. *Journal of Marriage and the Family* 29: 227–244.

Michelson, William. 1985. From sun to sun: Daily obligations and community structure in the lives of employed women and their families. New Jersey: Rowman and Allanheld.

Miles, Angela. 1985. Economism and feminism: Hidden in the household. A comment on the domestic labour debate. In *Feminist marxism or marxist feminism*, ed. Pat Armstrong et al. Toronto: Garamond.

Miller, Joanne, and Howard H. Garrison. 1982. Sex Roles: The division of labor at home and in the workplace. *Annual Review of Sociology* 8: 237–262.

Miller, S. M. 1971. The making of a confused middle-aged husband. *Social Policy* 2: 33–39.

Mindel, Charles H., and R. Habenstein. 1976. *Ethnic families in America: Patterns and variations*. New York: Elsvier.

Mishler, E. G., and N. E. Waxler. 1968. *Interaction in families: An experimental study of family processes and schizophrenia.* New York: Wiley.

Model, Suzanne. 1981. Housework by husbands: Determinants and implications. *Journal of Family Issues* 2: 225–237.

Monahan, Thomas P. 1970. Are interracial marriages really less stable? *Social Forces* 48: 461–473.

———. 1971. Interracial marriage and divorce in Kansas and the question of instability of mixed marriages. *Journal of Comparative Family Studies* 2: 107–120.

———. 1973. Marriages Across racial lines in Indiana. *Journal of Marriage and the Family* 35: 632–640.

———. 1976. An overview of statistics on interracial marriage in the United States. *Journal of Marriage and the Family* 39: 223–231.

Morgan, D. H. J. 1985. *The family, politics and social theory.* London: Routledge and Kegan Paul.

Morgan, S. P., R. R. Rindfuss. 1985. Marital disruption: Structural and temporal dimensions. *American Journal of Sociology* 90: 1055–1077.

Morgenthaler, E. 1979. Sweden offers fathers paid paternity leaves; about 10% take them. *The Wall Street Journal* (January 29): 23.

Morosinsi, Giuseppe. 1962. Osservazioni su alcuni aspetti sociologici dell' immigrazione in una area metropolitana. In Centro di ricerche industriali e sociali di torino, *Immigrazione e industria,* 295–304. Milano: Edizioni di comunita.

Moss, Howard A. 1967. Sex, age, and state as determinants of mother-infant interaction. *Merrill-Palmer Quarterly* 13: 19–36.

Mowrer, E. R. 1927. *Family disorganization.* Chicago: University of Chicago Press.

———. 1932. *The family.* Chicago: University of Chicago Press.

Mowrer, E. R., and Harriet Mowrer. 1951. The social psychology of marriage. *American Sociological Review* 16: 27–36.

Moynihan, D. 1965. *The Negro family: The case for national action.* Washington, DC: Government Printing Office.

Muncy, R. 1974. *Sex and marriage in utopian communities.* Baltimore: Penguin.

Munro, B., and G. Adams. 1978. Love American style: A test of role structure theory on changes in attitudes toward love. *Human Relations* 31: 215–228.

Murdock, G. 1934. *Our primitive contemporaries.* New York: Macmillan.

———. 1937. Comparative data on the division of labour by sex. *Social Forces* 15: 551–553.

———. 1949. *Social structure.* New York: Macmillan.

———. 1957. World ethnographic sample. *American Anthropologist* 59: 664–687.

Murphy, D. C., and L. A. Mendelson. 1973. Communication and adjustment in marriage: Investigating the relationship. *Family Process* 12: 317–326.

Murstein, Bernard I. 1970. Stimulus-value-role: A theory of marital choice. *Journal of Marriage and the family* 32: 465–481.

———. 1972. A thematic test and the Rorhschach in predicting marital choice. *Journal of Personality Assessment* 36: 213–217.

———. 1973. A theory of marital choice applied to interracial marriage. In *Interracial Marriage,* ed. Irving Stuart and Lawrence Abt. New York: Grossman.

———. 1974a. Clarification of obfuscation on conjugation: A reply to criticism of the SVR theory of marital choice. *Journal of Marriage and the Family* 36: 231–234.

———. 1974b. *Love, sex and marriage: Through the ages.* New York: Springer.

———. 1976. *Who will marry whom?: Theories and research in marital choice.* Springer.

———. 1980. Mate selection in the 1970s. *Journal of Marriage and the Family* 42: 772–792.

Muus, Rolf E. 1968. *Theories of adolescence,* 2d ed. New York: Random House.

Myrdal, Gunnar. 1944. *An American dilemma.* New York: Harper.

Nag, M. 1972. Sex, culture, and human fertility: India and the United States. *Current Anthropology* 13: 231–237.

National Council of Welfare. 1975. *Poor kids.* Ottawa: Supply and Services Canada.

———. 1988a. *Poverty lines.* Ottawa: Supply and Services Canada.

———. 1988b. *Poverty profile 1988.* Ottawa: Supply and Services Canada.

Navran, L. 1967. Communication and adjustment in marriage. *Family Process* 6: 172–184.

Nett, E. 1982. A critical comment on Eichler's "The inadequacy of the monolithic model of the family." *Canadian Journal of Sociology* 7: 309–315.

———. 1983. The family. In *Essentials of sociology,* 2d ed., ed. R. Hagedorn. Toronto: Holt, Rinehart and Winston.

———. 1988. *Canadian families: Past and present.* Toronto: Butterworths.

Nettler, Gwynn. 1982. *Killing one another.* Cincinnati: Anderson.

Neugarten, B. L., et al. 1965. Age norms, age constraints, and adult socialization. *American Journal of Sociology* 70: 710–717.

Neulinger, John. 1981. *To leisure: An introduction.* Boston: Allyn and Bacon.

Newcomb, P. M., and G. Svehla. 1937. Intra-family relationships in attitude. *Sociometry* 1: 180–205.

Newcomb, P. M., and M. D. Bentler. 1978. Longitudinal study of marital success and failure. *Journal of Consulting and Clinical Psychology* 46: 1053–1070.

Newcomb, P. M., and Peter Bentler. 1980. Cohabitation before marriage. *Alternative Lifestyles* 3: 65–85.

Newman, Graeme. 1979. *Understanding violence.* New York: Lippincott.

Niemela, P., et al. 1985. A new approach to remarriage. In *The aftermath of divorce—Coping with family change,* ed L. Cseh-Szombathy et al. Budapest: Akademiai.

Niemi, R. G. 1974. *How family members perceive each other: Political and social attitudes in two generations.* New Haven: Yale University.

Nimkoff, M. 1965. *Comparative family systems*. Boston: Houghton Mifflin.

Nkwi, P. 1987. The changing role of women and their contributions to the domestic economy in Cameroon. In *Transformations of African marriage,* ed. D. Parkin and D. Nyamwaya. Manchester: Manchester University Press.

Nock, Steven. 1979. The family life cycle: Empirical or conceptual tool? *Journal of Marriage and the Family* 41: 15–26.

Noller, P. 1984. *Nonverbal communication and marital interaction*. New York: Pergamon Press.

Norton, Arthur J., and Jeanne E. Moorman. 1987. Current trends in marriage and divorce among American women. *Journal of Marriage and the Family* 49: 3–14.

Norton, Arthur J., and Paul C. Glick. 1986. One Parent Families: A Social and Economic Profile. *Family Relations* 35: 9–17.

Norton, R. 1983. Measuring marital quality: A critical look at the dependent variable. *Journal of Marriage and the Family* 45: 141–151.

Nuss, S. 1982. Women in political life: Global trends. *International Journal of Sociology of the Family* 12: 1–10.

Nye, F. Ivan. 1976. Family roles in comparative perspective. In *Role structure and analysis of the family,* ed. F. I. Nye et al. Beverly Hills: Sage.

———. 1978. Is choice and exchange theory the key? *Journal of Marriage and the Family* 40: 219–233.

———. 1979. Choice, exchange, and the family. In *Contemporary theories about the family,* vol. 2, ed. W.R. Burr et al. Glencoe, IL: Free Press.

———. 1980. Family mini theories as special instances of choice and exchange theory. *Journal of Marriage and the Family* 42: 479–489.

Nye, F. Ivan, and A. E. Bayer. 1963. Some recent trends in family research. *Social Forces* 41: 290–301.

Nye, F. Ivan, and Felix Berardo. 1973. *The family its structure and interaction*. New York: Macmillan.

O'Brien, John. 1971. Violence in divorce prone families. *Journal of Marriage and the Family* 33: 692–698.

O'Connell, Martin, and Carolyn C. Rogers. 1984. Out-of-wedlock births, premarital pregnancies, and their effect on family formation and dissolution. *Family Planning Perspectives* 16: 157–162.

O'Neill, N., & George O'Neill. 1972. *Open marriage*. New York: M. Evans.

Oakley, Ann. 1974. *Housewife*. London: Allen Lane.

OECD. 1980. *Women and employment: Policies for equal opportunities*. Paris: Organisation for Economic Co-operation and Development.

Ogburn, W. 1933. The family and its functions. *Recent social trends*. New York: McGraw-Hill.

Ogburn, W., and M. Nimkoff. 1955. *Technology and the changing family*. Boston: Houghton Mifflin.

Olson, Jon L. 1977. Women and social change in a Mexican town. *Journal of Anthropological Research* 33: 73–88.

Oppenheimer, Valerie Kincade. 1982. *Work and the family: A study in social demography*. New York: Academic.

Orthner, Dennis K. 1975a. Leisure activity patterns and marital satisfaction over the marital career. *Journal of Marriage and the Family* 37: 91–102.

———. 1975b. Leisure styles and family styles: The need for integration. In *Leisure today: Selected readings,* American Association for Leisure and Recreation.

———. 1976. Patterns of leisure and marital interaction. *Journal of Leisure Research* 8: 98–111.

Osberg, Lars. 1981. *Economic inequality in Canada*. Toronto: Butterworths.

Osipow, S. H. 1983. *Theories of career development*, 3d ed. Englewood Cliffs, NJ: Prentice-Hall.

Osmond, Marie Withers. 1987. Radical-critical theories. In *Handbook of Marriage and the Family,* ed. Marvin Sussman and Suzanne Steinmetz. New York: Plenum.

Osterreich, Helgi. Geographical mobility and kinship: A Canadian example. In *The Canadian family,* ed. K. Ishwaran. Toronto: Holt, Rinehart and Winston.

Ovid. 1957. *The art of love,* trans. Rolfe Humphries. Bloomington: Indiana University Press.

Oxford Analytica. 1986. *America in perspective*. Boston: Houghton Mifflin.

Park, R. E., et. al. 1925. *The city*. Chicago: University of Chicago Press.

Parke, Ross D., and Douglas B. Sawin. 1976. The father's role in infancy: A re-evaluation. *Family Coordinator* 25: 365–371.

Parker, Stanley R. 1976. The sociology of leisure. Allen and Unwin.

Parkin, D., and D. Nyamwaya, eds. 1987. *Transformations of African marriage*. Manchester: Manchester University Press.

Parsons, Talcott. 1942. Age and sex in the social structure of the USA. *American Sociological Review* 7: 604–616.

———. 1943. The kinship system of the contemporary United States. *American Anthropologist* 45: 22–38.

———. 1949a. *Essays in sociological theory: Pure and applied*. Glencoe, IL: Free Press.

———. 1949b. The social structure of the family. In *The family. Its function and destiny,* ed. Ruth Anshen. New York: Harper.

———. 1951. *The social system*. Beverly Hills: Benziger Bruce and Glencoe.

———. 1954. The incest taboo in relation to social structure and the socialization of the child. *British Journal of Sociology* 5: 101–117.

———. 1955. The American family. In *Family, socialization and interaction process,* ed. Talcott Parsons and R. Bales. Glencoe, IL: Free Press.

———. 1964. *The social system*. New York: Free Press.

———. 1971. The normal American family. *Readings on the sociology of the family,* ed. Bert Adams and Thomas Weirath. Chicago: Markham.

Parsons, Talcott, and Robert F. Bales. 1955. *Family, socialization and interaction process*. New York: Free Press.

Patton, D., and E. Waring. 1985. Sex and marital intimacy. *Journal of Sex and Marital Therapy* 11: 176–184.

Paydarfar, Ali A. 1975. The modernization process and household size: A provincial comparison for Iran. *Journal of Marriage and the Family* 37: 446–452.

Pearce, W., and V. Cronen. 1980. *Communication, action and meaning.* Praeger.

Pederson, F. 1976. Does research on children reared in father-absent families yield information on father influences? *Family Coordinator* 25: 459–464.

Pedrick-Cornell, Claire, and Richard J. Gelles. 1983. Elder abuse: The status of current knowledge. In *Marriage and family,* ed. Ollie Pocs and Robert Walsh. Guilford, CT: Dushkin.

Peres, Yochanan, and Hamma Meivar. 1986. Self-presentation during courtship: A content analysis of classified advertisements in Israel. *Journal of Comparative Family Studies* 17: 19–32.

Peres, Yochanan, Liora Meisels, and Ruth Frank. 1980. Commercial matchmaking in modern Israel: A case of dubious rationality. *Journal of Comparative Family Studies* 11: 475–484.

Peristiany, J., ed. 1966. *Honour and shame,* Chicago: University of Chicago Press.

Person, E. 1980. Sexuality as the mainstay of identity: Psychoanalytic perspectives. *Signs* 5: 605–630.

Peter, Karl A. 1983. Religion, community relations and self-identity among Hutterites. In *The Canadian family,* ed. K. Ishwaran. Toronto: Holt, Rinehart and Winston.

Peters, Evelyn. 1984. *Native households in Winnipeg: Strategies of co-residence and financial support.* Winnipeg: University of Winnipeg. Institute of Urban Studies.

Peters, J. R. 1985. Adolescents as socialization agents to parents. *Adolescence* 20: 921–933.

Peters, John F. 1976. A comparison of mate selection and marriage in the first and second marriage in a selective sample of the remarried divorced. *Journal of Comparative Family Studies* 7: 483–490.

———. 1987. Changing perspectives on divorce. *Family matters,* 141–162. Toronto: Methuen.

———. 1988. Divorce and remarriage. *Marriage and family in Canada today,* ed. G. N. Ramu. Toronto: Prentice-Hall.

Peters, John F., et al. 1978. High school dating: Implications for equality. *International Journal of Comparative Sociology* 21, No. 3.

Peterson, E., and E. Nett. 1982. Sexuality in the classrooms of teachers with various sex role orientations. *Theory and Research in Social Education* 10: 29–40.

Petherick, T. and R. M. A. Sametz. 1984. Household structure and the use of time. Paper presented at the Fourth Canadian Congress on Leisure Research, Trois-Rivieres, May.

Petras, I. 1973. *Sexuality in society.* Boston: Allyn and Bacon.

Philbert, Michael, A. J. 1962. The emergence of social gerontology. *Journal of Social Issues* 21: 5.

Piddington, Ralph. 1976. A study of French Canadian kinship. In *The Canadian family,* ed. K. Ishwaran. Toronto: Holt, Rinehart and Winston.

Pike, Robert. 1975. Legal access and the incidence of divorce in Canada: A socio-historical analysis. *Canadian Review of Sociology and Anthropology* 12, No. 2.

Pines, Ayala, and Elliot Aronson. 1981. Polyfidelity, An alternative lifestyle without jealousy? *Alternative Lifestyles* 4: 373–392.

Piotrkowski, Chaya S. 1979. *Work and the family system.* New York: Free Press.

Piotrkowski, Chaya S., and Rena L. Repetti. 1984. Dual-earner families. In *Women and the family: Two decades of change,* ed. Beth B. Hess and Marvin B. Sussman. *Marriage and Family Review* 7, Nos. 3/4. New York: Haworth.

Piven, Frances Fox, and Richard Cloward. 1971. *Regulating the poor: The functions of public welfare.* New York: Vintage.

Pleck, J. H. 1979. Men's family work: Three perspectives and some new data. *Family Coordinator* 28: 481–488.

Pogrebin, Letty Cottin. 1974. Toys for free children. In *Sexism and youth,* ed. Diane Gersoni-Stavn. New York: Bowker. Reprinted from *Ms.* 11, No. 6 (December 1973).

Pollack, J. *Connecticut Mutual Life Report on American Values in the 80s.* 1981. New York: Research and Forecasts, Inc.

Porter, John. 1957. The economic elite and social structure in Canada. *Canadian Journal of Economics and Political Science,* 23.

Powell, Brian, and Jerry Jacobs. 1984. Gender differences in the evaluation of prestige. *Sociological Quarterly* 25: 173–90.

Prakasa, V., and Rao, V. 1979. Arranged marriages: An assessment of the attitudes of the college students in India. In *Cross-cultural perspectives of mate-selection and marriage,* ed. G. Kurian. Westport, CT: Greenwood.

Pratt, William F., et al. 1984. Understanding U.S. fertility: Findings from the national survey of family growth, cycle III. *Population Bulletin* 39, no. 5: 1–42.

Price, R., and S. Vandenberg. 1980. Spouse similarity in American and Swedish couples. *Behavior Genetics* 10: 59–71.

Price, R., et al. 1981. Model of spouse influence and their application to smoking behavior. *Social Biology* 28: 14–29.

Prince, P. 1965. The Tibetan family system. In *Comparative family systems,* ed. M. Nimkoff. Boston: Houghton Mifflin.

Queen, S., and Habenstein, R. 1967. *The family in various cultures.* Philadelphia: J. B. Lippincott Company.

Rabin, A. I. 1982. *Twenty years later: Kibbutz children grown up.* New York: Springer.

Radcliffe-Brown, A., and D. Forde, eds. 1950. *African systems of kinship and marriage.* London: Oxford University Press.

Radecki, Henry, and B. Haydenkorn. 1976. A member of a distinguished family: Polish. Toronto: McClelland & Stewart.

Radhill, Samuel X. 1974. A history of child abuse and infanticide. In *Violence in the family,* ed. Suzanne K. Steinmetz and Murray A. Straus. New York: Dodd, Mead.

Rallings, E. M., F. I. Nye. 1979. Wife-Mother employment, family, and society. In *Contemporary theories about the family,* vol. 1, ed. W.R. Burr et al. Glencoe, IL: Free Press.

Ramu, G. N. 1973. Family structure and entrepreneurship: An Indian case. *Journal of Comparative Family Studies* 4: 239–256.

———. 1977. *Family and caste in urban India.* Delhi: Vikas.

———. 1983. Courtship and marriage. In *The Canadian family,* ed. K. Ishwaran. Toronto: Holt, Rinehart and Winston.

———. 1988. Marital roles and power: Perceptions and reality in the urban setting. *Journal of Comparative Family Studies* 19: 207–227.

Rapoport, Rhona, and Robert N. Rapoport. 1978. Leisure and the family life cycle. London: Routledge and Kegan Paul.

Rapoport, Rhona, Robert N. Rapoport, and Ziona Strelitz. 1977. Fathers, mothers and others. London: Routledge and Kegan Paul.

Rapp, R. 1978. Family and class in contemporary America. *Science and Society* 42: 278–300.

———. 1979. Anthropology. *Signs* 4: 497–513.

Raschke, H. J. 1977. The role of social participation in post separation and post divorce adjustment. *Journal of Divorce* 1: 129–140.

Rees, B. J., and M. F. Collins. 1979. The family and sport: A review. In *Leisure and family diversity,* ed. Ziona Strelitz. UK: Leisure Studies Association.

Reiss, Ira L. 1960. Toward a sociology of the heterosexual love relationship. *Marriage and Family Living* 22: 139–145.

———. 1965. The universality of the family: A conceptual analysis. *Journal of Marriage and Family Living* 2: 443–453.

———. 1976. *Family systems in America.* 2d ed. New York: Dryden Press.

———. 1980. *Family systems in America,* 3d ed. New York: Holt, Rinehart, and Winston.

———. 1981. Some observations on ideology and sexuality in America. *Journal of Marriage and the Family* 43: 271–283.

Reiss, Paul J. 1959. *The extended kinship system of the urban middle class.* Harvard University. Unpublished Dissertation.

———. 1962. The extended kinship system: Correlates of attitudes on frequency of interaction. *Marriage and Family Living* 24: 333–339.

Rheingold, Harriet L., and Kaye V. Cook. 1975. The contents of boys' and girls' rooms as an index of parents' behaviour. *Child Development* 46: 459–63.

Rheinstein, Max. 1972. *Marriage stability, divorce and the law.* Chicago: University of Chicago.

Rhyne, Darla. 1984. *Marital satisfaction in Canada: A descriptive overview.* Toronto: Institute for Social Research, York University.

Rice, F. P. 1987. *The adolescent: Development, relationships, and culture,* 5th ed. Boston: Allyn and Bacon.

Richmond, Marie LaLiberte. 1976. Beyond resource theory: Another look at factors enabling women to affect family interaction. *Journal of Marriage and the Family* 38: 257–266.

Richmond-Abbott, Marie. 1983. *Masculine and feminine: Sex roles over the life cycle.* Reading, MA: Addison-Wesley.

Riehl, Wilhelm H. 1855. *Die Familie.* Stuttgart: Cottascher.

Rindfuss, Ronald R., A. Parnell, and Charles Hirschman. 1983. The timing of entry into motherhood in Asia: A comparative perspective. *Population Studies* 37: 253–272.

Riskin, J., and E. E. Faunce. 1972. An evaluative review of family interaction research. *Family Process* 11: 365–455.

Ritzer, George. 1988. *Sociological theory,* 2d ed. New York: Knopf.

Roberts, Kenneth. 1981. *Leisure,* 2d ed. London: Longman.

Robinson, Clyde C., and James T. Morris. 1986. The gender-stereotyped nature of Christmas toys received by 36–, 48–, and 60–month-old children: A comparison between nonrequested vs requested toys. *Sex Roles* 15: 21–32.

Robinson, John P., Philip E. Converse, and Alexander Szalai. 1972. Everyday life in twelve countries. In *The use of time,* ed. Alexander Szalai. The Hague: Mouton.

Rockwell, R. C. 1976. Historical trends and variations in educational homogamy. *Journal of Marriage and the Family* 36: 226–231.

Rodgers, R. H. 1973. *Family interaction and transaction.* Englewood Cliffs, NJ: Prentice-Hall.

Rodgers, R. H., and G. Witney. 1981. The family cycle in twentieth century Canada. *Journal of Marriage and the Family.* 43: 727–740.

Rodman, Hyman. 1967a. A comparison of power structure and marital satisfaction in urban Greek and French families. *Journal of Marriage and the Family* 29: 345–352.

———. 1967b. Marital power in France, Greece, Yugoslavia, and the United States. *Journal of Marriage and the Family* 29: 320–324.

———. 1970. The study of family power structure: A review 1960–1969. *Journal of Marriage and the Family* 32: 539–552.

———. 1972. Marital power and the theory of resources in cultural context. In *Comparative perspectives on marriage and the family,* ed. Eugen Lupri and Gunter Luschen. Special issue of the *Journal of Comparative Family Studies* 3 (Spring) 50–69.

Rogler, Lloyd H., and Mary E. Procidano. 1986. The effect of social networks on marital roles: A test of the Bott Hypothesis in an intergenerational context. *Journal of Marriage and the Family* 48: 693–701.

Rollins, B. and H. Feldman. 1970. Marital satisfaction over the family life cycle. *Journal of Marriage and the Family* 32: 20–27.

Roopnarine, Jaipaul L. 1986. Mothers' and fathers' behaviors toward the toy play of their infant sons and daughters. *Sex Roles* 14: 59–68.

Rosaldo, Michelle Zimbalist, and Louise Lamphere. 1974. *Woman, culture, and society.* Stanford: Stanford University Press.

Rosenblatt, Ellen, and Cyril Greenland. 1974. Early identification of child abuse. Paper presented to the Annual Meeting of the Canadian Public Health Association.

Rosenkrantz, Paul, et al. 1968. Sex-Role stereotypes and self-concepts in college students. *Journal of Consulting and Clinical Psychology* 32: 287–95.

Rosenthal, Erich. 1970. Divorce and religious intermarriage: The effect of previous marital status upon subsequent marital behaviour. *Journal of Marriage and The Family.* 33: 435–440.

Roser, Colin, and Christopher Harris. 1965. *The Family and Social Change.* London: Routledge and Kegan Paul.

Rosow, Irving. 1957. Issues in the concept of need-complementarity. *Sociometry* 20: 216–233.

Ross, Catherine E. 1986–87. The division of labor at home. *Social Forces* 65: 816–833.

Roszak, Theodore. 1969. *The making of a counter culture.* Garden City: Doubleday.

Rothbart, Mary K., and Myron Rothbart. 1976. Birth order, sex of child and maternal help giving. *Sex Roles* 2: 39–46.

Roussel, Louis and Patrick Festy. 1979. Recent trends in attitudes and behaviour affecting the family. *Council of Europe Population Studies,* no. 4.

Rowntree, B.S. 1941. *Poverty and progress: A second social survey of York.* London: Longmans.

Roy, Prodipto. 1961. Maternal employment and adolescent roles: Rural-urban differences. *Marriage and Family Living* 23: 340–349.

Ruben, D. 1969. *Everything you always wanted to know about sex.* New York: McKay.

Rubin, G. 1975. The traffic in women. In *Toward an anthropology of women,* ed. R. Reiter. New York: Monthly Review Press.

Rubin, Lillian Breslow. 1976. *Worlds of pain: Life in the working-class family.* New York: Basic.

Rubin, Z. 1973. *Liking and loving: An invitation to social psychology.* New York: Holt, Rinehart and Winston.

———. 1976. The measurement of romantic love. *Journal of Personality and Social Psychology* 16: 265–273.

Rubin, Z., and G. Levinger. 1974. Theory and data badly mated: A critique of Murstein's SVR and Lewis' PDF models of mate selection. *Journal of Marriage and the Family,* 36: 226–231.

Rubinson, R. 1986. Class formation, politics, and institutions: Schooling in the United States. *American Journal of Sociology* 92: 519–548.

Ruble, Thomas L. 1983. Sex stereotypes: Issues of change in the 1970's. *Sex Roles* 9: 397–402.

Russell, C.S. 1974. Transition to parenthood: problems and gratifications. *Journal of Marriage and the Family* 36: 294–302.

Russell, Graeme, and Jacqui Smith. 1979. "Girls can be doctors ... can't they?": Sex differences in career aspirations. *Australian Journal of Social Issues* 14: 91–102.

———. 1983. *The changing role of fathers.* Milton Keynes: Open University Press.

Ryan, William. 1971. *Blaming the victim.* New York: Random House.

Safilios-Rothschild, C. 1972. Answer to Stephen J. Bahr's comment on "The study of family power structure: A review 1960–1969." *Journal of Marriage and the Family* 34: 245–246.

———. 1976. A macro- and micro-examination of family power and love: An exchange model. *Journal of Marriage and the Family* 38: 355–362.

———. 1977. *Love, sex, and sex roles.* Englewood Cliffs, N.J.: Prentice-Hall.

Sanday, Peggy R. 1973. Toward a theory of the status of women. *American Anthropologist* 75: 1682–1700.

———. 1974. Female status in the public domain. In *Woman, culture, and society,* ed. Michelle Zimbalist Rosaldo and Louise Lamphere. Stanford: Stanford University Press.

Sapiro, Virgina. 1986. The women's movement, politics and policy in the Reagan era. In *The New Women's Movement,* ed. D. Dahlerup. Beverly Hills: Sage.

Scanzoni, John. 1970. *Opportunity and the family.* New York: Free Press.

———. 1972. *Sexual bargaining.* Englewood Cliffs: Prentice-Hall.

———. 1978. Sex roles, women's work and marital conflict. Lexington, MA: D.C. Heath.

———. 1979a. A historical perspective on husband-wife bargaining power and marital dissolution. In *Divorce and separation,* ed. George Levinger and Oliver C. Moles. New York: Basic Books.

———. 1979b. Social processes and power in families. In *Contemporary theories about the family,* vol. 1, ed. W. R. Burr et al. Glencoe, IL: Free Press.

———. 1987. Families in the 1980s. *Journal of Family Issues* 8: 394–421.

Scanzoni, John, and Greer Litton Fox. 1980. Sex roles, family and society: The seventies and beyond. *Journal of Marriage and the Family* 42: 743–56.

Scanzoni, John, and Maximiliane Szinovacz. 1980. *Family decision-making.* Beverly Hills: Sage.

Scanzoni, Letha D., and John Scanzoni. 1988. *Men, women and change: A sociology of marriage and the family.* New York: McGraw-Hill.

Schachter, J., and J. Singer. 1962. Cognitive, social, and physiological determinants of emotional state. *Psychological Review* 69: 379–399.

Scheuch, Erwin K. 1960. Family cohesion in leisure time. *Sociological Review* 8: 37-61.

Schiller, Bradley. 1976. *The economics of poverty and discrimination.* Englewood Cliffs: Prentice Hall.

Schlesinger, B. 1974. *One-parent families in Canada.* Toronto: University of Toronto Press.

———. 1975. One parent families in Great Britain. *One parent family,* 3d ed. Toronto: University of Toronto Press.

Schumacher, Edward. 1978. *The Philadelphia Inquirer* (November 20).

Schuman, Wendy. 1984. The violent American way of life. In *Marriage and the family 84/85,* ed. Ollie Pocs and Robert H. Walsh. Guilford, CT: Dusking.

Sebald, Hans. 1977. *Adolescence: A social psychological analysis,* 2d ed., New York: Prentice-Hall.

Seccombe, Karen. 1986. The effects of occupational conditions on the division of household labor: An application of Kohn's theory. *Journal of Marriage and the Family* 48: 839–848.

Segalen, M. 1983. *Love and power in the peasant family.* Chicago: University of Chicago Press.

———. 1986. *Historical anthropology of the family.* Cambridge: Cambridge University Press.

Serbin, Lisa A., et al. 1973. A comparison of teacher response to the preacademic and problem behavior of boys and girls. *Child Development* 44: 796–804.

Shamir, Boas. 1986. Unemployment and household division of labor. *Journal of Marriage and the Family* 48: 195–206.

Shamir, Boas, and Hillel Ruskin. 1983. Sex differences in recreational sport behaviour and attitudes: A study of married couples in Israel. *Leisure Studies* 2: 253–268.

Shannon, C., and W. Weaver. 1949. *The mathematical theory of communication.* Urbana: University of Illinois Press.

Shaver, P., and I. Freedman. 1976. Your pursuit of happiness. *Psychology Today.*

Shaw, Susan M. 1984. The measurement of leisure: A quality of life issue. *Society and Leisure* 7: 91–107.

Shibutani, Tamotsu, and Kian M. Kwan. 1965. *Ethnic stratification.* Macmillan.

Shlapentokh, Vladimir. 1984. *Love, marriage and friendship in the Soviet Union: Ideals and practices.* New York: Praeger.

Siegal, Larry J. 1983. *Criminology.* New York: West.

Silverman, William, and Reuben Hill. 1967. Task allocation in marriage in the United States and Belgium. *Journal of Marriage and the Family* 29:353–59.

Simmel, G. 1904. The sociology of conflict. *American Journal of Sociology* 9: 490–525.

———. 1921. Sociology of the senses: Visual interaction. In *Introduction to the science of sociology,* R. Park and E. Burgess. Chicago: University of Chicago Press.

———. 1955. *Conflict and the Webb of group affiliations.* Trans. Kurt H. Wolff and Reinhard Bendix. Chicago: The Free Press.

Sinclair, Deborah. 1985. Understanding wife assault. Toronto: Ontairio Ministry of Community and Social Services, Family Violence Program.

Sinclair, Stuart. 1978. *Urbanization and labour markets in developing countries.* New York: St. Martin's.

Singer, Benjamin D. 1986. *Advertising & society.* Don Mills, ON: Addison-Wesley.

Singer, M. 1968. The Indian joint family in modern industry. In *Structure and change in Indian society,* ed. M. Yinger and S. Cohn. Chicago: Aldine.

Skinner, D.A. 1982. The stressors and coping patterns of dual career families. In *Family stress, coping and social support,* ed. H. I. McCubbin, et al. Springfield: Charles C. Thomas.

Skipper, James K., Jr., and Gilbert Nass. 1966. Dating behaviour: A framework for analysis and illustration. *Journal of Marriage and the Family* 28: 412–420.

Skorepa, C.A., et al. 1963. A study of friendship fluctuations of college students. *Journal of Genetic Psychology* 102: 151–157.

Slater, M. 1977. *The Caribbean family: Legitimacy in Martinique.* New York: St. Martin's.

Slevin, Kathleen F., and C. Ray Wingrove. 1983. Similarities and differences among three generations of women in attitudes toward the female role in contemporary society. *Sex Roles* 9: 609–624.

Smith, Audrey D., and William J. Reid. 1986. *Role-sharing marriage.* New York: Columbia University Press.

Smith, Caroline, and Barbara Lloyd. 1978. Maternal behavior and perceived sex of infant: Revisited. *Child Development* 49: 1263–65.

Smith, Daniel S., and Michael S. Hindus. 1975. Premarital pregnancy in America: An overview and interpretation. *Journal of Interdisciplinary History* 4: 537–570.

Smith, Dorothy. 1981. Women's inequality and the family. In *Inequality,* ed. Allan Moscovitch and Glenn Drover. Toronto: University of Toronto Press.

Snow, Margaret Ellis, et al. 1983. Sex-of child differences in father-child interaction at one year of age. *Child Development* 54: 227–232.

Spanier, G. B. 1976. Measuring dyadic adjustment: New scales for assessing the quality of marriage and similar dyads. *Journal of Marriage and the Family* 38: 15–28.

Spanier, G. B., and P. C. Glick. 1980. Mate selection differentials between whites and blacks in the United States. *Social Forces* 58: 707–725.

Spencer, Herbert. 1876–1886. *Principles of sociology* New York: D. Appelton.

Spiro, M.E. 1956. *Kibbutz: Venture in utopia.* Cambridge: Harvard University Press.

Spitze, Glenna D., and Linda J. Waite. 1981. Wive's employment: The role of husband's perceived attitudes. *Journal of Marriage and the Family* 43: 117–124.

Sprey, Jetse. 1969. The family as a system in conflict. *Journal of Marriage and the Family* 31: 699–706.

———. 1979. Conflict theory and the study of marriage and the family. In *Contemporary theories about the family,* vol. 2, ed. W.R. Burr et al. Glencoe, IL: Free Press.

Stacey, Judith, and Barrie Thorne. 1985. The missing feminist revolution in sociology. *Social Problems* 32: 301–316.

Stack, Carol. 1974. *All our kin: Strategies for survival in a black community.* New York: Harper and Row.

Staines, Graham L., and Joseph H. Pleck. 1983. *The impact of work schedules on the family.* Ann Arbor: Survey Research Center. The Institute for Social Research, The University of Michigan.

Standing Committee on Social Development. 1982. *First report on family violence: Wife battering.* Toronto: Queens Park.

Statistics Canada. 1984a. *Lone parent families,* Catalogue 99–933. Ottawa: Ministry of Supply and Services.

———. 1984b. *Living alone,* Catalogue 99–934. Ottawa: Ministry of Supply and Services.

———. 1984c. *Fertility in Canada: From baby-boom to baby-bust.* Ottawa: Ministry of Supply and Services.

———. 1985. *Women in Canada.* Ottawa: Ministry of Supply and Services, Ottawa.

———. 1986. *Family characteristics,* Catalogue 71–533. Ottawa: Ministry of Supply and Services.

———. 1986. Marriages and divorces, 1985. *Vital Statistics* 11: 84–205. Ottawa: Ministry of Supply and Services.

———. 1987. *Families: Part I,* Catalogue 93–106. Ottawa: Ministry of Supply and Services.

Steady, F. 1987. Polygamy and the household economy in a fishing village in Sierra Leone. In *Transformations of African marriage,* ed. D. Parkin and D. Nyamwaya. Manchester: Manchester University Press.

Steele, Brandt, and Carl B. Pollack. 1968. A psychiatric study of parents who abuse infants and small children.

In *The battered child*, ed. Roy E. Helfer and Henry Kempe. Chicago: University of Chicago Press.

Stein, Peter J. 1984. Men in families. In *Women and the family: Two decades of change*, ed. Beth B. Hess and Marvin B. Sussman. *Marriage and Family Review* 7, Nos. 3/4. New York: Haworth.

Steinmetz, Suzanne. 1977. *The cycle of violence: Assertive, aggressive and abusive family interaction*. New York: Praeger.

———. 1981. Battered parents. In *Social problems: The contemporary debates* ed. John B. Williamson et. al. Toronto: Little, Brown.

Steinmetz, Suzanne, and Murray A. Straus. 1974. *Violence in the family*. New York: Dodd, Mead.

Stephen, T. D. 1984. A symbolic exchange framework for the development of intimate relationships. *Human Relations* 37: 393–408.

———. 1985. Fixed-sequence and circular-causal models of relationship development: Divergent views on the role of communication in intimacy. *Journal of Marriage and Family* 47: 955–963.

Stephen, T. D., and H. Markman. 1983. Assessing the development of relationships: a new measure. *Family Process* 22: 15–25.

Stephens, William N. 1963. *The family in cross-cultural perspective*. New York: Holt, Rinehart and Winston.

Sternbieb, George, and James W. Hughes. 1986. Demographics and housing in America. *Population Bulletin* 41: 1–35.

Stockard, Jean, and Miriam M. Johnson. 1980. *Sex roles: Sex inequality and sex role development*. Englewood Cliffs: Prentice-Hall.

Stoffle, Richard W. 1977. Industrial impact on family foundation in Barbados, West Indies. *Ethnology* 16: 253–267.

Straus, Murray A. 1964. Measuring families. In *Handbook of marriage and the family*, ed. Harold Christensen. Chicago: Rand McNally.

———. 1964. Power and support structure of the family in relation to socialization. *Journal of Marriage and the Family* 26: 318–326.

———. 1973. A general systems theory approach to theory of violence between family members. *Social Science Information* 12: 105–125.

———. 1977. Societal morphogenesis and intrafamily violence in cross-cultural perspective. *Annals of the New York Academy of Science* 285: 719–730.

Straus, Murray A., and Richard J. Gelles. 1986. Societal change and change in family violence from 1975 to 1985 as revealed by two national surveys. *Journal of Marriage and the Family* 48.

Straus, Murray A., et. al. 1980. *Behind closed doors: Violence in the American family*. New York: Anchor/Doubleday.

Strauss, Anselm. 1946. The ideal and the chosen mate. *American Journal of Sociology* 52: 204–210.

Streib, Gordon. 1978. An alternative family form for older persons, need and social context. *The Family Coordinator* 27: 413–420.

Streib, Gordon, and Mary Anne Hilker. The cooperative family. *Alternative Lifestyles* 3: 167–184.

Stroebe, Wolfgang, et al. 1971. Effects of physical attractiveness, attitude similarity, and sex on various aspects of interpersonal attraction. *Journal of Personality and Social Psychology* 18: 79–91.

Strohmenger, C., and Y. Lavoie. 1982. L'infecondité au Canada: Niveau et tendances. Paper presented at 50 ème Congrès de l'association Canadienne-francaise pour l'avancement des sciences.

Strong, Bryan, et al. 1983. *The marriage and family experience*. New York: West.

Stryker, Sheldon. 1968. Identity salience and role performance. *Journal of Marriage and the Family* 30: 558–564.

Stymeist, David. 1975. *Ethnic and Indian: Social relations in a Northwestern Ontario town*, Toronto: Peter Martin Associates.

Super, D. E. 1957. *The psychology of careers*. New York: Harper & Row.

Sussman, Marvin B. 1953. The help pattern in the middle class family. *American Sociological Review* 18: 22–28.

———. 1959. The isolated nuclear family: Fact or fiction. *Social Problems* 6: 333–340.

———. 1971. Themes for the 1970s. In *The Canadian family*, ed. K. Ishwaran. Toronto: Holt, Rinehart and Winston.

Sussman, Marvin B., and Lee Burchinal. 1962. Kin family network: Unheralded structure in current conceptualizations of family functioning. *Marriage and Family Living* 24: 231–240.

Sussman, Marvin B., and Suzanne Steinmetz, eds. 1987. *Handbook of marriage and the family*. New York: Plenum.

Swagar, Amy, and Lauren Fishbein. 1988. A tool for equality. *Leader in Action* Summer, 7–14.

Sweet, James A., and Larry L. Bumpass. 1984. *Living arrangements of the elderly in the United States*. Center for Demography and Ecology, University of Wisconsin, Working Paper, 84–11.

Szalai, Alexander, ed. 1972. The use of time: Daily activities of u]rban and suburban populations in twelve countries. The Hague: Mouton.

Szinovacz, Maximiliane E. 1984. Changing family roles and interactions. In *Women and the family: Two decades of change*, ed. Beth B. Hess and Marvin B. Sussman. *Marriage and Family Review* 7, Nos. 3/4. New York: Haworth.

Talmon, Yonina. 1962. Social change and family structure. *International Social Science Journal* 14: 468–487.

Tanfer, Koray, and Marjorie C. Horn. 1985. Nonmarital cohabitation among young women: Findings from a national survey. Paper presented at the annual meetings of the Population Association of America in Boston, March, 27–29.

Tavuchis, Nicholas. 1979. Ethnic perspectives. In *Courtship, marriage and the family in Canada*, ed. G. N. Ramu. Toronto: Macmillan.

Teachman, J. D., and Polonko, K. A. 1985. Timing of the transition to parenthood: A multidimensional birth-interval approach. *Journal of Marriage and the Family* 47: 867–880.

Theodorson, G. 1965. Romanticism and motivation to marry in the United States, Singapore, Burma, and India. *Social Forces* 44: 17–28.

Thibaut, J., and H. H. Kelley. 1959. *The social psychology of groups.* New York: Wiley.

Thomas, Darwin, and Jean Edmondson Wilcox. 1987. The rise of family theory. In *Handbook of Marriage and the Family,* ed. Marvin Sussman and Suzanne Steinmetz. New York: Plenum.

Thomas, W. T., and F. Znaniecki. 1918–20. *The Polish peasant in Europe and America,* 5 vols. Boston: Badger.

Thorne, Barrie, and Marilyn Yalom, eds. 1982. *Rethinking the family.* New York: Longman.

Thornton, Arland, and Deborah Freedman. 1983. The changing American family. *Population Bulletin* 38: 1–44.

Thornton, Arland, D. F. Alwin, and D. Camburn. 1983. Causes and consequences of sex-role attitude change. *American Sociological Review* 48: 211–227.

Thrasher, F. M. 1927. *The Gang.* University of Chicago Press: Chicago.

Tien, H. Yuan. 1983. China: Demographic billionaire. *Population Bulletin* 38: 1–43.

Tiffany, S. 1978. Models and the social anthropology of women: A preliminary assessment. *Man* 13: 34–51.

Tiger, Lionel, and Joseph Shepher. 1975. *Women in the kibbutz.* New York: Harcourt Brace Jovanovich.

Tilly, Louise A. 1985. Family, gender, and occupation in industrial France: Past and present. In *Gender and the life course,* ed. Alice S. Rossi. New York: Aldine.

Tilly, Louise A., and J. W. Scott. 1978. *Women, work, and family.* New York: Holt, Rinehart and Winston.

Tomeh, A. K. 1978. Sex-role orientation: An analysis of structural and attitudinal predictors. *Journal of Marriage and the Family* 50: 341–354.

Totman, Jane. 1978. *The murderess: A psychological study of criminal homicide.* San Francisco: Reed and Eterovich.

Townsend, Peter. 1957. *The family life of old people.* Glencoe, IL: Free Press.

Tracy, Dyanne M. 1987. Toys, spatial ability, and science and mathematics achievement: Are they related?. *Sex Roles* 17: 115–138.

Trost, Jan E. 1979. *Unmarried cohabitation.* Vasteras, Sweden: International Library.

———. 1981. Cohabitation in Nordic countries, from deviant phenomenon to social institution. *Alternative Lifestyles* 4: 401–427.

———. 1985. Remarriage. In *The aftermath of divorce—Coping with family change,* ed. L. Cseh-Zombathy, et al. Budapest: Akademiai.

Turner, Ralph. 1970. *Family interaction.* New York: Wiley.

U. S. Bureau of the Census. 1972. *Census of population, 1970,* PC. 2–4C. Washington D. C.: Government Printing Press.

———. 1973. *Census of population, 1970, Subject Reports, Final Reports, PC. 2–4B,* Washington, Government Printing Office.

———. 1977. Marriage, divorce, widowhood, and remarriage by family characteristics. *Current population reports,* series P-20, no. 312, August.

———. 1984. *Statistical Abstracts of the United States.* Washington: US Bureau of Census.

———. 1985a. Household and Family Characteristics: March 1984. *Current Population Reports,* series P-20, no. 398, April.

———. 1985b. Households, Families, Marital Status, and Living Arrangements: March 1985. Advance Report. *Current Population Reports,* series P-20, no. 402, October.

———. 1987. *Statistical abstract of the United States 1987, 107th Edition.* Washington, D.C.

U. S. Commission on Civil Rights. 1978. *Battered women: Issues of public policy,* Washington, D.C.: Government Printing Office.

U. S. National Center for Health Statistics. 1985. Advance report of final divorce statistics, 1983. *Monthly Vital Statistics Report,* vol. 34, no. 9, supplement, December.

———. 1986a. Advance Report of Final Marriage Statistics, 1983. *Monthly Vital Statistics Report,* vol. 35, no. 1, supplement, May.

———. 1986b. Births, Marriages, Divorces, and Deaths for February 1986. *Monthly Vital Statistics Report,* vol. 35, no. 2, May.

———. 1986c. Advance Report of Final Natality Statistics, 1984. *Monthly Vital Statistics Report,* vol. 35, no. 4, supplement, July.

Udry, J. Richard. 1963. Complementarity in mate selection: A perceptual approach. *Marriage and Family Living* 25: 281–289.

———. 1965. The influence of the ideal mate image on mate selection and mate perception. *Journal of Marriage and the Family* 27: 477–482.

———. 1971. *The social context of marriage,* 2nd ed. Toronto: Lipsett.

Ungar, Sheldon B. 1982. The sex-typing of adult and child behavior in toy sales. *Sex Roles* 8: 251–260.

United Nations. 1968. *Demographic yearbook, 1967.* 1969. *Demographic yearbook, 1968.* 1984. *Demographic yearbook, 1982.*

———. 1983. *Demographic yearbook.* New York: United Nations.

Urberg, Kathryn A. 1982. The development of the concepts of masculinity and femininity in young children. *Sex Roles* 8: 659–668.

Ussel, J. Van. 1970. Afscheid van de sexualitect. The Hague: Baaker.

———. 1975. *Intimitect deventer.* Van Loghum Slaterus.

Valentine, Charles. 1968. *Culture and poverty: Critique and counter-proposals.* Chicago: University of Chicago Press.

Vallee, F. 1971. Kinship, the family and marriage in the Central Keewatin. In *The Canadian family,* ed. K. Ishwaran. Toronto: Holt, Rinehart and Winston.

Vanderwiele, M., and J. Philbrick. 1983. Attitudes of West African students toward love and marriage. *Psychological Reports* 53: 615–621.

Vanek, Joan. 1980. Work, leisure and family roles: Farm households in the United States, 1920–1955. *Journal of Family History* 5: 422–431.

Vanier Institute of the Family. 1981. *A mosaic of family studies.* Ottawa: The Vanier Institute of the Family.

Veevers, Jean. 1979. Voluntary childlessness: A review of issues and evidence. *Marriage and Family Review* 2, No. 2.

———. 1980a. Childless by choice. Toronto: Butterworths.

———. 1980b. Voluntarily childless wives: An exploratory study. In *Family in transition*, 3d ed., ed. A. S. Skolnick and J. H. Skolnick. Boston: Little, Brown.

———. 1983. Voluntary childlessness: A critical assessment of the research. In *Contemporary families and alternative lifestyles*, ed. Eleanor Macklin and Roger Rubin. *Beverly Hills: Sage Publications.*

Verdon, M. 1980. The Quebec stem family revisited. In *Canadian families: Ethnic varieties*, ed. K. Ishwaran. Toronto: McGraw-Hill Ryerson.

Vickers, Jill. 1986. *Women's involvement in political life.* Ottawa: Canadian Research Institute for the Advancement of Women.

Visaria, Pravin, and Leela Visaria. 1981. India's population: Second and growing. *Population Bulletin* 36, no. 4: 1–56.

Vreeland, Rebeca S. 1972. Sex at Harvard. *Sexual Behaviour* (Feb) 4–10.

Waite, Linda J., and R. M. Stolzenberg. 1976. Intended childbearing and labour force participation of young women: Insights from nonrecursive models. *American Sociological Review* 41, No. 2.

Wakil, P. 1971. Marriage and family in Canada: A demographic-cultural profile. In *The Canadian family*, ed. K. Ishwaran. Toronto: Holt, Rinehart and Winston.

Walker, Kathryn E., and Margaret E. Woods. 1976. *Time use: A measure of household production of family goods and services.* Washington: American Home Economics Association.

Walker, Lenore E. 1984. The battered woman syndrome study: Psychological profiles. Paper presented to The Second National Conference for Family Violence Researchers, University of New Hampshire.

Waller, Willard. 1937. The rating and dating complex. *American Sociological Review* 2: 727–735.

———. 1951. *The family: A dynamic interpretation*, rev. Reuben Hill. New York: Holt, Rinehart and Winston.

Wallerstein, Judith S., and Berlin Joan Kelly. 1980. *Surviving the breakup: How Children and parents cope with divorce.* New York: Basic.

Walstedt, Joyce Jennings. 1978. Reform of women's roles and family structures in the recent history of China. *Journal of Marriage and the Family* 40: 380–382.

Walster, Elaine, and G. William Walster. 1978. *A new look at love.* Reading, MA: Addison-Wesley.

Walster, Elaine, G. William Walster, and Ellen Berscheid. 1978. Equity: Theory and research. Boston: Allyn and Bacon.

Wargon, S. T. 1979. *Children in Canadian families.* Cat. 98–810 Occasional. Ottawa: Statistics Canada, Minister of Supply Services.

Warner, Rebecca L., et al. 1986. Social organization, spousal resources and marital power: A cross-cultural study. *Journal of Marriage and the Family* 48: 121–128.

Wasserman, Sidney. 1967. The abused parent of the abused child. *Children* 14: 175–79.

Wearing, Betsy. 1984. *The ideology of motherhood.* Sydney: Allen and Unwin.

Weber, Max. 1947. *The theory of social and economic organization.* New York: Oxford University Press.

———. 1949. *The methodology of the social sciences.* Trans. E. A. Shils and H. A. Finch. Chicago: Free Press.

Weisner, Thomas, and Joan C. Martin. 1979. Learning environments for infants: Communes and conventionally maimed families in California. *Alternative Lifestyles* 2: 201–242.

Weiss, Robert S. 1975. *Marital separation.* New York: Basic.

———. 1979. *Going it alone: The family life and social situation of the single parent.* New York: Basic.

Weitzman, Lenore J. 1985. *The divorce revolution: The unexpected social and economic consequences for women and children in America.* New York: Free Press.

Wellman, Barry. 1977. *The community question: Intimate ties in East York.* Research Paper No. 90, Centre for Urban and Community Studies, University of Toronto.

———. 1985. Domestic work, paid work and network. In *Understanding personal relationships*, ed. Steve Duck and Daniel Perlman. London: Sage.

West, P., and L. C. Merriam. 1969. *Camping and cohesiveness: A sociological study of the effects of outdoor recreation on family solidarity.* Minnesota Forestry Research Notes, No. 201.

Westermarck, E. A. 1981. *The History of human marriage.* London: Macmillan.

Westley, William, and Elkin, Frederick. 1957. The protective environment and adolescent socialization. *Social Forces* 35.

Westoff, Charles F. 1974. Coital frequency and contraception. *Family Planning Perspectives* 3: 136–141.

———. 1978. Marriage and fertility in the developed countries. *Scientific American* 239, no. 6 (December): 51–57.

Westoff, Charles F., Gerard Calot, and Andrew D. Foster. 1983. Teenage fertility in developed nations: 1971–1980. *Family Planning Perspectives* 15: 105–110.

White, G., S. Fishbein, and J. Rutstein. 1981. Passionate love and the misattribution of arousal. *Journal of Personality and Social Psychology* 41: 56–62.

White, J. M. 1987a. Marital perceived agreement and actual agreement over the family life cycle. *Journal of Comparative Family Studies* 18: 47–59.

———. 1987b. Researching developmental careers: The career conformity scale. *Journal of Family Issues* 8: 306–318.

White, L. K., and D. B. Brinkerhoff. 1981. Children's work in the family: Its significance and meaning. *Journal of Marriage and the Family* 43: 789–798.

Whitehead, A. 1979. Some preliminary notes on the subordination of women. *I.D.S. Bulletin* 10: 10–13.

Whitehurst, Cliff. 1984. I'm afraid of my own child. In *Marriage and the family*, ed. Ollie Pocs and Robert Walsh. Guilford, CT: Dushkin.

Whitehurst, R. 1974. Violence in husband-wife interaction. In *Violence in the family*, ed. Suzanne K. Steinmetz and Murray A. Straus. New York: Dodd, Mead.

Whitehurst, R., and G. Booth. 1980. *The sexes: Changing relationships in a pluralistic society.* Toronto: Gage.

Whiting, Beatrice B., and John W. M. Whiting. 1975. *Children of six cultures: A psycho-cultural analysis.* Cambridge: Harvard University Press.

Whyte, Judith. 1985. Reducing the waste of womanpower. *Quarterly Journal of Social Affairs* 1: 193–210.

Whyte, Martin King. 1979. Revolutionary social change and political residence in China: *Ethology* 18, No. 3 (July): 211–227.

Wiebe, Paul D., and G. N. Ramu. 1971. Marriage in India: A content analysis of matrimonial advertisements. *Man in India* 51: 111–120.

Wilkinson, M. 1978. Romantic love and sexual expression. *The Family Coordinator* 27: 141–148.

————. 1981. *Children and divorce.* Oxford: Basil Blackwell.

Will, Jerrie Ann, Patricia A. Self, and Nancy Datan. 1976. Maternal behavior and perceived sex of infant. *American Journal of Orthopsychiatry* 46: 135–39.

Williams, John E., and Deborah L. Best. 1982. *Measuring sex stereotypes: A thirty-nation study.* Beverly Hills: Sage Publications.

Willie, Charles A. 1981. *New look at black families,* 2d ed. Bayside, NY: General Hall.

Wilson, Margo, and Martin Daly. 1987. Risk of maltreatment of children living with stepparents. In *Child abuse and neglect: Biosocial dimensions,* ed. Richard J. Gelles and J. Lancaster. New York: Aldine.

Wilson, S. J. 1986. *Women, the family and the economy,* 2d ed. Toronto: McGraw-Hill Ryerson.

Wilson, William Julius. 1987. *The truly disadvantaged: The inner city, the underclass, and public policy.* Chicago: University of Chicago Press.

Winch, R. 1955. The theory of complementary needs in mate selection final results on the test of the general hypothesis. *American Sociological Review* 20: 552–555.

————. 1958. *Mate selection: A study of complementary needs.* New York: Harper and Row.

————. 1967. Another look at the theory of complementary needs in mate selection. *Journal of Marriage and the Family* 29: 756–762.

————. 1971. *The modern family.* Holt, Rinehart and Winston, New York.

Wolfe, D. M. 1959. Power and authority in the family. In *Studies in social power* ed. D, Cartwright. Ann Arbor: University of Michigan, Institute for Social Research.

Wright, J. D. 1978. Are working women really more satisfied? Evidence from several national surveys. *Journal of Marriage and the Family* 40: 301–313.

Yang, C. K. 1959. *Chinese communist society: The family and the village.* Cambridge, MA: MIT Press.

Yarrow, Leon J., et al. 1975. *Infant and environment: Early cognitive and motivational development.* New York: Wiley.

Yllo, Kersti Alice. 1978. Non-Marital cohabitation beyond the college campus. *Alternative Lifestyles* 1: 37–54.

Yogev, S. 1981. Do professional women have egalitarian marital relationships? *Journal of Marriage and the Family* 43: 865–870.

Young, M., and P. Willmott. 1957. *Family and kinship in East London.* London: Routledge and Kegan Paul.

————. 1975. *The symmetrical family.* Middlesex: Penguin Books.

Zaretsky, Eli. 1977. Capitalism, the family and personal life. In *Woman in a man-made world,* ed. N. Glazer and H.Y. Waehrer. Chicago: Rand McNally.

Zhangling, Wei, 1983. Chinese family problems: Research and trends. *Journal of Marriage and the Family* 45: 943–948.

Zimmerman, Carle C. 1947. *Family and civilization.* Harper.

Zimmerman, Laconnie. 1975. Family systems in Latin America. *Sociological Internationalise* 13: 161–169.

Zuckerman, Diana M., and Donald H. Sayre. 1982. Cultural sex-role expectations and children's sex-role concepts. *Sex Roles* 8: 853–862.

INDEX